"This Culture of Ours"

Intellectual Transitions in T'ang and Sung China

"THIS CULTURE OF OURS"

Intellectual Transitions in T'ang and Sung China

Peter K. Bol

Stanford University Press
Stanford, California 1992

Stanford University Press
Stanford, California
© 1992 by the
Board of Trustees
of the Leland Stanford
Junior University
Printed in the
United States of America

CIP data are at the end
of the book

Preface

Perhaps in no other country would an intellectual history of six centuries be simultaneously a political history, a history of social elites, and a study of literary values. I am writing at the interface of these, from a conviction that intellectual, political, social, and literary history as separate disciplines are all necessary to understanding intellectual change during the T'ang and Sung dynasties. I am also writing about the intellectual life of the T'ang and Sung from the inside, using terms and ideas from the time. Translation is not a transparent medium, but the interpretation of writings in context enables us to see how the questions scholars asked changed and how their approaches to shared questions diverged, thus bringing us closer to accounting for historical change.

In the study of Chinese history, it is still possible to dare to write a book that sweeps through several centuries. I did not begin with a book of this scope in mind. The present work has its origins in a study of Su Shih and his circle and further research on eleventh- and twelfth-century intellectual culture. A search for the sources of Northern Sung elite culture drew me back into the latter half of T'ang history; to assess those developments, it was necessary to establish a contrast with early T'ang scholarship. As I began to see how the intellectual creativity of the late T'ang and Northern Sung was related to the demise of T'ang aristocratic culture, it became possible to see what made the Neo-Confucian movement different. The result is a work longer and broader than I had anticipated. It remains, however, a discussion of selected figures and texts from particular moments undertaken in support of certain arguments—too much writing has been left unread and too many figures have been left unmentioned for this to be a survey of intellectual culture.

I owe a special debt to the scholars of Chinese history and literature whose research during the past decade has made it possible to think about the six centuries discussed here. Without David McMullen's study of

T'ang scholarship, Steven Owen's writings on poetry, and studies in social history by John Chaffee, Patricia Ebrey, Robert Hymes, and David Johnson, this work would not have been possible. I have also profited greatly from conversations with Michael Fuller and Steven Owen over the years and from the comments of Albert Craig, Patricia Ebrey, Ronald Egan, Michael Fuller, Philip Kuhn, David McMullen, and Denis Twitchett. I have appreciated John Ziemer's work as an editor and, especially, his suggestions as a critical reader. Finally, I thank the Fellowship in Chinese Studies Program of the Wang Institute of Graduate Studies for the grant that made a year's leave possible.

P.K.B.

Contents

Chinese Dynasties
and Various Rulers

The first sages of tradition
  (Fu Hsi)
  (Shen Nung)
  (Huang ti)
  Yao
  Shun
  Yü

The "Three Eras" of antiquity
  Hsia
  Shang
  Chou
    Western Chou 11th century–771 B.C.
    Eastern Chou 770–256
      Spring and Autumn Period 722–481
      Warring States Period 403–221

The first imperial state
  Ch'in 221–207
  (Western) Han 202–A.D. 9
  Wang Mang's usurpation: the Hsin dynasty 9–23
  (Eastern) Han 25–220

The Three Kingdoms 220–80
(Western) Chin 266–316

Period of Division 316–589
  The Northern and Southern Dynasties 317–589

In the north, 386–581: (Northern) Wei 386–534, which divided into the Eastern and Western Wei, which were succeeded by Northern Ch'i and Northern Chou

In the south, 317–589: Eastern Chin 317–420, followed by Sung, Southern Ch'i, Liang, and Ch'en

Unification of north and south
  Sui 581–618
  T'ang 618–907
    T'ai-tsung 626–49
    Kao-tsung 649–83
    Empress Wu 684–705: the Chou dynasty 690–705
    Hsuan-tsung 712–56
    Su-tsung 756–62
    Tai-tsung 762–79
    Te-tsung 779–805
    Shun-tsung 805
    Hsien-tsung 805–20

The Five Dynasties and Ten Kingdoms period of north-south division
  The five dynasties of the north 907–60: Later Liang, followed by Later T'ang, Later Ch'in, Later Han, and Later Chou

  The ten kingdoms included in Szechuan the state of Shu and in the southeast Southern T'ang, Wu-Yueh, and Min

The Sung dynasty and the non-Han dynasties of the north
  the Liao dynasty of the Khitans 916–1125

  Northern Sung 960–1127
    T'ai-tsu 960–76
    T'ai-tsung 976–97
    Chen-tsung 997–1022
    Jen-tsung 1022–63
    Ying-tsung 1063–67
    Shen-tsung 1067–85
    Che-tsung 1085–1100
    Hui-tsung 1100–25
    Ch'in-tsung 1125–27

  the Chin dynasty of the Jurchens 1115–1234

Southern Sung 1127–1270
  Kao-tsung 1127–62

the Yuan dynasty of the Mongols 1264–1368

The later empires
  Yuan 1264–1368
  Ming 1368–1644
  Ch'ing 1644–1911
  People's Republic of China 1949–

"This Culture of Ours"

Intellectual Transitions in T'ang and Sung China

Introduction

> When under siege in K'uang, the Master said, "With King Wen dead, is Culture [*wen*] not here with me? Had Heaven intended that This Culture of Ours [*ssu-wen*] should perish, those who died later would not have been able to participate in This Culture of Ours. Heaven is not yet about to let This Culture of Ours perish, so what can the men of K'uang do to me?" —*Analects* 9.5

This Culture of Ours, Confucius notes, has survived the death of the Chou founding king, posthumously known as King Wen. This fact is both a sign of Heaven's regard for this culture and a guarantee of Confucius's safety, as a participant and carrier of that culture. But what is *wen*? Does it survive in Confucius as the arts and traditions of the Chou dynasty he has mastered? Is it, as many later commentators supposed, a reference to the writings of the ancients they believed Confucius edited and transmitted as the Classics? In the *Analects*, the term "wen" can mean external appearances and forms in general as well as normative patterns and models whose authority derived from their Chou dynasty origins. But in this account of Confucius in K'uang, we do not need to know the exact meaning of wen to see that Confucius is making two claims: participating in *ssu-wen*, "this wen" that has survived King Wen's death and is esteemed by Heaven (This Culture of Ours), continues the legacy of the Chou founder and accords with Heaven's will.

By T'ang (618–907) times, ssu-wen had come to refer first to the textual traditions that originated in antiquity, when the sage-kings translated into human institutions the patterns of heaven, now taken as "heaven-and-earth" or the natural order. By extension, This Culture included the traditions of proper forms in writing, governing, and behaving that men believed stemmed from the ancients and had been preserved and refined by Confucius in the Classics. T'ang and Sung dynasty (960–1279) scholars "participated in This Culture of Ours": they mastered the traditions, they imitated them in practice, and they continued and elaborated on them with their own scholarship and literary writing. They could claim, as Confucius had before them, that by maintaining This Culture of Ours as a cumulative tradition they were according with the natural order of things and continuing the legacy of antiquity.

Heaven and antiquity or "heaven and man," the natural realm in which heaven-and-earth brought things into being and the historical realm in which humans created institutions, came to stand for the two greatest sources of normative values. This Culture of Ours could stand for the idea of a civilization that combined the two, a civilization based on both the models of the ancients and the manifest patterns of the natural order. But T'ang and Sung scholars also saw that at moments of political crisis This Culture could perish. To save it, and to save the times, scholars could always return to antiquity and the natural order as the grounds for shared norms. In the early T'ang the historical and natural were not seen as incompatible. Seventh-century T'ang scholars sought to reintegrate the diverse strands of tradition, and thus to establish a cultural synthesis that would support the newly unified empire. For them the patterns of the cosmos and the civilization of the ancients corresponded. But in the latter half of the eighth century, as the T'ang coped with decentralization and rebellion, the literary intellectuals who tried to save This Culture began to speak of the "way of the sage" (sheng-jen chih tao) and the "way of the ancients" (ku-jen chih tao). The sages in this case did not take their guides from the cosmos; their eyes were on "human affairs," and they looked to the common needs of the people and responded to them. Scholars supposed that they could infer values for the present from the sages' actions and writings, that they could manifest these values through writing in an ancient style (ku-wen), and that they could put these values into practice through government. Attempts to formulate persuasive understandings of the Way and the sages continued through the Northern Sung (960– 1126), inspiring a diverse and competitive intellectual culture. In the eleventh century such ideas justified far-reaching efforts to change the relationship between government and society. But the turn away from heaven, the patterns of cosmic process as the ultimate grounds for moral life, also made for a more uncertain world, where normative models were at best provisional and the intentions of the sages were a matter of interpretation. A challenge to the focus on human affairs emerged late in the eleventh century and came to dominate intellectual life in the Southern Sung (1127–1279). The moral philosophers who established Tao-hsueh (the "Learning of the Way"), Neo-Confucianism in a narrow sense, contended that each individual was innately endowed with the patterns of the integrated processes of heaven-and-earth. It was only necessary, then, that men realize the "pattern of heaven" (t'ien-li) that was in their own nature, for this was the real foundation for a moral world.

An account of the shifting grounds for values in T'ang and Sung intellectual life is a vital part of the story this book tells. But to discuss this alone would obscure a far larger change in how scholars conceived of values. Put most simply, early T'ang scholars supposed that the normative models for writing, government, and behavior were contained in the cumulative cultural tradition. Debates over values were arguments over the proper cultural forms. But by the late Sung, thinkers had shifted their faith to the mind's ability to arrive at true ideas about moral qualities inherent in the self and things, and the received cultural tradition had lost authority. Between the early T'ang faith in the ability of the cultural tradition to provide the models necessary for a unified order and the late Sung belief that real values were innate principles came a period of extraordinary intellectual diversity that began in the latter half of the T'ang and continued into the Northern Sung. An erosion of faith in the possibility of guiding the world by defining correct appearances marked this period. Nevertheless, the most famous scholars during this transitional era insisted that the individual could apprehend an underlying *tao* with his own mind from the writings and accomplishments of the ancients. This Culture of Ours, as the formal traditions stemming from antiquity, mattered still as the source from which normative ideas could be inferred, even if the ideas transcended the particular forms whence they were known. Intellectual life was beset by a creative tension between a commitment to formal cultural continuity, to maintaining the wen of the past, and a search for the ideas that had guided the sages, to discovering the tao of the ancients. But for the Tao-hsueh thinkers of the Sung the task of the individual was to learn to behave according to the norms innately endowed in all things by heaven-and-earth. In contrast to early T'ang scholars, for whom the received cultural tradition had authority by virtue of its origins, and scholars during the transitional period, for whom the textual traditions of Our Culture were the source from which normative ideas could be inferred, the Tao-hsueh school held that the foundation for true ideas about how to act existed independently of culture. Yet few scholars were unaware of the need to establish something others could share, whether it be correct cultural forms, ideas about correct values, or doctrines about how to learn for oneself. The Sung Tao-hsueh thinkers may have rejected the notion that there was a cumulative tradition of cultural forms scholars had a duty to continue; yet in denying an equation between the received culture and true values, they did not give up a claim to be saving This Culture of Ours. Paradoxically, in their effort to save society by shifting the focus of learning away from cultural activities to the cultivation of ethical behavior, they created a new body of texts, doctrines, and practices that would define This Culture well into the seventeenth century.

But whose culture was it? For the men who figure in this book, it belonged to that small, elite group in Chinese society known as the *shih*, and that remained the case even as the role of the cultural tradition was transformed. During most of the six centuries dealt with here, those who called themselves *shih, shih-jen,* and *shih-ta-fu* dominated Chinese politics and society. As shih they were members of the elite rather than of the commonalty (*shu*) or of the populace (*min*). As a group their function was to "serve" (*shih*) in government rather than to farm the land, work as craftsmen, or engage in trade. And they supposed that they had the education and talent necessary to serve in government and guide society.[1] Yet the identity of the shih changed with time. In the seventh century, the shih were an elite led by aristocratic great clans of illustrious pedigree; in the tenth and eleventh centuries, the shih were the civil bureaucrats; and finally, in the Southern Sung, they were the more numerous but rarely illustrious local elite families who provided bureaucrats and examination candidates. The next chapter will trace this transformation and offer explanations for the demise of the aristocracy, the re-emergence of the shih as civil bureaucrats, and the transformation of the shih into local elites in the Sung. I shall argue there that office holding, pedigree, and learning were primary components in the corporate identity of the shih. This implies, I think, that for the shih learning was an area within a broader set of concerns, that it was something shih did as part of their shared identity, and that the values articulated and debated through learning were related to the political and social aspects of shih life. For the moment I note only that I do not think it makes the intellectual life of the shih less valuable to suppose some relation between intellectual change and the rather successful efforts of the shih to dominate Chinese society, politics, and national culture.

The aim of this book is to determine what changed in elite thinking about values, or how the shih changed "that culture of theirs," between the reunification of north and south into a single empire during the late sixth and early seventh centuries and the consolidation of local elite power in the twelfth century. At the same time I wish to account for the changes that took place. Certainly Tao-hsueh was the greatest legacy of the twelfth-century intellectual world. But following the transformation of intellectual life from the aristocratic culture of the early T'ang to the Neo-Confucian culture of the Southern Sung is not easy. Tao-hsueh was not, in my view, a necessary or logical outcome of earlier trends, although it clearly was indebted to earlier developments. The intellectual history examined here begins with early T'ang court scholars as representatives of the medieval world, and it ends with the emergence of Sung Tao-hsueh, the form of learning that dominated intellectual culture until the seventeenth century. But most of this study is devoted to what came between, with a particular focus on the emergence of ku-wen as an intellectual and literary style for the shih in the late eighth century and its great flourishing in the eleventh. In fact, almost half of this book deals with the great intellectuals and statesmen of the eleventh century. In a very general sense I see Northern Sung intellectual culture as the playing out of the tension in ku-wen between individual cultivation and sociopolitical responsibility—a tension apparent in the writings of Han Yü, the founder of ku-wen in the T'ang. Ou-yang Hsiu is a pivotal figure in the eleventh century, I think, because he himself gave full expression to this tension both by harkening to Fan Chung-yen's call for the transformation of the sociopolitical order through institutional activism and by maintaining a view of culture and morality as the products of individual creativity. It is simplistic, but not misleading, to see the next two generations after Ou-yang as choosing for one side or the other. Wang An-shih and Ssu-ma Kuang, the leading political thinkers and statesmen of their day, both addressed themselves to the sociopolitical order and arrived at very different conclusions; the two greatest intellectuals of the next generation, Su Shih and Ch'eng I, turned toward problems of individual cultivation and creativity and reached equally contradictory conclusions.

At the most general level, I am interested in what the shih of a given time thought of as *hsueh* ("learning"). Shih learning was a historical entity, constituted by men who read many of the same texts, shared many assumptions about the value of what they were doing, and established identities with reference to each other. It was their intellectual culture. More narrowly, I ask for particular moments during the T'ang and Sung, how some thought others ought to learn, how they justified their claims, and how others responded. There were usually several possibilities available to those who wished to influence others. I view intellectual change as resulting in general from some persons persuading others that one possibility among the available choices is better than the rest. An alternative slighted during one period may continue on the margins and later capture the center. I also think that in making a case for neglected ideas, scholars make them speak to the present by transforming them. To see how an old idea can be transformed into something more persuasive, I have tried to ask how certain scholars, literary men, and philosophers established links between learning, the grounds of values, cultural forms, and the political and social concerns of the shih as the elite. The most interesting intellectual figures in this context are those who come to be seen as speaking for something different, who persuade others to choose one view at the expense of another. I have given far less attention to their imitators, although without them the marginal could hardly become central. Similarly, I have inquired into those moments of greatest change, the moments of intellectual crisis when shih found themselves in the uncomfortable position of having to choose between incompatible alternatives.

On at least four counts this study departs from what might be asked of a

book on T'ang and Sung intellectual history. First, it is not a history of
Confucianism. Second, it fails to deal seriously with Buddhism. Third, it
grants literature a central role and treats a number of major thinkers as primarily literary men. Fourth, it ignores most of the early Neo-Confucian
moral philosophers. To some extent these decisions stem from my conviction that the history of philosophy does not always represent the
history of intellectual culture or adequately describe and account for the
ways we establish shared values. More detailed explanations for these
choices follow later in this chapter. Now, however, I claim an author's
prerogative and set the issues in a manner that will, I hope, incline readers
to accept my arguments. To do this, I compare two books on family life,
one from 590 and the other from 1190. They are emblematic of the
aristocratic and Neo-Confucian ages, the two worlds between which this
book falls.

The Cultural and the Ethical:
From the Sixth Century to the Twelfth

Yen Chih-t'ui's (531–91) *Family Instructions for the Yen Clan* and Yuan
Ts'ai's (fl. 1140–95) *Precepts for Social Life* may seem unpromising candidates to illustrate an intellectual transformation. The compilation of official commentaries on the Five Classics begun under the Sui dynasty (589–
618) might be a more appropriate subject for the medieval world, and the
works of Chu Hsi (1130–1200), the great tao-hsueh thinker, would be a
more obvious choice for the twelfth century. Yen and Yuan are useful for
my purposes, however, because each wrote about family life from the
intellectual perspective of his age. They illustrate the convergence of
social and intellectual history.[2]

As a member of the Lang-yeh Yen clan, Yen Chih-t'ui had an illustrious
pedigree. His twelfth- and eleventh-generation ancestors had established
the clan's dual heritage of service and scholarship at their home base of
Lang-yeh in eastern Shantung. They had served the state of Wei (220–65)
as prefectural administrators and selectors of personnel in the "nine-rank"
system of appointments and had specialized in studies of certain Classics.
In the early fourth century, Yen's ninth-generation ancestor had moved to
Nanking with the Chin (317–420) court; his descendants continued as
courtiers of the Southern Dynasties that followed the Chin. Yen's father
was a leading court scholar under the Liang (502–57), one of the most
cultured of the Southern Dynasties; his grandon, Yen Shih-ku (581–645),
would become a court scholar under the T'ang and write an authoritative
commentary on Pan Ku's *History of the Han*; Yen Chen-ch'ing (709–84), a
later descendant, would become a leading scholar and calligrapher. Yen
Chih-t'ui himself became a court scholar under the Liang dynasty; how-

ever, he was captured and taken north, where he served the Northern Ch'i (550–77), Chou (557–81), and finally Sui (589–618) dynasties.[3] The Lang-yeh Yens were an aristocratic clan. Although the family did not produce a string of truly powerful bureaucrats in the T'ang, as did the Po-ling Ts'uis (some of whom Yen knew) or the Chao-chün Lis, it was probably in-cluded on the lists of great clans that defined the aristocracy of the South-ern Dynasties.[4]

Yuan Ts'ai lacked illustrious ancestors. His family lived in Ch'ü prefec-ture in Liang-che East Circuit (modern Chekiang). Ch'ü was home to a number of shih families, producing almost 600 degree holders during the Sung, with a number of very successful shih lineages or descent groups (40 percent of those degree holders came from 24 lineages). Some of these descent groups had been known as shih-ta-fu since the tenth and eleventh centuries, and some continued to produce degree holders well into the thirteenth century. Yuan studied at the Imperial University (T'ai-hsueh) in Hang-chou in the 1150's and took a degree in 1163, but only two of his relatives are known to have passed the examinations. In contrast to Yen Chih-t'ui, who served at court, Yuan Ts'ai began as a local administrator and served only once at the capital. He stood out through his scholarship, writing several practical works for local government and society.[5] In his own way he is as representative of the successful shih of his day as Yen Chih-t'ui was of his: he entered official service through the examination system and spent most of his time in local government; his family main-tained itself in its locality, and the lack of a court career did not keep him from writing and publishing.

Both men were concerned with the future of the shih family of their day and wrote about how members should act to preserve it. Moreover, both placed family interests above official service. This meant different things to each. For Yen Chih-t'ui, it was important not to become too involved in politics.

I have always thought that in a family of twenty mouths the male and female slaves should not at most exceed twenty persons, with ten *ch'ing* [160 acres] of good land and a house just good enough to keep away wind and rain; a carriage and horse simply to take the place of a walking stick; a reserve of some 10,000 coins for the expenses of lucky, unlucky, and urgent circumstances. . . . It is safe for an official to stand in a position of middle rank with fifty persons he can see in front and another fifty in the back, a sufficient number to protect him from insult and danger. In case of a position superior to this, you should courteously decline it and retire to your private home.[6]

Yen did serve and he expected his sons to serve; the issue was serving on their own terms, to the extent possible, so as to maintain the honor of the clan.

My brothers and I should not have entered government service, but because of the decline of our clan's fortune, the weakness of our family members, the lack of someone to take responsibility within our branch,[7] our scattering outside our native country leaving no influential man to help you, and my fear lest you should be debased to the level of servants and bring disgrace upon your ancestors, I therefore have brazenly taken a public post, hoping to preserve [the family status] from fall. Moreover the political ethos in the north is so strict that no one is allowed to withdraw.[8]

He ended his "last will" by calling on his sons to "make continuing the patrimony and glorifying the name [of our family] your concern."[9] The Lang-yeh Yens could hardly have maintained their status through the previous centuries without being willing to serve any dynasty they found themselves under, as Yen Chih-t'ui did under four dynasties. Nevertheless, it is important to Yen to insist that he still believes that the honor of the clan can be distinguished from official service and is more important than it.

Yen saw that war and conquest made his family's future uncertain; yet he assumed that if his sons wished to serve, they could. Yuan Ts'ai also sees the future of shih families as uncertain, but in his day officials were rarely able to secure official careers for their descendants. Fate plays a larger role. "That worldly affairs often change is the principle of heaven [t'ien-li]. . . . There is no need to look far for proof of this; just compare your community of ten or twenty years ago with the same community today. There has never been any fixed direction to success and defeat, rise and decline."[10] The "wealth and honor" (fu kuei) that come with an official career are gained by fate, not calculation.[11] And they are exceedingly difficult to preserve across the generations. In a world where service cannot be relied upon as the family occupation, occasional service can make it more difficult to maintain the family position. Yuan explains:

The family of a man of high rank is even more difficult to preserve [than the family of a rich man]. As soon as he attains position and prominence, even if he is awaiting assignment, his salary will be substantial, the largess [he receives] will be much, and his attendants will be numerous. All of these come from the prefectural treasury. The clothing, food, and utensils, although they are of the utmost extravagance, are not paid for from the family assets. After his death, when they lack the salary, largess, and attendants of before, all the expenses of daily life will have to come from the family assets. How much worse when they divide one family into several families while their rate of consumption remains the same. How can this not lead to bankruptcy?[12]

Yuan assumes that the sons of officials are unlikely to gain office themselves. The conclusion he draws is not that shih should not serve in government, but that they must take care to prevent official success from interfering with the long-term need for sound family management. The economic well-being of the family, an issue Yen Chih-t'ui gives scant attention, matters greatly. But Yuan also sees that shih want to remain shih. Those who cannot depend on others for support should seek careers worthy of their status. Education for the official examinations is the best means to such careers, but, failing that, anything that will help the family survive honorably is acceptable.

For sons and younger brothers of shih-ta-fu, if they lack a hereditary stipend [i.e., access to rank through relatives] to maintain themselves or real estate to rely upon and wish to make plans for serving their parents and raising their offspring, the best thing is to be a *ju* [scholar]. Those of admirable talent who can train for the examinations, in the best case, may take a degree and attain wealth and honor or, failing that, may set themselves up as teachers and receive tuition income. Those [educated but] unable to train for the examinations, in the best case, may devote themselves to brush and paper and [become] employed preparing documents for others or, failing that, may practice punctuating and reading aloud and become tutors to children. If they are not able to be ju, then they may do anything that can provide support without disgracing their ancestors—becoming a doctor, clergy-man, farmer, merchant, or specialist of some sort.[13]

In Yuan's day, shih families had come to accept a variety of occupations beside office holding as means of supporting themselves, and the voca-tional distinction between shih families and others had blurred. Some struggled to maintain the distinction nevertheless. Lu Yu (1125–1210) surmised, for example, that shih created charitable states to ensure that their descendants would not sink to becoming craftsmen, merchants, clerks, or clergy.[14]

Yen Chih-t'ui and Yuan Ts'ai address different audiences; Yen instructs his sons, and Yuan sets forth precepts for those families in his jurisdiction that pursue wealth and honor. They conceive of the shih quite differently. For Yen the shih-ta-fu are families like his; "our family has made scholar-ship its occupation for successive generations." They are a hereditary elite, but each generation must strive to avoid slipping to the level of common people (*fan-jen, hsiao-jen*)[15] by maintaining the family's learned traditions, which Yen discusses at length. He distinguishes true shih clans from the militaristic, uncultivated, and often non-Han clans dominating govern-ment in the north and from the various servitors whose families have been hsiao-jen or commoners for generations.[16] He uses the device of instruct-ing his sons to persuade his peers not to forsake their traditions. Their learning gives them their respectability, and ultimately their learning is why those in power value them.

For Yuan Ts'ai the shih are not a hereditary elite, the shih-ta-fu families he speaks of are part of a larger group, which he refers to as "families of wealth and honor," "rich families," and "honored families."[17] He does expect his audience to educate their sons and to take part in the examinations, although he envisions little chance of their attaining official rank,[18] but he is not speaking only of families with officials. Yuan is addressing the pool of locally dominant families, I think, from which officials are drawn and to which their descendants will return. The basis of their position is not the learned tradition of the family and its pedigree but a mixture of wealth, status, and education. He is alert to the ways of preserving the place of the family in local society: a family should educate its members, strive to maintain harmony, keep good but formal relations with local officials and other leading figures, and carefully manage the family assets, real property, tenants, and servants. Its basic concerns are typical of families whose fortunes are tied to their local position, for whom the well-being of family members is more vital than the honor of the family name.

The social worlds of the shih in the writings of Yen and Yuan are different, and accordingly, they have different ideas about what it means to preserve the family. Yet both tell their peers how to act and in both cases "learning" is essential to their strategies of family preservation. But the kinds of learning they urge are not the same, and in the differences we see intellectual worlds far apart.

The style of writing is one indication of the difference. Yen's erudition and literary sophistication contrast with Yuan's more direct and simpler style.[19] The topics they take up are a further illustration. Yen deals with learning, literary composition, philology, phonology, Taoism, Buddhism, and the miscellaneous arts in addition to family ritual and social custom; Yuan divides his work into sections on getting along with relatives, regulating personal conduct, and ordering the family. Neither is particularly antagonistic toward Taoism or Buddhism, although Yen, who actually writes about them, accepts Buddhist rather than Taoist teachings.[20] Both are schooled in the Chinese textual tradition and the Classics.

Yen brings a "cultural" perspective to bear on almost everything he discusses, from remarriage and the family to learning and literary composition. He stresses broad acquaintance with the Classics, histories, various philosophers, and belles lettres, taking issue with those narrow ju who read only the Classics. All shih-ta-fu, he contends, need to learn if they are to survive changes in political patronage, gain true knowledge of how the world really works, and fulfill their administrative duties successfully. Those of greatest talent compose admirable works in the various genres of prose and poetry that, Yen holds, have evolved out of the Classics. His vision of learning is literary, and the terms he uses to refer to the most accomplished scholars are not ju or *ju-shih* but those commonly associated with literary men: *wen-shih* (literati), and *wen-hsueh chih jen* (men of literary learning). He expects learned men to be accomplished in calligraphy and painting as well as in archery, medicine, mathematics, and the lute, although he warns against being so skilled that superiors treat one as a mere expert.[21] The mastery of texts and literary composition, he warns, will not improve "ethical conduct" (*te-hsing*) or social customs.[22] When he turns to issues such as family relations, however, where we would expect discussions of ethical norms, we find instead analyses of family culture, regional variations, and historical examples, not moral universals. His "ordering the family" compares the position and customs of aristocratic women in north and south. His "what the age calls the customs of the shih-ta-fu" delves at length into the proper forms for addressing others and for using names, as well as situational variations and regional differences.[23] This is important, for he holds that the ritual maintained by a family combines common rules from the *Book of Rites* with the particular family tradition.[24] Yen's foundation for good behavior is cultural, not philosophical. It is not surprising that he is most rigorous on matters of spoken and written language.[25]

Yen Chih-t'ui's literary-historical mode of learning was part of the tradition of court scholarship, with its Classical studies, historiography, ritual scholarship, and love for literary elegance. His learning enabled him to bring the past to bear on his official duties through writing that related actual affairs and manifested their "normative patterns" (*li*) with elegance and meter.[26] For Yen, maintaining the cultural tradition was also a responsibility of shih families irrespective of political authority and provided a justification for the continued existence of the Lang-yeh Yens as a shih-ta-fu clan that was a model of decorous and proper behavior for all who would be civilized. Yen also tells us, however, that his peers were willing to sacrifice their standards, and he attacks aristocrats who place office and privilege above scholarship and culture, who pursue military careers, who seek the favor of barbarian powerholders, and who doubt that learning really makes a difference.[27]

Against Yen Chih-t'ui's view that culture was crucial to shih social status and political success, compare Yuan Ts'ai's concerns, as his friend Liu Chen introduces them:

Thinking about how to do good and, further, thinking about how to get others to do good is what the ethical man [*chün-tzu*] puts his mind to. Mr. Yuan [Ts'ai] Chün-tsai of San-ch'ü is of sufficient virtue and in conduct complete, of broad learning, and rich in the literary. With the air of one who "deliberates and thinks" and "presents and offers compositions,"[28] he has taken on the direction of a subprefecture. His is an administration of one "learned in the Way who loves his fellow men"; "the stringed instruments and singing [Confucius heard at] Wu-ch'eng" could not have surpassed this.[29] One day he showed me a book in several chapters he had written and said, "This can strengthen human relations and improve customs; I intend to publish it here. . . ." [Having read it, I conclude that] if the residents [of Yuan's subprefecture] put its words and intents into practice, they can be filial and fraternal, loyal and reciprocal, good and decent, and have the conduct of a shih with ethical standards. But this book is not to be applied only to Le-ch'ing [subprefecture], it can be extended to all within the four seas; it is not to be put into practice only in this one time, it can be a model to later ages. The Gentleman is so earnest in governing a single subprefecture, wishing to use what is "for himself" "for others,"[30] that we may know he will have a mind that will think about how to "make all under heaven good,"[31] when later he will bring the ruler to benefit the people.[32]

Liu saw Yuan's book as an attempt to persuade others that ethical precepts were primary and universal values.[33] Yuan's answer to the question of how shih families should secure their fortunes in the long term is as simple as Yen's, but quite different: to survive they must conduct their relations ethically.

This answer suggests the kind of learning associated with the great moral philosophers of the day, Chu Hsi and Lu Chiu-yuan (1139–93), although Yuan's realism and pragmatism varies from Chu's philosophical arguments and avoidance of appeals to self-interest.[34] The point I wish to make is more general. Both Yuan and the moral philosophers were part of a sea change in shih thinking about values that began in the late Northern Sung and dominated self-critical shih learning by the end of the twelfth century. In this period intellectuals increasingly forsook the literary-historical perspective of the past for an ethical-philosophical perspective. As the focus of scholarly writing shifted to ethical issues, the appreciation of the place of culture in shih life weakened. Liu's preface alludes to that past by suggesting that Yuan's book is also a literary piece meant to show Yuan Ts'ai's promise as an official and scholar. Many of Yuan's contemporaries treated the increased concern with ethical behavior as a proper balance to the traditional literary learning required by the examinations, but for Yuan and the moral philosophers of his day ethical conduct was more important. I do not mean that Yuan was a moral philosopher. The moral philosophers explained why the ethical was the basis for a moral society; Yuan assumed it. The philosophers argued that moral principles are real and universal, endowed in human beings as creatures of heaven-and-earth, which they must apprehend with their minds in themselves (tzu-te) and realize in daily practice (jih-yung). In this respect Yuan is quite different, as he explains in his introduction:

The elder teachers and ju of recent generations have frequently collected their words into "records of speech" to pass on to scholars. It must be that they wish to share with the whole world that which they have apprehended in themselves [*tzu-te*]. But in all [records of speech] the ideas are so subtle that scholars whose cultivation is not yet perfect will not be enlightened, even if they diligently recite and deeply ponder them—how much less average men and below. As for the likes of "small talk" [i.e., the notebooks and miscellanies popular among the literati] and notes on poetry, they are only for those wiser than oneself; they do not add anything to moral instruction.[35]

As I read it, Yuan Ts'ai sides with goals of the moral philosophers, whose "records of speech" he finds so abstruse, against merely literary amusements, even if he doubts the value of the philosophers' methods.

Yuan Ts'ai starts, one might say, from the ground up, from actual human behavior. His *li* are not moral patterns but principles of social dynamics, as in the oft-repeated phrase, "If you are able to know this principle, then you will be at peace in your breast."[36] For example, concerning relations within the family, he presumes that understanding why conflicts emerge enables one to avoid the kinds of emotional involvement that keep one from acting as an ethical person.[37] Yuan's discussion of family relations is interesting because he deals with the tension between his assumption that ethical norms are universal and his recognition that men and women frequently stray. In short, he writes about the problem of being ethical in an imperfect world: "The moral natures [*te-hsing*] of men come from what heaven endows; each has a certain bias. The ethical man is conscious of his bias and therefore makes up for it through what he practices, he then becomes a man of complete virtue. The common man is not conscious of his bias; he acts directly and emotionally according to his bias, and therefore often fails."[38]

Without claiming a perfectly moral nature, Yuan still reflects a basic ideal of the new age: the true worth of an individual should be measured in terms of ethical conduct. Yuan's insistence that wealth and honor are matters of fate leaves ethical standards as the only true measure of human worth. People should strive to meet them as an end in themselves, rather than seeing them as a means to wealth and honor.

Ethical conduct [*ts'ao lü*] and social status are two separate paths. We may not say that correctness of ethical conduct naturally leads to honor or that incorrectness in ethical conduct leads to suffering. . . . Now, ethical conduct is certainly something that we should put into practice, but we may not require that it have an effect on external things. If we expect it to have an effect and it does not, then our ethical conduct will necessarily be lax and our standards may change, and we would then join the ranks of unethical men [*hsiao-jen*].[39]

On the other hand, Yuan sees that continual striving for wealth and honor do quite literally, make the world go around.

Wealth and honor are themselves allotted. The Maker of Things, having set fixed allotments, has further made an unfathomable mechanism [for assigning wealth and honor]. This makes everyone in the world chase after [them] day and night; they grow old and die without ever becoming self-aware. If it were not thus, then there would be no problems at all in man's life between heaven and earth, and [the Maker's] art of constant transformation would be exhausted.[40]

Yuan Ts'ai's ideal shih is an ethical man rather than a cultured one in Yen Chih-t'ui's sense. As Yen Chih-t'ui pointed out, literary learning does not improve ethical conduct, and Yuan has nothing to say about education for the literary examinations except that it does keep one's sons too occupied to misbehave.[41] Perhaps this also explains Yuan's lack of interest either in the family traditions of the shih or in the ways in which they are culturally distinct from those who are merely wealthy; he is interested in standards that everyone can realize in daily life. He writes in his postscript:

Long ago Tzu-ssu discussed the Doctrine of the Mean. "The initial stage [of that Way is something] all ignorant husbands and wives can share knowledge of and all unworthy husbands and wives can practice. Taken to its utmost refinement even a sage cannot understand and practice it, yet it can be seen in heaven-and-earth."[42] Now, on the matter of taking what is seen in heaven-and-earth and expressing it in terms of man, the "records of speech" of the elder generations certainly have already filled pages. I have instead taken what husbands and wives share knowl-edge of and are able to practice and have said it in terms of the customs of the age, so that farmers and village elders and secluded wives and daughters will all be clear in their perception of it. Some may not share my likes and dislikes. Even as they find this wrong and that right, certainly there will be one or two things that match their minds. That will be enough to quell disputes and reduce punishments; customs will return to purity and strength, and when sages re-emerge, they will not set me aside.[43]

Yuan's goal is to explain how a universal morality applies to society by beginning with that which is common to the experience of every-one.

Just as Yen Chih-t'ui, speaking in a time when learning implied cultural traditions, judged his contemporaries in terms of culture, so did Yuan Ts'ai ask men to judge themselves in terms of the ethical concerns that were coming to define learning in his day. And just as Yen faced a time when he thought the great clans were forsaking their culture in an effort to advance themselves with the powerholders, so did Yuan face an age when he thought local elites were forsaking ethical standards in order to increase their share of local wealth and power. Why shih abandoned Yen Chih-t'ui's cultural learning in favor of Yuan Ts'ai's ethical concerns is the subject of this book.

Some Methodological Choices

Shih Learning or Confucianism?

The use of "Confucian" and "Confucianism" as general terms for the Chinese political elite and their values obscures distinctions among men and changes over time. The learning associated with being a ju, the most obvious Chinese equivalent of "Confucian," was not constant; few Han and T'ang scholars would have agreed with Sung Tao-hsueh thinkers that it meant the "learning of Confucius and Mencius." But, as we shall see, even the equation of ju with what T'ang men sometimes called the "learning of scholar-officials" (chin-shen chih hsueh) is problematic.[44] Let us begin instead with the broader category of elite learning, and ask, first, where shih located it in the spectrum of their shared concerns and, second, how they divided it up before the emergence of Sung Tao-hsueh.

One of the most frequently used taxonomies of elite concerns was the "four fields" (ssu k'o) of the Analects: te-hsing (ethical conduct), yen-yü (speech), cheng-shih (affairs of government), and wen-hsueh (culture learning).[45] By T'ang times each field represented both a value in itself and a category of activity for which historical models existed, and thus each was an area in which men could make reputations. The ideal man was virtuous in family matters, meritorious in official service, eloquent and proper in speech and conversation, and learned and literary in writing. At the very least, the three fields of ethics, government, and learning corresponded to family, politics, and culture as concerns integral to elite life in the T'ang and Sung. The use of this taxonomy dates at least to the fifth century.[46] The four fields figured in the T'ang recruitment and selection process.[47] They also were recognized in the state cult, as when Confucius's "teachings in the four fields" were lauded in establishing a temple to Confucius and the Duke of Chou in 619, and when the "Ten Wise" (shih che), the ten disciples associated with the fields, were enshrined in the temple in 720.[48] The meaning of the fields as values was raised in the Three Teachings (Buddhism, Confucianism, Taoism) debate of 827,[49] and they were used again in 863 in arguments for enshrining Han Yü (768–824) in the Confucian Temple.[50] They continued to be used in the Sung.[51] The relative value of these categories was debated. Some spoke of excelling in all four fields; others doubted it was possible; the Duke of Chou himself was reputed to have advised against demanding "completeness" of others.[52] The importance of the category wen-hsueh was not constant. The great northwestern clans instrumental in the T'ang founding placed less store on it than did the great families of the south and northeast, and its importance to attaining high office might vary even within a single reign.[53] For some, te-hsing and wen-hsueh were necessary training for official service, as when T'ang T'ai-tsung (r. 627–49) noted that in seeking the right men for office "we must make ethical conduct and learned knowledge the basis."[54] But it was also possible to follow Confucius and insist that learning wen was secondary to ethical behavior, a view echoed by T'ang T'ai-tsung (who murdered his brothers and forced his father's abdication) when he rejected the suggestion that his literary writings be compiled with the comment, "Being a ruler depends only on ethical conduct; what need is there to devote oneself to *wen-chang* [literary composition]?"[55] Reliance on literary examinations in recruitment, particularly with the advent of blind tests in the Sung, made it apparent why shih devoted themselves to wen-chang. It also prompted others to warn that ethical conduct was being ignored.[56]

In the ssu k'o taxonomy, ethical conduct is separate from learning (hsueh), and learning is linked to wen (literature and literary form, the textual tradition, culture). This formulation was not seriously challenged until the Sung moral philosophers asserted that te-hsing was the true object of learning.[57] But the use both of "wen-hsueh" to refer to learning in general and of "wen" as the object of learning allowed various possibilities. At least from the Han dynasty on, it was common to distinguish between wen-hsueh as a term for learning and wen or wen-chang (literary compositions) and *wen-tz'u* (literary elaborations) as terms for literary composition.[58] In fact, "wen" could refer to both the textual-cultural tradition and belles lettres, just as it could be used both by those who stressed orthodox models and the Classics and by creative literary men.[59] It is in this context that the T'ang use of the term "ju" should be understood. Confucius was a ju and a shih and a man with wen-hsueh; those called ju in the T'ang were also shih who studied wen. Confucius was at the center of official T'ang ideas about learning, as the controversial decision to remove the title of "former sage" from the Duke of Chou and bestow it upon Confucius in 628 and to grant Confucius's earlier title of "former teacher" to Yen Hui, indicated.[60] The powerful Ch'ang-sun Wu-chi (d. 659), a defender of this change, articulated the early T'ang image of Confucius: "At the end of the decline of Chou, Confucius saved wen [the textual-cultural tradition] from perishing.[61] He 'related the traditions of Yao and Shun, he illuminated the models of [the Chou kings] Wen and Wu,'[62] he amplified the sages' instructions through the Six Classics, and made clear the ju ethos [*feng*] for a thousand generations."[63] This is the Confucius of the state cult, the savior of a cultural heritage of normative models and the patron saint of a state education program in which the study of the Classics was paramount.[64]

Like the T'ang version of Confucius, the early T'ang ju were also men schooled in the ancient textual tradition, and the government patronized them for it. In 628, for example, "ju-shih" were summoned to the capital and rewarded, students thoroughly trained in a single classic were given office, teachers were appointed, ju-shih "from the four quarters" contributed books, and *ju-hsueh* flourished as never before.[65] Court patronage of the ju was also recognition for ju political morality. Because previous dynasties had inadequately patronized the *ju-feng* (ethos), the T'ang was reviving the "teachings of the Duke of Chou and Confucius" (*Chou K'ung chih chiao*), for "benevolence, duty, propriety, wisdom, and trustworthiness" are of great benefit in governing. "I now intend," the emperor announced in 624, to "honor the ju tradition [*ju-tsung*], to open the eyes and ears of those born later, and carry out the lessons of the Former Kings. For although the Three Teachings are different, the good that results is the same."[66] But the early court was less committed to bringing ju scholars into government than such announcements suggest, prompting one scholar to request more patronage, for "ju are the basis for transformation through instruction and the source of scholars. If the *ju-chiao* does not flourish, customs will deteriorate."[67]

In the context of a Three Teachings (*san chiao*) typology, all shih scholars are ju. But among the shih, terms such as "ju-chiao," "ju-hsueh," and "ju-shih" sometimes gave way to "wen-chiao," "wen-hsueh," and "wen-shih."[68] Such terms may have seemed less narrow than their ju counterparts; at the very least there were precedents for using them.[69] The rationale behind the subcommentaries on the commentaries of the Five Classics, for example, was that "there are many sorts of wen-hsueh."[70] Even if some equated wen-chiao and wen-hsueh with ju-chiao and ju-hsueh, there was a clear difference between wen-shih, who had a talent for literary composition, and ju-shih, who were men of scholarship but not necessarily literary skill.[71] Here we are concerned with two different ways of being "one who learns," a division reinforced by the biographical division between wen and ju scholars in the dynastic histories and the court's recruitment policies for scholars.[72] Yet each group claimed ssu-wen, This Culture of Ours, and traced its expertise back to antiquity. The fact of the difference is apparent in early T'ang attempts to achieve a synthesis by applying the term "wen-ju" to the greatest scholars, as when T'ai-tsung established the Hung-wen kuan (College for Amplifying Culture) and selected "wen-ju" to serve as academicians,[73] or when the eighth-century chief minister Chang Yueh furthered the careers of *wen-ju chih shih* (shih who were both wen and ju).[74] But tensions were also possible, as when Liu Hsu (897–946) lamented in the [*Old*] *T'ang History*:

"Recent times have valued wen and denigrated ju."[75] The existence of wen and ju perspectives on learning leads me to resist typing all shih as Confucians and shih learning as Confucianism.

Buddhism and Shih Learning

With the publication of David L. McMullen's *State and Scholars in T'ang China*, an extraordinary survey of official scholarship and intellectual trends, it is no longer possible to suppose that the flourishing of Buddhism in the T'ang meant that "Confucianism" was moribund before the rise of Tao-hsueh. When an intellectual history of all modes of thought and practice in the T'ang and Sung is written, we may see that leading scholars in all traditions influenced each other and that intellectual change did not respect boundaries. But an analysis of how intellectual Buddhist monks or doctrinal texts influenced shih thinking requires first that the changes in shih intellectual culture be clearly delineated.

The careful maintenance of the distinctiveness of the three traditions is a historical reason for believing that it is possible to discuss shih learning without giving an account of Buddhist and Taoist developments. The Three Teachings debates held at the T'ang court throughout the dynasty made all three traditions partial contenders for the patronage of an imperial house unwilling to subordinate itself to the moral authority of any one.[76] The imperial favor shown Taoists and Lao-tzu, concomitants of the imperial claim to descent from Lao-tzu, illustrates this. Enlarging the Taoist church, while increasing its dependence on the throne, on the one hand countered Buddhist patronage requests and on the other hand gave the ruler a house sage to offset the sage-kings and Confucius of the ju, as became increasingly clear under Hsuan-tsung (r. 712–56).

This Three Teachings typology is misleading, however, insofar as it implies that those who wore the garb of ju, monks, and Taoist masters were equal in relation to political power. Irrespective of how the emperor wanted to see things, shih scholars were officials who claimed to represent the state. Patronage of their scholarship was thus bureaucratic patronage of other bureaucrats. In contrast, the Buddhist church, which was double the size of the Taoist church in the eighth century,[77] insisted upon its independence from the state; indeed, the existence of a state to be independent from was in a sense necessary to the clergy's moral identity. In the early T'ang a majority of leading officials did believe that the community of Buddhist monks should be allowed its independence.[78] But the church-state relationship was not one of equals, and as long as the government could determine how many of its subjects might take vows, the clergy were not the equals of officials. The Taoist establishment, far more dependent on imperial patronage than the Buddhist, had less independence.

Public and private patronage of Buddhist and Taoist institutions, the elite's use of clerical services in mourning rites, and their respect for the abilities of monks and adepts suggests that shih generally were not narrow dogmatists. Thus the fact that a wen-ju such as Liang Su (753–93), Liu Tsung-yuan (773–819), or Po Chü-i (772–846) paid serious attention to Buddhist learning need not have made him a "Buddhist," just as a monk with a reputation as a *ju-seng* ("Confucian monk") need not have been a "Confucian." To label such men by faith is to assume that ideology was the key to identity. This is anachronistic in the case of men who conceived of the world in terms of received models and traditions, each with its own domain, although it may be appropriate to those who identified their cultural selves in terms of ideas. Hierarchy and status mattered in the T'ang, and distinctions in roles were obvious. A monk was not a shih, and an official was not a *tao-shih* (Taoist priest); changes in status were possible, but the legal hierarchies were discrete. We need to ask what elite scholars who followed Buddhist teachings were learning and why they thought it important. So too we should ask why some clergy schooled themselves in ju-hsueh and wen-hsueh. I suspect that the intellectual interchange was not constant over time, that moments of general social and political crisis affected all who benefited from the patronage that came with stability and prosperity, and that people were more likely to seek answers outside what they already knew when they were confused about what they should do.

Possibilities for mutual influence were furthered by the fact that in the sixth, seventh, and eighth centuries, leading clergy were often not socially distinct from leading officials. Sons (and daughters) from the great clan families became Buddhist monks (and nuns), gained leading roles in the Buddhist community, interpreted Buddhist teachings in ways compatible with their social background, and used their social and political connections to secure patronage for their sect.[79] Similarly, Taoist sects and scriptures in the fourth and fifth centuries had been the work of men from aristocratic families, and here too political issues had been involved.[80] Whether or not the scions of the best families continued to dominate the intellectual elite of the Buddhist and Taoist communities during later centuries, the offspring of both the illustrious and the obscure continued to become monks and tao-shih.[81] Other traditions had to remain distinct, of course, if they were to serve as alternatives, even when individuals aspired to political success. Wu Yun (d. 778) began as a ju-shih, failed the examinations, became a tao-shih, and then, having achieved a reputation for literary talent, was summoned to court by Hsuan-tsung and given a position in the Han-lin Academy.[82] Wei Ch'ü-mou (749–801), of the Ching-chao Wan-nien Wei clan, was a shih who returned to the ranks, or "resumed official garb." He studied the Classics and histories in his youth, became a tao-shih and then a Buddhist monk, and finally acquired civil rank by serving as a military governor in 784. He ended up at court, where he served as one of the most eloquent and literary representatives of the ju position in the Three Teachings debate of 796.[83] More common, I suspect, were those like the great Buddhist polemicist Tsung-mi (780–841), who came from a provincial elite family and prepared for the examinations before turning to Buddhist teachings but made connections with famous scholar-officials of his day.[84]

One of the grounds for intellectual exchange was the existence of three discrete, cumulative textual traditions. The reading, interpretation, and writing of texts required training and expert knowledge. The early T'ang court organized the shih textual legacy and encouraged Buddhists and Taoists to maintain their textual traditions. In the T'ang, at least, the translation of Buddhist scriptures into Chinese seems to have taken place mainly, and perhaps exclusively, under imperial sponsorship.[85] The imperial house also funded work on the Taoist canon, including, for example, the copying of all scriptures into 7,300 chüan (scrolls) and the preparation of a catalogue and encyclopedia in 675.[86] The lost Pearly Flowers of the Three Teachings (San-chiao chu-ying) in 1,300 chüan, compiled under Empress Wu (r. 684–705), brought out the separateness of these traditions in attempting to put them together.[87] Textual traditions and writing may have been important to a tradition's identity, but they were not necessarily equally important in the practice of the faith. Similarly, the formulation of doctrinal positions was not equally important in all traditions. Part of the problem in accounting for these differences is that no tradition was ever a single ideology or unified set of practices. Even within the court's narrow confines, for example, Taoists specialized in many different things: scriptural traditions, rituals, music, immortality practices, and alchemy. The abundance of Buddhist doctrinal writing and the philosophical sophistication of some monks raises the question of why Buddhists thought it important to write on doctrine and who their intended audiences were. Buddhist polemics often spoke to other clergy on matters internal to the Buddhist tradition.[88] When an external audience was addressed, was the goal conversion or patronage? In Stanley Weinstein's account of the T'ien-t'ai, Fa-hsiang, and Hua-yen schools, for example, imperial patronage looms large in explaining why erudite clerics promoted particular sutras over others and wrote synthetic accounts of Buddhism.[89] Even schools with less scholastic interests such as the Pure Land, Ch'an, the Esoteric, and Disciplinary, also relied on imperial patronage to gain an initial foothold.[90] An eventual explanation for the seventh-century Buddhist clerical elite's pursuit of competing accounts of doctrinal coherence might well be useful in accounting for the same phenomenon in shih intellectual culture in the eighth and eleventh centuries.

Part of the reason shih scholars in the early T'ang were not troubled by the coexistence of the Three Teachings, I suggest, was that each tradition claimed responsibility for different areas of human experience.[91] Erik Zürcher has suggested that the activities of the Buddhist clergy as a whole may have been closer to those associated with Chinese religion than to the textual scholarship upon which studies of doctrine depend: communication with deities and the dead, revelation, spirit writing, possession, exorcism, prognostication, messianism, control over natural events, magic, and so on.[92] These were activities of the tao-shih as well. A general distinction between the realms of experience that shih scholars addressed, on the one hand, and monks and tao-shih dealt with, on the other, is suggested by those Taoists and Buddhists who, by their own account, were expert in the realm of the hsuan (the hidden and mysterious) and in matters that were fang-wai ("beyond the bounds" of political and social life). This could include the unseen forces of heaven-and-earth, the ghosts-and-spirits, the many worlds of Buddhism, the journeys of the soul, and the like. Such matters were taken seriously at the highest levels of the T'ang government, as well as by local officials. The appointment of court clerics, the creation of national networks of monasteries and temples, the granting of ordinations, and all manner of public and private patronage secured the services of clergy as expert mediators between the social-political realm and supramundane mysteries. This left the mediating of human relations to officialdom, and the realm of human affairs was the main focus of elite scholarship.

In one respect, attention to Buddhism is crucial to this account. If early T'ang scholars generally did not see principled anti-Buddhism as essential to their tradition of learning, any change in that attitude needs to be accounted for. And their attitude did change with the deterioration of the T'ang order in the eighth and ninth centuries. When shih sought an all-encompassing tao that could provide all necessary values, other schools of thought became unnecessary. Han Yü's essay "Finding the Source for the Way" ("Yuan tao") exemplifies this with its attack on Buddhist and Taoist traditions for obscuring the true values of the sages. Han Yü turned back to the ancients of his tradition, but for others the existence of ways "beyond the bounds" promised an escape from the burden of conventions. As Ch'üan Te-yü (759–818) put it: "There are shih who pursue the traces of what is beyond the bounds and regard social norms as fetters; otherwise they must proceed along the path of literary composition [wen-chang]."[93] The desire for a single foundation was the problem of the age. It is illustrated by Tsung-mi's "On the Origin of Man" ("Yuan jen lun"), possibly a response to Han Yü, which begins by asserting that there is a single real "origin" and that a coherent morality can only be founded on that basis.[94]

The institutional difficulties of the state destabilized its relation to monastic institutions, as the great persecution of the Buddhist church in 845 makes clear. It aimed to reduce Buddhist activities to a token presence, after a phenomenal expansion of the clergy and monastic institutions—an expansion driven by sometimes lavish imperial patronage, the massive selling of ordination certificates by central and local authorities, and the incentive of tax and service exemptions for clergy. It is said that 700,000 people declared themselves monks and nuns in 830, during an amnesty program to control the numbers of men and women leaving lay life. A group of this size exempt from legal and fiscal obligations lessened the government's ability to survive. They constituted over 2 percent of the population, they were likely to be educated and well-informed, and they absorbed wealth without producing revenues. T'ang monks and nuns owned land, slaves, currency, grain, animals, and more, in many cases being the owner of record of the family estate. The social standing of the clergy is suggested by the court's decision in 842 that in confiscating personal property it would allow monks to retain one male slave and nuns two female slaves. The laicization of over 250,000 monks and nuns in 845 was accompanied by the confiscation of 150,000 slaves, some 4,000 monasteries, 40,000 chapels, and untold acres of land.[95] The effectiveness of the persecution indicates a shift in bureaucratic attitudes, or at least a belief that the survival of the T'ang was more important than personal sympathies. Those who let personal sympathies interfere with duty were criticized. Ennin records the edict condemning the minister Wei Tsung-ch'ing for daring to submit his own writings on Buddhist texts to the emperor in 843. Being a high official, Wei was told, "you ought to stay with the ju legacy. . . . How can you transmit a teaching from outside. . . . You are a pure ju among the shih, an official from an illustrious clan, yet you are unable to promote Confucius and Mo-tzu and instead are mired in trusting Buddha."[96] And yet, within a few years the court reversed itself; temples were rebuilt, and the Buddhist community restored. The persecution did not mean that the T'ang had become less "Buddhist," but ideas denying the necessity of Buddhism to a civilized society were becoming part of shih claims about learning.[97]

The Literary as Intellectual

Intellectual history is easiest when scholars write about ideas directly, and thus scholars active after 755 have been the subject of numerous studies.[98] They were intellectuals, men in conscious tension with society and the state, for whom the idea of the tao was a means of challenging the status quo. They were interested in reading the ancient philosophers, whereas early T'ang scholars had spoken of the Hundred Schools of the Warring States period as one-sided. Yet in most instances they were thought of as writers rather than as thinkers. They promoted their ideas through literary writings, they generally were famous as wen-shih, and they most obviously influenced the way men wrote.

The study of Han Yü (768–824) illustrates the problem. In intellectual history he has been treated as a leader of the "Confucian revival" and even as a founder of Neo-Confucianism. Historians of Chinese literature, however, see the "ku-wen movement" and Han Yü as promoting a literary change that influenced Northern Sung writing. Similar comments could be made about the treatment of Han's contemporary Liu Tsung-yuan. The problem is that Han Yü, by envisioning a resolvable tension between wen (the literary) and tao (moral-philosophical interests), combined what academic disciplines prefer to keep separate.[99] Some historians of Chinese philosophy find little of philosophical importance in Han Yü's work and treat his influence as merely literary.[100] Others see his transformation of literary style as the consequence of his desire to express his ideas about Confucian revival and Confucian orthodoxy.[101] I would simply reiterate a point made by Yao Chi-kuang in his 1947 article "The Scholarly Thought of T'ang Dynasty Wen-shih": T'ang intellectuals wrote in a world in which wen was still integral to learning.[102] The ku-wen "movement" was a literary-intellectual movement in which self-conscious thinking about values played a central role.

In the history of Chinese literature, ku-wen is often said to begin with Ch'en Tzu-ang (661–702) and the group around Li Hua (ca. 710–ca. 767) in the mid-eighth century.[103] This is anachronistic. The precedents for the stylistic moves associated with ku-wen—the break with the parallel style in non-poetic genres and the appeal to antiquity to justify being different are frequent examples—are different in nature from Han Yü's self-conscious use of "ku-wen" as a term for a morally superior way of learning and writing in the 790's. This is an example of the tension between literary and intellectual history.

From a literary perspective, the stylistic change—not the intentions it was meant to serve—may be more important. It is possible to see ku-wen as another case of what Stephen Owen calls the fu-ku literary sentiment of opposing the style of the times and returning to antiquity.[104] This preference for ancient models over modern practice and for the substantial, simple, and moral over the refined, brilliantly crafted, and sensuous is evident in Li O's letter in the 580's to Emperor Wen of the Sui (r. 581–605) demanding that wen-chang promote ethical conduct, Ch'en Tzu-ang's claim to be saving wen-chang after 500 years of decline, and Yuan Chieh's (719–72) stylized archaic pieces. For an intellectual historian, however, stressing ethical values and the larger sociopolitical functions of wen-chang (Li O) differs from calling for a break with recent tradition and a new beginning (Ch'en Tzu-ang), as well as from startling men into awareness through unconventionality (Yuan Chieh). Similarly, one might note that "antiquity" can refer to "extreme antiquity" (*t'ai-ku*) for Yuan, the Han dynasty for Ch'en, and the era of the sage-kings for Li. The use of historical terms for descriptive categories creates debates over the way we should employ the category. I prefer to explore when and why a term such as "fu-ku" was used as a concept. Under Hsuan-tsung, for example, Yuan Chieh writes, "Today the state is seeking to return to pure antiquity," possibly a sardonic reference to the grand ritual program of the late 740's.[105] After the suppression of the An Lu-shan rebellion in 763, the term may have been used to characterize attempts to restore the status quo ante, although in Li Kuan's (766–94)[106] reference to "the ruler who returns to *ku*," for example, "ku" refers to antiquity rather than the recent past.[107] In any case, we find the term being used before and after the 790's, for a political program, a literary program, or both.[108] Yet if "fu-ku" did not become as specific a term as ku-wen, it is certain that ku, antiquity, was a political and literary value of the highest order both before and after 755.[109]

One immediate problem in speaking of ku-wen is its translation as "ancient[-style] prose." For Sung, Ming, and Ch'ing anthologists, "wen" could mean prose as opposed to poetry, and it is often assumed that in the T'ang it referred to a new, discursive style of prose writing that broke with the demanding craft of parallel prose. In fact, "ku-wen" in Han Yü's day meant "literature of antiquity" or "ancient literary style" and included poetic and non-poetic genres.[110] I have yet to find convincing evidence that writers thought in terms of an overarching dichotomy in literature between prose (wen) and poetry (shih) before the end of the tenth century, and even then "wen" continued to be used for literary writing in all genres.[111] By the early eleventh century, some used "ku-wen" to refer to a variety of new non-poetic and non-parallel genres for writing about intellectual and political issues.[112] Given the importance of shih poetry in the eighth century, a movement aimed at transforming learning by changing the way men wrote could hardly afford to ignore poetry.

A prose/poetry dichotomy would not have been necessary if each genre (and sub-genre) had had its particular conventions of subject matter and format. In addition to the shih poem, *fu* (rhapsody), *lun* (essay), and *ts'e* (treatise) employed in the *chin-shih* examination, a variety of genres had to be learned by those seeking literary offices and reputations for writing.

Why then did a prose/poetry dichotomy eventually emerge? A desire for fewer constraints in writing may have made appealing more discursive genres (the preface, essay, record, letter, and stele inscription).[113] There was also debate over the value of various genres, evident in the dropping of the shih and fu from the chin-shih examination between 781 and 785.[114] But in the late eighth and early ninth centuries some also tried to use ideas about basic purposes to define broad categories of literary composition. For example, Yen Chen-ch'ing evaluated a man's work in terms of how he "related events," "did shih," and "elaborated on language" (tz'u yen; i.e., composed the instructions of the chief minister into formal documents).[115] In another example, Liu Tsung-yuan argues that "wen has two tao": to give commands and to praise and blame; and to guide the expression of emotions and to criticize. The first is based in narrative (chu-shu), which in turn stems from the Documents, Change, and Spring and Autumn Annals, and the second in comparison and affective image (pi-hsing), which stems from the Songs.[116] Given the affective character of Liu's landscape prose, I am not sure that he was dividing prose from poetry. However, a dichotomy between writing that inculcated values and writing that articulated the author's emotional responses could correspond to a prose/poetry division.

The supposition that the ku-wen style was the by-product of attempts to develop a manner of writing that better served to express ideas—an aim that later times assigned ku-wen with the Sung phrase "literature is a vehicle for the tao" (wen i tsai tao)—can be challenged. In fact, some of the early ninth-century critics of ku-wen writers faulted them for making an issue of the style of writing rather than stating ideas clearly.[117] Ku-wen did break with parallelism, but, as I see it, the issue was not the search for a better means of expressing ideas but the values attached to a stylistic choice. Some saw in the ornateness and surface decoration of parallelism the style of an age in decline, a contrast with the firm simplicity of the ancient. Yet another issue in the choice between a parallel and non-parallel style was the particular logic of argumentation. Consider two passages, both written before Han Yü appeared on the scene, by men attached to the idea of antiquity. The first passage, in parallel style, comes from the preface for a stele at a Buddhist temple. The author is Fang Kuan (697–763), who in 756 disastrously imitated the Spring and Autumn period use of oxcarts in battle.

> [1a] At the beginning the tao was present, and men were
>   harmonized,
>   [1b] The supreme ruler drew on [its] images and realized its plan.
> [2a] In middle antiquity its effectiveness fluctuated, and men
>   separated,

[2b] The Eastern Chou produced the rites to discipline their
actions.
[3a] In later eras [it] so degenerated that mankind was lost,
  [3b] From the West conversion to Buddhism spread and their
  moral sense was restored.
Now,
[4] Activity and rites are at odds,
[5] Tranquillity and tao agree.
[6a] The principles of the *Songs* and *Documents*,
  [6b] value the quality of seeing and hearing above all,
    [6c] yet they become distorted through activity.
[7a] The goal of the Buddha [vehicle and the precepts]
  [7b] is to turn away from looking and listening;
    [7c] yet they become appropriate through tranquillity.
Thus,
[8a] The books of the Former Kings,
  [8b] are they perhaps not complete?
[9a] The tao of the [Enlightened One],
  [9b] is it perhaps without superior?[118]

Compare this with the following passage, written in the 770's, from Li
Hàn's (fl. 750–70) preface to Tu Yu's (735–812) great review of institutions throughout history, the *Comprehensive Canons* (*T'ung tien*).

Now with the writing of the *Comprehensive Canons* are not the many who have
gone astray startled into awareness with great clarity? It holds that for the superior
man:

realizing his use lies in ordering the state,
  ordering the state lies in accomplishing things,
    accomplishing things lies in learning from the past [*ku*],
      learning from the past lies in changing with the times.
One must examine what was appropriate in past and in present,
fully grasp the subtleties of endings and beginnings.
[Then] at the beginning it will be possible to calculate the ending.
[Then] the past can be practiced in the present.

Inquire of it—it will be as orderly as a string of pearls;
Practice it—it will be as certain as hitting the bull's-eye.
This being so,
Turn it into literary learning, and one can be a comprehensive ju,
Turn it into government policy, and one can establish the august
  ultimate.[119]

Both pieces express ideas, or at least opinions, quite directly; both make
arguments. In both the argument dominates surface embellishment. Yet

the dualistic argumentation of the first belongs to an intellectual universe very different from that of the chained, linear argumentation at the heart of the second. Fang Kuan's traditional manner illustrates what Han Yü called ju using Buddhist language to speak to Buddhists. Li Han's exposition, although not without parallelism, recalls Chou and Han dynasty exposition. Fang's world is balanced, accommodative, and cumulative. It has a beginning with the tao of heaven-and-earth, a middle with the creation of social guides, and an end with Buddhism. Buddhism has compensated for the historical decline, but Fang only suggests that the Buddha's tao is ultimate and the Classics inadequate, he does not insist. Li Han wants necessary conclusions, clear starting points, certainty. There has been a decline; men must recover from it. There is a source of answers. One thing is supposed to follow from another; the reader is to keep to the path of Li's assertions, his string of pearls, and not stray. History and antiquity tell us what to do. As Li writes later in the preface, Tu Yu "has not accepted that which negates the books of the sages or distorts the subtle points of the sages"; there is no need to find a place for heaven-and-earth, an ultimate tao, or tranquillity. Yet if the lesson of antiquity is to "change with the times," we are left to wonder what is certain. Is Li's style really better suited than Fang's to the expression of ideas, or does it convey a different kind of sentiment, one appropriate to the ideas he is setting forth?

The ku-wen movement was an intellectual movement that saw literary change as integral to changes in public values and whose leading "thinkers" were literary men. In my view, the intellectual culture of the T'ang was still a "literary" culture, in which forms of scholarship were thought of as works within a larger field of "literature." Edwin Pulleyblank speaks of a new approach to the study of the Classics represented by writings on the *Spring and Autumn Annals*, which influenced Liu Tsung-yuan and others, and of the "neo-legalism" represented by Tu Yu's institutional studies, but I see little evidence that Classical and historical studies defined the center of elite learning in the T'ang. Some scholars did take up Li Han's challenge to turn the historical and institutional studies of the *T'ung tien* into wen-hsueh, and some did pursue historical scholarship, as the creation of an examination field on the three Han histories indicates.[120] But literary composition was the most common way of connecting learning, values, and social practice, and changing the way men wrote was the common way of influencing intellectual values.

Neo-Confucianism and Sung Thought

The historical importance of Neo-Confucianism in later imperial China is such that the study of Sung thought has largely been a discussion of

Sung moral philosophy and its origins. For many, it suffices to treat Sung intellectual culture in terms of the thinkers who provided the philosophical foundations for the Tao-hsueh movement. This narrow view, in which Ch'eng I (1033–1107) and Chu Hsi define the center, has the virtue of recognizing the importance of philosophical thought. Some scholars, however, have taken a broader view, which recognizes the importance of other intellectual trends in the T'ang and the eleventh century but suggests that they culminated in or had their essential aims finally realized by Tao-hsueh. Scholars have often taken Neo-Confucianism to refer to those figures who are the subject of both the narrow and broad accounts. Neo-Confucianism would not be an issue and the term would not exist without the Tao-hsueh of the Ch'eng-Chu school; extending this term back to Han Yü transforms him into a precursor of something he had not imagined. Such an approach obscures historical change and lessens the need for explanations. Its larger consequence for the study of Chinese thought during this period has been confusion about the intellectual character of the times.[121]

Were the conflict between broader and narrower accounts merely a difference between taking philosophy as the center and wanting to see the intellectual character of the times, I would not object. What I wish to warn against is an approach to the larger intellectual context that assumes the inevitability of Tao-hsueh. The problem goes back to Chu Hsi himself, but it has entered into modern scholarship most directly through Ch'üan Tsu-wang's (1705–55) enlargement of Huang Tsung-hsi's (1610–95) *Case Studies of Sung and Yuan Learning (Sung Yuan hsueh-an)*, the most comprehensive study of Sung thought yet written. I will note briefly Chu's approaches to the rise of Tao-hsueh and their effect on the *Case Studies*.

Taking a narrow view, Chu Hsi held that the most important intellectual development since the death of Mencius had been the recovery of the transmission of the "learning of the tao."[122] Chou Tun-i (1017–73) recovered the tao that had not been transmitted since Mencius and passed it on to the brothers Ch'eng Hao (1032–85) and Ch'eng I. They shared their more perfect understanding with their uncle Chang Tsai (1020–77). This scheme Chu called the *tao-t'ung*, the "unified succession of the tao" or "line of continuity with the tao."[123] Participation in the tao-t'ung made one a successor to the moral authority of the sages. The concept surely came from the term *cheng-t'ung*, used for a line of legitimate dynastic succession, but it denied the paramount importance of political institutions.[124]

Chu Hsi helped transform Tao-hsueh into an influential movement in which this narrow view of the origins was an item of dogma. In conversation, however, Chu Hsi sometimes adopted a broader perspective in which a group of men who came to national attention in the mid-eleventh century appeared to be on the right track. For example:

Someone asked, ". . . how could the flourishing of Tao-hsueh in this dynasty be a sudden event?

The Teacher [Chu Hsi] said, "There was also a gradual aspect to it. Beginning with Fan [Chung-yen] Wen-cheng, there were good [essays of] opinion. For example, in Shantung there was Sun [Fu] Ming-fu, in Ts'u-lai there was Shih [Chieh] Shou-tao, and in Hu-chou there was Hu [Yuan] An-ting. Later there were the Masters Chou, Ch'eng, and Chang. Therefore the Masters Ch'eng never dared forget these several gentlemen and always honored them. As for such as Yang [I] and Liu [Yun] who composed in an ornate parallel style, they were no comparison.[125]

These men were not necessarily at odds with true learning, Chu suggests. But how did Fan Chung-yen (989–1052), Sun Fu (992–1057), Hu Yuan (993–1059), and Shih Chieh (1005–45) contribute to it? Here and elsewhere they are placed in the context of literary developments (their essays in ku-wen style) as well as later philosophical developments. Yang and Liu were famed literary men of the early eleventh century, whose literary model Fan, Sun, Shih, and others rejected in favor of the work of Han Yü. They were still concerned with writing, Chu admits, but the writing of such men as Hu, Sun, Ch'en Hsiang (1017–80), and others pointed in the direction of the Ch'engs.[126]

Chu's broader, historical view is in service of a narrow point. The same can be said of the *Case Studies* account of Northern Sung intellectual trends. It does not begin with the tao-t'ung, yet its premise is that Sung Learning began to flourish once Tao-hsueh was established. It begins with two chapters on the Northern Sung thinkers Hu Yuan, Sun Fu, and Shih Chieh.[127] Ch'üan Tsu-wang justifies devoting his first chapter to Hu and his followers on the grounds that Hu and Sun "were the first stream in the rise of Sung Learning. Both Master Ch'eng and Master Chu said so." The *Case Studies* quotes a statement from one Liu I (1017–86) that has Hu defining the tao in terms of "substance, function, and literary manifestation" (t'i, yung, and wen). I do not think this scheme should be used to divide up eleventh-century thought.[128] Hu comes first because he was "more pure" and recognized the quality of Ch'eng I, but Hu, Shih, and Sun were supporters of the more influential Fan Chung-yen, the subject of the third chapter. Fan is here because Chu Hsi included him when he "determined the origins of scholarship."

Ch'üan notes that the inclusion of Ou-yang Hsiu (1007–72; chap. 4) is debatable, for many thought he "saw tao through wen," but adduces a quote from Ch'eng I's disciple Yang Shih (1053–1135) to justify Ou-yang's inclusion. In the 1040's Fan Chung-yen claimed that Ou-yang was the authority for ku-wen. He did "see tao through wen," but who among these early figures did not? Ch'üan uses Ch'en Hsiang (1017–80) and others (chap. 5) and various regional teachers (chap. 6) to suggest that the first generation had its echo. None of them were terribly influential. He includes Ssu-ma Kuang (1019–86; chaps. 7–8) and Shao Yung (1011–77; chaps. 9–10) because Ch'eng I pronounced both to be "unadulterated." Their numerological studies are introduced (chaps. 8, 10) but said not to be their real contribution. Shao, in contrast to the figures named above was a very marginal figure (and interesting because of that). Ssu-ma was both the greatest historian in the Northern Sung and a chief councillor in 1086. He patronized Ch'eng I without apparently agreeing with his philosophy. Shao was befriended by Ch'eng, Ssu-ma, and others in Lo-yang in the 1070's.

Chou Tun-i (chaps. 11–12) is the first to "truly enter the sage's room," although Ch'üan notes evidence against Chu Hsi's assertion that the Ch'engs began from Chou's ideas. With Ch'eng Hao (chaps. 13–14) and Ch'eng I (chaps. 15–16), we have now reached the two men in Northern Sung free of error. Chang Tsai (chaps. 17–18) was not always on the right track, but he shared the same basis as the Ch'engs. Chu Hsi had Chang Tsai learning from the Ch'engs; the reverse is more likely. Having reached the correct thinkers, Ch'üan turns in chapters 19–31 to those who followed in their footsteps. At the end of the book, he introduces Wang An-shih (1021–86; chap. 98) and the Su family (chap. 99): Su Hsun (1009–66) and his sons, Su Shih (1037–1101) and Su Ch'e (1039–1112). They are at the end because they opposed that to which men of true goodwill would "return."

Ch'üan Tsu-wang's account of the rise of Sung Learning is retrospective. He treats eleventh-century intellectual developments in terms of their contribution to the emergence of the Ch'eng-Chu school or their affinity with it, justifying his inclusions by adducing positive comments by members of that school. In my view, the *Case Studies* cannot serve as a reliable account of the intellectual history of the eleventh century. Yet its schema helps explain why many have lumped earlier figures together in the broad categories of Neo-Confucianism and Sung Learning and why accounts of Sung intellectual history usually begin in the early 1030's. Because we would not speak of Neo-Confucianism or Sung Learning were it not for the triumph of Tao-hsueh, it is anachronistic to speak of earlier figures as Neo-Confucians.[129]

The notion that a "correct learning" or "Confucian revival," led by Hu Yuan, Sun Fu and others, began trends leading to the Ch'eng-Chu school has been widely accepted.[130] Important aspects of both the narrow and broad views have been challenged, however. It is clear that the tao-t'ung thesis of transmission from Chou to the Ch'engs is neither historically tenable, as Ch'üan Tsu-wang noted, nor philosophically plausible.[131] Indeed, careful analysis of the so-called Tao-hsueh masters of the eleventh century has demonstrated that they lacked a shared philosophical system.[132] Some surveys have recognized that the *Case Studies* is inadequate as an account of who was influential and representative. This is especially true for the late eleventh century, a time of both intellectual debate and political factionalism, when Wang An-shih, Ssu-ma Kuang, Su Shih, and Ch'eng I all thought of themselves as teachers to all the shih, as some surveys recognize.[133]

The eleventh-century intellectuals that later generations defined as participants in the tao-t'ung did not constitute a single, self-conscious school. Nor were they the only intellectuals that influenced their times. Ch'eng I, historically the most important philosopher of the Northern Sung period, was in his own day one of several men with persuasive ideas. The story of Sung thought need not begin with Hu Yuan and Sun Fu simply because Ch'eng I spoke well of them. As James T. C. Liu has shown, Fan Chung-yen and Ou-yang Hsiu were intellectually prominent in the 1030's, well before Hu and Sun were summoned to teach at the capital.[134] An even larger issue is whether the perspective of Tao-hsueh is useful in considering any early figure. Ch'ien Mu, for example, notes that the early Sung intellectual world included educators, poets, historians, classicists, idealists, activists, and recluses. Compared with the later adherents of Tao-hsueh, they were far more engaged in literature, political reform, and wide-ranging scholarship.[135] In the study of Sung intellectual change, we need to account for these interests, if only to understand why they were challenged and why the center of intellectual life shifted to the philosophical and ethical concerns of Tao-hsueh.

2 The Transformation of the Shih

The T'ang dynastic order was built upon pre-existing interests and imposed upon them the hierarchies of political, social, and ritual authority necessary to create a unified system and preserve the dynastic house.[1] The fracturing of political authority in the eighth and ninth centuries, however, brought with it new administrative structures, different relations between political power and private wealth, and a new array of participants in struggles for power. The gradual collapse of the T'ang order meant the disintegration of national hierarchies of power, status, and wealth upon which the shih, who had begun the dynasty as an assemblage of aristocratic clans, had come to depend. The interests from which the Sung founders molded their state were no longer those that the Sui and T'ang had found at the end of the sixth and beginning of the seventh centuries. When the shih re-emerged as the social and political elite in the Northern Sung, they were no longer an aristocracy. This chapter will pursue three questions. Why did the shih as aristocratic great clans fail to outlast the T'ang after surviving the fall of earlier dynasties? Why did the shih re-emerge as a national elite of scholarly civil bureaucrats in the early Northern Sung? And why, in the course of the Sung, did the shih become local elites of literati?

"Shih" was a concept used to think about the sociopolitical order; at the same time, it referred to an element in that society. "Shih" as a concept was a socially constructed idea that those who called themselves shih held. The transformation of the shih thus can analytically be separated into changes in the way shih conceived of being a shih and shifts in the social makeup of the men who called themselves shih. As a concept, being a shih meant possessing qualities thought appropriate to membership in the sociopolitical elite. The concept changed when the qualities thought to make men shih changed, through addition and subtraction, through redefinition of a particular quality, or through a shift in the relative value of constituent qualities.

Between 600 and 1200, the three most important categories for defining the qualities that made men shih were culture, birth, and office holding. In 600 good birth meant having a good pedigree; that is, being born into a clan with a pedigree of high officeholders. In practice, good birth outweighed whatever at that moment counted as culture, and pedigree was the normative ground for gaining high office. By 1200 the quality of birth had been redefined, and an illustrious pedigree was no longer important. In 1200 "culture" outweighed birth (although what being cultured meant in 1200 was quite different from what it had meant in 600), and education was the normative ground for gaining high office. Similarly, the meaning and importance of government service relative to culture and birth were not constant.

Changes in the conception of shih were further complicated by disagreements over the content of the idea. For example, Yen Chih-t'ui's polemical contention that culture should matter more than government service was aimed at men with illustrious pedigrees who he believed were selling out to conquerors who cared little about culture. In order to make clear when and how the term is used in various documents, and as a reminder that the term itself allowed those who called themselves shih to see greater continuity with the past than was warranted, I do not translate it. Were I to translate the concept, I would need to take into account the dominant quality in the prevailing conception of shih and thus render it "aristocrat" from the Period of Division into the ninth century, "scholar-official" from the ninth century into the late Northern Sung, and "literatus" from the late Northern Sung on.

As a social group, the men who called themselves shih, together with their daughters and wives, were for most of the period the primary elite in the polity, thanks largely to their success in dominating the administrative apparatus. Members of this elite distinguished themselves from other kinds of people in numerous ways and sought to ensure that their offspring would continue to be seen as shih (or would continue to be seen as possessing the qualities of shih). A high birthrate and limited official posts probably made it impossible for them to prevent all their descendants from sliding into the ranks of the general populace. However, analysis of the kinship relationships of those recognized as shih over the generations leads to the conclusion that there was great continuity for extended periods. The shih were a self-perpetuating set of families, from which members fell but into which relatively few men from non-shih families climbed. There were exceptions to this. When the central government was weak and local power was in the hands of non-shih, during the late T'ang and the Five Dynasties period, for example, two things happened to a greater extent than usual. First, shih families in many places lost their standing as the primary elite, and the idea that the shih were the superior

TABLE I
The Transformation of the Shih

	T'ang	Northern Sung	Southern Sung
Quality of the elite	Aristocrats (birth)	Scholar-officials (service)	Literati (culture)
As social element	Great clans	Civil-bureaucratic families	Local elites

group in society ceased to be true in practice. Second, with their loss of command over economic and political resources, they lost the ability to prevent others from claiming to be shih as well. Government institutions could also encourage (or discourage) changes in both the social group and the conception. As a term for the social element, "shih" can be translated "great clans" for most of the T'ang, "civil bureaucratic families" for the Northern Sung, and "local elites" during the Southern Sung.

These transformations in the dominant quality in the prevailing conception of the shih and in the nature of the shih as an element in Chinese society can be represented through translation as shown in Table 1. This schema must be taken with many qualifications, both those alluded to in the preceding paragraphs and those that will become evident in the course of this chapter. These intellectual and social changes are connected to institutional developments that are related to formal changes in dynastic rule, but they should not be correlated exactly with dynastic transitions. Nevertheless, this represents my understanding of the transformations of the shih during the six centuries from the T'ang dynasty through the Sung.

In this chapter I am concerned with the conception of shih as a group within society and the position and makeup of the shih as a group. I try to define the changes that took place and account for them. At moments of social dislocation and political change, the concept "shih" was most fluid, and references to being a shih abound in writings. But a change in conception may not entail a change in membership. For example, there are good reasons to think that most of the local elites of the Southern Sung descended from the "civil bureaucrats" of the Northern Sung. Nevertheless, even if it could be demonstrated that all shih families of 1200 descended from the shih clans of 600, a change in the qualities that constituted the conception of shih—who they thought they were and why they thought they were it—has a direct bearing on the role those families played in society, the attitudes that guided the political actions of officials, and the culture they created for themselves. The conception of shih was, in essence, the definition of the shared values of the shih as a social group.

The need for an integrated intellectual and social history of the shih is evident in the fact that being a shih involved both conceptions of elite status and the social and political realities of elite life. Yet the study of Chinese history has amply demonstrated that it is possible to approach either in isolation. A single chapter treating social change through six centuries, apart from the intellectual developments examined in the seven chapters that follow, does little to redress the lack of integration in historical studies.

A note on the three concerns that have prompted me to separate the social from the intellectual will help explain the role of the present chapter. The first is a practical issue: dividing this discussion into chronological segments suitable for inclusion in later chapters would obscure the account of long-term social change and thus make the explanations for those changes difficult to follow. Second, the explanations proposed here for social transitions, in which the elite's concern with maintaining shih status is a major factor, do not adequately account for intellectual change. Moreover, although I see important connections between social, political, and intellectual developments, I do not suppose that social interests determine ideas or that ideas determine social interests. Seeing the ku-wen idea that shih could figure out overarching values through learning as one possible response to the breakdown of T'ang unity and the failure of the great clan system, for example, does not explain why ku-wen leaders were so concerned with literary style. Similarly, seeing that greater involvement in the local community was one possible implication of Tao-hsüeh teachings does not explain why Southern Sung local elites devoted so much energy to the examination system. By explaining social change separately, I hope to avoid reductionist and determinist explanations of intellectual life. This brings me to the third and most crucial issue. The research of others on T'ang and Sung elites and institutions has made it possible to write on the social transformation of the shih at a fairly high level of generalization. But laying the groundwork for new generalizations about intellectual developments has entailed the research on T'ang and Sung intellectual culture detailed in later chapters. There is an inevitable imbalance, thus, between the level of discussion of intellectual and social history. This imbalance is increased once we attempt to account for intellectual change, for understanding what scholars intended and how they interpreted the particular scholarly trends and political events they were responding to involves inquiring into the lives and works of individuals. Once the course of intellectual history in the T'ang and Sung is established, it will become possible to show in a general sense how intellectual trends were related to social transformations. Later chapters will return to these social transformations and the explanations for them proposed below.

Aristocracy and Its Demise in the T'ang

The clan as a form of social organization was common to both the Chinese elite and foreign conquering minorities. The early T'ang political leadership was largely an oligarchy of great clans from the northwest, with sinified foreign clans and mixed Chinese-foreign clans (the imperial clan being an example) as well. The T'ang inherited a society in which the shih as the Chinese elite existed as clans of various levels of importance. The *Sui History* tells of the situation in the north.

When the Later Wei [386–534] moved [the capital] to Lo[-yang, thus beginning the Eastern Wei (535–50)], there were eight lineages [*shih*] and ten surnames [*hsing*], all from the imperial clan [*ti tsu*]. Further there were the 36 clans [*tsu*], all of the states [*kuo*] following the Wei, and the 92 surnames, [of those] serving as hereditary chiefs of the subtribes [*pu-lo ta-jen*]. All became Ho-nan Lo-yang men. As for the Chinese *shih-jen*, [the Wei] ranked their clan status [*men-fa*]. There were the great surnames of the nation [*ssu-hai ta-hsing*], the commandery surnames, the prefectural surnames, and the subprefectural surnames. When T'ai-tsu of the Chou [506–57] entered the pass, all those descendants of the various surnames that had merit [in the campaign against the Western Wei (535–56)] were ordered to become their clan leaders [*tsung-chang*] and, further, to write their genealogies to record their descent. In addition, he made the various prefectures [in the territory] within [i.e., west of] the pass their place of registration.

In other words, the Wei formally recognized clans, making a general distinction between those affiliated with the imperial clan, those of its non-Han allies, and those of the shih. The Wei ranked the shih surnames by associating them with various administrative levels from state to subprefecture. The Chou founder rewarded his meritorious supporters by recognizing them as heads of their clans, formally establishing their genealogies, and giving them (new) choronyms.[2]

Irrespective of how non-Chinese the early T'ang may have been, however, the ruling house did not see itself as foreign and did not, in contrast to earlier dynasties in the north, defend the privileges of a conquering ethnic minority. But like the Wei and Chou rulers, T'ang emperors claimed the right to rank the great clans. There is evidence that the T'ang saw the shih and the great clans as one and the same; hence, its national clan rankings simultaneously served to list those clans it recognized politically and to distinguish the shih from the commonalty. To ask why aristocracy declined is, in effect, to ask how the equation of the great clans with the shih broke down.[3]

"Aristocracy" as a term is useful for its implication that social worth and the right to govern come by virtue of birth. By and large the T'ang founders accepted the idea of aristocratic clans with the right to political office. Following the Sui practice, the T'ang insisted that in principle this right existed at the court's pleasure, that in contrast to pre-Sui tradition the court would decide who would gain office and title, and that the prestige of the clans would depend upon what their members did for the empire.[4] In effect, it worked to make the survival of aristocracy a function of bureaucracy. For example, the T'ang "nobility" inherited noble titles from an ancestor who gained it by virtue of his service to the dynasty or close imperial kinship.[5] T'ang officials of the fifth rank and above in the nine-rank system had the right to make sons and grandsons eligible for appointment to office, but the appointment required that the son pass the selection process of the Ministry of Personnel. Such social and economic privileges as tax and labor service exemptions could be inherited, but in theory this right was limited to those whose father and/or paternal grandfather had held office.[6]

Yet, as David Johnson has shown, the medieval Chinese oligarchy of great clans continued in the T'ang. The *New T'ang History* calculates that the 369 T'ang chief ministers were descended from only 98 clans (*tsu*). And while editor Ou-yang Hsiu is anxious to make clear that the rise and fall of families "also depended on their descendants," he acknowledges that ministers were concerned with maintaining their family traditions and prided themselves on the prestige of their clans.[7] Government, it seems, recognized that social status was not simply a function of office holding. A lower percentage of the highest civil offices was held by members of the great clans in the T'ang than in dynasties during the Period of Division, but the percentage was still so high, about 60 percent,[8] that we may easily grant the two possibilities implicit in Ou-yang Hsiu's comments: the most illustrious families were better able to produce men with the traits thought desirable for the highest officials, and high social standing was of great value in rising to high office.

By the end of the eighth century, however, the situation had begun to change, and the nature of the T'ang system was interpreted variously. Liu Mien (d. ca. 806), who wanted to see a return to the ancient model of esteeming virtue and moral instruction in choosing officials, contrasted the valuing of surname and clan in the Period of Division with the T'ang's continuation of the Sui practice of "valuing the way of administration" and "honoring official rank."[9] In contrast, his contemporary Wang Yen preferred to raise aristocratic self-consciousness. In a stele for his eighteenth-generation ancestor, he boasted that when "the Later Wei defined the shih clans, all thought T'ai-yuan Wang was the foremost choronym in the world." As advice for his own times, he cited a Chin ancestor's admonition that if for three generations they should "neither serve nor learn nor tend to their clients, fail to marry [with the right families] and maintain the genealogy, fail to hold proper burials and maintain the graves, and not cultivate benevolence," they would sink to being *hsiao-jen*.[10] Wang Yen's efforts turned out to be in vain, although they probably struck a chord for many in his day, because in the process of perpetuating the medieval oligarchy the T'ang had also transformed it.

A T'ang great clan existed as a collection of families (*chia*) sharing the combination of what Johnson has called choronym, placename, and surname, such as T'ai-yuan Wang, Chao-chün Li, and Po-ling Ts'ui. Families belonged to a clan because they could trace descent from a common founder. The T'ang clan did not itself hold real property as a corporate entity, it did not have a single graveyard, it did not live in one place, and it was unlikely to have an ancestral temple for the clan as a whole. The first official ranking of clans, the *Great T'ang Record of Clans* (*Ta T'ang shih-tsu chih*), a 200-*chüan* work compiled in 638, recognized 293 choronyms and 1,651 families. It is not certain what "family" meant as a unit of the clan. Possibly it referred to the existing "mourning circles" (*wu-fu*), the group of kin included within the five degrees of mourning relative to a particular individual. Because the mourning circle did not extend beyond five generations, the clan would segment further and new "families" would appear with each new generation after the fifth.[11]

The lack of interest in providing for the welfare of all descendants distinguishes the great clan from the "lineages" that began to emerge among Sung shih-ta-fu. As Patricia Ebrey's study of the Po-ling Ts'uis and David Johnson's of the Chao-chün Lis indicate, the constituent families of T'ang great clans no longer had a common home base of extensive landholdings to fall back on, much less a body of armed retainers.[12] T'ang great clan families did not need to think about such matters as long as they could be fairly sure that their males were likely to have bureaucratic careers. Service meant income, both salary and land grants; thus the assumption of continued service made corporate property unnecessary. But since service required submitting to the selection process at the capital, families tended to move to Changan and Loyang. Finally, since service was essential to maintaining the prestige of the choronym, those families that failed to place successive generations of males in bureaucratic careers and had to live off the land, for example, tended to lose their presence in the clan until such time as they regained official careers. Nevertheless, the clan did hold a form of common property with a negotiable value: its pedigree. The concrete means with which families in a great clan perpetuated their pedigree was the shared genealogical record, which gave descent lines, noted officeholders and their ranks, and recorded marriages. It was a selective record, however; families failing to attain office and establish notable marriage alliances could disappear from the records. [13]

The continued value of a great clan pedigree depended upon others valuing the families who had it. Clearly the T'ang government, led by the imperial Lung-hsi Li clan, did value pedigree in practice. Independent of political authority, however, great clan families had long had ways of maintaining their exclusivity and making further distinctions of worth among themselves. The most obvious mechanism for doing so was to maintain marriage alliances with families like their own. The Po-ling Ts'uis, one of the famous four clans "east of the mountains" in Hopei, drew the great majority of their known marriage partners from a group of 29 families with pedigrees going back to the Northern and Southern Dynasties. For emperors concerned with their authority and the supremacy of their court in the sociopolitical world, exclusive marriage alliances were a social, and thus political, insult. [14] At the same time, as funerary inscriptions make clear, great clan families insisted that their worth derived from the ability of their members to maintain their family's high standards of learning and morality. They were the best, in other words, because they were best at preserving and continuing cultural traditions. Inscriptions praised the subject for "not losing the learning of ju," for achievement in "wen-hsueh," for "maintaining ju conduct," and so on, and observed that the shih of the day admired the man in question. [15] Similarly, the Po-ling Ts'uis reminded others that their members were worthy because of their learning, literary accomplishment, and high standards of ethical conduct. [16] At least in the early T'ang and before, when cultural continuity did depend on family continuity to a great extent, this was a well-grounded justification.

With hindsight it seems clear that the creation of an enduring political order required placing the institutional interests of the state above clan interests and forcing those with political roles to act accordingly. The T'ang took over a social world represented by clusters of great clans from the northwest (Kuan-chung), the northeast, northern Shansi, and the south. It also inherited the effort to increase the court's leverage over clans through clan rankings and the control of office holding. [17] To a greater extent than the Sui, however, the T'ang made a point of accommodating great clans from all areas. An attitude of aristocratic collegiality pervaded Kao-tsu's (r. 618–26) court. [18]

Given the existing strength of great clans, it is not surprising that the imperial court saw the value of bringing all interests into a single sociopolitical hierarchy. The creation of national clan rankings suggests, I think, that the imposition of a centralized bureaucracy, which reserved to itself the power of appointing men to ranked office, was not by itself adequate for this purpose. The first ranking—the *Great T'ang Record of Clans*—appeared under Emperor T'ai-tsung (r. 626–49), at whose behest the rankings were revised to give greater weight to service to the T'ang. This list of 293 great clans and their 1,651 constituent families included the shih-ta-fu of all regions and thus, it was said, distinguished the shih from the commonalty, but it also graded those clans into nine ranks, paralleling the nine ranks of office.[19] Later rankings continued this trend. The 659 list, for example, was formulated according to the criterion that "those who have attained a fifth-rank office [and above] under this dynasty shall all be elevated into the shih stream [*shih-liu*]," although we are also told that the "refined shih-ta-fu" objected to this standard on the grounds that it included those who had risen to high office through military accomplishments alone. Interestingly, the 659 list reduced the total number of clans from 293 to 235, perhaps a sign that some traditionally esteemed lines had fallen from favor, yet increased the number of families from 1,651 to 2,287.[20] The clan lists thus cut both ways, recognizing certain families as having a claim on political power by virtue of their pedigree while diluting the pool with outsiders who had attained status by rising to high positions at court. Whether the most prestigious clans cared to have the court rank them or not, the court had the power to do so. It was probably better to be on than off the list in any case. We can speculate that treating high officials from obscure backgrounds as shih allowed those whose social status was not in question to marry with the newly risen without being accused of adulterating their family line with commoners.

In the 638 and 659 lists, the shih were a very select group of families, smaller than the total number of families providing officials. In the 659 list the "shih stream" is limited to those families with members who had attained office sufficiently high to qualify for the *yin* privilege to place the current generation of sons in the bureaucracy. It is possible, given the common distinction between those serving at court and those serving in the provinces, that in 659 those in lower-ranking provincial posts were thought of as shih only if they also could claim membership in a ranked clan. But if the term "shih" was still reserved for aristocrats in the seventh century, in the eighth century men from "provincial" families had begun to insist that they were shih as well.[21] Institutionally imperial policy did nothing to discourage this trend, for the T'ang did promote men of obscure origin. Greater inclusiveness, as in 713, allowed the court to have it both ways: it accommodated new men while asserting the importance of great clan status. Still, the line between official and aristocrat serving as official was beginning to blur. There was a reaction against the trend under Hsuan-tsung (r. 712–56), whose chief minister Li Lin-fu defended aristocratic privilege. Yet even Li expanded the list to 398 clans in 749.[22] The unified national ranking of clans apparently ended within decades of the An Lu-shan rebellion of 755.[23] The clan rankings helped maintain an aristocracy, but the inclusion of those with bureaucratic and scholarly merit and the ranking of old families by service to the T'ang undermined the idea that pedigree was the basis of worth, a notion essential to conceiving of a social elite independent of the dynasty.

What did the great clans gain from a dynasty that so valued bureaucratic service that it threatened the value of pedigree? The answer, I believe, is that the short-term interests of great clan families were served by the prospect of official service for future generations, and in return they acquiesced to the central government's control over the distribution of office. The Po-ling Ts'uis, for example, did perpetuate themselves in office.[24] An examination of T'ang institutions in the 730's shows that perpetual service was theoretically possible for many clans.[25] A review of these institutional arrangements will also show how the equation of shih with aristocrat was undermined.

The great clans could make government service their occupation for successive generations thanks to the structure of the T'ang administrative apparatus and a system of official statuses that existed alongside that apparatus. The administrative apparatus was a pyramid with four levels, the top three of which were interconnected. A man could be promoted within his level, he could transfer from a lower to a higher level, and according to his position he could place his descendants at a lower rung in his own level or in the level below. He might also be able to place descendants in one of the official status groups, many of which had no substantive role in the administrative apparatus but through which one could become eligible to enter the top level of the administrative apparatus directly. Entering the top level of the administrative hierarchy required having "eligibility" or ch'u-shen, gained either through yin privilege, service at a lower administrative level, or membership in a non-administrative official status group. I shall regard "honorable" service as service in a lower administrative level provided it fed into the top level or membership in a formally recognized group that resulted in eligibility to enter directly the top of the administrative apparatus.

The apex of the administrative pyramid was composed of "officials in the stream for promotion" (liu-nei kuan), the officials in the nine ranks usually thought of as "the officials." In 737 this group numbered 18,805, having grown from about 14,000 in 657. Being a liu-nei kuan was the highest achievement in service. Within the nine ranks there were three distinct groups. About 200 men, those in the third rank and above, had the privilege of making their sons, grandsons, and great-grandsons eligible for appointment within the lower reaches of the nine ranks. About ten times as many occupied the fourth and fifth ranks; they had similar privileges for their sons and grandsons. The total of 2,200 in the first through fifth ranks corresponds roughly to the 2,620 men serving in metropolitan positions in 737.[26] Those in the first five ranks held "pure" offices (leading positions in central organs, major scholarly offices, and the most important prefectural posts). All the immediate descendants of this group could serve, either by entering directly into the nine ranks or by becoming a member of a guard, whence they gained eligibility to "enter the stream" (*ju liu*) after a period of service. (Guard service, nominal in many instances, is an example of membership in a non-administrative status group; it carried with it legal privileges.) The total number of those entering the nine ranks through *yin* privilege in the 730's is unknown, but 10,000 descendants of officials (*p'in-tzu*) in the first five ranks had gained eligibility through guard status in 737.[27]

Below the first five ranks were some 16,000 officials in the sixth through ninth ranks. The majority of them would have held the 16,185 local-government positions existing in 737 for officials in the stream. Their sons were not eligible for selection and appointment to an office within the nine ranks. They could, however, place sons in nominal and substantive posts in various kinds of guards, the most elite being the personal guards of the emperor and heir apparent (for rank six and above) and less elite prefectural detachments of guards (especially for officials of the eighth and ninth ranks).[28] Men in these positions also became eligible to enter the stream after a period of service. The eligibility list of 737 notes about 40,000 men in such positions, although the proportion from official families is unknown. Thus ranked officials could ensure that their immediate descendants would serve as well.

Those in position to become eligible to enter the stream far exceeded the 500–600 needed annually to keep the nine ranks at full strength, a number already achieved as early as 657 and 681.[29] Eligibility did not guarantee appointment. The Ministries of Personnel and War held selection examinations for those who had gained eligibility. The selection examination tested, in order of importance, the candidate's appearance, speech, calligraphy, and ability to compose a formulaic legal decision. But the vast majority had to be turned away, in spite of the creation of supernumerary positions.[30] Losers could, however, continue to enjoy their existing status.

The administrative apparatus, however, was not limited to the nine ranks. Of particular importance was the group of senior clerks and administrators known as "officials outside the stream for promotion" (*liu-wai kuan*). They were formally selected, served in formally defined posts, usually in capital organs, and had their own system of ranks. Liu-wai kuan became eligible for transfer to low-ranking positions "within the stream" after a period of service, although in theory they were ineligible for promotion to the higher "pure" offices. The eligibility list of 737 does not refer specifically to officials outside the stream, but since the 6,000 men in clerical positions it notes were in organs where liu-wai kuan served we may assume they belonged to that group.[31] Officials outside the stream had administrative responsibilities. Of the 222 positions at the Ministry of Revenue, for example, 10 percent were for officials within the stream, 77 percent were for those outside the stream, and 13 percent were for lower-status "special-duty officials" (*fan-kuan*).[32] Service as a liu-wai kuan may have provided sons of ranked officials unable to enter through the yin privilege a means of staying in government and entering the stream on their own. It also provided other families with a means of gaining a foothold in government.

Beneath the liu-wai kuan ranks was another group, the clerical service, working mainly in the prefectures and subprefectures and commonly known as fan-kuan. At one time a first-grade prefecture, with a complement of eighteen officials within the nine ranks, was entitled to make 150 such appointments, or 65 percent of its staff, whereas a major subprefecture could appoint 77 fan-kuan, or 72 percent of its total staff. Presumably the 57,416 "clerks" (*li*) recorded in 733 were what other sources call fan-kuan.[33] The social background of these special-duty officials is unknown. They were locally appointed and were literate; it is likely both that they came from leading local families, perhaps from provincial clans, and that some families used this kind of service to enter the bureaucracy. The fan-kuan were probably a major source of officials outside the stream. Beneath the fan-kuan were the special-duty employees (*fan-i*), scribes, runners, tax hasteners, and so on. Although the legislated number of fan-i was less than special-duty officials, they totaled nearly 300,000 in 733.[34]

Thus of the 370,000 men directly involved in the administrative apparatus in the 730's, about 70,000 were *kuan* (officials) in some sense, with the lower 50,000 having some hope of entering the nine ranks. Clerical positions could provide a cushion for a family in decline and a springboard for its re-emergence, as Ebrey's study of the Po-ling Ts'ui illustrates.[35] It also provided career opportunities for non-shih provincial families. But those gaining eligibility to enter the nine ranks through professional administrative careers were a minority of all those eligible to do so. By the 730's these statuses together were pouring applicants into the selection process at the rate of about 2,000 annually, in spite of the lack of vacant offices. It is not clear which group had the greatest advantage, although some have held that the liu-wai kuan may have.[36] By Tu Yu's estimate, eight to nine men were competing for every vacancy within the stream.[37]

In the list of 737, those in eligible categories total 137,000 men. These included 10,000 sons of ranked officials, 40,000 guards, 8,000–16,000 civil and military clerks, and over 60,000 students.[38] Thus the larger T'ang official system could indeed absorb the offspring of the great clans, given the numbers on the lists, although it could not place them all in the nine ranks. However, the same institutional arrangements that provided categories of service and eligibility for the sons of good families also allowed the sons of other families to enter some form of service and rise through the ranks. The T'ang system thus opened the possibility that membership in an eligibility group and lower-level service would allow one to claim to be a shih. There is evidence that in the late 730's some in government were promoting the view that shih were to be distinguished from farmers, artisans, and merchants as all those drawing an official salary or preparing for a civil or a military career.[39] The clans could be the best shih but, by the 730's, they were no longer the only ones who could consider themselves shih.

The category of 60,000 registered "students" is of particular interest. As a recruitment mechanism, the T'ang examination system was of minor importance. The prestigious literary examination (*chin-shih*) rarely graduated more than 30 men a year; by Twitchett's calculation it could hardly have staffed more than 2.5 percent of the ranked positions in 737; the Classics examination (*ming-ching*) produced about twice as many. At its height, in the ninth century, degree holders may have totaled 15 percent of officials within the stream.[40] Passing the examinations was not an easy way to gain eligibility compared to other kinds of service and status-group membership,[41] but a degree made passing the Ministry of Personnel's selection examination and being appointed to office fairly certain. Moreover, although prefectural students might be disadvantaged relative to students from the capital, they did get to attend the metropolitan examination and make connections with the powerful.[42] A degree also made one eligible for "pure" offices, usually reserved for men of good birth, thus helping provincial families break out of the rut of low-ranking provincial service.[43] Even such families whose clan status was not in doubt, such as the Po-ling Ts'uis, found that the examinations gave them an edge in competing against the offspring of similar families.[44] We may speculate that being a registered student was valuable even when a student did not get a degree. It could have been a holding pattern for the sons of all families of means, a way of acquiring a bit of capital culture, and, above all, a means of forging connections. Achievements in learning could be demonstrated whether one passed or not and attract those seeking men for staff positions. However we account for the pool of students, its existence is a sign that many thought being a student had social value.

Valuing a talent for learning was understood to challenge the claim that pedigree alone could qualify men for office. It had also become a factional issue under Hsuan-tsung.[45] During the first half of Hsuan-tsung's reign, for example, literary scholars like Chang Yueh held leading offices at court. Chang's biography records that he "brought in shih who were cultured ju" to raise the political ethos and denigrated those officials who lacked learning and literary talent.[46] Given the numbers eligible to enter the stream of ranked officials in 737, any favor shown to men whose claims rested on learning alone could come only at the expense of those who, having entered through privilege, claimed pure office by virtue of their pedigree. This had begun to happen, as suggested by the inclusion of the families of those with scholarly attainment, in addition to the good families, on the clan list of 713. Once culture was no longer exclusive to some great clans, it was possible to think of a shih as one who had acquired or was acquiring the learning necessary to serve in government, irrespective of family background.

The institutional arrangements allowed great clan families to perpetuate themselves as the elite, without being able to guarantee office in the nine ranks to their descendants. At the same time, these institutions created a formally recognized pool of the politically involved that was many times larger than the body of officials in the nine ranks. The proportion of the 137,000 listed in 737 that came from families on the clan lists is unknown, but it is hard to see how the 398 clans listed in 749, even if they included several thousand constituent families, could have accounted for the total number. If those in this pool could think of themselves as shih, without belonging to a ranked family, then great clan status and shih status were no longer the same. With so many oriented toward state service and capable of filling administrative and cultural roles in the state, claims to pedigree could appear as little more than self-serving justifications for the monopolization of power by aristocrats in general or by any one group among the aristocracy. The attributes that once had set the great clans apart—their political and administrative traditions, their culture, and their ethical standards—were no longer unique to them. The An Lu-shan rebellion and the rise of provincial power released this pressure and eventually made the claim to pedigree irrelevant.[47]

How this happened can now be stated quite briefly. The rise of provincial power, in particular the rise of independent governors whose power rested on their control over troops and local revenues, the growth of the armies, and the increasing importance of fiscal organs with the power of appointment offered opportunities for the many whose talents exceeded their positions. Often independent, frequently unsympathetic to the interests of the court and regular bureaucracy, provincial governors regularly usurped the power of appointment, assigning substantive functions to local men and army officers outside the T'ang recruitment system.[48] The An Lu-shan rebellion immediately deprived the court of its major revenue base, the taxpaying households: in 755 there had been about nine million; in 760 the court could not claim even two million.[49] The provincial governors' claims on local resources further hindered fiscal recovery. The state's inability to control trade or landholding left the private accumulation of wealth and land unrestrained, undermining its tax base. This further disturbed the social order, as new families used wealth to compete with the old, and it undermined political authority, as families found that they could gain wealth without first gaining political acceptance. The powerful financial commissions tried to adjust to the new realities by taxing commerce and total family wealth and, in so doing, allowed the privatization of the economy to continue. In addition, they created their own semi-autonomous bureaucracies. During the century after the rebellion, then, the court's bureaucratic hierarchy ceased to correspond to the realities of political power and the distribution of wealth in the empire.[50] Finally, although the provincial governors did not deny T'ang sovereignty, the area over which the court had substantial influence was greatly reduced. The northeastern governors, for example, maintained their autonomous control over much of the North China plain after the rebellion was suppressed. Increasingly the court, in the northwest, depended on Huai-nan, the area south of the Huai River, and Chiang-nan, the vast region south of the Yangtze, now the destination for a refugee stream of rich families, bureaucrats, and aristocrats.[51]

No doubt some of the men who found careers under provincial power-holders came from families outside the pool of traditional servitors, but the frustrated excess sons with little prospect of rising to central positions and the special-duty officials locked into ignominious provincial careers were a more likely source. In any case, the decentralization of power meant the end of a single national bureaucratic hierarchy dominated by families with a pedigree. A plethora of provincial hierarchies, led by governors whose survival depended on the loyalty and competence of their subordinates, came into existence alongside the court-based hierarchy. In this context the prestige of a man's choronym had far less value. At the court men from great families dominated the highest positions to a greater extent than before 755,[52] but the place of their families in the larger world of the T'ang was limited by the narrow authority of the court itself. Great clan families who worked for provincial powerholders were not helping preserve aristocracy; they were securing their own fortunes. Without a local economic base, independent military power, or special abilities, the great clans could exist as a uniquely privileged group only as long as the court controlled office and wealth. For a social elite to have substance, there had to be a social hierarchy. For some, to be sure, the survival of the T'ang court represented the possibility of restoring that hierarchy with the great clans as its apex. The fall of the T'ang in 907 left men who valued their pedigree at the mercy of rulers who did not share their pretensions. Yet both the idea that there should be shih and a social group of families with educated men oriented toward state service survived.

In his study of the Chao-chün Lis, Johnson argues that the Lis survived so long after they had lost their independence because the great clans represented an idea of social order. "So in a sense the Chao-chün Lis continued to exist because contemporaries, in their need for a clearly defined social elite, would not let them disappear. The old social system, in which status was determined by both family and office, had not yet been wholly replaced by the new system, in which office alone built up high status. As long as the old attitudes persisted, there was a need for 'great clans.' "[53] The great clan itself was a cultural construct, and this, Johnson points out, was its greatest weakness. "Yet the clan—the clan as an idea rather than as a biological entity—was vulnerable just because in the end it was no more than an idea. It was an idea without strong institutions to embody it. And it was an idea which had never developed an ideological foundation."[54] Ebrey, in her study of the Po-ling Ts'uis, points to a different side of this. Aristocrats became vulnerable because they claimed to be the elite by virtue of their achievements rather than through "overt glorification of their birth." Thus they opened the way for others to imitate them.

Another ideal frequently evoked was that of the *shih-ta-fu*, the cultured gentleman official. In the Southern Dynasties the aristocrats considered themselves the *shih*, giving the term exclusive and hereditary connotations which the Northern aristocrats continued to make use of in the Sui and T'ang. Yet *shih* remained an ambiguous term; it referred to the highest social stratum, but how narrow a stratum was open to changing perceptions. Unless the aristocrats could prevent others from imitating their ways, reference to their cultural excellence was an inadequate source of legitimacy. Others could also claim to be *shih*.[55]

In this view aristocrats as shih were engaged in a basic contradiction: they wished to be seen as the best families because of their cultural attainments, but by basing claims to status on culture they allowed others to claim they were just as good.

But perhaps the clan as idea did have an ideological justification, although not a moral-philosophical one, and clan families did have a source of legitimacy even when those without their pedigree rivaled their cultural attainments. The issue is the same in both cases. What justified the distinct status of the great clans was the value government and society attached to a long and illustrious pedigree. But the attachment to pedigree was simply a particular manifestation of a more general attachment to "tradition" that pervaded T'ang politics, society, and culture and was equally true for the "Confucian" shih, Buddhist monks, and Taoist priests. An attachment to tradition implied that the past should guide the present and that men with the longest and best pasts would be the best guides for the present. Scholars from such families could generalize the value of scholarship, as Yen Chih-t'ui did, while still claiming that men like him, by virtue of their family traditions, had received the standards by which cultural attainment was to be judged. The problem was that the T'ang, although a conservative dynasty, created a unified sociopolitical order that would preserve tradition, refine it, and extend its goods to all. In a sense, it shifted the focus from preserving tradition to acquiring traditions, so that even men without pedigree came to think that they could share the traditions of the shih.

From this vantage the diminution in the value of pedigree was part of the general erosion in the value attached to tradition. The military governors that arose were, at worst, hostile to tradition and all it entailed and, at best, far weaker than the court in their commitment to it. But after the rebellion scholars also questioned the value of continuing their political, social, and cultural traditions, just as new Ch'an sects in Buddhism questioned the value of tradition within Buddhism. The demise of T'ang brought to a close the medieval world that had begun in the Wei-Chin period. The Five Dynasties made a return to that world impossible, while leaving open the door to the creation of a new order in society and state.

The Sung Founding and The Re-emergence of the Shih

By the first decades of the eleventh century, the shih had become the sociopolitical elite of the Sung. But in the 930's, in the midst of the Five Dynasties in the north and the Ten Kingdoms in the south, this could not necessarily have been predicted. The Sung founders singled out the shih, among all the groups involved in government and politics, as the recipients of their special favor and institutionalized that patronage. To understand why the founders patronized the shih, we need to know both their aims and what had happened to the shih as a conception and as a social group once good pedigree ceased to be a negotiable commodity.

The Sung founders, the brothers Chao K'uang-yin (Emperor T'ai-tsu, r. 960–76) and Chao K'uang-i (Emperor T'ai-tsung, r. 976–97) were military men, their most important allies were military men, and they had matured in a world in which a man's political power was closely and obviously connected to his control over military forces. Wang Gungwu and Edmund H. Worthy, Jr., have demonstrated that some of the political institutions most vital for the unification of north China originated in provincial military governments or in organs that had allowed non-bureaucrats to usurp bureaucratic authority. Wang has shown how the military governors who became Five Dynasties emperors transformed the retainers used to manage the provincial administration into palace commissioners with wide-ranging civil and military authority. He has also traced the transformation of the governor's private army into the Emperor's Army (*shih-wei ch'in-chün*), capable of absorbing the armies of other military governors, and the creation of the Palace Corps (*tien-ch'ien chün*) under imperial control to defend against the threats of the Emperor's Army.[56] Pursuing the history of these two developments into the Sung, Worthy has shown how the two Sung founders, having usurped power from the Later Chou dynasty (951–60) yet following its policies, succeeded in establishing direct control over these central institutions. With this base, they then conquered the independent states of the south and north and reasserted central control over local government and finances.[57]

Sung T'ai-tsu emerges from these events as a man remarkably adept at protecting his hold on power while increasing his exercise of it. His control over the military illustrates this. Having usurped the throne through his control over the Palace Corps, T'ai-tsu made sure no future Corps commander could copy his actions. He achieved this not by creating a new army organization but by restructuring the chain of command in the military, by leaving key posts vacant or appointing to them men of relatively low rank, and by siphoning off the best provincial troops.[58] He personally screened his officer corps and demanded that they control their subordinates. Campaign strategy was drawn up at the capital, and the expeditionary forces charged with the campaign were amalgams of forces from different commands, with supervisors reporting to the emperor independently of the field commanders.[59] The policy of dividing authority was implemented at court as well: the Bureau of Military Affairs (*Shu-mi yuan*), the pre-eminent palace commission of the Five Dynasties period, was deprived of its authority in civil affairs, and the chief ministers were denied the right to participate in military decisions.[60] Rather than dismiss the 40-odd military governors (*chieh-tu shih*) who remained, he transferred them to new regions and gradually deprived them of their subordinate prefectures; the office was soon reduced to a nominal title.[61] Worthy makes a convincing case for doubting the traditional perception of the initial stage of the Sung founding as the triumph of the civil (*wen*) over the military (*wu*), for T'ai-tsu was not reducing the military side as much as he was using the power to reward and appoint to control it. He preferred practical to cultured men, and the armies were a major source of eminently practical men of proven achievement. And yet, as Worthy points out, when his brother T'ai-tsung took the throne and completed the conquest, he showed a marked preference for the "civil."[62] He, more than T'ai-tsu, helped bring about the return of the shih.

To see why T'ai-tsung equated the "civil" with the shih and why the shih might have seemed likely candidates for institutionalizing Sung rule, we need to see where they fit in the political world of the Five Dynasties period. First, in the north, in spite of the increasing centralization of authority, men from a wide range of backgrounds rose to high political positions through various routes: personal and family connections, military service, wealth, local dominance, administrative expertise, and education were all used by those who wanted to share in political authority. Warfare and frequent changes in power, both at the level of military governor and at the center, helped keep offices open and ensured some mobility among powerful families. Prosopographical studies based on the T'ang, Five Dynasties, and Sung dynastic histories both illustrate this mobility and demonstrate that the majority of men who rose to power held military positions and came from families with traditions of military service.[63] Second, those forebears of prominent Northern Sung shih-ta-fu who held office in the late T'ang and Five Dynasties periods tended to be low-ranking local officials, prefectural staff officials, and scholar-bureaucrats at various courts. In other words, there appear to have been families, distinct from military families, at the court and prefectural levels with traditions of holding scholarly and administrative positions that required education and literary ability.[64] Third, men who by virtue of examination degrees or education held what were regarded as civil offices were regarded as shih-ta-fu and distinguished from the sorts of men holding military posts and commission appointments, although military men and commissioners had a direct say in civil affairs. In particular, military leaders saw the shih as a distinct group.[65]

But who were these shih? Many, we may assume, came from families that had produced T'ang officials, and some of these were great clan families. But with the exception of a brief attempt in the Later T'ang (923–36), a Sha-t'o Turk dynasty, there is no evidence that political authorities during this period tried to establish hierarchies of great clans.[66] The virtual disappearance of genealogies and genealogical writing indicates that even if the shih of this period did think of themselves as descendants of great clans, they saw little point in creating the records necessary to document such claims. Those in power did not see gaining the support of great families as a necessary part of establishing order, in contrast to the courts of the Northern and Southern Dynasties, which had regularly marked changes in power with the collection of genealogies and creation of new clan lists.[67] The numbers of high officials who claimed descent or can be shown to have descended from the great clans of the T'ang declined abruptly and greatly.[68] It is possible that many great clan families had been destroyed during the course of rebellions, warfare, and natural disasters or had so little access to office that they turned to other occupations. But it is just as possible that their constituent households survived but ceased to value genealogy because pedigree no longer had a negotiable value. I do not know if it is possible to demonstrate overwhelming social discontinuity on the basis of biographical records. The lack of information on distant ancestry and the failure to use old choronyms (which rarely reflected actual residence in any case) may be a function of the failure to maintain genealogies.

If the shih were not seen as a social elite of ancient families, neither were they now the leading element in politics. What gave them a separate identity? The only answer for which there is substantial evidence is that men were seen as shih by virtue of their culture and education. Nishikawa Masao, in an effort to show that the position of civil officials rose over the course of the Five Dynasties, adduces numerous textual examples supporting his equation of shih-ta-fu with *wen-ch'en* (civil officials) and *wen-jen* (literary men). The texts he cites use terms such as "shih," "shih-ta-fu," "wen-shih" (literary shih), "ju" (Classical scholar), "ju-shih," and "wen-ju" interchangeably. In the eyes of many non-shih there was a certain respectability to being a shih and there are examples of merchants, palace commissioners, and military men having their sons trained in literary and Classical learning. Some even thought the shih-ta-fu exceptional because they maintained unusually high ethical standards. There is also evidence that toward the end of the Five Dynasties those in power were encouraging men to pursue an examination education and were making more effective use of degree holders as tools of central authority.[69] Yet there are also examples of powerful men humiliating men of learning and cases of civil officials becoming military men.[70]

Thus the shih as a concept and as families of a certain kind survived through a combination of education and service, but now service tended to be limited to less powerful civil positions gained by virtue of a literary education. The shih had become a kind of cultural elite, a living remnant of the bygone T'ang perhaps, composed of families that set some store in maintaining learned traditions. They had political ambitions, but, lacking political power, their means of effectively excluding others from their ranks was limited.[71] They were of use to men with power who lacked their literary talents, knowledge of history, and repertoire of classical forms. They were good subordinates, willing to let their political aspirations depend upon those above. The existence of military families did much to set the shih apart, so much so that shih who pursued a military career, for example, lost their claim to being shih. Perhaps we should see being a shih as a career option for ambitious men who lacked armed forces or the family power to dominate the locality. In some places they were welcomed; the elegant, literary court of the Southern T'ang (937–75) is a famous example. As the Southern T'ang poet and courtier Feng Yen-chi cautioned his brother, "When shih embellish their person with wen and attend to their office, reward and honor will come; why pursue danger in the search for a salary?"[72]

When the first Sung emperors patronized the shih, I suggest, they did so because the shih were willing subordinates, without independent power, who depended on a superior authority for their political position, and who brought to their duties a commitment to the civil culture invaluable to the institutionalization of central authority. Using the shih to govern was an example, I suggest, of the imperial desire to use men with ability but without a power base. As past experience had shown, military men were useful but potentially dangerous. Retainers and commissioners were bound to their superiors by personal connections; governing an empire with them meant using the retainers of others. Finally, the continued use of the locally powerful as subprefectural officials in their native places, common practice during the Five Dynasties period,[73] could thwart measures to reassert central control over local resources. Moreover, to realize their political and social ambitions, the shih depended upon the ability of a higher authority to re-establish a national sociopolitical hierarchy and put them at its apex. Among all political elements, then, their interests came closest to the emperor's interests: both believed they would gain by the centralization of authority.

The Sung founders were probably not far off in thinking that re-establishing the imperial system was the only viable option for attaining stability and unity. Nor were the shih necessarily wrong when, after the fact, they concluded that by virtue of their moral and cultural superiority they were the only ones who could secure the Chao brothers' dynasty. Such a judgment required a rewriting of the history of the dynasty's origins to claim T'ai-tsu as one of their own, as the ruler who saw the value of wen, ju, and shih.[74] In fact, T'ai-tsu did not single out the shih-ta-fu for favor, but he created the conditions and the precedents that partially explain why his successor T'ai-tsung did advance shih interests.

Among these conditions was the dramatic increase in Sung territory, population, and administrative units. In 960 there were 111 prefectures and 638 subprefectures with a total of 967,353 registered households. In 976, the year of T'ai-tsu's death, there were 297 prefectures and 1,086 subprefectures with 2,508,960 registered households. In 982, under T'ai-tsung, there were 328 prefectures with over 1,200 subprefectures and over three million registered households.[75] T'ai-tsu moved immediately to secure control over local administration. In 962, for example, he re-established the civil administrative office of subprefectural sheriff (*hsien-wei*), a role hitherto filled by the local garrison commander. In 963 he began appointing metropolitan officials as subprefects and broadened the use of prefectural co-administrators (*t'ung-p'an*) with the specific aim of removing fiscal authority from military officials. In 962 he ordered that death sentences be reviewed at the capital.[76] When these measures were taken, the conquests had not yet begun: the court consisted of slightly over 200 civil and military officials, and control over the territory of the Later Chou was at stake. But the conquests made it impossible for T'ai-tsu to keep track of local administrative units and personally scrutinize new appointments. We do not know how many official positions there were during the first two reigns, but a well-argued estimate calculates a minimum of 1,884 and a maximum of 5,755 in 976.[77]

T'ai-tsu filled some key prefectural positions with trusted subordinates, but for the more numerous subprefectural positions he kept on the officials of the surrendered states, at times reassigning them to units in other states.[78] This was expedient, but if the government was not willing to grant prefectural officials and governors the power of appointment, new recruitment mechanisms were necessary. It is doubtful that the yin privilege could have provided enough men, given the small size of the court bureaucracy, but in any case T'ai-tsu was inclined to reduce yin and restrict the influence of the court he had inherited. Transfers from the metropolitan clerical service were still taking place, but T'ai-tsu was suspicious of the senior clerks and reduced their numbers.[79] The first emperor wanted men of ability, with experience in practical affairs, and he proposed to get them through a system of recommendation from the local level. The edict inaugurating this system in 970 reads in part: "Prefectures of all circuits are to look for those among the common people [*min*] of known filial piety, fraternal respect, and illustrious ethical conduct with reputations in their villages acknowledged by both shih and commoners. [Prefectures with] more than 15,000 registered households may recommend one man. If there are men of unusual talent and exceptional conduct, this quota may be exceeded."[80] In 975 subprefects were ordered to "look for those among the common people who can be employed, men who are filial and fraternal, who work hard at farming, and are either of unusual talent and exceptional conduct or [have knowledge of] the civil constants and military strategy."[81] Yet in 971 some 800 vacancies were reported.[82]

Because it cannot be assumed that the shih-ta-fu dominated the local scene in the 970's, we cannot assume (as we could if this edict had appeared in 1070 or 1170) that those to be recommended were from shih families. Indeed, the aim of this policy was to find men without official status who were not shih, although the opinions of shih families did count. In part this was because T'ai-tsu already had an institution specifically aimed at selecting shih to become officials: the examination system.[83] T'ai-tsu's examination policies did claim to end past abuses and to bring in scholars who lacked wealth and family connections. The institution in 973 of the Palace Examination gave the emperor the prerogative of deciding who would pass, thus wresting control over the exams from court bureaucrats intent on building their own patronage networks.[84] The policy was but another example of T'ai-tsu's attempt to centralize authority. The Palace Examination was expressly intended to establish that degrees were received from the emperor, so that those who thus became eligible for promotion to higher civil positions at court would know that he was their patron, not the chief examiner or high civil ministers. But his failure to increase the number of graduates suggests that T'ai-tsu did not see the examination system as a useful means of recruiting men to staff local government.[85]

T'ai-tsung, however, saw potential in the examination system. In 977, after announcing his intent to use the candidates as "tools for bringing about order," he immediately passed 109 chin-shih. Two days later he re-examined failed candidates in the various other fields (chu-k'o)—less prestigious tests of memorization of certain Classics, histories, ritual codes, and so on—and passed 207. He then ordered that 184 men who had failed any exam at least five times be given degree-holding status.[86] Moreover, he set the precedent of granting the top candidates "capital" rank and appointed them as prefectural co-administrators; he promised choice postings to the rest.[87] This was an extraordinary act. First, while maintaining the Five Dynasties policy of sending degree recipients to local government posts, he had set a precedent of granting the best of them rank within the stream eligible for promotion, which by now meant status as a "ranking official at capital and court" (ching ch'ao kuan), instead of ranking them as "men eligible for selection" (hsuan-jen), who faced the daunting task of gaining promotion into the higher stream eligible for further promotion. (The background to this was a change in the civil-bureaucratic rank structure under the provincial governor system. The old division between provincial and metropolitan careers within the nine ranks was replaced by a division between an "administrative class" of all those in the nine ranks of offices and an "executory class" of hsuan-jen, men eligible for selection into the higher group, who filled the majority of local posts.[88] The ratio of administrative to executory officials corresponded to the ratio in the 730's between metropolitan officials, generally those in the first through fifth ranks, and provincial officials in the remaining ranks.) Second, T'ai-tsung had set a precedent for making the kind of degree (chin-shih being the best) and the rank of passing an automatic basis for assigning official rank and substantive office. This meant that Sung degree holders, in contrast to their T'ang predecessors, no longer had to satisfy the demands of the Department of Personnel. The shih responded. In 977 only some 5,000 men had attended the departmental examination; in 982 over 10,000 appeared, and in 992 over 17,000.[89]

The expansion of the examination system that began in 977 and continued into the following reigns was unprecedented in Chinese history. At the same time T'ai-tsung moved to close down other routes into civil office and to raise the status of degree holders and civil officials within the bureaucracy as a whole. First, the program of recommendation from local government was ended. In 976, the year T'ai-tsung took the throne, the 740 men recommended that year under T'ai-tsu's recommendation policy were "examined on what they had studied" and none were found acceptable. The thirteenth-century historian Ma Tuan-lin comments that this showed that the road to official service was closed for those who were "simple and without wen."[90] Transfers from the clerical service came to a virtual halt, and in 989 clerks were forbidden to take the examinations; as the ruler declared: "The examinations were set up for the shih stream." This made the division between civil officials and those in the clerical service so great that anyone from a shih family who entered the clerical service lost the right to enter the ranks of regular officials.[91] At the same time the political role of men with military rank was increasingly restricted. While maintaining the division between the chief councillors and the commissioners of the Bureau of Military Affairs at court, T'ai-tsung began to appoint degree holders to the Bureau and placed the military under the supervision of civil officials. In the provinces military officials continued to hold posts in the civil administration, but now these were very low posts, such as tax stations, and subordinate to civil officials.[92] Finally, as the prestige of the military ranks fell, the possibility of transfer from military to civil rank was restricted.

The consequences of these measures were clear. With civil officials as the dominant political grouping and the shih, defined by examination learning, as the almost exclusive source of civil officials, the shih were once again at the top of the hierarchy of prestige and power. Those with political ambitions now had a reason to pursue an education. We should be cautious, however, in assuming that T'ai-tsung patronized the cultured out of necessity. A cynical explanation would be that, not being above suspicion in the death of T'ai-tsu and in his claim to the throne, the new emperor needed to recruit as his own men those regarded as representing a more ethical style of politics. Expediency would not, however, exclude the possibility that T'ai-tsung, seeing the preservation of political order rather differently from his brother, believed in the promise of learning and civil culture. The case for this must wait for a later chapter.

Suffice it to say that the re-emergence of the shih as the dominant element in the polity took place within a generation of T'ai-tsung's succession. This is clearly illustrated in Table 2, which compares the number of degrees granted against the probable numbers of civil officials at various points during the first century of the Sung. But the table also holds some rather unexpected, and perhaps unwanted, news for those who have assumed that all Sung civil bureaucrats passed the examinations.

During the reigns of T'ai-tsung and Chen-tsung (r. 997–1022), the examination system passed more men than the known total of civil officials. The first decades of the eleventh century thus experienced a glut of civil officials.[93] But the proportion of civil officials who could have held examination degrees declined thereafter. The main reason for this decline is not hard to find: the expansion of the yin privilege, the right to make a relative eligible for rank and appointment. According to Umehara Kaoru, beginning late in T'ai-tsung's reign the right to extend yin to relatives was broadened (eventually including sons, grandsons, brothers, cousins, nephews, and grandnephews—both agnates and affines—and in some instances family tutors) and the occasions upon which this privilege could be used were increased.[94] For example, from 996, yin could be used annually on the occasion of the emperor's birthday, a practice that, when it was abolished in 1056, was adding 300 men to the roster annually. In addition, yin was granted on the occasion of the triennial sacrifices. Although the number of officials eligible to exercise this privilege was small as a proportion of all officials, by the 1040's it included men in the sixth and seventh ranks. Thus over the long term this small group was able to secure rank for many times their own number. Moreover, the number of relatives for whom an official could secure rank and the distance of the kinship of those for whom he could secure it increased with his rank. Although the position an official held corresponded roughly with his rank, rank promotions often continued for court officials even when they no longer held leading positions at court. Thus there were always more men with ranks that entitled them to yin than the number of leading positions at court would suggest, because yin was tied to rank rather than actual position and was used by those in temporary retirement. This meant that if promotions into the higher ranks increased, the number of men using yin increased as well, in spite of attempts to restrict

TABLE 2

Number of Civil Officials vs. Number of Degrees Granted, 997–1067

Year	Number of civil officials[b]	Regular degrees Number[c]	Regular degrees As percentage of civil officials	+ Facilitated degrees[a] Total[c]	+ Facilitated degrees[a] As percentage of civil officials	Exam period
997	1,884–5,735	5,159	274/90%			977–92
1004–15	5,000	8,017	160			992–1012
		10,922	218			983–1012
1023–31	9,400	3,831	40	4,444	47%	1012–30
		5,559	59	6,172	65	1002–30
1046	12,700	5,388	42	9,411	74	1027–46
		6,236	49	10,379	82	1019–46
1064–67	12,800	4,794	37	7,722	60	1046–63
		6,159	48	10,029	78	1038–63

SOURCES. Examination degree totals: Chaffee, *Thorny Gates*, pp. 192–95; for civil officials in 997: Furugaki, "Tai-so Tai-sō jidai," pp. 107–10, estimate; for numbers of civil officials after 997: Li Hung-ch'i, "Sung-tai kuan-yuan shu te t'ung-chi"; Lee also gives these figures in *Government Education and Examinations*, p. 225; Chaffee, *Thorny Gates*, p. 27; and Lo, *Szechwan*, p. 79.

[a]Facilitated degree holders are problematic. In the Southern Sung, they were registered with the selection bureaus even if they were not automatically appointed to local government posts.

[b]The figures given in the sources refer not to available positions, but to those registered as eligible for appointment. Those holding civil rank (*wen-kuan*) were either court- or capital-rank officials (the nine ranks of old) or "executory class" officials (*hsuan-jen*). The actual number of posts in the civil administration is unknown, and some of these were filled by men with military rank. However, the 977 estimate is based both on assumptions about the number of positions commonly held by civil officials and some references to the total number of men holding different ranks. The figure for 1004–15 is half the known total of 10,000 eligible civil and military officials. The figure for 1046 includes 2,700 court/capital-rank officials and 10,000 executory officials. For 1023–31 there is a figure of 2,000 court/capital-rank officials; supposing that the rate of increase from then to 1046 was the same for executory officials allows an inference of a total of 9,400. For 1064–67, there is a reference to 2,800 holding court/capital ranks, and the executory class is not thought to have grown much beyond 10,000 until the reign of Hui-tsung (1100–1125).

[c]Calculations of available degree holders assumes an average career length of 30 years. I also give totals for 20-year periods.

its use. This inflation, particularly from the late Northern Sung on into the Southern Sung, was encouraged by the use of yin to secure promotions for relatives already in the bureaucracy.[95]

The use of the yin privilege by civil officials was not originally intended to have such consequences for the civil bureaucracy. With the exception of the very highest ranks, yin was most commonly exercised for appointments to military ranks (which made the recipient eligible for appointment to minor positions in the civil administration). But by the 1020's requests that yin beneficiaries receive civil appointments were allowed. However, military officials continued to receive yin benefits in the form of military rank, and the grants of yin to imperial clansmen and the imperial in-laws, which at times involved over 100 men, generally took the form of military rank. Thus the yin system reflected the growing division between the civil and military bureaucracies.

It is important to keep in mind that the expansion of the yin system followed the expansion of the examination system and the emergence of degree-holding civil officials as the dominant element in politics. Thus, rather than being a mechanism that enabled non-shih men already in government in the 970's to secure civil office for their descendants, the use of yin helped shih families, who had entered through the exams, to perpetuate themselves in government service. We can see these developments, I suggest, as a deal T'ai-tsung was striking with the shih: in return for their support of central authority, he would see to it that they had exclusive rights to political leadership and that they, like their T'ang predecessors, could once again make government service the family occupation for generations. A later anecdote has T'ai-tsung proclaiming to his ministers: "We are also making long-term plans for our descendants, so that the imperial house will be fortunate forever, while you ministers will have salary and position for successive generations. Let each of you think only of how to aid me."[96] The increased use of yin and the attitude in this comment suggest that the shih families who had established themselves at the top of the political structure moved quickly to secure their place and to exclude others. Was a new aristocracy beginning to take form? Why this did not happen, and what happened instead, is discussed in the next section.

From Bureaucrats to Local Elites

The T'ang founders accommodated the great clans because they were powerful; the T'ang also undermined their independence. In contrast, the circumstances of the Sung founding favored the shih because they were relatively powerless and dependent, yet by the end of the twelfth century the shih had far more independence and local power than they had had at the start. Some change in the balance of power between imperial authority and the bureaucracy was predictable, given that the shih were allowed to become the exclusive source of civil officials. The examinations of 1057, with Ou-yang Hsiu as director of the Department of Rites examination, illustrates this shift. T'ai-tsu had established the Palace Examination to assert the supremacy of the emperor in the selection of shih for office; he and his successors had given substance to this institutional will by consistently failing as many as one-quarter of those who passed the examination at departmental level. In 1057, however, when Ou-yang changed the criteria to favor those whose "language and principles were closer to antiquity," all those he chose passed the Palace Examination.[97] In spite of their growing power, the recruitment practices and bureaucratic arrangements created to patronize the shih exclusively had the contrary effect of thwarting their efforts to perpetuate their descendants in office. Even as the emperor was losing direct control over the bureaucracy, the bureaucrats were losing their power to coordinate the institutional interests of bureaucracy with family interests. As a result, the shih increasingly depended on domination of local society to maintain the well-being of their family and on examination education as the necessary qualification in their self-definition as shih. On the one hand, their independence was not a direct threat to the survival of the dynasty, as the independence of the great clans had been, but on the other hand, their independence meant that political institutions had less leverage over local affairs. How did this happen?

Those Japanese historians who have distinguished the Northern Sung from the T'ang on the grounds that in the Sung office holding was the basis for social status have spoken of the Northern Sung elite world as a "bureaucratic society" (kanryō shakai).[98] Indeed, there were famous shih families in the Northern Sung that produced successive generations of high officials. Robert M. Hartwell identifies about 50 such families as forming the core of an eleventh-century "professional elite" whose representation in policymaking organs far exceeded their place in the bureaucracy as a whole.[99] Consider, for example, the Lü family, studied by Kinugawa Tsuyoshi.[100] Lü Meng-cheng (946–1011) became a chief councillor in 988, as did his cousin's son Lü I-chien (978–1043) in 1029, and I-chien's son Lü Kung-chu (1018–89) in 1086. The Fan family is another well-known case.[101] The Northern Sung focus on serving in government pervaded intellectual culture, and the most influential intellectual figures were also influential political figures, as the careers of Fan Chung-yen, Ou-yang Hsiu, Wang An-shih, and Ssu-ma Kuang illustrate.[102]

The Lüs and other great bureaucratic families, many of whom had residences at the capital, were unique in the frequency with which their members attained high court office. Yet there appears to have been a general belief in the Northern Sung that to be a shih meant to serve in government and that the goal of a family, once one member gained office, was to ensure that there would be officials in later generations. In a series of regional studies of Northern Sung officials, Aoyama Sadao has provided numerous examples of less well known yet successful bureaucratic families, particularly in the south, and has argued that the bureaucracy was "consolidated" by the end of the Northern Sung.[103] Aoyama's findings suggest the possibility of a strengthening of local elites of shih families. That is, with time, those chosen to serve as officials from a particular place tended to come from families that had produced officials in the past. Robert P. Hymes's study of the elite of Fu-chou, in Chianghsi, shows exactly this. A relatively small group of shih families could dominate the prefectural examinations and thus supply a disproportionate number of the local men who became officials. If we ask only where the bureaucrats came from, it appears likely that during the first century of the Northern Sung it was still possible for families that had not produced officials in recent memory to establish themselves as shih. But as time went on, this pool of families succeeded in shutting out newcomers to a considerable extent. As Hymes points out, the fact that over 50 percent of those passing the examinations of 1148 and 1256 were not directly descended from officials in the three previous generations, taken by E. A. Kracke, Jr. as evidence for a high rate of social mobility, may not be significant if collateral lines and affines are taken into account.[104] For my purposes, however, asking where the bureaucracy came from is less germane than asking how families were able to establish themselves as bureaucratic families, why the descendants of officials were in the end unable to maintain themselves as bureaucratic families, and how, under these circumstances, they managed to maintain themselves as shih.

I shall try to answer these questions, and thus show why the shih became local elites, through a discussion of the rise and fall of the Ch'aos, a successful bureaucratic family for whom it is possible to reconstruct a relatively detailed genealogy spanning ten generations from the tenth century into the thirteenth (see the Appendix for the family genealogy). The Ch'ao family, with residences in Kaifeng and nearby Chi prefecture, was in many ways similar to the Lü and Fan families, although it produced only one member of the Council of State, and then only an assisting civil councillor (ts'an-chih cheng-shih).[105]

Like many who established successful bureaucratic families in the early Northern Sung, the Ch'aos came from the north, as did all but eleven of the 103 members of the Council of State during the first three reigns (960–

1022).[106] Ch'ao Tsung-ch'ueh in Branch B, for example, served as an assisting civil councillor from 1040 to 1042 under Lü I-chien. As is the case with a number of families that first produced well-known officials in the Sung, the history of the family during the Five Dynasties is obscure. Nothing is known of family founder Ch'ao Hsien, aside from his name. His son, Ch'ao Ch'üan (ca. 904–?), however, was remembered for having moved from Ch'ing-feng in Shan-chou (Shan prefecture) in Ho-pei East to P'eng-ch'eng, the seat of Hsu-chou in Ching-tung West. The court career of his second son, Ch'ao Chiung (951–1034), allowed some of the family to establish residency at the capital, Kaifeng; others bought land at Chü-yeh in Chi-chou, also in Ching-tung West. Chü-yeh was about 150 kilometers from Kaifeng, on a lake with a river link to the capital. Eventually members of the family acquired land and residences in the subprefectures of Chin-hsiang and Jen-ch'eng in Chi-chou as well.

The success of Ch'üan's second son, Ch'ao Chiung, in the chin-shih examination of 980 and Chiung's speedy rise through literary and scholarly offices at court suggest that the father was a man of some learning himself and that the family had already acquired or had maintained the civil-literary education associated with the shih during the Five Dynasties period. Chiung was a favorite of Emperor Chen-tsung. His son, Ch'ao Tsung-ch'ueh, also rose through literary offices. Tsung-ch'ueh never took an examination degree. However, he used literary scholarship to advance his career. As a reward both for being his father's son and, in imitation of his father, for repeatedly submitting literary pieces eulogizing the dynastic achievements, he was granted chin-shih equivalency. His son, Ch'ao Chung-yen (1012–53), also gained office through yin and also received chin-shih equivalency, in his case through a special examination.

The Ch'ao strategy for securing official careers for descendants was typical in its use of both examination degrees and yin privilege. Ch'ao Chiung reached high court office through his literary gifts, extensive knowledge of ritual under an emperor who saw ritual as a means of bolstering the prestige of the dynasty, and personal relationship with the ruler. With high office came the right to secure rank for relatives, as Chiung and then Tsung-ch'ueh did. In general, when sons could enter office through yin, they did so.[107] However, to encourage the shih to serve the Sung in the first place, the rules for promotion and assignment had been geared to discriminate against those who gained rank through yin and to favor degree holders. As court officials saw that their use of yin diminished the career prospects of their sons, they looked for ways around these restrictions. One solution was the creation of various means for granting degree equivalency, thus giving the subject access to career tracks for degree holders.[108] The granting of chin-shih equivalency to

LIAO

HSI HSIA

Hsi Hsia

TURFAN

Ho-pei tung

Ho-pei hsi

Ho-tung

Yellow R.

Yung-hsing

Ching-tung tung

Ch'in-feng

Shan

Chi

Ching-tung-hsi

Hsu

K'AI-FENG

Huai R.

Ching-hsi pei

Huai-nan tung

Li-chou

Ching-hsi nan

Huai-nan hsi

Yangtze R.

Cheng-tu fu

Chiang-nan
tung

HANG-CHOU

Tzu-chou

Ching-hu pei

Liang-che

K'uei-chou

Hsin

T'ai

Fu

Chiang-nan hsi

Ching-hu nan

TA-LI

Fu-chien

Kuang-nan tung

Kuang-nan hsi

Hai-nan

Ts'ung-ch'ueh and Chung-yen made them eligible for higher promotions and assignments, making it more likely that they too would gain access to considerable yin rights. For those who were not eligible for yin, or who thought they could make it on their own, it was always possible to persist in the quest for a degree, as Ch'ao Tsung-chien (d. 1044) did. In some cases a man with rank through yin went on to take a degree; Chung-yen's son, Ch'ao Tuan-yen (1035–95), is an example. The Ch'aos were somewhat unusual in apparently not using the "various fields" degrees awarded for memorization of the Classics, although generally even holders of these degrees had advantages over men entering through yin.[109] This forbearance may have been because the family tradition esteemed literary scholarship, which, on the whole, came to be dominated by southerners during Chen-tsung's reign.[110]

Once they were established as a shih-ta-fu family, ensconced in a mansion in Kaifeng given to them by the emperor, and favored by Chen-tsung and Jen-tsung (r. 1022–63), the Ch'aos expected their sons to serve. The funerary biographies for the men of the first generations speak of their young sons as "not yet serving," on the sound assumption that a son of the Ch'ao family would. This did not always happen. Ch'ao Chung-hsun of Branch C, for example, spent a decade at the Imperial University without passing the examinations and returned to Chü-yeh to work at creating wealth. The youngest member of his generation and from a less successful line, he may have had little choice but to pursue the examinations. Yet quitting was not an easy move; Chung-hsun's biography tells that he felt he was ceasing to be a shih, for creating wealth was not the "filial piety of shih" but of a commoner. The commitment to holding office was strong.

For the bureaucratic families of the Northern Sung, political success was the basis for social relations. The Ch'aos maintained close relations with their peers in the bureaucracy. Their friendship with the Lü family began when Tsung-ch'ueh served under Lü I-chien and continued to the end of the Northern Sung. Above all, they married the daughters of officials and married their daughters to officials.[111] Even the wealthy Ch'ao Chung-hsun, who gave up the pursuit of office, married all six of his surviving daughters to officials. They did not begin this way. Ch'ao Chiung and Ch'ao Kou in the second generation married Changs; Kou's wife, possibly kin to Chiung's, was of a local Chü-yeh family without a record of official service. The next recorded instance of a Chü-yeh marriage occurred in the fifth generation (Ch'ao Tuan-pen), but in this case the woman's father was an official. The shift to national bureaucratic marriage was in place by the third generation when, for example, Ch'ao Tsung-ch'ueh married a Wang, of the family of the illustrious Later Chou and early Sung court scholar Wang P'u (922–82) of T'ai-yuan. There were probably more cases of marriage alliances than the record reveals. Branch A made several marriages with the Tus: daughters of Chung-ts'an and Tuan-pen married the high official Tu Ch'un (1032–95) and his son K'ai, and Ch'ao Pu-chih married a Tu daughter. All three branches married with the Lü-ch'ius (Tsung-ko, Tuan-chung, Sun-chih, and three daughters of Chung-hsun). Ch'ao marriages extended beyond the north. Another of Chung-ts'an's daughters married Fan Ch'un-ts'ui (1046–1117), the fourth son of Fan Chung-yen of Su-chou; Ch'ao Tuan-jen married a Yeh of Hang-chou; and Ch'ao Tsung-ko's oldest daughter married Tseng Kung (1019–83) of Chien-ch'ang prefecture in Chiang-nan West. In short, the Ch'aos illustrate the pattern of national rather than local marriages that Hartwell and Hymes have identified as typical of Northern Sung bureaucratic families. National marriage was, in effect, bureaucratic marriage, networks of allies were indispensable for families that made official service their occupation.[112]

To some extent bureaucratic success in successive generations required that families produce sons with the kinds of talent the government found useful. Although some Ch'aos had reputations as administrators, judges, and fiscal managers, the career path of choice in this family was literary scholarship. As Ch'ao Pu-chih recalled at the end of the eleventh century, Ch'ao Chiung and Tsung-ch'ueh, known in the family by their posthumous titles Wen-yuan and Wen-chuang, established themselves at court with their command of "literary learning and the affairs of government."[113] The Ch'aos also amassed one of the largest private libraries in Kaifeng.[114] The Ch'aos' success in garnering chin-shih degrees, evident in the fifth generation, had much to do with this tradition. Literary scholarship traditionally had been a route to court posts and policymaking positons; T'ai-tsung, Chen-tsung, and Jen-tsung had made a special effort to promote literary talents. The family reputation helped: Ch'ao Tsung-ch'ueh, for example, was appointed to the prestigious post of rescript writer (*chih-chih-kao*) over more qualified candidates in imitation of a T'ang precedent of a son succeeding his father in this post.[115] References to the family in the late twelfth and early thirteenth centuries, when the family had little political strength, also stress its tradition of literary achievement. This tradition was still alive in the Southern Sung when Ch'ao Kung-wu of the seventh generation wrote his famous annotated bibliography.[116] There were other career specializations in Sung; Hartwell has argued for the existence of a fiscal career path, for example.[117] Not all leading bureaucratic families had scholarly traditions, and not all scholarly families were as literary as the Ch'aos. The scholarly tradition of the Lü family, for example, was at first more oriented toward administrative concerns, although by the Southern Sung its reputation for scholarship had surpassed its political clout.[118]

The crucial element in the Ch'aos' success was a lasting commitment to family solidarity in theory and practice. It has been pointed out that the lineage orientation of Sung shih-ta-fu involved believing that the descent group should include all kin, irrespective of political achievement.[119] The theoretical commitment is apparent in the naming system the Ch'aos maintained for all known descendants in nine generations after Ch'ao Hsien. The common genealogy, a necessity for this naming system, was known well by Northern Sung Ch'aos, for they referred to each other both by name and by the numerical designations that identified seniority within a particular generation and they avoided duplicating names at least until the eighth generation.[120] The most famous example of the practical commitment to providing for future generations of kin was Fan Chung-yen's creation of a charitable estate to aid all descendants.[121] There is no record of the Ch'aos' trying to place land in a trust, but they did aid their kin in both Kaifeng and Chi-chou and those with yin rights used them for collateral kin as well. The family was much larger than the genealogical chart in the Appendix suggests, for Ch'ao Pu-chih contends that there were 500 people (including wives and daughters) as of 1107.[122] They knew each other and looked out for each other in the Northern Sung; although some were known as Chü-yeh Ch'aos and others as Kaifeng Ch'aos, they were self-consciously one family.[123] They also remembered how they had risen, for almost every biographical record of a later descendant in all three branches recalled the greatness of Ch'ao Chiung and Ch'ao Tsung-ch'ueh as the founders.

The attitudes and practices that helped the Ch'aos perpetuate their bureaucratic success were not unique. It is also true, of course, that unless the bureaucracy grew apace, their continued success took positions away from other aspirants to office. The potential for conflict between institutional process and family interest was inherent in the limited number of offices available. Before turning to this, however, I want to digress briefly to introduce what I think is a red herring. The most successful bureaucratic families in the Sung bear certain similarities with the great clans of the T'ang, although they did not dominate the court to the same extent. Robert Hartwell has suggested that they were in fact trying to perpetuate the T'ang tradition: "Whether the claims of the professional elite to distinguished ancestry were fictitious or real, these lineages attempted to perpetuate the T'ang tradition. They used choronyms, practiced status group endogamy, emphasized affinal relationships . . . and, most important, specialized in government service." For Hartwell, claiming "pre-Sung great clan ancestry" is a criterion for defining professional elite families,

together with capital residence, national intermarriage, successive generations of officeholders, and periodic control of the government between
980 and 1100. Hartwell goes on to list a series of examples, identifying
each by a T'ang great clan choronym: "They included lineages such as the
T'ai-yuan Wang of Lo-yang and K'ai-feng, the Ho-nei Hsiang and Ho-
tung Chia of K'ai-feng, the Hung-nung Yang."[124] The Ch'aos could not
claim great clan ancestry—Hartwell has not included them as an example
in any case—but it is certainly true that claims to descent from T'ang
ministers with great clan status were made, as Aoyama Sadao's studies of
Northern Sung officials and Kinugawa Tsuyoshi's study of the first 40
Sung chief councillors reveal.[125]

Does this mean that by the middle of the eleventh century the most
successful bureaucratic families saw themselves as continuing the T'ang
great clan aristocracy? The fraudulence of claims to great clan ancestry
may itself suggest the attraction of the aristocratic sociopolitical vision
and even an effort to recreate that idea in practice. This would imply that
in the concept of shih held by the most successful families good birth as a
quality outweighed merit gained through service and culture, the reverse
of what is commonly thought to have been the Sung attitude. The failure
of an aristocracy of great clans to re-emerge is not, after all, evidence that
some did not try to recreate one. But on further investigation it appears
that successful bureaucratic families of the eleventh century generally did
not see themselves as an aristocracy of great clans descended from the
T'ang. First, with rare exceptions Sung bureaucratic families did not use
T'ang great clan choronyms, nor did they think of their lineages, descent
groups, or mourning circles as constituent elements in a larger entity
identified by a great clan choronym. Moreover, scholars with a historical
sense of medieval aristocratic society understood that it was beyond
recovery in the very different world of the Northern Sung.[126] Second,
claims to great clan ancestors were a subset of the more widespread
phenomenon of claiming officials as ancestors. It was customary in Sung
funerary writing to identify those Sung and pre-Sung ancestors who had
held leading positions in government in an effort to define the moment
when the family of the official in question began to produce officials or
gain fame as shih. More common than claims to a great clan choronym or
descent from an official known to have been a member of a T'ang great
clan were claims to descent from late T'ang and Five Dynasties period
officials.[127] Yet, as eleventh-century scholars frequently noted, few families could document distant genealogical claims.[128] Third, in many instances claims to illustrious T'ang ancestors often appeared generations
after the family became established as a shih family in the Sung, and the
number of claims rose markedly from the middle of the eleventh century

on. In some cases, particularly when distant ancestors were adduced, the claims are fictitious; in others, when writers fail to give the full line of descent from a relatively recent ancestor, it may be because what had once been considered trivial information was now seen as relevant but families had only rough knowledge of their lineage. The completion, in mid-century, of the *New T'ang History*, with eleven *chüan* of genealogies of T'ang chief ministers, provided much information for families desiring illustrious ancestors.[129] All these points are dealt with in Johnson's study of the Chao-chün Lis. Furthermore, I have found no evidence that the Sung government engaged in extensive genealogical research or took an interest in ranking great bureaucratic families.[130] The Ch'aos are an exception that proves the point. As far as they knew in the eleventh century, they lacked illustrious T'ang ancestors: they cited Ch'ao Ts'o of Western Han as the only famous man with the surname in the previous eleven centuries. By the beginning of the thirteenth century, however, some members had discovered Wei and T'ang forebears worthy of inclusion in the records.[131]

A search for officials as ancestors, as evidence of shih ancestry, appears to be the issue here, not great clans and aristocracy. This focus marks an increased preoccupation with family identity. What was the situation that prompted such concerns in the first place? To gain insight into this question, we need only return to the history of the Ch'ao family for what it can tell us about the problems bureaucratic families began to face during the latter half of the eleventh century. This will bring us to the emergence of local elites and, along the way, suggest one explanation for why men claimed illustrious ancestors.

Writing in 1107, Ch'ao Pu-chih contrasted the growth of his family, 500 souls in the seventh generation, with its increasing political insignificance. The memory of the founders of the lineage was still strong—although few of those alive had met them—and the cultural traditions of the family were still maintained. But the Ch'aos were not producing high-ranking court officials. The shift from entry by yin to entry through the examinations, fully evident in the sixth generation, is a sign that Ch'ao sons now had to fend for themselves in competition with others. Although they were still competitive, the proportion of Ch'aos known to have held office fell sharply. With fewer men in office, the chances of a Ch'ao rising high enough to gain significant yin privilege decreased and further reduced the number of men in office. In addition, because some Ch'aos were visible opponents of Wang An-shih's New Policies, those in office had a more difficult time rising through the ranks. Thus, as the Ch'aos were increasing as part of the general population, their representation within the ranks of shih notable enough to be recorded was decreasing. The lack of references to Ch'aos in state and private historical sources suggests that from the fifth generation on their representation in the pool of officials was declining. During the first half of the eleventh century, we can trace the creation of new households with every generation, but with the sixth generation the number of households with descendants of whom we know nothing increases greatly, a decline that predates the loss of the north in 1126.

If the Ch'aos had planned for their descendants to remain shih-ta-fu by holding office, they were in trouble. Like other families that had risen to high office in the late tenth and early eleventh centuries, they had bene-fited from the initial expansion of government, but later expansions did not keep pace with the growth of the family. The problem was simple, and simply insurmountable: there were not enough positions to absorb all the sons of successful shih families.

The Ch'aos could do little about the shortage of posts. Had the Sung followed the T'ang in establishing an oligarchy based on pedigree and past service, the Ch'aos could well have maintained themselves in the bu-reaucracy. But the government did not do this. Instead, the court main-tained the arrangements that had originally favored the recruitment of shih for office, although now they worked against the interests of the most successful bureaucratic families. The division between clerks and regular officials now meant sons without access to yin or examination degrees had no lower-level governmental career to fall back on—at least if they ever hoped to become regular officials. Similarly, the division be-tween military and civil ranks, restrictions on transfer from the military to the civil service, and the general disregard for the military made military office less attractive.[132] The Sung did not create a status group of respect-able guard positions for the sons of officials, although the yin privilege was used for military titles in some instances. No doubt some sons did become clerks or, having acquired military rank, served as tax collectors or even army officers, although there is no record of Ch'aos doing so.[133] The rules on fairness in the examinations, intended to end nepotism in the early Sung, and the holding of qualifying examinations in the prefectures only served to encourage more men of talent to attempt the examinations. The examination system did offer the sons of officials certain advantages, of which Ch'ao Pu-chih availed himself, but these were not great enough to help all the Ch'aos of his generation.[134]

Moreover, during the course of the eleventh century the court gave in to pressure to stop the growth of yin privilege and, in the 1050's, to cut it back. It also began to limit the number of promotions from hsuan-jen status into the ranks of court and capital officials, which made men eligible for further promotions and thus led to access to yin privilege, and reduced the annual rate of promotions from 250–300 men to 100 in 1066.[135] Promotion to metropolitan rank required the sponsorship of higher officials—five in most cases—but the rules of sponsorship were changing as well. The right of officials at the capital to sponsor men was gradually reduced in favor of those serving in senior local government posts, and family connections to high court officials began to matter less than the ability to be useful to administrative superiors.[136]

The plight of northern bureaucratic families, who by mid-century had been placing men in office for several generations, was exacerbated by the court's willingness to allow the examination system to make the bureaucracy as a whole and the court itself more representative of Sung regions. New men were entering the upper reaches of the bureaucracy throughout the eleventh century, although how many is not clear.[137] More certain is the growing representation of the south, and of descendants of the southern kingdoms' civil officials.[138] The growing proportion of officials from outside the North China plain in the civil bureaucracy was reflected in the leadership of the Council of State: one-fifth of Chen-tsung's chief councillors were from the south, as were two-fifths of Jen-tsung's and four-fifths of Shen-tsung's.[139] Hartwell has found that under Shen-tsung the proportion of southern incumbents in policymaking and fiscal offices matched the south's share of the total population.[140] Moreover, southerners initially entered the bureaucracy more frequently through the prestigious chin-shih examination than did northerners, and thus were bound to gain career advantages. John W. Chaffee has documented the rise of the south in the examinations, from 30 percent of chin-shih degree recipients under Chen-tsung to 50 percent under Jen-tsung to 60 percent under Shen-tsung.[141] Almost all southern officials who achieved prominence did so through the civil bureaucracy; the less prestigious military, however, remained in the hands of northerners.[142] As the number of southerners in the bureaucracy increased, the number of northerners decreased.[143] The success of the south affected the Ch'aos in another way as well, for southerners successfully competed with northerners for literary positions at court. The sixth-generation Ch'ao Pu-chih was unusual in making his way through literary achievement.[144]

The effect on Sung politics of the growing number of aspirants for office and the competition for court office among those already serving is evident in the factional disputes that marked the two periods of institutional reform, Fan Chung-yen's abortive Ch'ing-li reform of 1043–44 and the New Policies regimes of 1069–85, 1093–1100, and 1101–25.[145] For example, in 1036 the southerner Fan Chung-yen accused the Chief Councillor Lü I-chien of favoritism in the promotion of officials; at court Fan tried to restrict yin privilege.[146] Fan's allies included southerners and such northerners as Han Ch'i (1008–75) and Fu Pi (1004–83). His supporters came not from leading bureaucratic families but from families with traditions of lower-level service. Of course, once high office and yin rights were attained, erstwhile reformers became the founders of bureaucratic families. Hans and Fans would eventually find themselves allied to Lüs and Ch'aos in opposition to the southerner Wang An-shih and his New Policies, along with many others from already established families. The successive New Policies regimes expanded government activity and created more jobs. In 1119, under New Policies adherent Ts'ai Ching (1046–1126), the number of military officials doubled to 30,000, and the number of lower-level civil officials (hsuan-jen) increased from about 10,000 to 16,000.[147] But this did little to help the Ch'aos and other opponents of the regime. The purge of 1093 was followed in 1102 with another purge, and leading opponents and their descendants were prohibited from entering the capital, thus making active officials ineligible for promotion to capital posts and their sons unable to attend the examinations. Ch'ao Pu-chih was included on the official blacklist; his cousin Ch'ao Yueh-chih and nephew Ch'ao Kung-mai were removed from office as well. By Hartwell's calculation, it was precisely during these years that the great bureaucratic families began to disappear from policymaking and financial posts.[148]

As competition increased, those in power at court defended their position. Under Chen-tsung, for example, Chief Councillor Wang Tan (957–1017), a northerner, objected to the elevation of Wang Ch'in-jo (962–1025) to Council membership on the simple grounds that southerners should not be allowed to lead the government.[149] Northerners objected that southern scholars were too literary and lacked the concern with "ethical conduct" they associated with old families. This was a recurring theme, one that could be used to contrast the old and conservative with the new and radical. It had already appeared in 993, for example, when Chief Councillor Lü Meng-cheng persuaded T'ai-tsung to block the rise of Chang Chi, "the best of the shih-jen from Chiang-tung," because he valued literary learning above "ethical conduct."[150] Later, similar conservative complaints would be heard from Ssu-ma Kuang and Ch'eng I. Men from established families also tended to have doubts about the favor shown degree holders in assigning positions within the bureaucracy. When Ch'en P'eng-nien (961–1017), another southerner blocked by Wang Tan, spoke in his brief history of the examinations of the advantages of using literary talents and avoiding nepotism, he was responding to those who saw the prestige of the chin-shih degree as a threat to the career chances of sons who entered service by other means.[151] Objections to the examinations continued through the Northern Sung. Some protested that

exams encouraged men who were not shih to act like shih; others argued
that anyone who passed deserved to be considered a shih.[152] On the eve of
the New Policies, Ssu-ma Kuang proposed to allow only candidates
recommended by court officials to sit for the degree, a sure way of
favoring well-established families.[153] Wang An-shih proposed instead to
create a graded school system to feed men into office, a way of ensuring
that the larger pool of shih would have some chance of success.

In short, the Sung dynasty failed to recreate the system of official
statuses and administrative levels that enabled T'ang families to perpetuate
themselves in state service. Sung institutions encouraged increasing numbers to aspire to office, yet ultimately thwarted attempts to make bureaucratic service the family occupation. The problem for such families was
how to remain shih when their sons did not serve. Consider the following
statements. Wang An-shih writes in a funerary biography: "[The gentle-
man] had three sons . . . none of whom he would let work at [agricultural]
production. He said, 'To be poor yet a shih is better than being an artisan
or merchant but rich.' All three sons passed the local qualifying examination, and Shen became the judge of T'ai-p'ing prefecture." The philosopher Yang Shih (1053–1135) writes about himself: "My family has made
being ju its occupation for generations; its name has not been listed with
farmers, artisans, and merchants." The administrator and military strate-
gist Cheng Kang-chung (1088–1154) writes about a man who liked to
show his writings to shih-ta-fu: "As for what we today call the four kinds
of subjects: the shih have learning, the farmers have fields . . . but only the
artisans and merchants roam the four quarters." Finally, the great literary
scholar Lu Yu (1125–1210) writes in a commemorative record for the
Ch'en family charitable estate: "When we infer the intentions of earlier
generations, we find that they have been one and the same: they cherished
their children and wished to see that their food and clothing were sufficient and marriages were made at the right age; they wished to have them
be shih, they did not wish to have them slide off into being artisans and
merchants, to descend to being clerks, or to depart to be the followers of
Taoists and Buddhists."[154]

It seems to me that claims to official ancestry—particularly shaky
claims to high official ancestry in a distant past—reflected the insecurity
many families felt about their continued status as shih. A claim to illustrious official ancestry many generations previous did imply, however,
that the family could remain shih without always serving.[155] This is
evident in Fan Chung-yen's composition of a genealogy, something that
had not interested previous generations of Fans. On the one hand, his
claims to both the northern origins of the Fans and descent from a T'ang
chief minister responded to court hostility to allowing upstart southerners

to make national policy. On the other hand, by reminding his own descendants that they had survived both migration and periods without office, he pointed out that it was possible for the Fans to remain a shih family by virtue of mutual support and education. In 1050, when he wrote the rules for his charitable estate, Fan did not expect all his descendants to serve. In 1073, when his son appended further rules, it had become necessary to institutionalize financial rewards for family members who became candidates for the examination. It is possible, although the sources do not speak of it, that bureaucratic families like the Fans and the Ch'aos were finding it difficult to keep their young men oriented toward service in such a competitive world.[156] Not everyone saw a need to claim official ancestors. Ou-yang Hsiu and Su Hsun prepared family genealogies explicitly intended to be models for other shih-ta-fu families, that went back only four generations. As Su Hsun explained, there was no need for men who had risen to wealth and honor to be ashamed of their background; they should worry about their descendants. A genealogy should provide a foundation for the future. Descent group solidarity, as Morita Kenji has argued, was the goal.[157]

Maintaining lineage solidarity helped families continue to claim to be shih when few males served, for it enabled all kin to share in the unquestioned status of those who did. But a re-evaluation of the qualities inherent in the concept of shih to place less of a premium on official service helped the family as well. By the end of the eleventh century, more men had begun to insist that a good shih put ethical standards before service or that a life of study made holding office unnecessary.[158] Above all, the examinations provided shih families with a means of recertifying themselves as shih, for those studying for the examinations could claim that they were on the path to service, whether they passed or not. The importance of having the culture of a shih is evident from popularity of the examinations: although only 500 some degrees were given at each triennial examination, by the end of the Southern Sung there were 400,000 prefectural candidates.[159] In Fu-chou in Fu-chien, 17,000 took the prefectural examinations, although the prefecture had only 300 registered students.[160] Yet if the possession of an examination education helped men think they were shih, the lack of office made it difficult to perpetuate the shih as a social group. Preparing sons for the exams was, after all, a drain on a family's finances. The emphasis on exam education went together with a social transformation of the shih into local elites, whose survival depended not on official income but on dominating the economy, institutions, and cultural activities of the locality.

The turn toward localism is evident in the failure of shih families to support Wang An-shih's New Policies. Wang's attack on families that used their wealth to dominate their locality (see Chapter 7) was balanced by his vision of a T'ang-style system in which all shih would serve in some formal capacity, even as clerks, without losing their claim to being shih. But he was too late.[161] By the 1070's too many families of officials had come to depend on independent economic means. In the Northern Sung there were those who like Wang believed that official service should be the family occupation of shih. Having entered the bureaucracy, some even left their collateral kin to take care of themselves and moved away from their native place. In spite of the strictures of Su Hsun's genealogy, Su Shih planned to retire outside his native Szechuan and Su Ch'e did. In contrast, some bureaucratic families that had placed all males in government for several generations realized the need to re-establish a home base and purchased land to that end. The family of Ch'eng I was one such case. Others came from families already well established locally; they did not see themselves as "founders" of the family fortunes, and they defended the right of rural elites to dominate the local scene; Ssu-ma Kuang is a case in point. Families that had never risen high enough to gain yin rights, probably the majority of shih families, were not likely to have entertained the prospect of making government the family occupation. The Ch'aos established their independent economic base in Chi-chou at the same time that they were becoming a bureaucratic family. Without it, they could not have held their kin together during the latter half of the eleventh century.

In the Southern Sung, too, a family that gained high office could place kin in office through protection, special examinations, and so on. As Richard Davis has shown, the Shih family, source of two Southern Sung chief councillors, was highly successful, indeed far more so than the Ch'aos.[162] The possibility of becoming a bureaucratic family still existed. It seems, however, that few Southern Sung families were as successful as the Shihs, whereas many Northern Sung bureaucratic families equaled the Ch'aos and many more aspired to. Great bureaucratic families disappeared, Robert Hymes has argued, because families of officials changed their strategies for maintaining elite status in the face of the new situation. Those who survived were those who had entrenched their families in the prefectures and, in collaboration with similar families, dominated local society. Southern Sung governments, focusing on the problems of defense, were less interested in directing local affairs and perhaps too willing to let local shih take responsibility for local order. The most telling symptom of this shift in focus from the national level to local society was a change in marriage patterns. In the eleventh century Ch'aos married with other bureaucratic families, irrespective of region, and this was true for officials from the Fu-chou area in Chiang-nan West that Hymes treats. In the Southern Sung, he demonstrates, even officials made their marriage alliances locally, a sign that they no longer believed the family fortune depended on government service.[163] In the eleventh century Tseng Kung, for example, had married a Ch'ao daughter. In the Southern Sung the Tsengs married Fu-chou families. The Lou family of Ning-p'o, studied by Linda Walton, also followed the new mode. Even in the twelfth and thirteenth centuries, when the Lous were unusually successful in gaining chin-shih degrees and entering office, they held onto their base in Ming-chou, intermarried with other local shih lineages, and established charitable estates. They did not establish themselves at the capital or leave their local base for their less successful members.[164]

Shih families that hoped that their descendants would not decline needed an independent economic base if they could not count on government salaries; to keep that base secure without automatic access to the privileges that came with office, they needed to solidify their position in the local community. Examination education was a useful investment: it distinguished shih families from those who were merely rich or powerful. They still aspired to office, at least in name, and they expended the effort to maintain the cultural education required of the civil officials they were unlikely to become.[165] As local elites, they needed a mechanism that allowed them to claim membership in the Sung national sociopolitical elite. This was the world at which Yuan Ts'ai directed his *Precepts for Social Life*. Nonetheless, Yuan's and more scholarly thinkers' concern with the cultivation of the moral self reminds us that some thought culture alone would not show men how to act responsibly. As long as examinations were seen as the path to office, it did not matter that examination education had little to do with personal conduct, for political institutions served to guide the behavior of officials. When the examinations became one means for legitimating local dominance, the lack of relevance of that education to the private conduct became obvious, and the situation was set for a redefinition of the nature of culture as a quality of the shih.

An account of the fortunes of the Ch'aos in the Southern Sung will bring this story to a close. Thanks in part to the great scholar Lou Yueh, a Lou of Ming-chou, we know something of what happened. Perhaps, if the north had remained under the Sung, the Ch'ao family would have ended up marrying other Chi-chou families and acting as a local elite there. They did not get the chance. Chi-chou was lost when the Jurchens conquered north China. It is possible that several hundred Ch'aos were captured as they fled to a Shantung port for the voyage south.[166] Those who survived in recorded history lived in the south.[167] They did not, however, establish a common home base. As of 1207, according to Lou Yueh, family members resided in Chiang-hsi, Liang-che, and Szechuan. This is quite likely. Ch'ao Pu-chih's son Kung-wei was serving in T'ai-chou in Liang-che when he lost his post in a scandal (his wife had taken bribes from the family of a criminal sentenced to death); Ch'ao Kung-wu and Kung-su served for extensive periods in Szechuan; Ch'ao Ch'ien-chih held a post at court and retired to Hsin-chou in Chiang-nan East; Ch'ao Kung-mai and his sons settled in Fu-chou in Chiang-nan West, and Ch'ao Kung-o was buried there. We know about the eighth and later generations only through accounts of the seventh.

In the last records the Ch'aos are treated as the remnants of an illustrious and highly cultured family. But they are seen as remnants, their glory in the past. Why do we not learn more about the Ch'aos? Why did they not revive in the south? Fortuitously some ended up in Fu-chou, but these Ch'aos, like other northern refugees, failed to transform themselves into long-term members of the Fu-chou elite. First, they were apparently unable to join the marriage network of the local shih families, even though they were well educated and were officials. This failure was linked to a second factor: they were unable to establish a firm property base.[168] Without property and social connections, the Ch'aos lost out. Other families led the community, built the schools, and put their sons through the examination system. Education and even office were no longer enough to secure the family fortunes. The Ch'ao family prestige could matter only if those with influence in Fu-chou wanted it to matter. The obvious conclusion is that those who had wealth and power did not want to share it with outsiders; they had enough trouble parceling it out among themselves.

Throughout the transformations of the shih from aristocrats to civil bureaucrats to local elites, culture and learning remained a quality of being a shih. The chapters that follow treat learning as part of the conception of the shih and thus as one of the ways in which the shih as a social group defined their common values. Learning and intellectual culture were not merely the pastimes of creative minds, divorced from issues of political responsibility and social privilege. Nor were attempts to guide others and set standards merely camouflage for self-interest, to be accounted for through functional explanations. In inquiring into the diverse possibilities that emerged between 600 and 1200 and by analyzing the role of the shih in Chinese history, this study attempts to realize one of the tasks of intellectual history: to clarify the connections between changes in intellectual values and changes in practices in such a manner that both thought and the historical world in which thought took place are illuminated.

3 Scholarship and Literary Composition at the Early T'ang Court

Within five years of the T'ang founding, the court had begun commissioning scholars to review the history, literary writing, rituals, and Classical studies of the past in order to establish models for the present. Yen Shih-ku (581–645), grandson of Yen Chih-t'ui, was one of these scholars. In his youth Yen had gained a reputation for being broadly acquainted with the textual tradition, learned in Classical exegesis, and talented in literary composition. He understood the political goals of the dynasty and was politically well connected; T'ang Kao-tsu (r. 618–26) entrusted Yen with the task of writing crucial edicts during the struggle for power, and T'ai-tsung (r. 626–49) turned to him to establish definitive editions of the Classics. Yen's talents also extended to history—he wrote the most important commentary on the *Han History*, the dynasty the T'ang saw as its model—and he was known for his expertise in state ritual.[1] In short, he had a firm command of the scholarly and literary traditions of This Culture of Ours and put them to work in service of the consolidation of imperial power and the restoration of a unified empire.

The subject of this chapter is the view of the cultural tradition and the role of literary compositon in it shared by early T'ang court scholars. Because they tried to synthesize traditions from the previous centuries and anchor them more firmly in antiquity, I shall call their attitudes "medieval"; because these traditions were carried on by great clan families, they were also "aristocratic." The characteristic assumption of this medieval aristocratic worldview, as I interpret it, was to think of values as cultural forms (wen in a broad sense). "Hsueh," learning as a moral activity, meant mastering the appropriate cultural forms so well that one could reproduce them and vary them to fit the situation. "Cultural forms" is an awkward rendering of much that came to be implied by the term *jen-wen* (human culture), as used in the phrase "contemplate jen-wen to transform the world." It includes, for example, all that belongs to the category of "ritual," the textual legacy of the past, and literary composition (wen-chang). Written language had to be put into the proper cultural form to be effective; it had to be "said with wen."[2]

The medieval view assumed that cultural forms served as models, even as they changed over time. Medieval scholars did not argue whether cultural forms should or could serve as guides; they assumed that they did influence behavior, for better or for worse. Behind the belief that cultural forms were real lay, I think, two closely related assumptions. First, the models and forms that made up culture were elaborations, imitations, and variations on forms from the past; the new had been built upon the old in a cumulative fashion to create a tradition that stretched back to the beginning of civilization under the Former Kings, a beginning still accessible through the Classics. Second, the original creations from which the cumulative tradition arose replicated and continued the manifest patterns of heaven-and-earth. Just as the workings of the cosmos revealed constant patterns (li), medieval scholars held, the cultural forms created by the Former Kings manifested patterns for human society. In building upon these cultural foundations in composing wen-chang, later men were thus continuing a culture that originally corresponded to the integrated organization of heaven-and-earth.

Early T'ang scholars did not say, for example, that rites or poems can be normative if the designer or author has first grasped the proper ideas, or that culture is a medium or device through which values can be communicated. Such statements are characteristic of later times, when scholars would distinguish the ideas behind the forms from the forms themselves. For later eras, maintaining formal continuity with the past would matter less, but in the medieval world continuity with tradition was crucial to the possibility of a moral order in the world. Yen Chih-t'ui's *Family Instructions* illustrates this aristocratic view.

This did not mean that all cultural forms were equally good, appropriate, or successful as models for society. Early T'ang scholars reflecting on the preceding centuries said that endless elaboration and refinement had led to cultural works that were so "floating and ornate" (*fu-hua*) that the connection to simpler and more substantial origins had been lost. Moreover, various ancient traditions had been taken in directions that were not conducive to a unified empire. We may say, therefore, that early T'ang scholars were concerned with "values" in the sense that they thought about choosing traditions to encourage and reconnecting traditions that had separated. What we cannot say, in my view, is that they tried to influence their times by speaking about values as "ideas" or, as would be the case later, as a tao that could be followed without adopting the wen that had originally manifested it. Learning in the early T'ang was wen-hsueh. It was congruent with the ritual endeavors thought vital to the working of the polity.[3] The radically changed intellectual world discussed in Chapter 4 suggests that aristocratic learning collapsed when scholars came to believe that for cultural forms to be normative one had to find true ideas to put into them. When culture lost its efficacy and scholars began to search for ideas as the ground for creating their own wen, a return to the medieval world became impossible.

Defining the Cultural Tradition: The Institutions of Court Scholarship in the Early T'ang

In the early T'ang, during the reigns of Kao-tsu and T'ai-tsung, court patronage played an essential role in promoting learning and scholarship. In *State and Scholars in T'ang China*, David McMullen has set out in some detail the court institutions in which scholarly activity took place, the projects scholars worked on, and the disciplines involved. Closest to the emperor were the advisory colleges of the inner court. Created to provide the ruler with scholarly consultants, secretaries, and literary companions, these colleges sometimes served as schools for small numbers of students and centers for compilation projects. These included the Hsiu-wen kuan (College for Cultivating Wen) later known as the Hung-wen kuan (College for Amplifying Wen), founded in 621, and the Ch'ung-wen kuan (College for Honoring Wen), founded in 639 as part of the crown prince's establishment. In the titles of these institutes, "wen" refers both to the textual tradition and to literary endeavor. In the eighth century two more institutes were established: the Chi-hsien yuan (Office of the Assembled Wise) in 725 and the Han-lin yuan (Office of the Forest of Brushes) in 738. The latter, once it gained control over rescript writing, became the preeminent scholarly institution of the inner court.

In the outer court, the premier academic institution was the Kuo-tzu chien (Directorate for the [Education of] the Sons of State), with three schools preparing sons of officials of different ranks for examinations and official careers, as well as specialized schools in law, orthography, and mathematics. Under T'ai-tsung as many as 3,000 students attended the Directorate. The T'ai-ch'ang ssu (Court of Sacrifices) was responsible for the state ritual program; the Shih kuan (Office of Historiography), a T'ang innovation, saw to the compilation of a historical record; and the Pi-shu sheng (Imperial Library) maintained the library, composed official documents, and oversaw the Bureau of Astronomy. The government recruited some scholars through examinations. In its final form under Hsuan-tsung (r. 712–56), the chin-shih required literary composition in poetry and prose genres in addition to the rote knowledge of one or two Classics required for the *ming-ching* ("elucidation of the Classics") examination. The T'ang also recruited men through frequent "decree examinations" (*chih-k'o*) in various categories, all of which required literary training; in many instances serving officials took these examinations as a means of qualifying for further promotion.[4]

Scholars benefited from these institutional arrangements in several ways. They gained access to the emperor and policymaking, they acquired a role in recording and prescribing imperial and court conduct, and through the colleges they educated the sons of court bureaucrats and thus perpetuated the scholarly community. A review of the projects they worked on will give us some sense of the traditions of learning they valued.

Classics. Between 631 and 653, the project, begun under the Sui dynasty, of an authoritative edition of the Five Classics (*Book of Change, Book of Documents, Mao Odes* or *Songs, Book of Rites,* and *Spring and Autumn Annals*) was completed by committees led at various points by Yen Shih-ku, K'ung Ying-ta (574–648), and T'ai-tsung's brother-in-law Ch'ang-sun Wu-chi (d. 659). The result was the *Wu ching cheng-i* (The correct significances of the Five Classics). For each Classic the compilers chose a definitive commentary from the range of possible Han and post-Han commentaries and appended subcommentaries to elucidate the Classic, elaborate on the main commentary, note alternative views, and generally survey the exegetical tradition that had grown up around each Classic. Later intellectuals would unfairly derogate this work as mere textual exegesis (*shun-ku*) that ignored the "greater principles" (*ta-i*) of the sages. In fact, the introductory essays spelled out the unique and enduring value of the Classic and the commentaries discussed the significance of the text; yet the *Wu ching cheng-i* was above all a sorting out of traditions of scholarship on texts fundamental to civilized life. While recognizing the diversity of past scholarship, it identified some commentaries and modes of interpretation as most authoritative and brought northern and southern traditions of interpretation together. In short, it integrated, ranked, and summarized an extensive tradition in a single set of works. It was a kind of encyclopedia of Classical studies.[5]

Histories. Between 623 and 636, standard histories of three northern dynasties (Ch'i, Chou, and Sui) and two southern dynasties (Liang and Ch'en) were written. In 656 ten treatises covering these five sixth-century dynasties treated in the histories were finished; these were eventually included in the *Sui History.* Later came the *History of the Northern Dynasties* and the *History of the Southern Dynasties* and a new *Chin History.* These were works by committees; some men worked on several histories, and some made use of earlier drafts. Here again scholars attempted to sort out the legacy of an era of division and turmoil, recognize the achievements of the various northern and southern, Han and non-Han states, and identify what was worth continuing in the past and what should be avoided. Later intellectuals, who would object that these histories failed to judge past men as a way of warning and admonishing the present, passed over the willingness of these scholars to accept the diversity of the recent past, a willingness born perhaps of their own confidence in T'ang's ability to maintain political unity.[6]

Ritual and Law. Following Sui models, new codes for ritual and law were formulated under T'ai-tsung. The *Chen-kuan* [*Reign Period*] *Ritual*, now lost, defined 150 rituals in six categories. The *T'ang Code* discussed the general principles of criminal law and specified offenses and penalties. Intended to be universal and comprehensive, both codes were updated in later reigns, another illustration of a desire to accommodate change.[7]

Literary Compendia. Court scholars organized and digested the literary heritage in several compilations. Still extant is the *I-wen lei-chü* (Categorized selections from literature) in 100 *chüan*. Its 46 categories and 727 subcategories cover the realms of heaven, earth, and man, following each "affair" (*shih*) with explanatory quotations from the Classics, histories, and other writings, and then present selections from various genres of literary writings (poems, rhapsodies, prefaces, inscriptions). The much grander *Wen-ssu po-yao* (The wide-ranging and essential in literary thought), in 1,200 *chüan*, is lost. A surviving preface indicates that it too drew on a wide range of texts to elucidate a broad range of subjects.[8] The *Wen-ssu po-yao* probably incorporated earlier compendia. Short or long, such works provided a variety of past models and possibilities for thinking and writing about affairs. They were not totally inclusive, however, as the addition of sections devoted to Buddhist and Taoist topics in the great compendium of Empress Wu's reign, *The Pearly Flowers of the Three Teachings*, illustrates.[9]

Classical exegesis, historiography (of which ritual and legal codes were a subdivision), and literary writings were discrete textual traditions and disciplines, each with its own genres, established procedures, and past models. In fact, in the fifth-century Sung dynasty, separate schools had been created for Classical studies, historical studies, literary studies, and what has come to be called Neo-Taoism (*hsuan-hsueh*, or learning that fathomed the unapparent patterns).[10] Disciplined scholarship did not mean career specialization, however; a scholar could serve on commissions in different fields. Compilation projects continued in most fields through Hsuan-tsung's reign. Literary compendia seem to have been particularly numerous, possibly in an attempt to absorb increased literary production; Classical exegesis in the form of new commentaries, however, appears to have been moribund.

Organizing the Cultural Heritage:
The "Treatise on Bibliography"

Works that reviewed, ordered, synthesized, and compiled the textual legacy of the past involved choices of what texts to include and how to rank them. I will use one such work, the "Treatise on Bibliography" ("Ching-chi chih") from the *Sui History* of 656, to elucidate the vision of the cultural tradition that such choices reflected. The compilers made a point of explaining their priorities and their categories in the general introduction, in summary evaluations at the end of each major division, and in the discussions of each subdivision. Indeed, they faulted previous bibliographers for failing to explain the intent of their particular arrangements.[11] Their most general distinction was between traditions that stemmed from the Former Kings of Chinese antiquity and those they classed as "outside the square" or "beyond the bounds" (*fang-wai*).[12] The Buddhist and Taoist scriptural traditions were "teachings from beyond the bounds"; although the "Treatise" reviews their historical development and organization, it does not list the titles of books on these subjects in the imperial library. Without rejecting these teachings out of hand, the compilers warn that "common shih" who do not "comprehend their purport" will go far astray in studying them.[13] This distinction appears within the bibliography proper as well. The ancient Taoist philosophical texts (as distinct from Taoist scriptures), whose great popularity is granted, are said to represent attempts to fathom the "mysterious" (*hsuan*) realm of tao as cosmic process. Such matters, the compilers assert, the sages placed "beyond the bounds" for fear that men would be confused.[14]

What the compilers considered their cultural tradition was thus within the bounds, *fang-nei*, at least in origin, for minor streams did sometimes cross the boundary. They divided this textual tradition into four major divisions: the Classics (*ching*), histories (*shih*), philosophical schools (*tzu*), and literary collections (*chi*), each of which stemmed ultimately from the sage-kings. The earliest precedent for the quadripartite organization was Hsun Hsu's (d. 289) bibliography from the early Chin dynasty, and there was an alternative, the sevenfold division created by Liu Hsiang (80–9 B.C.), adopted in Pan Ku's (d. A.D. 92) *Han History*, and revised more recently with the *Ch'i lu* (Sevenfold record) of the Liang dynasty, all of which the compilers noted. A comparison of the *Ch'i lu* and the "Treatise" reveals an attempt to reduce the status of what had hitherto been important fields of study. Aside from the removal of Taoist and Buddhist texts, the major change was the disappearance of the separate division for the occult arts of prognostication, divination, astrology/

astronomy, apocryphal writings, medicine, the Five Phases (*wu hsing*), and calendrical studies. The new bibliography explicitly deprecated apocryphal texts and placed them at the end of the Classics division; most of the other subjects were relegated to the philosophical-schools division. Prognostication and divination texts, which the government was seeking to suppress, were not even granted a separate subsection. Military texts, given equal status with the various schools in the *Ch'i lu*'s "Schools and Military" division, were reduced to a section within the schools division. The section on ghosts and spirits in the *Ch'i lu*'s historical division disappeared entirely.[15] The compilers also changed the organization of earlier quadripartite schemes so that the historical division preceded the section on philosophical schools.

In discussing the historical development of the textual tradition in whole and in part, the compilers repeatedly made a larger point: the cultural tradition had been in decline. The decline of the ancient Chou dynasty (*Chou chih shuai*) had been a decline in the traditions of producing texts to serve as models for a unified order. The Western Han had stopped this decline to a degree in its effort to reconstitute ancient texts, but decline set in again in the Eastern Han and worsened during the Period of Division. Political order and textual order were one and the same, a unified culture was a moral culture.

The decline in Classical studies began with the Warring States, when "the canonical wen were discarded and the ju of the Six Classics, being unable to fathom the guiding purport," gave themselves over to lengthy elaborations that further obscured the original models.[16] After the Ch'in dynasty (221–207 B.C.) burned the books, the scholars "lost the original Classics" and depended on "oral transmissions"; when the Classics were restored to written form, they appeared in variant versions. The rise of apocrypha in the Eastern Han and the "language of mystery" (*hsuan-yen*) of the Chin period marked a second stage of decline, when on top of endless elaboration and diversification, men sought meanings outside language and tradition. This perverted the "correct canons of the Former Kings," for "when the sages set forth teachings to restrain human desire, they necessarily based them on human affairs and adjusted them to the central tao. They had little to say about the decree of high heaven; they certainly never addressed the patterns [*li*] of what is outside the square."[17] Historiography had declined as well; after the Han dynasty, historians failed to produce reliable and coherent views of a period and no longer "knew previous sayings and past actions, detected the patterns of heaven-and-earth, or grasped the guidelines for human affairs"; their works could not serve to guide rulers and the bureaucracy or set out models of good and bad.[18] Each of the various philosophical schools was based on one aspect of the sages' teachings and government; each had some value, but without a larger unity to incorporate them, their contending claims were divisive. The ju school was included in this indictment.[19] Finally, literary composition, which stemmed from the sage-kings as well, had lost its original function of "making the language clear" and "relating affairs and tracing emotional responses," becoming instead ever more complex, ornate, and self-referential.[20]

As a work by and for scholars, the "Treatise" defined "our" tradition of learning as originating in antiquity, connecting to political and social affairs, and developing through cumulative change and diversification. Each division had a general function, although the compilers had little use for philosophical schools. The Classics served as the foundation from which the other divisions had developed, so that ching-chi (Classics), the title of the first division, included the other three and the whole was called the "Treatise on Ching-chi." The whole was unified by its shared origin. Stemming the decline in all fields required re-establishing continuity with the ancient models, but the compilers also insisted that continuity involved transforming them while being guided by a commitment to the common and constant. For, as the general introduction contended, in writing scholars were "instituting what is proper according to the times, employing the refined and the substantial in alternation, responding with continuation and transformation, and continuing and transforming on the basis of centrality and constancy. What has centrality and constancy can last; what continues and transforms can grow large. The teachings will have their objects; their employment will be inexhaustible. In fact, the mold of benevolence and righteousness; in truth, the bellows of the tao and virtue."[21]

The message to the scholarly community, I think, was that it could perpetuate the cultural tradition by producing works truly continuous with its origins and thus the larger purposes those origins realized. There were boundaries scholars should not cross easily and priorities they should not ignore, yet they could hold all the parts together while accommodating changing circumstances.

The court scholars also had a message for political leaders, one made on behalf of the scholarly community as a whole: the textual tradition was the moral-cultural legacy of civilization, and men learned in it were necessary to political unity.

Now as for the ching-chi [the Classics and the textual tradition], [they are] the subtle pointers of the spiritual and the possible affairs of the sagely; [they are] that with which one makes constant heaven-and-earth, regulates yin and yang, corrects social guidelines, and promotes virtue; without, they make apparent benevolence for benefiting things, and within, they store practices for being good oneself. Those who learn them will grow; those who do not learn them will fall. When [the ruler who is engaged in] the great enterprise honors [these texts], he completes his imperial virtue; when a common fellow can recite them, he wins the respect of nobles. What King has not proceeded along This Way of Ours [ssu-tao] to establish his influence, spread his title, glorify his transforming power, and change customs? Thus it is said, "When, as a man, he is compliant and sincere, it is the teaching of the Songs; when he comprehends widely and knows what is far off, it is the teaching of the Documents; when he is accommodating and harmonious, it is the teaching of the Music; when he is reverent and respectful, it is the teaching of the Rites; and when he composes and draws analogies, it is the teaching of the Spring and Autumn Annals."[22]

"This Way of Ours"[23] is "This Wen of Ours," the Classics. A century later, in 733, an imperial pronouncement on learning put it this way: "The tao depends on wen."[24] The rhetoric is serious.

The "Treatise on Bibliography" exemplifies the task its compilers charge scholars with: to reverse the decline of culture—to change from the present course of writing, which lacks substance and is fu-hua—by bringing their work back into line with ancient models, the "correct canons of the Former Kings."[25] The decline, I would stress, is seen as resulting from the manner in which cultural forms have been continued and transformed and not, as later intellectuals would have it, from a failure to apprehend the tao of the sages with one's mind. For the court scholars it followed that ending the decline depended on changing the way men continued culture through their own wen.

Writing as Culture

Like Yen Chih-t'ui, T'ang court scholars saw writing as both a public matter—it had direct bearing on the quality of the polity—and an individual's affair—it demonstrated his achievements, responded to the times, and established a public presence. In a well-known passage, Ts'ao P'i (187–226), Emperor Wen of the Wei, had written: "I would say that wen-chang is the great enterprise of ordering the state [or: the great enterprise of the well-ordered state], a splendor that does not decay."[26] Ts'ao was speaking of wen-chang as literary composition—he mentions memorials, letters, inscriptions, and poems—but he cited as evidence for his proposition the Book of Change of King Wen of the Chou and the Rites of the Duke of Chou.

It is possible to translate "wen" as the "literary" and mean the "merely literary," much like those historically minded T'ang court scholars who objected to wen that appealed because of the power of its language to evoke effects but had no socially redeeming purpose. In their view, however, this was something that could happen to wen and wen-chang, not a definition of wen. Wen includes the surface and appearance of a thing, specifically a patterned surface and appearance, but it also includes writing, the writing of China invented by the sages as the first step in civilization, and both the resulting textual tradition and its legacy of cultural forms. For the court scholars, even those who objected to embellished writing, wen was a matter of first importance. Wen-chang, as a term for the various genres of "literary composition" in collections of belletristic writing, was part of wen. This is to say, the "literary" and even the "merely literary" were part of wen, but they did not subsume wen. Histories of Chinese literature generally discuss wen as a concept that bears on "literature," but they are not histories of wen. To a considerable extent, the court scholars saw the importance of wen-chang in terms of the role it played as part of wen.

The term "wen-chang" antedates literary composition as an activity, yet its original meaning can apply to literary composition. In an oft-cited passage, Confucius speaks of the unnameable greatness of the sage-king Yao, who took his measure from Heaven; the loftiness of his accomplishments is paralleled by "the brilliance of his having wen-chang."[27] Given the older uses of the terms "wen" and "chang" for a manifest pattern and a pattern created through the use of different colors, respectively,[28] and the use of "wen-chang" to refer to an army standard or blazon (an identifying colored pattern),[29] it is possible to see Yao's "having wen-chang" as his possession of some formal display that represented to others the man and his achievements. We need not assume that Confucius thought Yao had written anything, yet Confucius did suppose the wen could be acquired and passed on. His disciple Tzu-kung said that it was possible to hear Confucius's wen-chang (but not his views on nature and the way of Heaven),[30] perhaps referring to mottoes or sayings as Confucius's models for behavior.[31] Words and sayings, and eventually literary compositions, gave the pattern of the man and his achievements; they fit well with the old sense of wen-chang. Confucius associated wen with learning, but did not consistently equate it with writing, much less with writing as literary art. Yet he recognized that wen as surface adornment could be appreciated and copied precisely because it was attractive.[32] Later men thought Confucius had taught from and transmitted texts, however, and they supposed ancient court officials had composed literary pieces.[33] They saw a parallel between their own writing as a way of manifesting their character and achievements in learning and the idea that Yao had had wen-chang.

By T'ang times written texts were essential to learning, and specialists in texts began to suppose that civilization began with writing. The Sui-

T'ang scholar Yü Shih-nan (558–638) states, for example, "Writing [*wen-tzu*] is the basis of the arts of the Classics and the beginning of Kingly government."[34] Perhaps in early times an interest in well-crafted writing as a mark of learning was supported variously by belief in word magic, by the experience of using artful language in persuasion, and the uncanny ability of those with literary skill to evoke images and emotional responses in others. One thinks, for example, of the *Ch'u tz'u* (Songs of Ch'u), of the "roaming persuaders" of the Warring States Period, and so on. The rise of wen-chang as literary composition is easier to trace. One of the seven divisions of Liu Hsiang's bibliography was devoted to lyric poetry (*shih*) and rhapsodies (*fu*), and although Pan Ku does not use the term "wen-chang" in his comments on this section, he issues a typical criticism of the authors of the merely literary: "They compete to compose verbal elaborations that are ornate and prolix and [poetry's] duty to criticize is lost."[35] In the Han it became possible to make a reputation for composition rather than for political achievements, as Pan Ku implies and as Ssu-ma Ch'ien's biography of Ssu-ma Hsiang-ju (d. 117 B.C.), the great rhapsody writer of Emperor Wu's reign, demonstrates. The *Later Han History* recognized this new career option and path to fame opened to scholars in the Eastern Han by creating a division of biography for writers, the *Wen-yuan* (Park of literature), an addition to the existing *Ju-lin* (Forest of ju) section, used in Ssu-ma Ch'ien's *Records of the Historian* for scholars. Henceforth histories would contain both a *Ju-lin* and a *Wen-yuan* or, in some cases, a *Wen-hsueh* section.

The popularity of the literary endeavor is evident in the proliferation of genres in addition to the rhapsody and lyric poem. Ts'ao P'i's early third century "Discourse on Wen" notes four pairs of genres: the memorial and deliberation, the letter and treatise, the lyric poem and rhapsody, and the inscription and dirge.[36] By the time of Hsiao T'ung's (501–31) *Wen hsuan* (Selections of wen), it was possible to list 37.[37] Genres gave "being good at wen-chang" specific historical content; their development meant being able to compose specific kinds of wen-chang. In the Eastern Han, according to the early T'ang "Treatise on Bibliography," it became customary to assemble such writings by individuals in *chi* (collections). In the early T'ang 437 such collections, principally from the Chin, Sung, and Liang dynasties, were extant (of a total of 886 then known to have existed at some point). Anthologies appeared as well, apparently beginning with Chih Yü's (d. 312) *Wen-chang liu-pieh chi* (Collection of diversified wen-chang; *or* Literary compositions according to genre). In the early T'ang, 107 anthologies were extant (of a total of 249 known such collections).[38]

The central place of literary composition in the sixth-century courts of the south was well known in the early T'ang. Historians noted that past rulers had patronized literary composition and treated literary craft as the pre-eminent achievement of learning.[39] At southern courts ornate literary accomplishment became the mark of being cultured.[40] This was an elegantly polite form of learning, which asked men to study the appropriate way of composing in a particular genre, the genre appropriate to the particular occasion, and the properly refined way of handling any subject.[41] As Confucius's disciple Tseng-tzu said: "A gentleman makes friends through wen and looks to his friends for support in benevolence."[42] Southern courtiers perhaps did not think it possible to make friends without wen. Although the northern courts set less store by learning, when they wished to have the best of learning, even they patronized men good at wen-chang such as Yen Chih-t'ui. Before the T'ang, then, wen-chang had come to be seen as the aristocratic means of demonstrating the acquisition of culture. Literary endeavor allowed men to participate in This Culture of Ours as individuals; it did not require court office or a tedious commitment to scholarship. In practice literary composition was by far the most popular field of learned endeavor, as David McMullen has pointed out.[43]

Yet the rise of wen-chang carried with it a dilemma. Wen and by extension wen-chang came to be seen as necessary to a civilized order, yet the justifications for the literary enterprise also justified an open-ended process of refinement and change that some found dangerous. Early T'ang scholars took note of the necessity of the literary by repeatedly citing two passages that gave it a rationale and a purpose. The first passage implies two ideas: that the "pattern-tradition-culture-literature of man" (jen wen) was parallel to the "pattern of heaven" (t'ien wen), the manifest pattern of cosmic process; and that to transform human society into a properly ordered world, one had to take guidance from the wen of man. The two sentences in question appear in the Pi hexagram of the Book of Change: "Contemplate the wen of heaven to detect changes in the seasons. Contemplate the wen of man to transform all under heaven [kuan jen-wen i hua-ch'eng t'ien-hsia]."[44] Hsiao Kang (503–51), the future Emperor Chien-wen of Liang (r. 549–51), explained jen-wen in his preface to his brother Hsiao T'ung's collection. In defense of the proposition that "the significance of wen is great and far-reaching," he cites this passage and, after elaborating on the cosmic order, turns to the wen of man. "Then writing [wen-chi] came into being, and books were made; songs arose, and hymns began. [The ancients] perfected filial piety and reverence in the human relationships; they shifted customs toward Kingly governance. The tao extended to the ends of the eight directions and the normative patterns [li] penetrated through the nine levels, bringing the illumination of the spiritual into action and the bells and chimes into harmony. This is what is meant by the wen of man."[45] Wen is, then, the root of civilization and the embodiment of the cosmic pattern. It has the power to guide and stimulate.

The second passage is from the *Tso chuan*, where it is attributed to Confucius. Here the idea is that to realize intent in action requires the mediation of wen between language and practice. "The language is to be adequate to what one is intent on [*chih*] and the wen is to be adequate to the language. If he does not use language, who will know what he is intent on? If the language lacks wen, it will not go far [*yen chih wu wen, hsing erh pu-yuan*]."[46] Court scholars quoted only the last sentence, usually replacing the conjunction *erh* in the last clause with the object signifier *chih*, so that the sentence reads: "When one puts [the intent] into language without wen, then when he puts it into practice it will not go far." Saying what one means is not enough. Language must be made wen before it can serve as an enduring guide to practice.

But the reasons why wen is vital also validate efforts to improve the wen that mediates between heaven and man, ruler and subject, language and action. By T'ang times a long tradition of writing about literary composition accepted this. Examples include Ts'ao P'i's "Discourse on Wen," Chih Yü's "Collection of Literary Compositions According to Genre," Lu Chi's (261–303) *Wen fu* (Rhapsody on literature), Liu Hsieh's (ca. 465–ca. 522) *Wen-hsin tiao-lung* (Elaborations of the cultured mind), and Hsiao T'ung's preface to the *Wen hsuan*.[47] This was at the root of scholarly discomfort, for it seemed that what society saw as the best wen was also, in one view, the kind of highly refined writing least appropriate to transforming all under heaven into a single empire and setting standards for practice conducive to unity.

The debate was well established before the T'ang. To see the two sides of the argument, consider, first, the *Wen hsuan* preface as a justification for continued refinement. Hsiao T'ung suggests that literary composition is the best of the textual tradition that includes Classics, histories, and philosophical schools and that its ongoing refinement makes it the ultimate sophistication of civilized life. As David Knechtges, a translator of the *Wen hsuan*, notes, Hsiao T'ung "comes close to conveying the idea of 'pure literature.'"[48] In this he was, perhaps, approaching a description of the actual situation. The preface begins on a dark historical note.

> Let us examine the primordial beginning,
> And distantly observe those shadowy customs—
> Times when men dwelled in caves in winter, nests in summer,
> Eras when people consumed raw meat and drank blood.
> The age unadorned, the folk simple,
> This Culture of Ours was not yet active.

This depiction of a crude antiquity when men were little better than the animals they ate set the stage for the essential point: wen transforms men into civilized beings.

> Then when Fu Hsi came to be king to all under heaven,
> He began by drawing the eight trigrams and by creating writing
> To replace governance through knotted ropes.
> It was out of this that the textual tradition came into being.

Now we have the advent of civilization, that is, the appearance, first, of the trigrams as images corresponding to the forces operating in heaven-and-earth and, second, of writings as the means by which the king's policies would be recorded and transmitted. The textual tradition thus begins from the records of the sage-kings' government and instruction. All this is perfectly correct from the early T'ang view, as is the following.

> The *Change* says, "Contemplate the wen of heaven
> To detect changes in the seasons.
> Contemplate the wen of man
> To transform all under heaven."
> The temporal significance of wen is far-reaching indeed.

Wen was brought into being with the eight trigrams and writing as the medium through which the ruler's will was communicated. Thus did writing become both the medium and the record of civilization. It is that to which the later ruler looks to transform the world. (The author, as crown prince, expected to inherit the throne and become the sage-king of the day himself.)

At this point in the preface, Hsiao introduces the idea of cumulative refinement. What was regarded as valuable in the past appears crude when compared to the refined forms of the present. When something becomes more intense, it is no longer what it was originally.

> The crude cart is the beginning of the Imperial Conveyance,
> But does the Imperial Conveyance have the simplicity of the crude
>   cart?
> Thick ice is formed by accumulated water,
> But accumulated water lacks the cold of thick ice.
> Why is that?
> Let me suggest:
>   Continuing the affair [in the first case] added ornament,
>   Changing the original [in the second case] increased intensity.
> Since this is so for things,
> It ought to be so for wen as well.
> Having changed and altered with the times,
> It is difficult to describe in detail.[49]

In my view, the preface invites the reader to continue a process that is both historical and natural by participating in the ongoing refinement of wen through literary composition. The literary is the refinement and inten- sification of This Culture of Ours, even though it appears to be a small and less significant part of the textual tradition as a whole.

In the *Wen hsuan* preface, the refinement of language and expression and a concern with surface and affect are positive values. Those who continue the development of wen-chang are improving on the ancients. We can find an early T'ang version of this attitude in the literary encyclopedia *I-wen lei-chü.* Its preface contrasts its use of the "affairs" of the realms of heaven, earth, and man as organizing categories and the *Wen hsuan's* organization around genres. Yet it still represents each affair, from celes- tial bodies to insects, through its cumulative elaboration in the entire textual tradition (from the Classics on) and faults earlier encyclopedias that merely "wrote directly on the affair." Each entry concludes with the quotation of several wen-chang, the ultimate refinement of man's appre- ciation of the world.⁵⁰

The opposing view did not doubt the transformative powers of wen- chang; what it did not want was the refined sophisticates of the southern courts. T'ang court scholars found one example of this view in Li O's letter to Emperor Wen of the Sui (r. 589–605) calling for enforcement of the prohibition of 584 against the ornate southern style of wen-chang.

I have heard that when the wise kings of antiquity transformed the people, they necessarily changed what [the people] saw and heard. They curbed the people's sensual desires, and they blocked the people's impulse to abandon themselves to evil; they showed the path of simplicity and harmony. The five teachings [on the five human relationships] and six kinds of conduct [filial piety, friendliness, etc.] were the basis for instructing the people;⁵¹ the *Songs, Documents, Rites,* and *Change* were the gate to moral duties. Thus, for enabling families to restore filial piety and parental love and men to know how to be polite and courteous, and to rectify customs and harmonize manners, nothing was more important than these. All those who did present memorials and offer rhapsodies, compose elegies and engrave inscriptions, did so to praise virtue and give precedence to wisdom, to illuminate merit and set forth the normative pattern [*li*]. And even if they were not admonishing and encouraging, there was real significance.

Descending to later ages, customs and teachings gradually declined. The three rulers of Wei valued literary elaborations [*wen-tz'u*] one more than the other. They ignored the great way of being ruler to men; they liked the minor art of "insect carving."⁵² Those below followed those above, much as an echo or a shadow; competing for ornamented appearance [*wen-hua*] consequently became the cus- tom. In the southeast in Ch'i and Liang, it spread so completely that noble and base, wise and foolish, all devoted themselves solely to verse. In consequence, once more men omitted normative patterns and preserved what was exceptional;

they sought the empty and chased the minute. They competed over the originality of a single poem and contested the cleverness of a single word. Poem after poem and document after document never got beyond describing the moon and dew; tables were heaped and chests filled with nothing more than the appearance of wind and clouds. Society ranked men by such [endeavors], and the court picked shih on this basis. Once the path to salary and advantage [through the literary] had been opened, the feeling of attachment became even more intense.[53]

Li goes on to assert that, having stopped paying attention to the texts of the sages, men devoted themselves to embellishment with the result that "the literary brush became ever more lush and government ever more chaotic."

The *Wen hsuan* preface and Li O's letter suggest opposing views of the history of culture and the meaning of being civilized. In the first, culture is a cumulative, open-ended enterprise. The past is being improved upon, and in the process the original (undesirable) substance is transformed. Scholars should rework the tradition into something new. In the second, the history of culture is the decline of culture: refinement obscures the original models that restrained men with ethical duties. Scholars should aim at giving contemporary form to the original models. Yet both Li and Hsiao operate within the same intellectual universe. Both claim to be continuous with the past in various ways, both ultimately ground culture in the cosmos, and both assume that wen-chang provide models for the present. Both positions locate the normative patterns of li in wen. But Li O, who argues that it is possible (though not desirable) to omit li, insists that there is a particular set of cultural forms in which normative patterns are manifest. By T'ang times a polarity between "wen" and "tz'u" (elaborated language) and "li" had become a standard part of thinking about wen. Both wen and li can mean "pattern." This allows for various kinds of correspondences: wen is human, whereas li is of heaven-and-earth; wen is manifest, li is hidden; wen is particular and historical, li is general and constant; wen is literary and li is ethical.[54] The use of this polarity signaled a recognition that the elaboration on past models was, in fact, indeterminate and that there was a need for some term to refer to the constant in a world of change. T'ang court scholars shared Li O's sense of cultural decline. As Wei Cheng (580–643) explained in his introduction to the *Ch'ün shu chih yao* (The essentials of governing from the many books), wen-chang had drifted along without returning; the ever more elaborate it had become in its attempts to distinguish all things, "the ever more it had lost the source for writing."[55] Yet scholars sought a synthesis of the two views, not a simplistic, authoritarian resolution.

Before turning to that synthesis, I would observe briefly that those who were concerned with wen thought they were addressing an issue raised by

Confucius. Confucius had spoken of *ssu wen* and of the Chou being "resplendent in wen, having before it the example of the two previous dynasties. I am for the Chou."[56] But the *Analects* also warns that concern with wen alone is not sufficient. To make his point, Confucius proposes a polarity: "When there is a preponderance of native substance [*chih*] over acquired refinement [*wen*], the result will be churlishness. When there is a preponderance of wen over chih, the result will be pedantry. Only a well-balanced mixture of wen and chih will result in gentlemanliness."[57] By T'ang times, numerous polarities were associated with wen and chih: acquired/innate, frivolous/substantial, refined/simple, surface/depth, gaudy/plain.[58] Whereas the *Analects* suggests that one could favor chih or wen, in the T'ang wen and chih had become a polarity within wen–chang itself.

For Confucius the problem was to find something that would bind the open-endedness implicit in valuing wen: "The gentleman widely versed in wen but brought back to essentials by the rites can, I suppose, be relied upon not to turn against what he stood for."[59] In one instance he insists that ethical behavior is the primary concern: "A young man should be a good son at home and an obedient young man abroad, sparing of speech but trustworthy in what he says, and he should love the multitude at large but cultivate the friendship of his fellow men. If he has any energy to spare from such actions, let him devote it to learning wen."[60] And he distinguishes the cultural forms for cultivating the self from the ethical norms of social relations.[61] For in the end, he is concerned with how men act: "If a man who knows the three hundred *Odes* by heart fails when given administrative responsibilities and proves incapable of exercising his own initiative when sent to foreign states, then what use are the *Odes* to him, however many he may have learned?"[62] T'ang court scholars shared his concern, but they lived in a world where it was possible to think that how men acted depended on the cultural forms they had acquired.

The Mission of Wen-chang

In the introductions to the chapters of literary biographies in the eight histories of the Period of Division and in other writings, the T'ang court scholars set out their vision of wen-chang, its mission, why that mission was possible, and what was necessary to accomplish it.[63] The similarities in their various statements make it possible to speak of a shared credo for the learning and culture of the shih. To make their case, they argued from wen as a general category that included all learned activity to wen as the narrower enterprise of literary composition, assigning it a crucial responsibility in resurrecting a cultural tradition in decline and in securing the unified political order of the T'ang. As a bibliographic tradition, literary collections were of secondary importance. Reflecting the attitudes found in past prefaces to literary collections, the compilers of the "Treatise on Bibliography" saw literary collections as a resource for appreciating the character of their author and for following changes in styles of literary expression.[64] But, as the eight histories recognize, literary composition is the form in which the larger cultural tradition is brought to bear on any moment in history. This gives the wen-shih a vital role in state and society. Moreover, although the ju were more committed to the authority of the Classics—and the court scholars certainly were insisting on the primary importance of the Classics—they saw that literary scholars had an interest in the entire textual tradition.[65]

The eight histories regard the wen and ju traditions as different but compatible. Both share an origin in the ancient creation of writing and government and a common responsibility for the perpetuation of all that these represent. The ju are important because the Classics are invaluable; they are heir to the exegetical tradition and must keep the Classics accessible as sources of models. But writers of wen-chang have equally indispensable tasks, one of which is to bring those ancient models to bear on the present.[66] The early T'ang court scholars note times (the Wei-Chin period, the Liang dynasty) and places (the southeast, Loyang) at which the wen side flourished more than the ju, but generally they commend those rulers and courts that saw the value of both. For example, the Liang founder is said to have valued both ju-ya (ju correctness) and wen-chang; the Northern Ch'i founder aided in the restoration of wen-chang, rites, and music; and the Chou founder saw the value of ching-shu (the methods of the Classics) and hsueh-i (the learned arts).[67] T'ang T'ai-tsung, in an introduction to a collection of his poems, provided a more recent example of this effort to hold the two together. His interest in i-wen (literary composition) was, he claimed, informed by his desire to know the character of past rulers (and make it possible for later rulers to know him) yet grounded in standards of sage-king correctness drawn from the wen-chiao as he found it in the Six Classics and balanced by a concern for "martial virtue."[68]

The histories, like the "Treatise on Bibliography," make cultural decline the central theme of their reviews of the wen and ju traditions. After the Han dynasty, neither sustained its ancient functions. In part this was the fault of rulers, who were not consistent in supporting or listening to scholars. At the same time those who represented the ju and wen modes of learning, when left to their own devices, had tended to be consumed by parochial concerns. The ju, for example, instead of teaching others to employ the teachings of the Classics—the wen-chiao, ju-chiao, or ching-

shu—in the tasks of government, drifted into exegetical studies of the texts. Scholars of wen also drifted into partial, parochial interests, and became mere *tz'u-jen*, men skilled in verbal elaborations. Just as the ju devoted themselves to writing about the language rather than the teachings of the Classics, so did tz'u-jen devote themselves to refining the literary surface in search of personal recognition. Skill and ornament won out over substance; the personal and sensual overrode the common and constant. Although the histories of the northern dynasties held that northern rulers gave inadequate attention to wen, they were especially critical of southern rulers who knew that wen did indeed matter but patronized the merely literary.[69]

The court scholars thus needed to explain what kind of wen the T'ang should patronize and, because they were asking scholars to change from recent practice, they needed to justify their views. Their accounts of the correct form of wen-chang as part of wen, however, offer a view far more complex than a simple return to the authoritative models of antiquity. The complexity stems from an effort to show that wen does, in fact, hold everything together. It has cosmic grounds, in the tao of heaven-and-earth, but it also has historical grounds, in the works of the sage-kings and later writings. It not only sets out models for all under heaven from above, but it also manifests the emotional responses to the times and the character of individuals below. These issues will first be treated separately.

Wen and the Tao of Heaven-and-Earth

The introductions usually begin with some version of the patterns of heaven and of man. The *Chou History* notes: "The two forces [i.e., yin and yang] were fixed, and the sun and moon flashed with light; the pattern [*wen*] of heaven was manifested. The eight trigrams were set forth and written records were created; the pattern [*wen*] of man was detailed."[70] Writing began with the schematic representation of the interaction of natural forces. The court scholars also noted the more elaborate accounts of this in the *Hsi-tz'u chuan* (Commentary on appended verbal elaborations) of the *Book of Change*. Fu Hsi, contemplating the images (*hsiang*) of heaven and their parallels on earth, observing the tracks (wen) left by birds and beasts, and drawing on his body and on things, created the eight trigrams "to bring into circulation [*t'ung*] the power of spirit illumination and categorize the actualities of the ten thousand things."[71] One official view, however, adopted the idea that the eight trigrams came from the *Ho t'u* (River chart), a figure on the body of a dragon that rose out of the Yellow River.[72] Whether wen was a human artifact or simply presented itself to human notice in a mysterious way, both versions suppose that wen manifested patterns of heaven-and-earth and things as an order that existed before human society.

In this regard some scholars of Chinese literary thought have made a point of signal importance to the understanding of medieval culture: that culture rested on the assumption that there is no necessary disjunction between the human realm and the realm of heaven-and-earth; the patterns of human cultural creations can thus be identical to the patterns of the cosmos. In contrast, traditional Western theories see literature in terms of mimesis, as an always imperfect attempt to represent and imitate the truths of a separate realm. Greek views of literature thus begin from a conviction that it is fiction. T'ang (and earlier) attempts to understand the nature of wen begin from the assumption that it is veracious. As Pauline Yu writes with reference to the tale of Fu Hsi, "Mimesis is predicated on a fundamental disjunction between two realms of being, one of which is replicated in the verbal product, regarded by Plato, for example, as but a pale shadow of some timeless truth. In contrast, implicit in the Great Commentary [Hsi-tz'u chuan], as in the Great Preface to the Classic of Poetry, is the assumption of a seamless connection, if not virtual identity, between an object, its perception, and its representation, aided by the semantic multivalence of the term hsiang [image]."[73]

T'ang scholars did claim that wen originally replicated the pattern of heaven-and-earth in forms that served as guides for man; they recalled, for example, that Yao took his standards from heaven and had brilliant wen-chang.[74] The greatest wen "is in perfect agreement with heaven-and-earth; it creates instructions and sets forth models."[75] From this, it follows that wen can also provide a guide to the workings of heaven-and-earth. For example, because Confucius's inherent character partook of the tao of heaven, his editing made it possible for the Six Classics to "give the scope of heaven-and-earth."[76] And wen can "make accessible the typical responses [ch'ing] of the hidden and apparent and illuminate the conjunction of heaven and man."[77] The Former Kings and sages had availed themselves of heaven-and-earth's guidance directly and personally. The T'ang preface to the Book of Change asserts:

When Kings acted, they necessarily took the standard from the tao of heaven-and-earth so that not a single thing failed to fulfill its nature. When they moved, they necessarily accorded with yin and yang so that not a single thing was harmed. Therefore, since they were able to hold together the cosmos and respond to the spirit light, the royal altars were never exhausted and their reputations never decayed. This was only possible because [their] tao attained the ultimate of the mysterious and subtle [hsuan-miao].[78]

There is that which is "mysterious and subtle," but the sages had perfectly realized it.

The claim that wen-chang originally looked to the tao of heaven-and-earth might imply that latter-day composers of wen-chang should also seek to penetrate the realm of the mysterious. This was a difficult point for the court scholars. They were not about to give up such an important argument that literary composition should reflect timeless norms, but they also saw heaven-and-earth as "outside the square" and contended that there was a necessary connection between the *hsuan-hsueh* of the Wei-Chin period and literary decline. Scholars of the period had become mere tz'u-jen, who "all desired to match the process of spontaneous creation [*tsao-hua*], to have brilliance rivaling the sun and moon."[79] Superficiality and embellishment were the consequence of trying to give form to the mysterious instead of taking guidance from ancient models.[80]

Lu Chi's *Wen fu* (Rhapsody on literature), from A.D. 303, illustrates what the court scholars objected to, even if they did not deny his achievement.[81] Lu confronted the disintegration of a unified political culture, and like other scholars associated with "studies of the mysterious," he supposed that the truly constant was no longer manifest. The sociopolitical world was not predictable; for guidance men depended on their own insights. For Lu Chi wen-chang made it possible to reconnect mysterious constants and visible models.[82] Wen was the counterpart of what was hidden in the mind and the real order that was obscured by the unreliable workings of external phenomena.[83] Writing was public and fixed, it provided others with access to what was hidden, it revealed the writer himself, and it captured something true about the things being discussed. It was a way of *t'i wu* ("giving the normative form of a thing"), an approach to wen-chang T'ang scholars associated with this period in particular. Lu's rhapsody might be said to give the normative form of wen as literary composition. As he notes in introducing his subject, "I constantly fear my conceptions not being equal to the thing, and my wen not being equal to my conceptions."

In fact, Lu spoke of the composer as one who not only "took a position at the hub of things and contemplated in the mysterious [*hsuan*]," but also "roamed through the forest of wen-chang," and who then "might express himself in *ssu-wen*." The writer "traps heaven and earth in the cage of form; he crushes the myriad things under the tip of his brush" and "may depart from the square and deviate from the circle; for he is bent on exploring the form and exhausting the image." But in the end he returns to order: "When the heavenly arrow is at its fleetest and sharpest, what confusion is there that cannot be brought to order?" The result was a work of real value, for "the function of wen is surely to serve as that through which the many normative patterns [are manifested]." And thus, Lu concluded, true wen-chang could "travel endless miles . . . span innumerable years . . . bequeath patterns to the future . . . preserve the tao of [Kings] Wen and Wu . . . be like spirits and ghosts in bringing about metamorphoses . . . and be new always."

In more recent times Liu Hsieh had made similar claims in his *Wen-hsin tiao-lung*. His first chapter, "The Origin in Tao" ("Yuan tao"), has been used to great effect by Stephen Owen to explain why literature could be seen as that "in which the 'aesthetic pattern' [*wen*] of the universe becomes manifest."[84] Liu begins by elaborating on the idea of the wen of heaven and proceeds to argue that wen-chang, as the wen of man, is the manifestation of the human mind, which is itself of the "mind of heaven-and-earth." Literary composition, as practiced, made this more than a conceit. The parallelism and internal organization of the composition reflected the bipolar organization of the cosmos; the configuring of things and the implication of larger categories that followed from the juxtaposition of opposites and creation of parallels corresponded with ideas about heaven-and-earth, as did the sense of movement and transformation that resulted from the accumulation of lines. Liu Hsieh, however, makes a point of insisting that access to the ultimate tao is mediated by sages and language: "Thus we know that tao has proceeded through the sages to manifest wen and that the sages have illuminated tao through wen. [Their wen as the manifestation of tao can be] extended in all directions without being retarded, employed daily without being exhausted. The *Change* says, 'Stimulating the activity of all under heaven depends upon the elaborations of language [*tz'u*].' That which enables elaborations of language to stimulate all under heaven is the wen of tao."[85] T'ang court scholars encouraged a further retreat from the search for personal access to the hsuan.[86] They were calling, after all, for a return to shared models for a unified state. The tao of heaven-and-earth and the li of things was adequately manifested in the wen of antiquity. There was no need then, personally to go beyond the bounds of man's wen and enter the realm of the hsuan in learning; yet through the appropriation of ancient models, wen continued to embody the tao of heaven-and-earth.[87]

Wen and the Legacy of Sages and Former Kings

Typically, having cited heaven-and-earth, the court scholars immediately claimed that wen as *the* textual tradition began with the records of the words and deeds of the ancients.[88] The ancient texts had mediated the relationship between man and cosmos by making heavenly norms guides for human affairs. The manifest patternings of heaven-and-earth guided the sages in "establishing the words for transforming the world."[89] The *Chin History* gives a standard account of the original function: "Then the tao of written records arose, the wen of bells and chimes spread; bringing customs under Kingly transformation, honoring filial piety and respect in the social bonds. They gave woof and warp to *ch'ien* and *k'un* [yang and yin], they joined together [*mi-lun*] center and periphery. Thus we know how great and far-reaching is wen as a standard for the times."[90] Once records were transmitted, the "surviving influence [of the sages] could be transmitted," making it possible for later men to learn from the past and prepare models for the future. The *Chou History* explains:

Thus the Duke of Chou, he of many talents and arts, reflected on the two eras [of Hsia and Shang] to make [wen's] root correct; and Confucius, he whose inherent character partook of Heaven's tao, edited the Six Classics to support its branches. Therefore they were able to give the scope of heaven-and-earth and set the measures for human relations. Fathoming spirits and understanding transformation, the very best of a thousand years past; ordering the state and regulating customs, containing what shall be employed for a hundred generations hence. Perfect indeed; such was the writing of the sages.[91]

Recorded in writing, these expressions became the wen of man; they enabled later men to use past achievements as guides and provided models for their own wen. It is also in this sense that the introductions to literary biographies use the saying "If he puts [what he is intent on] into language without wen, then when he puts it into practice it will not go far."[92]

The court scholars were in full agreement about the need to keep wen grounded in this historical tradition of wen both as normative models for society, which men would accord with, and as the legacy of past models in reference to which the current ones should be composed. Like it or not, those who composed wen-chang were thus responsible for "aiding the tao of kingship" and providing the "means by which he above spreads his teachings to those below," for nothing was more important than "regulating rites and music, ordering human relations, comprehending past and present, and relating good and bad."[93]

But, having said this, the scholars proceeded to point out how the tz'u-jen of later times concerned themselves with literary embellishment, drifted ever farther away from the original models, lost touch with the sources, and thus could not produce wen capable of showing the way to a moral order.[94] From the perspective of the court scholars the substantial, less embellished models of antiquity truly had *wen-ya* ("cultural correctness" rather than "literary elegance").

Wen and Human *Ch'ing* and *Hsing*

The court scholars hold that the Former Kings created wen, overarching models for a unified polity patterned on the natural order, and they conclude from this that those who compose wen should share the purposes of the Classics in form and function. Had the scholars rested with this "top-down" view, they would merely be saying that writers should serve larger moral-political purposes. They go beyond this, however, by recognizing the validity of belletristic literary writing as a historical tradition they trace back to both the Classics (the *Songs* and *Documents*) and Ch'ü Yuan (332–295 B.C.) and the Ch'u poets.[95] In this tradition wen-chang is writing that expresses the individual's emotional responses to particular circumstances (*ch'ing*) and thus reveals his nature or inherent character (*hsing*). Yet for the eight histories there is no necessary contradiction between wen as normative models and wen that "subtly expresses the personal nature [*hsing-ling*]," although these can be different enterprises in practice.[96]

The idea of grounding poetry and literary composition generally in the individual can be traced back at least to the Han. For T'ang scholars it began with the "Great Preface" to the *Songs*, which they ascribed to Confucius's disciple Tzu-hsia, and the T'ang preface to the *Book of Songs* elaborated on this. In "Discourse on Wen," Ts'ao P'i had made the influential statement that "in wen, vital energy [*ch'i*] is the most important thing," a claim that located the ultimate grounds of wen in the individual as part of the natural order. The grounding in the individual is also a vital part of the mix for Lu Chi and Liu Hsieh.[97] For the court scholars, the idea that the literary expressed the self is true for all genres; it is not simply a theory of poetry. To quote the *Chou History*:

> If we trace back to the origin of the writing of wen-chang, it is based in *ch'ing-hsing*. With deep thinking, the transformations are limitless; taking form in language, the diverse streams spread out. Although the lyric poem and rhapsody proceed separately from the memorial and proposal and the inscription and dirge travel apart from the letter and discourse, when we get down to their essentials and raise up their whole, then ch'i is the important thing in all, and all transmit conception [*i*] through wen.[98]

The diversification of forms of expression, evident in the proliferation of genres, results from a common process, the authors contend, that is itself determined by the ch'i of the author and thus necessarily reflects what he has his mind on. The issue here is the significance of literary style and form, how men write as a revelation of what they think and feel rather than what they say.

For the court scholars, both the style of expression and the desire to express oneself were connected to an understanding of emotional response that antedated the T'ang and would eventually be incorporated into Sung moral philosophy. The basic premise is quite simple: when external events impinge on the self, they provoke feelings within. The T'ang preface to the *Songs* put it thus: "The six emotions are calm within, the hundred things stir without. The emotions move according to things; things provoke the emotions to shift."[99] For better or worse, an emotional response is a disturbance in the calm state that is original and natural to man's internal being. This disturbance or agitation is inevitable, unless one closes oneself off from the external world or finds some other way of suppressing the emotions. The second assumption made is that when things stir up emotional responses, men will lose control over their actions, unless they have a way to keep a sense of proper measure. They will be controlled by things, and as the T'ang preface to the *Book of Rites* pointed out, the social order will disintegrate into the pursuit of selfish desires.[100] That preface cites the most famous formulation of this, the passage from the "Record of Music" in the *Rites* translated below (passages in parentheses paraphrase the T'ang subcommentary).

A man is born calm; this is his nature [*hsing*] from heaven (i.e., this is what he obtains from what is so-by-itself [*tzu-jan*]). He is stirred by things and set in motion; this is the desire of his nature. When he is consciously aware of everything that comes, then his likes and dislikes will become apparent (for he will like those things that fit his conceptions and dislike those that do not). When his likes and dislikes have no proper measure within (because he relies on his own feelings), and when his conscious awareness is enticed from without (because his mind follows the things he sees outside and desires arise), he becomes unable to turn back to himself (and stop his emotional desires), and thus the heavenly pattern [*t'ien-li*] (i.e., his nature) is destroyed (for things never stop coming and stirring him). When things stir a man endlessly and when his likes and dislikes have no proper measure, then when things come he is transformed according to those things (so that when good things come he does good and when evil things come he does evil). When a man is transformed according to things, it destroys the heavenly principle (i.e., the pure and calm nature from heaven), and he follows human desires to their limit. Then there will be recalcitrant and deceitful attitudes and licentious and destructive affairs. Thus the powerful will coerce the weak, the many will exploit the few, the clever will deceive the foolish, and the brave will intimidate the timid. The infirm and ill will not be cared for. The old and the young, the orphaned and the widowed, will not attain their places. This is the path to total chaos. Therefore the Former Kings instituted rites and music, that men would take their measure from them.[101]

The aim of the "Record of Music" is to demonstrate that ritual is necessary: it provides the public standards for determining socially acceptable responses. As "things," the rites serve both as objective models of appropriate behavior and simultaneously stimulate correct emotional responses. "Ch'ing" refers to both the emotional responses and the real, actual "circumstances" and objective conditions that provoke those responses. In this sense, ch'ing do not lie, although they may be unwelcome; they accurately reflect the state of affairs that prompted the response as well as the particular character of the man responding.

Wen fits this paradigm easily: proper forms provide both the social models that stimulate correct responses and the forms of expression through which men should respond. Wen-chang makes for a more complex case, for writing takes form variously, in a manner that serves to vent the author's emotional response to his circumstances. As such it can substitute for action. As the T'ang preface to the *Songs* holds: "Although he expresses himself without doing anything, it benefits his soul" [*sheng-ling*].[102] But the quality of the response reveals not only the character of the author but also the quality of the world he is responding to. The "Great Preface" to the *Songs*, which accounts for the origins of poetry as the manifestation of intense emotional response, argues that poetry has value precisely because it is true. The tone of poetry reflects the quality of government, it may be the "sound of" an ordered state, a chaotic age, or a state about to perish.[103] The T'ang preface states: "The six emotions are calm within, the hundred things stir without. The emotions move according to things; things provoke the emotions to shift. When government is pure and harmonious, then [the responses of] pleasure and delight will spread over court and country. When the times are cruel and sullied, then resentment and criticism will appear in chant and song."[104]

Both court and scholars could see the value of wen-chang as a vehicle for influencing others, whether subjects below or rulers above, but for different reasons they also could value wen-chang as the spontaneous response of the author. For the court the tone of writing revealed the effects of government on the governed, and for the writer it was a means of making his frustrations heard. The eight histories contended that wen-chang should be informed by the normative wen of the ancients, but they also held that it should give form to emotional responses. The frivolous literary embellishment that marked polite wen-chang in the Southern Dynasties, they concluded, was in fact the sound of a state about to perish. By avoiding writing that suggested unpleasant and intense emotions, the southern courtiers neglected the duty of literary composition to criticize.[105] There was, therefore, nothing reprehensible about writing that was grounded in ch'ing-hsing. Such a view implied that feelings of conflict and frustration were latent, at the very least, in authentic literary expression. At the same time, the decision to express the self implied a desire to find some way of ameliorating internal conflict and restoring harmony with the world, a motive that was not at odds with the idea of setting forth models for a harmonious society. The *Sui History* explains:

Thus the functions of wen are great indeed. It is that with which the one above spreads his virtuous teachings to those below and those below get across their emotional responses and individual will [*chih*] to the one above. The greatest [function of wen], by giving woof and warp to heaven-and-earth, creates instructions and sets out models. The lesser [function of wen], the airs and tunes and the songs and hymns, corrects the ruler and harmonizes the people.

Sometimes it is a banished minister slandered and exiled, or a homeless shih at the end of his road—the path is tortuous and [his patron] not yet found, his will is repressed, and there is [no one] to express it to. Indignant in his misery, he speeds his wen to the palace; he springs free of the mud and reaches the blue clouds. Time and again they have been saved from drowning in the space of a morning and left a reputation lasting a thousand years. This is why superior men of all kinds put their minds to it.[106]

Wen-chang makes it possible for men to do many things at once: to rechannel frustration, to express their views, to break out of isolation and make contact with those above, and to establish a lasting reputation, in the process.

The court scholars were not grudging in their acceptance of the self-expressive role of literary composition. Yet they were quick to assert that those who had reduced the task of wen to "describing their feelings and giving form to the thing" were being socially irresponsible.[107] The problem, I think, was that even if self-expressive functions of wen shared grounds in the natural order of things with the moral-political models of the ancients, it did not follow that the writer who was venting his feelings was according with the models of the ancients. The *Ch'en History* confronts the problem and proposes that the expression of individual character should be dependent upon the proper form: "When the wen and the normative pattern [*li*] are clear and correct, [the wen-chang] expresses individual character [*hsing-ling*]."[108] The court scholars did not wish to base larger models directly on heaven-and-earth, ignoring ancient traditions; neither were they willing to say that in writing one needed only to release the emotions without reference to traditions of literary expression.

Wen and Literary Craft

The Tang preface to the *Documents* asserts that genre, style, and craft have figured in the history of wen since the sage-kings and are crucial to the successful functioning of wen-chang in society.[109] The eight histories relate the emergence of genres and the importance of style and craft to the expression of emotional responses, as the *Chin History* notes in introducing the diverse achievements of Chin literary figures. "Preferences come into being from the emotions; yielding and firmness are based on the individual character [*hsing*]. Where the emotions are heading is expressed in song. Yet there being no fixed form to stimulation and response, the style and rules [of composition] are variously created."[110] The diversity of genres and styles emerged out of the need to give particular form to the internal states that resulted from involvement in the world. This process was cumulative: the manners of those most successful at expressing their emotions were imitated; imitation led to diversification. The *Chou History* is typical in seeing the rhapsody as the beginning of this process and treating as the first figures of note such early writers as Ch'ü Yuan, Sung Yü, Hsun-tzu, and Chia I. "All shaped and cast individual character [*hsing-ling*] and wove together criticism and correctness; truly, the creation of embellished rhapsodies was their crowning achievement. After this, writing grew abundant and the form of composition was no longer one."[111]

However, the cumulative diversification of belles lettres is not to be seen as an arbitrary process. As I understand them, the court scholars were also arguing that wen as the formal patterning of emotional responses is inherently normative because the process through which the emotions are expressed as form is itself orderly. The editors of the *Northern Ch'i History* wrote, "Thus, as for that from which wen arises: the emotions are expressed within. Man has six emotions, and he is endowed with the refinement of the five constants [i.e., Five Phases]. The emotions stimulate the six [corresponding] ch'i and accord with the order of the four seasons."[112] The emotions stimulate the ch'i, an entirely natural and fundamentally regular process, and thus there is pattern and structure to expression. The T'ang preface to the *Songs* makes this more explicit. "The emergence of joy and sorrow is hidden in what is so-by-itself [*tzu-jan*], the starting point of happiness and anger does not proceed from human affairs. . . . Thus the origins of the inherent pattern [li] of poetry are one with the opening and shutting [of yin and yang], while the function of the traces of poetry change with the cycle [of dynastic rise and fall]."[113] Thus because the process of emotional response is natural, poetic structure has inherent (and thus normative) pattern, yet at the same time the actual poems men write are tied to the historical moment. By sticking to the framework of the generic traditions of the past, men are according with the natural order.

And yet the histories depicted a cumulative historical tradition of increasing complexity, propelled by men who sought to distinguish themselves through composition. By and large they condemned post-Han developments for superficial concern with appearances while recognizing achievements in literary craft. They noted that wen-chang had become the means through which the emotions were translated into socially acceptable forms and an individual identity made public. Men of learning were now expected to be able to express themselves as well; as the *Northern Ch'i History* advised, those who lacked natural genius should study extensively and practice at length.[114] Yet they are ambivalent. They appreciate the ritual function of literary forms as appropriate modes of expression, but they object that by providing forms for self-expression the tradition of literary composition rewarded skill in the manipulation of the forms alone at the expense of strong personality, moral commitment, and intense emotions. Their views, it may be noted, do describe court poetry as it was practiced at the time.[115]

Their resolution of this conundrum was not a one-sided rejection of literary craft or a demand for intensity. Rather, they proposed a synthesis of what they saw as the dominant polarities within the historical tradition. The *Sui History* presents this in terms of styles of wen-chang in south and north.

To the west of the Yangtze [in the south] melodies spread; they valued the pure and finely woven. North of the Yellow River the language and principles were true and firm; they stressed energy and substance [*ch'i chih*]. With energy and substance, normative patterns [*li*] dominate the language [*tz'u*]. With purity and fineness, the appearance [*wen*] surpasses the conception. Pieces in which the pattern is profound can easily be put into practice; pieces in which the form is ornate are appropriate for singing. This is the general difference between the achievements of southern and northern tz'u-jen. If one can take the pure tones of the one and cut out the awkward sentences of the other, getting rid of the weaknesses of each and combining the strengths of both, the form and substance will be properly balanced, and [the result] will be fully good and fully beautiful.[116]

What this synthesis of north and south represents, I think, is a synthesis of the various concerns discussed to this point: the universal grounding in heaven-and-earth, the authoritative models of antiquity, the intensity of real emotion (now directed toward social and political matters), and literary craft. All of them can be brought together in wen-chang.

The Mission of Wen-chang Accepted

The early T'ang court scholars neither turned away from literary composition as a scholarly activity nor questioned its value for the polity. They rejected what they saw as a one-sided concern with appearances and literary embellishment by articulating a larger vision of wen in which this concern was only a part of the whole. In effect, they provided a new set of justifications for wen-chang, justifications that encouraged later T'ang scholars to continue to believe that literary composition was the highest achievement of learning as a moral enterprise. As they presented it, the mission of wen-chang was to save This Culture of Ours after its long era of decline. Saving it meant restoring unity, and scholars could play their part by weaving together interests that otherwise tended to diverge: constant norms and historical experience, past models and present intentions, expressions of common standards and expressions of personal will, moral commitment and individual talent. Wen-chang allowed all learned men to participate in the T'ang imperial project of incorporating diverse interests in a single polity.[117] This was a cultural project, in which the manifest patterns of and for cosmos, state, and individual inhered in the cultural forms that mediated relations between heaven and man, ruler and ruled, and individual and society. These cultural forms kept men focused on the realm of society and politics, within the bounds of tradition, while allowing them to claim that heaven-and-earth and the internal life were being incorporated. It was up to scholars to show that the cultural tradition, with all its diversity, was a whole of complementary parts by representing this in their own writing. If it could be done in wen-chang, it was possible in practice as well. The survival and great achievements of the T'ang state could be seen as proof of their accomplishment.

But this depended on convincing new generations of scholars to adopt the court scholars' goals and perspectives. There is evidence that later generations were persuaded to locate wen-chang in the larger enterprise of wen as the manifestation of cosmic order and legacy of ancient models, to note the development of the textual tradition, to recognize the importance of style and craft and the grounding in the self, and to claim responsibility for saving culture from its long decline. Three scholars who gained reputations under Kao-tsung (r. 649–83) and Empress Wu (r. 684–705) can serve as examples: Lu Chao-lin (ca. 630–ca. 685), Wang Po (647–75), and Yang Chiung (650–ca. 693).[118]

Yang Chiung's preface to Wang Po's collected works begins by noting the wen of Heaven and of man, the beginning of the textual tradition, the appearance of Confucius, and the division between wen and ju with the emergence of the self-expressive literary tradition. With the Ch'in, he continues, Heaven let This Culture of Ours perish, and Han writers were unable to fully restore its tao; scholars during the period of division either pursued "insect carving" or simply echoed former practices. Wang Po, however, was able to rejoin these interests and speak to all concerns. The Wangs—the T'ai-yuan Wangs in fact—had a family tradition of learning (the famous teacher and scholar Wang T'ung was Po's grandfather), and Wang Po in his youth was already a good student of recent historical and Classical scholarship. In office he produced works on command, when he traveled the compositions he wrote manifested the "inherent patterns of natural creation." Everyone paid attention to his writings; his stele text for a temple to Confucius is an example. Yang then launches into an elegant discussion of Wang's impact on court literary circles, arguing that in 661 there was a return to highly ornate writing and an exclusive concern with appearances. Wang was part of a new generation, encouraged by older court scholars, that changed this style. "Thereupon, they set their minds drumming and dancing, put forth their usefulness, so that all within the eight points of the compass gathered headlong through their thoughts, while myriad ages appeared and disappeared under the tips of their brushes. . . . And in these mighty mirrors men found the true hegemons, powerful but not empty, strong but able to enrich, ornamented but not precious, stable and growing ever sturdier."[119] But Wang was not concerned solely with style, he aimed to grasp matters of enduring value in past and present, to pursue the patterns of the sages and the conjunction of heaven and man. He wrote a commentary on the *Change*, and through this he gained insight into the realm of the hsuan. He wrote on the *Analects* and on Wang T'ung's writings, and he completed various works of his own in addition to his occasional writings and commanded works.[120] In short, Yang Chiung presents Wang Po almost as a model of the kind of man the court scholars of Kao-tsu's and T'ai-tsung's reign thought scholars should be; indeed, he has Wang fighting the very same fight. Not surprisingly we find that Yang shared these views himself.[121]

Wang Po did indeed claim that he aimed to restore This Culture of Ours, after a millennium of decline, by returning to the true mission of wen-chang as that by which the polity was guided and the individual will expressed, "great principles illuminated and branch streams corrected." Wang takes the view, in fact, that the fortunes of the polity depend upon whether the tao of wen-chang is practiced or not. They are not merely a reflection of the quality of government.[122] When Wang received a scholarly appointment at court, he was ordered to produce a set of ten normative statements on political conduct. The only entry that concerns learning is appropriately entitled "i-wen." It begins:

The *Change* speaks of contemplating the wen of heaven to detect changes in the seasons. The [*Tso*] *chuan* speaks of language without wen not going far when put into practice. Therefore, [as Ts'ao P'i said,] wen-chang is the great enterprise of ordering the state, a splendor that does not decay. But what the superior man turns his mind and spirit to should be the great and far-reaching. [Wen-chang] is not only to trace the emotions and give forms to things; it is not only the lesser art of insect carving.[123]

As Yang notes, Wang could see this approach as part of his family tradition through his grandfather Wang T'ung. Today we think of Wang T'ung as a Confucian ju, but for Wang Po the boundaries were not as clear as they are for us. He treats Wang T'ung as a man concerned with wen; indeed, Wang Po claims T'ung located himself as a successor to Confucius with the phrase "With King Wen dead, is wen not here with me [i.e., Wang T'ung]?" His preface to T'ung's continuation of the *Documents* (a preface to a similar continuation of the *Songs* is lost) is yet another example of the scholarly credo. T'ung had collected a series of Han through Chin documents; Po's preface defines the criteria that make wen-chang of later times equal to the documents of the sage-kings: they "harmonize ch'ing-hsing and regulate the state, spread moral relations, and relate the essential way."[124]

Most of my examples come from prefaces to literary collections; it is also in prefaces that Lu Chao-lin takes his stand.[125] The similarities between these prefaces and the introductions to the literary biography sections in the eight histories are quite obvious. We find the same key passages, the same review of the historical tradition, and the same conclusions about the need to realize both the political and the individual functions of wen. It may well be that the authors took the introductions and prefaces to court compilations as their models. By adopting the early T'ang credo as a way of introducing the wen-chang of recent individuals, these men were doing more than merely claiming that they thought wen-chang ought to be like this; they were arguing that the works of the men in question contributed to the program. A generation later Lu Ts'ang-yung would make an even more forceful claim along the same lines for Ch'en Tzu-ang (661–702) as the man who saved the tao of This Culture of Ours after five hundred years of decline.[126] High T'ang poetry, which in Owen's account marks a transition from "poetry as social gesture to poetry as an art with cultural and personal dimensions that transcended the social occasion," has its roots in the court scholarship of the early T'ang.[127]

The early T'ang court scholars had created a vision of This Culture of Ours, of the textual and literary traditions of the past, that could serve as the model for a unified and civilized empire, and they had showed how individuals could participate in it. The T'ang was successful in establishing and maintaining that empire; it could justifiably claim to have both reversed the process of historical decline and matched the Han and ancient Chou. The belief that learned men could hold traditions together in an accommodating whole was shared by many. The 60,000 registered students of Hsuan-tsung's reign stand as evidence that the number of participants in This Culture was steadily increasing; it was no longer limited to scholars at court and aristocrats with a scholarly tradition. The breakdown of the T'ang order after 755 harmed not only the immediate interests of those whose fortunes were tied to the state but also their faith in the correctness of the early T'ang cultural synthesis.

4 The Crisis of Culture After 755

Few contemporaries denied that the An Lu-shan rebellion of 755 had resulted in an institutional crisis. The subjects of this chapter, however, believed that the rebellion and the inability of government to re-establish central authority fully was linked to a more profound crisis of culture and wen-chang, one that antedated 755. Reluctantly, I shall forgo any attempt to trace the development of intellectual life from the early T'ang through the reigns of Empress Wu and Emperor Hsuan-tsung. Suffice it to say that later men believed that literary culture had prospered. As Po Chü-i wrote in the ninth century, "The state has transformed all under heaven with literary illumination [*wen-ming*] and rewarded the shih for literary learning [*wen-hsueh*]. For over two hundred years wen-chang has been brilliant."[1] After the rebellion, particularly during the Chen-yuan and Yuan-ho reign periods (785–820), the court resumed its patronage of the literary as the pre-eminent civil art.[2] But now when emperors "valued wen" and tried to "use the wen of man to transform the world,"[3] they were also declaring an intent to rein in the military and return to a situation in which "the civil [wen] is ruler over the military [*wu*]" or "to bring military affairs to an end and practice the *wen-tao*."[4] A policy of valuing wen over wu was given substance by imperial interest in wen-chang, by the use of literary ability as an important criterion in evaluating shih, and by the giving of political authority to *wen-shih*.[5] The increasing importance of the Han-lin Academy, a center of literary scholarship, and of the posts of chief examiner and rescript writer was symptomatic of this policy.[6] The idea of a civil/military dichotomy was not new in Chinese history—it has its origins in the use of the Chou founding kings Wen and Wu as contrasting models—but it had not figured in early T'ang discussions of wen. Its use in the eighth century went together with calls to restore civil order during a time of military affairs under the leadership of men with literary and cultural attainments.

It was not lost on some that the patronage of the literary merely because it was wen was camouflage for the court's failure to reassert central authority and, as one man put it, to realize the model of heaven-and-earth and the Former Kings.[7] Some saw Hsuan-tsung's (r. 712–56) imitation of ancient cultural models as vainglorious. His reign had failed, despite a ritual program intended to bring the T'ang into harmony with heaven-and-earth and show the emperor as one who, like the Former Kings of antiquity, "responded to tao"; despite attempts to reorganize the bureaucratic system according to the *Rites of Chou*; and despite Fang Kuan's use of Spring and Autumn–era techniques to battle the rebels. Rituals would not save the dynasty, some intellectuals pointed out; nor would the resurrection of ancient models.[8]

The crisis of culture in scholarship appeared initially as a conviction that the cultural models of the past had not worked as intended. Some men claimed the right to do something about this state of affairs, not by denying the importance of wen, but by seeking to recover its original moral efficacy by changing the way men composed wen-chang. Gradually a far more enduring crisis of culture began to take shape, one that would consume the energies of intellectuals for the next three centuries: a crisis of faith in the ability of culture to influence human behavior. And it was created by the very men who sought to save This Culture of Ours.

The assumption that, for better or for worse, wen did influence behavior had given early T'ang scholars a reason to synthesize the traditions of the past in support of the newly unified empire. The figures discussed below, however, no longer assumed this. In arguing that they could change the way men behaved by "restoring" the transformative influence of literary composition, they admitted that wen did not, in fact, necessarily influence conduct. The theoretical gap continued to widen. The literary intellectuals who believed that for writing to have social value it had to be grounded in a personal understanding of tao in effect separated "thinking about values," to translate the nature of their interest in tao, from thinking about cultural forms. Knowing what was good and doing good were matters not of knowing the right forms to imitate but of having the right ideas in mind. This effort, which made ideas more real than culture and which required that each man think for himself and write in a style true to his understanding, thus undermined the goal of a shared, normative culture to serve as the basis for civil order. As long as the excitement of breaking with convention and several hundred years of cumulative tradition lasted, only a few worried about the consequences of doing away with universal cultural models, for the new ideas about learning promised to enable all shih to transform themselves into self-conscious, morally independent men of intellectual integrity.

The men who led the way were mostly from great clans, although not necessarily from the strongest branches, and they were well schooled in the literary habits and assumptions of the past. Yet their work helped destroy the aristocratic culture of medieval China and introduce an era of self-conscious inquiry and debate over ideas. To show how this happened, I shall discuss two sets of men. The first was active during the four decades after the rebellion. It helped establish the pattern of literary men claiming authority over learning without the sanction of court sponsorship. The second set consists of men born around 770, for whom Han Yü's ideas about wen and tao were of the greatest consequence. Here I shall treat only those of the 770 generation who helped make the idea and practice of *ku-wen*, or ancient-style writing, an intellectual movement among the shih. The great danger in telling the story of the emergence of a new, creative, and variegated intellectual culture between 755 and 820 is that we may read back into it the later claim that "literature is to convey moral truths" (*wen i tsai tao*) and conclude that matters of literary form had become irrelevant. Some authoritative reference works attribute this phrase or the idea to Han Yü. Han did not say it—it appears in the writings of the moral philosopher Chou Tun-i in the eleventh century— but the mistake suggests the need to view the eighth century from the perspective of the T'ang past rather than of the Sung future.

The Restoration of Wen-chang (755–793)

In the aftermath of the An Lu-shan rebellion, as a means of contributing to the restoration of order, a number of scholars began to call for a change in the practice of wen-chang. Some of them were court officials; others were refugees who had found safety outside the capital and did not return to court. Their views gained adherents over the course of the next several decades, and by 802, when Ch'üan Te-yü (759–818) was appointed director of the examinations, they had become part of the mainstream. Li Hua (ca. 710–ca. 767), a Chao-chün Li, identified his late friend Hsiao Ying-shih (717–59), of the Liang imperial clan, as saving wen-chang in the face of decline.[9] Li's friend Tu-ku Chi (725–77), of the great Turkic Tu-ku clan, adopted this view, crediting Li, Hsiao, and Chia Chih (718–72), a Ch'ang-le Chia, with the "restoration of wen-chang," and placed himself as their successor.[10] When Tu-ku died, others in turn identified him as the successor to Li, Hsiao, and Chia.[11] One of them, Tu-ku's student and literary executor Liang Su (753–93),[12] became a leading intellectual at the capital and advised Lu Chih (754–805) on candidates at the examination of 792. After Liang's death, Ch'üan Te-yü claimed the mantle. He placed Liang as a successor to Li and the rest as men who "had exercised authority over wen" without high office.[13] Ch'üan himself had connections to the Li and Tu-ku families, became chief examiner, and served briefly as a chief minister.[14] The writings and ideas of Li Hua and his successors set the stage for the rise of ku-wen, yet neither Han Yü nor his followers chose to acknowledge the debt.[15]

The post-rebellion restorationists echoed several early T'ang attitudes. They spoke of the decline of wen after the Han and the authority of ancient models, deprecated literary embellishment, and stressed the social and political roles of writing. More directly they found precedents for their views in the figures of Ch'en Tzu-ang (661–702) and Chang Yüeh (667–730). Lu Ts'ang-yung had made Ch'en Tzu-ang's claim—"The tao of wen-chang has declined for five-hundred years"—the premise for his preface to Ch'en's works. Chang Yüeh, the great patron of scholars as a chief minister to Hsuan-tsung, had restated much of the early T'ang credo in a stele for one of Lu Ts'ang-yung's ancestors. Chang's protégé Chang Chiu-ling (678–740) credited Chang Yüeh with saving This Culture of Ours after several hundred years of decline.[16] Ch'en Tzu-ang, the outsider who claimed personal responsibility for saving wen from decline, was an important precedent for Hsiao Ying-shih, Li Hua, and others who felt themselves to be outsiders—men outside the capital, from weaker branches of old clans, who lacked high position.[17] Before 755 Hsiao Ying-shih had, Li Hua later wrote, "taken wen-chang and institutions as his personal responsibility." Although there is little evidence to support Li's assertion that "all the men of the time allowed him this," the rebellion created an audience for those prepared to claim such responsibility. Moreover, the chin-shih examination system provided those with persuasive definitions of "good" wen a ready mechanism for influencing elite values. The T'ang examinations were not blind tests, especially after 755, when the additional writings candidates submitted to the examiners and influential officials at the capital and the letters of recommendation they collected greatly affected the outcome. A change in literary values could affect these extra-formal requirements, if those in authority chose to prefer certain kinds of writing over others.[18] The story of intellectual change between 755 and the 820's can be told, then, as a tale of cultural politics, in which scholars sought to change the way men acted by changing the way they wrote and thought.

Hsiao Ying-shih, Li Hua, and Chia Chih

Common to Hsiao Ying-shih, Li Hua, and Chia Chih was the conviction that it was necessary to break with current ideas about "good" wen-chang. One of the few surviving pieces of Hsiao's work contains this statement: "Whenever I compose wen, my meter is not close to the conventional; in all the proposals I draft, I necessarily look to the ancients. I have never paid much attention to [writing] after the Wei and Chin, much less the petty and insignificant judgment form [used by the Ministry of Personnel]—how could such ever attract the steadfast will of a full man."[19] Lu Hua's preface to Hsiao's collection gives a more elaborate account of Hsiao's assessment of literary history. In essence, Hsiao held that there had been writers as late as the Wei-Chin period who composed poems and rhapsodies that were still in line with the *Songs* and stayed close to the "source of Kingly transformation" in their expositions. He commends Ch'ü Yuan and Sung Yü of the Warring States period, who produced *wen* that was "heroic" but not to be taken as constant models (*ching*). Among Han dynasty writers, he praises Chia I, whose *wen-tz'u* were the most correct and close to the normative form for order; Mei Ch'eng and Ssu-ma Hsiang-ju, who were talented men but whose writings were not close enough to the admonitory (*feng*) and rectifying (*ya*) qualities of the *Songs*; Yang Hsiung, who made thoughtful use of his conceptions; Pan Piao, who had a good sense of pattern; and Chang Heng, who had great breadth. In the Wei-Chin period, he singles out Ts'ao Chih, Wang Ts'an, and Hsi K'ang. But between them and Ch'en Tzu-ang, whose "wen form was most correct," he saw nothing worth mentioning.[20] Hsiao thus held that to restore the moral function of wen-chang it was necessary to return to those writers whose literary composition still evidenced moral concerns. He called for a synthesis based on individual writers as models, as opposed to the early T'ang synthesis of Northern and Southern Dynasties literary trends. Yet he saves wen-chang from within the tradition of literary composition. He is speaking not of "values" as a category but of styles of writing that evidence a concern with existing (but often ignored) norms.[21]

Li Hua envisioned a more radical possibility. He began an essay on friendship with the claim that "high antiquity did not have wen." Dismissing traditional justifications for the historical existence of literary composition as a discrete tradition—its source in the Former King's creation of wen after the pattern of heaven-and-earth, the normative wen of antiquity collected in the Classics, and the self-expressive literary composition of later ages stemming from Ch'ü Yuan and Sung Yü—he makes moot the idea of finding proper models within this tradition and turns instead to the "teachings" of the Former Kings.[22] In another instance, he asserts that although Confucius's wen-chang were transmitted and the writings of his followers through Mencius were "the continuation of the Six Classics," with Ch'ü Yuan and Sung Yü the "tao of the Six Classics" became concealed.[23] The desire to ground wen-chang in textual traditions other than belles-lettres is evident in his call for a change in examination standards: "I humbly think that seeking to achieve order begins with studying the Classics and histories. Mr. Tso's *Kuo-yü*, the *Erh-ya*, the *Hsun-tzu*, and *Mencius*, and such schools are aids to the Five Classics. Put them into practice in the world as if they were medical prescriptions. The examining officials and candidates should employ them. The other theories of the hundred schools and the apocryphal books are to be preserved but not employed."[24] Li's own wen-chang accord with this advice: they are informed by his historical scholarship and knowledge of the Classics, and they speak thoughtfully and directly to issues of politics and morality. In the central terms of Li's own theorizing, his work stresses "substance" (*chih*) rather than surface embellishment (*wen*). With examples from the Classics and Han history, his essay "On Chih and Wen" (or "On Making Wen Substantial"), from which the passage above comes, argues that wen and chih are a polarity of unequal parts: "wen is not as good as chih," but if the imbalance in favor of wen is too great, merely increasing chih will not save it. Restoring order depends upon re-establishing a simpler and more moral way of life that all can practice. For the ruler, "cultivating virtue to order the world lies in neither cunning nor [military] achievement; rather, it requires being chih yet having institutions; the institutions simply are not to be complex."[25]

Li Hua's position is not incongruent with the study of institutions as in Tu Yu's *T'ung tien*.[26] But I am not sure Li agreed with Tu's contention that "the basis of transformation through instruction lies in creating a sufficiency of food and clothing," not in ritual.[27] Li Hua was not a ritualist, but he was a moralist for whom virtue and personal behavior had priority over institutions. He is a literary scholar of a new sort: a critical analyst, moral teacher, and literary persuader; joining polite society and using literary talents to glorify the state and spread the ruler's transforming influence are not his goals. Before 755 he had written that for "transforming the world, nothing is superior to wen."[28] After 755 he reflected that it was possible for great literary achievements to go together with evil conduct: an abundance of literary talent had not made the "generals and ministers" act correctly, and others had taken a cue from their conduct. The union of the literary and the ethical was necessary to "give form to tao," he wrote, but "among the disciples of the Master there were [men excelling in] ethical conduct, speaking, the affairs of government, or literary learning, yet no one combined these four. Even though ethical conduct is more revered than the arts, it is still difficult to be complete."[29] Yet a unity of wen-hsueh and ethical behavior was necessary.

It seems to me that Li Hua pointed the way toward a solution in which the burden of uniting wen and ethical behavior depended upon the individual's self-conscious choice of values. Alluding to the *Songs*, he argued that the Classics showed that the guiding values (the "will") of the writer or "creator" (*tso-che*) of wen-chang could be distinguished from his emotional responses to the events of the day, which determined the literary tone of the work and linked it to the times.

Wen-chang is based on the writer, whereas sorrow and joy are linked to the times. [A case of wen-chang] being based on the writer is the will [*chih*] that [guided Confucius in creating] the Six Classics. [A case of its] being linked to the times is the joy of [poems responding to the Chou founding kings] Wen and Wu and the sorrow of [poems responding to Chou's decline under kings] Yu and Li. [With wen-chang the ancients] established themselves and made their names known, and [thus] there were states and families. [With wen-chang] they transformed men and perfected customs, [yet some states and families] succeeded and [others] failed.

Wen-chang has real consequences but, Li asserts below, its value depends on the nature of its creators' will. The literary aspect of writing, the vehicle of the emotions, is secondary.

Seen from this perspective, what is proclaimed by the will is called language. What embellishes and perfects it is called wen. The wen of the virtuous is credible [as a standard for practice]. The wen of those without virtue is false. . . . Confucius's wen-chang were transmitted by Yen Hui and Tzu-hsia. After their deaths, Tzu-ssu and Mencius created [wen-chang] that are the continuation of the Six Classics. But Ch'ü Yuan and Sung Yü [also men of virtue writing at the time] never went beyond [merely expressing] their endless pain [at the decline of virtue], and thus [with their wen-chang] the tao of the Six Classics became concealed. . . . When wen agrees with conduct and conduct with wen, is that not akin to the ancient.[30]

For Li Hua the need to find grounds for a unity of cultural form and personal conduct required narrowing the textual tradition to a line of morally correct writings. In doing so he insisted that what men said, "the language," mattered more than how they said it, "the wen." The implication of this, I think, is that things have value because they agree with a tao, not because they are part of wen.

   Chia Chih, the third figure Tu-ku Chi credited with the "restoration of wen-chang," became a court official under Hsuan-tsung, accompanied the emperor on his flight to Szechuan during the rebellion, and served again at court in the 760's. He knew Li Hua and Hsiao Ying-shih, having passed the chin-shih examination together with them in 735, and was admired by Li Hua.[31] He differed from Li by accepting the origins of the literary traditions in high antiquity and in the patterns of man and heaven. Like Hsiao he held that the transformative function of wen-chang had been lost after the Han dynasty. Only men deeply schooled in the Classics who unified wen-hsueh and ethical conduct, he thought, would save This Culture of Ours.[32]

In Chia's view, the way to do this was to change the public definition of good writing by changing examination standards. In 763 Yang Wan proposed scrapping the literary aspect of the chin-shih examination and forbidding the practice of gaining eligibility by submitting writing samples. Instead, Yang proposed the T'ang should restore the "ancient system" of the Han, in which men of "ethical conduct" were recommended by local officials and then tested on a Classic of their choice. He sharply attacked "valuing wen-tz'u" in selecting shih for office, arguing that since the introduction of occasional genres (tsa-wen) in the examinations students had merely studied poetry and the literary collections of a handful of writers, ignoring the Six Classics, the Three Histories, and the tao of Confucius and Mencius.[33] Chia's defense of a literary examination swayed the court. He began by claiming that wen was the greatest of overarching values, a kind of conduct in fact.

"The policy of the Hsia dynasty was to value loyalty, the policy of the Yin dynasty was to value reverence, and the policy of the Chou dynasty was to value wen."[34] Thus wen, as with loyalty and reverence, is [a manner of] conduct that unifies men. Moreover, of the posthumous titles that describe [a man's] conduct, the most admirable is wen. When wen flourishes, then loyalty and reverence are preserved with it. Therefore when earlier periods used wen to select shih, it was based on wen [as a form of] conduct. If one peruses conduct through tz'u [elaborated language], then it pertains to tz'u [as skill in language, not as conduct].[35]

In antiquity the relation between the literary text and conduct was not problematic, Chia continues. Wen served as models for conduct from above and evidence of the conduct of those below, and the Songs played a crucial role in orchestrating social harmony. But now T'ang examiners look to the "lesser tao" of wen, namely, memorization and literary craft. Because those in authority do not value wen as a means of transforming men, students neglect the tao of the Former Kings in favor of literary skill and slide into immoral behavior. Of all groups in the population, the shih are most susceptible to transformative influence from above (feng-hua), he notes. The T'ang has created a vicious circle: the court officials responsible for setting standards for shih learning have themselves lost sight of the "large and far-reaching" issues of a moral order. Never having acquired the principles of ethical behavior, the shih lacked the wherewithal to stay firm in the face of the An Lu-shan and Shih Ssu-ming (d. 761) rebellions. An Lu-shan "gave one shout and all within the four seas were disturbed." Abolishing the literary examinations is, Chia concludes, a false solution. Saving the state requires transforming shih learning, not forsaking it. Moreover, in the aftermath of rebellion, there are few shih left in the countryside, and official families have scattered. Better to work at reestablishing schools and improving the salaries of teachers.[36]

Hsiao Ying-shih, Li Hua, and Chia Chih represented a critique of wen-chang from within the larger tradition of literary learning. Aware that institutional restraints had weakened, they charged the individual with responsibility for his own conduct. In their view the best way to accomplish this was to change the way men thought about literary composition. They helped inaugurate the new, post-rebellion intellectual culture in which, as David McMullen has shown, scholars would determine the intellectual issues of the day through informal writings and make the concept and practice of wen the most widely discussed of all issues.

Tu-ku Chi: "Giving Form to the Will"

Tu-ku Chi promoted the idea that Hsiao, Li, and Chia had effected a "restoration of wen-chang" and that Li Hua was the model scholar. In elaborating on the role of the individual's "will," Tu-ku broke out of the circularity of having wen agree with conduct and conduct agree with wen.[37] Tu-ku's preface to Li Hua's collection presents his account of what the restoration of wen-chang means and Li's role in it. To do this, Tu-ku advances a tripartite relationship among literary forms, language, and the "will."

The will [chih] is given form only through language [yen]; the language is manifest only through the literary form [wen]. These three are interdependent, just as getting across the river depends on making use of boat and oars. Once [such genres as] the Canon [tien] and Counsel [mo] [of the Documents] were neglected and the Rectitude [ya] and Eulogy [sung] [of the Songs] became dormant, the tao of society deteriorated and wen also declined. Therefore writers often put the written words [of the Classics] first and [the intended use of the words] to compare [pi] and stir [hsing] last. This manner spread, and [writers] did not turn back. And so it went till there were even those who embellished on their words [tz'u] while ignoring their intent, so that the more skillful the glossy appearance, the greater the loss of content. At the point of greatest ruin, parallel couplets aligned the branches and paired the leaves; the "eight faults" and "four tones" became fetters. It was as if [the rule of composition] were laws to be obeyed, so closely were they held to. Then, when men heard the works [of the ancients],[38] they laughed till breathless; everyone was the same, as if swept away by wind and clouds. The wen was not adequate to the language. The language was not adequate to the will. It was like using a magnolia petal as a boat, kingfisher feathers as oars—one plays with them on dry land; they are no use in crossing the river. The pain of it: the wash of custom deluding men for so long.[39]

Tu-ku's proposition throughout the piece is that language and literary forms (i.e., genres of literary composition) should be seen as means of expressing the will. As his next paragraph (quoted below) will show, the "will" represents a general moral concern that is inchoate and indefinite.

The will becomes particular only when the individual says something in response to affairs, but what he says must further be put into a recognizable format. The unannounced term here is *hsing* (practice), for Tu-ku is elaborating on the passage in the *Tso chuan*: "When one puts [what he is intent on, i.e., the will] into language without wen, then when he puts it into practice, it will not go far."[40] In antiquity language and literary form were adequate to the will, but once the ancient literary forms ceased to be employed, society and culture declined. Tu-ku's thesis is that the course of decline was exacerbated by efforts to recover the order of antiquity by imitating and elaborating on the wen of the ancients. Thus, first the principles of the *Songs* were lost, then the intention of the ancients' words was lost, and finally the rules of parallel composition became so strong that literary forms thwarted the expression of language that manifested the will.[41]

The T'ang founding halted this decline, Tu-ku's preface continues. Ch'en Tzu-ang returned to the Rectitudes in verse and then Li Hua, Hsiao Ying-shih, and Chia Chih began to "promote the manner of mid-antiquity [when Confucius edited the Classics] to further broaden the wen-virtue [of the early T'ang]." In short, some T'ang scholars had sought to make wen and language capable of expressing the will by breaking with modern forms and returning to the ancient ones. But Li Hua approached this in the correct manner. He first had the will, then he spoke to the occasion out of moral concern, and finally his words were given form in various genres.

His Honor's *tso* [acting and creating writings] was based on the Kingly tao; in general he took the Five Classics as the source. He described his feelings to lodge his censure, and after that there were songs and chants. He praised transformation through instruction and offered admonitions and criticisms, and after that there were rhapsodies and eulogies. He made his own judgments to dispute what everyone else held to be right and wrong, and after that there were expositions and proposals. And in creating records and prefaces, inscriptions for tripod and stone, he rectified praise and blame by selecting [for inclusion] affairs [*shih*] [his subject] had effected. He wrote only on that to which Confucius had pointed. Thus the purport of the Airs and Rectitudes, the roots of punishment and policy, and the great constants of loyalty and filial piety are all manifest in his words.[42]

Literary scholars followed this line, Tu-ku continues, and within twenty years a majority of scholars had been influenced. "What the knowledgeable called a restoration of wen-chang was in fact begun" by Li Hua. At this point the preface takes up Li's career and selected compositions in various genres as manifestations of Li's will. Li's narrow view of what was right did not prevent literary creativity; his writings were "ripples and waves in a myriad transformations, yet always rooted in the

Canons and Counsels." At the same time they revealed Li's true character, "Perusing his wen, you will know his substance; it does not depend on seeing his appearance and hearing his voice."[43] The promise of a unity of morality and culture lies in this claim that Li's wen truly reflected the qualities of the man.

I do not think it is overly interpretive to see in Tu-ku's model a universal claim that writing has value if it is an authentic expression of individual will, a view that can include different value orientations, and a more particular claim that the values that are worthwhile are derived from the Classics. Thus, on the one hand, it is crucial that all scholars see literary endeavor as the task of manifesting their own attitudes; on the other hand, they should have a particular attitude drawn from the ancients. The last is vital, for it is Li Hua's commitment to the Kingly tao that makes his writing an expression of the great moral constants of antiquity and thus justifies his criticisms of his times.

Not all scholars adopted Li Hua's approach as Tu-ku interpreted it,[44] but Tu-ku's own views attracted some in the highest circles.[45] He also attracted students. As one explained, Tu-ku understood why wen-hsueh was central to the polity, and he made clear the "root and source" for the tao of a literary learning capable of guiding men to the recovery of a unified polity.[46] Tu-ku Chi's success was a sign, an admirer wrote, that "heaven must have wished to revive This Culture of Ours."[47] Tu-ku's best student was Liang Su.

Liang Su: Wen Based on Tao

Liang Su was the first truly post-rebellion scholar of the line that began with Hsiao Ying-shih and Li Hua. Liang wrote at a time when the court was "transforming the world with the wen of man," as he put it, rather than relying solely on military means.[48] Yet if antiquity showed that it was possible to integrate wen-chang, political policy, and social practice, the days were gone when rulers and ministers could harmonize government with nature and their songs could "seep into the minds of men so that the minds of men, finding joy in them, were at peace, and [could] permeate social customs so that social customs, according with them, were fortified."[49] The burden now fell to scholars; they had to create "ssu-wen adequate to revive the times, enduring brilliance adequate to leave for successors."[50]

In prefaces to the collections of Li Hua's nephew Li Han and Tu-ku Chi, Liang set forth his view of how the literary enterprise could create a culture capable of reviving the times. He begins the first with a statement of the purposes of wen: "As for the creating of wen: first, it is how one expresses tao and rectifies the guidelines of the inherent nature [hsing-

ming]. Second, it is how one refines the institutional models [*tien-li*] and fortifies the duties of the five human relationships. And third, it is how one makes clear moral analogies and establishes a center for all under heaven."[51] The wen created by the ancients, Liang continues, combined all three: individual nature, political and social models, and adjustments to change through analogies and provisional standards. But with the decline of the Chou, wen declined as well, and these three purposes divided into separate streams. The Han saw a revival of two of the three purposes: the wen of the Han historians preserved the sociopolitical models of the Former Kings, whereas the wen of the rhapsody writers continued the third purpose, associated with the feudal hegemons of the Chou's decline. This duality continued into the Period of Division, taking shape as the tension in literary creations between wen and li, embellishment (from the rhapsody writers) and normative pattern (from the historians). Liang accounts for the decline as follows: "Therefore [originally] wen was based on tao. When they lost tao they broadened [wen as received] with *ch'i* [vital energy]. When ch'i was inadequate, they decorated [the wen that had been broadened] with elaborated language. Now, tao can include ch'i and ch'i can include elaborated language, but when the elaborated language is not appropriate wen is defeated."[52] The cumulative tradition had been somewhat efficacious, Liang allows, but it had not realized the first purpose of wen (to express tao). Eventually it became so elaborated that wen lost its normative function. The T'ang scholars' remedy for this had occurred in three stages: from Ch'en Tzu-ang to Chang Yueh, and then to Li Hua, Hsiao Ying-shih, and Chia Chih, and finally to Tu-ku Chi, who saw that achieving a personal connection to tao was a prerequisite for reviving culture.[53]

For Liang, tao appears not to be the historical tao of the Former Kings but something beyond culture. Nor, despite his references to "Heaven's tao," does he appear to mean the tao of heaven-and-earth. Similarly, for Liang "hsing-ming" is not the personal character and the emotions that served traditionally as grounds for literary expression. Rather, he uses the term in sympathy with Buddhists and Taoists, who as "men outside the square," were presumed to have ways of establishing connections between the individual and the ultimate tao. Li Hua, Tu-ku Chi, and especially Liang Su all reflected on Buddhist and Taoist teachings.[54] Liang saw value in Buddhist ideas about the mind and human nature and Buddhist practices aimed at enabling men to detach themselves from the phenomenal world, and they informed his use of tao as a concept.[55] Tao was the ultimate source; mysterious and ineffable; it was "without bounds," "without name"; it made the Buddha as sage possible; it was that with which the "perfected man who is without mind" was constantly one; and so on.[56] Liang was persuaded more by Buddhist than by Taoist views.[57] True immortality, he explained, required ending the false action that leads to birth. "The sage [Buddha] knew that [man's] basis was empty and his form nonexistent. He set forth the great tao so that [man] would bring his emotional responses back to the nature [literally: to *hsing* his *ch'ing*], so that he would not go astray but return them to their basis there."[58] This was not unprecedented; others believed that Buddhist teachings had "restored the emotional responses" of men, teaching them to feel moved by good and bad.[59] This is the tao Liang sees as the key, I think, to giving writing real value, for it is the ultimate basis for the individual.

Liang's most serious discussion of the inherent nature (*hsing*) is his account of the T'ien-t'ai sect's *chih kuan* meditation doctrine, which he held fit with Confucius's idea of illuminating tao by avoiding entanglement in external things.[60] In his lyrical "Inscription for an Intuition" ("Hsin-yin ming"), he speaks of the Buddha mind as he experiences it, in which self and things, Heaven and man, the internal and external, change and transformation, all come together in an ineffable unity as man responds to the external world with perfect appropriateness.[61] With reference to Buddhist texts, Liang comments at one point that "one proceeds through the language yet leaves the language behind, turns to the image yet forgets the image."[62] I think that Liang, rather than keeping the Buddhist and ju separate, was willing to bring this view of tao to bear on This Culture as well.

Tu-ku Chi was an example, Liang held, of one who made tao his grounds and aim in writing. But the commitment to tao did not mean that wen was irrelevant, as his preface to Tu-ku's collected works explains. The theme in this case is taken from the thirty-eighth chapter of the *Tao-te ching*: "Hence when tao was lost there was virtue [*te*]; when virtue was lost there was benevolence; when benevolence was lost there was rectitude; when rectitude was lost there were the rites."[63] This was appropriate, for Tu-ku had passed the examination in Taoist texts under Hsuan-tsung. Liang writes: "Now the greatest of all is Heavenly tao, next is human wen. In the past the sage-kings used it to regulate the hundred measures, and ministers below used it to further the five teachings [on moral virtues]. When virtue further declined, censure took form in songs, and criticism was manifested in the records. Therefore, tao and te, benevolence and rectitude, will not be illuminated except by wen; ritual and music, punishment and policy, will not be established except by wen. The importance of wen depends on the success of government, but the quality of wen depends on the talent of individuals." Tao and te do not make themselves manifest; men manifest them through wen. Men must first find a connection, as Tu-ku did. "When His Honor did it, he grasped tao and te as the [internal] basis and treated ritual and music as hat and girdle [i.e., external form]. He took the essentiality and principles of the *Change*, the rectitude and stirring of the *Songs*, the praise and blame of the *Spring and Autumn Annals*, and joined them in elaborated language [*tz'u*]. Therefore, his wen was accommodative yet simple, frank yet pleasing, distinguished yet unadorned, full yet lofty. Free of empty praise in discussing men, true to the facts in drawing analogies. All trembled, as once again they gazed upon the tradition [*i-feng*] of the two Hans."[64] Tu-ku made tao and te his basis, but at the same time he followed the Han view of the Classics in writing. As Tu-ku did in discussing Li Hua, Liang combines the universal—but replacing the "will" with tao te—with particular models. The result was a man whose conduct and writing manifested the norms of antiquity yet in every instance pointed men toward tao.

Tao gave [Tu-ku] purity; heaven bestowed te on him. Perceptive and intelligent, intrepid and correct. He proceeded inside and returned on his own, his tranquillity and activity could be taken as standards. Filial piety and fraternal respect accumulated to make the basis for conduct; literary art was completed through extra strength. Whenever he established language worthy of emulation [*li yen*], it was always of the great constants of loyalty and filial piety, of the great plans of kings and hegemons, of the great principles of the expedient and the normative, of the great models of past and present. In its midst, although waves broke and thunder shook, rising and falling in a myriad variations, the diverse streams all uniformly converged to focus on tao.[65]

And, Liang concludes, "Did Heaven perhaps bestow authority over transmitting and creating to our Master? If not, how is it that we here can now come across This Culture of Ours [in his work]? . . . [Whenever he spoke,] he always put tao and te first before wen-hsueh."[66]

Liang Su takes the post-rebellion departure from the early T'ang cultural synthesis to a deeply problematic extreme. Living in a time that took wen to stand for civil order, cultural tradition, and normative models, these men saw their role as scholars as deriving from their wen-hsueh, their ability to learn from the textual traditions and models of the past while responding as morally concerned individuals to the times through their writing. Their doubts about the belletristic tradition and supposition of a narrower tradition of morally authoritative wen-chang was similar to yet different from early T'ang views. First, in their desire to show how literary writing could guide social behavior, they admitted that it did not. Second, as they tried to understand how to do this, they further eroded the assumption that cultural forms had real value. By treating wen as merely the embellishment on the language one wished to speak and supposing that one's moral purpose or will should determine what one had to say, Li Hua and his successors in effect separated morality and culture. This separation was foreign to the early T'ang, when it was held that in its inception and through its continuation the cultural tradition reproduced the constant patterns of the cosmos. Liang Su is extreme because he accepts the possible conclusion that since the cultural tradition is separate from the basis for morality it can be connected to it only incidentally; thus any morally valid wen-hsueh and wen-chang require thinking grounded in an ultimate source of moral ideas existing outside tradition. This, however, leads to further conclusions: if the wen of the cultural tradition does not inherently have value, then real values cannot necessarily be known through wen-hsueh, and the enterprise of literary composition does not necessarily matter. But for T'ang scholars to have accepted such conclusions would have entailed denying that they and their kind of learning had any special claim to moral authority in T'ang society.

With Liang Su's death in 793, the story divides. The line I have been following to this point continued at court with Ch'üan Te-yü, a sometimes chief examiner and chief minister, who claimed authority over wen in the line of Li Hua, Tu-ku Chi, and Liang Su. Ch'üan kept to the idea that wen was necessary to transform the world and that political authority should be guided by the creators of ssu-wen in the present. However, the idea of the decline and restoration of wen was becoming conventional, and Ch'üan's writings suggest he helped deprive this challenge to the status quo of its critical power.[67]

The other line, pursued below, begins with men who found themselves on the outside in the 790's. Although they did not acknowledge it, they were indebted to Liang Su and his predecessors for establishing the precedent of individuals' saving society through restoring wen-chang, and they were inspired by the idea that to have real value writing had to be based on a tao the author found for himself.[68] But they were also men who felt they were not getting a chance to realize their will, men for whom the court's claim to be transforming all under heaven with the wen of man rang hollow. These lines from Meng Chiao (751–814) make the point:

> The mood of killing is not on the frontiers,
> It's an icy chill, this autumn in the heartland.
> Roads' dangers are not in the mountains—
> There are smashed carriage shafts on the plains.
> Even Ho-nan raises troops,
> Streams pure and foul are jointly locked.
> Not simply private troubles for the wanderer,
> Boats on official journeys too are delayed.
> Worse still, cut off from my duties as a son,
> So far from home I'm completely blocked off now.[69]

We turn now to Meng Chiao's friend Han Yü and to some of Han's contemporaries.

The 770's Generation:
The Problem of Wen and Tao

The restoration of wen-chang called on individual scholars to take responsibility for public morality through their own literary writing. The literary intellectuals of the 770's generation agreed that the literary enterprise had to be a moral one, but they did not adopt Liang Su's idea of tao. What was the basis for public and private morality? they asked. How should the individual gain access to it? How was it related to the textual legacy and to their own literary composition? In the early T'ang vision the tao of heaven-and-earth was manifest patterns perfectly imaged by the historical wen of the sage-kings. Now there emerged a vision of the unity of the tao the individual knew and experienced for himself and of the wen as the style and oeuvre the individual had to develop for himself. The demand that individuals know for themselves and transform themselves made it difficult to agree on what men should value in common. At the same time, valuing the personal acquisition of moral ideas over the imitation of good cultural forms made it increasingly difficult to see how values could be shared, for imitation was now a sign that one had not seen for himself. The men of this generation saw that they did not agree. Po Chü-i (772–846), writing in 806, draws an analogy between his times and the contending and one-sided philosophical schools of the Warring States period.[70] Li Ao (774–836) lists six mutually exclusive ideas about the standards for good wen.[71] In his examination questions of 803, Ch'üan Te-yü recognized the lack of intellectual unity.[72] There were clusters of scholars in the new generation, each with its own program. Han Yü (768–824), for example, found admirers in Li Ao, Huang-fu Shih (777–830), and Chang Chi (768–830). Liu Tsung-yuan (773–819) had much in common with Han Yü, but was also associated with Lü Wen (772–811), Liu Yü-hsi (772–842), and students of the *Spring and Autumn Annals* such as Lu Ch'un (?–ca. 806). Po Chü-i and Yuan Chen (779–831), who applied the restorationist ideas to poetic genres, represent yet another intellectual center. For many of these men, continuity with antiquity was a matter of continuing values, the tao of the ancients.

The transformation of intellectual values is evident in the new account of the decline and restoration of culture that emerged from Han Yü's circle: the story of the decline and recovery of the tao of the sages. His defenders audaciously claimed that Han was the first in the millennium since Mencius and Yang Hsiung to hold to the true way. This credo, which ignored all T'ang figures before Han, appeared in a letter from Chang Chi to Han Yü commonly dated to 798.[73] It was included in funerary inscriptions for Han Yü by Li Ao and Huang-fu Shih[74] and restated in the preface to Han's literary collection by Han's son-in-law. Such a partisan view could not serve as grounds for a new consensus among scholars, although in almost every generation thereafter some did harken to it and many more studied Han's works.[75] Its greatest impact was on eleventh-century intellectual culture. And when the philosopher Ch'eng I concluded that true learning was not wen-hsueh, he created a new version of the decline and restoration. According to this version, his brother Ch'eng Hao was the first since Mencius to know tao. Han Yü cannot be taken as the voice of his generation, but he marks a turning point in intellectual life, and the problems he addressed and the issues he created were of enduring consequence.

What Made Han Yü Different?

Han Yü's pronouncements on wen and tao, the subject of this section, do not exhaust Han Yü the man.[76] Through his writings, whether on the loftiest matters of state, on the small events of daily experience, or even on the fanciful, he established a personality that was plausible as a real person. His work is interesting. Han's moral seriousness is accompanied by an appreciation of literary play and a willingness, in the midst of high seriousness, to be personal. The language is fresh yet replete with ancient echoes.[77] His writing helped to create a lasting new language, one scholars would use for centuries to come. He revealed a self subject to foibles and errors, whose moral will and emotional responses were not always in accord. This Han Yü, so evident in Stephen Owen's study of his poetry, makes it difficult to see the man as a simple moral didact. In his poetry, Han's ambitions run up hard against the realities of court politics, revolts, and social disintegration. He breaks with polite conventions[78] and makes a point of showing that old assumptions no longer work for him. Others might see a normative order of heaven-and-earth; Han experienced the cosmos as irregular and dissonant.[79] Some could suppose the ancient texts clear and sufficient; Han Yü at times found them confused and misleading and inadequate as guides to antiquity.[80] Han Yü's poetry illustrates the breadth of his interests, his range of innovation, and his willingness to take on past and present as he found them. His identity emerges through an emotionally involved engagement with the world; it is not a narrowly constructed doctrinal image. And yet a combination of detachment and engagement imbues his writing with self-consciousness, and his self-consciousness enables him to laugh at his seriousness without retracting it.[81] His poetry conveys serious conviction—his insistence that one becomes a moral man through learning, not by noble birth, being an example—but it is not dogmatic.[82]

Han Yü was part of late eighth-century scholarly culture, of course, and he was well aware of Li Hua's circle, as well as of Liang Su and Ch'üan Te-yü.[83] Still, as Han himself wrote, only the unusual is remembered and cherished, and we can well ask how Han Yü distinguished himself from both the restorationists and the contemporary literary mainstream.[84] In essence, Han used his idea of ku-wen to redefine "good" wen. Han supposed, as had the restorationists, that changing how shih wrote was a means of changing how they acted. But Han went beyond this. What made ku-wen as a style of wen-chang different from merely imitating morally correct ancient models, he believed, was that doing it necessitated thinking for oneself. At the same time Han was proposing new standards for literary practice, he was redefining "good" learning to mean thinking about values, specifically the values that had guided the sages, the *sheng-jen chih tao* (the way of the sage),[85] as they could be inferred from the textual tradition.

The two sides of wen-hsueh, learning as the effort to know values and literary practice as the effort to represent values, were coordinate yet distinct. Han writes in 804: "One reads books to do *hsueh* and strings together words to do wen, not to boast of how much [he has read in learning] or compete over embellishment [in writing]. For hsueh is how he does tao and wen is how he does li [normative pattern]."[86] Han Yü believed he could hold the two together, but an integral and necessary connection was not easily made. The problem was this. A good scholar was supposed to think about values for himself and manifest what he had apprehended through wen. But by accomplishing this through a style of writing that was ancient and a language that defined the sheng-jen chih tao, the scholar was effectively claiming that his wen-chang manifested true values. In the context of T'ang intellectual culture, it was easy for scholars who aspired to being seen as moral men to draw the conclusion that they were thinking and acting like the sages merely by imitating Han's language and style. Han was caught in contradictions: between a conviction that men had to think for themselves and a belief that values had to be drawn from the cultural tradition and between an awareness of the need to create wen that could guide others and his rejection of the idea that cultural forms were normative. Ku-wen can be seen as a way out of this thicket. As a style that was ancient, it was a personal way of writing rather than a claim that good writing imitated or elaborated on ancient wen-chang. In this it was parallel to Han's sense of the sheng-jen chih tao, for the tao was a kind of mental style—the values that guided the ancients in responding to affairs—rather than normative patterns and rules of conduct explicit in the Classics.

The Sheng-jen Chih Tao

In an exchange of letters in 798, Chang Chi asked Han Yü to stop writing frivolous compositions and turn his literary talent to writing a tract about the tao of the sage to teach others. Han Yü declined both requests. For Chang Chi, Han's position implied an exclusive choice. Han, who had been discussing his ideas about the tao of the sage with his circle, saw little to be gained by saying it in writing. Chang's summary is the earliest account of Han's ideas.[87] It is a new version of the theme of decline and restoration in which, for the first time in the T'ang to my knowledge, the decline is not treated in terms of the ever more superficial elaboration of wen. Han's new paradigm is Mencius's defense of the tao against the inroads of the teachings of the individualist Yang Chu and the utilitarian Mo Ti.

Customs have declined and do not match those of antiquity; this must be the result of the tao of the sage having been cast aside. After Confucius passed away, Yang Chu and Mo Ti magnified the odd and put forth different explanations to confuse what men heard. Mencius created a book and corrected them; the tao of the sage again was preserved in society. The Ch'in dynasty destroyed learning. On top of this, the Han dynasty used the techniques of Huang-Lao [Taoism] to instruct men, causing men gradually to become confused. Yang Hsiung created the *Exemplary Sayings* [*Fa-yen*] to dispute them; the tao of the sage was still clear. Once Han declined, the dharma of the Buddhists from the West entered the Central States. Generation after generation the men of the Central States translated and disseminated it; the techniques of Huang-Lao gained in its trail. And anyone who spoke of the good was one of these two sorts.

Long ago, because the tao for continuing life in the world had been neglected, the sages made the uses of medicines and metal, wood, fire, water, and earth into things to fortify [the tao of life]. Because men depended on the good, they clarified the virtues of benevolence and righteousness to instruct them, so that men would have constants. Therefore political order and the process of living preserved each other and were not at odds. Today what society depends upon for life are all the devices and usages of the sages, but when it comes to how men feel [*jen-ch'ing*] we are mired in different learnings [*i-hsueh*] and do not proceed through the tao of the sage. This causes the duties of ruler and minister, father and son, husband and wife, and friend and friend to be lost to the age, and the state and family to continue in disorder. Certainly this pains the benevolent man.

In the nearly thousand years since Yang Hsiung created the *Exemplary Sayings*, no one has spoken of the tao of the sages. The only one to speak of it is you. When those who practice the conventional [*su*] hear [your words], most find them bizarre and do not believe, seeing them only as cause to slander [you]. In the end [merely speaking without writing] does not aid instruction. You are most intelligent about wen-chang, resembling Mencius and Yang Hsiung. Why not do one work to revive and preserve the tao of the sage, so that the men today and men later will know that you have distanced yourself from what [those who follow] the different learnings do. . . .

What you have to say about wen-chang is not at variance with the ancients, but what you are doing now at times does not go beyond those who keep to convention. In my opinion [such writing] has not yet got it. I hope you will end such pastimes, reject substanceless chatter, be broad in receiving all shih, be a successor to Mencius's and Yang Hsiung's creations, and dispute the theories of Yang and Mo, Lao[-tzu] and Shakyamuni, so that the tao of the sage will appear again in T'ang.[88]

Chang Chi depicts the sheng-jen chih tao as the moral ideas that can guide men's emotional responses in a manner congruent with the material and institutional legacy of the sages. He charges that his contemporaries have the sages' institutions but not their values.

Although Han Yü turned aside Chang's criticism of his literary pursuits, he did not take issue with this description. Like Mencius, he saw the need to dispute, even if he would not write. "It is not so that I like having my own tao prevail. My own tao is the tao passed down by Confucius, Mencius, and Yang Hsiung. If it does not prevail, there will be nothing with which to do tao [wei tao]."[89] The tao they transmitted is the sage's tao, the proper object of learning. One of Han's examination questions asks students, said to be "learning the tao of the sage," to draw an analogy between Mencius's combating Yang and Mo and the present.[90] Han's famous "Discourse on Teachers," from 802, speaks of "making tao my teacher." Here, as above, tao is something that can be passed down, preserved, and heard, and anyone in whom it is "preserved" is worthy of serving as a teacher to others, regardless of social status.[91] Han Yü's views may owe much to Mencius and Yang Hsiung, but in the T'ang context the idea that something called the sheng-jen chih tao was the ultimate source of values and the object of learning appears to have been Han Yü's own invention.[92]

The tao of the sage provided Han with the grounds for values. Putting it into practice was a moral reason to serve government; studying it and writing with it was a moral purpose for those outside government. Propagating it justified "being broad in receiving shih" and gave Han a reason to speak out on behalf of all those scholars who had studied it but fallen out of favor. As Han pointed out, this kind of learning provided a standard for judging men independently of family status.[93] By displacing wen as the focus of learning, Han in effect denied that the possession of aristocratic culture made a man worthy. "The Master's tao is great and inclusive," Han wrote at one point, but his own followers had had only partial visions of it.[94] Yet Han was reluctant to say that Confucius or his followers had exclusive knowledge of it, or even that he himself "knew" it. It had some of the qualities of a cumulative tradition that could be transmitted and contributed to. For example, he later decided that Mo-tzu's teachings could supplement the teachings of Confucius.[95] When he finally read the *Hsun-tzu*, he decided that it fit in somewhere between Mencius and Yang Hsiung, though it needed editing to remove what did not conform to the tao.[96] Eventually he also decided that Yang Hsiung was not completely acceptable either, thus leaving Mencius as the last one who came close to comprehending the tao fully.[97] The "Discourse on Teachers" takes a broad view: "A sage has no constant teacher." Confucius studied with men not as good as himself, even with Lao-tzu.[98] But the sage Lao-tzu of the imperial cult and the sage Buddha of the monks were not part of it this "ancient tao" or "the tao of the ancients." It came from China's antiquity; to share it one had to value that antiquity. Clearly Buddhism did not. Institutional critiques of Buddhists as subverting familial and political hierarchies had seen Buddhism as a danger to something that existed. But from Han's perspective, Buddhism had in fact won; it had persuaded people that the tao—the real tao—was not part of the sages' creation of a moral order.

Han does not elaborate on the contents of the sheng-jen chih tao. As he explains at one point, he takes not the words but the *i* (intent, conception, idea) as his teacher.[99] The sheng-jen chih tao is in part the intention to guide how men respond, I think, much as earlier scholars had spoken of "contemplating the wen of man" to transform society. It underlies This Culture of Ours; it is the values congruent with the institutions the sages created and, as such, "our" way of living a complete and coherent life. Han Yü's most important account of his understanding of morality is his essay "Finding the Source for Tao" ("Yüan tao"), which would become one of the most influential texts in later Chinese thought.[100] It is, at once, a 'claim for the completeness of the tao of the sage, an attack on Buddhism and Taoism, an account of the parts that make up the whole, and an example of reconnecting culture and value in the microcosm of a wen-chang. It is an account of how the world ought to be and an explanation for why it is not so. The essay allows us to draw some conclusions about the idea of morality Han has in mind.

"Finding the Source for Tao" begins with definitions that make clear Han Yü's premise: tao and te do not have an existence independent of culture and history; they are ideas created by men.

To love broadly is what is meant by *jen* [benevolence]. To practice this yet do so appropriately is what is meant by *i* [righteousness]. Proceeding from here to go there is what is meant by *tao* [path or way]. Being capable/sufficient of oneself without depending on externals is what is meant by *te* [virtue or internal guides].

"Jen" and "i" are defined terms [*ting-ming*]. "Tao" and "te" are empty positions [*hsu-wei*]. Thus, for tao there are the [paths set by] the superior man and the lesser man; for te there are [capabilities that have results] unfortunate and fortunate. . . . When referring to what I call "tao" and "te," I am speaking of them in conjunction with jen and i.[101]

Han has brought tao and te back "within the square." His argument is simple. Tao and te are categories without normative content. They refer, respectively, to proceeding (or acting) toward an end and being capable of doing so autonomously. They are "empty positions" that must be defined before action can be morally guided, in the same sense that the idea of a hexagram is meaningless until the six "positions" are filled with either broken or unbroken lines. For their content, Han appropriates two pre-eminent moral terms of the cultural tradition: "jen" and "i." Note, however, that he defines these terms as ideas as well. They are the intentions necessary for the integrated order discussed in the essay: caring for all in a manner appropriate to the situation. What men need to learn is how to proceed on their own toward accomplishing this.

The essay sets out to persuade the reader that men can learn from the tradition of the sages, and that the tao and te in Taoist and Buddhist traditions are alternative and less substantial definitions of these "empty positions," rather than insights into the true nature of tao and te. This is said first with reference to the *Lao-tzu*, which makes tao and te things in themselves, existing independently of and having priority over jen and i, and Han implicitly takes issue with Yang Hsiung for granting this.[102]

The "decline" is now given as the story of how Taoism (or, to use Han Yü's term, Huang-Lao) in the Han dynasty and Buddhism thereafter, as the Yang Chu and Mo Ti of later times, made it impossible for men to see a connection between jen/i and tao/te, reduced Confucius to a secondary figure, and established two new sets of moral instructions (*chiao*) in competition with the shih. To explain what jen and i meant in practice, and to show that his gloss on these terms is essential to the cultural tradition, Han turns back to antiquity and gives an account of the sages' creation of civilization, drawing on a variety of texts.

How did the sages decide what to do? How did it come about that civilization was created? Han answers that they looked to the needs and desires of men and created institutions that satisfied their desires in a way that led them to care for each other. Han simply ignores the old idea that the sages reproduced the patterns of heaven-and-earth in human institutions. Taoists, he goes on, think the effort to establish institutions and guide men created problems. In fact the sages created rulers and armies to drive out the vermin and beasts that harmed men, and they located men in the central land. Men were cold, so they made clothes; hungry, so food; subject to the elements, so houses; and so on till there were artisans and traders, doctors and medicine, rites and music, policy and punishments, weights and measures, and walls and guards. Without the sages, humanity would not have survived. The Buddhists think purity requires doing away with political and social obligations. In fact, the sages created a hierarchical order, in which rulers commanded, ministers effected their orders, and the people produced, crafted, and circulated goods, to ensure that human needs would be provided for. The Taoists treat simplicity and ease as the single standard of value, Han continues, but the one standard of sagely wisdom is whether the action is appropriate to the situation, not whether it is simplest. The Buddhists think that ordering the mind requires treating society and state as external to the mind, but the point of "correcting the mind and making intentions sincere" is to "accomplish something" (yu wei) in society and state. Taking guidance from either tradition is to impose the "barbarian" on what is "Chinese" (chung-kuo), for what it means to be Chinese is to follow the instructions of the Former Kings. In short, those traditions make it impossible for "us" to truly be ourselves.

Han then runs through a summary of the "instructions of the Former Kings," their wen (the Songs, Documents, Change, and Spring and Autumn Annals), their methods of governance, classes of population, social roles, clothing, housing, and foodstuffs. Their tao is easy to illumine, he asserts, and their instructions easy to practice. Moreover, this tao is fully adequate for self and for others, for the mind, for the state, and for society. This tao was passed down from Yao through the sage-kings to Confucius and Mencius. Hsun-tzu and Yang Hsiung did not get to its essentials. After the Duke of Chou, those who passed it on held the role of minister, not ruler; they could only talk about it at length, not put it into practice. What is to be done? he asks. Destroy the institutions of Buddhism and Taoism, guide men with the tao of the Former Kings, and then all those who suffer will be nurtured.

Some conclusions. First, the essay is in a new style of writing. It exemplifies the idea of the individual's constructing a picture of the whole for himself. It is written in a language of Han Yü's own making, in which numerous allusions to past texts and archaic terms and formulations serve to make reading different from the conventional. It is organized around an argument, rather than elaborating an ancient theme or passage or refashioning a particular ancient wen-chang (although Han composed such works as well). Finally, in the context of its times, it is combative to the point of rudeness—it calls for the dismantling of the T'ang status quo.

Second, a perusal of the Ch'üan T'ang wen (Complete T'ang prose) suggests that this essay was unprecedented in the T'ang. I have found no earlier examples of a literary composition that sketches a complete vision of the moral order created by the sage-kings, accounts for its creation, lays out the history of civilization, and attributes its decline to the adoption of particular ideas as values. Its impact is evident in the innumerable imitations, variations, and alternative visions that were written thereafter. By the same token, these copies make it difficult to keep in mind that "Finding the Source for Tao" was once new, unusual, and entirely unorthodox.

Third, and most important, is the understanding of morality in this piece. Han argues that human desires are not an obstacle to creating a moral world. Civilized institutions make it possible for men to satisfy their desires, needs, and interests in a socially constructive manner. The virtues of jen and i are defined by this. That is, from the sages' actions we see that these virtues mean caring about others but wanting to see that their interests fit into an integrated order. These, and not loyalty and filial piety, for example, are now held forth as the arch-virtues of civilization. This view contrasted with the prevailing ethics of the day, which held that morality and human desires were inimical and that external things were a threat to ethics.[103] From this vantage, Buddhist ideas about cultivating the mind, stopping desires, and separating oneself from society are at odds with "our" morality. The goal of "our" internal cultivation, Han contends, is yu-wei, accomplishing things in society. It follows that to be a moral man is to be engaged with the world of human interests—there is no value in isolating oneself to preserve one's integrity. Being a paragon of ethical standards, indeed "ethical conduct" as a category, is less important than using government to change the world and benefit it. Nor is "restoring wen-chang" necessary to realizing morality. What, then, was the point of Han Yü's ideas about wen-chang?

Ku-wen

In 798 Chang Chi spoke of a tension between what he saw as Han Yü's literary pastimes and his doctrinal claims. Liu Tsung-yuan too thought that a man with Han's interests should not write such frivolous and "bizarre" pieces as the "Biography of Fur-point" (on the rabbit hairs in a brush), at least until he saw its serious purport.[104] Han Yü did not desist. In fact, much more than the restorationists, Han valued the literary.[105] Literary men, even if they were interested only in poetry, could be the modern equivalents of the sages, philosophers, and historians of the past. In his farewell preface for Meng Chiao (803), he constructs a unified intellectual-literary tradition on the basis of the idea that men "sound forth" in speech and song when things impinge upon them and upset their internal equilibrium. The great texts in all four divisions of bibliography resulted as men "sounded forth" in ways appropriate to different circumstances. Han lists the sage-kings and ministers of the Three Eras (Hsia, Shang, Chou); Confucius and his followers; various schools of the pre-Han period including followers of Yang Chu or Mo-tzu and the Taoists, Legalists, and strategists; Li Ssu in the Ch'in; and Ssu-ma Hsiang-ju, Ssu-ma Ch'ien, and Yang Hsiung in the Han. He notes but does not name men of ability in the Wei-Chin period who did not match antiquity. Finally, for the T'ang, he credits Ch'en Tzu-ang, Su Yuan-ming, Yuan Chieh, Li Po, Tu Fu, and Li Kuan with "sounding forth as best they could," but makes Meng Chiao the first to truly sound forth in poetry, a category in which he includes his followers Chang Chi and Li Ao as well.[106] They all responded to the world by sounding forth because of an internal imbalance.

In this view even the best writings are partial, imbalanced responses to the imperfect world of a particular time; none is a fully adequate or permanent model. To sound forth from a state of imbalance is to be "ancient." But the ancient is also "natural." The natural internal state of equilibrium is disturbed by external things, compelling an emotional response colored by personal character and an outflow of ch'i. Sounding forth is a natural response, an attempt to rebalance the world and regain the natural state. This allows for a larger distinction between those who allow themselves to respond to things and those who try either to suppress their feelings or, in the manner of polite letters, to write to create a (false) sense of balance and harmony. But if the acceptance of emotional response allows Han to distinguish his intellectual tradition from that of the Buddhists, for example, it does not lead to proper values. Yang and Mo are as much a part of the tradition of sounding forth as Mencius and Confucius. Knowing what to value thus can require the replacing of natural internal equilibrium with the tao of the sage as an intellectual construct, a self-conscious sociohistorical version of the balanced whole that serves as both the mirror reflecting the imperfect world and the filter defining one's response. One can "fill" the self through learning from the sages. "Therefore, those who depart from the sage even slightly and those who apprehend only one part of the whole have not completely 'fulfilled their bodies.'" The internal thus becomes the basis for external expression; as Han puts it, one is "making full the substance and then blazing forth."[107]

Han took both positions, as two prefaces for Buddhist monks illustrate. For a monk enamored of calligraphy, Han argues that one who tries to keep thoughts from arising in the mind cannot bring forth great calligraphy. He will be limited to copying the traces of past masters. To equal them, he must share their mind of sounding forth out of imbalance.[108] This is the naturalistic view. For a monk who "likes wen-chang," Han summarizes the tao of the sage as found in "Finding the Source for Tao." When we write for monks, he explains, we should stop speaking about Buddhist teachings. Wen-chang is part of our tradition; we should explain the ideas it rests upon and tell them of "that which makes us different from the birds and beasts" to enlighten them.[109] This is the moral, historical view. Yet in either case it can be true that the substance inside one determines the external manifestations; in this sense the style of expression, the wen, is also internal. "Now, as for what is called wen, you must have it inside you. That is why the superior man is careful about his substance [shih]. The quality of the substance will not be hidden when it is expressed. When the roots are deep, the branches flourish; when the body is large, the voice is ample. When conduct is lofty, the language is rigorous; when the mind is pure, the ch'i is harmonious."[110] Being true or sincere (ch'eng) arises as an issue for Han because he wants to make the forms of expression a function of what is inside himself rather than taking his models from received external forms.[111]

Writing ku-wen promises to resolve the tension between the given self that cries out when upset and the self constructed out of ideas about how one ought to feel. Doing ku-wen involves seeking a coherent understanding of ancient texts, learning to write in an ancient manner, and being able to act in accord with ancient values. Han commends the student for whom he wrote the "Discourse on Teachers" as follows: "He likes ku-wen. He has comprehended [t'ung] all the Six Classics and the commentaries. In practicing them, he is not constrained by the times. I applaud his being able to practice the ancient tao [ku-tao]."[112] Han understood that equating stylistic values with moral superiority encouraged imitation of ancient wen without a commitment to living by the ku-tao. Some had difficulty understanding this, for Han had to explain several times that ku-wen was based on first understanding the ku-tao, not on simply analyzing the manner in which the ancients wrote.[113] Demanding that the language come from the individual was a way of countering this trend. "In antiquity," he writes, "all phrases came from the men themselves"; in contrast, later men have simply plundered the language of the past until the tao was obscured.[114]

The possibility of imitation arose from supposing a necessary equivalence between the tao a man had inside and the wen he created outside. How could Han deny that imitation of past forms or his own style led to apprehending tao yet suppose that the wen truly represented tao? The conclusion I draw from Han's most famous account of his own ku-wen, his "Reply to Li I," is that what he had inside himself was in fact a personal version of the tao of the sage. In other words, although that tao was something larger and constant, it was always understood in a personal manner; the wen that resulted was a true representation of what was inside, but to imitate the wen of another was to fail to acquire a personal basis for oneself. Li I had sent Han examples of his own work and inquired about how to say something worthy of being remembered (li yen). Han asks: Is your will focused on those who said something worth remembering in antiquity and nurtured their roots before getting the fruit, or on getting ahead in the present? For two decades, Han goes on, he has aspired to the ancients. He began, he writes, by reading works of the Three Eras and the Han dynasty exclusively, keeping only those that fit "the will of the sage." Then he went through a period of confusion. When he "took something" from his mind, and put it into writing, he sought only to get rid of the old clichés; as a result he produced works difficult to read. He showed them to others, "without realizing that others' not laughing at them" was a sign that they still fit too well with conventional expectations. He then realized that he still had to distinguish the "correct" from the "artificial" and "not fully correct" in ancient books and get rid of all that was not correct. Han had reached his own conclusions about the tao of the sage, I take it, and knew what writing fit that tao. Now, he goes on, when he drew on his mind to write, words flowed out, and when others criticized his works, he was happy. Praise, he now saw, would mean he was still "preserving the theories of others" in his own works. He continued like this, the work flowing ever more freely, yet still laboring to make his work fully pure and unadulterated. Then when his work reached this point, he could let himself go.

Although this is so, I must still cultivate [my wen and my mind]. I shall make it travel along the path of jen and i, swim in the source of the Odes and Documents, without ever becoming cut off from the source to the very end of my days. Ch'i is water. Language is something floating. When the water is great, all things great and small will float. Such is the relationship between ch'i and language. When the ch'i is full, both the length of the phrases and the level of the tones will be as they should be.

He is not, Han explains, claiming perfection, but he is not concerned with whether others accept him and his work, for waiting on them is to depend on others. For Han, practicing the ku-tao meant establishing a personal moral foundation independent of society.

The superior man is not like this. He has his tao for organizing his mind, he has his measure for conducting himself. If employed, he applies them to others; if left out, he passes them on to his followers. He sets them out in his wen, and they serve as models for later ages. Is such enough to feel joy? It is not. There are few whose will is set on antiquity. Those whose will is set on antiquity will necessarily be left behind by the present. I find my true joy in them, yet I grieve for them.[115]

The individuality of Han's understanding leads to an external mani-festation in writing that necessarily varies from the conventional. It is individual yet not without its normative quality. The question, I think, is what comes to serve as a model: the style, particular values, or the intention of the man to be moral through the literary enterprise? Another of Han's letters speaks to this. Take the sages and worthies of antiquity as your teachers in literary practice, he charges a petitioner, but learn from their intentions, not their literary elaborations. Do not ask whether wen should be easy or difficult; do whatever is right. But, he continues, citing several great Han writers, if you want your work to be noticed and remembered, it must differ from the usual productions of the age. Even if what you say is not fully right, as long as you model yourself on the intentions of the sages and worthies, you are still better than those who follow convention. And, as long as society continues to believe in the value of wen, such men are useful. "As for the tao of the sage, if wen is not necessary to it, then there is nothing more to say. But if it is, then we must value those who are able at it. Those who are able at it are none other than those who are able to establish themselves without following others. Since there has been writing, who has not engaged in wen? But what has survived to today is necessarily from those who were able at it."[116] Virtue, Han had written in "Finding the Source for Tao," is being able to rely on oneself. Ku-wen, I would argue, was Han's version of the wen that went with relying on oneself. Yet, because it rested on the individual's discov-ery of the tao of the sage as the guide to a moral society through the wen of antiquity, and because it was expressed in a manner that recalled the ancients, it was not incongruent with the cultural tradition even while it broke with present convention. Yet Han has acknowledged another pos-sibility: that wen is not necessary at all; men who know the truth need only to act. Han does not reach this conclusion, I would suggest, not only for the obvious traditional reasons but also because he had to test the ideas and attitudes he equated with the tao of the sage through personal experi-ence in responding to circumstances. The credibility of his views de-pended on demonstrating that he could respond to the actual world with them. He could do so in public and, persuasively, through writing. As long as absolute certainty about what was moral remained elusive, wen had a necessary role to play.

With Han Yü what it meant to learn changed. As his son-in-law Li Han wrote in his preface to Han Yü's collection, being immersed in "This Way of Ours" became the grounds for wen, and yet wen is the device with which men *kuan tao* ("thread tao"). This refers to Confucius's enigmatic claim that "my tao is thread on a single strand,"[117] and the example of wen that does this is the Classics as elaborated, edited, created, and employed by Confucius. The point is not that wen is a vehicle for tao, but that wen is the device with which the ideas that constitute morality are linked together coherently.

Wen is the device for threading tao. Those who are not deeply immersed in This Tao of Ours will not attain this. With the *Change* he [Confucius] interpreted the lines and images [of the hexagrams]. With the *Spring and Autumn Annals* he recorded affairs. With the *Songs* he chanted and sang. With the *Documents* and *Rites* he pared away the false. Were not all these cases of being deeply immersed? Before the Ch'in and Han their *ch'i* was complete and one. Such [Former Han men] as Ssu-ma Ch'ien, Ssu-ma Hsiang-ju, Tung Chung-shu, and Yang Hsiung may still be called men who were outstanding. By the Later Han and the Wei dynasty of the Ts'aos, the manifestations withered. From the Ssu-mas [of the Chin] on, the norms were upset totally. They said, from the *Change* on down is ku-wen, plagiarizing and stealing is craft. Wen and tao were obscured and blocked, and no one, in their obstinacy, knew it.

The gentleman [Han Yü] was born in 768. . . . From when he knew how to read books and do wen, he recorded several thousand words a day. When mature, the Classics were memorized and understood. He harshly rejected the Buddhists. The histories and many schools were searched through so nothing was concealed. . . . The brilliance of the sun, the purity of jade, the sentiments of [the Duke of] Chou and the thoughts of Confucius, a thousand attitudes, a myriad appearances, yet all in the end enriched with tao and te, jen and i. Of penetrating insight into antiquity, yet full of care for the present, he then revived the ruined tradition and taught others to do [wen] for themselves. His contemporaries were shocked at first; then they laughed and pushed it aside. The gentleman became even more adamant, and in the end all followed him and fixed upon it.[118]

Han Yü, Li implies, is the successor to Confucius. He showed the way to a new beginning.

Other Voices

The idea that literary endeavor became a moral enterprise only when the writer personally comprehended the tao of the sage and creatively brought those values to bear on experience spread among the literary intellectuals of Han Yü's day. Not everyone thought of the tao of the sage in Han's terms. Some, Han's follower Li Ao and Liu Tsung-yuan, for example, spoke of the way in which the sages had, by gaining personal access to something real and universal, arrived at ideas fitting to the particular, historical circumstances of their day. The idea of knowing for oneself by thinking like the sages kept at bay the danger of transforming ku-wen into a meaningless literary convention. At the same time, individuality and moral autonomy raised the specter of a world without shared norms, in which scholars could not claim the role of guides. To some degree Li Ao and Liu Tsung-yuan confronted these uncertainties and accepted them. Others who did backed away; Liu Mien and Lü Wen, for example, illustrate the desire to say what was right and wrong for all.

Li Ao and the promise of coherence. In language that mimicked Han Yü's, Li Ao claimed: "This tao of mine is not the tao of a particular school. It is the tao through which the ancient sages proceeded. If this tao of mine is blocked, the tao of the superior man will cease. If this tao of mine is clear, then the tao of Yao and Shun, Wen and Wu, and Confucius will not yet have been cut off from the age."[119] In another letter he tells his nephew to "learn the tao of the sage," instead of trying to find powerful patrons, and to manifest it in wen to show others what you have understood.

Do not believe those who label wen-chang one of the arts. Now what is called one of the arts is the wen that convention likes or [the wen of] those of great fame in recent times. [Wen] that is able to attain [that of] the ancients [ta ku-jen] is the elaboration in language of jen and i. How can it be named one of the arts? Confucius and Mencius have been dead for over a thousand years. Although I will not get to see them as men, I have been able to know their sageliness and worthiness by reading their elaborations in language. We cannot make predictions about those who will come later, but how do we know that they will not read my elaborations in language and know that which my mind preserves? They should not be misled.

But, Li immediately continues,

I have yet to see a man whose innate nature [hsing] is of jen and i who lacks wen. Nor have I ever seen a man who has wen that is able to attain [the ancients] who does not work at jen and i. [If one] proceeds from jen and i to wen, it is [due to] the innate nature. [If one] proceeds from wen to jen and i, it is [due to] practice. This is like the mutual dependence between sincerity [ch'eng] and clarity [ming] [in the "Doctrine of the Mean"]. Honor and wealth depend on the external world. I cannot know whether you will have them or not, for they are not something we can attain by seeking. So why should we be so caught up with them? Jen and i and wen-chang come into being internally: we know when they are there; we can seek to fill them out. Why should we be afraid to do so?[120]

Both of these letters were written to justify independence from society. In one case, Li Ao stands apart to ensure that the tao of the sages is preserved for the world, for his "is not the tao of a particular school." In the second case he asserts that the purpose of writing is to be remembered as an individual. Yet this is not good enough; a writer's wen must show that he shares the sages' values yet still be truly his own. The passage ends with a quasi solution, let both the tao and the wen come from within.

The last passage suggests a certain longing to be self-contained and self-sufficient, as well as a desire to be remembered. The next recalls that wen is supposed to guide others. "The moral force [ch'i chih] and language expressed by men is the wen of man. If the moral force cannot fill up heaven-and-earth and if language cannot serve as the basis for transformation through instruction, then the wen of man is in error. . . . When the wen of man is in error, we lose the means of establishing [man] between heaven and earth. Therefore we must be careful about wen." But how is one to achieve this? Li continues by envisioning a universal basis.

[Everything] necessarily has a center [chung]. If one resides at the center, then although lengths, sizes, and heights are not one, their centers are one [i.e., the fact of centrality is constant]. Thus, in putting forth language, [when it comes from] one who resides at the center, it is the wen of the sage; from one who inclines toward the center, it is the wen of imitating the sage; from one who is close to the center, it is the wen of the worthy; and from one who turns away and departs, it is the wen of the mediocre man. From middle antiquity to here and now, few among those who have engaged in wen have not turned away and departed from the center.[121]

In a relative world the phenomenon of centeredness is constant. But why is it the true standard? Because, Li argues, possessing chung as the central, pivotal, and internal constant is something heaven-and-earth and man have in common.[122]

Li Ao strikes me as someone who envisions various possibilities and tries to satisfy many demands at once. But his desire to find grounds for moral certainty and for his own worth as a man is certainly a frequent refrain. Li's essay "Returning to the Innate Nature" ("Fu hsing shu") pursues the possibility of grounding being a sage in heaven-and-earth. Timothy Barrett has argued convincingly that Li wrote for friends favorably inclined toward Buddhism and Taoism in an effort to capture the language of internal life from those traditions.[123] Li objected to Buddhism. Any teaching that could not be practiced fully by everyone, he argued, could not be regarded as "the tao of the sage."[124] As a means of finding the true nature, Li's treatise raised the "Doctrine of the Mean" as an alternative to the practice of T'ien-t'ai meditation proposed by Liang Su, whom Li otherwise admired. As I understand the work, Li argues that "The Mean" shows how the sages arrived at universally valid ideas through their ability to mentally illuminate the processes of heaven-and-earth and harmonize themselves with them. The "external" view of the early T'ang, in which the sages created the wen of man imaging the patterns of heaven-and-earth, is now internalized and individualized. At first glance Li seems to be adopting a Buddhist line: true insight requires arriving at "emptiness" and blocking the rise of emotional responses. In fact, Li is arguing that the

Buddhists stop short of the real basis. Emptiness is simply a stepping-stone, the ineffable state of *ch'eng* (sincerity) that makes insight into universal process possible. The mind, by becoming detached from the world, is able to see what is so-of-itself and universally true of the world. Li's argument is hard to follow, and his connections seem forced, but he attempts to bring together heaven-and-earth, human institutions, the mind, nature and decree, language, and morality. His goal is to establish that human nature is originally good and that any individual can realize that goodness and thus gain both moral autonomy and moral authority. The approach seems to be a combination of meditation and reflection; one cuts off emotional responses to things in order to attain a natural ability to respond to things correctly.

Li's work may have been something of an experiment; he does not develop these views in his other writings. But the concept of mental access to universals remains an interest of his. He uses the idea to claim that men like him are morally superior to those in power and that his pronouncements on right and wrong are truly "common to all under heaven," even when they are at odds with the majority view.[125] It allows him also to assert that in putting his judgments into writing, he is being a Confucius—citing "With King Wen dead, is not wen here with me?" and "I wish not to speak, Heaven does not speak"—as well as being a Mencius and a Ssu-ma Ch'ien.[126]

Li's well-known "Letter to Chu Tsai-yen" suggests that he tried to put all this together through literary practice.[127] It speaks to the problem of how one can identify fully with the tao of the sage, as something norma-tive and universal, while still establishing an individual identity in wen. In Li's terms, he is showing that the tao of the ancients is fully in accord with two principles of good wen: "fabricating conceptions" (*ch'uang-i*), to make a work unique in appearance; and "creating the language" (*tsao-yen*), so that it is said in a new manner. The "great principle of fabricating conceptions" is that basic commonality can be diversely expressed; in other words, the many can be manifestations of the one. Its realization depends, however, on a chain of connections: "When the principles are profound, the conceptions will be far-reaching; when the conceptions are far-reaching, the inherent patterns [*li*] will be distinguished, . . . the ch'i will be straight, . . . the elaborations in language will be full, . . . the wen will be skillful." Li then turns to "creating the language." Although the language that arises in this manner is informed by principles and inherent patterns, "if the literary elaborations are not skillful, they will not form wen." The basis for ideas is separate from the criteria for judging the quality of the wen as literary writing, and this implies that there is no necessary form for wen that is truly based on tao. I am fairly sure that Li is saying this, but he works hard to avoid the conclusion that the wen of the past is irrelevant. What we learn from history, he argues, is that it is still necessary to form "the wen of a single school" (*i-chia chih wen*), and he lists 22 literary and philosophical masters from the period after the Classics as evidence. This, he contends, is what Confucius meant by saying, "If it is said without wen, it will not go far in practice." Those who can "combine wen, inherent pattern, and principles will be able to stand alone in their age, and they will not disappear in later periods." Against "six ideas about wen-chang today," Li argues that the only measure of literary value is one's success in creating a coherent, self-contained, and independent corpus of writing. The creation of a coherent style thus manifests the intellectual search for a self-contained, coherent vision of tao, and the coherence of the literary work replicates the coherence of heaven-and-earth. In attaining i-chia chih wen, he is fundamentally continuous with all the great thinkers and writers of the past, and although his tao may not be particular, his wen becomes his own.[128]

This points toward the conclusion that morality is defined by coherence; there are no pre-existing external standards. But at the very end of the letter, Li criticizes Chu Tsai-yen for using incorrect forms in referring to his peers. The objection is prefaced by the following: "The reason I do not go along with the times but learn ku-wen is that I enjoy the conduct of the ancients. One who enjoys the conduct of the ancients will cherish the tao of the ancients. Therefore in learning their language, I have to practice their conduct; in practicing their conduct, I have to give weight to their tao; in giving weight to their tao, I have to accord with their rules of propriety."[129] This suggests to me Li's uneasiness with the implications of what he had written.

Liu Tsung-yuan and being centered. It has been argued that the statecraft-oriented study of the *Spring and Autumn Annals* of the late eighth century was the intellectual background to Liu Tsung-yuan's thought. By the time Liu came into contact with these scholars, however, it seems that he already knew Han Yü and that some *Annals* scholars had already adopted the rhetoric of wen and tao.[130] It has also been argued that Liu turned away from literary practice and helped free the Confucian revival from literature.[131] In 810, however, Liu admitted that in the years leading up to 805, when he was exiled for his role in the abortive reform coup, he had concerned himself with bureaucracy and memorials: "I had not yet understood the tao of doing wen." But while in exile, having read the works of the hundred schools, he has began to know the standards for wen-chang.[132]

"Establishing language [worthy of being remembered] depends on what is inside," Liu notes in 810; in this sense, literary composition is secondary for shih, although it has a certain usefulness in the examinations. But it is not at all a secondary matter when wen-shih concern themselves with establishing order by "drawing directly on the tao of Yao and Shun and the will of Confucius," and then clarifying it and expressing it, instead of relying on "old books and aged students."[133] In a famous letter to Wei Chung-li (dated 813), Liu further sets out his understanding of the relation between wen and tao. Wen is not about reviving ancient forms, he asserts, nor is it merely skill in the elaboration of language, as he had thought in his youth. Now he knows that "wen is to illuminate tao" (wen i ming tao). This places him on Han Yü's side, but Liu makes a point of disclaiming certainty. He knows what wen should do, he explains, but he is not certain how close he himself has come to tao; only when those who "like tao allow my wen" is he inclined to believe he is on the right track.[134] This is more than a polite statement; the content of Liu's tao did not translate into doctrine.

Liu was uneasy with much that can be seen in Han Yü: the exclusion of Buddhism, claims to authority, the conspicuous assertion of differences with contemporary standards, and pointed insults to polite conventions. Liu's ambivalence about "establishing the language and setting forth the wen" as a means of illuminating tao stems,[135] I think, from Liu's willingness to equate the tao of the sage with the "tao of [great] centrality," as a real state of mind that had guided the sages in responding to things.[136] He seems not to have thought of this in terms of heaven-and-earth, for he rejected all practices that implied human reliance on heaven-and-earth or thinking about universals in terms of yin-yang and the Five Phases.[137] He did not, however, object to Buddhist teachings about mental cultivation.[138] He envisioned this tao as ultimate and transcendent, yet he was equally convinced that men had to rely on their own efforts and their own mind to restore order in the world.

The duty of scholars, Liu eventually concluded, was to create the wen that would lead men to "enter" the tao of the sage on their own. In introducing his essays "Criticizing the Kuo-yü" ("Fei Kuo yü") from 808–9, he spoke of the need for men to "proceed through centrality and constancy [chung-yung] and enter the tao of Yao and Shun."[139] In letters discussing his aims in criticizing the Kuo-yü, Liu explained that "this small work I have forced myself to write" was written on the basis of "what I have apprehended with a will focused on centrality," in protest against the "conventions of the times," for men who "proceed in the way of centrality" [chung-tao]. No longer being in a position to put it into practice, he wrote it as a literary work so that it may survive and "the tao of aiding the age and extending [benefit] to things" will be known to the future, for few engaged in government at present "proceed through great centrality."[140]

Liu's tao is realized by bringing it to bear on human affairs, if not in government then in scholarship. As far as I know, however, although Liu adopted the concept of "centrality" from the "Doctrine of the Mean," he did not explore or elaborate on that text.

In a rhapsody written while in exile, Liu reflected on how he had arrived at his tao. He began to learn, he writes, when he saw the difference between past and present. He then turned to antiquity, taking Yao and Shun as his teachers. But antiquity would not become clear to him, and later times, being marked by self-serving partiality, offered no guidance either. Thus he turned to other schools, "seeking what was appropriate to great centrality." He concluded:

> Tao has image [hsiang],
> But has no set form [hsing].
> Extend variation and make use of the [changing] times,
> Keep the will responsive.
> Not reaching [the center] is dangerous,
> Overstepping loses the good.
> Diligently guard centrality
> And go along with the times.
>   . . . .
> Raise the able and suppress the crooked,
> White and black, muddy and pure [clearly divided];
> Treading the great square,
> Things cannot entangle me.[141]

Tao was something to be envisioned with the mind and had no definite form. It allowed for flexibility and responsiveness yet was a constant standard. Having understood this, he continues, he turned back to the ancient texts, and everything became clear. He concludes that his misfortune had been connected to this. He became too willing to rely on his own ideas exclusively, and because he was concerned only that his integrity (ch'eng) be "unified," he had ignored the threat of the petty-minded who had exiled him.[142] His misfortune was, in a sense, the price he had to pay for his autonomy.

The issue for Liu, I think, is engagement; "centrality" has no specific content, but it can be brought to bear on affairs (chi wu, "extended to things") in responding to and acting on the world. Although Liu rarely becomes dogmatic in discussing intellectual matters, he has much to say on the question of how a commitment to this idea of centrality goes together with an involvement with things. The sages practiced centrality. Their tao is both the idea of that centrality as an ultimate value and the true way to practice centrality in the world. Centrality was inherently an accommodative stance, however, and some thought Liu was telling men to go along with the times. This was not so, he wrote one man: "It is the tao through which Yao, Shun, Yü, T'ang, Kao-tsung [Wu-ting of the Shang dynasty], Wen and Wu, the Duke of Chou, and Confucius proceeded."[143] To say, as he had, that one should "be square within and round without,"[144] meant "internally to preserve your tao and externally to practice it," just as a square cart rolls with round wheels. "When things that are external summon, you then respond to them. When you respond to them appropriately in every instance, it is called 'timely centrality,' and one attains the name of a superior man. . . . I see firmness and yielding as being of the same form. Only by responding to change as if [he himself is spontaneously] being transformed is he able to keep the will focused on tao."[145] Liu's suggestion that centrality involves being "square within" is interesting, because it suggests that he conceives of centrality/internality (both, after all, are *chung*) as having specific content. In fact, as the analogy to the cart makes clear, the square cart provides the space that can be loaded.

In exile, Liu concluded that through wen he could illuminate this tao for others. This required a mode of writing that would attract attention while turning that attention toward practicing the tao of the sage. It had to be unique, different from the conventions of the day, yet guide others.[146] There was a risk in this: by attending to the literary aspect, he invited others to think learning was merely a literary project. He writes to an imitator:

You certainly are interested in the language of the sages, but the language of the sages was aimed at illuminating tao. Those who learn should seek it in tao and leave their elaborations in language behind. Those elaborations in language passed on to the age must go through writing. Tao makes use of elaborations in language and is illuminated; elaborations in language make use of writing and are passed on. The essential thing is simply to get to tao. When tao is reached, simply extend it to things. This is drawing on the internal aspect of tao. Those today who devote themselves to writing because they value elaborations in language—for whom a seductive appearance is skill, for whom being esoteric is ability—are they not external? . . . I have been learning the tao of the sage, and although I am in a difficult situation, my will to seek it has not ceased, so that I am practically at the point that I can converse with antiquity. . . . Now what you seek in tao is external, and what you look to me for is even more external.[147]

His letter to Wei Chung-li, he told others, contained his best account of what he did to ensure that his writing would serve to illuminate tao.[148] The conclusion I draw from this letter is that Liu's tao was an array of good qualities, qualities of character that he saw in the ancients. The letter distinguishes several aspects. There are the psychophysical attitudes necessary to "aid tao": seriousness and rigor, a purity and freedom from arrogance. Liu aims for profundity and clarity, comprehensiveness and measure, and transparency and weight. Then there are his means of "drawing on the source of tao." For this he turns to the Five Classics, not for their language or ideas but for qualities of manner: substance, constancy, appropriateness, decisiveness, and activity. To manifest this in wen, however, he draws on various modes of expression from the larger textual tradition: the *Ku-liang* commentary to the *Spring and Autumn Annals* to intensify the ch'i; the *Mencius* and *Hsun-tzu* to extend the branches; and so on for the *Lao-tzu* and *Chuang-tzu*, the *Kuo-yü*, the *Li sao*, and Ssu-ma Ch'ien. This is done in the hope that such an assemblage will result in work of lasting value. The idea of centrality fits in here as an ultimate organizing principle; one should have a center from which one can include different parts in constructing a balanced, unified whole.

In Liu's hands the textual tradition becomes qualities to be embodied in thought and expression. The tao of the sage does not translate into a doctrinal statement; rather, it is to have the qualities that constitute good character, qualities one might look for in an official and a judge. This tao can be illuminated through writing as the scholar's way of responding to affairs of the world. This Liu did do, writing about history, contemporary society, and nature as he experienced it. It may well be that Liu believed the style of his expression vouchsafed the morality of his responses and judgments.

Liu Mien and dogmatism. "Wen and moral instruction have divided into two," Liu Mien (?–ca. 806) wrote; from Ch'ü Yuan on literary learning has not served moral purposes.[149] The T'ang had not changed the situation, it had simply followed the Sui in valuing office above virtue; its men lacked honesty and shame.[150] "The superior man learns wen to practice its tao," he tells one official.[151] To another: "The functions of the ju are what is meant by wen."[152] Current literary composition represented the decline of true wen; it was not to be valued. Those who made it their calling were not to be honored.[153] For although "to speak yet be incapable at wen is not to be a superior man and ju, to be able at wen yet not to know tao is to be neither a superior man nor a ju."[154] Insistence on being a ju implied a narrow concern with the Classics, yet Liu was not advocating traditional mastery of the commentaries. Scholars should return to the Classics, he tells a doubtful Ch'üan Te-yü in 806, but they can "illuminate the tao of the sage" without knowing the commentaries. Those who "illuminate the principles of the Six Classics and are in accord with the tao of the Former Kings are superior men and ju; they are the basis for instruction."[155]

But what Liu sought in the Classics was a set of rules to follow. The superior man learns from the sages in order to "know the tao" and thus to make the rules of the past clear to the present. "When he speaks, [his words] will be Classics, when he acts, [his actions] will be moral instructions." He must speak, as Liu insists on doing, of the "great tao" only, without introducing "minor tales" (the *hsiao-shuo* material that Han and Liu frequently used in their writing). "Taking the sages as teachers," however, opens the way for multiple interpretations. Liu responds: "Those who take the sages as their teachers must have rules [*fa*]." These rules are hard to know and even harder to make wen, Liu grants, but he knows when someone has not done it. For "seeking the tao of the sage depends on seeking the mind of the sage, and the mind of the sage depends on writing according to the rules [*fa*] of the sage."[156] Men who try to "see the mind of heaven-and-earth, know the basis of *hsing-ming*, and maintain the capability for intuitive insight" undermine those rules. He objects that such an approach to knowing tao denies the reality of emotional response and thus undermines ritual, for ritual came from human emotions and moral instruction proceeds from ritual.[157] What Liu fears, I think, is that the personal search for ultimate values leads men to devalue public, external standards. Accordingly he narrows wen, in contrast to the innovative freedom of his cousin Liu Tsung-yuan and Han Yü, and he reduces tao to something knowable and definite.

Lü Wen and ethical standards. Lü Wen (772–811), his friend Liu Tsung-yuan said, "was good at speaking about tao."[158] But for Lü, the tao of the sage made it unnecessary for men to encounter ultimate tao. He writes in his "Rhapsody on Finding Joy in Ordering the Mind" that "tao has no image, Heaven has no voice; had the sages not created things, how could we contemplate transformation [through the wen of man]." One forms character according to what the sages created and expresses it externally: "One begins by accumulating within and expressing without, filling up the nature and nurturing the emotional responses."[159]

The "tao of learning" was lost 800 years ago, Lü writes, when the transmission through teachers was lost. To save the age, men must learn the ethical norms of the Classics. "Now those who learn do not merely receive the commentaries. One must seek the means to transform men. 'Renewal every day, and renewal again.'[160] Instruction does not mean extensive writing; one must base [one's writing] on loyalty and filial piety, extend it with ritual and righteousness, strengthen it with good faith and observance of procedure, and stir it with honesty and shame."[161] Scholars must avoid the faults of the Wei-Chin period, both the desire for unique insight ("taking singular learning as innate knowledge") and the mere memorization of the Classics, for they resulted in a loss of knowledge of the "subtle purport of the sages and worthies, the great basis of transformation through instruction, the rules of human relationships, and the root and source of the Kingly tao." For Lü the Classics were not books, things to be read through commentaries, as much as guides to the purports and functions of the things with which the sages transformed men. The *Rites*, for example, are not the rituals of social life but "must be how one regulates *ch'ien* and *k'un*, cycles yin and yang, manages human emotions," and so on. The Classics are sources for ideas for a normative program for re-establishing morality.[162]

Lü's views are broader than Liu Mien's, but he shares the desire for fixed public standards. Only writing that inculcated those standards deserved to be called wen, he concludes in his essay "On Transformation Through the Wen of Man." Here the "wen of man" becomes the ethics necessary for institutions to restore social order. The wen of the family: "the husband dominates with firmness, the wife establishes herself through yielding; the father is caring and instructs, the son is filial and admonishes." The wen of the court: "the ruler directs ministers with benevolence, the ministers serve the ruler with righteousness." And so on, for the wen of bureaucracy, of punishment and policy, and of transformation through instruction. Lü's wen is a normative culture, yet he insists that his definition takes the literary and emotional aspects into account: it weaves together various accomplishments and embellishes human feelings so as to create an appealing, patterned appearance (wen). He contrasts this with the current understanding of the wen of man: "Sycophantic ministers of recent times, because the ruler of the day is incompetent, image *ch'ien* and *k'un* and relate Yao and Shun in creating wen for 'transforming the world,' thinking that emblazoned flags and ritual clothes, the commentaries and literary skill, are the wen of man. They cause the ruler of men to lose the basis completely while feeling entirely self-satisfied as he seeks perfect order through enlarging the display of majesty and awaiting peace by singing while he sits."[163] If this is what man's wen means, Lü continues, then all dynasties can claim to be wen, no matter how poorly they fared. If wen is something of social value, in other words, it must be redefined so that only cultural forms with correct values will be thought of as wen.

From the 770's generation I shall leap over a century and a half to the Sung. The men who set the course for intellectual culture in the Northern Sung found their goals and questions in the writings of this generation. The blossoming of innovative writing and intellectual inquiry that began in the late eighth century continued, although some who gained fame for wen rejected it. But the promise that had sparked it—the idea that by grasping the tao of the sage men could transform the world—kept becoming ever less credible as the political situation deteriorated and men whose position depended upon scholarly attainments had ever less influence over political events. The Sung unification made it possible to value wen once again and, eventually, to think that men whose wen illuminated tao should guide the state.

The latter half of the eighth century saw the demise of the early T'ang view that wen was always effective for better or for worse, because men acted according to what they saw and heard, and thus the end to the early T'ang approach to establishing a normative culture through the selection of appropriate models and the synthesis of diverse traditions. Scholars who thought in terms of models appropriate to a newly unified empire and of a synthesis of the various strands of tradition did not need to ask what principles should guide thought or how men could know values. The "restoration of wen-chang" had envisioned a recovery of the unity of wen-chang and behavior, at least for the individual, and had sought to guarantee that men would behave ethically by demanding that they return to normative models of wen. Yet, the premise for the restoration of wen-chang was the insight that literary forms had, in fact, failed to function as normative models!

But the restorationists set in motion a shift from adopting the right wen to seeking the right values. Aristocratic medieval culture died when the shih had to think about what they should value. This did not put an end to wen-chang. But as the rise of ku-wen makes clear, it opened the way for new kinds of individual writing, in which what men wrote and how they wrote represented the writer's own views on enduring values. To a great degree the tao of the sage was an empty category each person had to fill in his own way. In contrast to the early T'ang, the literary intellectuals of the latter half of the eighth century saw themselves as being in tension with the political order and their culture. Ku-wen encouraged this attitude and justified it. A Han Yü or Liu Tsung-yuan could be part of the system while still claiming the high ground from which to criticize it. The idea that individual scholars could find a tao of the sage gave scholars grounds for claiming responsibility for transforming society. The capital, court, and emperor might still be the center of culture, but they and their culture had lost moral authority.

5 Civil Policy and Literary Culture: The Beginnings of Sung Intellectual Culture

The wen of the T'ang was a political and scholarly model. For the government of the Sung founders, emulating it meant unifying the empire under civil rule, restoring the civil (wen) after a century dominated by the military (*wu*). But the T'ang's wen had two answers to the question of what scholars should do. Early T'ang court scholarship told them they should glorify the reunification and reverse the cultural decline of the Five Dynasties through the compilation and synthesis of cultural traditions and forms. But the late T'ang ku-wen intellectuals told them they should establish the independence of the scholarly community against the currents of the times and speak for morality and the common interest. That these answers were understood to have different implications for learning and writing is clear from the works of both spokesmen for ku-wen and proponents of literary synthesis. There was no true return to the early T'ang equation of value with cultural form—after the intrusion of ku-wen ideas into consciousness such an equation would have been forced at best—but many early scholars did combine an accommodative and eclectic appreciation of the broader cultural heritage with talk of the tao of the sages.

The scholarly community agreed upon the larger political issues during the first few decades of the dynasty: the survival of the dynasty and the restoration of the shih to political leadership. Similarly, intellectual differences, however real, were irrelevant unless it was first established that, in the words of early scholars, "man's possession of wen is the great tao of ordering and regulating," "wen is the emblem of the state and treasure of the nation," and "wen is the pre-eminent value for the age."[1] The intellectual history of the Northern Sung has its origins in the conviction of these first decades that wen was a value common to the realms of both politics and learning. But it also has its origins in the difference between the synthetic style of court scholarship and the moral outspokenness of ku-wen.

The process of questioning and debate that marks Northern Sung intellectual history began in full force during the third decade of the eleventh century, when it was certain that the Sung civil order would endure. It was at this point that some younger scholar-officials began to ask, in effect, What is there left to do? What should our purpose be now? They found their answer to that question in the works of the T'ang ku-wen writers who urged them to stand apart from the times, to aspire to the tao of the sages, and put that tao into practice. Putting it into practice required gaining power at court, establishing wen that was true to the tao of the ancients, and transforming society accordingly. For Fan Chung-yen and his supporters, the idea of overthrowing those in power was a purpose that was exciting—if only because it was so obviously a perilous choice for an official—and yet the righteousness of their cause was vouchsafed by the sages themselves. Even in retrospect it is hard to account for Fan's confidence, yet he did succeed for a brief moment in 1044.

This chapter will trace the unfolding of early Sung scholarship through Fan Chung-yen's victory at court. Ku-wen learning and the role of the ku-wen writer as agitator for political and social transformation set the basic agenda for Sung intellectual culture during the eleventh century. Later chapters will demonstrate this, while examining how some of the most influential scholars grappled with the problems inherent in the ku-wen view of learning. The questions intellectuals spoke to changed with time; younger generations took up new issues, political disputes brought latent differences into the open, and age and experience occasionally prompted changes of heart. But by and large the eleventh century was still a time when the great writers were also the great thinkers, when intellectuals supposed that values were to be known from the cultural tradition and given persuasive form through wen.

Yet attempts to establish a culture grounded in the universal values of the sages' integrated social order did not lead to a durable consensus. The era of intellectual ferment that began with the advent of ku-wen ended with thinkers who did not believe that wen was essential to knowing or realizing real values. The Tao-hsueh movement that would dominate intellectual culture by the end of the twelfth century looked back to the moral philosophers of the eleventh, men such as Ch'eng I, whose answer to the question "Is doing wen harmful to tao?" was "It is harmful," and his disciple Yu Tso (1053–1127), who interpreted Confucius to mean "It is better to have no wen at all than to learn it without a basis."[2]

But at the founding of the dynasty all this lay far in the future. In the story of Sung intellectual history, the advent of Tao-hsueh was a radical change in course, and it redefined the questions intellectuals asked. In considering why people came to change direction, we need to see what

course they had been on. Given the T'ang past, it is not surprising that
ideas about wen defined learning in the early Sung. Here we shall ask how
and why they did, and then why intellectuals began to take up the ku-wen
cause. My account is guided by the introduction to the collected biographies of literary men from the *Sung History*.

It has been so from old that in the case of a founding and unifying ruler one could
predict the pattern of an entire era from what his times valued. When the Great
Ancestor [T'ai-tsu; r. 960–76] changed the mandate, he first gave employment to
wen officials and took power away from military officers. The Sung's valuing
wen [the literary/civil] had its roots in this. While still heirs-apparent, T'ai-tsung
[r. 976–97] and Chen-tsung [r. 997–1022] already had reputations for loving
learning. Once they took the throne, [the Sung] became more wen by the day.
Through the successive reigns of their descendants, all those above who acted as
rulers of men were constantly engaged in learning, and all those below who acted
as ministers, from the chief councillors down to the local officials, were selected
through the examinations; and so within the four seas wen-shih who combined
substance and refinement appeared in droves.
    At the beginning of the dynasty, Yang I [974–1020] and Liu Yun [chin-shih 998]
were still imitating the tonal rules of T'ang writers. Liu K'ai [947–1000] and Mu
Hsiu [979–1032] were committed to changing [literary style to that of] antiquity,
but their strength was not equal to [this goal]. Then Ou-yang Hsiu [1007–72] of
Lu-ling appeared and led with ku-wen. Wang An-shih [1021–86] of Lin-ch'uan,
Su Shih [1037–1101] of Mei-shan, and Tseng Kung [1019–83] of Nan-feng arose
and harmonized with him. Day by day the wen of Sung inclined more toward
antiquity. After the move south, the wen energy did not match that of the Eastern
Capital [at Kaifeng in the Northern Sung]. Surely [wen] is sufficient to observe
changes in times, and so we have composed the "Park of Literature Biographies."[3]

The early Sung court promoted wen. It promised to establish a civil (wen)
order by employing men who proved their wen-hsueh in examinations.
But soon a division emerged between men such as Yang I, who favored
T'ang traditions of literary accomplishment, and men such as Liu K'ai,
who called for a return to the T'ang ku-wen tradition. In the end, we are
told, the ku-wen road was taken thanks to the leadership of Ou-yang
Hsiu. I shall begin with the question of how the Sung court promoted
wen and how scholars responded.

Civil Policy and Literary Scholars Before the 1020's

T'ai-tsung and Chen-tsung, the first Sung emperors to patronize learning
extensively, imitated the early T'ang model with court projects to sort out
and synthesize the cultural tradition. Early Sung scholars also looked back
to T'ang traditions of learning, but they included the writings of Han Yü's

generation in their scope and brought its distinction between wen and tao to bear on learning. It was no longer possible to think that one could find the right way by finding the right models; it was also necessary to speak of the sages and their tao.

The Court

For men in the last decades of the tenth century, anxious to show that military rule had come to an end, T'ai-tsung's use of literary learning to recruit shih, to "broadly draw in the shih through wen,"[4] and the employment of shih to restore civil authority over military men were entirely of a piece. As Ssu-ma Kuang (1019–86) later noted, T'ai-tsung intended to "restore the wen teaching [wen-chiao] and suppress military affairs."[5] The use of "wen" for civil made promoting the literary an aspect of establishing a civil order, as when T'ai-tsung renamed the academic institute's library the Court for Esteeming Wen (Ch'ung-wen Yuan)[6] and produced a book of his own under the title When Wen Is Illustrious, Governance Transforms (Wen ming cheng hua).[7] The civil-military dichotomy was raised in the examinations as well. The essay theme for the palace examination of 980 was: "Wen or wu, which is primary?" The responses may not have been entirely in accord with the imperial will, which had another northern campaign in mind, for three years later the theme was the declarative "Wen and wu flourish together." The theme for the rhapsody in the examination of 1000 suggests where the court ended up: "Contemplate the wen of man to transform all under heaven."[8] Yao Hsuan (968–1020), in a 1011 preface to his anthology of late T'ang writing, explains the success of the Sung founding as a "clear result of valuing wen and honoring learning."[9]

As in the T'ang, valuing wen and encouraging wen-hsueh were not incompatible with esteeming ju and harkening to ju teachings. In giving due attention to the Classics, taking advice from scholars, establishing a ritual system for the dynasty, and sorting out the legacy of the past, Sung T'ai-tsung was acting as the patron of the cultural tradition and civil values in general.[10] Eleventh- and twelfth-century works, while overstating his older brother T'ai-tsu's commitment to learning, at least make a plausible case for T'ai-tsu as a sometime patron of scholars. They note, for example, the emperor's visits to the Directorate of Education in 960 and 963, his order to military ministers to "read books and value understanding the tao of governing" in 966, his interview with a private scholar in 968, his announcement that chief councillors should henceforth be "men who read books," and his own study of the Former Kings in the Documents in 968.[11] T'ai-tsung did much more. He continued the program of book collecting begun in 966, annexing the libraries of conquered states and rewarding donors with degrees, promotions, and cash. The collection, moved to the newly constructed Court for Esteeming Wen in 978, was supposed to contain all the works listed in the T'ang *K'ai-yuan Four Category Catalogue*. Yet T'ai-tsung's rationale for collecting books also struck a late T'ang note: "The state is diligently seeking the ancient tao and opening up the source of transformation." Books made this possible: "Where else besides books will we be able to find models pertaining to the basis of transformation through instruction and the sources of order and chaos." But he collected more than books; soon he expanded the program to include calligraphy and painting and instructed local officials to purchase rubbings.[12] Anything that was wen could be collected.

T'ai-tsung's court also continued several Five Dynasties printing projects. Beginning in the late 980's, it issued definitive printed versions of the T'ang Five Classics first collated and printed between 932 and 953 and, then, again building on earlier efforts, turned to commentaries and subcommentaries for the *Ku-liang* and *Kung-yang* commentaries of the *Spring and Autumn Annals*, the *Ceremonial* (*I li*), the *Rites of Chou*, the *Classic of Filial Piety*, the *Analects*, and the *Erh-ya*. These, known as the Seven Classics, were finished in 1000. In 1011 an edition of the *Mencius* was also published.[13] Editions of Ssu-ma Ch'ien's *Shih-chi* and the two Han histories were also prepared and printed as part of a project, lasting from 994 to 1061, to publish all seventeen dynastic histories. Other historical works were made available as well: a revision of the *Collected Documents on T'ang Administration* (*T'ang hui-yao*) was submitted to the throne in 961 and an edition of Tu Yu's *Comprehensive Canons* (*T'ung tien*) was finished in 1000. The *History of the Five Dynasties* was completed in 973. Dictionaries were also issued: a new edition of the *Shuo-wen chieh-tzu* was printed in 986; the *Kuang yun*, a revised and enlarged version of the *Ch'ieh yun*, was finished in 989. The Buddhist *Tripitaka* was printed in 971–83 in Szechuan.[14] Beginning in 990, the court also sponsored editorial projects for Taoist texts, culminating in a revised manuscript version of the Taoist Canon in 1016.[15]

Little in this was original, but the Sung was outdoing its Five Dynasties predecessors in making the cultural tradition available through modern technology and in spreading learning (many of these standard texts were distributed to the prefectures and subprefectures). The great court compilation projects, however, showed that the Sung had inherited the responsibility for the cultural tradition and had succeeded to the Han and T'ang; the projects also provided jobs for scholars. Although the compendia made free use of earlier compilations, the Sung projects aimed at being comprehensive, providing all the cultural tradition had to offer on everything important to know about heaven-and-earth and, especially, human affairs. The *T'ai-p'ing Imperial Reader* (*T'ai-p'ing yü-lan*; 1,000 *chüan*, preface dated 983), named after the T'ai-p'ing hsing-kuo reign period (The Flourishing of the State in Great Peace; 976–83) of T'ai-tsung, categorized material under the general divisions of heaven, earth, and man. The *T'ai-p'ing Extended Record* (*T'ai-p'ing kuang-chi*; 500 *chüan*, preface dated 978) did the same for materials that dealt with the "mysterious" side (ghosts and spirits, immortals and adepts, monks and priests, doctors and shamans) and with "minor tao," such as painting and chess. The *Finest Blossoms from the Park of Literature* (*Wen-yüan ying-hua*; 1,000 *chüan*, preface dated 987) anthologized past wen-chang by genre following the model of the *Wen hsüan*. The *T'ai-p'ing Prescriptions by Imperial Grace* (*T'ai-p'ing sheng-hui-fang*; 100 *chüan*, preface dated 992) provided medical prescriptions taken from public and private records. Finally, the *Ts'e-fu yüan-kuei* (1,000 *chüan*, preface dated 1013) provided a comprehensive account of government affairs in a topically arranged chronological survey.[16]

In part the court was investing in the symbolic value of the compilation projects. Chen-tsung's preface explained that he had ordered the compilation of the *Ts'e-fu yüan-kuei* to show that he shared T'ai-tsung's "will" (*chih*) in sponsoring the earlier compilations: "to promote This Culture of Ours."[17] Even if Sung scholars did not find the compilations they produced terribly relevant, they were helping the Sung rulers show they differed from the illiterate rulers (and ministers) of the recent past. T'ai-tsung portrayed himself as a ruler-scholar. Having ordered the compilation of the *Imperial Reader*, he announced a program of daily reading to finish it within a year. He employed learned advisors, appointed lecturers on the Classics and histories beginning in 987, and made use of his new library.[18] He was a wen-ju who took responsibility for the survival of the cultural tradition and claimed to transform men through education. As Chen-tsung later noted, "the use of wen-chang to transform men began with T'ai-tsung."[19] T'ai-tsung's activity as a calligrapher illustrates his avowed commitment to wen. Throughout his reign, he distributed samples and copies of his own calligraphy to favored ministers, famous mountains and monasteries, and reclusive scholars. His assembled works occupied thousands of scrolls.[20] As "ruler to the world," how could he justify the time and effort? "In my heart I am devoted to [calligraphy] and cannot give it up. After years and months I have fully grasped these styles. But the thorough learning of the small cursive script is difficult, and few are skillful in the flying-white style. By mastering these forms, I have kept them from disappearing."[21] He was helping preserve This Culture.

In being a patron of scholars and as a scholar himself, T'ai-tsung allied the imperial house with the shih and their interests, and shih with merit in learning could look to the emperor for support. The imperial patronage of the civil was given its greatest substance by T'ai-tsung's decision to expand the examination system into the pre-eminent mechanism for recruiting civil officials. The examination requirements continued those of the Later Chou dynasty, which in turn copied the late T'ang. Chin-shih candidates composed a *shih* poem, a rhapsody, and an essay (*lun*) on set themes. At the departmental examination they also wrote treatises (*ts'e*) on policy questions. They were tested on memory knowledge of the *Analects* and asked ten factual questions on the *Spring and Autumn Annals* or *Book of Rites*, for example, the commentary's gloss on a certain passage or the personage being referred to in a particular line.[22] The literary composition requirement made the chin-shih unique. At its best it encouraged mastery of the cultural heritage and creative thought, but standards were lower in practice and candidates were likely to spend more time on the rhymes for the poetry sections, for these determined success or failure.[23] The chin-shih remained primarily a test of literary skill until 1071, when poetic forms were dropped in favor of questions testing an understanding of the meaningful principles inferred from a particular Classic.[24]

The various other examinations produced the majority of degree holders until the 1040's, when the balance shifted in favor of the chin-shih. They were abolished after 1073. Each of the eight "various fields" (*chu-k'o*) tested memorization and factual knowledge of the required texts. The number of degrees within these fields is known only for a few years. In 973, for example, a year with 26 chin-shih degrees, 5 degrees were awarded in the Five Classics field, none in the Nine Classics, 38 in the Three Rites (*Record of Rites, Ceremonial, Rites of Chou*), 26 in the Three Commentaries (on the *Spring and Autumn Annals*), 7 in the T'ang *K'ai-yuan Ritual Code*, 3 in the Three Histories, 18 in Thorough Learning (*hsueh-chiu*) in the Classics, and 5 in Understanding of the Law (*ming-fa*).[25] In 1057, in an attempt to promote the study of the Classics as a source of values, an Understanding the Classics (*ming-ching*) field was added, with the idea of eventually replacing the various fields and returning to the dual-track T'ang system of chin-shih and ming-ching degrees. The ming-ching was envisioned not as a memorization test but as a test of the ability to discuss the "principles" of the Classics chosen for study.[26] Before this, candidates in the various fields were expected to have only full passive knowledge of the texts (and commentaries) in question. They were not asked to express opinions or demonstrate original talent; none of these fields equaled the chin-shih in prestige.

The examination system did not encourage the kind of learning associated with ku-wen; rather, it continued the T'ang court tradition of wen-hsueh, of text learning and literary composition. I assume that the shih found this an acceptable way of being selected for office because it was close enough to how they conceived learning. If anything, the procedures to ensure fairness that began in the 990's made texts and writing even more important, for in an effort to be fair examiners were denied knowledge of the candidate as a man.[27] Some objected that candidates were being told that wen-chang alone mattered for scholars. There was some truth in this. In 980, for example, when a candidate announced himself in the field of One Hundred Poems, a degree not offered in decades, he was passed "to encourage learning," although his poems were judged unacceptable.[28] The reasoning was dubious, but the intent accorded with policy. And the policy was a success: 5,200 shih attended the departmental examination in 977, 10,200 in 983, and 17,300 in 992.[29] The scholars who gained prominence under T'ai-tsung and Chen-tsung may have disagreed with each other over policies and taken issue with the imperial will on occasion, but they had no problem agreeing that the Sung was right to value wen.

Scholars

Of the many shih who gained reputations for writing and scholarship during the first three Sung reigns, some were Five Dynasties court scholars absorbed into the Sung court, others were court scholars who held Sung examination degrees, and still others spent most of their career in local government.[30] Few were willing merely to ornament the retinue of the powerful and gloss over crass political decisions, but they were expected to provide some embellishment, their literary praise pleased the imperial eye and ear and promised to ensure that the future would see the Sung in the best possible light, and they were rewarded for appropriate flattery.[31] A career in scholarly office allowed them, if they chose, to speak out on issues of the day; it almost always led to several terms as a prefect. They saw themselves as contributing to the creation of a lasting civil order and offered T'ai-tsung various programs for achieving it.[32] They remonstrated with the emperor as well.[33] In some cases, for example in 986, we find them joining together in defense of civil interests against the expansion of military activity, in this case the effort to recover sixteen northern prefectures from Liao control. At times their advice and remonstrance may have been for show,[34] but sometimes they bluntly contradicted imperial claims to civil order and "great peace."[35] No doubt the emperor was showing that he would take advice from scholars—a sign, history told, of a great ruler—and certainly both ruler and minister self-consciously imitated the relation between T'ang T'ai-tsung and his scholarly ministers.[36] But scholars also tested the limits of remonstrance, and found them.[37]

The scholarly attainments of the most influential men were largely on the literary side. With few exceptions specialists in the Classics were relatively obscure and uninfluential.[38] Literary intellectuals spoke to the vital questions of state and rose to higher office. Many proceeded along an emerging scholarly "fast track" that began with a high ranking on the chin-shih examination, a stint in local government, appointment as an academician, tenure as rescript writer and Han-lin academician, and sometimes membership on the Council of State.[39] Nor did achievements in wen-hsueh preclude appointment to the Bureau of Military Affairs or the Finance Commission. Literary intellectuals had personal contact with the emperor and an inside knowledge of court politics. They provided the voices that gave the Sung court its culture, and their presence associated the Sung state with wen.[40] Some of them had promoted the idea of wen as the guiding value for the polity before the Sung founding. They were patrons themselves of ambitious younger men seeking to rise through learning and writing. They were expected to promote wen-hsueh among the shih, to explain the importance of wen, and to provide models of cultural accomplishment after a century of decline in education and cultural standards. As Chen-tsung said in 1009: "Ministers responsible for writing are the primary teachers of those who learn."[41]

Although the outlook of early Sung court scholars was not uniform and the attitudes of individuals varied, they sought to promote the civil and literary over military interests. In contrast to the partisanship of later intellectuals, they envisioned a literary culture that by accommodating diversity would help secure the Sung unification. Three examples will illustrate this and, at the same time, provide a sense of how some men understood learning.

Hsu Hsuan: civil order and the literary man. Hsu Hsuan (917–92) was the greatest Five Dynasties scholar to find a place at the Sung court and gain the attention of T'ai-tsung. Hsu had served the Southern T'ang; by 975, when it submitted, he had become one of the most influential ministers at the elegant and literary Southern T'ang court. He had long spoken for the value of literary learning. In 938, for example, he envisioned a society in which the political relationship between ruler and ruled would be established through the persuasive literary expression of values and consciousness. Following the Great Preface to the *Songs* and Po Chü-i's ideas, Hsu held up the model of an antiquity whose rulers inculcated values in their subjects and learned of the sentiments of those below through poetry. This is why the tao of the Former Kings offered an alternative to military force, he wrote; although this "tao is not yet practiced," men should pursue literary learning in the hope of realizing it.[42] By 957 he was calling for shih with literary merit to be given political responsibility. Man's ability to express his emotional responses to things distinguished him from animals, he argued, and literary men were best at setting forth their emotions. Thus, he concluded, testing wen was also the best way of selecting shih to serve as officials and making known "what the state valued."[43] Implicitly Hsu contrasted those who manifested desires and feelings through writing with military men who acted to get what they wanted.

Hsu's sense of the connection between literary learning and the civil state fit well with opinion at T'ai-tsung's court. He was also appreciated for helping save This Culture of Ours when it was about to perish, a mission Hsu had taken upon himself as a Southern T'ang minister.[44] In 989 Hsu was serving the Sung, convinced that wen had been accepted as the basis for the new political order and that now, as in antiquity, it was possible for the superior man to "save the age" while "getting ahead in the times." There was no longer an antithesis between the ideal and the practical; men with cultural accomplishment could join together in serving the state while realizing the ideal.

The tao of the superior man is expressed in individual [conduct] and extended to things. It proceeds from inside and reaches full development outside. Language is the means of putting it into practice, and wen is why the practice extends far. Thus wen is of pre-eminent value for the age. Even though past and present differ in form, north and south vary in tone, its essentials are simply to broadcast the kingly beneficence and transmit the emotional responses of those below and, without departing from the tao of the sage, to accomplish the common goals. As for [the stylistic values of] lofty tenor with untrammeled force, brief phrasing with subtle import, a tone melodious and an embellishment luxuriant, such are secondary achievements.[45]

For Hsu, a unified land under civil rule was the common goal. Like the early T'ang court scholars, he sought to accommodate north and south and synthesize the normative and expressive functions of wen while cautioning against literary craft (although he was quite skilled himself). But he also added the later T'ang idea of taking the tao of the sage as the test of value. Hsu thus placed the scholar at the center, between political power and its subjects and between utility and moral norms.

T'ien Hsi and Chang Yung: the unity of culture and tao. For scholars who came to maturity under Sung rule, passed Sung examinations, and served T'ai-tsung and Chen-tsung, wen was an officially sanctioned value. T'ien Hsi (940–1003), from a northwestern family that had migrated to Szechuan, for example, passed the K'ai-feng prefectural examinations on the theme "Transform all under heaven with the wen of man."[46] For Chang Yung (946–1004), a northerner, it was a given that political order depended on "shih who learn from the past and are free of self-interest."[47] To a greater extent than Hsu apparently, T'ien and Chang were alert to the diverse and potentially divisive possibilities within the cultural tradition. T'ien and Chang knew each other; both served as academicians at court and as successful prefects in the provinces; both were outspoken men of strong will (T'ien Hsi was particularly famous for his critical memorials) and would inspire eleventh-century intellectuals.[48]

Both believed that learning was integral to the enterprise of establishing a unified sociopolitical order; wen was not only a matter of refinement or self-expression.[49] Serving in Szechuan, for example, Chang Yung set about persuading the learned among the local shih to attend the examinations and enter state service. As Chang explained to a student: "The task of ju is wen." Heaven-and-earth had done their creative work; the sages had appeared and established ritual and righteousness, the five relationships, and the Classics. Men of the present who "made language wen" and grasped the tao of the sage could give form to social roles, define rituals, set the principles for policy, and more.[50] The "brush of the wen-shih deliberates in the middle," Chang told Chen-tsung, mediating between the sage ruler above and those below, proclaiming morality and extending transforming influence yet also returning to antiquity (fu-ku) to show how this was to be done.[51] Chang at times adopted the stance of one studying the past rather than seeking to get along with the present.[52] It is not coincidental that these sentiments echoed ku-wen themes; by his own account Chang had studied Han Yü and Liu Tsung-yuan.[53]

T'ien Hsi spoke of "taking the methods of the ju as his personal responsibility and the tao of antiquity as his enterprise," instead of seeking power and wealth. This tao meant several things, T'ien explained. Expressing opinions about the worthiness of men in power was tao; aiding "all under heaven so that not one thing loses its place" was also tao. It was possible to practice this tao, he went on, with either the "conduct of the superior man" or the "wen of the superior man." To do both was best, but the conduct was essential.[54] T'ien also presented himself as a student of the late T'ang, listing Han Yü and Liu Tsung-yuan, Li Po and Tu Fu, Po Chü-i and Yuan Chen, Lü Wen and Lu Chih, among others, as a range of appropriate models for scholars aiding a ruler intent on returning to the institutional models of antiquity.[55]

Chang and T'ien presented themselves as proponents of the ancient tao and spoke of unifying wen and tao, but they also took tao as something that could not be narrowly defined and cast themselves as advocates of an inclusive vision of wen. For Chang the idea of an ultimate common tao freed the present from particular past models, and he was notorious for his dislike of ritual and the ritually minded. It was not style—ancient or modern—that made a work "wen," he wrote; rather, a work was wen because its author possessed the tao of the sage. "Elaborations in language may differ, but tao may not differ."[56] Elsewhere Chang explained that one grasped tao in the mind and then, having a broad acquaintance with past traditions, found a way to create wen-chang that could guide the present. Those who composed the works that "illuminate the right and redress error" were men who "appropriate the mind of creation [tsao-hua]" and "put forth the blossoms of the canon."[57]

T'ien Hsi developed the idea of combining personal intuition of tao with the mastery of the broad cultural tradition more fully. His efforts to transform the present through composing wen-chang and practicing "loyalty and good faith" were possible, he contended, because he included the Classics, histories, philosophical schools, and literary collections within his vision of learning the tao of the sage. When Chen-tsung came to the throne, T'ien proposed the compilation of a new *Imperial Reader* with selections from all four categories of texts in 360 *chüan*, one chapter for each day of the year.[58] Opposed to dividing the textual tradition into works reaffirming the Classics and those departing from the ancient norms, T'ien proposed distinguishing between works emphasizing continuity and those representing creative variation. The former are the "normal form" of wen; the latter the "variations of wen." But just as heaven-and-earth had their "constant patterns" (ch'ang-li), there were inevitable variations and unexpected events. Both were necessary, since This Culture of Ours could survive only if allowed to change with the times. Han Yü and Liu Tsung-yuan were concerned with the orthodox, he wrote, yet in appreciating Li Ho's songs they showed that "sensual songs did no harm to correct pattern." The aim was the creation of wen, for "man's possession of wen is the great tao of regulating and ordering; one who has apprehended this tao can control the process of transformation through instruction."[59]

In a letter to Sung Po, an older scholar and a leading literary man at the court, T'ien set forth his theory for "threading on one strand" creativity and tradition. Tao is that which functions "so-of-itself" (tzu-jan). The literary creator gains direct but momentary access to tao as the so-of-itself process of creation whence all things come into being. In these moments of intuition, his emotional responses to things (ch'ing) become one with his own innate character or nature (hsing), and his nature, which normally limits his capability, becomes one with tao. In a spontaneous, creative, and unpredictable manner, tao affects his nature and emotional response leading to an orderly, integrated, and thus moral expression of wen, just as "a small wind sets the water rippling." In the context of composing wen-chang, T'ien argues, one should not give primacy to any particular one of the possibilities represented by the T'ang masters. Instead, mastering all to a degree, the writer draws on tao to compose works that integrate aspects of past compositions. The works are emblems of creative unity and integration in the human realm that transcend the limitations of the writer's individual nature. They become "living" things, imbued with spirit and containing the "spring of creation." In contrast to a landscape painting, which lacks the living quality of the scene it depicts, a wen-chang thus produced is a true creation with a life of its own. In the end, he concludes, "I do not know whether wen has me or I have wen."[60]

I would suggest that for Chang Yung and T'ien Hsi, and for a number of younger men not discussed here, wen as literary composition was not a set of normative models or a vehicle for doctrine, but the emblem of the individual's ability to integrate strands of past culture into a whole. Tao, a somewhat indistinct idea of heaven-and-earth or the ancient sages, promised a natural foundation on which modern men could unify ideas about antiquity and the sages without becoming beholden to a particular doctrine. They wanted a synthesizing, inclusive moral basis for domestic unity at a time when the Sung was solidifying its conquest, reaching a political consensus on making peace with the Khitans, and struggling to avoid factionalism.[61] Thinking about the grounds of harmony also fit well with Chen-tsung's desire to believe that his reign, its cession of territory to Liao in the treaty of 1004 notwithstanding, was securing the Sung's possession of Heaven's mandate and, with the restoration of the great Feng and Shan sacrifices in 1008, ushering in an age of great peace.

Literary Refinement Versus Ku-wen: The Emerging Division

Within the accommodative view of wen and learning evident in the writings of Hsu Hsuan, Chang Yung, and T'ien Hsi can be found the faultline for a debate over literary and intellectual standards that by the 1030's would begin to divide scholars. Hsu, T'ien, and Chang tried to hold together the tao of the sage and the ku-wen style with the idea of a unity of literary and textual traditions grounded in an ultimate natural tao. Literary standards mattered as competition for examination degrees increased. Students wanted to know how to pass the exams, and scholarly officials watched what kind of literary accomplishments were rewarded. Those who asked how diverse interests could be held together while raising the level of quality could see literary sophistication as a means of demonstrating both cultural breadth in learning from the past and creative skill in interweaving those strands into a form suitable to the present. The idea of raising literary standards was approved in an imperial edict of 1005 on the "encouragement of learning" that noted the dismal standards of many candidates and repeated instances of cheating.[62] The growing influence of Yang I under Chen-tsung was a sign that this view was persuasive for many at court. At the same time some objected to the emphasis on literary breadth and refinement and called for the exclusive study of the Classics following what they understood to be Han Yü's views on ku-wen and tao of the sage. Liu K'ai and Wang Yü-ch'eng, early proponents of ku-wen, made a point of denying that the merely literary had value in itself. There is evidence that others continued to espouse similar views through Chen-tsung's reign; for example, an imperial edict in 1009 spoke of "This Culture of Ours returning to antiquity" and called for a less embellished style fit for moral instruction. Chen-tsung's court thus recognized a difference of opinion, but generally it held to the more inclusive literary and cosmic tao of ministers such as Wang Ch'in-jo (962–1025) and Ting Wei (962–1033). They also encouraged Chen-tsung to ever greater involvement in the mysteries of tao, providing him with letters from Heaven, auspicious omens, divine ancestors, and great sacrifices.[63]

Yang I: wen as the refinement of man. Yang I (974–1020) was straightforward in his preference for literary sophistication. He issued eight literary collections during his lifetime, some of which were printed.[64] His extant writing is finely and intricately constructed, loaded with allusions, and skillful in its evocation of scene and his response to it. His prose, which he preferred to compose in parallel style, is by far the most difficult of all the early Sung figures discussed here. Yang certainly recognized the ku-wen current, although he did not use the term. He notes, for instance, that a desire to "illuminate the tao of the sage" fits the imperial interest in "returning to the system of the Three Eras," and he does not belittle those court scholars of the 990's who, as "leaders of the alliance of literary composition" (*wen-chang meng-chu*), sought to make wen the vehicle for inculcating moral values.[65] But for himself, in his own role as literary scholar and patron to others, writing that "gives the form of the thing and traces the emotional responses" (*t'i-wu yuan-ch'ing*) and "sings of the individual character" (*yin-yung hsing-ch'ing*) holds greater interest.[66] From his perspective such work was not at odds with antiquity, and there was nothing wrong with "carving and engraving" in a world seeking to rise above the crudeness of the recent past.[67] Yang simply was not persuaded that men should make promoting the ancient tao the purpose of literary writing or should exclude particular schools from their reading.[68] The examination questions he wrote suggest he did not believe there was a simple answer to the question of what all shih should value.[69]

Yang I outlived the best-known early opponents of literary refinement. In about 1007 he put together an anthology of poems written during the compiling of the *Ts'e-fu yuan-kuei*, which was immediately recognized for its high level of refinement and embellishment. The "Hsi-k'un style" of wen-chang, named after the title of this collection, was a sign for some that the Sung had risen above the crude and vulgar qualities of Five Dynasties writing, but by the end of Yang's life some had begun to decry Yang's influence openly. In the 1030's Shih Chieh (1005–45), for example, launched a famous attack on Yang I and Hsi-k'un as the enemy of true learning.[70] Yang himself was an admirer of Li Shang-yin (813–58), the great T'ang prose stylist and poet. Li had not been an advocate of antiquity, nor did he accept the notion that the sages of the Classics had a privileged claim to tao.

It was not necessary to adopt the parallel style of Yang I to be a proponent of literary refinement. For some the point of valuing literary skill was to affirm the duty of scholars to serve the interests of a court that was, after all, serving the larger interest of securing a civil order. Hsia Sung (984–1050), who passed the decree examination in 1007, is a case in point.[71] Hsia wrote in an elegant but "ancient" style and claimed the mantle of the Classics, sages, and tao, while arguing that the flourishing of wen as literary writing made the Sung better than the Han and T'ang. His "Ode on Extending Wen" made a direct connection between the raising of literary standards, the revival of This Culture of Ours, the dawning of an age of great peace, and the proposal to re-establish the rituals of antiquity and carry out the Feng and Shan sacrifices in 1008.[72] Another rather clever piece argued that the Ch'in's burning of the books was really a good thing, for it taught that wen was vital to the survival of the polity: "When a state perishes, wen perishes first; there has never been a case of preserving wen yet not being able to save [the state] from perishing."[73] Like Yang, he was responding to a time when, in Hsia's words, "the emperor is expecting transformation through the wen of man."[74]

Liu K'ai and Wang Yü-ch'eng: ku-wen and true values. The northerner Liu K'ai (947–1000) never became a court scholar, although he corresponded with many at court and took the chin-shih degree. He was one of the first prefects appointed when, in about 986, the emperor decided to appoint shih with literary talents to places traditionally run by military men.[75] Liu is often treated as the first Sung ku-wen scholar and self-proclaimed successor to Han Yü. Although it is now clear that Han already was a well-established model, Liu was unusual in claiming that Han Yü's ku-wen alone taught men how to realize true values.

Accounts of the Sung ku-wen movement typically depict Liu K'ai as a simple, sincere man struggling to find the right way. Liu K'ai's two autobiographical accounts, however, suggest he self-consciously created a literary persona for himself, first as the successor to Han Yü and then as a sage in his own right. The first, the "Biography of the Rustic from Tung-chiao," discusses his choice of his first adult name of Chien-yü ("supporting Han Yü") and the honorific Shao-hsien ("continuing the predecessor" [i.e., Liu Tsung-yuan as a lesser Han Yü]).[76] As "the Rustic," he wrote an *Unofficial History*, in 30 *chüan*, on events in his native Ta-ming. But then he shifted from history to the Classics and, in imitation of the Sui-T'ang scholar Wang T'ung's continuation of the Classics, composed pieces to fill in the lost portions (*pu-wang*) of the *Songs* and *Documents*. In recognition of his achievement, he wrote a new autobiography, called himself Master Fill-in-the-Gap (Pu-wang hsien-sheng), and took the name K'ai (to open the tao of the ancient worthies and sages for the present) and honorific Chung-t'u (on the right track or on the road to authority). Having appre-hended the tao of the sage himself, he claimed, he was "opening the road" for his times, "so that past and present proceed through me."[77]

For Liu K'ai, the road led from Han Yü to himself as a sage or at least as the spokesman for the tao of the sage in the line of Han, Mencius, Yang Hsiung, and now Wang T'ung.[78] What he learned from Han Yü, Liu explained in a 970 preface to Han's collection, was that one who possessed the tao could act and teach through the device of literary composition; it was not necessary to write books. Before leaving for the capital and the examination of 973, Liu explained in a series of letters how he could be equal to the sages and produce wen-chang equal to the Classics.[79]

In contrast to the limited, candle-power vision of the common man, Liu argues, the sage comprehends all sides with the illuminating power of the sun and, seeing the whole, is free to change his focus according to the situation without slipping into partiality. Because whatever comes to his mind is in perfect agreement with tao, his spontaneous responses to things help them realize their role as part of the whole. Wen-chang is his device (*ch'i*) for affecting things. As the product of his mind, it is in perfect agreement with tao. It is, however, merely a device; the sage does not think about the literary surface through which he works. But later men, Liu explains, can learn how to be sages from the surviving devices of the sages (the texts) if they learn to look past the literary aspect to the ideas in the sages' minds: benevolence, righteousness, propriety, wisdom, and trustworthiness. Liu defines these familiar virtues as natural aptitudes of mind and sentiment: for example, benevolence is the ability to have the familial feeling that keeps humans from separating, and righteousness is the systematic organization of affairs necessary to establish proper mea-sures. The tao of the sage is a set of ideas for guiding the creation of an integrated order. Sages were "born knowing it," Liu admits, but it can be learned from teachers as long as one avoids laboring endlessly over the Classics and commentaries or seeking normative patterns (*li*) in the elabo-rated language of the Classics. The Classics, after all, are merely the product of the sages' bringing integrative attitudes to bear on affairs through wen-chang. Moreover, this is a natural process: to "bring to life" is to accord with heaven's tao; to imitate tradition and convention is not natural. Indeed, the proof that Mencius, Yang Hsiung, Wang T'ung, and Han Yü did accord with the heavenly and sagely tao is their ability to break with the conventions of wen-chang, for that could only have come from relying on tao directly and speaking from their own minds. Wen-chang, Liu concludes, are the "fish-trap of tao." One who wishes to catch tao must attend to the device, but it is a means, not an end.[80] Only one who shares the mind of the sages can compose works that are efficacious in governing. "The mind and wen are one," Liu contended. The internal mind is the master of its external manifestations; wen as an external appearance thus has an internal structure. A correct mind means correct wen, and the wen can guide those who subscribe to it to correctness and gradually persuade those who do not. Including language from the Classics, histories, and hundred schools to unify culture is unnecessary. Moreover, borrowing the language of others means not expressing one's own mind directly, which is what it means to be truly ancient.[81]

Some objected that Liu was narrowly learned and that his denial of the value of the larger textual tradition in favor of Han Yü was divisive.[82] Such an objection overlooked Liu's claim that the mind possessed universal guides to an integrated order that transcended cultural forms and justified change. His call on Chen-tsung to fully reorganize the political system and "establish a new policy" (li hsin fa), an idea that would appear a century later with Wang An-shih, is an example of this.[83] Yet Liu was not about to forsake a claim to tradition. As he explains in his famous "Response to an Accusation," his wen and tao were the wen and tao of the sages.

You accuse me of liking ku-wen. What do you mean when you say ku-wen? Now, ku-wen does not depend on the elaborations being so difficult or the language being so demanding that others have difficulty reading and reciting it. It depends on making ancient the patterns and lofty the intent, determining length according to what one has to say, creating a structure in response to change, and conducting affairs as did the ancients. This is called ku-wen. If you are not able to appreciate my writing and take my meaning, it is because you look at it from the present and recite it in the present. You do not use the ancient tao to contemplate my mind; you do not use the ancient tao to contemplate my will. My wen is without error. Were I to follow the wen of the age, how could I set forth instructions for the common folk? And I would feel ashamed in my own mind. If one wishes to practice the ancient tao but instead is of a kind with the wen of people today, it would be like mounting a thoroughbred to sail the seas. . . . My tao is the tao of Confucius, Mencius, Yang Hsiung, and Han Yü. My wen is the wen of Confucius, Mencius, Yang Hsiung, and Han Yü. You have not thought about what you are saying and wrongly accuse me. To accuse me is permissible, but if you accuse my wen and tao, then you are my enemy.[84]

In being self-consciously narrow and different, Liu K'ai claimed to be the true heir to the sages and thus morally independent of contemporary society. He also isolated himself from those in power at court.

Hsia Sung showed that it was possible to advocate literary refinement without writing in a difficult style; Wang Yü-cheng (954–1001) illustrated that it was possible to promote ku-wen as a moral enterprise without isolating oneself. A northerner, a court scholar, and an outspoken political critic, Wang was also well connected to such older court scholars as Hsu Hsuan and Chang Yung. A case has been made for seeing Wang as rounding off the hard edges of ku-wen, avoiding the pitfalls of Liu K'ai's dogmatism, and making more room for both aesthetic interest and individual expression.[85] Still, Wang broke with prevailing opinion in claiming that only writing based on the Classics and five constants deserved to be called wen.[86] He rejected all attempts to incorporate the ideas of the hundred schools into writing, arguing that only when men based their wen-hsueh on the Classics would their governance be benevolent and righteous.[87] Yet a broad appreciation of T'ang writers did not harm "learning the tao of the sage."[88] Moreover, he saw the need to influence others. "Wen is to transmit the tao and make clear the mind," he explained; writing that became abstruse in an effort to be unconventional defeated the purpose of wen.[89]

Men who sought to be singular in order to prove they were more anxious to be moral than to get along with the times risked losing the attention of the powerful under Chen-tsung.[90] But the idea persisted that ku-wen represented an alternative to both the intellectual eclecticism and literary refinement of the day. For example, Yao Hsuan's anthology of largely post-rebellion T'ang writing, the Wen ts'ui (The best of literature; completed 1011), was presented as an alternative to the literary models of the Wen hsuan and, implicitly, to the newly compiled Finest Blossoms of the Park of Literature, which was modeled on the Wen hsuan. It proclaimed Han Yü the greatest of all literary figures, and singled out Liu Tsung-yuan, Li Ao, and Huang-fu Shih as Han's allies in making the tao of the former sages and Confucius clear. Yao limited his selection to those T'ang worthies who attained the tao of antiquity rather than those who excelled in literary craft. Wen is still an overarching value—"For 300 years the T'ang used wen to order the world"—but achieving order depends upon wen that favors antiquity.[91]

A second example is more unusual. The monk Chih-yuan (976–1022) was active as a teacher of ku-wen to other monks.[92] He describes ku-wen, which he equates with "learning ju," as an activity discrete from Buddhism.

What is called ku-wen establishes language worthy of being remembered according to the ancient tao, and the language must illuminate the ancient tao. What is the ancient tao? It is the tao the sage-teacher Confucius practiced. Long ago Confucius related the affairs of Yao and Shun and took Wen and Wu as models; the Six Classics were then complete. His fundamental precepts were simply benevolence and righteousness and the five constants. If you aspire to This Culture [ssu-wen], you must really master the tao of the five constants. Do not lose the center yet change with the times, change but maintain continuity [with the ancient], for what is continuous endures and what endures agrees [with the tao]. Once you have apprehended the tao in the mind, let it come out by doing wen-chang and spread it as transformation through instruction [chiao-hua] [thus to save the age and set forth the kingly way, etc.]. . . . This should be the goal of doing wen. The creation of ku-wen truly is complete in this. Were ku-wen merely writing without parallelism and creating sentences difficult to read, . . . then the books of the heterodox—Lao-tzu, Chuang-tzu, Yang Chu, and Mo-tzu—could also be seen as ku-wen since they are neither rhymed nor parallel, and that should not be.[93]

Although Chih-yuan could hardly be as totalistic as Liu and Wang, he too saw that ku-wen was not merely a literary style but also a commitment to manifesting moral ideas others could share and live by. The acceptance of ku-wen by monks who did wen is probably evidence of its growing acceptance among the shih. And this helps explain, I think, why with the inauguration of a new reign in 1022 Fan Chung-yen was able to rally others to his cause.

Fan Chung-yen and the Rise of
Ku-wen in Politics and Learning

Chen-tsung died in 1022. Jen-tsung came to the throne in his thirteenth year under the empress dowager as regent; he ruled from 1032 until 1063. A change in imperial leadership could open the way for other changes at court. Fan Chung-yen (989–1052) began to agitate in the mid-1020's. His views did not move the court, but he gained a following among younger officials. Entangled in a major crisis on the northern frontier in the early 1040's, the court gave Fan and his allies leading positions in an attempt to unify domestic politics. For a brief moment, in 1043–44, Fan's group set policy. Fan Chung-yen's rise marked the emergence of a self-conscious political opposition with a well-articulated policy program; it also helped create an intellectual world that defined itself against political authority. The political aspects of the Ch'ing-li reform are well known.[94] Less well studied is Fan's adoption of the rhetoric of "restoring wen-chang" as

found in the writings of Li Hua and Tu-ku Chi and eventually of the ku-
wen political and intellectual ideals of Han Yü's "Finding the Source for
Tao."

Attacking the Court

Fan put himself in the public eye in 1025 with a letter to the empress
dowager and emperor telling them that their first concern should be "to
save This Culture of Ours."[95] This goal requires bringing into government morally committed scholars who will speak frankly about what the
"Sage Dynasty should, but has not yet, put into practice." The first thing
such men will address is the tao of wen-chang, for wen is both a sign of the
quality of governance and the chief influence on the quality of the age. The
current state of wen—the embellished literary style popular under Chen-
tsung—is a sign of moral decay, and it must be changed. "The weakness
of wen-chang is the concern of the superior man," Fan explains, for it
makes it impossible for the ruler to extend his "transforming influence"
and thus sets the stage for the founding of a new dynasty. It follows, then,
that saving the dynasty depends on raising men who will break with
convention and do morally substantial wen on the model of antiquity.

> I humbly hope that Your Sagely Kindness will discuss the tao of wen-chang with
> the great ministers and learn from the suasion of [the sage-kings] Shun and Yü.
> How much more the pity that, with the once in a millennium occurrence of a sage
> dynasty, we do not pursue the loftiness of the Three Eras but value the pettiness of
> the Six Dynasties. Yet what period has not had men in the ranks of wen-chang? It
> must be that what the age values cannot be changed singlehandedly. Who is not
> swayed to follow the commands of the great ruler? You might instruct the
> ministers responsible for composition to restore the ancient tao and invite erudite
> shih, placing them in advisory positions, in order to save This Culture of Ours and
> strengthen transforming influence.[96]

In other words, if the dynasty is to survive, it must make sure that the wen
that mediates between the ruler's will and the polity at large is ancient, and
thus it should turn to men like Fan.

In 1027 Fan followed this with a longer letter to the chief councillors,
audaciously writing about affairs of state while in mourning, urging them
to fulfill their responsibility for civil and military affairs and for local
government in particular and act on behalf of "all living things under
Heaven."[97] Again he raised the issue of wen-chang, telling them to change
the examination system so as to wean shih from the literary styles of later
times and turn them back to the canons of the Former Kings. Presuming
that questioning candidates on the "great essentials" of governance would
ensure a gradual return to the ancient tao, he called for evaluating candi-

dates on the basis of the treatise and the essay rather than on the poem and rhapsody sections.[98] He repeated his views a year later, asking the court to encourage learning that took the Six Classics as the guide to institutions, strategic planning, moral judgments, and so on, thus preparing shih to act in the present as the sages had in the past. The various philosophical schools and histories were "not where one seeks tao." The tao to be sought was not a transcendent cosmic tao but, as Fan put it, "the tao of the wen of the former sages."[99]

Fan was anxious to get ahead in the world. His advocacy of the Classics and criticism of the "southern" wen of the Six Dynasties, for example, show that as a southerner he was not a client of the southern leaders Wang Ch'in-jo and Ting Wei, whose interest in the cosmic tao and literary elegance had marked Chen-tsung's reign.[100] Called out of mourning in 1027 to teach at the school built by the sympathetic Yen Shu (991–1055), Fan showed himself somewhat more willing to compromise with the system than his earlier pronouncements suggested, for he did prepare students in current literary standards.[101] Still, Fan found opportunities to oppose the court. Yen recommended Fan for a post as academician in 1028; the next year Fan objected to the empress dowager's treatment of the emperor and was demoted. Fan was trying to create a division; he was not just seeking fame. In a letter to Yen Shu in 1030, he justified himself. The shih could be divided into two "factions," he explained. There are those who say, "When I express myself, what I say will always be lofty yet at risk; and when I establish myself, what I do will always be lofty yet at risk. The tao of the king is correct and straight; there is no need for circuitousness." The other faction, of course, seeks to get along, find agreement, and avoid trouble. Because those who speak out are punished, they learn to keep quiet, thus letting careerists who do not benefit the state win by default. He, however, would not "stay out of harm's way to keep the body whole." He would speak frankly, in order to keep the government from "harming the people."[102] By refusing to follow the convention of shutting up about politics when punished, Fan claimed to be setting the stage for the victory of the truly moral, if they would but follow his example.

With the exception of Hu Yuan (993–1059) and Sun Fu (992–1057), neither of whom sought political power, Fan attracted men about fifteen years younger. In 1033, when Fan was called back to court as a policy critic, Ou-yang Hsiu (1007–72) and Shih Chieh (1005–45) wrote urging Fan to speak out.[103] The furor aroused by Fan's demotion in 1036 for accusing Chief Councillor Lü I-chien (978–1043) of filling the court with his own clients necessitated an imperial edict warning officials against factionalism and forbidding them to address matters beyond their responsibilities.[104] Fan and his allies claimed the high ground of loyalty to an emperor whose ministers were keeping him from fulfilling his responsibility to be active in using government to transform society. Fan himself wrote a series of essays at the time to make this point. The following comes from "On the Values of Emperors and Kings."

Lao-tzu said, "I do not act [wu-wei], and the people transform themselves; I value tranquillity, and the people correct themselves; I have no desires, and the people enrich themselves; and I do not try to do anything, and the people make themselves simple."[105] [Lao-tzu] was speaking of the customs of antiquity to caution a time of many problems. But the Three Eras differed from that more ancient period. Kings over all under heaven personally led [the effort of] transformation through instruction, to make the people pursue goodness. Therefore the *Rites* says, "The ruler is attentive to what he likes and dislikes. If the ruler above likes it, the people will follow it."[106] Confucius said, "When the one above likes the rites, none of the people will dare be irreverent; when he likes what is right, none of the people will dare be insubordinate; when he likes trustworthiness, none of the people will dare be insincere."[107] The point is that sage emperors and insightful kings cannot be free of likes; it simply is a matter of [whether what they value] is correct.[108]

For the emperor to become involved, given that some of his ministers were telling him to be like the sage-king Shun and practice "non-action," he should replace his current ministers with men who knew what a good ruler should like.[109]

Fan's demotion in 1036 offered his adherents a chance to stand up for principle. Ou-yang Hsiu, for example, wrote an outrageous letter to the policy critic Kao Jo-na: I have considered your conduct on this and previous occasions, Ou-yang wrote, and your failure to defend Fan Chung-yen now confirms what I have suspected: "You are not a superior man."[110] The letter, of course, meant demotion and fame for Ou-yang Hsiu. The southerner Ts'ai Hsiang (1012–67), a literary scholar who would serve as a policy critic in 1043–44, then wrote a long poem attacking Kao and eulogizing Fan and his leading defenders, Ou-yang, Ou-yang's friend the northern ku-wen writer Yin Shu (1001–46), and the southern policy critic Yü Ching (1000–1064).[111] The next year Li Kou (1009–59), a southern scholar preparing for the examinations, wrote in support.[112] Two years later Su Shun-ch'in (1008–48), a literary scholar and grandson of a chief councillor from Szechuan, joined in.[113] They were betting, I think, that by sacrificing their immediate career prospects for the sake of reputation they were assuring themselves of greater authority in the future, for any decision to employ them in policymaking offices would mean that the court accepted their ideas.

Fan himself admitted to the emperor in 1043 that he and his followers formed a faction. What drew them to Fan? Simple deterministic explanations seem not to work very well; that is, age, region, and social background alone did not make the faction.[114] All had or would gain reputations as literary intellectuals, but perhaps because they were on the winning side in the end, most of the surviving collections from this generation are from men associated with Fan.[115] What they clearly shared were ideas.

First, against the passive approach to governing by "non-action"—minimal government interference in society, attention to problems only after they arose, and concern only for the state's institutional need for revenues, labor supply, and security—Fan and his allies called for an active government that materially benefited local society. Second, against what they saw as the careerism of their fellow officials, they argued that the shih should take as their purpose "being for all under heaven" and "saving society." In other words, men should self-consciously and publicly put the interest of the whole before self-interest. Third, they objected to the acceptance of Buddhism and Taoism as ethical teachings and called on the government to concern itself with local education. This meant transformation through instruction (chiao-hua), teaching that the ethical relationships taught by the sages (those, for example, between ruler and minister, husband and wife) and the guiding values of the sages' tao (benevolence and righteousness) were what "being good" meant. True morality was not quietistic. Perhaps more important was their program for establishing local schools for both descendants of officials and upwardly mobile commoner families. The latter were, as Yü Ching put it, "the shih of the future."[116] Fourth, against the view that learning was the process of acquiring the textual knowledge and literary skills necessary for examination success, they insisted that shih should take the tao of the sages as the focus of learning and treat writing as part of the effort to put the tao into practice.

Into the 1040's many of them claimed to "know tao" and supposed that this tao could be effected irrespective of historical conditions. The supposition that tao was not problematic led to simplistic demands: the government should practice the tao of the sage; men committed to this end should have the power to effect policies that benefited all; the government should teach everyone what the sages taught so that they would support activist policies; and shih should promote these goals through their wen-chang. Men such as Shih Chieh, Sun Fu, and Tsu Wu-tse (1006–85) tended to tie the parts together rather dogmatically.[117] Others, Ou-yang Hsiu being the best example, were more aware of the complexities.[118]

The tao of the sage provided a simple, common idea for setting norms for government, social life, and learning. But it was also divisive, for it allowed Fan's adherents to divide the political world into morally superior men (*chün-tzu*) like themselves and morally corrupt men or lesser men (*hsiao-jen*) who opposed them. It could make moral commitment more important than talent, as Yin Shu once argued it should,[119] and it justified making having the right values a standard for selecting shih for office, as Fan himself had proposed in calling for examination reform. It is perhaps not surprising that some suspected Fan's group of putting the realization of their ideals before the interests of the dynasty.[120]

How was the court supposed to deal with men who promoted antiquity and morality and claimed to be immune from bureaucratic rewards and punishments? One solution was to co-opt them. This was not sheer opportunism on the court's part. In 1038 the chief of the Tanguts, a tribal people on the northern border to the west of Liao, proclaimed himself Emperor of Great Hsia and proceeded to attack the Sung. The court sought both political unity at home and military success abroad. Although its armies did not fare well before Hsia offered peace in 1043, Fan and Han Ch'i (1008–75) had taken major responsibilities in the war zone. They were rewarded with court appointments and brought to the capital for the peace negotiations. But placing Fan, Han Ch'i, and Fu Pi on the Council of State and Fan's followers in positions of influence meant allowing them to propose their ten-point program.

1. Changing the merit rating system for civil and military officials so as to ensure the promotion of capable men. The goal was to reduce the impact of the seniority system to the advantage of activist officials.

2. Reducing yin privilege and ending the practice of using yin rights to gain status as an academician for relatives already in office. The goal was to favor holders of examination degrees and make it difficult for men who entered office through privilege to rise to leading court positions.

3. Reforming the examination system to ensure that candidates would be men whose conduct was "ethical" and whose learning was oriented toward statecraft. The aim was to disadvantage mere literary skill and favor ku-wen-type learning with its focus on principled behavior and politicial idealism.

4. Instituting a sponsorship system for assigning men to posts in local government instead of following the seniority system. The aim was to ensure that local administration would be in the hands of competent men concerned with the general welfare.

5. Providing office-land for local government posts, thus providing local officials with adequate income and reducing corruption.

6. Increasing agricultural production through officially sponsored water conservancy and land reclamation projects.

7. Strengthening national defense by improving the quality of the soldiers, military leadership, and planning.

8. Reducing rotating compulsory service in local administration by landowning families by decreasing the number of administrative units, thus spreading the burden for tax collection and transport, clerical support, and so on over a greater number of families.

9. Gaining popular support by carrying out past amnesties for criminal violations and canceling tax arrears from the previous reign.

10. Requiring that imperial edicts and laws be obeyed, thus ensuring that the policies adopted would be followed by the bureaucracy.[121]

Fan envisioned changing the mores and makeup of bureaucracy to ensure that officialdom would actively work to improve economic welfare, reduce burdens on the population, and strengthen the state militarily. His program required more government-directed activity yet promised that an improvement in the general welfare could be attained without increasing burdens on the population. In contemporary terms, he defined the activist (yu-wei) approach to governing.

In accepting his appointment, Fan was, we might say, taking the bait. He did not have full control over the Council of State or the imperial mind.[122] Some of his followers objected that he had retreated from his institutional goals and was selling out.[123] It really did not matter; imperial support for Fan's domestic program did not go far beyond allowing him to propose it. Once the terms of peace with the Hsia were agreed upon, Fan and his allies were forced from office, and his program was abandoned. But the court had profoundly miscalculated if it thought it could manipulate Fan and his followers, for the credibility of their ideas depended not on imperial favor but on their success in persuading the shih. And they had been working at this for over a decade through their active support of local schools.

Transforming the Shih Through Schools

At the same time Fan and his protégés had been challenging the court, they had been speaking to the shih, both officials and prospective officials. Sun Fu had understood that Fan Chung-yen's goals went beyond government policy and extended to transforming the political elite as a whole. As he wrote to Fan, you would "cause the learning of Our Sung to become the learning of Shun and Yü, of Wen and Wu, and cause the sons of Our Sung officials to become the sons of the officials of Shun and Yü, of Wen and Wu."[124] Beginning in the 1030's, Fan's group actively promoted the establishment of local schools as a means of transforming elite learning and thus, they hoped, the shih themselves.

To an extent, simply being for the creation of local schools was enough. The court and local officials had not been terribly interested in local schools; after all, local schools aimed at preparing students for the examinations could only create more competition for successful bureaucratic families, who could see to the education of their own either at the capital school or through private studies. Occasionally local officials, working with local families, had obtained the necessary court permission and even grants of land for endowments. Schools at least introduced families of low-ranking officials, men with shih backgrounds but no recent office-holding forebears, and powerful local families that sought greater respectability to current examination models. Under Jen-tsung local and bureaucratic interest in schools increased dramatically. We know of only 16 prefectural and 32 subprefectural schools founded during the 60 years between 960 and 1021; during the next 40 years 80 prefectural and 89 subprefectural schools were established. There are reports of construction of at least 34 schools in 1022–40.[125] Fan and his followers were party to at least 16 schools between 1035 and 1045, most of which were new and over half of which were in the south, and they applauded local officials who recognized that schools were, as Yü Ching put it, "the basis for governing."[126]

The rhetoric of school inscriptions was intensely moral. Education was to transform men. How did this fit with the (presumably) practical motives of, for example, the shih of Ou-yang Hsiu's own Chi prefecture, who contributed 1.5 million cash to the establishment of a school? Surely they expected that someone would pass the exams? From Ou-yang's perspective, and this is echoed in the inscriptions penned by others in the group, the importance of the school lay elsewhere. A school was the ancient means of governing by transformation through instruction; it was supposed to change the customs of the local shih.[127] For Tsu Wu-tse, writing as an exam candidate about a new school in his native Ts'ai prefecture, it meant that those who "wore ju clothes" in this northern place would, on learning the teachings of Confucius, abandon their "barbarian" and "Buddhist conduct," adopt the ethical practices of the sages, and become defenders of "ritual and righteousness."[128] Han Ch'i, writing for a school he founded after the reform, argued that changing and unifying local values had a direct bearing on the survival of the state: people who believed that the relationships between ruler and minister, father and son, and so on were paramount would "be content with their role" (and not rebel). Human nature could be guided, he insisted; if learning brought real growth only to those with better natures, others still depended on learning to know what to fear.[129] As Yin Shu explained it, to build local schools was to believe that government did not have to proceed through coercion; it said that the "governance [through example and persuasion] of the Three Eras" was preferable to the purely administrative concerns of the Han and later times.[130] Such language reminded people that success in the examinations was not the only purpose of learning (for few would pass) and offered them another prospect: through their studies they could share the culture of the men who were writing the inscriptions.

Schools were thus a vehicle for realizing the ku-wen vision of making the tao of the sage a real basis for social life and a shared culture. Even those not party to Fan's reforms—for example, the southerner Sung Ch'i (998–1061)—could see that there was little connection between the values of officials and local customs and that as long as officials did not concern themselves with transforming the area under their jurisdiction, the Sung would remain a land where "within a hundred li the moral tone is not the same and within a thousand li customs are not the same."[131] Few in Fan's group had grown up at court; their family memories of making the transition from local society to full participation in governing were more recent, and some of them were still trying to break in. They were aware that shih came from different regions and that a common culture and a common morality could not be assumed. As a group made up of northerners and southerners, scions of court families and men from non-bureaucratic families, they could see themselves as evidence that acquiring a common culture was possible. But they wanted more than the spread of wen; they wanted common values.

At court in 1043–44 Fan and his allies moved quickly to support local schools. A modest proposal to grant all requests from local administrators to found schools soon gave way to a policy of requiring them to establish schools.[132] But schools alone, it was argued, would not lead to a new generation of shih united around a common purpose and program. Yin Shu warned, for example, that students did not always follow their teachers and that the program did not include measures to transform men entering through the yin privilege.[133] A change in examination standards was essential: if the examination did not test what the schools taught, students were unlikely to make the sage's tao the focus of learning. As Li Kou complained to Fan in 1037, those devoted to the sages' "purpose" who pursued the "ancient tao" were disadvantaged by a system that passed only those who strictly adhered to the set forms for poetry and that, being a blind test, made practicing the ethical precepts of the sages irrelevant. The message most candidates would receive, Li contended, was simply that "the tao of learning brings no increase."[134]

With this in mind, Fan and his allies took an older idea a step further. Earlier regimes had legislated, apparently ineffectively, that greater attention be given the prose sections of the chin-shih test in sifting candidates.[135] They now pushed through a policy of grading the prose sections first and making the initial cut on that basis, simplifying the set forms for the poetic sections, and requiring questions on the "greater significance" of passages from the Classics in the various memorization fields.[136] Questions for the treatise and themes for the essay could be set to compel candidates to pursue the kind of learning they themselves practiced. They were, however, a minority on the committee that composed the new rules, and the published version of the rules had far more to say about the technical rules for grading papers than about the program of study or the contents of the examination. In addition, while allowing all those of good character entry into local schools, the new regulations required a guarantee that those candidates sent to the capital neither be of merchant or artisan background nor have ever belonged to the clergy.[137] Fan's group could hardly fault the exclusion of former clergy, but committee member Ou-yang Hsiu did object to the exclusion of artisans and merchants; keeping the shih a discrete social group was less important, he argued, than promoting the idea that attainments in learning determined the social worth of the individual.[138] The new rules shifted the issue away from ideology, but they were in any case rescinded once the reformers were ousted. Changing the examination standards to transform shih values would be tried again in 1057, but for the moment the proponents of antiquity had to fall back on less institutional forms of persuasion. They already had an audience anxious to hear what they had to say, and they found that there was much to debate.

6 Thinkers and Then Writers: Intellectual Trends in the Mid-Eleventh Century

The abolition of the Ch'ing-li reforms in 1044 halted efforts to establish an activist policy until the accession of Emperor Shen-tsung in 1067 and the promulgation of the New Policies. Intellectual culture during the middle decades of the eleventh century saw the maturing of the younger generation of Fan Chung-yen's followers, men born around 1005, and the emergence of Ou-yang Hsiu (1007–72) as the most important literary intellectual among them after 1044. It was also during mid-century that two generations of future intellectuals appeared, each of which responded to the ku-wen program of its day. Wang An-shih (1021–86) and Ssu-ma Kuang (1019–86), leaders of the two great political camps of the 1070's and 1080's, began their careers on the eve of the Ch'ing-li reform. In the late 1050's, when followers of Fan Chung-yen regained power at court and Ou-yang Hsiu directed the examinations, Su Shih (1037–1101) and Ch'eng I (1033–1107), who would become the most influential intellectuals of their generation in the 1080's, were at the capital trying for examination degrees. The paths of all the major figures of Northern Sung thought cross during these years.

Rather than surveying intellectual life, this chapter deals with the problem, articulated by Fan's followers in the late 1030's, that came to define the center of debate for their own and succeeding generations of intellectuals. These men had found a common intellectual purpose in the search for a tao that would provide the foundation for politics, society, and culture. Scholars should seek to know the tao of the ancients, they contended, and the wen would follow. This confident formulation of intellectual priorities turned out to be far more problematic than they first had thought. What was this tao? Where was it to be found? How could it be known? What did it include and what did it leave out? Fan's followers did not reach common conclusions in the search for values; neither did successive generations.

Within this framework it is still possible to identify changes in focus. Initially Fan's followers spoke of establishing that the search for tao was the most important thing in "doing wen." But as the ku-wen literary style became the language of morally engaged learning, the decision to write in the ku-wen style lost its partisan flavor. The generation of Wang An-shih and Ssu-ma Kuang was concerned less with how shih should write than with the political question of using the tao of the ancients to transform state and society. For Su Shih and Ch'eng I in their youth, however, the focus had shifted from the institutional to the more personal search for the style of thought that would enable one to respond to things as the sages had. The drift away from literary solutions is evident in this. The priority ku-wen writers gave intellectual inquiry over literary effort thus created a paradox of sorts. It was precisely because literary activities were thought to be vital to establishing shared values that ku-wen writers like Ou-yang Hsiu had been able to establish themselves as intellectual leaders, but the implication of the search for values was that wen was not, in fact, of vital consequence. We shall see that this was not a conclusion that was easily accepted.

I have threaded together the sections that follow around Ou-yang Hsiu, both because of his influence and because of his awareness of the extremes. One-sidedness in the natural world, he once explained, leads to the best of things and to the worst of things; the middle is secure but never extraordinary.[1] Ou-yang's own one-sidedness tells us something about what ku-wen thought left out; his willingness to adopt a reasonable middle ground tells us something about the tensions intellectuals were trying to resolve. To a great extent I see the ku-wen movement of mid-century through his eyes. As a thinker and as a writer, he exemplifies the tension between cultural tradition and universal values.

Ou-yang Hsiu and His Generation

For Fan Chung-yen's followers, giving priority to values meant intellectual effort was the necessary grounds for literary accomplishment. In their terms it was a matter of learning tao before wen. As Ts'ai Hsiang (1012–67) explained in 1037 in criticizing a man for attempting to imitate Han Yü's style:

[My earlier letter said that] when you proceed from tao to learn wen, then tao is attained and wen is also attained. Those who proceed from wen to tao and have difficulties with tao are many. This is why tao is the basis of wen, and wen is the function of tao. It is more important to attract others through tao than through wen. In your previous letter you spoke in terms of literary elaborations, that is why I said this. It is not that I am deprecating literary writing, but that there is a necessary sequence to things.[2]

Ts'ai's correspondent demurred: by studying the right wen, he was acquiring its tao as well.[3] Ts'ai wrote back, explaining, "What I meant was that scholars should put learning tao first and learning wen second. Yet you say that the tao of the Six Classics all proceeded through wen in order to become clear and that you have never heard of men who began through the wen [of the Classics] and lost tao. You have missed the point of my earlier letter."[4] The fact that it was possible to distinguish between external forms and moral ideas one sought implied, however, that the individual needed to have both and that giving priority to tao did not relieve him from the need to compose works that would be seen as wen. Tsu Wu-tse (1006–85) recognizes this in 1043, in his preface to the late ku-wen writer Mu Hsiu's collection. "What is accumulated inside is called tao. What is expressed outside is called wen. When there is tao and there is wen, then one can be a superior man."[5]

The idea that tao had priority over wen went together with the conviction that if one had tao, wen would follow. True scholars were to be thinkers and then writers. As Ou-yang explains to a student in 1040:

Now, scholars have always been doing tao, yet few have attained it—not because man and tao are separated, but because scholars have gotten stuck in something along the way. We can say of wen that it is something hard to do skillfully yet something one likes [doing]; it is easy to enjoy yet it makes one feel self-satisfied. Scholars today frequently get stuck in it. As soon as they are skilled, they say, "My learning is adequate." Some even go so far as to cast aside all other affairs, attending not at all to them, and say, "I am a wen-shih, my job is wen, and that is all." This is why few attain it. . . .

Although the wen of the sages cannot be matched, generally tao won out and the wen came by itself without difficulty. Therefore Mencius did not spend any time on writing books; Hsun-tzu probably wrote only late in life. Only the likes of Yang Hsiung and Wang T'ung had to work to imitate the language [of the sages]. They are cases of men whose tao was inadequate who had to force the language. Those who were confused in later generations saw only that the wen of earlier generations was transmitted and thought that being a scholar was wen and nothing more. . . . I am one who learns tao but has not attained it, but fortunately I am not caught by what gives me pleasure and do not become stuck where I pause.[6]

In this instance Ou-yang makes the literary enterprise the problem. It gets in the way, it distracts, it mediates. Wen, however, is something Ou-yang enjoys; he must force himself to care more about seeking tao. By his own later account, Ou-yang had erred prior to 1036 by valuing literary embellishment, a taste evident in some of his writings from 1030–33, while on his first post in Loyang.[7] It is good to keep this in mind, for although Ou-yang converted to ku-wen and the views of Han Yü, he brought his past with him.

Some of the promise that learning the tao of the ancients held is expressed by Yin Shu (1001–46), the man who turned Ou-yang toward the ku-wen camp. Having the tao in mind, Yin explained, enables one to manage affairs (in government) and say things of value (in writing), for it makes it possible for one to act independently and to see the patterns of things. It results in achievements and wen-chang of real value.

One who is committed to antiquity can set aside so-called wen-chang and reputation for achievement and devote himself to seeking the tao of antiquity. The tao of antiquity is distant. One can apprehend it only in the mind. If the mind is not lax about it, one can regulate affairs. If the mind is unclouded about it, one can say things worthy of note. It is because it is not lax that one is able to treat success and failure as external to oneself and believe in what one maintains [within]. It is because it is unclouded that one is then able to see deeply into what is most hidden and fully arrive at the inherent patterns [li]. Believing in what one maintains stems from honest purity; fully arriving at the patterns comes from clarity. Being pure and clear is arriving at what the ancients arrived at. When one has gone as far as one can go, then wen-chang and a reputation for achievement will follow.[8]

But the tao was distant and difficult to define. Still, as Ts'ai Hsiang wrote in 1037, if one did have a glimpse of it, he could trust his judgment.

Now tao is the largest [of things] and the most impartial. Because it is the largest, no scholar can comprehend all its essentials. Thus different opinions and one-sided ideas arise. The superior man fears that tao will not be clear; so he proceeds to say that the right is right and the wrong is wrong. Because [tao] is the most impartial, when the superior man says the right is right and the wrong is wrong and all [his judgments] are alike in being appropriate, he cannot give way [to the opinions of another] on personal grounds.[9]

On the one hand, because no one can see the whole, there will be partial opinions; on the other hand, because it is still necessary to make judgments, it is necessary to say what one believes to be right. Ou-yang Hsiu, joining in this discussion, made a salient point: one should not object to being criticized by others, he argued, for the goal was to join in "figuring out tao."[10]

The question was how to define tao. For Ou-yang the tao to be figured out lay within the realm of human affairs. Guides for human behavior were not to be found in heaven-and-earth, divination, and the innate characteristics of man. As James T. C. Liu's study of the man and as Ou-yang's writings from the late 1030's—his history of the Five Dynasties and writings on the *Spring and Autumn Annals* and the *Book of Change*—make clear, his tao of the sage pertains to social and political affairs.[11] The

rhetoric of the 1044 edict on examination reform—"Ju who comprehend
the patterns of heaven, earth, and man and have insight into the sources of
order and chaos in past and present can be called broad"—was not his.[12]
Writing in 1033 in response to a student's submission of his prose, Ou-
yang notes what he found correct—opposition to convention, concern
with antiquity and tao, and a desire to "pluck up the present and return it
to antiquity"—but, he warns, "You speak of the tao of the Three August
Ones of high antiquity [Fu Hsi, Shen Nung, and Huang Ti], you discard
the near for the distant, and you are concerned with lofty language at the
expense of the practical. In this you go somewhat too far." The tao of the
ancients was practical.

> In learning the superior man is concerned with enacting tao [wei tao]. For enacting
> tao, he must seek to understand antiquity. When he understands antiquity and
> illuminates tao, he then practices it in his own life and effects it in affairs. He
> further expresses it through manifestation in wen-chang in order to gain the trust
> of later ages. His tao is the tao that men such as the Duke of Chou, Confucius, and
> Mencius constantly practiced and effected. His wen-chang are what have been
> conveyed by the Six Classics and trusted to the present. Their tao is easy to
> understand and can be imitated. Their words are easy to illuminate and can be
> practiced. When those who make grandiose claims speak of them, they take the
> obscure and empty as tao, the vast and sketchy as antiquity. Their tao is difficult to
> imitate; their words are difficult to practice.
>   When Confucius spoke of tao, he said, "Tao is not distant from man."[13] He who
> spoke of centrality [chung] with constancy [yung] said, "What guides [human]
> nature is called tao." He said further, "What can be departed from is not tao."[14] . . .
> What is referred to in these instances is the tao of the sage. This is what is possible
> to practice in one's personal life and effect in affairs. . . . What is meant by
> "antiquity" are the affairs of ruler and minister, superior and inferior, rites and
> music, and punishment and policy.[15]

To seek the lofty and distant, he continues, is to seek values that cannot
serve as a common standard. The sages cared only about what was useful
to society.

After Confucius, Mencius was the one who knew tao best, but his words did not
go beyond teaching men to plant mulberries and hemp, to raise chickens and pigs.
He thought caring for the living and seeing off the dead was the basis for the kingly
tao.[16] Now, the wen of the two canons [of Yao and Shun] are certainly wen and
Mencius's words are certainly tao. Yet that his concerns are easy for people today
to understand and are near-at-hand is because he attended to the practical. Scholars
today do not take them as a foundation to any extent but prefer the words of those
making grandiose claims. They imagine the undifferentiated mess of the ancient
beginning and take what has no form as the perfect tao. What is neither lofty nor
low, neither distant nor close; what the worthy are capable of and the foolish can

reach by trying; what is uniformly based on great centrality, for which there is neither surpassing nor coming up short and thus can be practiced without change for a myriad generations—these they say are not worth doing. They concern themselves with the doing of the lofty and distant and seek to surpass others with the useless theories of those who make deceitful claims. [Good] scholars do not devote their minds to such.[17]

Ou-yang is going to an extreme of the practical and common here, but he was consistent in demanding that men think about values in terms of what he saw as the actualities of human existence.

But within the ku-wen camp some did believe they could link the lofty and distant tao of the primordial beginning with the practical. Shih Chieh (1005–45), who passed the examinations with Ou-yang in 1030 and pledged his support to Fan in 1033, was a great admirer of Han Yü and Liu K'ai.[18] Now, he writes in 1033, that the rulers have improved institutions so that it is possible to change the values of society through education, the duty of scholars is to change how men write, for "the defect of the present time lies in wen." Unless something is done to "save This Culture of Ours," all institutional reforms will be for naught. To act as a sage or worthy is to end the literary writing that "takes wind and clouds for the structure, flowers and trees for the images, ornate elaborations of language for the substance, rhymed phrases for the meter, tonal rules for the basis." In this case Shih proposes to conceptualize wen as all-encompassing and all-defining cosmically based moral culture.

Now, there is heaven and earth, and therefore there is wen. "Heaven is honorable and earth is lowly; ch'ien and k'un are fixed. The low and high are set forth; the noble and humble have their roles. Movement and tranquillity are constant; firm and yielding are divided."[19] . . . Through this did wen come into being. "Heaven hung forth images, manifesting the auspicious and ominous, and the sage imaged them. The Yellow River produced the Chart, the Lo River produced the Diagram, and the sage took them as standards."[20] Through this did wen become apparent. "Contemplate the wen of heaven to detect changes in the season. Contemplate the wen of man to transform the world."[21] Through this did wen become useful.[22]

This follows the early T'ang view of a cultural tradition grounded in the patterns of heaven-and-earth. Shih goes on to assert the compatibility of the "great tao" of Fu Hsi, Shen Nung, and Huang Ti (which Ou-yang placed beyond the bounds) with the "constant tao" of the later sage-kings. The great tao and the constant tao are that by which the cosmic and human pattern (wen) were manifested; the Classics were that by which the wen was written. And, he goes on:

Therefore, the two forces [yin and yang] are the structure of wen, the three relationships are the images of wen, the five constant [virtues] are the substance of wen, the nine regions are the numbers of wen, morality is the basis of wen, rites and music are the adornment of wen, filial piety and fraternal respect are the beauty of wen, achievement is the visage of wen, transformation through instruction is the clarity of wen, administration is the net of wen, and commands are the sound of wen. The sage is he who administers wen. The superior man illuminates it. The common people proceed through it. . . . [When all the aspects of wen given above are realized,] there will be models for honorable and lowly, there will be rules for superior and inferior, noble and humble will not disturb each other, inner and outer will not harm each other, customs will be fortified again, human relations will be corrected, and the kingly tao will be fulfilled.[23]

Shih Chieh's mission in his writing was to repeat and insist that there was only one tao and one teaching: that passed down by the sages and carried forward by Mencius, Yang Hsiung, Hsun-tzu (sometimes), Wang T'ung, and Han Yü.[24] He must combat Taoism and Buddhism, he writes, for they teach men that modes of behavior inimical to this tao are also moral, and he must attack the literary style of Yang I, for it keeps men from seeing the tao of the sage.[25] In his later writings, Shih did not rely on the idea of a tao of heaven-and-earth; he writes in 1037 that the tao of the sage is better than heaven-and-earth, because whereas nature is irregular, this tao is unchanging.[26] Ou-yang focused on the practicality of the various concerns of antiquity; Shih insisted that the key issue is the systematic and coherent arrangement of those concerns into a single system.[27] This was an exclusive system: it had to be taken as a whole, and it required the scholar to persuade others that the idea of a perfectly integrated system was the true heritage of China's antiquity.

From Ou-yang's perspective, Shih Chieh represented the self-isolating self-righteousness of those whose claim to singular knowledge of tao licensed breaking with tradition. The two had at each other in an exchange of letters in 1035 over an inscription in Shih Chieh's idiosyncratic calligraphy.[28] I am told, Ou-yang writes, that you "simply wish to be different from the age. Now I have heard that in learning the superior man [seeks] to be right and that is all. I have never heard of him being different." Shih's calligraphy illustrates the consequences of trying to be unique: it ignores past standards and fails to provide a model for others.

How much more so in the case of this calligraphy. On the one hand, it does not take the past as its teacher; on the other hand, it is inadequate to serve as a model for the future. Even if everyone liked it, one still should not do it. How much more so when everyone says it is wrong. Why then do you alone do it? Is it really that you like being different in order to be loftier than others? Yet I had heard that you were able to get others to praise you. Is this because you walk the middle tao and hold fast to constant virtues? Or is it because you boldly make yourself different and shock contemporaries? . . . You are instructing others and acting as a teacher, yet you rush to make yourself different. What will scholars have for a model? And if, unfortunately, all scholars follow you, will you really be uniquely different anymore? If you do not quickly stop, I fear that later, when students are accused of preferring the strange, the blame will be traced to you.[29]

In return Shih Chieh accuses Ou-yang of being concerned more with the cultural arts than with tao. "My mind is able to focus solely on the correct tao . . . my wen does not go against the inherent pattern or harm instruction."

Now what orders the age is tao. Calligraphy is simply to transmit the tao of the sage. If it can transmit the tao of the sage, it is adequate. Why must there be a model [for that calligraphy] in antiquity or a teacher for it in the present? Why are you so concerned about this? . . . Do you think the state has established schools and education officials to teach men calligraphy or to teach men the tao of the sage? Am I not to teach men loyalty and filial piety? Am I not to teach men benevolence, righteousness, ritual, wisdom, and good faith? You charge me with being incompetent in calligraphy. How could I deny this? But I fear you are not charging me with what is truly urgent.[30]

But, Ou-yang replies, if your defense is that you have not mastered calligraphy, then you in fact grant my point. Superior men need not devote themselves to calligraphy. The question is the proper attitude toward something as secondary and unimportant as calligraphy. There have been rules for written characters ever since their origin, and to learn from antiquity means also to learn the purposes things such as characters were created to accomplish and the historical rules that have been developed to ensure that it remains possible to attain those ends. "Now you turn verticals into slants, squares into circles, saying, 'I am practicing the tao of Yao, Shun, the Duke of Chou, and Confucius.' This will not do at all. . . . You also say, 'There are things in which I really differ from the age, for I detest Buddha and Lao-tzu and reject wen-chang that are embellished.' This will not do in the slightest. Now, Buddhism and Taoism are things that those who are confused do. Embellished compositions are something those who are superficial do. . . . For shih-ta-fu not to do Buddhism and Taoism or embellished compositions is like being a clerk and not taking bribes. This is how it should be; it is hardly enough to use to claim to be a worthy."[31] Ou-yang, it seems to me, wanted to see Fan Chung-yen's group gain power and influence, and for this merely claiming to be right was not quite enough.

But for some of Fan's followers being right was more important than success. Sun Fu (992–1057) was a teacher of some influence. His career illustrates that it was becoming possible in the 1030's to gain fame through writing without having an official position. Sun also aimed to "save This

Culture of Ours," opposed Buddhism and Taoism as the barbaric enemies of the Chinese tao of the sage, subscribed to the idea of a lineage of sages and worthies, and admired Liu K'ai.[32] After failing the examinations, he established himself as a teacher, erecting a lecture hall at his home at T'ai-shan in 1040 and lecturing at court in 1043–44.[33] Earlier, perhaps in response to failing, he had built a Hall of Faith in Tao, for which he wrote an inscription proclaiming that for one who had faith in the tao of the sages and worthies, learned it, and enacted it, social success was irrelevant.[34] He was also renowned for his studies of the *Spring and Autumn Annals*, which made the *Annals* speak to current issues in the tradition of Tan Chu and Lu Ch'un of the T'ang.[35] Sun held that the literary enterprise should be the modern equivalent of the Classics. The Classics "are all wen"; they are "called *ching* [Classics/constants] simply because the final version comes from the hand of Confucius." But this did not mean that men were free to formulate their own ideas.

Later men are weak; they cannot be successors [to the sage]. They should only support ethical instruction [*ming-chiao*] and assist the sage. They may set out the subtle points of the sage, or label the other starting point of the many philosophers, or express what has not been understood for a millennium, or correct the failings of the day, or announce the great constants of benevolent government, or object to the secondary techniques of utilitarian achievement, or promote the fame of the sages, or describe the anger and sorrow of the populace, or point out the state of relations between heaven and man [i.e., comment on the significance of natural disasters], or relate the strategic situation of the state. In all instances they must address affairs and take up what is real, writing when they are moved. Although the genres are many—they write essays, proposals, memorials, songs, poems, appreciations, eulogies, admonitions, explanations, inscriptions, and persuasions—when they alike return to tao, all [their writings] are called wen. If they turn their thoughts to the vacuous and write about the formless, it is useless absurdities, not wen.[36]

Ou-yang Hsiu could agree with much of this, I think, but he preferred to see the individual be true to the intentions of the sage while having his own tao and his own wen. He writes Tsu Wu-tse in 1040: "One who learns ought to take the Classics as his teacher. To take the Classics as his teacher, he must first uncover their intentions. When their intentions are apprehended, his mind will be settled; when his mind is settled, his tao will be pure; when his tao is pure, what fills him inside will be substantial; when what fills him inside is substantial, then what is expressed as wen will be dazzling."[37]

Fan's circle as a whole combined the call for taking "transformation through instruction" (*chiao-hua*) seriously with a demand for activist government to integrate and materially benefit society. Ou-yang Hsiu's

1042 essay "On the Basis" is an example of this.[38] Still, individuals tended toward different poles. For Shih Chieh and Sun Fu, the tao of the sage was a doctrine of universal ethical standards. Li Kou (1009–59), on the other hand, stressed material benefit. "May we speak of profit? I say, men cannot live except for profit; why may we not speak of it? May we speak of desire? I say, desire is an emotional response of humans; why may we not speak of it? To speak of them but not accord with ritual leads to greed and lust; that is criminal. But to say one may not speak of them, even if neither greedy nor lustful, is nothing other than robbing man of life and going contrary to human feeling. This is why the age does not appreciate ju."[39] Li had become famous well before receiving an office in the 1050's. He had attracted the attention of Fan Chung-yen, Ou-yang Hsiu, and others and around 1041 had been recommended for a decree examination. Between 1031 and 1043 he wrote over a hundred chüan of essays and remarks, including theoretical pieces, discussions of the Change and Rites of Chou, and plans for "enriching the state, strengthening the military, and pacifying the people," and he regularly sent copies to the men he admired. He concerned himself with using wen to order the world. "How the spirits created the myriad things and how the worthies ordered the myriad things are ultimately one. For the enterprise of the worthy, nothing has greater priority than wen." And he presented himself as a student who "recites ancient books and does ku-wen," following Han Yü and Liu Tsung-yuan.[40]

"On Ritual," a set of seven essays Li wrote in 1032, identifies the concerns of the sages, envisions a system, and articulates general principles. "On Ritual" is about the idea of an integrated social order, and Li Kou uses the term li ("ritual" or "rite") to refer to that whole. Ritual is a concept: "Li is an empty term, a general name for institutions,"[41] and "what is meant by li is to enact and to regulate."[42] Its "basis" is to provide the food, clothing, shelter, and utensils necessary for life; clarify the social distinctions and roles necessary for orderly relations within the family, community, and state; and maintain connections to the dead through mourning and sacrifice. Its "extensions" are harmonizing and regulating through music, directing the idle through policy or administration, and frightening the recalcitrant into compliance through punishment. Its "other names" are the ethical values of benevolence, righteousness, wisdom, and good faith. These values are defined, however, in terms of the "basis": benevolence, for example, also means to see that food and clothes are sufficient by not taking the farmers away from agriculture.[43] The essays treat these three areas—socioeconomic life, public institutional activity, and ethics—as aspects of a single, unifying concept of ritual as "the standard for the tao of man and the main principle of instructions for the age." "The means whereby the sages ordered society [t'ien-hsia], state, and family, and cultivated the person and rectified the mind were none other [than this]: they were unified by ritual."[44] Li denies the implication that the test of value is integration and coherence; his ideas are apprehended from the sages; he is not making them up himself.[45] "Ritual" as a term for an integrated order, he insists, refers to a system such as his that has been modeled on antiquity; it is possible for socio-economic life, institutions, and ethics to operate in a "non-ritual" man-ner.[46] "Ritual" is a functional term applicable to any inclusive, coherent system and a normative term for the true system of antiquity.

In "On Ritual" Li points out that he limits himself to the realm of human affairs. He ignores what is innate to man as the basis for an integrated order, he writes, in favor of learning from the actual affairs of the sages.[47] He will not debate whether human nature is good, bad, or mixed.[48] He refuses to treat "the teachings of former ju" as authoritative, but judges them for their contributions to what he knows.[49] He treats heaven-and-earth and yin and yang as irrelevant to the creation of an integrated order.[50] Finally, he does not concern himself with historical change since antiquity. The Han and T'ang do not provide worthwhile models, Li contends, for they failed to establish the institutions of the Former Kings and allowed Taoism and Buddhism to rise. Ou-yang could agree with all of this except Li's desire to ignore history, and this may explain why Ou-yang did not try to conceptualize a perfect order.

Li's lack of interest in the internal life was controversial. Sometime around 1046, another ku-wen writer, Chang Wang-chih, a nephew of the anti-reform chief councillor Chang Te-hsiang, attacked Li's essays on ritual on the grounds that ritual was an "external" affair, an attempt to guide men through institutions. For Chang a true moral order had to be founded on some internal and ethical basis.[51] This objection came in fact from the monk Ch'i-sung (1007–72), whose ku-wen writing brought him into contact with men like Li Kou, Chang Wang-chih, and Ou-yang Hsiu.[52] Ch'i-sung defended Buddhism against the claim that the tao of the sage was totally adequate to teach men how to be "good." His claim that true values were ultimately internal kept a place for Buddhist insights and practices and provided grounds for his contention that the tao of Bud-dhists and of the ju were "thread by a single strand."[53]

For some it was necessary to show that the ku-wen program was at least not incompatible with ideas about the internal and natural foundations for morality. Hu Yuan (993–1059), whose teaching encouraged students to find connections among their studies, national politics, and their own private lives during these years, would later try in his lectures on the *Change* to fit heaven-and-earth and human nature into his practical vision of the sage's tao.[54] Ou-yang Hsiu, however, denied that men are morally self-sufficient.

I have been troubled by how many scholars today speak of *hsing* [nature]; therefore I always say, hsing is not something scholars should be urgently concerned with; it is something the sages spoke of rarely. . . . The fact that the *Doctrine of the Mean* says, "Heaven's decree is what is meant by hsing, guiding[55] hsing is what is meant by tao," makes clear that hsing lacks constancy and there must be something to guide it. . . . Is hsing really not worth studying? I say, hsing comes into being together with the physical body and is something all men have. Those who act as superior men simply cultivate their person and govern others. The goodness and badness of hsing need not be investigated. If hsing were in fact good, the person would still have to be cultivated and others governed. If hsing were in fact bad, the person would still have to be cultivated and others governed. If one does not cultivate his person, then even if he is a superior man, he will be a lesser man.[56]

Precisely such views prompted Ch'i-sung to argue that Han Yü, the source of so much ku-wen thought, had misled ju into thinking that their tradition was external.[57]

Ch'i-sung's diatribe against Han Yü, a work in 30 parts, aims to show that Han Yü was wrong.[58] This attack on Han was, of course, directed against all those who looked back to him, including Ou-yang Hsiu, Ts'ai Hsiang, and Yin Shu.[59] Ch'i-sung could, however, use the fact that the same ku-wen writers were concerned with morality to build a bridge to his own position, as his distinction between "human wen" and "language wen" (*jen-wen, yen-wen*) illustrates. Ethical values are "human wen"; the ku-wen writing of the day is "language wen." He records a visit from Chang Wang-chih, who brought new writings by Ou-yang Hsiu.

A student, one of the guests, broke in: "When wen [like Ou-yang's] flourishes, the whole world will be in order." Master Hidden [Ch'i-sung] told the guest: "The wen of Mr. Ou-yang is language wen. Order for the whole world depends on the flourishing of human wen. Human wen makes use of language wen for expression, and language wen relies on human wen to serve as its source. Benevolence, righteousness, propriety, wisdom, and good faith are human wen. Sentences and writing are language wen. When wen-chang apprehends the basis, then that whence it comes forth will be correct of itself. As Mencius said, 'He finds its source wherever he turns.'[60] Mr. Ou-yang's wen for the most part is based on benevolence, good faith, propriety, and righteousness. You ought to admire Mr. Ou-yang's source; that is all right."[61]

Ch'i-sung's recasting of the ku-wen distinction between wen and tao in terms of a tension with wen itself allowed him to avoid granting Ou-yang Hsiu's claim to tao.

With the failure of the Ch'ing-li reform, Ou-yang, Fan Chung-yen,

Han Ch'i (1008–75), and others were demoted to the provinces. In reply, Fan claimed that political failure could not undo their moral victory in establishing ku-wen as the dominant mode. Fan's party quickly moved to write the history of the rise of ku-wen. In 1046 Fan himself penned what would become the textbook account in his preface to Yin Shu's collection, and Han Ch'i incorporated it into Yin's "grave declaration." Fan reflected on how difficult it was to ensure that wen-chang would serve the tao of the sage, as it had in antiquity. Han Yü had appeared in the T'ang to take charge of wen so that the ancient tao flourished once again, but it had declined during the Five Dynasties. Liu K'ai had led Sung men to learn from the Classics and seek tao, but Yang I had influenced scholars to pursue ornate writing and treat the ancient tao as too impractical to be worthy of study. Yin Shu followed Mu Hsiu and devoted his strength to ku-wen. But then, writes Fan (and Han), Yin Shu found Ou-yang Hsiu. Ou-yang "greatly revived [wen] and through this the wen of the world has been transformed completely."[62]

Thus by 1046 the two highest-ranking reform politicians had given their imprimatur to Ou-yang Hsiu as the proper model for the scholars of the day. This made it easy to forget that Ou-yang Hsiu's "grave record" for Yin pointed out that the story was not historically accurate. Moreover, Ou-yang announced, he did not agree that ku-wen was right and ornate writing wrong. The issue was not literary style but the agreement between what one wrote and inherent patterns (li); writing in parallel style that accomplished this was just as good.[63] The man who was now seen as the model for ku-wen had apparently decided to abandon the idea that one manner of writing was inherently moral and true to the tao of the sage. Ou-yang had argued early on in his career that the value of writing ought to depend on the credibility of what one was saying.[64] As he wrote in 1040, "The tao of great centrality means to know what we can know."[65]

The Next Generation

Fan Chung-yen was not entirely wrong in thinking that "the wen of the world" had changed during the 1030's and early 1040's. With two exceptions, the seventeen literary collections from the generation of students born around 1020, most of whom began their careers either shortly after or before the Ch'ing-li reform (there were examinations in 1042 and 1046) support his view. The occasional writings of this generation are very much in the ku-wen style; literary embellishment is not a value. Moreover, these men speak to larger issues of politics, thought, and culture and put forward their own ideas.[66] When Ou-yang's generation prepared for the examinations, many of their elders still believed that raising the level of literary accomplishment was integral to establishing a civil order in the

Sung.[67] The generation of 1020 grew up in a world in which the most vocal scholars called for writing to speak to tao; they themselves tended to discuss the ideas themselves rather than the need to have ideas. Not everyone adopted the ku-wen program, yet even opponents wrote in the ku-wen manner and addressed the issues raised by reform intellectuals.

To illustrate this, I will mention only two men from this age, Ssu-ma Kuang, chin-shih of 1038, and Wang An-shih, chin-shih of 1042; they received their first appointments in 1042. Ssu-ma was the son of a high-ranking northern court official and gained rank through yin privilege before taking a degree. Once he was posted to the Directorate of Education in 1046, he stayed in metropolitan posts for most of the next 25 years. Wang An-shih, from a southern family of lower-ranking local officials, served mainly in the provinces until the late 1060's. Both sought recognition among high-ranking officials by sending them samples of ku-wen writing.[68] As Ssu-ma explained to a possible patron, his writing would show that he was "superior man, concerned with knowing what was greater and more far-reaching."[69] Ssu-ma's patrons, appointments, and writings, however, placed him in the anti-reform camp.[70] Wang An-shih was recommended to Ou-yang Hsiu and Ts'ai Hsiang in 1044 by his cousin Tseng Kung (1019–83) as one whose "wen is ancient and whose conduct matches his wen."[71]

For Wang the ku-wen promise was simple: common values result in a common culture. He writes Tseng Kung in 1044: "We learn from the sages and that is all. When we learn from the sages, our friends and teachers will necessarily be men who also learn from the sages. The words and actions of the sages are uniform; of course [our friends and teachers] will resemble each other."[72] Being the same is good; shared ideas should lead to shared conclusions. As Wang wrote in 1045: "I believe only in the sages. When I heard that in antiquity there were a Yao and a Shun and that their tao was the great central, perfectly correct, and constantly practiced tao, I obtained their books, shut the door, and read them. I lost any sense of both anxiety and joy. I threaded together top and bottom; I immersed myself in their midst. The smallest, seamless; the largest, boundless; I sought only to fathom them as one."[73] Writing to Tsu Wu-tse the next year, Wang set out his conclusion: the tao, the sages' mental apprehension of it, their actions and teachings, and the written record thereof were all in perfect agreement; any apparent contradictions were merely situational variations that could ultimately be resolved into a unity. Wang argues from this that coherence in writing is a sign that one has grasped what is fundamental and primary. "Therefore if one writes it on wooden slips and it is good, then when it is applied to all the people it will always be good. . . . Under different circumstances it will also be good."[74]

The conclusion he draws in 1047 is that men should work to bring about "perfect order" (*chi-chih*), by using government to work for the welfare of all the people. In antiquity each was assigned his proper place and all shared in the benefit, so that even "the blind and the deaf, the pygmy and the dwarf, each was able to use his talent to draw support from the appropriate office."[75] The sages were activist rulers. "They connected the roads and rivers. They organized paddy fields and mulberry [plantings]. They erected dikes, dug irrigation canals, and dredged out rivers to prepare against flood and drought. They established schools and assembled the people together to practice rituals and music in them, thus bringing them to submit through transformation. These they enjoined [upon men] as priorities and are clearly easy to know."[76] Ku-wen and the Ch'ing-li reform helped Wang see what he should be doing as a scholar and as an official; he would pursue this vision all the way to the chief councillorship.

Ssu-ma Kuang's first ku-wen essays date from 1042 and 1045, just before and after the Ch'ing-li reform. Ssu-ma was influenced by the writing of men like Ou-yang, but he did not seek them out as mentors.[77] Ssu-ma did not present himself as traditionalist; being a ju was not a matter of adhering to the commentaries on the Classics or ritual decorum. But in contrast to Wang he stressed the importance of behaving ethically over transforming society. The man who lives by the moral standards of the Classics can measure others against his own standards; he then makes his praise and criticism known through his wen-chang and in that sense is revealing the tao of the sages.[78] His essays elaborate on this. "On the Ten Worthies," written in 1042, gives priority to "ethical conduct" among the four fields on the grounds that it alone involves knowing the good; in contrast the affairs of government, literary learning, speaking are merely talents that can be used for any end.[79]

Ssu-ma was particularly critical of the idealization of antiquity as a source for government policy. It was simply another style of wen-chang and harmful because it claimed knowledge of good ends. Too often men had idealized antiquity at the expense of working to secure the dynastic house, a surer basis for political order.[80] In 1045 Ssu-ma refused to glorify reformers as magnificent failures and martyrs to ideals. Do not credit attempts to restore "ritual and righteousness," "perfect impartiality," "policy and instruction," and the "great tao," he explained; instead ask how men served their ruler, benefited their state, and nurtured the people.[81] Activist rulers threatened the survival of the dynasty.[82] Changing political course was not wrong, Ssu-ma argued, but one needed to consider the motives of those who sought to change things: Were they not really aiming to further their own careers?[83] Proposing to refashion the world according to an ideal model distracted attention from the immediate tasks of government; it discouraged men from judging a policy by its likely consequences.

Ssu-ma Kuang's writings from the 1040's strike me as the work of a man who knows what he is supposed to be doing. His task is to serve in government and concern himself with making the system work. Ssu-ma is a Han-T'ang man; the history of the Han and T'ang dynasties tells him the typical problems of a political order and the outcomes of possible solutions. For Ssu-ma, the insider, the ku-wen vision is neither new nor admirable; it is merely irresponsible. Wang An-shih, on the other hand, is attracted to the ku-wen program precisely because it promises to tell him what he and all shih ought to be doing. Wang is an outsider to court politics, of course, but his desire to find something to believe suggests a sense that nothing in the present has real value. He wants more than an official career. He has gone to an extreme; his test of value is to want something that will be good for everyone and that everyone can share.

Ou-yang Hsiu in His Maturity

Ou-yang Hsiu's mature views on learning appeared in the late 1050's, just as another generation was emerging. His writings from this period, his most important since the 1030's, are worthy of consideration in their own right. But Ou-yang's views on what and how shih ought to learn are also important because they speak to larger questions and intellectual di- lemmas. From the comments on wen and tao of Ou-yang's own genera- tion, it is already evident that there were different ideas about the kinds of common values being sought and the kind of society that they should lead to. Was the tao of the sage a matter of "human affairs" or did it require grounding in human nature and the cosmos? But whether men should have recourse to transcendent ideas in guiding state and society was also at issue, as Ssu-ma Kuang's alarmed response to the Ch'ing-li reform illus- trates. What role would proponents of the tao of the sage grant learning from imperial history? Finally, ku-wen writers still faced a problem that stemmed from supposing both that there was one correct tao and that wen-chang reflected the tao the writer had acquired within himself. As Wang An-shih saw, these propositions taken together legitimated calls for uniformity. What justification was there, then, for valuing creativity and individuality in wen-chang? What need was there, in short, for a literary culture?

Ou-yang Hsiu was writing in the late 1050's as part of the court. Two old allies of Fan Chung-yen, Fu Pi (1004–83) and Han Ch'i (1008–75), had been brought back and given leading roles on the Council of State, thus ending over a decade of anti-reform government. Although Fu and Han did not pursue an activist reform program, they maintained some interest in transforming shih learning and appointed Ou-yang Hsiu director of examinations for 1057. After the fact, it was asserted that thanks to Ou-yang: "The wen style changed and returned to the correct."[84] Ou-yang failed many of those who had been expected to pass, and an angry crowd of disappointed students demonstrated in the streets. The court stood behind him: in a break with precedent not repeated until the 1070's the emperor passed at the Palace Examination everyone Ou-yang had passed at the departmental level.[85] Ou-yang said he favored passing those who "comprehended the methods of the Classics and wrote ku-wen."[86] His three questions for the treatise section supposed that students had been trained to find larger ideas in the Classics and express them in the ku-wen style, something not all students were prepared for, and he quite possibly decided to fail those unable to answer his questions.[87]

Ou-yang's three questions asked candidates for ideas about water conservancy to be abstracted from the "Tribute to Yü" chapter of the *Documents*, the proper relationship between government and society as revealed by the *Rites of Chou*, and the authorial intent behind the inclusion of four mutually exclusive explanations of the provenance of the eight trigrams in the *Commentary on Appended Verbal Elaborations* (*Hsi-tz'u chuan*) of the *Change*.[88] These were polemical, like most examination questions, yet they also hint at the style of thought Ou-yang represented. That not all shared Ou-yang's values is evident from the court's decision to bring in the older Hu Su (996–1067) to direct the examinations of 1059. Hu had no truck with ku-wen, and his questions for the treatise section repudiated both the form and content of Ou-yang's questions.

The first question illustrates the use of antiquity and the Classics to address modern issues. Ou-yang begins from the text. There was a great flood under Yao, and Yü controlled the waters. The "Tribute of Yü" relates how Yü proceeded, discussing geography, relative advantages and disadvantages, and his methods. This text should be studied, Ou-yang asserts, as the beginning of the tradition of expertise in water control and as a guide to policy in this area, for the inability of the present government to solve problems associated with the Yellow River is to be contrasted with Yü's success. Ou-yang offers two possible explanations to account for the modern failure. It is either a personnel problem—that is, the court has not found men competent in water conservancy—or it is due to a lack of interest on the part of scholars in the "learning of the 'Tribute of Yü'"—that is, they do not know about the nature of rivers and the methods for channeling them. This provides the rationale for discovering whether students have in fact studied this text, because as long as there are men with the knowledge it will be easy to solve the personnel problem.

He begins with a practical issue: What were the relative elevations of the nine regions into which the document divides China and with which rivers did Yü start his work? He then gives a hint: one can infer from the record of Yü's deeds that he began with larger rivers and then turned to the smaller, connecting them or blocking them as need be. Ou-yang suggests that this evidences a general principle of governing: begin from the large and the small will follow. He then turns to historical knowledge: How did the names for the larger rivers mentioned in the text change over time? He ends by speaking to those who doubt that antiquity has a bearing on policymaking. Determining relative benefit and harm, he contends, requires precisely the sort of information necessary to understand the essentials of Yü's method for controlling the waters: topography, the appropriate sequence of work, the amount of effort involved, and so on. [89]

Ou-yang's questions are oriented toward selecting individuals who studied the Classics for the conceptual skills necessary to deal with similar affairs in the present, as a source of general principles necessary for the task of government, and as part of traditions of factual knowledge. Learning is a multi-sided affair, requiring knowledge of principles and facts, the constants and the contexts, and governing depends on educated men. The two other questions also ask students to take the Classics seriously. Candidates are asked to consider whether the *Rites of Chou* does in fact support the idea of activist government, portrayed negatively here as burdensome government, one that places so many demands on the populace that it is unlikely to be happy. Is there a way out, Ou-yang asks; is it possible that if we correctly understood the proper sequence of the "method of effectuation" in the text, we could see how a "great peace" can be achieved without making too many demands? Ou-yang's question on the eight trigrams is, to my mind, an attempt to subvert attempts to find sources of values outside human affairs. What is the "deeper significance," he asks, of including mutually exclusive explanations of the origins of the trigrams (i.e., as resulting from cosmic process, miraculous appearances, mystical intuition, or the depiction of natural phenomena)? Do not discuss divination or debate the validity of competing claims, he tells students; explain what the author intended.

Interpretations of antiquity and the Classics are the foundations for thought in Ou-yang's questions. Continued resistance to this approach is evident from Hu Su's questions of 1059. For Hu, the ultimate model for an ordered world is heaven-and-earth, and the sources of particular ideas for policymaking are Han and T'ang precedents. Hu was known for his interest in connecting yin-yang and five phases theory with policymaking. [90] He began his first question (on the best time for carrying out death sentences): "The tao of heaven and yin and yang actually comprehend the affairs of government."[91] Government activity should accord with the ch'i of the trigram sequence and the mind of heaven, he contends; he then asks for a discussion of Han and T'ang precedents and historical variations in the calendar. Similarly, his third question takes up the significance of the eight trigrams and nine sections of the "Great Plan" section of the *Documents* as evidence for the unity of heaven and man.[92] Both the *Change* and the "Plan" help in understanding "nature and decree" (*hsing-ming*) and in predicting the consequences of actions, he asserts; Why then do Wang Pi's commentary on the *Change* and K'ung An-kuo's on the *Documents* stop at "human affairs" and ignore earlier ju insight into heaven's tao? Since later times have ignored the cosmic side, what can be done to restore this kind of learning?[93] Within this heavenly framework, the test of policy is benefit and loss, not the virtues of those who govern. Hu's fourth question, for example, tells students to adduce historical evidence to show that the founding of states depended on the strategic location of the capital rather than on personal virtue.[94]

Hu Su's questions represented a different tradition of thought, although he suggests it is not popular. But his questions may have satisfied some of the failures of 1057 on literary grounds: his questions were written in parallel style, not in discursive ku-wen, and presumably required answers in the same style. Yet we shall see that some candidates sympathetic to the idea that heaven-and-earth was the source of values shared Ou-yang's concern with what the individual thought.

The two major scholarly projects occupying Ou-yang during the 1050's provide a fuller sense of what he believed men should think and how he viewed the roles of antiquity, the Classics, and history in learning. The first, his contributions to the revision of the *T'ang History*, reveals his sociopolitical ideas. The second, a commentary titled *The Original Significances of the Songs*, bears on morality and literary composition. Ou-yang was brought into the history project in 1054 to revise the basic annals, tables, and treatises. His appointment may have owed much to intellectual politics. The *T'ang History* revision project was not a reform idea, in spite of the precedent of Ou-yang's private rewriting of the *History of the Five Dynasties* in the late 1030's. The anti-reform chief councillor Chia Ch'ang-ch'ao initiated the project in 1045. The assignment of scholars not part of the Ch'ing-li reform group (Sung Ch'i, Chang Fang-p'ing, and Wang Yao-ch'en) suggests an aim of establishing the T'ang dynasty (rather than antiquity) as the model for the Sung. Ou-yang was appointed to bring the project into line with the new regime, I suspect. He replaced Chang and Wang and, at one point, was told to revise Sung Ch'i's revision of the biographies to bring them into line with the views he had set forth in the other sections, a commission he declined. The work was completed in 1060.[95] I shall limit my interpretation to Ou-yang's treatises.

Ou-yang begins the treatises of what is now known as the *New History of the T'ang*[96] with a new definition of the decline from antiquity in terms of unity and duality, in contrast to the early T'ang view of decline in terms of wen and to the later view in terms of the decline of tao.[97] With this he gets at two fundamental intellectual problems: finding a unitary intellectual basis for politics and morality and overcoming the disjunction between antiquity and later history. His analysis of the decline is given in the first treatise, "Rituals and Music."

Through the Three Eras order came from unity [*i*], and ritual and music extended to all under heaven. After the Three Eras order came from duality [*erh*], and ritual and music were empty terms.

The ancients used palaces and conveyances for abodes, garb and headgear for clothes, sacrificial vessels for utensils, and natural materials for music. Thus did they attend the sacrifices and approach the court, serve the spirits and order the populace. Their annual and seasonal assemblies took place as audiences and visitations; their happiness and social intercourse took place as archery contests and communal feasts. They gathered the masses to undertake projects, creating [everything from] hunting parks and schools down to hamlets and paddy fields. Whether auspicious or ominous, sorrowful or joyous, all the affairs of the populace came as one out of ritual. When through this they taught their populace to be filial and caring, to be friendly and fraternal, to be loyal and trustworthy, and to be benevolent and principled, they did so entirely within the context of household life and work, clothing and food. For it must have been that everything they did, at every moment, was done in this way. This is what it means to say that order came from unity and that ritual and music extended to all under heaven. If all under heaven learned it and practiced it, they would not have known why they were being moved toward the good and away from crime, and it would have become conventional behavior.[98]

When the Three Eras had already disappeared, [the world] went through the Ch'in's change of the ancient. Those who [possessed] the world after that followed the Ch'in in everything, from the titles and ranks of the son of heaven and the many officials to the institutions of state and the palaces, vehicles, clothes, and utensils. Although some rulers desired order and thought to make changes, they were unable to transcend the times and return to the Three Eras. They were caught up in the conventions of the day, making a few changes here and there but generally content with just getting by. Administration, judicature, and national defense were the first concern in whatever they were doing. They said, "This is doing policy; this is how to govern the populace." As for the rites and music of the Three Eras, they kept all the names and objects stored away with the responsible office and brought them out from time to time for use at sacrifices and at court. They said, "This is doing ritual; this is how to teach the populace." This is what it means to say that order came from duality and that ritual and music were empty names. But when they used them at sacrifices and at court, even the high officials who attended to these matters had no idea what they were doing, while everyone else under heaven grew old and died without seeing them. How could they then wish to know the glory of ritual and music, perceive their intent, and be so subjected to their transforming instruction that it became conventional behavior.[99]

Antiquity represents the unity of the moral and social with the political and institutional. The decline is the splitting apart of the original unity and the emergence of a world of duality, in which political-institutional interests and moral-social concerns are regarded as separable. Antiquity as unity had disappeared before the Ch'in, but by creating a new set of political institutions and accompanying devices the Ch'in "changed antiquity" (*pien-ku*) and made impossible a true "return to antiquity" (*fu-ku*). Once the institutional means for governing without ritual were created, the rites and music of the Three Eras became nothing more than surviving remnants of the ancient way of establishing order. The state of duality had emerged.

Ou-yang is not saying that the restoration of the unity of antiquity is possible. The ancients were in fact teaching certain moral values, but in antiquity morality was embedded in daily social life. For the political elite and the common people life was rite; no one conceived of the moral as something separate from actual existence. Ou-yang's antiquity was a world without self-consciousness, in which there was no distinction between forms and values or the moral and the actual.

A return to the unity of antiquity is impossible, for the simple reason that it is possible to see the "unity" of antiquity only from the vantage of "duality." In other words, self-consciousness—knowing that the present is different—puts the unself-conscious state of antiquity beyond recovery, even if it were practical to discard modern institutions. In the 1030's Ou-yang had grappled with the contradiction between being moral yet involved in politics.[100] In 1042, in the essay "On the Basis," Ou-yang had somewhat shallowly toyed with the idea of returning to the integrated order of antiquity by reviving ritual and activist government. I interpret his introductions to the T'ang treatises as an explanation of how he can accept the impossibility of returning to antiquity without sacrificing the idea of unifying politics and morality.

His introduction to the first treatise continues by ruling out the idea that one can recover the unity of antiquity through the imitation of ritual forms. To live in a world of duality requires making a distinction between the form (wen) and the intent (*i*). Earlier men who had tried to return to unity by imitating ancient ritual had failed to make this distinction. "They used the utensils but did not know their intent. They forgot the root and preserved the branch. And even then they were unable to be complete."[101] The T'ang had continued along the same lines, the one difference being that the T'ang had aimed at completeness, a reference to the great state ritual program of Hsuan-tsung's reign: "This may also be called glorious, but [the T'ang] was not able to attain the magnificence of the Three Eras, for it had all the forms but the intentions were not there. This is what it means to say ritual and music had become empty names."[102] The T'ang approach is not an adequate model. The present can share the intent to unify politics and morality without adopting the ancient forms.

Ou-yang's introductions to the other treatises show a way to aim for the unity of the political and moral without giving up historical self-consciousness or denying the institutional changes that led to the present. He creates a dialectic between an inquiry into the institutional concerns that began in antiquity and changed over time and an inquiry into the intentions behind those concerns and the alteration and realization of those intentions through time. This is neither easy nor simple. Making government a moral enterprise requires knowledge; one must trace the historical development of institutions while keeping in mind their possible functions and purposes and sharing the larger intention of ancient ritual to create an integrated social order. One must, Ou-yang shows, proceed case by case to fathom the relationship between ancient and later and evaluate relative benefit. It is up to present scholars to determine how the parts have emerged over time and to fit them together into a whole.

As he had in the New History of the Five Dynasties, Ou-yang warns against seeking authority outside the human realm: "Human affairs are heaven's intent."[103] Now, in treatises on the calendar, astronomy, and the five phases, he launches into a more detailed critique. Heaven-and-earth are not constant, he argues; rather, their apparent constancy is an artifact of the "numerology" (shu-shu chih hsueh) with which men describe heaven-and-earth. "Numbers are the functioning of what is so-by-itself; their functioning is inexhaustible and is without incoherence." But history shows that calendrical systems have in fact changed because heaven-and-earth changes.[104] Calendrical and astronomical studies have their place, and although this cumulative tradition remains murky, it contains worthwhile knowledge.[105] Ou-yang objects to the use of the five phases to classify natural phenomena and assign moral significance to irregular natural events. At most, great natural disasters can be taken as a general sign of misgovernment, but any attribution to specific political acts is unreliable.[106]

The history of human affairs, Ou-yang notes, offers an alternative to seeking an integrated moral order. The T'ang, like its predecessors, sought territorial expansion, military power, and greater wealth, but history also shows that these utilitarian goals can ultimately lead to the destruction of the state that pursues them.[107] A state may be smaller, less powerful, and less wealthy, yet it can measure itself in terms of ideal domestic sociopolitical relations rather than its position vis-à-vis other states. Within this context, Ou-yang evaluates the intentions and forms of institutions through history. Some institutional forms he traces to antiquity; others are new yet realize ancient intents.[108] Some have developed to the point that the original intention is supplanted.[109] Some have remained fairly constant and can be maintained still.[110] Some must be changed as historical or cosmic circumstances change.[111] The question is not whether change is good, bad, or inevitable; rather, it is a matter of knowing what parts need to be changed and how to go about deciding when and how to change them. Ou-yang is not calling for a wholesale reform of the system, nor is he saying that men should be cautious about changing anything, as Hu Su insisted in 1059.[112] Instead, he proposes a case by case evaluation of existing structures. He thinks in terms of revising and emending rather than transforming.

Ou-yang does not doubt the need to work through government institutions, but he does see that men need something more than historical knowledge. They must be able to transcend self-interest and see beyond the institutional interests of government.[113] They need what Ou-yang calls "virtue" (te). The ancients sought to expand virtue, not territory, knowing that preservation of unity depended on this.[114] When men guided by virtue govern, penal codes and armies—institutions that are necessary when morality and politics are separate—will cease to be the basic concern of government.[115]

Ou-yang Hsiu rearranged the treatises of the T'ang History so as to begin with the essay "Ritual and Music" and had discussed how ritual satisfied men. The old history had begun with "Ritual and Ceremony," with ritual's function being to limit human desires as a threat to order.[116] (The Sung History would begin with "Astronomy," or "the wen of heaven.") Ou-yang's treatises supplemented his account of the ancient intent of ritual with detailed accounts of how T'ang institutions worked and what interests they realized. His decision to place the "Treatise on Biography" last was intended, I think, to make the point that although secondary to action, writing was also, in the end, the source of moral and historical knowledge, the knowledge of purposes and the knowledge of means. Ultimately, he argues, although all four categories of bibliography have value, for true guidance scholars must seek the "original authenticity [pen-chen] of the Classics." The tao of the Classics was substantial, comprehensive, and enduring.[117] For Ou-yang, the Classics have value not because the sage-kings were perfect or imitated the tao of heaven, but because they have survived, in spite of the Ch'in's burning of the books and the errors of Han exegesis. As such, they are the starting point for all who do wen in the present. Ou-yang has come full circle; his introduction to the first treatise was an example of beginning from the tao of the Classics.

Ou-yang's Original Significances of the Songs (Shih pen-i), completed in

1059, illustrates how he interpreted the Classics.[118] More than that, it bears on what Ou-yang means by the tao of the Classics and, because he is commenting on the *Songs*, it speaks to the role of literary composition as a moral enterprise. In his writings on the *Change* and *Spring and Autumn Annals* in the 1030's, Ou-yang rejected the idea that the sages relied on the realm of heaven to plot their course in the realm of man. In arguing this, he insisted on reading the texts for himself, free of the exegetical tradition that began in Han.[119]

The *Original Significances of the Songs* was Ou-yang's most detailed study of any Classic. In it he addresses both the hermeneutics of interpreting the original text and of evaluating later exegesis. Its concern with intentions and later interpretations resembles his concern with the original intentions and the cumulative tradition in the *T'ang History*. In an appended essay, "On Root and Branch" ("Pen mo lun"), Ou-yang defines four levels of understanding corresponding to four historical stages. The "original" historical stage, the period of the poems' creation, is also the "fundamental" level of understanding. "These poems were created thus: [the authors] met affairs and were stimulated by things. They gave a patterned appearance [*wen*] [to their responses to things] with language, treating as good what they found attractive and criticizing what they disliked, in order to express their praise and resentment through their mouths and to channel the sorrow and joy, happiness and anger, in their hearts. This was the intention of the poet."[120] The poems, then, are nothing more than the responses of men to their circumstances, an idea well established by the "Great Preface" to the *Songs*. Once poems appeared, they were collected by officials, recorded, and turned over to the Music Master to be set to music. At the second stage, they were classified, ranked, and stored away for the proper occasion.

With these first two stages, Ou-yang has argued that the original poets did not compose poems with the intent of their being collected, and that the officials of the second stage collected, classified, and used whatever they could find without having particular moral purposes in mind. The poets did not write to inculcate moral virtues; they responded with their personal likes and dislikes. The intent of the poet was to express his response to the particular thing that aroused him. "He creates this poem relating this affair; the good he praises, and the bad he criticizes. [This is] what I call the intent of the poet."[121]

Once the collection and classification procedures had fallen into disarray, the third stage began. Confucius responded to the "ruin of ritual and music" by correcting and editing the poems and including them in the Six Classics. "He made manifest what they found good and bad so that they would encourage and warn. This was the purpose [*chih*] of the sage."[122] In other words, as the moral culture failed, it became necessary to persuade men to be good by showing them the difference between the moral and the actual. To accomplish this, Confucius used the poems, seeing in them the naive (but correct) moral responses of the ancients. This third stage was a time when men had to think about morality. The "purpose of the sage" was a self-conscious attempt to appropriate the unself-conscious response of the poet for the purposes of defining models of morally correct responses to things.

The fourth stage was the emergence of the exegetical tradition. After the Chou declined, the cultural tradition was no longer transmitted through schools. Other ideas had appeared, and the Classics were, through the Ch'in's work, reduced to fragments. "Teachers of the Classics" appeared who tried to reconstitute the texts. Ou-yang presents himself as part of this fourth stage, and as its greatest critic. The basic error of the "former ju" was to try to discern the significance of the poems and the sages' purpose by investigating the second stage. They sought hidden meanings in the arrangement of the poems within the Classic. Ou-yang's premise is that there is no moral significance in the arrangement of the poems and that information on classification had long been lost (perhaps even before Confucius). To base an understanding of the moral significance of the Songs on what cannot be known, he concludes, is to miss the moral significance that can be inferred from what is knowable.

What can be known is the fundamental and original point that the poet relates the affair and his response to it. Moreover, to know this is also to have "apprehended the purpose of the sage," a conclusion that follows from the historical stages Ou-yang has set out.[123] The task of modern teachers of the Classics is to recover the intent of the poets; this is the "original/fundamental significance of the Songs," and the purpose of the sage. The Songs thus makes it possible to see the particular instantiations of the moral values Confucius believed were integral to the ancient order.

Understanding the poems as simple, naive works of praise and criticism that the sage sampled to represent a normative moral attitude, Ou-yang is prepared to judge the interpretive efforts of the exegetical tradition. He does not try to undo that tradition—it has, after all, preserved the texts. A wholesale rejection of past interpretations would be tantamount to setting up a separate school, precisely the error that results from speculative interpretations, and to denying history. Thus, as Steven Van Zoeren has shown, Ou-yang does both. He draws on earlier allegorical interpretations (in fact he finds little that is new) while shifting the focus from the interpretation of allegorical meaning to the speech act of the poet. He does not accept the "Great Preface" as the work of Confucius's disciple Tzu-hsia, yet he allows that the text does stem from the sage's ideas. His criteria for rejecting interpretations are internal inconsistency and so much disagreement with the normative patterns of the sages that "harm is done to the Classic."[124] His inclination is to revise and emend, not to break with the past.

Ou-yang sees the poets as men like himself, responding emotionally to events and thus always making judgments. The poem is an event in context; it is by nature a coherent expression, to be understood in terms of how men respond to a given situation. The poems record *jen-ch'ing*, emotional responses to the actualities of human life.[125] This Classic reveals the tao of the sage not as a set of universal principles but as the sage's understanding that morality consists of typical emotional responses. As Ou-yang writes elsewhere: "The order of Yao, Shun, and the Three Kings was necessarily based on jen-ch'ing."[126] This brings us back to Ou-yang's treatises for the *New History of the T'ang*, for the effort to bring about a world in which men once again respond morally to events depends on those with political responsibility thinking about what they can do to move the present in the direction of a world in which politics and morality are one. But this brings us back to the *Songs*; to become men who respond morally, they, as individuals, must realize that the "purpose of the sage" was for them to share the "intents of the poets." The *Songs* makes it possible for them to acquire the sensibility of the ancients. From this vantage, the task of those who compose wen-chang is to respond to affairs themselves with a sensibility cultivated through the study of antiquity and later history.

In his maturity Ou-yang traded the voice of self-righteous opposition for the accommodative tone of one who believed he could hold the center. He offered a model of thinking about values that turned attention back from the search for a universal dogma and reaffirmed the importance of wen. In effect he was lowering intellectual horizons while increasing the responsibility of learning. The general could exist only in response to the particular; the ancient had to be taken together with the cumulative traditions that led to the present. Ou-yang's writings imply that "returning to antiquity" and "the tao of the sage" are empty slogans. The response of the new generation of intellectuals emerging in the 1050's was decidedly mixed.

The Response of a New Generation

Two men who would become the most important intellectual figures of their generation appeared on the scene in the 1050's: Su Shih and Ch'eng I. Both Su Shih and his brother Su Ch'e (1039–1112) passed the 1057 examination under Ou-yang Hsiu. Su Shih was very much a student of his father, Su Hsun (1009–66), and Ou-yang Hsiu. Ch'eng I failed the palace examination in 1059, but his brother Ch'eng Hao (1032–85) and uncle Chang Tsai (1020–77) passed in 1057.

The Sus and Ch'engs were very different families. The Ch'eng brothers descended from a line of northern officials going back to the Five Dynasties. The Ch'engs made extensive use of yin privilege to keep family members in state service, but in the 1050's circumstances forced the brothers to rely on the examinations. Through family connections, they were, however, able to enroll at the Directorate of Education, a proven way of nurturing successful candidates.[127] Unlike their forebears, the Ch'eng brothers' interest in intellectual matters was serious, and at least Ch'eng Hao was initially drawn to the idea of an activist state. Both were influenced by Hu Yuan, who had returned to active service around 1052 and had, in 1056, been put in charge of the Imperial University.[128] In contrast, the Sus were new. When their father brought Su Shih and Su Che to the capital from Szechuan in 1056, Su Hsun's older brother Su Huan (1001–62) was the only relative in office, and he was only a local official of no great note. By Su Hsun's own account, they were a prominent local family, with wealth and some education, but his father had not been a shih-ta-fu. Su Hsun was determined to achieve an illustrious career through ku-wen. For two decades he was not successful, failing the chin-shih examination of 1038 and a decree examination in 1047. But in 1056 he gained Ou-yang Hsiu's attention.[129] Sensitive to questions of status, Su Hsun saw in reform thought the idea that being a shih was a matter of learning rather than social background,[130] an idea the Ch'engs found less attractive. For Su Hsun and his sons, Ou-yang Hsiu was both a model and a patron.

In 1057 Su Shih and Ch'eng I had some things in common. Their teachers were leading Ch'ing-li intellectuals, they wrote in the ku-wen style, and they cared about antiquity and the sages. In particular they shared Ou-yang's concern with how individuals could cultivate an ability to respond morally and went beyond it to envision how a man could learn to be a sage himself. Yet in thinking about what it meant to be a sage they focused on different aspects of what it meant to be human.

Su Hsun and Su Shih: The Sage and Human Emotional Response

I will introduce Su Shih through a discussion of Su Hsun's "On the Six Classics," a set of six essays Ou-yang described as "the wen of Hsun-tzu."[131] They do bear on Su Shih's thinking, my primary concern, but I include them here to demonstrate as well how far some took the idea that values are a social construct. Su Hsun first wrote to Ou-yang Hsiu in 1056 and applauded the new regime as the revival of the Ch'ing-li reform; Ou-yang's praise of Su Hsun brought Su immediate fame.[132] His six essays, like his writings on political strategy, suppose that individuals can influence the course of events, the "force of circumstance" (*shih*) that leads logically to predictable consequences, through the use of *ch'üan* to "balance" the one-sided tendency of the moment and thus redirect the course of events. "Ch'üan" can be translated as authority, power, deviation from the constant, and expedience, but the model is the ch'üan as steelyard, which allows one to control a heavy object with a fractional move of the counterweight. For Su Hsun actions are always contingent on historical circumstances, as George Hatch has pointed out, yet the circumstances are themselves the result of past attempts to deal with the one-sided effects of earlier actions. Su sees the Classics not as a source of timeless norms but as evidence of how the sages persuaded men to accept civilization and of how the role of those who follow the sages has changed over time.

Why were people persuaded to accept the unnatural imposition of social hierarchy and organized activity when they lived in a state of equality and provided for their needs through their own efforts? Su finds his answer in four of the Classics, the *Ritual*, *Change*, *Music*, and *Songs*, which he sees as the legacy of four constant activities (*ching*) that persuaded men that the sages' rules were not at odds with their own feelings and desires. His analysis proceeds through a dual logic: one action creates a one-sided effect that must be countered by another; together they bring about a situation that requires a further pair for balance. For Su the sages' efforts to benefit humanity replaced the original "oneness" of undifferentiated unity with a world of dualities.

The first four essays proceed as follows. People were first persuaded to accept the sages' social, political, and economic institutions by weighing the profit of fulfilling their needs without bloody competition against the loss of their primitive leisure; they instinctively disliked death more than they liked ease. Since the sages knew that people would feel that a conclusion reached by simple calculation was not awe-inspiring, they appealed to heaven-and-earth, yin and yang, and the ghosts-and-spirits to make the source of the tao of the sage mysterious and themselves unfathomable. "The sages created the *Change* to mystify [*shen*] the eyes and ears of all under heaven so their tao would then be honored and not set aside. This was a case of sages using their expedient power [*ch'üan*] to get hold of the minds of all under heaven and to ensure that their tao would last forever."[133] But making the institutions work required that people acknowledge the authority of their rulers, fathers, and elders. How did the sages persuade men to accept the inequality of ritual? Having mystified the people into accepting their authority with the *Change*, they made a point of treating as their equal only those who imitated them in the physical acts of paying obeisance to rulers, fathers, and so on. They took advantage of the primitive desire to be equal to train men to treat others as superiors. At the same time people saw that hierarchy decreased violence and served life, and ritual thus directly served their own desire for life.[134]

But in the now peaceful world men could break the rules without dying. The sages cogitated: "What I told people about the necessary pattern [that lacking social distinctions, you will struggle and kill each other] was so. [At the time] the facts bore this out, and thus they found it credible. I knew the pattern, and they all knew the facts. Now if the facts do not necessarily turn out that way, then the pattern will not be enough to redirect what everyone is saying. This is something that cannot be dealt with through proclamations." So the sages invented music to make men want to honor their superiors. People would then say, " 'Ritual certainly is something my mind possesses'; then how could they not believe the sage's persuasion?" Ritual was imposed on man from outside, music made him feel it was inside him. But as a result people began to suppress feelings of resentment and lust. So the sages created songs so that feelings could be vented before they exploded into destructive behavior. "The teaching of the *Songs* was to avoid having human emotional responses go so far that they cannot be overcome."[135] This final part was necessary to ensure that men would feel inclined to accept the unnatural restraints of civilization. This Culture of Ours, these essays imply, was the by-product of attempts to make a connection between institutional authority and human feeling, *jen-ch'ing*. Without such a connection, men would not have accepted the sages' teachings.

But institutional authority and moral authority are not constants. Su's last two essays deal with the fact of irreversible historical change. In "On the *Documents*," he argues that eventually political authority began to justify itself, and that once it did it was impossible to return to a world where rulers could do as they wished.[136] "On the *Spring and Autumn Annals*" argues that Confucius brought about a similarly irreversible change in the relationship between scholars and political power. The first non-king to claim the authority (ch'üan) of the sage, Confucius showed that men who had tao but not position could, in the common interest, claim authority over politics.[137] Writing without office, Su Hsun is of course claiming knowledge of the tao of the sage and moral authority for himself.

Ou-yang Hsiu sponsored Su Shih for the decree examination of 1061. Su Shih submitted 50 essays, whose theoretical framework he set out in a three-part essay "On *Chung-yung*," or "On Centrality with Constancy," an analysis of the "Doctrine of the Mean."[138] This polemical piece rejects attempts to locate values in human nature and stresses active involvement in affairs.[139] But Su does argue that chung-yung is an overarching concept

that contains the three essentials "to which the Duke of Chou and Confucius adhered in order to become sages," requirements that former ju
missed by treating the "Doctrine of the Mean" as a treatise on nature and
decree (*hsing-ming*).[140] Su's essay displays attitudes he would maintain,
although he eventually turned away from the somewhat mechanical dualism in the universal method of being a sage outlined here.

The three essential requirements are in full accord with the cosmic tao.
To practice chung-yung is to realize the pattern of the cosmos: "What
antiquity called chung-yung was not to go beyond fully realizing the
pattern [*li*] of the ten thousand things."[141] One of Su's goals in the essay is
to establish that this pattern exists in man as a fundamental duality of
feeling; on reflection men will see that they prefer a balance of opposites to
one-sidedness. He notes the danger: claiming that an inherent sense of
ambivalence is the basis of being moral may lead one to think that since
there are two sides to everything, one is always doing good. Su acknowledges the similarities between "being chung-yung [and] what Confucius
and Mencius called being a village worthy," who thinks men should
accept conventions.[142] For Su, however, the idea is to be in the world yet
against the world at the same time, without being at cross-purposes with
oneself.

In brief, Su explains the three requirements of being a sage as follows.
First, one must embody the polarity of knowing what one should do and
wanting to do it.[143] One must see clearly what ought to be done (*ming*) and
desire to do it as if it were integral to one's own being (*ch'eng*). But only
proceeding from knowledge to sincerity makes sense to Su (contrary to
the "Doctrine of the Mean"); without external and historical circumstances there is nothing to be sincere about. Second, there is the sage's tao
of achieving this in every instance.[144] Using ritual as an example of
something men know they should do but find at odds with their own
feelings and desires, Su describes a process of reflection on ultimate
consequences leading to the conclusion that not following ritual is self-
destructive and, thus, that ritual does accord with human desires. "This is
not only so for bending and bowing; everything in the world that is called
'forcing men' must have [some similar circumstance] from which it came
into being. Understanding *ming* is simply a matter of distinguishing what
something is born from and extending it to its ultimate consequence."[145]
The basic pattern of man's nature and feeling is two-sidedness, and thus to
accept being two-sided accords with one's natural inclinations. This simple pattern is, however, often obscured by the multiplicity of forms in
which it can be manifested.[146] Third, one must learn to put chung-yung
into practice so as to be constantly centered.[147] The problem: "Having
apprehended one side of it but having forgotten its center, one is unable to

feel secure traveling the comprehensive path all day. Even if one desired not to quit, how could one succeed?"[148] The center between two sides, Su argues, is not a fixed position or a mean from which men should not veer. Su agrees with Mencius that "holding to the middle without ch'üan is no different from holding to one extreme."[149] *Chung*, Su explains, is created by an individual through one-sided movements between extremes. Partiality is not incommensurate with centrality. One creates a center by being prepared to take the opposite position, for either side can be correct depending on the circumstances and neither is sufficient alone. Only the practice of going to both sides can be fully right. This means, Su explains, that a man should be willing to do things that others regard as self-interested and cowardly, even though he himself knows that he is doing it to realize chung-yung and the tao of the sage. In the end, the motive of action determines its value. Does one practice centrality to serve oneself or in order to show that there is a common tao that all can share and all will benefit from? But Su admits that the difference between a moral man and others will not always be visible. Seeing the difference requires knowing the "taste"; it cannot be judged by outward appearances alone.[150]

There is a good bit of cleverness in Su Hsuan's and Su Shih's essays, but the point remains that they are trying to establish a role for scholars and culture that brings together political authority and the human condition in a manner that does not require the denial of the individual and his feelings and desires. For the Sus the sage responds to things flexibly, with knowledge of the situation and a sense of human feeling. There is a longing here, I think, for a tao that enables the individual to act spontaneously yet appropriately. This is most evident in what father and son have to say about wen. Su Hsun writes:

The *Change* [says], "The wind drives across the water. Dispersion." This is the most perfect wen under heaven. Yet these two things seek not at all to be wen. They do not [even] have any intention of seeking each other out. They come across each other unexpectedly, and out of that wen comes into being. So it is that when they make wen, it is neither the wen of water nor the wen of wind. These two things are not able to make wen, yet they are unable not to make wen. When things are acting on each other, wen comes forth in their midst. Therefore this is the most perfect wen under Heaven.

Now jade is wonderfully beautiful, yet it cannot be regarded as wen. Once carved and decorated, it is not that it is not wen, yet it cannot be judged in terms of the spontaneous [tzu-jan]. Therefore, under heaven it is only from wind and water that wen comes into being without purposeful effort.

In the past the superior man lived in the world without seeking meritorious achievement. When he could not stop himself [from acting], he achieved something and all under heaven regarded him as worthy. He did not seek to have anything to say. When he could not stop himself [from speaking], the words came out and all under heaven thought him to be one who spoke the truth.[151]

In this passage wen results when each of two parties acts according to its own proclivities without regard to the other. Wind across water creates perfect wen; men acting with intention on jade create a less perfect wen. Things of true value, Su Hsun opines, are created when a man responds to things without calculation and intent because he cannot stop himself from responding. The superior man acting on man can replicate this, even if it is not entirely spontaneous. There is a longing for the possibility that there are values one can embody so perfectly that all one says and does has value. Yet it is hard to imagine Su Hsun writing without conscious purpose—his essay "Techniques of the Mind" speaks of the need to be guided by principle (*i*) in one's mind[152]—and his longing for spontaneity may signal an unease with the calculated plotting of his essays.

In 1059, when the Sus, already aware of their literary reputations, were returning to the capital by boat, they compiled the poems they wrote along the way into an anthology. Su Shih wrote a preface giving his version of the idea of spontaneous response to circumstances. He distinguishes *wei wen* ("doing wen") from *tso wen* ("creating" it). The amusingly contradictory goal is to produce wen without intending to produce something that will be called wen, to be doing something of value without being motivated by a desire to do something of value.

Preface to the *Collection from a Journey South*

For those engaging in wen in the past, the skill lay not in being able to do it but in not being able not to do it. When mountains and rivers have clouds, when plants and trees have flowers, it is that the real content, having become full and tumescent, has been manifested on the outside. Even if they desired not to have them, would it be possible?

Ever since as a youth I heard my father discoursing on wen, I have thought that the sages of antiquity had things they created when they could not help it. Therefore, however much I and my brother Ch'e have done wen, we have never dared have the intention of creating wen.

In the year *chi-hai* [1059], we accompanied our father on a trip to the [southern] region of Ch'u. There was nothing to attend to on the boat, [yet] playing draughts and drinking wine are not the way for a family to enjoy itself. The beauty of mountains and river, the rusticity of local customs, the traces of worthy and superior men, and all that with which our eyes and ears made contact would, in various mixtures, collide inside us and issue forth as song. Now my father's creations and my brother's wen should all be here, a hundred pieces in all. We have called it *Collection from a Journey South*, for it captures the events of a moment for another day's musings. Besides, these were all obtained in the midst of talk and laughter, and they are not wen done out of purposeful effort.[153]

We see here more clearly the interweaving of two theories. One is the ku-wen idea of literary moral cultivation; accumulate values inside and express them outside. The other is Su Hsun's version of literary spontaneity: wen that comes forth through the unsought meeting with things. Su Shih's twist on this is to suppose that what is being expressed from inside is neither moral nor sentimental—indeed, Su seems to be posing as egoless—but is rather the particular conjunction of old and new experiences that accumulate inside him as he moves through the landscape. The self is merely the vessel in which a universal process of things meeting takes place and the means through which their particular pattern is expressed.

Su Shih would eventually learn to cope with his desire to be natural yet be right and, along the way, would establish himself as the greatest writer of his time. He would continue to believe what is already evident here: the tao of the sage was not a particular set of ideas and concerns but the style of thought that enabled one to respond in a moral or unifying fashion through literary and political action.

Ch'eng I and Ch'eng Hao: The Sage and Human Nature

The Ch'eng brothers arrived at the capital in 1056. In preparing for the examinations, Ch'eng I wrote an essay on the theme, apparently set by Hu Yuan, "What learning was it that Yen-tzu loved?" The essay is about learning. Like Su Shih, Ch'eng sees being a ságe as the goal. There is a method for attaining that goal; again like Su, he does not accept the view that sageliness is innate. But at the end of the essay, Ch'eng asks: If there is a method, why do men not follow it? He answers: "Later men did not understand; they thought sagehood was basically innate knowledge, not something to be attained by learning, and thus the tao of learning has been lost to us. Men have not sought it within themselves but outside themselves; they have treated extensive study and effortful memorization, clever literary form and beautiful diction, as skill and have ornamented their language. Thus few have attained the tao. Thus the learning of today is different from that which Yen-tzu loved."[154] Now although this is couched in the familiar ku-wen terms for criticizing literary craft, Ch'eng in fact was questioning whether any learning that proceeded through external sources, thus wen-hsueh in general, could guide one toward sagehood. Ch'eng I's alternative to text-based learning is "the learning that Yen-tzu alone loved: the tao of attaining sagehood through learning."

Can sagehood be attained through learning? I say, it can be. And what is the tao of learning? I say this: Heaven-and-earth accumulate essence, that which obtains the most refined [ch'i] of the five phases becomes man. His basis is pure and tranquil.

Before it is expressed, the five natures [*hsing*] are fully complete in [the basis]. These are humanity, righteousness, propriety, wisdom, and faithfulness. Once the physical form has come into being, external things jar his physical form and there is movement on the inside. When the inside moves, the seven emotional responses [*ch'ing*] come out. These are pleasure, anger, sorrow, joy, love, hate, and desire. When the emotional responses have intensified and become increasingly agitated, his [five] natures are depleted. This is why one who is aware restrains his emotional responses to make them agree with what is inside. He corrects his mind and nurtures his natures. Therefore we say he is making his emotional responses [agree with his] natures.[155] The stupid do not know how to control them. They loose their emotional responses and reach depravity; they fetter their natures and lose them. Therefore we say they are making their natures [agree with their] emotional responses.

The tao of learning is simply correcting the mind and nourishing the natures. When what is inside is correct and a man is sincere, then he has become a sage. For the learning of the superior man it is necessary to first make this clear in the mind and know what to nurture, then to work at practice in order to seek to arrive [at sagehood]. This is what is called proceeding from clarity [*ming*] to sincerity [*ch'eng*]. Therefore learning must fully occupy a man's mind. If it fully occupies his mind, he will know his natures. Knowing his natures, turning back and being sincere to them, he is a sage.[156]

Ch'eng asserts that man, as a creation of heaven-and-earth, has certain innate endowments that should guide his conduct. A man has to cultivate consciousness of these innate guides so that they can control his emotional responses to things; otherwise his emotional responses will damage his moral nature. Drawing heavily on the "Doctrine of the Mean," Ch'eng arrives at a vision of being a sage fundamentally different from Su Shih's. He opposes emotional response to a moral nature, and he posits an independently existing moral nature as a self-sufficient guide to ethical conduct. Men can destroy it, but they do not acquire it or accumulate it. Because it exists inside men, they can turn to it directly; it does not depend on convincing oneself of the validity of conclusions drawn from antiquity. Yet Ch'eng has put himself in something of a bind, for he must acknowledge that the disciples of Confucius did study the *Songs*, *Documents*, and the six arts, but he cannot explain how these are relevant to becoming a moral person.

This piece owes much to the ku-wen idea of the sage, but it is a radical denial of the ku-wen premise that values are a human construct. Instead, Ch'eng has resurrected ideas about heaven-and-earth, such as the correlation between the five moral values and five phases. Ou-yang Hsiu noted and ridiculed this aspect of classical five-phases theory, which dates from the Han, as the speculation of numerologists.[157] Liu Mu's (fl. early eleventh century) numerological study of the *Book of Change*, a work that had gained a certain popularity by this time and that did subscribe to this view,[158] had been sharply attacked by some ku-wen writers.[159] Ch'eng was not a numerologist, but he stood with those who cared about *hsing-ming*, a term that stems from the opening of the "Doctrine of the Mean": "What Heaven decrees [*ming*] is called the nature [*hsing*]. Following the nature is called the tao. Cultivating tao is called instruction." The tie to ideas about heaven-and-earth is fairly simple, for hsing-ming is from heaven, not culture.

Ch'eng's ideas were in a tradition that still had some currency, as Hu Su's examination questions from 1059 illustrate.[160] But Ch'eng sees heaven-and-earth as something internal to man as well. Heaven-and-earth as the external model for human order is not the issue here; thus Ch'eng does not depend on the supposition of a cosmic resonance that makes heaven and man interdependent and tells the ruler when he is going astray. This is an individual enterprise: every scholar should realize his moral nature in order to accord with heaven's tao.

In desiring to have something in himself to rely on, Ch'eng does not differ from Su Shih, but in his account learning can take place in isolation from society. In a letter to Chang Tsai in 1059, Ch'eng Hao, however, wrote of the need to combine the hsing-ming perspective with the idea of responding to things. After meeting Fan Chung-yen in about 1040, Chang spent much time before 1057 pursuing philosophical questions. It is clear that Chang thought he was discovering how an understanding of the tao of heaven-and-earth could lead to true conclusions about morality and the sages. A disciple later wrote—admiringly I think—that Chang's *Correcting Youthful Ignorance* "has what the Six Classics do not convey and the sages never spoke of."[161] Ch'eng Hao tries to persuade Chang that being moral does not require cutting oneself off from contact with external things, as Chang Tsai had supposed in vain attempts to "settle" (*ting*) his *hsing*. The internal and external should be one; the hsing should be "settled when active and settled when tranquil." It is not possible to maintain a constant state of moral equanimity if Chang thinks that with every response to things he is losing that state. The solution is to avoid an external/internal distinction and view the response to things as being of the hsing as well. The rationale for this view is: "The constancy of heaven-and-earth is due to its mind extending to all things yet its being without mind [i.e., selfish purposes]. The constancy of the sage is due to his emotional responses according with all affairs yet his having no emotional responses [i.e., selfish inclinations]. Therefore the learning of the superior man is broad and impartial; things come, and he responds accordingly."[162]

One who functions like heaven-and-earth is able to accommodate all things without partiality.[163] Men fail to act like this because their "emotional responses are obscured in some way; therefore they are unable to pursue tao. In general, the danger is in being partial [or, selfish] and being calculating. One who is partial is unable to see that being activist [*yu-wei*] is to respond to things. One who is calculating is unable to see that having true insight [*ming-chueh*] [into things] is to be spontaneous." The problem with the idea of responding to things spontaneously is that the response may simply manifest the partiality of the actor. But an effort to reflect before responding leads to being calculating. Both are inherently self-interested. Ch'eng Hao envisions a sage who has transcended partiality, whose responses perfectly fit the true interests of the thing he responds to. "When the sage is joyful, it is because the thing ought to be enjoyed. When he is angry, it is because the thing deserves anger. Thus the joy and anger of the sage are not tied to his mind; they are tied to things. If so, then the sage certainly does respond to things. How could he regard following the external as wrong and seeking in the internal as right?"[164] Eventually Ch'eng I would figure out how man's innate qualities made possible the spontaneous moral responsiveness Ch'eng Hao envisions here.

However different Su and the Ch'engs would turn out to be, in 1057 they share many of the same aspirations. They are interested in the sage as an individual who remains moral while involved in things. They are pursuing ideas about what all men can share that will guide them under all circumstances. They are trying to envision a perfectly moral but socially involved scholar. This amounts to a search for the grounds of moral autonomy for the individual. This was, to be sure, an important aspect of earlier ku-wen thought, but now the search for those grounds has become a serious intellectual goal. Perhaps, in 1057, they are simply reflecting current ideas about the kind of purpose appropriate for a morally ambitious young man. Certainly both share the mature Ou-yang Hsiu's concern with the individual. But if so, trends differ considerably from those of 1044, when Wang An-shih and Ssu-ma Kuang appeared on the scene and young men debated the possibility of transforming society through the institutions of government. In the 1050's Wang An-shih and Ssu-ma Kuang were steadily advancing in the bureaucracy and becoming known for their ideas about government. For Wang, the return to power of the Ch'ing-li reformers meant a court more likely to be receptive to his own ideas, which he urged on them in his famous "Ten Thousand Word Memorial" of 1058.[165] For Ssu-ma, the new regime's attitudes were disquieting, and he took pains in 1057 to disassociate himself from ku-wen.[166] The time for Ch'eng I and Su Shih was still in the future.

7 For Perfect Order: Wang An-shih and Ssu-ma Kuang

Wang An-shih (1021–86) and Ssu-ma Kuang (1019–86) were the most influential thinkers of their generation and the leaders of the two opposing camps in a political crisis that profoundly affected the subsequent political and intellectual history of the Sung. Wang and Ssu-ma were political thinkers in the broadest sense. That is, from the beginning of their careers in the early 1040's they were addressing the same problems: What was the proper relation between the state and society? What kind of learning would enable the shih to fulfill their responsibilities as the political elite? By the end of their careers, each was convinced he had discovered universal answers to these questions. They arrived at equally coherent visions of a perfectly ordered world in which many of the same institutional, social, and cultural elements were woven together. But these were irreconcilably different visions. "What I have said here runs exactly counter to your ideas," Ssu-ma once wrote Wang, who replied, we disagree "because the methods [shu] we have adopted are for the most part different."[1] The parallels between the New Policies crisis and China during the second half of the twentieth century are hard to miss.[2]

The intellectual careers of Wang and Ssu-ma are related to the rise of ku-wen thought in opposite ways. Wang An-shih adopted the view that scholars who understood the tao of the sage from the Classics could use government to transform society and attain perfect order under heaven. He had the answer to a question he once posed for students.

There were root and branch to the sages' ordering of the age. There was what came first and last in their putting it into practice. The problems of the world have been left uncorrected for a long time now; teaching and policy have yet to be made according to the intentions of the sages. We have lost sight of the root, seeking it in the branch; we have taken what should come last and put it first. And thus the world careens toward disorder. Now if it is so that the world will not be ordered except through the means the sages used to achieve order, then to be considered a true shih one must attend to how the sages achieved order. I want you gentlemen to relate in full the root and branch of how the sages achieved order and what they did first and last.[3]

This typifies Wang's intellectual style: one analyzes antiquity in order to uncover a universal program, whose elements are coherently connected as root to branch (*pen mo*), thus revealing those that are basic to others, and for which there is a logical sequence of steps from first to last (*hsien hou*) for establishing the basis. To a considerable extent Ssu-ma also believed that there was a necessary order to things, although in his case this could be illuminated only through the study of post-sage-king history. Ssu-ma's efforts are related to ku-wen, however, not merely because he reacted against the idealization of a classical sociopolitical order, but because the rise of ku-wen thought compelled him to do what otherwise would not have been necessary: justify in intellectual terms the Ch'in-Han tradition of imperial government.

The promulgation in the early 1070's of Wang An-shih's New Policies (*hsin fa*), as his program of institutional reforms and policy initiatives soon came to be called, was arguably the most important political event in Sung history, short of the restoration of the dynasty in the south after 1126. Wang gained power under the new emperor Shen-tsung (r. 1067–85), then in his twentieth year, who publicly supported an "activist" policy.[4] Wang promised a program that would eventually solve the increasing budget deficit without raising taxes[5] and strengthen the Sung against the Tangut state of Hsia in the northwest. He came to power after a decade of uninspiring political leadership. When, after long delay, Jen-tsung had adopted a successor, he chose poorly. By all accounts his nephew Ying-tsung (r. 1063–67) was a weak, unstable man. His reign was marked by an acrimonious debate among officials over whom he should call his "father," his natural father (Prince P'u) or Jen-tsung. The dispute revealed a divided court; the Council of State was dominated by men inspired by old allies of Fan Chung-yen who envisioned a government more responsive to the needs of the populace, but below them were academicians, censors, and policy critics like Ssu-ma Kuang, men long associated with opposition to institutional change.[6] Relatively speaking, Wang An-shih was a fresh voice; he had, by and large, steered clear of factional disputes at court, and he had something he wanted to accomplish. The New Policies did increase the wealth and power of the government, and although the program did not achieve perfect order, its adherents controlled the court for most of the five decades after Wang's final retirement in 1076. His partisans dominated the reigns of Shen-tsung, Che-tsung (r. 1085–1100), and Hui-tsung (r. 1100–25), except during the

Yuan-yu reign period of 1085–93 when the empress dowager as regent brought back Ssu-ma Kuang and the opposition. The Yuan-yu court abolished most of Wang's program; when New Policies advocates returned in 1094, they purged and eventually blacklisted their opponents, including Su Shih and Ch'eng I. The final rejection of the New Policies program and Wang's learning did not take place until the death of Ch'in Kuei (1090–1155), the major chief councillor during the Southern Sung restoration. The Sung government never again had the same degreee of command over society and shih learning.

Many have studied the New Policies in the context of Sung institutional, economic, and social history. There has been a tendency to argue that Wang's program was a function of the military, fiscal, and social problems it addressed, that it was an answer to and, in some sense, caused by larger problems of state and society. In fact the decision to try Wang's program was a political choice, one that involved rejecting Ssu-ma Kuang's program of bureaucratic reforms, which promised different solutions to all the same problems without requiring that the government reorganize society. Wang and Ssu-ma understood that a choice was being made, although each believed that his own scholarship demonstrated the correctness of his own position. Wang understood that his ideas, not the exigencies of the political situation, justified his political goals. He explained to the emperor in 1069: "I certainly wish to aid Your Majesty in accomplishing something [yu-wei], but today customs and institutions are all in ruin. . . . If Your Majesty truly wishes to use me . . . we should first discuss learning so that you are convinced of the necessary connections in what I have learned." Indeed, one of Ssu-ma Kuang's criticisms was that under the New Policies regime literary men were in charge of policy.[7] The emperor himself noted that some believed Wang's learning had not prepared him for practical leadership. But, Wang replies, "Learning from the Classics [ching-shu] is the means for correcting the problems of the age [ching shih-wu]. . . . The priority of the moment is to change customs [pien feng-su] and establish institutions [li fa-tu]."[8]

Wang and Ssu-ma shared the belief that a moral order in the world depended upon perfecting the institutions of government and that the principles for government could be known. Their principles were different, they drew their conclusions from different sources, and they arranged the pieces, many of which were the same, into irreconcilably different systems. Much has been written about Wang An-shih and his policies, and in recent years scholars have been less prone to dismiss Ssu-ma Kuang's criticisms.

One of the most apparent features of Wang's goals—at least in the eyes of some of his critics—was his desire to unify shih values and keep the shih tied to government. The New Policies regime expanded the school system and sought to impose a single national curriculum while creating more official positions and nearly doubling the size of the bureaucracy. Ssu-ma envisioned a more limited government that stalled social change, and although he believed the shih should be a fairly closed group with less competition for office, he also aimed to maintain them as a national elite oriented toward bureaucratic careers. But they rose to prominence as competition for office was making it more difficult for officials to ensure the status of their descendants, and, although Wang's party held power for fifty years, it failed to unify the shih or intellectual circles around his political vision. An understanding of the intellectual and institutional aims of Wang An-shih and Ssu-ma Kuang will be useful in later chapters in accounting both for Su Shih's defense of intellectual diversity and, I think, for Ch'eng I's success in formulating a way of thinking about values that would prove persuasive.

This chapter begins by establishing the differences between Ssu-ma's and Wang's political visions, as they expressed them in the late 1050's and early 1060's. It then turns to their intellectual careers. Finally it reviews the New Policies, Wang's defense of them, and Ssu-ma's critique.

Different Visions of Political Order

Both Wang An-shih and Ssu-ma Kuang began to call for political reform under Jen-tsung. In 1061, for example, in his role as a policy critic, Ssu-ma proposed a reform of the promotion system. He envisioned a twelve-grade system of assignments (*ch'ai-ch'ien*), covering everyone from chief councillor to subprefectural registrar, and new rules for determining assignment, tenure, and promotion. This reform was close to Ssu-ma's heart; he believed that correct bureaucratic management would enable government to ensure public well-being and secure the survival of the dynasty. Carrying out his proposal would require breaking with the established practices of tenure and seniority and end the tracking of officials by the rank of their examination degree and the nature of their entry into the civil service. The proposed system was intended to assign bureaucrats to posts they could handle and to promote them for real achievements. Ssu-ma was aiming at bureaucratic reform and rationalization; he believed bureaucratic procedures needed to be changed so as to realize the larger ends of the bureaucracy as the vehicle of government. Wang An-shih, a new appointee to the prestigious post of rescript writer, was called upon to comment on Ssu-ma's proposal. He dismissed it as a "petty reform that in the end offers no solutions to real problems and is not worth undertaking." Improving existing bureaucratic practice missed the point, Wang held, unless it was accompanied by a complete re-examination of the entire system. "If the court is committed to greatly perfecting institutions [*fa-tu*] and molding and ranking human talent," it should initiate a general discussion and invite all "shih with proposals" to participate.[9]

Wang could not object to the idea of employing men according to their abilities. But he could, and did, oppose efforts to improve the operation of government without first reconsidering its basic purpose. Ssu-ma was confusing the branch of administration with the root; he was putting secondary measures to improve bureaucratic processes before more primary tasks. Three years earlier, in his "Ten Thousand Word Memorial" presented to the emperor upon his appointment as supervisor of funds in the Finance Commission (*tu-chih p'an-kuan*) in 1058, Wang had explained that the true basis for order was increasing the pool of talent and that the primary task was revamping the education system. He repeated its essentials again in 1060 and 1061.[10] Ssu-ma's proposal of 1061 reflects his view that the changes men like Wang An-shih had in mind were misguided and unnecessary.[11]

Wang's memorial sets out a sequence of integrally connected policy goals, giving both a vision of the integrated order of antiquity and an explanation of how to restore that order in a radically different present. Wang begins by attributing the moral, financial, and foreign problems of his day to a failure "to understand institutions." If institutions are to lead to order, Wang asserts, they must "agree with the policies of the Former Kings." But imitating ancient institutions does not mean simply copying the traces of antiquity: "Imitating the policies of the Former Kings means we should simply imitate their intentions." The present should imitate the intentions of antiquity because they, rather than the institutions themselves, remained constant through historical change.

The two emperors [Yao and Shun] and the three kings [Yü, T'ang, and Wen] were removed from each other by over a thousand years. Order had alternated with chaos and splendor with decline many times. The changes they encountered and the situations they faced differed, and the measures they adopted varied as well. But their intentions in making society and government [*wei t'ien-hsia kuo-chia chih i*] were always the same in root and branch and [what they put] first and last. I therefore say: we ought simply to imitate their intentions. If we imitate their intentions, then whatever changes and reforms we make will not shock the people and cause complaint, yet they will surely be in agreement with the policies of the Former Kings.[12]

Wang claims that the intentions of the sages were consistent and formed an integrated whole that can guide policy in the present. Such policies can be put into effect without fear of the consequences.

But, the memorial continues, even if the ruler wishes to "reform all affairs under heaven to fit the intentions of the Former Kings, circumstances make this impossible. Why? Because the human talent in society [*t'ien-hsia*] is inadequate."[13] In other words, the government is not recruiting men capable of realizing the intent of the sages. Since the lack of the necessary talent is the problem, the root of government at this moment is to "cast and complete" talent. As the memorial proceeds to set out the sequence of priorities to accomplish this, however, it becomes apparent that Wang believes education cannot be detached from social, economic, and bureaucratic policy. The basis cannot be completed without creating an integrated system that takes itself as its own end.

The bulk of the memorial is devoted to a sequence of four requirements for ensuring that talent be adequate. First is "instruction" through state schools. Schooling in antiquity immersed men in the integrated system of the day. Students learned "the affairs of rites and music, punishment and policy," by living in an environment in which all that they saw and practiced were the "model sayings, ethical conduct, and intentions for ordering society of the Former Kings." Second is "nurturing." The ancients nurtured all the people, providing economic support, establishing rituals of passage and of daily life appropriate to their economic stations, and controlling them with penal law, thus "unifying social customs and bringing about order." Third is "selection." The ancient schools, which educated all and saw to the economic well-being of all, recommended the most wise and most able to the leaders, who might after examining their speech and conduct, assign them probationary employment and titles. Schooling and nurturing thus prepared men to take over the task of schooling and nurturing others. Fourth is "employment." Those who proved their competence were assigned ranks and responsibilities commensurate with their talents. Such officials were to be given long tenures and left unfettered by regulations so that they could develop and complete projects and do what needed to be done. Ssu-ma's first concern is Wang's last.

Wang's antiquity is a self-contained and self-perpetuating system. It is an organic whole in which all the parts function interdependently and talented individuals are circulated back into the system that molds them. It is holistic; it incorporates all aspects of life into a sum bigger than its parts, transcending any distinctions between government and society, the political and the cultural, or public and private spheres. And it is moral in that it is the framework in which things have value and purpose. There is hierarchy here, but hierarchical distinctions are relatively unimportant. The ruler and dynastic house are not functionally necessary.[14]

In what ways does the present not agree with ancient intent? Today "instruction" is incomplete, Wang argues, for it deals only with the civil and literary and ignores the military side. Salaries are too low to "nurture" honesty among officials, the rites fail to restrain men, and the law does not punish basic faults. "Selection" is based on literary skill and memorization; it fails to garner men of real use. "Employment" is determined by a seniority system that assigns men to positions beyond their competence. To realize the ancient, Wang concludes, government must first think out strategies and make precise calculations, then gradually put them into effect, and finally bring them to fruition. It can then offer rewards to those who further the cause and punish those who hinder it.

Wang's account of the inadequacies of the present suggest a program less grand than his model of antiquity would justify. He has shifted from a system including all the people to one in which the shih already exist as the elite and the immediate task is to apply the intents of the sages to the molding of the shih.[15] In Wang's system, government provides for the shih, and the shih are part of government at some level. Proper training and employment of the shih will enable the government to expand its activities to all men (thus creating and employing more shih). Still, he envisions a government with the power to command society through its molding of the shih as a national and local sociopolitical elite.[16]

The unification of shih values was, Wang believed, essential to transforming the world. This unity did not exist in 1058, as Wang explained to a friend: "The ancients 'unified morality and made customs the same [for all].'[17] Therefore when shih looked to what the ancients had accomplished for standards, there was no difference of opinion. Today families hold to separate tao and men to different virtues. Moreover, [the virtues] they hold are pressed by the force of degenerate customs, and they are unable to be like the ancients in every case; how can the difference of opinion be fully repressed?"[18] This made schools crucial—they could "unify all those who learn" so that the shih would know their true purpose[19]—and once Wang established a school system and curriculum in the 1070's, he thought differences of opinion should cease.

Although Ssu-ma Kuang and others would accuse Wang of demanding as chief councillor that others be the same as himself, Ssu-ma was no less certain of his opinions.[20] He was certainly right, however, in thinking that he had a very different view of what an ordered polity was. In contrast to Wang, who asked what government should do for the welfare of society, Ssu-ma asked how men should act to preserve the polity. Invited to set the question for the decree examination of 1052, Ssu-ma argued that the difference between antiquity and later times was simply that ancient dynasties lasted longer.[21] He saw no need for a fundamental restructuring. In 1056 he wrote: "It is not that what could be done in antiquity cannot be done in the present; it is that instruction [in the present] has not been perfected. Since the foundation in the present is correct, we need only to make an effort at the rest; there is no need to fear not matching antiquity."[22]

Ssu-ma's assertion that the present foundation was correct follows from his understanding of the nature of the polity the sages created to move men from the self-destructive state of "great antiquity," in which men lived like animals and struggled with each other to survive, to an orderly world.

The sages, grieving that it was thus, arose and ordered [the people]. They chose the worthy and knowledgeable to be rulers and elders to them; they divided the land and made boundaries for it; they gathered father and son, older and younger brother, husband and wife, and nurtured them; they effected their rites and music, policies and commands, and restrained them; they illuminated their tao and virtue, benevolence and righteousness, filial piety and paternal caring, loyalty and good faith, honesty and humility, and taught them. If there were still foolish and wild folk who resisted and did not go along, then with whips they awed them, with axes they executed them, and with soldiers they exterminated them. Thus the people were all secure in their respective roles and kept to the constant; they nurtured life and attended to the dead; they multiplied and lasted.[23]

Ssu-ma's antiquity is of a piece with the tradition of imperial governance, in which political stability required persuading and coercing the people to accept their allotted roles. Ssu-ma's world is marked by hierarchy, boundaries, and restraints; he does not share Wang's vision of a government that actively works to increase prosperity and teaches men how to rise in status.

In the 1050's and 1060's Ssu-ma was concerned primarily with rectifying the bureaucratic processes that most affected the fortunes of the state by explaining the principles to which they had to adhere. As he had written in 1045, "being principled" means "clarifying the great roles of ruler and minister, understanding the great principles of the world, and defending them to the death without changing."[24] He warned, for example, of the need to ensure that political institutions were kept "public" (*kung*); that is, they must always function in the interest of the state's survival rather than in the "private" (*ssu*) interest of those who governed.[25] This defense of institutional integrity was meant not to challenge or deny private interests but only to ensure that the boundary between the pursuit of self-interest and the public responsibilities of state service was maintained. Ssu-ma's collection of aphoristic comments, the "Impractical Writings" of 1057, suggests that for Ssu-ma the moral challenge for a shih was to learn to subordinate himself to his duties. Those who truly follow the "tao of the sage," he writes, will not try to change what they cannot control—intelligence and courage, rank and wealth—they will simply try to fulfill their given role. One who accepts his lot is free of the affliction of unfulfilled desires, whether idealistic or selfish.[26] And in 1057, at the time of his return to court, Ssu-ma composed a series of essays on the theme of making government work for the survival of the state.[27]

In the 1060's Ssu-ma used his post as policy critic to set out the general principles he believed would ensure dynastic survival. His memorials to the emperor from 1061 represent an alternative to Wang's memorial of 1058. Ten days after Ssu-ma proposed reforming the system of appointments, he submitted a memorial in five parts, "The Five Guidelines," as "the essential tao for preserving the state and [for dealing with] the pressing concerns of the moment."[28] These were the framework for the flood of programmatic memorials from Ssu-ma during his tenure as policy critic. They are directed at the emperor, the central and highest figure in Ssu-ma's scheme of things. He begins, in "Preserve the Patrimony," with a review of the rise and fall of dynasties. Why, he asks, have dynastic houses succeeded in maintaining the unity of the empire for only 500 years of the last 1,700 years? The responsibility lies squarely with the dynastic house and the adventurism and negligence of emperors. "Attend to the Moment," the second part, begins by denying any equation between the natural cycles of heaven-and-earth and political history. As he had written in 1056, "The teaching of the sages is order man, not heaven; know man, not heaven."[29] Dynastic houses rise through human actions—the first essay defines the dynastic founder's possession of "heaven's decree" as his having the intelligence and strength to outlast his rivals. Dynastic decline, far from being inevitable or natural, can be prevented through the proper methods. It is "simply like preserving a great house." The owner "must solidify the foundation, fortify the pillars, strengthen the beams, reinforce the roof, raise the walls, and tighten the lock. Once it is finished, he must also choose a good descendant and have him diligently maintain it." The owner is the ruler, and the house is the polity: "The populace is the foundation of the state [kuo], ritual and law its pillars, high ministers its beams, the bureaucracy its roof, the generals its walls, and the troops its lock." If the ruler carefully maintains it and "preserves the finished models of the ancestors," it can be held forever.[30]

Although mechanical and static, in Ssu-ma's analogy the polity is a coherent and inclusive structure in which the parts are integrally connected. Its survival depends on human choice and interest. The ruler's task is to keep men to their appointed roles. He does this out of self-interest—he wants his descendants to inherit his wealth—although by doing so all who play a role in the structure benefit. Here too the whole is greater than the sum of its parts. But it is also so that the common good results from serving the dynastic interest. The rest of the memorial is predictable. Rulers must prepare against foreign invasion and natural disasters by selecting good military and civil officials, training the soldiers, storing up grain, and ensuring effective local administration ("Long-range Planning"). The all-important process of making appointments requires noticing faults of character before they have a political effect ("Attend to the Incipient"). Finally, the ruler must take measures to ensure that the functions of government are accomplished in substance, not merely in appearance ("Be Concerned with Substance").

The ruler plays the central role in this scheme and bears primary responsibility for making it function correctly. In 1061 and then in memorials to every subsequent ruler he served, Ssu-ma offered the ruler two sets of instructions.[31] First were "the three great virtues of rulers: benevolence, knowledge, and militancy [wu]."[32] Benevolence Ssu-ma defined as transforming through instruction, improving administration, nurturing the populace, and benefiting all things. Knowledge meant understanding the principles of tao and being able to recognize security and danger, the wise and the foolish, and right and wrong. Militancy meant adamant support for decisions that accorded with tao, unconfused by slander and flattery.[33] Ssu-ma's second set of instructions takes up his greatest interest: personnel policy. "I have heard that the way of achieving order depends on but three things: first, the assignment of offices; second, trustworthy rewards; and third, necessary punishments."[34] The good ruler is the ultimate bureaucratic manager. He assigns officials according to competence, rewards achievement, and punishes failure.[35] Rewards and punishments are necessary, for as Ssu-ma wrote in "The Five Guidelines," few are truly able to be "concerned with the public and forget the private."[36]

Ssu-ma rarely envisions new tasks for government, arguing instead that problems arise because bureaucrats fail to fulfill functions that are already well defined. In the 1060's, for example, when he writes at great length on fiscal and military issues facing the dynasty, in every case he argues that better administration will resolve the most difficult problems.[37] If men are assigned according to their abilities, rewards and punishments will make them see that private advantage lies in fulfilling their public roles. For Ssu-ma men must always be restrained, for they tend to act out of self-interest. Wang An-shih's view, that "the sages' enacting of tao was human emotional response and nothing more,"[38] is congruent with a program that deals with desires by trying to satisfy them.

Ssu-ma Kuang's "great house" of the polity is hard to construct and comes apart easily; it requires constant management to keep the selfish interests of the various parts from causing the collapse of the entire structure. The difficulty, as Ssu-ma himself points out in a long memorial entitled "Be Careful About Habits" from 1062, is to get men to accept that they will be allowed to pursue their own interests only within the confines of the roles established for them.[39] The memorial sounds like a response to the objection that men are naturally inclined to resist such restraints. In brief, Ssu-ma argues that whether men are inclined to resist or accept subordination is all a matter of "habits" of behavior that have developed through history. It is up to the government, then, to reinforce those social values that will habituate men to subordination. At root there is one primary value: political authority must "make the people accustomed to the roles of superior and inferior" (shang-hsia chih fen). [40] This was the habit in antiquity. "Ritual" meant a hierarchy of authority from the son of heaven through the feudal lords down to the people. (Ssu-ma's Chou dynasty was a centralized state.) This "habit" was also the safety net of the polity. Ssu-ma supposes an instinctive human resistance to change that makes men reluctant to challenge authority and willing to follow it. History from the decline of the Chou on, he asserts, shows the erosion of this habit, although the survival of powerless Chou kings is evidence of its value. But with Han through T'ang history, when dynasties failed to restore "ritual," the habit of challenging superiors emerged. By the end of the T'ang, men no longer spoke of "the ranking of honored and humble or the principles of right and wrong," and the ephemeral states of the Five Dynasties period were the result. [41] The Sung is on the right track, for the founders "understood that all misfortune arises from the absence of ritual" and took measures to establish the authority of the ruler and withdraw authority from the provincial governors. They unified the hierarchy of authority so that it extended from the court to fiscal intendants (for Ssu-ma the modern equivalent of the feudal lords of the Chou) and thence to local officials and the people; "thus the ranking of superior and inferior was correct and rules and principles were established." [42] To stay on course, relations of authority should not be upset and men should not seek higher stations.

The historical view of this memorial is found in Ssu-ma's historical studies, as we shall see. Those works also contain the view, only implicit in the memorials, that the shih are a pre-existing social elite. Rather than encouraging men to become shih, the government should gain the support of the shih and, thereby, the support of the populace. [43] The desire to avoid both social and political change heightens the contrast with Wang An-shih's vision of a sociopolitical order in which the ambition for greater status and wealth is not harmful to the common good.

Learning

Wang An-shih knew what government should do. Ssu-ma Kuang knew how government should be conducted. There is, of course, a great deal of difference between saying what to do (tasks must be defined, institutions created or expanded to carry out those tasks) and saying how to act (roles and functions must be defined, ethical standards clarified). It is at this point that "learning" again comes into play, for each man, through his own learning, had arrived at conclusions about what shih should know that justified his way of thinking about government, and each produced a body of work to persuade the shih. Their intellectual careers were integral to their political programs.

Although both had literary accomplishments, they both distinguished between literary aims and the pursuit of values. Wang, for example, responded to a student's submission of a literary sampler by asking, "Do you wish to excel through literary writing?" Or "do you wish to illuminate tao?"[44] In a similar case Ssu-ma asked: "I do not yet understand your purpose. Is it the wen of antiquity or the tao of antiquity you wish to learn?"[45] But if Wang, as his own practice demonstrated, believed that doing wen could be commensurate with learning tao and accepted wen-hsueh as the basis for examinations,[46] Ssu-ma hoped to detach the literary enterprise from serious learning. In 1083 he entered the following in his "Appreciation of Non-action," a collection of aphorisms, under the title "The Harm of Wen." "Someone said to the Impractical Old Man, 'You have apprehended the beginnings of tao; it is a pity you lack the wen to express it.' The Impractical Old Man replied, 'That is so. The Superior Man has wen to illuminate tao; the lesser man has wen to express [or advance] his person. Who except a lesser man with wen would be able to turn white into black and south into north?'"[47] He explained to a leading literary man of the day that the wen-hsueh of the "four fields" of the *Analects* did not justify the wen-hsueh of his day, it meant the texts of the *Songs* and *Documents* and the forms and sounds of rites and music. When it came to making language wen, he pointed out, Confucius said only that "elaborated language [*tz'u*] is simply to get [the point] across."[48] This phrase was beginning to appear with increasing frequency. It supported an instrumental view of writing rather than the literary view associated with the lines so frequently quoted in the past: "If it is said without wen, practice will not extend far." Even Wang An-shih allowed that this was not the "basic intent" of doing wen.[49] Wen did have a place in Ssu-ma's scheme. Proper forms of expression were necessary to social life.[50] He also agreed that poetry was an appropriate mode for the literary presentation of one's individuality.[51] But literary activity had no real value in governing.

Part of the reason for Ssu-ma's hostility lay in the claim of literary men to be "creating" things of value. This implied that making ideas up was legitimate. But to think about tao, one had to take ideas from outside. Ssu-ma explains to a student:

Confucius described himself as "transmitting, not creating."[52] Thus the tao of Confucius was not found in himself. He must have been relating the tao of the three august ones, five emperors, and three kings. The three august ones, five emperors, and three kings did not find it in themselves either. They investigated the tao of heaven-and-earth and taught it. Therefore, if those who learn are focused on tao, then nothing is equal to grounding it in heaven-and-earth, examining it among the Former Kings, taking evidence from Confucius, and verifying it in the present. When the four are in perfect agreement and he tries to progress, then in whatever his knowledge reaches and his strength matches, no matter the distance or the size, he will not lose the correctness of tao.[53]

It is possible to know things, Ssu-ma asserts, that satisfy all the major tests of value. One who knows these things and has the strength to practice them can be sure of acting in accord with tao.

Wang An-shih once remarked that "those who act as *shih* today know they should learn, but some do not know how they should learn."[54] In my view Wang and Ssu-ma each believed the methods he used to reach his conclusions provided shih with a model of "how" to learn. This distinguishes them from Ch'eng I and Su Shih, each of whom explicitly addressed the question of how the individual could know values for himself. The discussions of Wang's and Ssu-ma's scholarship that follow are, among other things, concerned with their methods of learning (i.e., arriving at conclusions about what all shih should believe) and "from where" they learned. How did Wang, who gained a reputation as a Classicist, learn from the Classics? As he wrote a student, "If you wish to illuminate tao, then whatever departs from the Classics of the sages is not worth being illuminated."[55] Similarly Ssu-ma's accomplishments as a historian lead to the question of how he learned from history. As he wrote in his *Comprehensive Mirror for Aid in Government*, history is the "single starting point for ju."[56] Both men were less exclusive in practice than such assertions imply, yet in general Ssu-ma treated the Classics as the beginning of history, whereas for Wang history was a collection of data awaiting integration into the system of the Classics. Although some of the details of "what" they learned will be introduced, I am principally concerned with "how" they learned and shall argue that both men supposed that there was a method of learning that guaranteed the adequacy of the conclusions they reached.

Wang An-shih as a Scholar: The Coherence of the Classics

The material for Wang An-shih's intellectual life is plentiful, although much of it cannot be dated exactly. By the early 1060's, a collection of essays, the *Various Persuasions from Huai-nan* (*Huai-nan tsa-shuo*) and his *Commentary on the "Great Plan"* ("*Hung fan*" *chuan*) were in circulation.[57]

In power he contributed to the writing of official commentaries on the *Documents* and *Songs*, now extant only in remnants,[58] and wrote one himself, the *New Significances of the Institutes of Chou* (*Chou kuan hsin-i*), which is extant. After that he also wrote a dictionary, the *Explanations of Characters* (*Tzu shuo*), known now only from fragments. As did Ssu-ma Kuang, Wang wrote commentaries on the *Change* and *Classic of Filial Piety*, both lost,[59] and the *Lao-tzu*, which has been reconstructed in part.[60] Late in life he wrote on Buddhist texts, although his commentaries on the *Surangama Sutra*, *Diamond Sutra*, and *Vimalakirti Sutra* are now lost.[61]

There are about fifty undated essays in Wang's collection. Here I shall note recurring themes bearing on the search for values, beginning with Wang's attempt to resolve the tension between cultivating oneself and ordering society.[62] Being "for oneself" (*wei chi*) and being "for others" are equally one-sided, Wang contends in "On Yang [Chu] and Mo [Ti]." True learning begins with the self and ends with being able to guide others.[63] The tension is resolved by filling the self with ideas others can share. One must correct the self with the aim of being able to correct society. Wang argues against the view that when one has attained a pure state things will "correct themselves" spontaneously under one's moral influence. Rather, he corrects himself so as to "make things take their norms from me."[64] The scholar seeks to know what is right for everyone.

The individual who can find these ideas will have the means to become a sage through learning, gain a sense of moral integrity, and act in accord with tao, irrespective of social opinion and reward.[65] The ideas themselves have an ultimate foundation. In "Nine Transformations, Then Reward and Punishment Can Be Addressed," he finds an example in the sequence in the *Chuang-tzu* of nine stages from clarifying heaven and *tao-te* to determining right and wrong and applying rewards and punishments.[66] There is no contradiction between natural, cosmological, and innate and the system of sage government. That is why men can rely on the model of antiquity, a society in which those in power and those below have the same standards, worthy men are employed, and those who learn are rewarded.[67] Heaven-and-earth provide the beginning for the human world, Wang explains in the essay "Lao-tzu," but man has created things necessary to complete what nature has brought into being. "Thus in the past when the sages were in power and took all things as their responsibility, they necessarily instituted the four methods. The four methods are ritual, music, punishment, and policy; these are the means for completing things."[68] Attend to the intents of the sages' "methods," rather than the ultimate source of the things that the sages governed with their methods. "Great Antiquity," in the course of faulting those who defend non-action by imagining a pristine primeval human condition, concludes that what the present should be discussing is "the methods with which [the ancients] transformed men" from beasts to civilized beings.[69]

Wang recognized that some students wanted to "attain the relation between the sage and heaven's tao,"[70] but he had trouble seeing how that unity could be conceptualized.[71] The inclusive, natural tao could not be used to deduce normative principles for human affairs. "If we speak of the whole of tao, then it is present everywhere and does everything. It is not something those who learn can rely upon, nor should they keep their minds on it."[72] Following Han Yü, he denied that terms such as "tao" and "te" referred to inherently normative faculties, although he granted that the ancients used such terms in a normative fashion. He extended this to human nature as well. "It is all right to say that when one leaves the good for the evil, his *hsing* [moral nature] is lost. . . . One may say he has lost his hsing but may not say hsing has no evil. Confucius said, 'Hsing are close; practices are far apart.'[73] He was saying that hsing that are close to each other become distant from each other through practice, and thus practice must be carefully attended to; he did not mean simply that hsing were close to each other."[74] What is good must be determined with reference to social life. "Yang [Hsiung] and Mencius," for example, denies that Mencius meant human nature was only good, arguing instead that (as Yang Hsiung said), it is the source for both good and bad behavior. Knowing the "pattern of hsing and ming" was not adequate, Wang concludes, unless it is combined with an understanding of their proper directions; that is, of the ends self-cultivation should serve.[75] "On Hsing," "Hsing and *Ch'ing*," and "The Origins of Hsing" all can be read as refuting the moral sufficiency of human nature and the implication that talent, external standards, and emotional responses are irrelevant to being moral.[76] Yet Wang also defends a student he describes as "employing his mind on the internal" instead of seeking to get ahead in the world.[77]

Wang's essays are a justification for activism. His repeated objection to Buddhist and Taoist teachings is that they suppose that moral autonomy requires personal union with an ultimate reality and thus disengagement from society. They have not seen the values that enable an individual to transform society from within; they have failed to see the potential unity of self and society. Wang posits a middle level, between higher mysteries and the actualities of existence. This is the level at which the sages worked. Wang takes as an example Tseng-tzu's translation of Confucius's claim that "my tao is thread by one" into "loyalty and reciprocity." Some supposed Confucius's tao was "intuitive [*shen-ming*] and unfathomable." In fact, "loyalty capable of realizing the self and reciprocity capable of realizing things," Wang writes, was something "even the tao of Confucius could not improve on."[78] There are values and virtues that can be practiced all the time and they can be defined and ranked.[79]

The sages must have apprehended tao with their minds, Wang wrote in the 1040's, but they did things others could know. One did not have to be a sage himself. "The worthy is not always in agreement with the sage in [the matter of] conduct. It is simply that his knowledge is such that he can know the sage."[80] "On Chuang-tzu" takes this further. The sages intended to establish standards "the average man can meet" and discussed them in detail. They recognized standards beyond the ability of the average man, but these they mentioned only sketchily to keep the world from becoming confused.[81] There is nothing wrong with being a sage, but it is essential to know that the sages believed order could be based on what most men actually could do. "Relating the Mean" explains that Confucius did not demand too much of men. "The tao of the sage is simply based on the mean."[82] Assuming that there is a universal basis that allows for specific social guides, whether one draws on it instinctively or calculates acts with derived knowledge, the effect is the same, Wang contends in "Benevolence and Knowledge."[83]

The danger, Wang recognizes, is to equate enduring values with particular forms. He explains in "Bravery and Clemency" that righteousness is doing what is right, not sticking to received definitions of how the righteous man acts in the face of danger.[84] Similarly, in "King and Hegemon," the hegemon seeks a kingly reputation by imitating the affairs of the true king but fails to function as a king. The true king changes with time and thus has achievements truly equal to the ancients.[85] Elsewhere Wang distinguishes between the tao and the "traces" (chi), the recordable words and deeds. If the times are different, to imitate the traces is to lose the tao. "If the times are different and he insists upon doing it the same, then what is the same are the traces and what is different is tao. . . . For a long time the shih of the age have not known that tao cannot be made one [at the level of] traces. . . . The tao of the sages and worthies both come from one, but if they do not adjust in response to changes in the times they are not worth being called sages and worthies. The sage understands the greater adjustments; the worthy understands the lesser ones."[86]

For Wang three conclusions follow from this distinction between tao and "traces" or forms. First, it is not necessary to imitate piecemeal ancient models and precedents. Second, it is permissible to create new forms in one's own day for others to imitate. Third, it is legitimate to do away with received traditions that have resulted from imitating the traces of the past. The customs of the populace must be "corrected," he argues in "On Customs," if we are to provide them with security and prosperity.[87] In "Encouraging Habits" the inertia of habit is said to thwart the implementation of the "tao of the Former Kings."[88]

The point of learning is to find ideas one can extend from oneself to all of society. One can find these ideas in antiquity, for the sages sought to transform society by establishing models all men could adhere to. But how did the sages succeed in implementing their models? Wang's answer in "Rituals That Are Not Ritual" is that the sages "instituted ritual" *systematically* in response to changing historical circumstances and the social mores of the day.[89] The systematic institution of ritual is the true meaning of imitating antiquity, he asserts elsewhere, not the adoption of those ancient rituals that seem appropriate to the present.[90] This is why the Classics are the foundation for thinking about values, he explains in "The Master [Confucius] Was Wiser than Yao and Shun." All sages are equal, they are all on a par with heaven-and-earth and perfectly moral, but Confucius was more complete for he "collected all the affairs of the sages and greatly completed a system for a myriad generations." He could do this because by his time the major transformations in the instituting of systems (*chih fa*) in response to change had taken place. The Classics are simultaneously a cumulative record of historical change and a comprehensive, integrated system.[91] As Wang writes elsewhere, ritual is a coherent system that takes into account human needs and instinctive tendencies.[92]

The Classics provide Wang with the system for organizing everything into an integrated whole. He can then work from that basis to include everything that has emerged since antiquity. As Wang notes in "Selecting Talent," scholars must "comprehend past and present, acquaint [themselves] with rites and rules, the patterns of heaven and the affairs of man, and the changes in policy and instruction."[93] Eventually Wang went a step further. After leaving the chief councillorship, he wrote to his cousin Tseng Kung:

> For long the world has not seen the complete Classics. If one were only to read the Classics, it would not be enough to know the Classics. I thus read everything, from the hundred schools and various masters to [such medical texts as] the *Nan ching* and *Su wen*, the pharmacopeia, and various minor theories, and I inquire of everyone, down to the farmer and the craftswoman. Only then am I able to know the larger structure [*ta-t'i*] of the Classics and be free of doubt. The later ages in which we learn are different from the time of the Former Kings. We must do this if we are fully to know the sages.[94]

In other words, if Wang can see how everything can be put together into a whole, he has truly seen the system of the Classics.

Wang's ability to see the coherence of things, particularly the coherence in the texts of antiquity, came to represent his own unity with "the completeness of heaven-and-earth and the larger structure of the ancients."[95] His interpretations of the Classics supports this. His "method" is exactly what Ou-yang Hsiu rejected in his commentary on the *Songs*: using the arrangement of the text as the key to its intention. This passage from his "Explanation of the Sequence of the *Chou nan* Poems [of the *Songs*]" is representative.

> The governance of the king begins in the family. The orderly arrangement in the family is based in the correct [relationship] between husband and wife. The correct [relationship] between husband and wife depends on seeking a noble lady possessed of virtue as consort to pair with the superior man. Therefore [the *Chou-nan* sequence] begins with "The Ospreys." Now the reason a noble lady is possessed of virtue is that, in the family, her basis is in the affairs of woman's craftwork; therefore this is followed by "The Cloth-plant."[96]

Although the official commentary on the *Songs* is lost, Wang's preface claims that he has recovered the true meaning, lost since the time of Confucius. The *Songs* "are congruent with morality [*tao-te*] above and come to rest in ritual and righteousness below. By imitating the wen of their language, the superior man is stimulated; by following the sequence of their tao, the sage is completed."[97] The quotation above is an example of that sequence. Wang could, he wrote a doubter, use the *Songs* and the *Rites* to "explain each other," because in "such learning as mine . . . their pattern [*li*] is the same."[98]

The passage above illustrates how Wang justifies his interpretation of the intentions of the sages in the Classics. At first glance it seems that Wang is adducing, in an entirely ad hoc manner, moral commonplaces and interpretations to account for the sequence of poems in the *Songs*. In fact, I think that there is a dialectic in which Wang relies on the fixed sequence of the poems to ascertain which moral principle, among a wide range of possibilities, is intended. The coherence of the argument—that is, his ability to create a necessary or convincing sequence—thus demonstrates the validity of his choice. Because Wang supposes that a Classic contains at least the makings of a coherent system, he can conclude, for example, that in the integrated order of the ancients craftwork was the basis for a wife's virtue. Wang's essays on the *Change* similarly appeal to his ability to see an inherent coherence to the arrangement of the hexagrams, images, and so on, to justify the ideas he uses to account for the sequence.[99] When Wang claims for his commentary on the "Great Plan," another example of this procedure, that he has broken free of centuries of exegetical restraint and "comprehended its intent," he is asserting that he has arrived at its coherence.[100] The *Institutes of Chou*, which lent itself to this approach, represented "the presence of tao in the affairs of government,"[101] the *Songs* dealt mainly with ethical conduct, and the "Great Plan" put many of the pieces together.[102] The one Classic Wang excluded from the New Policies curriculum, the *Spring and Autumn Annals*, did not lend itself to this kind of programmatic analysis.

An extreme case (to my mind) is Wang's explanation of the *Ho t'u* and *Lo shu*, the [Yellow] River Chart and the Lo [River] Writing, which tradition held to be the divine origins of the *Change*.

Confucius said, "From the River came forth the Chart and from the Lo came forth the Writing; the sage took them as a standard."[103] That the Chart had to come from the River and [what came from] the Lo was not called a chart, whereas the Writing had to come from the Lo and [what came from] the River was not called a writing—I understand this. It was because a chart was to show the tao of heaven, and a writing was to show the tao of man. It must be that the River was what joined to heaven and a chart refers to images. What brings about an image is called heaven;[104] therefore a dragon was made to bear it on its back, and it came from the River, for the dragon excels at changing and the tao of heaven values change. The Lo was what was at the center of earth, and a writing refers to models. What imitates models is called man;[105] therefore a tortoise was made to bear it on its back, and it came from the Lo, for the tortoise is good for divination and the tao of man values divination. Such was the so-of-itself intention of heaven-and-earth and such was the reason the sage, in the *Change*, took his measure from [the Chart and Writing].[106]

Everything Wang says is, taken item by item, an acceptable common-place. The power of his comments lies in showing that the givens actually form an inclusive whole and thus reveal what they really mean. Wang's point is that this is what they really mean. Once he can locate his parts in his whole, he can assert that "such was the so-of-itself intention of heaven-and-earth and such was the reason the sage. . . ." The coherence of his inclusive arrangement is the grounds for determining real value.

Wang knew what he was doing. Moreover, he believed the coherence he saw corresponded to innate human qualities. In a school inscription from 1065, in the course of explaining why the Ch'in had been unable to eradicate ancient ideals, he asserts: "The morality of the Former Kings came from the patterns [*li*] of *hsing-ming*, and the patterns of *hsing-ming* came from men's minds. The *Songs* and *Documents* could accord with and reach [men's minds], [the Ch'in] could not take away what they had and give them what they did not have. Although the Classics were lost, what came from men's minds was still present."[107] Wang can think his sightings of the coherence in texts corresponds to their intention because coherence is of the mind and the Classics are in accord with the innate patterns of the mind. "On the Great Man" also makes a connection between transcendent intuition and social virtues. "The tao of the ancient sages always 'entered into the spiritual' [*ju yü shen*]. . . . Their tao existed in the midst of empty silence and invisibility; when it was present in a man, it was called virtue. Thus although the tao of man is spiritual, [men] could not refer to themselves in terms of the spiritual but in terms of virtues only."[108] In

"Ritual and Music" Wang uses the term *ching*, something essential and refined that can be distinguished from human culture but is necessary to it, to explain why there was no contradiction between the integrated order of antiquity and cosmic tao.

This is why the numerology of the calendar, the models of heaven-and-earth, and the abodes of men were all constructed by the sages of earlier times who attained the essential and loved learning. Later men preserved their completed models, but how were they to understand their origins from them? . . . Therefore, when the ancients spoke of tao, nothing was prior to heaven-and-earth; when they spoke of heaven-and-earth, nothing was prior to the person; when they spoke of the person, nothing was prior to the hsing; and when they spoke of the hsing, nothing was prior to the essential. The essential is that by which heaven is high and the earth is thick; it is that by which the sage is on a par with [heaven-and-earth].[109]

The essential is that which makes the unity of heaven-and-earth and man possible; without it men would not be able to continue the functions that the forms are intended to serve.

Wang's most philosophical essay, "On Attaining Unity," contends that there is a necessary dialectic between the analysis of phenomena and the spiritual fathoming of unity.[110] "Now one who cannot get the essence of all the significances [*i*] of all under heaven cannot enter *shen*. [But] if he cannot enter *shen*, then he cannot get the essence of all the principles under heaven. . . . This ought to be as one, but [the passage] must speak of it in dual terms simply because it is speaking about their sequences."[111] The sages can do both. The essay opens with what I take to be a straightforward claim for coherence as the test of meaning.

All the ten thousand things have an ultimate normative pattern [*chih-li*] to them. If one can get the essence of their pattern [*li*], he is a sage. The tao of getting the essence of their pattern lies simply in attaining their unity. If one attains their unity, then all things under heaven can be apprehended without calculation. The *Change* says, "Unity attained, yet a hundred considerations."[112] It is speaking of the hundred considerations all reverting to unity. If one is able to attain unity and get the essence of all patterns under heaven, then he can enter *shen*. Once he has entered *shen*, then [he has reached] the ultimate of tao. Now when thus, he is at a moment of "no thought, no action, tranquil and unmoving."[113] However, there are certainly affairs under heaven that can be thought about and acted on, thus he must "comprehend their causes."[114] This is why the sage also values being able to "attain practice."[115]

Attaining unity, seeing how things form a coherent whole, guarantees that one has determined the pattern for the things in question.

Learning is figuring out how things fit together in a coherent system; thus it is to know how things ought to be, to arrive at their normative pattern. The process Wang calls "attaining unity" thus reveals universal standards. For Wang the process of learning is universal: all things have their patterns, and the human mind has its innate faculties. In practice, however, Wang brings the process of learning to bear on wen, the textual tradition, rather than on things themselves. Wang's *Explanations of Characters* (*Tzu shuo*), the "dictionary" distributed to the schools as part of the New Policies curriculum, illustrates this. The work itself is lost, but he employs his method of character analysis in his commentary on the *Institutes of Chou*, from which I have taken the following example.[116] It occurs in a series of similar definitions of the characters used to refer to the bureaucracy; it explains "shih" (i.e., the elite), in this Classic a term for a lower-ranking officer.

The character *shih* 士 and *kung* [artisan] 工 and *ts'ai* [talent] 才 are all derived from *erh* [two] 二 and from *kun* [vertical stroke] |. The *ts'ai* [talent] extends to all places; therefore it extends out above and below 才. The *kung* [artisan] merely prepares human devices; therefore it extends out neither above nor below 工. If the shih is not a complete ts'ai, it would be proper also that he [like the artisan] would not extend out at all. However, being one who has set his will on tao, he therefore extends out at the top 士. The shih is one who *shih* [serves] 事 others. Therefore "shih" is also glossed as "serve." If he serves others, then he is not yet able to use knowledge to command others [thus he ranks below the grandee; this also explains why the vertical does not extend past the bottom horizontal], and he is not one whom others serve. Therefore, [one who is] not yet married is called a "shih" [this is another way in which the shih differs from the grandee].[117]

In these and other cases, Wang assumes the given referents of the terms discussed. His goal is to define the normative function of that thing in relation to other things, their roles as parts of an integrated system. The coherence of his account of a set of characters constructed from various arrangements of the same elements proves that he has gotten the essential principle for each one.

Wang is rectifying names, the first task of government in the *Analects*,[118] by using patterns inherent in written characters to define norms for the things the characters refer to. The premise of the *Tzu shuo* was that it had become necessary to recover the true, but lost, meanings. Wang took the *Tzu shuo* seriously, as Winston Lo has shown. Wang's introduction and memorial of submission explain that the particular structure of a character has "moral significance" (*i*) and is "based on what is so-of-itself" even though characters were "instituted by men." Writing began with the sages, and although the pool of characters grew and forms and pronunciation changed, the moral significance remained inherent in their structure. His purpose is just as clear: "to unify morality," just as the sages did by regularly systematizing the writing system. It is true, Wang admits, that the Ch'in's introduction of the clerical script was a radical break in terms of forms. "Heaven was allowing This Culture of Ours to be lost." Yet the deeper, meaningful pattern remained for him to recover. His introduction to the *Tzu shuo* concludes: "How could it not be but that Heaven plans to restore This Culture of Ours and is using me to aid its beginning? Therefore teaching and learning must begin from this. Those able to understand this will already have nine-tenths of the ideas of morality."[119] In the *Tzu shuo*, then, Wang An-shih thought he had at last begun the process of restoring This Culture of Ours, by finding in the written language the moral guides necessary for an integrated world.

I suggest that Wang An-shih was developing a way of learning that justified a way of governing he believed was true to tao. The material foundation for this way of learning was the Classics of antiquity as written documents; his learning was his method for deriving values from those documents. The texts and their writing occupied the middle ground between the unitary tao of the cosmos and social life because they were the traces of the sages as men whose minds realized tao. Studying antiquity was practice for governing and the source of necessary ideas for governing: it taught one how to integrate things and the inherent norms of things. At the same time, Wang saw integration and coherence as the natural processes of the human mind. In the dialectic between Our Culture and the mind, heaven and man became one, for the task of the mind was to recover the inherent coherence of a culture grounded in the natural coherence of the sages' minds. His vision of the unity of the tao of heaven-and-earth and the historical tao of the sages allowed Wang to suppose that he had a basis for instituting a new cultural order, one that did not need to continue past traces yet could claim true unity with antiquity.

Ssu-ma Kuang as a Scholar: The Consistency of History

Beginning in the early 1060's and continuing through his fifteen-year withdrawal from court (1071–85), Ssu-ma Kuang produced a series of historical works. The *Chronological Charts* (*Li-nien t'u*), in 5 *chüan* submitted in 1064, covered the 1,362 years from 403 B.C. to A.D. 959. Ssu-ma included the chronological summary of political events in the *Charts* in his *Record of Examining the Past* (*Chi-ku lu*), an extant work.[120] This version contains 36 entries in which Ssu-ma evaluates the various states and their rulers.[121] The *Charts* became the outline for the *Comprehensive Mirror for Aid in Government* (*Tzu-chih t'ung-chien*), the first section of which Ssu-ma submitted in 1066 as the *Comprehensive Treatise* (*T'ung-chih*), in 8 *chüan*, covering the years 403 to 207 B.C. With the *Treatise* Ssu-ma gained court support for work on the *Comprehensive Mirror*. This 294-*chüan* book, covering 403 B.C.–A.D. 959, was finally submitted in 1084, together with an "Examination of Discrepancies" and a "Table of Contents," each in 30 *chüan*. In 1081 Ssu-ma submitted the *Tables of the Hundred Offices (Pai-kuan piao)*. Commissioned by the court, this was meant primarily to explain the Sung bureaucratic system. Ssu-ma included the accompanying record of political events for the years 960–1067 in his *Record of Examining the Past*.[122] This he submitted in 20 *chüan* in 1086, making his chronology complete by adding a review of the period from the sage king Fu Hsi through 402 B.C. Thus he wrote a chronology of all of Chinese history. These works were officially recognized and, particularly in the case of the *Mirror*, produced with government financial support, although Ssu-ma maintained independent editorial control.[123]

Ssu-ma Kuang's intellectual interests during this period were not limited to history.[124] Probably in 1081 Ssu-ma finished a work now known as *Mr. Ssu-ma's Letters and Ceremonies (Ssu-ma shih shu i)*. The "letters" section gives the proper forms for memorials, private letters according to the relative status of the correspondents, and letters to family members according to their relationship. The bulk of the text is devoted to rituals of capping, marriage, and, in greatest detail, mourning.[125] In both regards Ssu-ma was drawing his material from historical traditions, adjusting it to better fit modern life. Ssu-ma also participated in various dictionary projects. Like Wang, he believed that words had normative significance, but for Ssu-ma their definitions could be based on earlier dictionaries.[126] On the lighter side was a small work entitled *New Rules for Pitch-pot (T'ou-hu hsin-ko)* of 1072, in which he encouraged shih to play pitch-pot as an alternative to chess. Chess taught men to value deceit; pitch-pot, he argued, came closest to the function of the ancient ritual of archery.[127]

He reviewed the writings of the "former ju" as well. Ssu-ma at first singled out Hsun-tzu and Yang Hsiung as the only two among the hundred schools to have apprehended the "correct methods of the tao of the Former Kings."[128] He rejected Mencius, however, writing in his *Doubts About Mencius [I Meng]* (1082–85) that Mencius encouraged men to disregard the principle of hierarchy Ssu-ma had come to see as the essence of the tao of the sage.[129] He also doubted Wang T'ung's importance, objecting for example that Wang undermined the idea of a necessary connection between the mind and the "traces" of the sage, a failing that allowed Buddha and Lao-tzu to be seen as sages as well. The popularity of Wang's *On Centrality (Chung shuo)* he credited to literary fashions.[130] Ssu-ma had no particular fondness for Han Yü, nor evidently for Ou-yang Hsiu, and certainly not for Wang An-shih.

Eventually Ssu-ma decided that Hsun-tzu was, like Mencius, "too narrow" to be taken as a true interpreter of the tao of the sage.[131] But he never lost his appreciation of Yang Hsiung.[132] He prepared a collected commentary on the *Exemplary Sayings* (*Fa yen*) and, in 1082, prepared one for the *Supreme Mystery* (*T'ai hsuan*), Yang Hsiung's more systematic alternative to the *Change*.[133] He was Yang's greatest defender at a time when Yang's ideas were losing appeal.[134] The *Supreme Mystery* was congruent with the Classics, he held; after Confucius Yang alone "knew the tao of the sage." Ssu-ma saw Yang as connecting political order and "mystery" (*hsuan*), which Ssu-ma took as the term for an ultimate cosmic source for ongoing creation. Yang had found the middle ground of principles that applied to both heaven-and-earth and the political order.[135] Eventually Ssu-ma began to work such matters out for himself with his own commentary on the *Change*, which asserted the systematic parity between heaven and man and the equivalence between the moral principles and numerology of the *Change*,[136] and his numerological-cosmological imitation of the *Supreme Mystery*, the *Hidden Vacuity* (*Ch'ien-hsu*).[137]

Ssu-ma Kuang was aware that his horizons had extended to include issues of heaven-and-earth and human internality.[138] His commentary on the *Change* stands in contrast to his fear in the mid-1050's of "getting stuck" in yin and yang and losing sight of "human affairs."[139] In 1049 Ssu-ma wrote that "the tao of the sages and worthies is entirely conveyed by books."[140] In "On the Origin of Destiny" ("Yuan ming") of 1056, he contended that the sages taught men to know and order man, not heaven, and objected to seeking heaven's intent before understanding the "pattern for man" (*jen-li*).[141] It is possible that Ssu-ma's friendships with Shao Yung, the Ch'eng brothers, and others in Loyang in the 1070's persuaded him to extend the boundaries of his claims to include heaven-and-earth.[142] Ssu-ma's later writing also evidences a growing interest in the mind and in internal cultivation. "The lesser man orders the traces," Ssu-ma wrote in 1083, "the superior man orders the mind."[143] This supported his conviction, consistent from the 1050's through 1085, that the relations between heaven and man meant one should be content with one's lot and work at being ethical; talent was given by heaven, and success was a matter of fate; there was no way to guarantee personal success.[144] The goal of cultivation was to attain a state in which one would not be disturbed and distracted by the enticements of social reward (or punishment) but would practice one's tao and be in accord with ritual.[145] Ssu-ma's writings in the 1080's on the concept of *chung-ho* (centrality and harmony) in the "Doctrine of the Mean" argue that chung-ho was at once the essential principle of heaven-and-earth, the core concept of the sages, and the foundation of ritual and order.[146] Yet the philosophical interest of this is questionable. "Centrality," he contended, referred to the virtue of "neither going too far nor not far enough," not to internality. The mind had to be fixed on some-

thing and ordered with something, not emptied or guided by nothingness. There was no "innate knowledge from heaven" that would emerge
by trying to empty the mind of knowledge and feeling. Keeping one's
thoughts on centrality at all times and moderating all daily activities
trained one to be spontaneously moderate and balanced in responding to
things.[147] Ssu-ma was averse to the "lofty theories" of his contemporaries.
His commentary on the *Tao te ching*'s opening line, "The tao that can be
spoken of is not the constant tao," is: "The tao can be spoken of, but it is
not what common men call tao."[148] One of the more philosophical lines
from the *Change*, "Fathom pattern [*li*] and realize the nature [*hsing*] to
arrive at the decree [*ming*],"[149] means simply "Right or not right is *li*.
Talented or not talented is hsing. Succeeding or not succeeding is *ming*."[150]
Ch'eng I's "investigating things" (*ko-wu*) was Ssu-ma's "fending things
off."[151] He insisted that he was not speaking of "having no mind," although mental equilibrium required "cutting off intention."[152] Internal
cultivation helped Ssu-ma stand by the ideas he had acquired. "Debating
Hsing" and "Debating Ch'ing" from 1066 are quite explicit and very
much in line with the *Hsun-tzu*: human nature is not originally good; that
is why one must learn. Seeing the patterns of the tao of heaven-and-earth
leads to behavior at odds with human feeling; that is why men should
follow ritual.[153]

Ssu-ma's ideas about the tao men can follow appear first in his historical
studies; his cosmological studies and his ideas about self-cultivation are
congruent with them. His contention that the past can guide the present
rests on a basic claim that the deciding factors in the creation and demise of
a polity are consistent throughout history. In the introduction to the
Chronological Charts, he phrases it thus: "The tao of order and disorder is
on a single thread [*i kuan*] through past and present."[154] In submitting the
Comprehensive Treatise in 1066, he wrote: "The sources of order and
disorder have the same structure [*t'i*] in past and present."[155] He could
explain why each state initially succeeded and why it failed. Numerous
variations and particularities revealed consistent principles. The major
tenets of Ssu-ma's political advice are also found in his histories.[156] "From
the beginning of man to the end of heaven-and-earth," he writes, "for
those who possess the state, although there are myriad kinds of variations,
they do not go beyond these."[157] This search for timeless principles recalls
Wang An-shih; yet if the test of Wang's conclusions was coherence, for
Ssu-ma the proof was consistency: through the millennia the principles
were the same.

But if all history teaches the same lessons, why is it necessary for Ssu-
ma Kuang to write his histories when he can distill their essence into
memorials? Here I see another parallel with Wang An-shih's efforts. Like

Wang, Ssu-ma supposes that the texts refer to something real, in this case the political history of dynasties. The principles he is finding are consistent through change, yet they are inherent in the phenomena he is studying. "What ought to be" is embedded in and derived from "what is." Ssu-ma's writing his own history is parallel to Wang's writing his own dictionary. In the process of studying it, the reader learns how to analyze things so as to determine their value (just as one learned Wang's method of character analysis) and, at the same time, what those particular values are (just as one learns the moral functions inherent in the particular characters). Still, there are differences. Wang's synchronic approach aims to include everything and to show how each part is interdependently related to other parts; his model is the unified system of the *Institutes of Chou*. Moreover, it insists that men turn their attention toward things and invites them to construct the parts into wholes for themselves, restrained only by the need to find a place for everything. Ssu-ma's diachronic study shows that there are necessary principles, but that human action is also constrained by circumstances. The model is the *Spring and Autumn Annals*, whose record of events was thought to reveal timeless principles of order. Men need a historical perspective on their own moment; although they cannot radically change the world, they can shift the direction of events if they act early enough. The *Chronological Charts*, for example, repeatedly notes the moment at which something was or should have been done to prevent the demise of a state and the point at which a dynasty could not be saved.[158]

The *Comprehensive Mirror* was Ssu-ma's greatest work. Much has been written about the procedures for writing it and his collaborators, Liu Pin (1023–89), Liu Shu (1032–78), and Fan Tsu-yü (1041–98).[159] But Ssu-ma was not willing to let the events speak for themselves. He interjects comments on dynasties in the *Chronological Charts* and the *Mirror* almost 200 times; about 80 of these interjections are Ssu-ma's own, and the remainder are quotations from other historians and writers.[160] The *Comprehensive Mirror* reveals the lessons of history. The objectivity of Ssu-ma's approach is not the issue. Ssu-ma was sure that history revealed constant principles; given that he chose to focus on the political history that supported his conclusions, he did his best to provide a comprehensive and impartial record that made his findings obvious. The interesting question, as many scholars have found, is not Ssu-ma's method of compilation but his meaning.[161] It is clear from Ssu-ma's memorials from the 1060's and the reappearance of the events and conclusions of the *Chronological Charts* in the *Mirror* that his ideas antedated his opposition to the New Policies. At the level of the particular there is little that is new, with the exception of passages that reflect his interest in heaven-and-earth and the mind.[162]

What seems to be more pronounced is a sense that dynasties exist to preserve order as Ssu-ma understands it and that the maintenance of order depends upon having the right ideas about what is necessary to it.

An argument about how Ssu-ma Kuang learned from history and what he learned, if it is to be persuasive, must take the *Comprehensive Mirror* into account. I shall make my case through a translation and analysis, supplemented with references to other parts of the text, of Ssu-ma's long comment on the first entry in the chronology.* The entry, for the year 403 B.C., the twenty-third year of the Chou king Wei-lieh, reads: "[Chou] for the first time commands the great officers of Chin, Wei Ssu, Chao Chi, and Han Ch'ien to serve as feudal lords." For Ssu-ma this one incident, the effective division of the state of Chin into three states, captures the essence of the "decline" of the Chou order. He uses it to explain the timeless principles of order, now being contravened in form as well as practice. Ssu-ma's comment begins:

Your Minister Kuang says, "Your Minister has heard that of the son of heaven's responsibilities [*chih*] none is greater than ritual [*li*], that in ritual nothing is greater than roles [*fen*], and that in roles nothing is greater than names [*ming*]. What is ritual? It is the guidelines [*chi-kang*]. What are the roles? They are ruler and minister. What are the names? They are duke, feudal lord, councillor, and great officer [*kung, hou, ch'ing,* and *tai-fu*].

Ssu-ma is using "ritual" in several senses. It is the division of authority between superior and inferior positions or ruler and minister. It is the cultural forms and practices (the rites and ritual paraphernalia) appropriate to various positions and duties (the "names") in the overall political structure. Ritual is both an idea and the cultural forms that manifest that idea. Ritual is also the *chi-kang* of the state, the rules that order relationships between men. For Ssu-ma the collapse of these rules makes political recovery impossible, as happened after the An Lu-shan rebellion when the ruler failed to "correct the ritual of superior and inferior."[163]

Ssu-ma next develops the assertion that ritual is the ruler's first responsibility.

Now, the reason that the [territory] within the four seas and the populace, although broad and multitudinous, took direction from a single man, so that even the exceptionally strong and extraordinarily talented dared not but to rush to serve, was that ritual served as the *chi-kang* for them. For this reason the son of heaven coordinated the three dukes, the three dukes led the feudal lords, the feudal lords directed the councillors and great officers, and the councillors and great officers ordered the shih and commoners. The noble oversaw the humble, and the

---

*Ssu-ma's comment is given in its entirety in the set-off block quotations that follow in the remainder of this section.

humble served the noble. Superiors directing inferiors was like the heart employing the limbs and the root and trunk ordering the branches and leaves. Inferiors serving superiors was like the limbs guarding the heart and the branches and leaves screening the root and trunk. Only then was it possible for superiors and inferiors to protect each other and for the state to be ordered and secure. Therefore I say, of the son of heaven's responsibilities nothing is greater than ritual.

Ssu-ma's ideal political structure is a combination of ancient feudalism and imperial centralism. It is a pyramid in which any two levels exist in a relationship of ruler/minister or superior/inferior. Responsibilities are delegated—the ruler does not direct the ministers of the feudal lords—but authority ultimately comes from the ruler, who must ensure that the structure is maintained. In his commentary on the *Change*, Ssu-ma treats this structure as the human version of the sequence in which the supreme ultimate (*t'ai-chi*) gives rise to the two, four, eight, . . . with the king being the supreme ultimate.[164] In fact, Ssu-ma has two ways of accounting for the political structure. On the one hand, the sages took their standard from heaven-and-earth; hierarchical authority is natural.[165] On the other hand, the Former Kings established the levels of authority because, in addition to "according with the inherent pattern," they grasped that human sentiment made men unwilling to take direction from others of the same rank. The populace needed *tai-fu*, who in turn needed feudal lords, who in turn required a son of Heaven.[166] Antiquity thus gave the basic structure; the problem for those who lived later was to unite existing powerholders and regions with that structure so that inferiors would follow superiors.[167] This had most recently taken place at the end of the Five Dynasties.[168] Without it no polity was possible. On this basis Ssu-ma denies that there can be a qualitative difference between the king and the hegemon; not only do they share aims and methods in maintaining a unified structure of authority, but also they succeed and fail for the same reasons.[169] This is the measure for evaluating a state; Ssu-ma disavows the traditional idea of defining a single, continuous line of legitimate dynasties through history.[170] Although the names may change, the effective and lasting structure of authority is the same throughout history. If later men understand this, they can act accordingly; as Ssu-ma puts it, they can restore the tao and ritual of the Former Kings.[171]

At the heart of this political structure are the roles of ruler and minister.

King Wen arranged the sequence of the *Book of Change* with the hexagrams *ch'ien* and *k'un* at the beginning. Confucius appended [an elaboration on the significance of this] saying, "Heaven is high and earth is low; *ch'ien* and *k'un* were fixed. Low and lofty were set forth, and the noble and humble had their positions."[172] He was saying that the positions of ruler and minister were as unchangeable as heaven and earth. The *Spring and Autumn Annals* degrades the feudal lords and honors the royal house. Even when the person of the king was insignificant, he was ranked above the feudal lords [as in the sequence by which the *Annals* gives the date]. From this we can see that the sage was never anything but attentive to the boundary between ruler and minister. If the [ruler] is not as cruel as the [evil last kings] Chieh or Chou or as benevolent as [the founding kings] T'ang and Wu, to whom men returned and heaven gave the mandate, then the roles of ruler and minister ought to be maintained to the death. So if Wei-tzu had replaced [his half-brother, the evil King] Chou, [their ancestor, the Shang founder King] T'ang would have [continued to receive sacrifices] on a par with heaven, and if Chi Cha had [accepted] rulership of Wu [from his brother], then T'ai-po [the ancestral founder of the feudal state of Wu] would have [continued to] consume the blood [of sacrifices]. Yet the fact that these two men preferred losing the state and did not act [as rulers] truly was because they held that the great standard of ritual must not be disordered. Therefore I say that in ritual nothing is greater than the roles.

The ruler/minister or superior/inferior relationship exists between all levels. But it is a reciprocal relationship, as between yang and yin, a point made in Ssu-ma's commentary on the *Change* as well.[173] It is entirely "natural," the human equivalent of the relations between heaven and earth. Elsewhere in the *Mirror* Ssu-ma equates it with the relation between husband and wife as the "tao of man" and the "great norm."[174] This is how various levels are bound together, for all except the ruler and the common people are rulers to some and ministers to others. It refers also to a division of responsibilities between various levels; one side should not interfere with the tasks of the other. Many of Ssu-ma's comments address this relationship, for it may be natural and vital to the survival of the overall structure but practicing it is hard.

The ruler/minister relationship, though complementary, is unequal. In the *Mirror*, as in his memorials, Ssu-ma stresses the ruler's use of "reward and punishment" in directing his ministers. Ministers who do not perform well can be dismissed, a principle of personnel management that is applicable to all levels.[175] Ssu-ma insists, however, that ministers, or those in subordinate roles, may not try to get rid of their ruler or superiors. The passage quoted above argues this in an extreme case: brothers of rulers who are begged to take power but refuse, even though it means the loss of the dynasty. And yet, again and again Ssu-ma depicts rulers as short-sighted, self-interested, uncaring, uncritical, and generally incompetent. Ssu-ma finds few positive models of rulers.[176] Ministers do have options. They can, as above, stand aside and watch the dynasty collapse. They do not have to serve a bad ruler, but they may not join in deposing him.[177] If a ruler is at all receptive to criticism, and Ssu-ma points out that many are not, ministers can try to show him the error of his ways. No one, not even the sages, is free of error.[178]

This creates an interesting tension. As subordinates to be managed through rewards and punishments, inferiors are presumed to be self-interested. But if they are good at being ministers, if they are truly "loyal," they must be public-minded. In his commentary on the *Change*, Ssu-ma suggests one resolution: it is all a matter of horizons; the self-interest of the sage includes all under heaven.[179] In the *Mirror*, however, he accepts the tension that comes from demanding that ministers be both independent of the ruler and subordinate to him.[180] Ministers choose to serve, after all; rulers are born rulers (Ssu-ma recognizes but does not dwell on the prevalence of hereditary offices in antiquity).[181] "The loyal minister," Ssu-ma writes, "sets forth the general structure [*ta-t'i*] to rectify what is wrong in the mind of the ruler."[182] Reward and punishment, Ssu-ma insists, must be based on an understanding of right and wrong.[183] As Anthony Sariti has argued, against the view that Ssu-ma is a proponent of autocracy, this shifts moral authority over politics from ruler to minister.[184] If not all ministers choose to fulfill this role—Ssu-ma does not idealize ministers either—they still share responsibility for knowing the structure and thus for determining right and wrong. The *Mirror* explains what that structure is. As far as I can tell, Ssu-ma sees no gray area in which the choice is morally ambiguous. The distinction between morally superior men and lesser men is real; superior men know what is right and wrong, work to get the ruler to see it, and maintain their autonomy.[185] One thing such men know is that the ruler is the supreme ultimate of the political structure. But they also know, or at least Ssu-ma knows, that there are always enough shih in the world to fulfill the role of loyal ministers and guide the ruler in attaining true order.[186] The conclusion Ssu-ma draws from this, in every instance, is that political failure is the fault of the ruler, the one responsible for choosing the men who tell him what should be done.

Ssu-ma next turns to the importance of names (*ming*) in maintaining distinctions in roles.

Now, ritual distinguishes noble and humble, ranks near and distant relatives, regulates the many matters, and structures all activities. Were it not for the names, it would not be apparent; were it not for the accoutrements [i.e., the "devices" for making clear rank and position], it would not be manifest. Only after there are names to command them and accoutrements to differentiate them will the proper places for superior and inferior be clear. This is the great constant of ritual. If the names and accoutrements are lost, how can ritual survive by itself? In the past, when Chung-shu Yü-hsi had been of service to Wei, he refused the city [offered as reward] and requested the ornamental trappings for his horse [that would mark him as being of a higher rank]. Confucius thought it would have been better to give him more cities, for names and accoutrements were not to be granted [unless one had attained that rank].[187] The ruler was responsible for this; once correct policy was lost, the state followed. When the ruler of Wei invited Confucius to make policy, Confucius wished first to rectify names. He thought that if the names were not rectified the populace would not know how to act.[188] Now ornamental trappings are a small thing, yet Confucius begrudged them. Rectifying names is a minor concern, yet Confucius put it first. Truly it was because once names and accoutrements were disordered superior and inferior would lack the means to protect each other. Now, all problems begin with something insignificant but culminate as something obvious. Because the sage considers the long-term [consequences], he is able to attend to what is insignificant and correct it. The awareness of the multitude is limited; therefore they always wait until it is obvious before trying to remedy it. Correcting the insignificant requires little strength, yet the achievement is great. Remedying the obvious takes all one's strength, yet one accomplishes nothing. When the *Change* says, "Hoarfrost underfoot; solid ice is not far off," and the *Documents* says, "In one or two days there may occur ten thousand springs of things," they refer to this sort of matter.[189] Therefore I say that in roles nothing is greater than the names.

This paragraph marks the transition to Ssu-ma's analysis of the significance of the events of 403 B.C. The collapse of the ruler/minister relationship and ritual as the political structure begins when inferiors encroach in minor ways on the prerogatives of their superiors. It may be cheaper in the beginning but, as Confucius saw, it is infinitely more costly in the end. For Ssu-ma reward and punishment is the ruler's office; a ruler whose rewards are both inappropriate to the deed and inconsistent with the basic principles of the polity has abrogated his most important responsibility.

The passage just quoted also illuminates Ssu-ma's attitude toward "culture." Names and accoutrements represent the wen of ritual. Elsewhere in the *Mirror* he explains: "Now, ritual and music have a basis, and they have a *wen* [external form]. Centrality and harmony are the basis. Appearance and sound are the extension. Neither side can be unilaterally disregarded. The Former Kings maintained the basis of ritual and music, and it never departed from their minds, even for an instant. They practiced the wen of ritual and music, and it was never distant from their body, even for a moment. It flourished in the inner apartments, it was manifested at court, it spread over the villages and neighborhoods, it extended to the feudal lords, and it flowed everywhere within the four seas. From sacrifices and the military to the daily necessities of life, ritual and music always included everything. So it went for decades and centuries, until the transformation through governance was complete and 'the male and female phoenix came with their measured gambolling.'[190] When there is no basis but only the extension, when it is practiced for one day and set aside for a hundred, it will truly be difficult to try to change customs. . . . Now, ritual does not mean majestic ceremonies, but without majestic ceremonies ritual cannot be put into effect. Music does not mean sounds and notes, but without sounds and notes music cannot be perceived. A mountain provides an analogy: it will not do to take a clump of dirt and a rock and call it a mountain, but if you get rid of all the dirt and rocks, where is the mountain? Thus it is said, 'Without a basis it will not be established; without wen it will not be practiced.' "[191] Ssu-ma distinguishes between the underlying values and the outward forms, the wen of ritual and music. When the forms embody the values, a defense of the forms defends the values. But the connection between culture and values is a possible, not a necessary or natural, connection. Once the connection is made, however, the continued existence of the polity depends upon maintaining the received culture.

Ssu-ma uses this understanding of cultural forms to analyze the decline of Chou and the reason for its political survival during four centuries of decline. This is background to the events of 403 B.C.

Alas. [The Chou kings] Yu [r. 781–771 B.C.] and Li [r. 878–828 B.C.] lost virtue, and the Chou tao had been declining day by day. The *chi-kang* was falling apart. Inferiors were encroaching, and superiors were being replaced. Feudal lords were launching punitive campaigns on their own, and their great officers were usurping state policy. Seven- or eight-tenths of the general structure of ritual had been lost. But [the reason] that the sacrifices to [the founding kings of Chou] Wen and Wu [were as continuous as] silken threads joined together must have been that the Chou descendants were still able to maintain the names and the roles.

Why can I say this? Before this, [the hegemon] Duke Wen of Chin, having been of great service to the royal house, requested of King Hsiang [r. 651–619 B.C.] the privilege of being carried to his grave through a subterranean passage. King Hsiang refused, saying, "This is a mark of kings. For there to be two kings before the virtue of one has been replaced is something you, Uncle, detest. Had you not known this, why would you have requested permission, since you have the land and the passage?"[192] Duke Wen was then fearful and did not dare disobey. Thus although Chou's territory was no greater than that of [such small states as] Ts'ao or T'eng and its populace no more numerous than that of [the small] Chu and Chü, for several hundred years it was the ultimate lord over all under heaven; even such powers as Chin, Ch'u, Ch'i, and Ch'in did not dare make themselves superior. Why? Simply because the names and the roles were still being preserved. Now, the Chi family in Lü, T'ien Ch'ang in Ch'i, Po-kung in Ch'u, and Chih-po in Chin all had the power to drive their rulers out and rule themselves. They did not do so, not because their strength was inadequate or their hearts unwilling, but because they feared that if they betrayed their names and contravened their roles all under heaven would join in executing them.

If roles and names are maintained, even if the structure of political authority has deteriorated, the dynasty and a good degree of political order can survive. Here and elsewhere in the *Mirror*, Ssu-ma reiterates a point made in his memorials: if the values necessary for order have become part of custom, the state can survive a period of poor rule.[193] The Spring and Autumn period of Chou history, alluded to here, provides Ssu-ma with a case for examining more carefully his assertion that ritual restrains desire. The sense of right and wrong, morality, stems from the ritual order that operates here. The subordinate feudal lords do want to encroach, but they know it is wrong and hesitate. The ruler knows it is wrong and refuses. And although the Chou ruler lacks his own means of coercion, the general political opinion that encroachment is wrong provides the threat of coercion.

Shared values are fundamental to order. By defending standards, the ruler makes it possible for good ministers to act to maintain order. This is why the government must always act morally rather than expediently, for ultimately the polity's survival depends upon its ability to demonstrate that standards exist. If it cannot demonstrate this, it cannot expect others to act correctly. Ssu-ma returns to this theme in various ways in the *Mirror*. Tao is more important than strategic advantage.[194] "Virtue," the ability to see what is right and stand by it, is more important than "talent."[195] Wrong methods should not be used to correct wrongs.[196] The advantages of good faith in dealing with family, state, and world outweigh the short-term rewards of deceit.[197] Good faith must be kept in relations with the barbarians as well.[198] "Although their *ch'i* is of a different sort, they are the same as human beings in choosing profit over loss and preferring life to death. If one gets the tao for controlling them, they will accord and submit. If one loses that tao, they will revolt and invade."[199] Acting morally toward others simply means fulfilling the responsibilities of one's role in the relationship and demanding of subordinates that they fulfill theirs. This, however, is what King Wei-lieh of Chou ceased to do in 403 B.C.

Now, at this time the great officers of Chin had violated and disregarded their ruler and divided the state of Chin. The son of heaven, since he was unable to punish them, instead gave them honorable status so that they ranked with the feudal lords. Here he was no longer able to defend these inconsequential names and roles so he threw them all away—at this point the ritual of the Former Kings was exhausted.

When the Chou king acquiesced to the demands of the officers of Chin, he gave up the last defense of his dynasty and opened the way to increasing disorder. The *Comprehensive Mirror* begins with this event because it marks the end of classical antiquity. Hereafter the ritual and morality of the sage-kings and a true and lasting political order would never be fully restored. In contrast to Wang An-shih, who saw the decline of the Chou as the result of men imitating past forms rather than instituting a new order on the basis of the ideas of an integrated order, Ssu-ma Kuang understood the decline as a failure to maintain formal standards. But was the Chou ruler really to blame?

Some think that at this time, the Chou house being weak and the three states of Chin being strong, even if he had wished to refuse permission it would not have been possible. This is not so at all. Now, being so strong, had the three Chin not been worried about being executed by all under heaven for contravening righteousness and encroaching on ritual, they would have established themselves without requesting permission of the son of heaven. Had they established themselves without requesting permission, they would have been rebellious ministers. Had there been lords such as [the hegemons] Huan and Wen in the world, they certainly would have honored ritual and righteousness and launched punitive campaigns. Now, for them to ask permission of the son of heaven and for him to grant it means they are feudal lords by the decree of the son of heaven. Who will be able to punish them now? Therefore, with the three Chin being ranked with the feudal lords, the three Chin are not destroying ritual, the son of heaven is destroying it himself. Alas. Once the ritual of ruler and minister was ruined, all under heaven competed for supremacy with cleverness and strength. At this point, even if the descendants of sages and worthies had been the feudal lords, the altars of the states would still have been extinguished and the populace brought close to extinction.[200]

It would have been better for the ruler to stand fast. Had he taken history as his mirror, he would have seen that by requesting permission the Chin officers were recognizing Chou authority. The ruler could not be certain that they would have disobeyed a refusal on his part or that feudal lords would not have punished them. But his agreement made it impossible for good men to act, for good ministers do not go against what their ruler has decreed. The ruler abandoned the moral authority of the Chou. Once that was gone, all restraints were lost. The *chi-kang* was destroyed, and the situation was beyond saving.

The *Comprehensive Mirror for Aid in Government*, as I read it, is intended to show that the idea of a unified hierarchy of political authority is the basic principle for the polity. It follows that the most pressing concern of government is the structure of political relationships. Ssu-ma's reading of history thus attends to the events that reveal how this principle is being realized and contravened, in particular the actions of men with political power in relationship to each other. Ssu-ma is not against laws and institutions; such "public tools of all under heaven" must be applied uniformly and without exception.[201] But they are instruments for maintaining order, not for organizing men to further the common welfare.

The ruler plays the most crucial role in this structure, prompting some readers of the *Mirror* to see Ssu-ma as an apologist for autocracy. Ssu-ma's comments, however, stress the problems rulers create. He notes many bad ministers yet shifts the blame for their misconduct to rulers. The failures of ministers are, by definition, failures of the one who employs them.[202] Emperor Shen-tsung's use of Wang An-shih was simply the latest case. Yet it is true that Ssu-ma's ruler is without equals and challengers. Ritual did not allow for usurpation. Yet Ssu-ma saw how poorly rulers had fulfilled their roles in the past. What was to be done about irresponsible rulers?

I think the *Mirror*, as a monumental effort to shape the opinions of readers, is part of Ssu-ma's answer. Using history to blame rulers for failures of government was a way of trying to make the ruler feel responsible by holding him responsible. Moreover, if shih opinion could be brought to share Ssu-ma's views, at least the emperor's ministers would be on the right track. Ssu-ma, I suggest, was coming to terms with a central political problem of the imperial system in a non-aristocratic world and seeking to find a way to constrain, if not box in, a sovereign with unprecedented power by holding him to extraordinarily high standards. The ruler had to make the right choices, admittedly a difficult task.[203] Ssu-ma could, however, use history to argue that there were fundamental values necessary for both ruler and the shih as responsible members of the state. To make these ideas work, they had to believe that those ideas were real, necessary, and practicable. In this light we may understand Ssu-ma's efforts to show that heaven-and-earth had a similar structure and that the mind could be kept focused on duty.

The New Policies

One of the great aspirations of eleventh-century intellectuals was to see what one had learned put into practice. Wang An-shih came to court in 1068 and proceeded to institute his program. He served as sole chief councillor in 1071–74 and 1075–76 but then retired. Ssu-ma Kuang left the court in 1070 over his opposition to Wang. When he returned in 1085, after the death of Shen-tsung, and became a chief councillor, he set out to abolish the New Policies and return government to its proper course. He died in office in 1086, half a year after Wang. Each man came to power after having argued through writing and scholarship for the larger justifications for his approach to government. Both were convinced that a moral order in the world depended on government, and yet the universality of their political theories not only made the irreconcilability of their approaches clear but also made government through compromise and accommodation an unacceptable alternative.[204]

In 1068 Wang called for immediate action on education, the civil service, agriculture, the military, and finances.[205] Beginning in 1069, he orchestrated the promulgation of policies that would address these problems. He made clear from the start that he would not be concerned with budget deficits, promising the emperor that the employment of men skilled in "managing wealth" would ensure that "revenues will be more than adequate without increasing taxes on the populace." Ssu-ma did not believe this, in part because he did not grasp that the economy could grow more quickly than the population: "The wealth and products that heaven-and-earth produce are of a fixed amount. What is not with the populace is with the government." For Ssu-ma more government revenues meant less for the people.[206] Wang, who seldom worried about this distinction, did increase government revenues tremendously, but it is generally thought that the period saw general economic growth as well.[207] In any case, Wang An-shih's definition of the priorities of the day—managing wealth, changing customs, and establishing institutions—prevailed over Ssu-ma's calls for restraint.[208]

The Major New Policies, in Chronological Order[209]

1. 1069/2 Finance Planning Commission, which drew up the plans for the key policies and circumvented the old bureaucratic leadership. In addition, commissioners were sent to investigate local conditions in agriculture, irrigation, and obligatory local service and to recommend action.

2. 1069/6 Administrative Regulations Commission, which planned the restructuring of the bureaucracy completed in 1082 and centralized financial, administrative, and military planning and operation under the Council of State. Hitherto organs in these three areas had reported directly to the emperor.

3. 1069/7 Equitable Transport Policy, which permitted certain fiscal intendants to meet government needs by buying and selling according to market conditions, rather than relying on fixed local quotas and transport obligations. This policy was replaced by the State Trade Policy in 1072/3.

4. 1069/9 Green Shoots Policy, which loaned money to farmers, and eventually to urban dwellers, at 20 percent interest.

5. 1069/11 Regulations on Agriculture and Water Conservancy, which set rules for recovering fallow land, carrying out local irrigation projects, and undertaking river conservancy.

6. 1070/12 Tithing Policy (*pao-chia fa*), which organized households into units of 10, 50, and 500 for mutual surveillance. Each household with two or more adult males supplied one member for local militia duty. Eventually the tithing units were charged with tax collection.

7. 1071/2 New examination system and policy for schools. The vari-

ous fields were dropped in favor of a single chin-shih examination. In place of the test in poetry, candidates wrote on the greater significance of ten items from the Classic of their choice (*Odes, Documents, Change, Rites of Chou, Book of Rites*) and from the *Analects* or *Mencius*. They also had to write one essay and three policy proposals. Education officials were to be appointed to all prefectures, with special provisions for the northern circuits (*lu*). Income-producing lands were ordered to be set aside for the schools. The long-range goal was to create a graded school system that would produce officials through the Imperial University.

8. 1071/10 Hired Service Policy, which abolished obligatory local service by hiring men to fill local sub-bureaucratic posts. Households paid a cash tax instead.

9. 1072/3 [State] Trade Policy, which established offices in major commercial centers to replace wealthy guild merchants as wholesalers, buying from and selling to smaller merchants and traders, and loaning money to smaller merchants at interest.

10. 1072/8 Land Survey and Equitable Tax Policies, a program to survey land according to standard units, assess the quality of land, and determine ownership, thus facilitating a regrading of households according to wealth and ensuring an equitable distribution of the new obligations.

11. 1073/3 Bureau for Commentaries on the Classics, which prepared commentaries on the *Odes, Documents,* and *Rites of Chou*.

The policies were interdependent: managing wealth required institutions whose effectiveness depended upon training officials and changing customary practices. Making these policies work required total control, and taken together, the policies put the government in command of society. From Wang's perspective, it was good to "unify morality and make customs the same," and he was confident that he knew how to accomplish this. Objections to his policies in part were "divergent opinions" (*i-lun*) that questioned the principles of the whole. As debate flared, leading bureaucrats quickly divided into opposing camps. One opponent described the situation in 1071:

[One] is secure in the constant and practices the old, happy when there are no problems. [The other] transforms the old and changes policy, pleased by the daring to act. . . . [The first] holds that in keeping to the successful policies of the [imperial] ancestors we only need follow those that are beneficial and, on the basis of traditional [policies], repair their deficiencies in order to achieve order. . . . [The second] holds that the [old] policies are rotten and the [old] way exhausted; without a great transformation, we will be incapable of managing things and realizing our purposes.[210]

Wang was immune to counter-arguments. To say that the people were unhappy did not count, for if the court "decided every matter according to moral principles [*i-li*], then popular sentiment (*jen-ch'ing*) ought eventually to change of its own accord."[211] Some objected that the policies ran counter to the patterns of human experience, but Wang was sure they accorded with the inherent patterns of things (*li*) and would necessarily work.[212] Others protested against the center's detailed rules, arguing that policies should be adapted to the local situation. But, said Wang, "heaven-and-earth create the myriad things, yet each thing, even something as small as a blade of grass, has its pattern [*li*]. In governing today, we should ask only whether the policies established harm man or not; we should not rescind them because they deal with the minute."[213]

Wang's educational policy was, as he had promised in 1058, intended to mold the shih. His memorial on the examinations ran: "The selection of shih in antiquity was rooted in schools in every instance. Therefore when morality was unified above, customs were perfected below and the talents of men were such that all were capable of accomplishing something [*yu wei*]."[214] Not all learned to think in the new way for themselves, however. "Eight- or nine-tenths of the shih have been transformed by the methods of the Classics," Wang commented, but just as many "have not sought mental comprehension."[215] The state schools were promising as a way to secure future officials of one mind and keep the growing number of candidates tied to government. Wang proposed to employ shih as clerks, for "when good shih are willing to serve as clerks, then clerks and shih may once again be united as one, as in antiquity. . . . This was a priority of the Former Kings."[216]

The New Policies immediately affected shih families whose wealth depended on the rural economy or commerce. In gaining control over the bureaucracy, Wang planned to manage the wealth of local elites as well, for "to manage wealth the ruler should see public and private [wealth] as a single whole."[217] The local rich might suffer, but, as Wang said, "Today in every prefecture and subprefecture, there are *chien-ping* [engrossing] families that annually collect interest amounting to several myriad strings of cash without doing anything. . . . What contribution have they made to the state to [warrant] enjoying such a good salary?"[218] The new institutions for managing wealth were intended to help the poor and provide funds for local economic investment and relief. They were also intended to remove those of independent means upon whom the poor were dependent. To benefit society (*li min, li t'ien-hsia*), Wang had to control those private interests that, by their very existence, threatened the government's command over society. Wang's logic might be stated in this fashion: for the people to receive benefits, they must be organized; to be organized, they must be willing to take direction from the government; to be willing to take direction, their material interests must depend upon their doing so. Those social elements that came between the people and the government—that is, those who used their wealth to make others dependent on them—were an obstacle to this end.[219] Wang called these elements *chien-ping*. With this term, translated sometimes as "engrossers," he meant all those who monopolized land and wealth and made others dependent upon them, in either agriculture or commerce. It is evident from his discussions with the emperor that Wang believed "suppressing *chien-ping*" was one of his and the sage-kings' most important goals. Without doing it, he could not "cause benefit to come from a single source."[220]

With his loans to farmers, a government trading policy intended to benefit small traders, and state organizations encouraging trade and agriculture, Wang was sure he was on the way to a government that would benefit everyone and integrate all into a single system. Any institution, it seemed, could ramify into related areas. For example, Wang saw the pao-chia system's ultimate goal as making "farmers and soldiers one."[221] Trained militia units would eventually become better, and cheaper, than the regular soldiers.[222] They would become a source of new community leaders, men who would command the respect of the militiamen and the community with their intelligence and prowess, who would lead the people in taking direction from the government.[223] The pao-chia offered an alternative basis for community, one that disregarded family ties and status and kept the people oriented toward the state. Wang soon concluded that the units could take on responsibilities for other policies; by 1075 they were charged with collecting the land tax, service tax, and Green Shoot loans. Using the people in many offices was, Wang asserted, the way the Former Kings employed the people.[224] Wang's policies gave substance to the promise he made the emperor in 1070: "Once the policies are in effect, everyone will be of use. We will be employing all the people under heaven to do all the affairs under heaven, and we will be free of the problem of useless people."[225] Perfect order was at hand.

Ssu-ma Kuang had a "divergent opinion" on the structure of the state, the organization and process of government, the relation between government and society, and the necessary order in society. For Ssu-ma order required a clearly defined political hierarchy and division of functional responsibilities; Wang broke down established divisions within government and integrated functional roles. Wang integrated institutional and social interests; Ssu-ma argued for a necessary boundary between the institutional responsibilities of government and the private domain in which men pursued their material interests. Wang attacked the power of private wealth in society; Ssu-ma defended the rich as socially useful and politically indispensable. Their foreign policies differed as well. Wang supported efforts to recover territory and absorb new population in the northwest. Ssu-ma favored a balance of power between the Sung and foreign states.

Once again Ssu-ma argued that the court was responsible for the general structure of the entire system and the overall definition of policy goals; below that were the organs responsible for overseeing policy in various areas and the several levels of local offices whose officials had responsibility for working out the details of policy according to local conditions. The faults of the old policies were to be remedied, Ssu-ma contended, through better personnel administration.[226] Wang might see himself as a Duke of Chou aiding a King Ch'eng, but he was merely someone who insisted that everyone share his opinions.[227]

Ssu-ma wanted to make the debate an argument over an issue of principle: Should the government be concerned with "profit" (*li*) or not? That is, as Ssu-ma explained it, should the government try to manage the wealth of society as a whole and, to accomplish this, interfere in the way the people realized their material interests, or should it let them pursue those interests for themselves? Ssu-ma did not think "managing wealth" was part of ancient government.[228] Government should ensure that its policies did not prevent the people from enriching themselves.[229] Taxation was only so that government could maintain order. The Green Shoots loans were destroying the necessary social function of the rich. The relationship between rich and poor was mutually beneficial: the hardworking rich lent to the slothful poor to enrich themselves, and the poor borrowed from the rich in order to survive. Bureaucratic management of credit, he explained at length, would lead to greater indebtedness and continual default. In effect the government was creating landless refugees, the source of rebellion, while giving up the fiscal means to cope with rebellion.[230] The institution of a service-exemption tax collected in cash, as well as cash loans, he argued, was changing the nature of the rural economy. Whereas previously taxes in kind had taken goods the people could produce through their own labors, the new system made producers dependent on the market to sell goods to acquire the cash to pay their taxes. The poor would suffer; they were easily harmed by price fluctuations.[231] Government trading offices reduced the profit margins in commerce, thus reducing the number of traveling merchants and harming the flow of goods.[232] Monetarization under the new tax system led to commercialization, destroying rural self-sufficiency, the basis for rural stability. The pao-chia policy forced the people to take on duties that interfered with agriculture without adequately training them. In sum, the policies to manage wealth forced the people into flight and banditry, and the pao-chia system taught the people enough martial technique to become bandits yet deprived local government of effective security forces.[233]

From Ssu-ma's vantage, the New Policies would lead inevitably to the collapse of the state. The rich keeping the poor in a state of dependency was in the interest of the state in some sense, for this made it possible for the ruler to order the people by gaining the support of the shih. For Ssu-ma it made no sense for the government to encourage more men to act as shih or to try to mold the shih through education. The ruler had to show the shih that he was worthy of their support. The shih existed already; they did not have to be nurtured and supported. Ssu-ma preferred to ignore state schools and prefectural qualifying examinations in favor of a recommendation system. The best way of staffing goverment, he argued, was to admit to the examinations only those men recommended by high officials (who would be free to recommend kin), giving preference to those with the greatest number of sponsors.[234] Government was an enterprise of the existing elite.

When Ssu-ma came to power, he moved immediately to rescind the policies,[235] restated his general principles on the roles of emperor, court, and bureaucracy,[236] and proposed measures to improve administrative process.[237] For the first time Ssu-ma Kuang argued that the only justification for the New Policies had been Shen-tsung's desire to extend the borders of the Sung to match those of the Han and T'ang. Placing the blame on the emperor was consistent with Ssu-ma's understanding of the ruler's role in the polity. He concluded that without a desire to "employ the troops" there was no rationale for any of the New Policies.[238]

The imposition of the New Policies divided the shih into opposing camps. Although the opposition controlled the court during the Yuan-yu reign period (1086–93), the partisans of Wang's policies and learning regained power in 1094 and largely remained in power until the loss of the north in 1126. Both Su Shih and Ch'eng I, members of a generation of intellectuals who matured during the first New Policies regime and experienced the opposition's failure to establish a political alternative, found intellectual grounds for rejecting Wang's style of learning. But they also forsook the premise under which Ssu-ma Kuang, like Wang An-shih, had been operating: that the unity of shih values and the harmony of the social order depended on political institutions. It seems to me that the success of Wang An-shih and Ssu-ma Kuang in arriving at coherent but mutually exclusive models of a world unified through government encouraged Su and Ch'eng to think that the grounds for unifying values lay elsewhere. Their search led them in very different directions, however. Su, the last great spokesman for the centrality of wen in intellectual culture, ended up questioning the need for any intellectual orthodoxy. Ch'eng, whose focus on moral self-cultivation opened a way of being a shih independent of achievements in both wen and government service, came to believe that he had discovered the one real basis for all thinking.

8 Su Shih's Tao: Unity with Individuality

After Ou-yang Hsiu's death in 1072, Su Shih (1037–1101) became the most influential literary figure of the day. His prose became a model for ku-wen writing, he was seen as a great poet, his calligraphy was valued, and his comments on painting were studied.[1] He has been and will continue to be a major figure in the history of Chinese literature and art. The concomitant of this view, however, has been a dismissal of Su as "merely" a literary talent, lacking a serious position on either political or philosophical principles.[2] This is not simply a historiographical problem created by reading back into the eleventh century the later centrality of Ch'eng I's intellectual legacy. When gaining Ou-yang's patronage in 1057, Su had every right to think that his kind of accomplishments in wen put him at the center of serious learning. But from the 1070's on, with Wang An-shih in power, Ssu-ma Kuang leading the opposition, and men like Ch'eng I gaining the attention of conservative leaders, some thought those who devoted their energies to literary pursuits had chosen merely to be wen-shih rather than to speak to "those who learned" about common values.

As intellectual leaders, Wang An-shih and Ssu-ma Kuang saw learning as illuminating the tao for the polity and the literary enterprise as a legitimate but secondary endeavor. Political visions that required intellectual conformity and the subordination of the self to institutional goals had nothing to gain by allowing the creativity and individuality associated with literary interests to be confused with political values. Men concerned with the natural foundations for ethics opposed the literary on other grounds. Chou Tun-i (1017–73) wrote in his *Comprehending the Change* (*T'ung shu*):

Wen is a means for conveying tao [*wen so-i tsai tao*]. If the wheels and shafts of a cart are decorated but men do not use them, they are mere decoration—so much more so when the cart is empty.

Literary elaboration [*wen-tz'u*] is art. Morality [*tao-te*] is substantial. When one is earnest about the substance [of morality] and one with art writes it down, then if it is beautiful it will be cherished. When cherished, it will be transmitted, and then worthies will be able to arrive at it by learning. This then becomes instruction. This is why [Confucius] said, "If it is said without wen, it will not go far in practice." However, the unworthy will not learn. . . . They do not know they should be concerned with morality. They instead regard literary elaborations as ability. They are being artful and nothing more. Alas, this defect has been with us for a long time.[3]

Chou is not arguing that language should be the transparent vehicle for ideas—he recognizes that the vehicle lasts by being artful—but he rejects the idea of making an integral connection between wen and morality and casts out those concerned with wen as morally unworthy. Ch'eng I, who met Chou in his youth, held that composing wen harmed tao. Doing wen required skill and concentration, but "if you concentrate, your will [*chih*] will be limited to this. How will you then share the greatness of heaven-and-earth?"[4] Here, attending to literary composition limits moral growth.

Where did this leave Su Shih? He distanced himself from both political idealists and moral philosophers. He objected in 1061, for example, that "all those who serve discuss the tao of the true king and transmit ritual and music. They wish to restore the Three Eras and strive to match Yao and Shun. . . . All those who learn discuss heaven and man and infer nature and decree [*hsing-ming*]"[5] Yet if he chose not to be either a political thinker or a moral philosopher, why was he important enough to become famous and influential? There were various answers to this in his own times. First, he was in many ways a spokesman for the wen-shih, still probably the largest group among the scholarly. His follower Li Chih (1059–1109), for example, records:

[Su] Tung-p'o once said, "The responsibility for wen-chang lies with shih who, famous in their time, make an alliance with each other. Then this tao will not decline. Today being a height of great peace, wen-shih are appearing one after another. The object is to make the wen of a single time have someone to take as an ultimate authority. In the past Ou-yang Hsiu turned this responsibility over to me. Therefore I have made the effort. At another time, when the leadership of the alliance of wen-chang will be charged to you gentlemen, it will be just as he passed it on to me."[6]

Yet Ch'in Kuan (1049–1100), another follower, responded to someone who admired Su and his family only for their literary art by arguing that the Sus had a philosophical side as well.

This is not the thing for which to acclaim the Sus. The tao of the Sus is most profound in matters of nature and decree and apprehending it in oneself [*tzu-te*].

Next is the fact that their capacities are sufficient to bear major responsibilities and their knowledge is sufficient to reach what is still far off. As for their expository compositions, theirs are among the most unpolished presently circulating. You judge the Sus, yet your discussion is limited to wen-chang. I gather you wish to honor the Sus; in fact you end up degrading them. . . . Among the three [Su Shih's] tao is like the sun, moon, and stars in weaving together heaven and earth; all that lives knows to look up to such lofty brilliance. . . . Go visit the two [brothers] at the capital, or instead take the writings they have composed, read them well, and think about them carefully, in order to imagine them as men.[7]

Ch'in's alternative seems to be to admire Su Shih as a man. This view, which could lead to the conclusion that Su was such a unique and exceptional individual that he could not be imitated, persisted in the scores of stories about Su Shih in twelfth-century miscellanies.[8] Still another view, put forward by Su Ch'e (1039–1112) in his funerary biography of his brother, argues that Su Shih was a great official, something he had to prove at his first post, where "the senior clerks, seeing him to be a man of wen, did not bother him with administrative affairs."[9] It is with this in mind that Su Ch'e relates in unusual detail Shih's achievements as a subordinate local official in the 1060's, as a vice-prefect and prefect in the 1070's and briefly during the Yuan-yu (1086–93) period, as a leading court official during the Yuan-yu period, and as an outspoken critic who was exiled to Huang-chou in 1079–84 and to isolated spots in Kuang-nan in 1094–1100 for his opposition to the New Policies.[10]

We have, then, a man who was admired as a person, was the foremost literary model of his day, and was a political figure of great stature. I shall argue, as others have, that Su was saying something he wanted others to share.[11] By his own account, he was in the tradition of Ou-yang Hsiu, and he praised Ou-yang in 1057 for saving ku-wen from the faults of misguided profundity and archaism and for going beyond Han Yü and T'ang ku-wen to draw upon the "wen inherited from the Former Kings" and to "enlighten those who learn."[12] While Ou-yang lived, Su wrote in 1072, "This Culture of Ours was transmitted, and those learned had a teacher. . . . [Now, with his death] This Culture of Ours has changed into a deviant way and those who learn have gone so far as to practice barbarian forms; the superior men take non-action as goodness, and the lesser men, in full flood, think their time has come."[13] In 1090, an intellectual leader in his own right, he insisted that Ou-yang's reputation would survive his critics of the moment and that he was Ou-yang's successor: "I see myself as incomplete, but that the shih of the world do not reject me, thinking instead that I can 'participate in This Culture of Ours,' is entirely due to Ou-yang Hsiu."[14] Like Ou-yang, and Confucius before him, Su Shih saw himself as the vehicle through which This Culture of Ours was continued. This was not a mere claim to literary authority. It challenged Wang An-shih's assertion, in his introduction to the *Explanations of Characters*, that Heaven was saving This Culture through Wang. The claims to This Culture and thus to moral authority, for that is what such claims meant, of Ou-yang, Wang, and Su Shih were recognized by those who sought to deny them. "Has This Culture of Ours been cut off?" asked the Tao-hsueh advocate Hu Hung (1105–55). No, he answered, the shih have granted it to the Ch'eng brothers, not Ou-yang, Wang, or Su.[15]

Thus I find it reasonable to suppose that Su Shih was speaking to issues of culture, politics, and morality. The question is what he had to say. To this inquiry I append another. Since leading figures had begun to doubt that the literary enterprise was part of morally serious learning, how did Su Shih rhyme his literary side with his ideas about values? My inquiry is guided by Su Ch'e's brief account of Shih's literary-intellectual career.

With regard to wen, the Gentleman obtained [his special talent for] it from heaven. When young, he and I both took our father as our teacher. At first [my brother] liked the writings of Chia I and Lu Chih. In discussing order and chaos in past and present, he did not speak emptily. But then he read the *Chuang-tzu*. He said with a sigh, "Previously, when I perceived something of what was within me, my mouth was unable to put it into words. Now I have seen the *Chuang-tzu* and grasped my own mind." Subsequently he produced [his three-part essay] "On Chung-yung." He discussed the subtleties, none of which had been explained by men in the past.

He once said to me, "In my view among those who learn in today's world, only you can be ranked with me." But when he had been exiled to Huang-chou, he shut his door and lived in seclusion. He raced on with brush and ink, and his wen underwent a complete transformation. It came to be like "a stream coming down in flood,"[16] and, overwhelmed, I was no longer able to keep up with him.

Our father read the *Book of Change* in his later years. He mused over the lines and images and apprehended the actuality of hard and yielding, far and near, happiness and anger, going with and going against, in order to contemplate its elaborated language, and then everything fell into place. His *Commentary on the Change* was not finished when illness overtook him, and he ordered the Gentleman [Su Shih] to complete his work as he had intended. In tears, [my brother] received that charge and ultimately produced the completed work. Only then did the subtle language from a thousand years past become clearly understandable.[17]

He further wrote *Explanations of the Analects*, in which he repeatedly brought out Confucius's concealed points in a timely way. At the very last, when he was living on Hai-nan, he wrote his *Commentary on the Documents* to clarify through inference the learning of high antiquity, which had been disrupted. Much of what he said had not been understood by former ju. Having completed the three books, he placed his hand on them and sighed, "Even if the present age is still unable to trust [me], if there are superior men in the future they ought to understand me."

As for his occasional poems, laments, inscriptions, accounts, letters, memorials, expositions, and proposals, they generally surpassed those of others. There are the *Eastern Slope Collection* in 40 *chüan*, the *Later Collection* in 20, the *Memorials* in 15, the *Inner Rescripts* in 10, and the *Outer Rescripts* in 3. His poetry basically resembles that of Li [Po] and Tu [Fu]. Late in life he enjoyed T'ao Yuan-ming and rhymed to almost all his [works], 4 *chüan* in all. When young he liked calligraphy, and when old he did not tire of it. He said of himself that he did not match the men of the Chin [in calligraphy] but that he had more or less come close to Ch'u [Sui-liang], Hsueh [Chi], Yen [Chen-ch'ing], and Liu [Kung-ch'üan] of the T'ang.[18]

Su Ch'e notes his brother's unique talent for wen, yet stresses his debt to literary and artistic traditions, measures him against them, and describes his achievements in terms of them. At the same time, he insists that Su Shih's learning surpassed that of his contemporaries, and here too he stresses Su Shih's grounding in tradition. Su understood "the learning of high antiquity, which had been disrupted," an implicit challenge to all other claims to knowledge of antiquity and transmission of the tao of the sage. A subtle point is being made with the statement that Su "clarified through inference" the learning of "high antiquity" (*shang-ku*); that is, he inferred from the Classics (works of mid- and later antiquity) the intellectual values that guided the sages in creating civilization, and he saw the cultural tradition in light of this original mode of thinking. Su was not a narrow ju; he was drawn to Chuang-tzu. He was not concerned merely with appearances; he studied the "Doctrine of the Mean." At the same time, he was an admirer of Han and T'ang proponents of institutional reform. But in his energy and creativity he was not easy to imitate.

The inquiry that follows is composed of sections on his essays for the decree examination of 1061, his response to intellectual trends he associated with the New Policies, his message in commentaries on the *Change* and the *Documents*, and his ideas about good wen. The portrait that emerges is of a man who is opposed to dogmatism in any form, who treasures flexibility, diversity, and individuality, yet who is consumed by the search for unifying values. As a literary man, Su Shih confronts the ku-wen tension between the search for moral universals and literary engagement; as an intellectual, he faces the ku-wen predicament of believing that one should know for oneself while seeking to know what all can share. I shall argue that Su Shih eventually resolved these dilemmas through his explanation of how the individual could make a connection between a belief in an ultimate unity of all things and his own responses to the particular events of a historical, changing, and always imperfect world. Su Shih's tao required individuality and diversity for the realization of the common interest. It was a universal way of thinking about values that did not require uniformity. Moreover, Su's tao finally explained how the wen men created could have real value without requiring that all share the same style or reach the same conclusions. In place of certainty Su held forth a vision of a culture that was cumulative, changing, and accommodative of a plurality of interests. Su Shih answered, I think, the questions that had stimulated intellectual life since the late eighth century. But by formulating answers others could and did share, Su also relieved his followers of the need to be thinkers themselves. In my view he was the last of the great literary intellectuals who, in the tradition of Han Yü, stood at the center of intellectual debate. But by disavowing the goal of creating a culture that transparently embodied moral universals, by concluding that humanity would always face an imperfect world, and by refusing to grant that there were normative standards that were correct under all circumstances, Su Shih turned away those who continued to insist on the possibility of moral perfection in self and society.

1061: Unity with Diversity

After Ou-yang Hsiu recommended Su Shih for the decree examination of 1061,[19] Su submitted 50 essays: "On *Chung-yung*," in three parts, 25 policy proposals, 20 discourses on historical figures, and the two-part "On the Great Minister." The concept of *chung-yung*, constantly creating a center through combining polarities, is the organizing principle both for the literary structure of the essays, as shall be demonstrated below, and for Su's ideas about government, learning, and conduct. The essays are also, as Su Ch'e's account of Shih's thought suggests, a synthesis of Chuang-tzu's relativism, Chia I's idealization of antiquity, and Lu Chih's pragmatic reformism.

Su Shih's goal in these writings is to show that it is possible to create a whole by balancing opposing interests. He writes, he explains in a cover letter, from a moral perspective for high officials who read from a political perspective.[20] Morality and politics are different—to try to be moral and politic simultaneously is self-destructive—yet necessary to each other.[21] The writings provide the common ground. Those in power can read his words for guidance in "controlling the times."[22] But they should also read them to see that the authorial qualities they reveal make Su precisely the kind of man the world needs. Political order depends on achieving a balance of "law" (rules, traditions, conventions) and "man" (human initiative). "If man dominates law, law becomes an empty device; if law dominates man, man becomes a position filler. When man and law both receive their due without one dominating the other, the world will be secure."[23] Today, however, law dominates, because men lack the "self-confidence" necessary to take initiative.[24] Su's essays will show that he has the necessary self-confidence.

In 1061 Su explains that his "self-confidence" (*tzu-hsin*) stems from his conviction that he can know the real values of all things as parts of an integrated whole. His concern with seeing a systematic whole is congruent with the views of Wang An-shih and Ssu-ma Kuang. He writes in another cover letter:

For fifteen years, since I began to engage in learning until today, I have held that the real problem in learning is to be free of partiality and that the real problem in being free of partiality is to comprehend the inherent patterns of all things [*t'ung wan-wu chih li*]. If one does not comprehend the patterns of all things, it is impossible to be free of partiality, even if one wants to be. If one thinks something good because one likes it or bad because one detests it—if I have confidence in myself on this account, then [I] will be deluded.

That is why, abiding in darkness and silence, I peruse the changes [*pien*] of all things. I fully exhaust the inherent patterns of their being so-by-themselves [*ch'i tzu-jan chih li*], and I judge them in my mind. Whatever does not accord with this, even if it be what in antiquity was called a theory of worthies, will not be fully accepted. Although it is on this account that I have confidence in myself, it is also on this account that I myself know that I will not be appreciated by the age.[25]

Su supposes that things have inherent patterns (*li*) that the individual can comprehend by examining their changes, variations, and permutations (*pien*). He can look to the things directly, at least in thought. By taking the inherent patterns of all things into account, he transcends partiality, although he does not claim perfect impartiality (*kung*). Knowledge is the basis for judging things and sifting received ideas.

Because Su's essays are so programmatic, it is possible to elucidate what "comprehending the patterns of all things" means in the practice of his writing. First, "things" (*wu*) are historical categories of human affairs. In the policy proposals, these include various roles within the government (emperor, court ministers, local officials), social groups (the shih, the common people, the military), the functions and responsibilities of these roles and groups, and, above all, the relationships between the various parties and the various functions. "All things" in this case is all parts of the polity, including the barbarians against which China defines itself. Second, the "changes" (*pien*) are changes in hitherto harmonious and productive roles and relationships. Changes in this sense occur when parties cease functioning in their roles, and the balance shifts. The ministerial usurpation of imperial authority is a *pien*, as is the fall of a dynasty. Less negative are the variations and permutations necessary to rebalance an out-of-kilter relationship. Third, "pattern" (*li*), often replaced by shih (Su Hsun's "force of circumstances"; see Chapter 6), refers to the unfolding of events along a particular course. The pattern of a thing is its necessary course of development given the circumstances. This usually has a logical conclusion, such as the self-destruction that results from unimpeded one-sidedness. Patterns are inherently so, they tend to be "so-by-themselves" and necessary (*pi-jan*). Patterns of development are predictable; they can be deduced through thought.[26]

Su wrote in "On *Chung-yung*" that "what antiquity called *chung-yung* did not go beyond fully expressing the inherent patterns of all things."[27] But the "pattern" of a thing is also its tendency to one-sidedness. Su gets around this by *t'ung li* (connecting the inherent patterns to each other). He sees that to function in a complementary fashion things must be juxtaposed as parts of a unity. *Chung-yung* involves recognizing that two sides are necessary. Each piece has its particular mode of functioning and direction of development. Left alone, a piece would become destructive; joined together with other parts, its natural tendencies are constructively channeled. The result is an organism of human creation. "For the disposition of forces in the world," he writes, "we can take as an analogy a single human body."[28] In fact Su means that the world can be governed so that it will be like the body: "When the sages order the world . . . they connect its joints and arteries with each other to form a unity. . . . Thus the world can be made to act as a single human body. . . . Today it is not so."[29] The task is to create a situation in which "ordering the world is analogous to controlling water. . . . [One] causes it not to become blocked, stagnant, and thus useless" so that one need only "expel the old and let in the new."[30] Su appropriately takes medicine as his analogy and speaks of restoring the body politic to a healthy equilibrium.[31]

The Method of the Policy Proposals

It is impossible to do justice to the 25 policy proposals as concrete suggestions for reform in a brief space.[32] Instead, I shall comment on the method used to justify the institutions and policy changes recommended in several of the proposals, for Su's reliance on a method in 1061 contrasts with his mature ideas. The proposals are organized into "Generalizations" (*lueh*) (1–5), "Particulars" (*pieh*) (6–22), and "Divisions" (*tuan*) (23–25), covering the political elite, the functions of government in managing the empire, and China and the barbarians.

The proposals form a hierarchy of nested pairs. The greatest opposition is between China (Proposals 1–22) and the barbarians (23–25). Su is concerned principally with revitalizing China as a prerequisite for regaining the initiative in foreign relations.[33] Within China a distinction is made between emperor, court ministers, and shih (lower officials) (the Generalizations) and the functions of government (the Particulars). The latter are further divided into the bureaucracy (6–11), the populace (12–17), wealth (18–19), and military power (20–22). The addition of a new topic complements the previous topic, those two in turn form a unit complemented by a third, and so on. For example, the Particulars section begins by creating an effective bureaucracy and then balances this with the populace; the bureaucracy and populace together organize wealth; to survive, a wealthy state needs military strength.

Within these general topics, essays are paired so that each pair treats a single problem in terms of two elements that, when rebalanced, together create a complementary duality. For example, in the section on relations with the populace, Proposals 12 and 13, entitled "Strengthening Transformation Through Instruction" and "Encouraging Familiality," deal with social mores; 14–15 are on creating wealth through agriculture; and 16–17 concern local security. Proposal 12 calls for officials to balance their unsuccessful inculcation of traditional norms by setting a personal example of adherence to rules by seeing that the state keeps its promises and limits its demands on the populace; Proposal 13 counters selfishness among the populace by imposing a clan organization that encourages self-reliance and mutual aid. In short, officials should adhere more to the rules and the populace should rely more on itself; this is to be accomplished by requiring that officials set a personal example and that the populace follow the rules of the clan system.

In fact, each of the seventeen Particulars posits some particular variation of the polarity between man and law as a general category, each rectifies an imbalance by going further in one direction, and in each pair of essays one party is more bound by rules and the other is given greater initiative. For example, bureaucratic malfeasance is addressed in terms of high- (6) and low- (7) ranking officials. High-ranking officials are allowed to act on their own initiative outside the rules, but if left to their own devices, they tend to usurp authority. Su's solution is to punish their abuses of privilege more severely, so that they will serve as an example for their subordinates. The low-ranking officials stick to the rules too closely because job competition keeps them from taking initiative for fear of mistakes, yet infrequent periods of service encourage graft. The solution: promote the low-ranking only for actual achievements, so that they see that it serves their interests to take some initiative. Su Shih is righting the balance, tightening the rules for those who have the most leeway while encouraging those hemmed in by rules to act on their own. One thing leads to the next. Reducing malfeasance is not enough, however; the next two essays discuss measures for ensuring effectiveness and competence (8–9). Finally, Su outlines a scheme to motivate men to maintain these qualities throughout their career (10–11). Su builds his state in this manner, ending with Proposal 22, in which the bonds between the populace and the political elite have become so strong that the populace will sacrifice itself in defense of officialdom.

The Particulars assume that all men are self-interested. Su constructs his body politic by creating circumstances in which the pursuit of self-interest serves the public interest. But his Generalizations on relations between emperor, great ministers, and shih (here low-ranking and prospective officials) (Proposals 1–5) assumes that men are also public-spirited. Here the problem is not law but man, for, as Su writes, the law is like notes in music; control over the effect lies not with the notes but with the musicians (3). When the three roles return to a state of energetic harmony, "each will be able to realize its separate function without disturbance" (1). Three of the five essays set out the independent function of each role, and two deal with the relationships holding them together. Briefly, the role of the ruler, once he has turned away from the lethargy of non-action, is simply to desire to "accomplish something" (*yu-wei*) (1); the ministers, once freed from the distraction of foreign affairs, need consider only ways of "acting on the world" (*wei t'ien-hsia*) (2); and the shih, told to avoid both setting themselves above social criticism and seeking safety in being like everyone else, need only achieve something at the local level (4). Su then considers how to harmonize the emperor and ministers (3) and emperor, court, and shih (5). If the ruler favors accomplishing something, he will encourage his ministers to speak their minds and will support them in fully realizing their plans (3). If the court (ruler and ministers) wants to act, it will learn what needs to be done from the shih who execute policy (5). Thus Su comes full circle: the shih who execute policy are ultimately the source of policy; in them knowledge meets action, and proposal execution. Su, of course, is writing as a shih.

Su combines something of Wang An-shih's organic holism and activism with Ssu-ma Kuang's limited government and distinct roles, without calling for uniformity of values in the manner of Wang or insisting on Ssu-ma's distinction between superior and inferior. Su does not reject shared values or hierarchical authority; he simply does not treat them as matters of first importance. Unity requires opposites and a state of balanced tension to thwart inherent tendencies toward one-sidedness. A unity of purpose coexists with a division of interests; staying whole demands finding a place for both sides.

The Perspective of the Historical Essays

The 20 essays on historical figures reverse the perspective from ways of structuring situations to guide individuals to the values with which past men have responded to their times. They provide polarities for the well-rounded man while sharply attacking attempts to create dogmas.[34] The essays are arranged topically rather than chronologically, although the first notes the beginning of civilization and the last the T'ang intellectual legacy. Su takes up governing (both the civil [Essays 1–4] and the military

[5–8] aspects) and learning the tao of the sage (9–13) and ethical conduct (14–17). He concludes with three essays against dogmatism (18–20).

Once again Su opts for two-sidedness. In discussing the affairs of government, for example, he begins from the polarity of benefit and ritual. The sages introduced tools for agriculture, hunting, and fishing, Su writes, that man might seek benefit and satisfy his desires without having to struggle with the animals for survival. But profit seeking opened the gate to deceit; so the sages balanced profit with ritual, that men would not only think of their own convenience. The error of the First Emperor of the Ch'in, the subject of Essay 1, was to choose his techniques solely on the basis of profit without regard for ritual. Similarly ministers who seek to persuade rulers must recognize a legitimate polarity between moral principles and self-interest (2. "On Kao-ti of the Han"). Knowledge of past models must be balanced with knowledge of the present, of the capabilities of the men who make up the political scene. Both are necessary to be "able to unify" (3. "On Emperor Wu of the Wei"). Expedient action must be balanced with an ability to transcend selfishness (4. "On I Yin"). These essays are far more interesting and nuanced than this summary suggests, but I shall focus instead on those that speak most directly to the search for values.

The five essays on learning the tao of the sage begin with Su granting supremacy to Confucius while doubting those who have tried to define the "tao of the Master" (9. "On Tzu-ssu"). He then takes up two styles of practicing this tao as a person (10. "On Meng K'o") and then the connection between the tao of the sage and government (11. "On Yueh I"). These are balanced by two essays on tradition, one on the correct attitude toward predecessors within the tradition that stems from Confucius (12. "On Hsun Ch'ing") and the other on those outside this tradition (13. "On Han Fei"). Su favors the "Confucian" tradition in that Confucius is his model of acting as sage but he treats the later ju as moral absolutists who lacked Confucius's ability to respond flexibly to all situations.

Su's basic distinction is between those who look to the tao of the sage and those with a "different starting point" (i-tuan), such as Lao-tzu, Chuang-tzu, and Lieh-tzu, who go outside the realm of man to find a starting point in the "non-existence of the phenomenal world" (wu-yu). They deny the reality of both social distinctions and human emotional response (jen-ch'ing) and thus, by encouraging men to suppress emotions, make them impervious to institutional constraints and social criticism (13. "On Han Fei"). But Su adopts a Taoistic critique of those ju who start from the human realm yet reduce the tao of Confucius to fixed principles. The first line of the Tao te ching, "The tao that can be spoken of is not the constant tao," seems to be in the back of Su's mind throughout, although he never cites it. Those who define human nature in moral terms tell men to ignore their actual sentiments—they thus end up quite like the "other starting point"—and their absolute distinctions between right and wrong keep men from seeing that the morality of an action depends upon the context. Su is a Confucian relativist, who claims a common starting point with moralists yet objects to Mencius, Hsun-tzu, and Yang Hsiung for trying to establish particular identities by creating narrow foundations with their respective theories of human nature as good, bad, and mixed (9. "On Tzu-ssu").

For Su the tao of the sage must be universal, all-embracing, and irre-ducible. "The tao of the Master can be proceeded through, but it cannot be [fully] known; it can be spoken of, but not debated. This was [because Confucius] did not vie to create a petty theory and thus open the starting point of [defining] right and wrong. For this reason he alone was never set aside."[35] But if this tao cannot be exactly defined, what can be said about it in practice? "What can be apprehended and spoken of is only [Confucius's] reverting to perfect appropriateness; it was simply for this that he was regarded as a sage."[36] Men should take their necessary standards (ch'ü pi) from the tao of the sage. Mencius, however, set standards on the basis of what men were capable of (a reference to the four beginnings of benevo-lence, righteousness, ritual, and wisdom) (9. "On Tzu-ssu"). Mencius's account is inadequate, however, not wrong. The value of his definitions is that they provide a test of those who claimed to be practicing the tao of the sage, for the sages did include what all men knew and practiced. But Su's Mencius went beyond these basic requirements and valued the flexi-bility of "appropriateness" above conformity to rigid doctrine in practice (10. "On Meng K'o"). Confucius, in contrast, aimed to incorporate the greatest possible amount of knowledge and talent; he was able to include everything by connecting all he learned together in a coherent whole. This is what he meant by "have one to thread all."[37] He was able to act appropriately in every case because he had included all that might prove useful in restoring a situation to its proper balance.

The contrast between meeting a universal minimum and reaching the highest level of attainment—the difference between Mencius and Confu-cius—has a parallel in government (11. "On Yueh I"). The "tao of the king" (wang tao) describes the achievements of the ancient sage-kings, but practicing it requires attaining the same level of learning as the sage-kings. This differs from the tao of the hegemon, but the real question is what one is capable of. Those able to be true kings transcend actual circumstances because all under heaven responds to them as one. A ruler who has not succeeded in unifying everything, however, will do well to respond to the actual circumstances and, in the manner of the hegemon, do his best to further political unity: "If you wish to be kingly, then be kingly; if you are not to be kingly, then examine the circumstances in which you find yourself. Do not cause yourself to fail in both respects, and be ridiculed by all."[38]

Su cautions, however, that the end of unity does not justify any means. There are traditions and bounds of civilized conduct, even in military affairs. Those who wish to include all and respond flexibly must take tradition into account as well. Su faults Hsun-tzu for rejecting Mencius and Tzu-ssu. Hsun-tzu showed that one could claim authority while rejecting much of one's tradition, and thus, Su claims, his student Li Ssu, as minister of the Ch'in, thought himself justified in the ultimate sacrilege: the destruction of the Classics, the record of the tao of the sage (12. "On Hsun Ch'ing").

Su elaborates on this theme in three closing essays. The commonality of man, the political unity of society, and the intellectual unity of learning do not require, he insists, presupposing a single moral human nature, a single moral politics, or a single doctrine as the tao of the sage. Commonality does not require uniformity; demanding that all men act alike does not serve the common interest.

"On Yang Hsiung" (18) refutes both claims that human nature is good, bad, or mixed and Han Yü's attempt to make these different claims compatible.[39] Su begins by asserting a distinction between "nature" (hsing) and "capability" or "talent" (ts'ai). For the first to be universal, he contends, it must be something common to the best and worst of men, something inescapable. Yet clearly men differ in talent. The relationship can be understood by analogy: the nature of trees is to flourish when nurtured, but material differences in size and hardness limit their possible uses. Those who fail to make this distinction impute to the nature of all men abilities particular to some, and they demand that all men act in ways suited only to some. Taking Han Yü as his example, Su develops a second theme: definitions of human nature create a false dichotomy between nature and human feeling (jen-ch'ing), leading men to think that their failure to live up to supposedly common standards is the fault of their emotions. In fact, the sentiments reveal what is common to all and what can be employed for moral ends. Su appeals to common sense: Who believes that the desire for food, shelter, and sex are not part of human nature? If these sentiments are common to man, Su proceeds, they are neither good nor bad. If the sentiments are part of the nature, good and bad cannot be in the nature. Rather, good and bad must be consequences of different ways of directing the sentiments, a point Su thinks Yang Hsiung approached when he related moral character to what one cultivated and noted that men were capable of both good and bad.

But how are good and bad to be determined and what is the role of common standards? The original point in making a distinction between good and bad was not to define norms for all men, Su explains, but simply to ensure that "the singular pleasures of a single man could not win out over that in which all men alike were secure." To keep exceptional men from generalizing from their own partiality, it was useful to equate the good with that which satisfied common sentiments. For Su, the fulfillment of human desires is the root of the good, and identifying things that satisfy all men is the role of the sage. Sages are not philosophers but acute observers of the social world: "When discussing human nature, the sages intended to fully express the patterns of all things and the common knowledge of the multitude in order to resolve the doubts of the world." In contrast, "Han Yü used the capability of one man to define the nature of all men." Thus by separating sentiments from nature, Su concludes, Han freed himself from having to consider the social world in arriving at notions of good and bad and thus "unconsciously drifted into Buddhism and Taoism"—the very things he wished to save the definition of human nature from.

"On Chu-ko Liang" (19) askes whether there is a single moral means to establish political unity. Su argues that Chu-ko Liang failed to unify the Three Kingdoms because he did not clearly distinguish between "benevolence and righteousness" and "deceit and strength" as the respective methods of king and hegemon. Either can be used to take or to maintain the state, but they cannot be used at the same time. Chu-ko had the talent to create a single state in which all men would feel secure. But, at the start, when he had the opportunity to succeed through moral suasion, he failed to persevere in benevolence and righteousness. Then, once at war, he failed to use deceit and strength in pursuit of victory. Chu-ko, Su explains, first tried to take the state by arousing the "mind of the world" with his own loyalty and trustworthiness and thus gaining the support of men of honor. If he had remained steadfast, particularly when his principles threatened his own interests, he would have succeeded. Losing the courage of his convictions, he lost the trust of others and had to fight. Yet once at war he tried to act honorably, refusing to corrupt his enemies. This was not moral behavior, Su argues, but an example of placing his own desire for reputation above the interests of those he had led into war. He was trying to do what he had already shown himself incapable of doing. "Not dividing the enemy when they could be divided," Su concludes, "was great righteousness when T'ang or Wu did it. But doing it when one is not a T'ang or a Wu is to lose an opportunity. This is the great danger for men of benevolence and superior men."[40] Su is not, I think, arguing that the ends justify the means. Political unity is good, and there are historically proven means to that end. These means are contradictory and mutually exclusive in practice; a man must decide on the one he is capable of and effect it coherently. The moral point has to do with the motives behind the choice: Chu-ko Liang subordinated the end of political unity as a common good to his singular desire for a good name; he lacked a moral end and thus the means failed him as well.

"On Han Yü" (20), the final essay, criticizes Han for valuing the name, but not the real substance, of the tao of the sage with his lofty theories, his loud reverence for Confucius and Mencius, and his attack on Buddhism and Taoism. Su has an analogy: the value of pearls and jades is an illusion created by social demand, whereas the value of food and clothing is understandable to everyone through the daily experience of use. Pearls and jades are beyond the reach of many. Han treated the tao of the sage as a priceless good, thus making it something few could hope to attain. Removing this tao from actual life led Han into error. First, Han saw benevolence in Mohist terms, as the same whether extended to men, barbarians, or animals. Not so: "What the sages do differs from the Mohists in that the sages make distinctions." Su explains: "Instruct them that they will have ability, transform them that they will have knowledge—this is benevolence when dealing with men. Not denigrating their ritual but affecting their sentiments, not censuring their departure but welcoming their arrival—this is benevolence when dealing with barbarians. Killing them in season and using them with restraint—this is benevolence when dealing with birds and animals. . . . Confucius did not love all equally."[41] Second, in a Taoist manner Han separated human nature and the emotions. Since the emotions and social distinctions are preconditions for ethics, Su claims, a denial of emotional response combined with a claim that morality lies in one's nature alone is tantamount to teaching men to be like Lao-tzu's passive infant. The tao of the sage is the middle way everyone can participate in; it does not require treating all things equally or blocking out the social world.

The two-sidedness, acceptance of human sentiment and desire, and advocacy of *jen-ch'ing* in these essays from 1061 fit Ou-yang Hsiu's perspective. Su's views were not without political meaning. The followers of Fan Chung-yen on the Council of State did not have the full support of the academic institutes and censorate, as the great ritual controversy of Ying-tsung's reign would soon make clear. (Ou-yang justified Ying-tsung's ritual recognition of his biological father as his father on the basis of *jen-ch'ing*, whereas the academicians argued that ritual and moral principle required the emperor to proclaim his predecessor Jen-tsung as his father.) Perhaps Su Shih was offering a rationale for a regime that favored making policy fit human sentiment and circumstance rather than moral doctrine.

Still, we can see something more significant than political support in these writings. Su is arguing, I think, that the unity of politics and morality does not mean that those who govern should adhere to fixed standards in responding to present circumstances to keep the polity in good health. Yet he agrees on the need for a common moral foundation of shared ideas that will help shih make the connection between learning and politics and get from what is so to what ought to be so. The tao of the sage may be nebulous, but it is a fairly clear attitude of mind. One tries to look at how men really behave and to satisfy their needs in the manner of Su's Confucius, who acted "appropriately" in whatever situation he found himself without claiming eternally valid rights and wrongs.

Su's idea of *chung-yung* as the balancing of two sides is his method for bridging the gap between human reality and the normative goal of an integrated polity. It includes his understanding of both organic process, as his analogy to medicine makes clear, and the nature of human sentiment. In his hands it becomes a device for holding together a variety of one-sided possibilities. All the methods, values, and strategies of the past can have a place, but none of them need be treated as an absolute. The balance of interests that forms Su's integrated order is always precarious. It cannot be maintained by an institutional structure or by fixed ethical standards. Rather, it depends on the constant attention of individuals, who must use the institutions and particular interests of others to create the circumstances that will incline men, for the moment, in the desired direction. Su, then, has shifted the burden to individuals who have learned how to keep the parts together. Neither a moralist nor an institutional reformer, he plots a course toward unity that accords with the fundamental dualism he ascribed to the human character in his essays on *chung-yung*.

Opposing Wang An-shih

Su Shih took up a local post after the decree examination, returned to Kaifeng in 1065 to test successfully for academic status, but left in 1066 when Su Hsun died. When he returned to the capital in the winter of 1068, the political situation had changed dramatically. The new emperor had turned to Wang An-shih. But if Su had distanced himself from moralistic conservatives in 1061, he soon found himself party to their opposition to the New Policies. His criticism of dogmatism could be directed at Wang as well. Although by the middle of 1069 Su had begun to oppose Wang's programs, he gained a highly visible appointment as judge of Kaifeng prefecture the same year. Su did not sway from his criticism, and within a year the court answered his letters and memorials to the emperor with a censor's charge that Su had in the past used government facilities for private commerce. As was expected in such cases, Su requested an appointment outside the capital. A year later he was dispatched to Hang-chou as vice-prefect. Promoted to prefect of Mi-chou and subsequently assigned to Hsu-chou and Hu-chou, he continued to serve until 1079, when he was arrested on the charge of slandering court policy and ministers in his literary writings. He was found guilty and banished to Huang-chou (Huai-nan West), where he remained until 1084.

With the exception of his comments on proposed reforms of the school and examination system, Su's objections to the New Policies were generally the same as Ssu-ma Kuang's, although in 1086 Su would oppose Ssu-ma's attempt to abolish the new institutions altogether. Su objected to the Finance Planning Commission, the appointment of commissioners for agricultural and water management projects, the "Green Shoots" loan policy, the institution of the hired-service tax, and the government trading policy. Like Ssu-ma he thought that the Planning Commission distorted bureaucratic procedures, that government loans and attempts to regulate the market would cause economic harm, and that the New Policies increased the wealth of the state at the expense of private wealth. Su had more to say about commerce than the rural socioeconomic order. A family history of commercial activity may lie behind his view that the distribution of goods, the commercial and urban economy in other words, should be left in the hands of private merchants and that urban dwellers should not be subject to the same tax obligations as rural households. Su did applaud policies of reducing support to imperial clansmen and the quotas for yin privilege; he liked the idea of toughening up the military until he saw that this meant leaving the old and feeble without support. It most ways Su was one voice in the chorus, a fine voice perhaps but not a soloist. He did not formulate an institutional alternative or offer a program for reducing the deficit, alleviating the suffering of the poor, or giving China greater weight in international relations. His strongest argument was simply that policy initiatives that provoked so much opposition were impractical and counterproductive—the axe that chopped against the grain (the "inherent pattern") would blunt before it split the log. And thus Su ended up in the perhaps uncomfortable position of having to justify inaction and conciliation, and consequentially, he acknowledged, foreign defeats and regular revenue shortfalls.[42]

Once it became clear, after the initial burst of protests, that the emperor supported Wang, opponents quieted. Su was no exception, but during the years leading up to his arrest he resisted in other ways, through informal prose and poetry. His writings had some effect, for the prosecutors at his trial based their case on the poetry and prose collected in a three-*chüan* work with the cumbersome title of *Academician Su Tzu-chan's Ch'ien-t'ang Collection: The Yuan-feng [Reign Period] Continuation.*[43]

Su's writings from the 1070's, such as *Ch'ien-t'ang Collection*, are not programmatic, and the methodical dualism of 1061 is absent. He is critical of the one-sidedness of current thought; he sees students moving between the extremes of slavish imitation and world-denying mysticism. His concerns have shifted to issues made pressing by the politics of the new regime. How, he asks, can men find it in themselves to resist the temptations of going along with power and wealth—how can they attain the independence necessary to resist the regime's demands—without having to withdraw from the world? How, in short, can one preserve one's integrity while still being socially responsible? The writings from the 1070's do not give a simple answer, but they do show Su Shih beginning to formulate the problem at a general level in terms of "self and things" (*wo wu*). Having a self capable of responding to things appropriately, in a manner that was in the interest of both things and self, was not easy. It required self-awareness, yet awareness revealed that one could never truly transcend the inclinations of personality and interest; it demanded an appreciation of things, yet he could not be certain that he saw things for what they were. There was no sure method. What Su could do, as his writings attest, was use himself to demonstrate that one could try to cope. If he had a solution in the 1070's, it was his creation of a literary persona for himself as a model for others. This section will follow Su as he hammered away at the various sides of the questions of the day, starting with his attack on the intellectual trends he associated with the New Policies.

Su responded to Wang's proposal of a national school system and unified examinations in a memorial in 1069.[44] First, he denied the practicability of Wang's goal. "Returning to the system of antiquity"—in this case a nationwide system of state schools that served as training centers for an activist bureaucracy—required changes too radical and fundamental to be acceptable. Construction expenses, salaries, and student stipends would create new burdens; to play a serious role in governance, schools would have to become involved in military and legal affairs. This was not likely to happen, Su argued, and the result would be a national school system that existed in name only.

Having dismissed Wang's proposal for a national school system, Su criticized the one-sidedness of various proposed alternatives to the current system of passing men on the basis of poetic composition. First, to admit men to the metropolitan examinations on the basis of "ethical conduct" would encourage excessive displays of self-sacrificing and poverty as shih competed to prove their incorruptibility and filiality. Second, if usefulness was the reason for dropping poetry in favor of prose, then all literary composition was indefensible; wen-chang in general was not directly applicable to the tasks of government. Furthermore, the supposition of a necessary connection between personal character and literary approach was not tenable. A master of literary embellishment such as Yang I, Su asserted, would make a better minister in the present than Shih Chieh and Sun Fu, whose prose gained them reputations for "comprehending the Classics and learning from antiquity." The poetry requirement had not been an obstacle to recruiting great ministers in the past; moreover, rigorous formal standards forced students to write carefully and allowed for objective grading standards. Third, a return to the T'ang system, in which candidates were known to the examiners, simply meant opening the gate to favoritism. Finally, requiring essays on the "greater signifi-cance" (ta-i) of the Classics would not increase talent, since the ability to discuss the Classics had little to do with official duties, but it would make men narrower. In Su's view, then, none of the suggested changes truly improved on the old system. Su did find one thing wrong with the way things were, however. He charged that students of the day were infatu-ated with Taoism, Buddhism, and discussions of nature and decree. This was potentially dangerous, he argued, for if shih were actually to think that life and death and high and low social position did not matter, it would be impossible to direct them through the manipulation of rewards and punishments.[45]

Although interests in innate qualities antedated Wang's regime, Su decided that there was a connection. As he wrote in the 1080's, "During the ten-odd years Master Ou-yang [Hsiu] has been dead, shih have begun to engage in [']new['] learning, disturbing the real substance of the Duke of Chou and Confucius with the semblance of Buddha and Lao-tzu."[46] In any case, in 1069 Su was struck by the incongruity: students who sought transcendent values beyond form were being examined on their mastery of literary forms to determine whether they had acquired the right values.[47] As a grader for the examination of 1070, Su found sycophantic imitation the rule of the day and protested by writing his own palace examination question and answer after the fact. Su was particularly in-censed by the success of a candidate who pandered to Wang An-shih's belief in his own rightness, a conviction enshrined in Wang's famous denial of the traditional grounds for political criticism: "Heaven's decree is not worth fearing, the opinions of the majority are not worth following, and the ancestors' rules are not worth using." To seek extraordinary achievement required an ability to discern the real qualities of others, Su commented; since Wang had failed to do that, he should stick to the standards that had guided the ancients and fear heaven, accept the major-ity view, and imitate the imperial ancestors.[48] Thus Su attacked from two different ends, accusing Wang of demanding uniformity in learning, on the one hand, and accusing students of seeking the ultimate and transcendent, on the other hand.

Uniformity and imitation were easy targets. In the following Su alludes to Wang's *Explanation of Characters*, required reading for students by the end of the 1070's.

When shih are not able to complete themselves, the problem lies with customary learning. The problem with customary learning is that it corrupts men's capabilities and blocks men's ears and eyes. They recite what their teacher said about the construction of characters and follow the customary wen. After only several ten thousand words of this is the task of being a shih finished.

Now, learning is to illuminate inherent patterns [li], and wen is to relate one's purpose. Thought is to interconnect what one has learned, and ch'i is to help one's wen. The men of the past guided their faculties of perception and broadened what they saw and heard; this was how they learned. They corrected their purpose and developed their ch'i; this was how they spoke.

The learning of Mr. Wang is exactly like striking prints: they come out according to [the image carved on] the block, and there is no need to decorate them before they are usable. How could they ever be made into rare and precious implements?[49]

Greater diversity and individuality are good, but having one's own ideas is not automatically good. Quality requires extensive knowledge, insight into patterns, and integration, and writing requires an independent sense of purpose. By demanding imitation, Wang prevented shih from learning for themselves and thus from having something worthwhile and unique to say.

Su would not grant the possibility of one mold for all shih. Soon after the fall of the New Policies regime in 1085, he writes his follower Chang Lei (1054–1114), charging his followers with making it possible for later men to see "the great whole [ta-ch'üan] of the ancients" by bringing out the diversity within the whole.

There has never been a decline in wen-tzu such as that of today. The source of this is really Mr. Wang. Mr. Wang's wen is not necessarily not good. The problem is that he likes to make others the same as himself. Ever since Confucius was unable to make others achieve the same benevolence as Yen Hui or the same courage as Tzu-lu, it has not been possible to move others toward each other. Yet with his learning Mr. Wang would make all under heaven the same. The goodness of the earth is uniform in bringing things into being; it is not uniform in what it brings into being. It is only on barren, brackish soil that there are yellow reeds and white rushes as far as the eye can see. This, then, is the uniformity of Mr. Wang.[50]

Locating the ultimate source of value in the process of creation itself was a key aspect of Su's later thought. For present purposes, the letter illustrates

Su's objection to uniformity. His examination questions make the point that any attempt to define ultimate values in language precludes universality. "Each saying of the sages has a method [*fang*], but if you have not caught on but hold fast to a single method, thinking it constant, the confusion in society will be insurmountable. . . . In these two [examples what the sage] says is the same, but can his reasons for speaking be made the same?"[51] Su's examination question for the Kaifeng prefectural examination in 1069 was pointed directly at Wang An-shih, who had been telling the emperor that "deciding on one's own" (*tu-tuan*) was a necessary virtue. For Su this was an easy target; his question simply adduced historical examples to show that "diligence, decisiveness, and self-confidence," the appparent virtues of a capable ruler, had on occasion led to disaster.[52]

Just as he retrospectively described Ou-yang Hsiu as the modern Mencius, defending the Confucian way from the extremes of Yang and Mo,[53] Su took it on himself to challenge the opposite extreme of uniformity: the search for an ultimate reality beyond the realm of historical knowledge. Here he is writing for a Buddhist temple and finding shih with a Buddhist fault.

Mutton and pork are used for viands. The five flavors are used to harmonize taste. Glutinous rice is used for wine, and yeast is used in making it. This is the same for all under heaven. The materials are the same, the water and fire are equal, and the temperature and humidity are one. Yet if each of two men prepares [the dish], the quality [of the meal] is not equal. Must it not be that what makes one better cannot be drawn from the quantities [given in the recipes]? However, those who made the recipes in antiquity never left out the quantities. The able went on from the quantities to get the marvelously subtle. The unable stuck to the quantities and ended up with an approximation. The point of departure was one, but there were the able and the unable; thus were the excellent and the crude manifested. When men see that this [point of departure] is one, then, seeking the excellence beyond the quantities and casting aside experience in pursuit of the marvelously subtle, they say, "I know what makes wine and food better." Then they ignore the proportions, set aside the quantities, thinking that [quality] does not depend on them. But if they create everything alike according to their own whim, then little [of what they create] will not be spit out by others.

Today our scholars have the same fault. Astronomy and geography, the calendar and music, building and clothing, the rules of capping, marriage, mourning, and sacrificing, what the *Spring and Autumn Annals* rejected and adopted, what ritual allows and the law forbids, why the successive dynasties rose and fell, and why some men are wise and others worthless, these are what scholars ought to work at. They say, "None of these are worth learning; learn what cannot be transmitted through speech and conveyed through books."[54]

There is a connection here, I think, between imitation and transcendence. When men find that the quality of the result depends upon the cook rather than the recipe, they will give up recipes and search for the secret to being a good cook; when scholars find that although everyone has imitated the proper model only some pass the examinations—that quality depends on individual ability rather than on what they are told to learn—they will give up learning entirely and search for the secret to ability. Better to encourage a broad range of learning from many sources than to teach a single model. Let me, Su seems to imply, learn how to create recipes by learning from past experience. Read slightly differently, this analogy makes the case for Su's own middle position. Received knowledge is useful—it enables men to roughly approximate the achievements of others—but the quality of the result depends on what individuals bring to it.

One of Su's most amusing accounts of the fallacy of trying to define the ultimate tao was written shortly before his arrest and cited, together with the piece on Buddhism, as evidence of slander.

On Finding an Analogy for the Sun

A man born blind did not know the sun and inquired of the sighted about it. Someone told him that the sun's shape resembled that of a tin pan, so he rapped a pan and heard its sound. Later he heard a bell and thought it was the sun. Someone told him the sun's rays were like a candle, so he fingered a candle and felt its shape. Later he handled a flute and thought it was the sun.

The sun is far removed from a bell and a flute, but the blind man did not know the difference, for having never seen the sun he sought it from others. Tao is more difficult to see than the sun, and while a man has yet to catch on, he is no different from a blind man. When someone who has caught on tells him, however clever his analogies and skilled his guidance, he still can do no better than pans and candles. From pan to bell, from candle to flute; a never-ending chain of images. Thus when men of our day speak of tao, some label it according to what they have seen and some, not seeing anything, imagine it. Both are errors of seeking tao.

Master Su says, "Tao can be brought on, but it cannot be sought after." What does "brought on" mean? Sun Wu said, "Those skilled at war bring the others on; they are not brought on by the others."[55] Tzu-hsia said, "The various artisans master their trades by staying in their workshops; the superior man brings his tao on by learning."[56] When it arrives on its own without anyone seeking it, is this not what "bringing on" is all about?

There are many divers in the south. They live with the water every day; at seven they can wade, at ten they can float, and at fifteen they can dive. Now diving is not at all something to be done carelessly; one must have gotten something of the tao of water. Thus when brave northerners, inquiring of the divers, seek how they dive and try it out in the Yellow River according to what they have been told, they always drown. So it is that all who devote themselves to seeking tao without learning are northerners learning diving.

In the past, when poetry was used in choosing shih, shih learned in an eclectic fashion but did not aim at tao. Today, when Classical studies are used in choosing shih, shih know about seeking tao but are not concerned with learning.[57]

Su was skilled at placing larger issues in the context of actual practice, but it was a skill born of the belief that abstract ideas were meaningfully experienced in the particular. Tao, as the ultimate source, can be intuited in experience but not defined; it can be realized by learning gradually and incrementally how to do something oneself, not by simply following a set of instructions. The danger is that shih will think tao can be known apart from things, as something transcendent. It is transcendent (and thus beyond definition), but it is also immanent in things and affairs. It combines the way something works and the way it ought to work, the normative and the descriptive. Given both tao and learning, ultimate value and actual things, the center lies with learning how to do things so that the tao of the affair will be realized. The upshot of this, I think, is the view that the relationship of primary concern is not between man and tao or man and heaven but between self and things.

Su has no doubt that the things and affairs making up the context of human life are real and that to get through this life successfully men must attend to them. He does see that the way men perceive things is variable. His famous "Account of the Terrace of Transcendence," from the mid-1070's, was an example of this. Against his brother's view that such a terrace allowed one to stand above it all, Su proposed to proceed both "within things," and thus appreciate any thing, and "outside things," and thus avoid being overwhelmed.[58] Keeping a distinction between self and things was crucial. Men cannot be satisfied if they measure their own worth in terms of having things; yet if they do not care about things, they will not be motivated to act responsibly. Men with standards so lofty as to make satisfaction impossible and men who try to keep things away have not found a way out; they simply make the world a source of anxiety, and their lives become a constant battle to avoid being overwhelmed. But things did not have to be at odds with self. If Ou-yang Hsiu collected "things"—even if the things were those others did not value—he could not, some argued, be legitimately said to have autonomy, to be "one who possessed tao."

Master Su says, Not so. To depend on holding onto these five things [Ou-yang collected] to be at peace is mistaken, but to depend on being free of the five things to be at peace is also mistaken. . . . Things are able to entangle the man because self possesses them. Self and things alike cannot help but receive form from heaven-and-earth; so who can possess them? Yet some think that they possess [things] themselves; if they get them they are happy, and if they lose them they are sad. Now, the Retired Scholar [Ou-yang] called himself Six-but-One, for his person and the five things as equals were one. He did not know whether he possessed things or things possessed him. The Retired Scholar and the things alike were not subject to possession; so who can make this an issue of gain or loss?[59]

From a perspective broad enough for a man to be conscious of himself and of things, he could convince himself that possession was not real in the first place; thus the prospect of not having things or losing them became irrelevant, and his appreciation of things would no longer be an obstacle.

In a more practical vein Su proposed an attitude of attachment grounded in detachment. In a famous piece from 1077, for his friend Wang Shen's art collection, he puts it like this:

The superior man may visit his intention [yü i] on things, but he may not leave his intention behind [liu i] with things. When he visits his intention on things, insignificant things can be a pleasure and the most precious of things cannot be an affliction. When he leaves his intention behind with things, insignificant things can be an affliction and the most precious of things cannot give pleasure. Lao-tzu said, "The five colors make man's eyes blind; the five notes make his ears deaf; the five tastes injure his palate; riding and hunting make his heart go wild with excitement."[60] However, the sages never did away with these four, it was simply that they visited their intentions on them. . . .

Of all things that can be enjoyed, enough to please men but not enough to change them, nothing compares with painting and calligraphy, but if one leaves intent behind and does not release it, then there may be misfortunes beyond saying. . . . When I was young, I did like these two things. What our family possessed, I only feared losing, and what others possessed, I only feared not being given. Then I laughed at myself, saying, "I set little store by wealth and honor and much by painting, I treat life and death lightly but take calligraphy seriously—I have really got things wrong, I am losing my original mind!"[61]

If men can see what they are doing, if they can gain the perspective on themselves that constitutes self-consciousness, they can create a center between being entangled by things and insulating themselves from the world. Intrinsic to that self-consciousness is a view on the nature of values. Why is it, Su asks in "Inquiring About Nurturing Life," that men spit out maggot-ridden food only when they have seen the maggots?

Let us examine whence this is born [sheng]. Someone discussing the eight delicacies will swallow; someone speaking of excrement will spit. The two not having come into contact with the self, whence is born the swallowing and the spitting? Are they born from things or are they born from the self? When one knows they are born from the self, then even if there is contact with them one does not change. This is truly being at peace. When [the self is] at peace, things affect the self lightly. When in harmony, the self responds to things suitably. The external being light and the internal being suitable, the pattern [li] of life [sheng] is complete.[62]

The pattern of life (and note Su's repetition of the word *sheng*) involves responding to things. But to keep that pattern complete, to maintain a balanced relationship between self and things, one must see that emotional responses to things come from the self. At times Su envisions a more difficult achievement: "Men and ghosts, birds and beast, presented in mixed array before me; sights and sounds, smells and tastes, intersecting in my body; the mind must have a tao, so that even if it does not rise [in response], all things will be in contact with it."[63] But in "Nurturing Life" he is content with the mediating power of self-consciousness.

But it is not easy to have a feeling of self-worth without reference to things, even if the values imputed to things come from the self. Men can learn to see that "possessing things" is self-destructive and that their emotional responses to things are grounded in their own minds, yet even the desire to be above it all and show a loftier intent is a symptom of the same problem. Su's "Account of Mr. Chang's Hall for Treasuring Calligraphy" (1072) begins:

All the men of the day craved fine food and drink, beautiful clothes, and sensual delights. There was a man who thought himself lofty and ridiculed them. He plucked the zither and played chess; he collected old calligraphy and paintings. Guests came, and he boastfully displayed [his possessions], thinking the utmost of himself. But one guest ridiculed him. "The way the ancients made themselves known to later ages," he said, "was through speech and literary composition; how could [objects such as] these be worth liking?" But a shih of the heroic sort ridiculed them both, holding that shih ought to be known in the age for great achievements, for [what Confucius spoke of as] "putting it into empty words rather than manifesting it in doing things" was something those who had no choice did.[64]

Su goes on to object to those who "ridicule the likes of others on the basis of their own likes" and adds an unsubtle dig at those young proponents of the New Policies whose idea of great achievement is to turn "untested learning" into policy, wasting people as a calligrapher wastes paper.

There is another side to this. Men may impute value to things, but things have something to them, they are real. Responding to things requires not only understanding the characteristics of human response but also knowing something about things. As Su noted in criticizing Wang An-shih, the object of learning is to illuminate inherent patterns. Yet precisely for those things in which a recognition of *li* is most vital—those things whose forms are most various and ephemeral—this knowledge is most difficult to assess.

In discussing painting, I have held that men and animals, buildings and utensils, have constant forms, whereas mountains and trees, water and clouds, although lacking constant forms, have constant patterns. When [a painter's depiction of] a constant form is off, everyone knows it; but when [a painter's depiction of] the constant li is inappropriate, even some who understand painting will not know it. Thus all who gain fame while deceiving the age are sure to rely on what has no constant form.

Although this is so, when a constant form is off, the loss goes no further; it cannot spoil the whole. But when a constant li is inappropriate, then it undoes everything. It is because their form is not constant that their constant li must be attended to with care.[65]

Better obvious mistakes of the surface than a misrepresentation of underlying truths. The problem lies in the difficulty of seeing the errors that really matter.

Nothing reduces to a simple formula. Learning about things is important, as Su argues strongly when faced with those he suspects of ignoring the phenomenal world. Knowing about things is, however, not easy. Misperception and deception are ever-present threats, and a truly impartial view of phenomena can lead one to think everything is hopeless. Human interests and purposes—the desire to serve the living and preserve the existing—should intrude.[66] Su himself contrasts his position with those who seek tao outside phenomena or rely on a fixed doctrine. I would add a contrast with those like Shao Yung who believe a systematic understanding of the phenomenal world is possible and necessary to knowing values. Shao writes: "Using things to contemplate things is nature [hsing]. Using self to contemplate things is emotional response [ch'ing]. The nature is impartial and clear; emotional response is partial and murky."[67] When one sees things in relation to each other, rather than in terms of the values men impute to them out of their own concerns, one can know the inherent value of each thing as a product of heaven-and-earth. In my view Su accepts "using self to contemplate things" while trying to avoid the danger of universalizing his own prejudices.

The phenomenal world matters, but there is no sure method for knowing the value of things. The self is important, but there is no sure method for ensuring its worth. Su's interest lies with life between the extremes of seeking tao and abject subjection to social pressure, and he gently reminds those who think they have figured everything out that they have forgotten the other side. He writes in 1079:

Chang Chih-fu of Chien-an built a room to the west of the main office and called it "Deliberate." He said, "I plan to spend mornings and evenings here. For all that I do, I shall always first deliberate and then act. You will write a record of this for me."

Aha. I am the most undeliberative and uncontemplative man in the world. When I happen on something, I respond; I have no time to deliberate. Were I to deliberate before I respond, the response would never get there. Were I to deliberate once I had responded, it would be too late. So I go through life, not knowing what to deliberate upon. The words respond in my mind and burst into my mouth. If I spit them out, I offend others; if I swallow them, I offend myself. I think it better to offend others; thus in the end I spit them out.

The superior man relates to the good just as he would to a pretty face and to what is not good just as he would to a foul smell. He does not have to look over the matter and then deliberate and, having calculated the degree of attractiveness, either avoid it or go after it. So it is that, facing a matter of principle, if one deliberates on benefits, righteousness will not be realized; and, facing a battle, if one deliberates on survival, the fight will not be vigorous. As for success and failure, gain and loss, death and life, and misfortune and fortune, these are my fate.

When young, I came upon a recluse who said, "To get close to tao, a Confucian lessens deliberation and reduces desire." I said, "Are deliberation and desire equal?" "[Deliberation] is worse than desire," he said. In the courtyard were two basins for storing water. The recluse pointed to them and said, "This one has an ant-sized drip; from the other we get rid of a pint a day. Which will empty first?" I said, "Certainly the one with the ant-sized drip." Deliberation and contemplation harm a man at a rate that is insignificant but ceaseless. What the recluse said agreed with my own mind.

Anyway, the pleasures of not deliberating cannot be named: to be vacuous yet clear, single yet comprehensive, secure yet unremitting, unfixed yet tranquil, drunk without drinking wine, asleep without closing the eyes—wouldn't it be misleading thus to commemorate the Hall of Deliberation? However, each thing that is said is appropriate to something. The myriad things are nurtured together yet do not harm each other; tao are practiced together without contradicting each other. As wise as he is, what Chih-fu calls "deliberation" can hardly be the restless attempt at deliberate contemplation of common custom. The *Change* says, "Without deliberating, without acting"; this is what I want to learn from. The *Songs* says, "Deliberation without perversity"; this is for Chih-fu. Recorded on the fourteenth day of the first month of the second year of Yuan-feng [1079].[68]

Su Shih was teasing, but only to an extent.

About one thing, however, Su Shih apparently was deliberate—the act of definition deprives the ultimate source of particular values of its universality. This is an attack on dogmatism of all sorts; it is also a valiant defense of the possibility of real grounds for human commonality. The "Colophon to the Ching-ch'i Outer Collection," here given in its entirety, illustrates this. The piece is undated, but the wording suggests Su had heard of the intellectual activity of such Loyang men as Shao Yung ("measures and numbers") and the Ch'eng brothers and their followers ("questioning and answering"), although the obvious referent for "mystery" (*hsuan*) is Buddhism. In making his point, Su refers to the famous passage in which Confucius spoke of threading his tao on a single strand. As Arthur Waley translates: "The Master said, Shen! My Way has one (thread) that runs through it. Master Tseng said, Yes. When the Master had gone out, the disciples asked, saying, What did he mean? Master Tseng said, Our Master's Way is simply this: Loyalty, Consideration."[69]

The learning that fathoms mystery [hsuan-hsueh] and the learning that defines moral principles [i-hsueh] are one. When an age has those who have caught on [ta], the learning that defines moral principles is all a "mystery." If they have not caught on, the learning that fathoms mystery is all "moral principles."

Recent generations of scholars have been competing for loftiness through the mysterious. They practice their separate approaches, and they exhaust their measures and numbers; questioning and answering in confusion, responding and agreeing without exhaustion. But when they come to a matter of life or death or are involved in some momentous undertaking, few are not defeated [in their attempt to remain above it all].

Confucius said, "A simple fellow put a question to me. It was as if he were empty. I kept hammering at both ends until I got everything out of him."[70] This generation having no Confucius, there is no one to hammer at it. Therefore the simple fellow is enabled to use his emptiness to cheat the age and pick up a name. This is ridiculous.

The Retired Scholar of Ching-ch'i has written several "Biographies of the Transmission of the Lamp." He promotes the learning that defines moral principles in order to make up for the failings of the mysterious. It is analogous to herding sheep: one looks for the ones at the back and whips them along; there are no constant sheep.

When Yen Yuan died, there was no disciple to whom could be given words of hidden significance. From Tzu-kung on, none heard about [human] nature and heaven's tao.[71] Only Tseng-tzu trusted to tao. He studied fervently and did not serve in government. He followed Confucius longest of all. In dialogues between teacher and students, "yes" was always said. But it was the "yes" of Tseng-tzu alone that is recorded in the Analects. Thus I know that the subtlety of Confucius is transmitted in a single "yes." The square peg and the round hole matched, not leaving space to admit a hair. Beyond the one "yes," mouth and ear are both lost. Yet the followers, so petty, wanted to know what he had meant. They were of the type that tries to tie the wind and catch shadows, whom it is not worth informing with the real. How grievous.[72]

Su Shih hammers away at both ends. Something unites the realms of moral principle and mystery, but those who "catch on" to this are few; most think only one side is adequate. I am not sure Su is entirely in sympathy with Ching-ch'i, a Buddhist layman who apparently favored the moral above the mystical side of Buddhism; not because Ching-ch'i was Buddhist but because his position implied there could be fixed constants. Su's own position is clear: hsuan-hsueh can include i-hsueh, but not the other way around. The last paragraph affirms this; anything more specific than an assent to Confucius's assertion that his tao is thread by one strand is false.

As readers, we may feel that we know Su as a man, we may believe that he was able to hold together mystery and history, self and things. But could Su do more than assent that there was one integrating strand?

A Sharable Ethic: Su Shih's
Commentaries on the Classics

Mencius said, "The reason for disliking those who hold to one extreme is that they cripple tao. One thing is singled out to the neglect of a hundred others."[73] If Su had not gone beyond objecting to those who held to extremes, it would be open to question whether he ever arrived at a sharable ethic.[74] In his commentaries on the *Change* and *Documents*, Su Shih did, however, propose a way of thinking about values others could share. He began the commentary on the *Book of Change* after being exiled to Huang-chou in 1079. He no longer wished to be seen as merely a critic, a reputation his writings had earned him—that was the "old me" he told an admirer, not the "present me."[75] Su wrote his commentary on the *Book of Documents* after Wang An-shih's successors returned to power in 1094 and Su was exiled to the remote south. Together with the lost commentary on the *Analects*, these works were meant, Su wrote, to "correct the mistakes of past and present" and "bring increase to the age."[76] Returning from Hainan island shortly before his death, he wrote: "Only when I regard these three books on the *Change*, *Documents*, and *Analects* do I feel this life has not been lived in vain. Nothing else is worth mentioning."[77]

In both commentaries Su arrives at the same conclusion: individuals can learn to respond creatively yet responsibly to a changing world. In Su Shih's terms, he is explaining what it means to act as a sage. He does this, however, in terms of two different realms. In writing on the *Change*, Su addresses attempts to ground values in innate human qualities and ideas about cosmic processes. In explaining how he understood the tao of heaven-and-earth and "human nature and decree" (*hsing-ming*), Su was showing that he could take into account the concerns of philosophical thinkers. This commentary is politically engaged—the interpretation of the hexagram texts reiterates his criticism of those who impose uniformity on the world or demand all agree with one man[78]—but it is in the commentary on the *Documents* that Su directly addresses political thought and statecraft. The *Documents* commentary lays claim to the model of ancient governance with which "scholars of recent times" or "the recent scholar" (presumably Wang An-shih) had justified coercive government.[79] Su was demonstrating that the sage of his vision could cope with the problem of governance. I think we should see Su's two commentaries as his means of establishing that there was a single way of thinking that not only applied equally to individual morality and public policy but also made unnecessary the two extremes he had noticed in 1061: attempts to equate human nature with a universal definition of morality and to equate the sage-kings' governance with a single political system.

In reading both Classics, Su's preference was for exploring the richness of a text from multiple perspectives,[80] but in writing Su also had arguments to make about what the sages, as actors, speakers, or compilers, meant. He was not, he was sure, forcing the text to fit his own ideas.[81] His interpretive approach differed considerably from Wang An-shih's efforts to establish meanings by supposing a coherent arrangement of the text. Su maintained a dialectic between inferring from the parts the larger meaning of the whole, the *ta-i*, and interpreting the parts as various aspects of that general meaning. The model here is the idea of the one and the many, in which the parts manifest diverse aspects of a unifying idea. Similarly, the *Change* and the *Documents* revealed to Su two aspects of a unitary tao of the sage.

Accounts of Su's commentary on the *Change* are available elsewhere; here I shall briefly recount the basic structure of Su's vision of the sage in that work.[82] Su saw the *Change* as a cumulative text, created by successive sages who worked to keep a connection between the "great whole of tao" and human life. The book can be used as a practical guide to dealing with human affairs, but one who has "caught on" (*ta-che*)—one who sees that how the sages created the book corresponds to how the tao operates in the realm of heaven-and-earth—can leave the book behind and act as a sage himself. Particularly in discussing the *Commentary on Appended Verbal Elaborations* (*Hsi-tz'u chuan*), Su's goal is to explain how it is possible for man to practice the tao (of the book, sages, heaven-and-earth, and *hsing-ming*). Su's basic model of the connection between tao and things in all realms reduces to the following. There is a unitary, inexhaustible source (tao in relation to heaven-and-earth, *hsing* in man) whence all things come into being. The process through which things come into being operates in a dualistic manner (e.g., yin and yang), but neither the one source nor the dual forces through which it operates can be known intellectually. All inherent patterns (li) are one li, but the "one" cannot be fixed and defined as something; yin and yang cannot be equated with tao.

Men generally lack an inclusive perspective. They live in a world of dualities, cut off from the source, and are always being carried "downstream" into a world that is becoming ever more complex and diverse with the creation of new things. Were a man able to tap into the common source and respond to particular events from their common basis, his responses would have real value. Thus he must work his way "upstream," as Su puts it. He can do this, as Su argues with reference to things as diverse as swimming, music, and the desires, by understanding intellectually the inherent patterns by which the thing or affair came into being. He can study the li of water (how one sinks and floats) and learn to swim; he can reflect on his feelings and see that there is something beyond desire whence desire comes. But in the end he makes a leap into an intuitive unity with the source or oneness with the thing. At this point he achieves spontaneity, and being one with water or with his own character, he can respond to it (or from it) without calculation. "Those in antiquity who were good at governing never competed with the people. Instead they allowed them to choose for themselves and thereupon guided them to it [their choice]."[83] Thus a man acts in a manner true to himself and to the thing he is responding to and brings into being things that have real value for that moment. Su's spontaneity is premised on knowledge, thought, and learning. His aim is to accomplish things of value. As he does so, he is exemplifying Confucius's claim that "man can broaden tao; it is not that tao can broaden man."[84]

In discussing the *Change*, then, Su interprets the issues of self and things as a problem of connecting the phenomenal world of diversity and change in human life with the one ultimate unitary source of values common to all things. To connect life and tao is to link the common interest and the particular, partial actions of the individual; the promise this holds is that it is possible to do things of real value.

In his commentary on the *Documents*, as in his commentary on the *Change*, Su infers and tries to clarify the source and process behind the exemplary models the sages present in the Classic so that the reader can practice it himself. Three themes in Su's treatment of the *Documents* are of interest here: Su's attack on the interpretation of the work to justify coercive government; his account of the benevolent government he believed the Classic was intended to present; and his conviction that behind this model of benevolent government lies a way of being that includes yet transcends the model. The first and second themes are surely in part a critique of attempts by the New Policies regime to force society to conform to its dictates. The third speaks to Su Shih's (and his age's) larger concern: how the individual can realize true values in learning and practice.

Coercive and Benevolent Government

Su's commentary on the "P'an-keng" chapter of the *Documents* is one of several that discuss how the government ought to proceed when compelled to make important changes.[85] In this case, the Shang king P'an-keng confronts popular resentment as he prepares to move the capital to Yin. Su comments:

Now the populace has gathered together and expresses its resentment. One suspects [P'an-keng] ought to establish new policies and effect expedient measures, using all his awesome might to control them. [But] P'an-keng was a man of benevolence. His sending down instructions to the populace was simply to "make constant the former affairs," meaning he did not create new laws, and to "correct the institutions," meaning he did not establish expedient measures. He was saying, "Let none of you dare to suppress the remonstrances of the lesser men." He feared that the various officers and responsible officials would draw inferences contrary to his intent and forbid the populace to speak. When P'an-keng moved [the capital] and Yin was restored, did he not employ this tao?[86]

P'an-keng understood that the prospect of moving the capital disturbed the people, but he did not force them to comply. Instead he ordered that their complaints be heard. Moreover, he made clear that however unsettling this change might be, his aim was to maintain and improve on the immediate past. The unbenevolent man, into whose mouth Su put sentences Wang An-shih had used, is quite the opposite.

An unbenevolent man despises the populace. He says, "The populace can share in success; it is difficult to plan the beginning with them." Thus in all aspects of governing, he is like thunder and ghosts, keeping the populace from knowing where [political change] is coming from. How would he be willing to reveal his true feelings and plan together with the populace? Now [P'an-keng] is saying, "I announce to the populace the measures that have been prepared; nothing is concealed. This is greatly respecting the populace. What is said can surely be practiced without going too far. Thus the populace will trust me and change to follow me."[87]

P'an-keng seems not to have gone quite as far as Su would have liked—he did not "plan together" with the people—but he was open about his intentions. On the other hand, Su continues, he also acted to keep popular resentment in check by reminding the leading families that they had a duty to persuade the populace to see the necessity of the move and warning them not to seek popularity by appealing to common resentment.[88] To keep the support of elite families and quiet the populace, Su explains, P'an-keng made clear he did not aim to deprive them of their wealth and avoided employing "men who liked material goods." He wished "rich and poor to live together supporting each other," thus "teaching the populace the tao of improving life."[89] P'an-keng was not Wang An-shih, then, but he was not perfect either.

Doing something anyway when the populace is not happy never happened with the Former Kings. . . . P'an-keng is forced to move, but when the Former Kings did this they made the populace act yet it was not frightened, and they made the populace labor yet it was not resentful. P'an-keng is the decline of virtue. His means of gaining the populace's trust were not perfect, therefore there was such protest. Yet when the populace expressed resentment and went contrary to his decree, P'an-keng was not angry. He took responsibility himself for having brought on the problem, allowed even greater freedom of expression, and over and again instructed and explained. In replacing battle-axe and halberd with mouth and tongue, he was the utmost in loyalty and integrity. This is why Yin did not perish but was restored. The superior men of later times who have oppressed the populace and relied exclusively on their own [opinions] have all used P'an-keng as an excuse. I must dispute.[90]

For Su the "intent" of this document is the idea that good rulers heed the opinions of their subjects rather than forcing others to obey.

The model of benevolent government Confucius created with the *Documents* is, in fact, a model for a fallen age. Su holds that Confucius chose the various documents of the Classic to serve as positive models.[91] Yet the Three Eras period is, from at least Shun on,[92] an age of ongoing "decline" (*shuai*). The ancient kings were better but not qualitatively different from later men; their faults were also those of the Han and T'ang rulers. When Ch'i, the Hsia founder Yü's son and successor, speaks of exterminating the entire clan as a means of punishing an evildoer in "The Speech at Kan," Su remarks: "Only Ch'i and T'ang [the Shang founder] speak of exterminating the clan. [Thus] we know that virtue has declined. But they only say it; there was never talk of their really having exterminated men's clans."[93] Surely King T'ang was a sage, yet T'ang does not represent perfect virtue.[94] Su's sage-kings accept the moral ambiguity of having to create evil precedents out of present necessity, a point Su develops explicitly with reference to the destruction of the evil king Chieh by T'ang, whose shame at behaving unethically did not stop him from doing what had to be done.[95] Su places King Wu, the Chou founder, in a similar situation.[96]

The benevolent government of the *Documents* is also dynastic government, and that, Su argues, creates an unavoidable tension between "man" and "law." Generally sage-kings and their ministers chose man over law, but they were always being driven toward law because of the contradiction between popular desire and the claims of the royal house to all under heaven as its own property. The rulers thus needed officials to administer the realm. Su notes that from Yao and Shun on the number of offices and bureaucrats kept increasing, so that "in later times virtue declined and governance degenerated even more. They trusted to man ever less, leaving everything up to law."[97] Relying on rules to keep control made crime inevitable and punishment necessary.[98] The sages at least understood the law's limitations; they "relied on man and law together yet relied on man to a greater extent. Therefore for the [criminal] code they set up only general principles [*ta-fa*]. The details of the severity [of punishments] they left up to men to propose according to the situation. . . . Therefore punishments were simple and governance was pure."[99] Still, the Former Kings did not make extensive use of capital punishment, penalize the kin of criminals, or destroy entire families.[100] Su thus contests those documents that appear to treat capital force as legitimate.[101] Being for "man" means allowing men to pursue their own interests and not sacrificing innocents on the altar of unchanging law.[102] It means never letting "terror" predominate over "love."[103] It means "forbearance" of the minor transgressions of the populace, not, as some would have it, "bearing" their suffering.[104]

The ancients wanted to convince the people that government would not harm their interests, for "the sages thought popular opinion determined whether [the state] would survive."[105] It respected and valued well-established families, for the "great lineages" (ta-tsu) and "families prominent through the generations" (shih-chia) were sources of the right kind of officials. Su does, however, reject hereditary office holding and points out the corrupting influence of families with great wealth and power.[106] But above all, Su insists that the sages understood that political policy had to have broad support among the elite. The significance of "The Canon of Yao," in which Yao chooses Shun as his successor, was not that power should be given to the most worthy instead of to kin but that Yao recognized that ultimately, however perfect his own knowledge, he could not force others to accept his unprecedented act of giving Shun the empire unless others concluded by themselves that Shun was the right man.[107] A sage does not confuse his own inclinations with what is good for everyone, as Su comments on the final document: "Confucius must have thought that the one sentence that could lose the state was this: 'All the people should be like me.' "[108]

Su's benevolent government includes much that had come to be associated with the "Confucian" side of the imperial system, although Su rarely makes an issue of doctrine.[109] There is a place for "rites and music." Ritual is an external, formal model to which men are expected to adhere, however, and as such it has something in common with law. "If one loses propriety [i.e., ritual], he enters [the domain of] punishment. Ritual and punishment are one thing."[110] Ritual is preferable as a way of molding men's behavior from outside: it appeals to a man's sense of honor rather than his fear of pain.[111] It is a better political standard than "profit" because it puts the preservation of social order before wealth and power, as the Duke of Chou taught King Ch'eng.[112] Citing T'ang history, Su contends that rulers concerned with finances will be manipulated by those with resources and lose their authority.[113] But ritual is a means of preserving the state, not an end in itself. Su recognizes that the ancients did make a connection between ritual-and-music and heaven-and-earth, but concludes that the loss of ancient music makes it impossible to recover the ancients' ability to tune in to the cosmos.[114]

Still, even if Su asserts both that government should "cultivate human affairs" rather than relying on heaven's mandate and that heaven's mandate correlates with the general will of the populace,[115] he allows that heaven-and-earth and the ghosts-and-spirits respond to human actions with natural events. Han dynasty excesses in interpreting portents should not lead men to ignore the evidence of omens in the *Documents* and *Songs*.[116] It is possible to infer the sources of events using the five phases of change, for "heaven and man are not far from each other" and "heaven and man have a tao that is mutually comprehensible."[117] But Su takes this only to a point. The "superior man must comprehend the tao of heaven" but he who has "caught on mentally comprehends" and avoids shaman-like communication with the ghosts-and-spirits.[118] Su was trying to save the political utility of cosmic resonance (which Wang An-shih denied), I think, for "the ruler fears nothing from all under heaven; only heaven can admonish him. Today he says, '[Explanations for] natural disasters cannot be sought through analogies [to political events]. I need merely see for myself that nothing is wrong.' There is no greater obstacle to governing the state than this; so I must dispute."[119]

Su does not deny the role of institutions, but he sees cultivating the self as a more pressing issue. Faced with Shun's instructions on various measures for suppressing the rebellious Miao people, Yü had doubts, Su thinks: "It seems that in his mind he did not entirely agree; he thought when [Shun's] person was cultivated all under heaven would submit of their own accord."[120] The Miao resisted because Shun "had not cultivated himself completely"; Shun ought to have "sought [the reasons for this] in himself."[121] The ruler who cultivates himself keeps "selfish desires" in check because they keep him from accepting criticism.[122] When rulers do not have fixed standards, "the shih who are intent on being of use" will be prompted to do their jobs well rather than trying to get ahead by appealing to the ruler's prejudices. Rectifying the mind is useful; it enables the ruler to "contemplate the real substance of gain and loss."[123]

Self-cultivation is not merely attaining a mental state of freedom from bias. The sages exemplified virtues of lasting value that men can learn. "All the virtues of the sages, such as benevolence, righteousness, filial piety, fraternal respect, loyalty, trustworthiness, ritual, and music can be learned."[124] One begins to integrate the virtues into the self by focusing the mind on them. "The virtues of the sages necessarily begin with mental concentration [*nien*]. . . . When a man reaches the utmost of concentration, then even when he lets go and does not concentrate they are always there. In the beginning he concentrates on benevolence and is benevolent;

he concentrates on righteousness and is righteous. On reaching the ultimate, he does not concentrate but is of himself benevolent and righteous."[125] For Su it also follows that what a man values is a matter of choice. "If the will is on benevolence, then everything he apprehends in learning will be benevolent. . . . If the will is on achievement and profit [*kung-li*], then everything he apprehends in learning will be achievement and profit."[126] As in his commentary on the *Change*, Su takes care to avoid equating the virtues with human nature, without denying that all virtues have a source inside man.[127]

Certain virtues are appropriate to benevolent government, Su agrees, but the list of particular virtues in one document was intended merely to aid those who "did not know men" and needed "rules to reduce mistakes."[128] "In the end there is no rule for knowing men," he writes.[129] Yet government must constantly seek the right men, and those in charge often lack the "tao" for knowing men.[130] Imitating set virtues is not enough. "What men desire is the same as the sages, but [men] do not cultivate the means to gain what they desire."[131] Su's commentary also speaks to how men can cultivate that means.

Going Beyond the Model

Su's commentary presents a choice. His readers can either adopt the true model of ancient government or cultivate their inherent ability to act as the sages did, for the model of benevolent government is simply the result of treating the sages' responses to an imperfect world as worthy of imitation. Su thus looks beyond the "traces" other men have imitated to the sources of the traces in the self. He finds there grounds for human commonality and individual autonomy. It is possible for men to respond to things as they themselves see fit yet realize the common good.

Su spells out his view of this internal basis in two passages. The first takes up the lines "The mind of man is unstable, the mind of tao is unapparent; be of true insight and maintain unity, hold fast to the mean [*chung*]."[132] Chu Hsi later used this "sixteen-character teaching" in arguing for an absolute distinction between heavenly principle and human desire. For Su the distinction is between the emotions and their source.

The mind of man is the mind of common men: [the emotional responses] such as pleasure, anger, sorrow, and joy. The mind of tao is the original mind [*pen-hsin*]: it is what is able to bring into being pleasure, anger, sorrow, and joy. Security and danger come into being out of pleasure and anger; order and disorder depend on sorrow and joy. The expressions of this mind have moved heaven-and-earth and harmed the harmony of yin and yang. It can be said to be unstable. As for the root mind, where is it in fact? Does it exist [phenomenally]? Or does it not exist? If it exists [as a phenomenon], then that which brings into being pleasure, anger, sorrow, and joy is not the root mind [i.e., if a particular thing, it cannot be the one source for many emotions]. If it does not exist, then what is it that brings into being pleasure, anger, sorrow, and joy? Therefore, the root mind is not something scholars can seek through effort, yet those who have caught on can apprehend it for themselves. Can it not be said to be unapparent? Shun is warning Yü, saying, "Would I have you follow the mind of man? The mind of man is unstable and cannot be relied on. Would I have you follow the mind of tao? The mind of tao is unapparent and cannot be seen." But how could the mind be two? [The appearance of twoness arises] because one lacks true insight [literally: does not see its essence]. If one has true insight, then it is one.

Su's point, I think, is that instead of tying emotional responses to particular affairs—that is, instead of establishing rules of good and bad—the sages were saying that responding appropriately depends on connecting the ultimate source within and one's feelings about things. He goes on to equate this with the idea of *chung* (the state before emotions are aroused) and *ho* (expression in proper measure) in the "Doctrine of the Mean."[133]

[The state when] pleasure, anger, sorrow, and joy are not yet aroused cannot be named and spoken of. Tzu-ssu named it *chung*, taking that as the manifestation of the root mind. Those who did tao in antiquity surely recognized this mind. If they nurtured it in the proper fashion, then it was obviously apparent in the midst [*chung*] of the most unapparent. If they saw this mind, then pleasure, anger, sorrow, and joy were all tao. This they called "harmony." Pleasure then became benevolence, anger then became righteousness, sorrow then became ritual, joy then became music. They accomplished affairs of flourishing virtue wherever they went. Why should it be found strange that they got heaven and earth into their proper places and nurtured the myriad things?

Making the connection, seeing that there is an ultimate common source, ensures that informed responses to things will be good. The values and practices associated with benevolent government were institutional translations of the emotional responses of men who maintained unity. "When the mind of tao is hidden and the mind of man rules, pleasure, anger, sorrow, and joy each follows its desires and the disasters [they cause] are beyond words. The mind of tao is the mind of man; the mind of man is the mind of tao. If one lets it go, it is two; if one has true insight into them, they are one."[134]

The second passage occurs as a comment on I Yin's advice "At last as at first be one, and all the time shall you be renewing every day" in the document "All Possessed One Virtue."[135] Here Su argues that having a "ruler within" allows one to respond to things according to the situation. "Being one" does not mean finding an unchanging standard.

[Some say that] "being one" means unchanging, for if a man is good and unchanging is that not good, and if he is not good and unchanging is that not close to being a Chieh? This is not what it means. When there is a ruler within [*chung yu chu*] it is called "one." When there is a ruler within, then things come and he responds. When things come and he responds, then he is daily renewing [things]. If there is no ruler within, then things will be in control. Pleasure, anger, sorrow, and joy are all things, but who is making them be renewed? Therefore I Yin said, "At last as at first be one, and all the time shall you be renewing every day."

I have said before that the sage is like heaven. He kills at the right time, and he brings into being at the right time. The superior man is like water. He takes form according to things. Heaven does not transgress against benevolence; water does not lose its levelness. Because it is one [i.e., because it has a ruler within], therefore it is renewing. Because it is renewing, therefore it is one. It is one; therefore it does not flow away. It is renewing; therefore it is not exhausted. This is the essential tao that has been transmitted since Fu Hsi. I Yin was ashamed that his ruler was not like Yao and Shun; so he instructed him herewith. The multitude says if a man renews he cannot be one [unchanging], and being one [unchanging], he is not renewing. I Yin is saying that oneness is that by which he renews. This means that "the myriad things are nurtured at the same time yet do not harm each other, and [the various] tao are practiced at the same time yet do not conflict with each other."[136]

There is no contradiction between change and constancy, then, if what is constant is the ruler within. This ruler cannot be defined, but its operations are analogous to those of something like water that can be constant yet take various forms. The ruler within makes possible the independence necessary to act as one sees fit.

The sages could deal with an imperfect world because, rather than sticking to a particular model, they were able to "respond to things" (*ying wu*), as Su notes with regard to the Shang and Chou founders.[137] Thus they did not try constantly to govern through either non-action or activism.[138] The world being imperfect and usually on the brink of imbalance, the sages did not try to have everything at once; they did what was most pressing, tacking and tilting as necessary.[139] Being able to respond thus requires a clear understanding of the situation and how things work. "The mind can be misguided or correct," Su writes, and "affairs can be right or wrong. Correct the mind and seek the patterns [*li*] [of affairs]; they can always be apprehended."[140] And "if a man enacts a virtue without knowing the li by which it is so [i.e., why it is virtuous], then his virtue is like borrowed goods; it is not something he himself possesses. If he himself cannot possess it, how will he be able to extend it to others?"[141]

I think Su Shih favors this tao because he sees that other choices lead inevitably to coercive government. To summarize his reasoning, men who rely on fixed models to know what is right, however good their model, will seek to be seen as fitting the ideal rather than acting appropriately in changing circumstances. In the long run problems will emerge, the discrepancy between the good and the actual will increase, and they will have little choice but to rely on force to restore order. On the other hand, those who try to keep received models relevant to a changing world by making the virtues of the sages into lofty abstractions make it difficult for others to think it possible to transcend self-interest and act like a sage.[142] The common man is thus left to pursue the wealth and honor society has to offer, similarly ignoring the common good and hastening decline; coercion will again be necessary to restore order.

Su finds his ideas about being able to respond to things at the heart of the "Great Plan" ("Hung fan"), which Wang An-shih had seen as revealing the coherent system of the ancient order. The title of this document means "great model" (ta-fa),[143] but the model was the product of practicing the "tao of being limitlessly ultimate [huang-chi]" at a particular time in history.[144] "The tao of being limitlessly ultimate is great," Su writes; "it accepts everything and finds nothing unacceptable."[145] He puts forward a vision of government that allows the participation of all men who claim to be of good will and uses each according to his talents.[146] His premise is that each man can respond to things within the area of his expertise. Government should not see this tao as a program of study; it should concern itself with "removing that which obstructs being limitlessly ultimate."[147] Taking note of the references in the "Great Plan" to heaven and the five phases, Su argues that his tao is in accord with "what is so-by-itself of heaven's pattern" (t'ien-li chih tzu-jan).[148]

Su's search in his commentaries on the Change and the Documents for a tao that included yet transcended the texts and institutions of the sages explains Su Ch'e's conclusion that Su Shih "clarified through inference the learning of high antiquity, which had been disrupted."[149] It was a view of learning that recognized the value of tradition—the source of moral models—and transcended it, for Su inferred from antiquity the tao that had guided the creative acts of the sages themselves. His vision of learning spoke to the shih as men who sought both to act with integrity as individuals in social life and to act responsibly as officials in politics. Su's commentaries work at two levels. They delineate advice for behavior in the hexagrams and norms for government of the Former Kings while simultaneously proposing a tao of acting as a sage oneself. But these two levels share a common basis, for both Su's reading of the behavioral and political norms of the Classics and his interpretation of how a sage is able to create models for others are guided by his belief that, because ultimately there is a unitary source for all things, it is possible to act in a manner that is in the real interest of the whole. To be a sage, one must believe that there is a real basis for unity.

But how, in fact, could shih learn to be sages? Su Shih's message was directed at men for whom maintaining one's integrity in the face of social pressure and doing well in official service were not enough. They wished to be remembered.[150] To them, and to many shih who would never pass the examinations or serve in government, Su argued that as individuals they could learn the tao of the sage and simultaneously accomplish things worthy of being remembered by others. They could do this in the realm of literature and art, through their own personal participation in wen.

A Place for Wen

The Su Shih depicted here invited men to transcend dogma and rely on themselves. They needed to know more than principles. Men had interests and desires; things had their inherent patterns. To coerce men into ignoring their desires and into operating against their tendencies would not work for long. Su thought they could seek out the patterns inherent in things that explained their development and variation. Yet all things were partial, even oneself; without some sense of commonality, taking the interests of others into account could be an excuse for pursuing selfishness. Su located the individual in the middle, between seeing things as they were and acting to help them be what they ought to be. Responding was interfering, and if the ultimate point of interfering was to keep things whole—to keep the self whole, the state whole, culture whole—then the individual had to be guided by an intuition of some fundamental unity, in which the patterns of things and the interests of the self were conjoined and the spring of a spontaneous response to things released. Su asked that men believe that however hard it was to be certain of how and why, the inherent interests of all things were connected.

Su articulates values that fit with his way of trying to be inclusive: breadth before narrowness, congruence with past accomplishments before radical departures from them, and creative flexibility before imitation and rigidity. In a world where not a few found teachers of dogmas, Su was unwilling to promise absolute certainty or an unreflective spontaneity. Living with uncertainty was hard work; spontaneity required study and thought. In place of certain total knowledge, he offered deeper, broader, and more nuanced awareness. Su's relativism was at best instrumental. Models existed; men could infer the basic strategies. The variations that emerged in individual practice were still variations; the swimmer would drown and the government would perish if the fundamental patterns of swimming and governing were betrayed. The water and the populace have wills of their own, so to speak, and can be advantageously channeled only by proceeding along the paths of their own inclinations. In the end Su makes practice the only way to demonstrate to oneself and others that one had truly combined a knowledge of things with an intuition of unity.

Su's ideas are woven through his comments on the literary enterprise.

Here I shall note three strands. The first concerns writing as the vehicle for expressing ideas about things. As he tells one inquirer: "Confucius said, 'Verbal elaborations simply get the point across.' Things certainly have this pattern [*li*]. Not knowing it is the problem. If one knows it, the problem is not being able to get it across in speaking and writing. Verbal elaborations are simply what gets this across."[151] Writing made possible the nuanced expression of ideas that were difficult to know and define.

Confucius said, "If it is said without wen, it will not go far."[152] [But] he also said, "Verbal elaborations simply get the point across." When verbal elaborations stop at getting the intent across, they are suspected of not being wen, but this is not so at all. I doubt you will find one in a million who seeks out the subtlety of a thing—like tying the wind or catching a shadow—and is able to make this thing be complete in the mind. How much less often is one able to make it be complete in speech and writing? This is what is meant by verbal elaborations getting the point across. When verbal elaborations reach the stage of being able to get the point across, then the wen cannot be exhausted.[153]

In effect this denied that one could claim to possess "wen" as a value through literary craft alone, although writing that expressed difficult ideas could make use of all that was associated with a cultivated literary aspect. Making the literary aspect the point was to miss the point, but to object to the literary aspect was to fail to see why it was there in the first place. Su turned Yang Hsiung's criticism of literary effort back against Yang himself.

Yang Hsiung liked to make his verbal elaborations difficult and deep in order to give an attractive appearance [*wen*] to his shallow and simple ideas. If he had said them straight out, then everyone would have known [they were shallow]. This is precisely what is meant by "insect carving." His *Supreme Mystery* [a book modeled on the *Change*] and *Exemplary Sayings* [in imitation of the *Analects*] are both of this ilk. Why did he regret only his rhapsodies? He carved insects all his life and, having only varied the melody, then called them Classics. Is this permissible? Ch'ü Yuan composed the "Li Sao." This further variation of the Feng and Ya [of the *Songs*] "can rival the sun and moon in brilliance";[154] may it be called "insect carving" because it resembles a rhapsody? If Chia I had gone to visit Confucius, he would indeed have been welcomed; yet [Yang] disparages [his writing] as rhapsodies and treats [Ssu-ma] Hsiang-ju in the same class. Hsiung's ignorance was thus in case after case; one can talk about it with those who know, but it is difficult to speak of it with the vulgar. I mention this since we have been discussing wen.[155]

What Yang Hsiung had to say was shallow. He simply camouflaged his shallowness with an appearance that made his ideas seem difficult.

But Su did not simply adopt an instrumental view of writing. The second thread emerges when Su notes that the media through which men express understanding are "things" themselves. This has subtly complex implications. Writing has particular genres, genres have their histories, they exist in relation to other genres within larger categories, and there is change and variation over time. Thus someone using writing for his own purposes should respect its patterns as well, for what he writes has significance as writing as well. This is particularly obvious when Su speaks about calligraphy. Men contribute to the tradition by mastering its conventions, grasping its inherent patterns through the study of the full range of genres, and finally contribute to it new things and new ideas. Su writes of Ts'ai Hsiang's "flying white"–style calligraphy:

A thing [i.e., category] is of one li. If you have comprehended its idea, then you can do any part of it. Doctoring by specialty is the downfall of medicine. Painting by subject is the vulgarization of painting. The doctoring of [the great doctors of the past] Ho and Huan did not distinguish between young and old. In painting, Ts'ao [Pa?][156] and Wu [Tao-tzu] did not select just men or just things [to paint]. It is acceptable to say that [the best painters and doctors] were strong in doing certain things, but it is unacceptable to say that they were able to do this but not able to do that. Those who do seal script today do not do the clerk and running styles as well, nor do they get to the cursive style. It must be that they are not yet able to comprehend their idea. With the likes of Chün-mo, [however,] formal, running, cursive, and clerk styles are like the idea [also: are as he intends]. His remaining strength and extra intent are transformed into the "flying white" style. It can be cherished, but it cannot be learned. If he had not comprehended the idea, could it have been thus?[157]

Su applies this view to what he saw as the four great divisions of cultural accomplishment: prose, poetry, calligraphy, and painting. This passage also suggests that guiding wen as a larger category required mastering the larger pattern of its historical development.

Those who know create things. Those who are able transmit them.[158] Things were not completed by one man alone. Regarding superior men in relation to learning and craftsmen in relation to crafts: having begun in the Three Eras and having passed through the Han, by T'ang times [the things created through learning and transmitted through craft] were fully available [pei]. Hence when poetry reached Tu [Fu] Tzu-mei, prose reached Han [Yü] T'ui-chih, calligraphy reached Yen [Chen-ch'ing] Lu Kung, and painting reached Wu [Tao-hsuan] Tao-tzu, then the variations of past and present and all possible affairs were fully available. Wu Tao-tzu painted human figures as if catching a shadow with a lamp. He accepted what came and allowed what went as it suddenly appeared or went off the side; horizontal, slanting, level, and straight—all were reinforcing each other. He grasped the number of what was so-by-itself and was not off by the tip of a hair. He put forth new ideas in the midst of rule and measure; he lodged subtle li outside daring carelessness. In past and present there has been only one man of whom it can be said, "A traveling blade with room to spare, a swinging axe that makes the wind."[159] With other paintings I am sometimes unable to determine authorship, but when it comes to Tao-tzu, I know whether they are authentic or not at a glance.[160]

Various inferences can be drawn from this brief history of literature and art. Su supposes that the processes of development are similar in all areas, with moments of creative change and periods of imitation. The claim that T'ang men realized all possible variations makes the point that it is possible to grasp the pattern of wen in its entirety by studying the T'ang. This, in turn, sets the stage for those who "know" to create things and bring about a further transformation. Wu Tao-tzu illustrates the point that the surface appearance should be integrally connected to an attempt to express how something really is. The creation of unique works and stylistic diversity only adds to the cumulative growth of a unified culture.[161]

These two strands come together in a third. For Su the cultural enterprise represents one possible way of practicing his vision of morally engaged learning. It is not the only way, and the prose, poetry, calligraphy, and painting that result are not of vital importance to human welfare or the most important qualities of an individual. But they do offer a terrain in which a student can learn to practice tao, and anyone who can learn to practice the tao in the area of wen can do it in other areas as well. Su explains to a Buddhist monk:

The sea of dharma of the Flower Garland is [as insubstantial as] a "grass hut"; how much more so poetry, calligraphy, and the zither. However, among those who learned tao in antiquity none began from emptiness. Wheelwright Pien chiseled wheels, and the hunchback caught cicadas [and, having done this all their lives, were regarded as being men of tao].[162] As long as one can develop one's cleverness and skill with it, nothing is too humble. If [Monk] Tsung apprehends tao, then both his lute playing and calligraphy will gain in strength, and his poetry even more. If Tsung is able to be like one mirror containing ten thousand, then his calligraphy and poetry ought to be even more unique. I shall peruse them, taking them as an indicator of the degree to which Tsung has apprehended tao.[163]

From this perspective, cultural accomplishment is a means through which the individual can pursue his interests and reveal to himself and others the stage of his development.

Su appreciates the man. He asks with reference to his cousin Wen T'ung (1019–79), renowned for bamboo painting, "Are there those who love his virtue as much as they love his painting?"[164] But Su can account for what makes his work important.

When bamboo first comes into being, it is only an inch-long shoot, but its joints and leaves are all there. It develops from [shoots like] cicada chrysalises and snake scales to [stalks like] swords rising eighty feet, because this development was immanent in it. Now when painters do it joint by joint, and add to it leaf by leaf, will this be a bamboo? Therefore, in painting bamboo one must first apprehend the complete bamboo in the breast. He takes up the brush and gazes intently; then he sees what he wants to paint and rises hurriedly to pursue it, wielding the brush forthwith to catch what he has seen. Like a hare leaping and falcon swooping—if he hesitates, it will be lost.

Yü-k'o [Wen T'ung] instructed me thus. I am not able to do so, but [my] mind discerns how it is so. Now when the mind discerns how it is so but one is not able to do so, inner and outer are not one, and mind and hand are not in accord. This is a fault stemming from not learning. Therefore, all who have seen something within but are not adept at executing it, will, in everyday life, see something clearly for themselves but suddenly lose it when it comes to putting it into practice. This is not true only with bamboo.

[My brother] Tzu-yu composed the "Ink Bamboo Rhapsody" for Yü-k'o, and said, "Cook Ting merely cut up oxen, but the nourisher of life chose him [as an example]. Now when you, Master, make use of this bamboo here and I think you are the one who has tao, am I wrong?" Tzu-yu had never painted; therefore he only grasped his intent. As for me, I have not only grasped his intent—I have grasped his method as well.[165]

Knowing the method of attaining tao was not, of course, the same as doing it in practice. Wen T'ung could practice it in painting, and Su could practice it in prose, poetry, and calligraphy. Su's famous description of his own writing takes his vision of learning as its premise.

My wen is like a spring with a ten-thousand-gallon flow. It does not care where; it can come forth any place. On the flatland spreading and rolling, even a thousand miles in a day give it no difficulty; when it twists and turns about mountain boulders, it takes shape according to the things encountered—but it cannot be known. What can be known is that it will always go where it ought to go and stop where it cannot but stop, that is all. Even I am not able to understand the rest.[166]

When spontaneity was achieved, real value was present. Su later recalled that "Ou-yang Hsiu spoke of wen-chang as being like pure gold and beautiful jade. The market has a fixed price. They are not things that men can fix the value of with their talk."[167] Wen could have real value, but it depended upon how men learned.

Su Shih defended the validity of the cultural enterprise in the shih world. He saw the importance of cumulative cultural tradition to thinking about values and believed literature, and art, provided the individual with a means of cultivating his ability to act responsibly. Su did not reduce wen-chang to a vehicle for moral ideas; instead he made it an aspect of learning as a universal process of uniting the interests of self and things, so that the diversity of culture became an emblem of human unity. Yet it is also true, I think, that Su Shih was the last great figure in the Sung to occupy a central role in both intellectual life and literary endeavor.

I suggest that Su Shih marks the close of two eras in Chinese intellectual history: the literary-intellectual quest to unite the search for universal values with cultural creativity, which began with Han Yü and continued into the eleventh century, and the much longer period, dating back at least to medieval times, in which thinking about values took the form of thinking about cultural traditions. In the medieval world the great task of wen-chang was to weave the diverse strands of textual-cultural traditions together into a whole that could represent the unified polity and the accomplishments of the individual. The early T'ang court scholars wrote:

When we examine their merits and fix their boundaries, [wen-chang have] collected the blossoms of the Six Classics and hundred schools, probed the secrets of Ch'ü Yuan and Sung Yü, Hsun-tzu and Yang Hsiung. When they are far-reaching in tone, profound in purport, fitting to normative patterns, and skillful in language, then, lustrous and fragrant, form and substance will be in suitable proportion, and ,the detailed and the summary will vary appropriately. They will gauge importance accurately; they will give both past and present their due. Harmonious yet strong, ornate yet normative, as brilliant as a design of the five colors, as variegated as a symphony of the eight tones. And when one is thus, he becomes what Ts'ao P'i called the comprehensive talent able to realize the normative form [of wen-chang] in all its aspects, what Lu Chi called one whose ability to overcome obstacles enables him to grasp the conception.[168]

By seeking the values that could guide the creation of a normative culture through literary effort, however, T'ang ku-wen writers undermined the medieval view. In place of cultural synthesis intellectuals began to seek the tao of the sage, and it became possible to see literary writing as a means of representing one's apprehension of values that could be conceived of apart from the cultural forms that manifested them. As Li Han wrote of Han Yü: "Wen is the device for threading tao. Those who are not deeply immersed in this tao of ours will not attain this."[169]

However, both medieval scholars and ku-wen intellectuals assumed that the textual-cultural tradition and the literary enterprise were necessary to their respective goals. The irony of Su Shih's position is that in order to explain how what an individual writes can have real value he settles on a way of thinking about values that does not in theory privilege the literary enterprise. Literary engagement could be a way of learning to take intellectual responsibility for oneself in an imperfect world and the spontaneity of literary creation could demonstrate one's mastery of the process of learning, but gaining knowledge requires thinking about things, rather than texts and doctrines. This view made Su part of a new intellectual era, but Su differed from Ch'eng I—the man to whom this new era turned for thinking about tao—by holding that the apprehension of values was mediated by culture and personality. For Su knowledge was not absolutely certain and even the most persuasive conclusions were always in some sense provisional.

9 Ch'eng I and the New Culture of Tao-hsueh

Ch'eng I (1033–1107) began the movement that led to the emergence of Tao-hsueh as the most important intellectual force in the twelfth-century Southern Sung. I shall argue that Ch'eng I disowned the cultural *problématique* that had engaged scholars for several centuries and that he and the Tao-hsueh movement he inspired constitute a radical break in shih thought. Ch'eng I's philosophical ideas substantiated his youthful vision of man as a creature with innate moral faculties endowed in him by heaven-and-earth. He was not the only one to pursue such issues, but after 1085 he became the leading proponent of this line of thought. Chou Tun-i died in 1073. Chang Tsai and Shao Yung died in 1077. In 1085, just as the opposition was returning to power, Ch'eng's older brother, Ch'eng Hao, died. Ch'eng Hao had spoken of "heaven's pattern" (*t'ien-li*) as the innate source of morality common to all; he had also attracted a number of students. Ch'eng I's appointment as lecturer to the emperor in 1086–87 gave him and his ideas—heretofore a teaching with a regional following—national visibility and far more credibility than they had enjoyed previously.[1]

Ch'eng I failed the palace examination of 1059 and then stopped trying for a degree.[2] He also decided not to pursue a career as an administrator in the family tradition, although eventually his father's access to yin privilege made this an option. As Ch'eng would later say: "Serving as an official plunders a man's will."[3] Ch'eng was not uninterested in politics. From the start he saw himself as belonging to the elite of the elite, first by virtue of his illustrious family tradition and then on the grounds of his learning.[4] Early in the 1070's the Ch'eng brothers and their father, Ch'eng Hsiang (1006–90), moved to Loyang. Resident in the Loyang area much of the time, Ch'eng I was in contact with, among others, Ssu-ma Kuang (1019–86) and his collaborator Fan Tsu-yü (1041–98), then finishing the *Comprehensive Mirror for Aid in Government*; the renowned statesmen and scholars Wen Yen-po (1006–97) and Fu Pi (1004–83); Lü Kung-chu (1018–89), son of the late Chief Councillor Lü I-chien (978–1043) and a patron of Ch'eng I since the 1060's (Lü would also become a chief councillor); and Han Wei (1017–98), a future chief councillor and one of the several illustrious sons of the late councillor Han I (972–1044).[5] These were potent social and political connections.

Lü Kung-chu and Ssu-ma Kuang arranged Ch'eng I's appointment as a lecturer to the child emperor in the spring of 1086. Criticized from various quarters for presumptuousness, rigidity, self-importance, and hypocrisy, and forced to defend the moral purity of his conduct to the empress dowager herself, Ch'eng I was eventually dismissed from his court appointment in the fall of 1087 and assigned to a teaching appointment at the Loyang branch of the Directorate of Education.[6] However, his service was enough to warrant his exile to Szechuan in the purge that followed the New Policies advocates' return to power. Ch'eng I lived long enough to see the second round of persecution; he was included in the official blacklist of 120 Yuan-yu reign period partisans in 1102—a list engraved on stelae erected throughout the land—and in 1103, when the writings of Su Shih and his circle were ordered destroyed, Ch'eng I's teachings were banned as well.[7]

The discussion of Ch'eng I that follows begins with his claim to exclusive authority over the search for values. In effect, Ch'eng redefined what it meant to be a ju by excluding from consideration those who identified learning with textual traditions. It then turns to his denial that culture played a necessary role in thinking about real values. For Ch'eng I real values stemmed from heaven-and-earth; they inhered in self and things and could be recognized directly by the mind, but they were not the creations of human thought and culture. The final issue in regard to Ch'eng I is his great philosophical achievement: to explain why shih should believe that the individual could apprehend real values directly with the mind without the mediation of culture and personality. Ch'eng denied that the effort to compose wen-chang that embodied values was necessary to the achievement of a moral society; he also challenged the priority of political institutions. Yet, as the last section of the chapter will demonstrate, the Southern Sung Tao-hsueh movement worked to create a new culture in which literature and government were subordinate to ethics. Ch'eng thus plays two roles in this account of intellectual history. Like Su Shih, his resolution of the search for values was to propose a way of knowing values, and thus he represents an end to a transitional period. But as the creator of a doctrine and founder of a school, he also represents the beginning of a new era of intellectual debate, one that developed from his ideas about the cosmos, the mind, human nature, and ethical conduct.

Ch'eng I Claims Authority

After Ch'eng Hao's death in 1085, Ch'eng I began to claim that he and his brother had recovered the learning of the sages and that no one after Mencius and before the Ch'engs had gained a true understanding. Because the rhetoric Ch'eng I employed came from Han Yü and the ku-wen tradition, we may surmise that Ch'eng was also insisting that Han and his successors were false claimants to the legacies of both This Tao of Ours and This Culture of Ours.

In "Finding the Source for Tao," Han Yü had contended that the institutions of the sages but not the values that had guided their use of institutions had survived. Ch'eng I adopted this distinction in his grave declaration for Ch'eng Hao, replacing Han's tao of the sage with "the learning of the sage," but he disputed the implication that the values that truly mattered (This Tao of Ours) had to do with government.

When the Duke of Chou died, the tao of the sage was no longer practiced. When Mencius died, the learning of the sage was no longer transmitted. When the tao was no longer practiced, there was no good government for a hundred generations. When the learning was no longer transmitted, there were no true ju for a thouand years. When there was no good government, shih were still able to illuminate the tao of good government by learning indirectly from others and transmitting it to later times.[8] But when there were no true ju, everyone was lost and no one knew where to go. Human desire went free and heaven's pattern [t'ien-li] was destroyed. The Gentleman [Ch'eng Hao] was born 1,400 years later. He apprehended in the surviving Classics the learning that was not transmitted; his will was to use This Tao of Ours [ssu-tao] to enlighten this people of ours.[9]

Knowledge about the proper political order is available to the shih, Ch'eng argues (perhaps a nod toward Ssu-ma Kuang), but without true ju to restore the transmission of the sages' learning, men cannot behave ethically. The issue is not whether government is good but whether people are good, and the problem in getting people to be good is to establish that there is a choice between t'ien-li and human desire. This view supports Ch'eng I's own decision not to pursue an official career: as a true ju, he was doing something more important.

In his "record of conduct" for Ch'eng Hao, Ch'eng I tells how his brother sought and found tao. It is clear that the tao in question refers not to the ideas of the ancients but to something that exists "outside the square" of history and culture, something that involves realizing the nature and fathoming the spiritual, matters typically associated with Buddhism and Taoism. His brother's achievement was to grasp that filial piety and respect for elders as virtues for the family and ritual and music as virtues for the state were the starting point for comprehending the mysterious.

The Gentleman engaged in learning from his fifteenth or sixteenth year. Once he heard Chou [Tun-i] Mao-shu of Ju-nan discuss tao, he rejected the examination enterprise and gave himself over completely to seeking tao. He did not yet know its essentials; he drifted through the various schools and was involved with [ch'u-ju] Taoists and Buddhists for several decades, before he turned back to seek it in the Six Classics and found it. He had insight into natural things [shu-wu] and detected human constants. He knew that fully realizing the nature to arrive at the decree had to be based on filial piety and respect for elders, that fathoming the spiritual and understanding transformation came from comprehending ritual and music. He discerned those errors of the heterodoxies that seemed to be correct; he resolved the delusions that had not been clarified for a hundred generations. Since the Ch'in and the Han no one had yet reached This Pattern of Ours [ssu-li]. He said that the learning of the sages was not transmitted after Mencius died, and he took reviving This Culture of Ours as his personal responsibility.[10]

I suspect Ch'eng is defending his brother from the charge of approaching ju values from a Buddho-Taoist perspective and imputing some of his own views to Ch'eng Hao (who did, after all, successfully pursue an examination degree). Be that as it may, he presents Ch'eng Hao as someone who did think the mysteries of human nature and the cosmic process were to be understood.

Ch'eng I named the kind of learning he and his brother had recovered Tao-hsueh, the "learning of the way."[11] In a commemorative text for a disciple in 1087, he writes: "When I and my brother promoted Tao-hsueh, the age was alarmed and doubtful; you and [your cousin] Liu Chih-fu were among those who have done the most to make those who learn see its effectiveness and believe [hsin-ts'ung]."[12] Ch'eng I is the first person dealt with in this book to demand explicitly that others "believe" his teachings in order to see the truth for themselves.[13] From his perspective, of course, it was foolish to ask others to develop their own ideas when true ones were available. Called to court in 1086, he announced himself as a ju who would "use Tao-hsueh to aid the ruler,"[14] for "I was fortunate in apprehending [the learning of the sage] in the surviving Classics, and without heed for my limitations, I have taken responsibility for the tao upon my own person. Although those who have ridiculed me are many, in recent years the believers [hsin-ts'ung-che] have also been numerous."[15] In his own eyes, then, his brother's death made Ch'eng I the sole authority over the learning that enabled men to know true values. As he wrote in a commemorative text for a disciple, "Sage learning has not been transmitted for a long time. I, born a hundred generations later, aspire to illuminate This Tao of Ours and revive This Culture of Ours after its being cut off."[16]

With his use of "ssu-wen" and "ssu-tao," Ch'eng I claimed the grandest terms in thinking about common values. He located himself and his brother as the first since Mencius to understand the learning of the sage, and he distinguished his way of learning by calling it Tao-hsueh. The Ch'engs stood alone in their times, in this view, as the true spokesmen for the ju tradition. It is common to see the Ch'engs as the Confucian response to the Buddho-Taoist challenge, a challenge met by using Buddhist and Taoist philosophical ideas to establish intellectually persuasive grounds for traditional Confucian morality. Ch'eng I could claim to be recovering the meaning behind the opening sentences of the "Doctrine of the Mean"—"What Heaven decrees is called the nature. Following the nature is called the tao. Cultivating tao is called the teaching"—in such a way that men who took this seriously would not need to turn to Buddhists for answers. As Ch'eng would later note: "Heaven has this pattern [li]; the sage follows and practices it; this is what is called tao. The sages made the basis heaven; Buddhists make the basis mind."[17] But Ch'eng I's Tao-hsueh was directed in the first place at what he saw as the mainstream of shih learning.

His rhetorical strategy was to suggest that no one else was concerned with morality in learning. "Those who learn today have divided into three. Those of literary ability are called wen-shih, and those who discuss the Classics are mired in being teachers. Only those who know tao are [engaged in] ju learning."[18] This is an attack on Classical studies and literary composition as the two kinds of examination education. Ch'eng had attacked literary composition in an essay on Yen Hui in 1056, and he restated his views at some length in a letter to the emperor in 1057.[19] In 1068 he wrote: "Later ju all took literary composition [wen-chang] and mastering the methods of the Classics [ching-shu] as their concern. Literary composition is nothing more than making words pretty and showy and ideas new and unique in order to please the ears and eyes of others. The methods of the Classics are nothing more than explicating the glosses and comparing the strengths of earlier ju in order to establish a different interpretation [shuo] as your own contribution. Can such kinds of learning actually arrive at the tao?" In its place he proposed to treat ethical conduct as the way to "illuminate tao." Some thought this meant nothing more than "cultivating the person and being attentive to conduct" by forcing oneself to adhere to external standards, but Ch'eng had something more in mind: "It is possible to say that what we look for in conduct can be achieved by forcing oneself. But is comprehending it in the mind possible through attentiveness and cultivation? Especially since if you do not have it inside, you will be unable to force it [to appear] on the outside. This is the basis for ju."[20]

In the old argument over the relative value of wen-hsueh (literary learning) and *te-hsing* (ethical conduct) for the shih, Ch'eng I chose conduct. As he explained to an official, "No basis of governance is more important than reviving the common people's conduct. When the customs of the common people are good, they will have adequate clothes and food; this has always been so. All natural disasters are brought about by being not good."[21] But Ch'eng went beyond this: by relating the ultimate goal of learning to ethical conduct, rather than to reflection upon the textual tradition, he challenged the tie between *wen* and *hsueh* and redefined *te-hsing* as a manifestation of one's knowledge of values. "Those who learn definitely should force themselves, but if they do not attain knowledge, how can they succeed in practice? How can you keep up what you practice by forcing yourself? The only thing to do is to illuminate the inherent patterns [*li*] clearly, and naturally you will find joy in according with the patterns. The nature is originally good; to accord with pattern and act, it is necessary to give pattern to affairs [*li shih*]."[22]

The implication of this unity of thought and ethical behavior was to deny that text-based learning was integral to knowing and realizing values. This left Wang An-shih, Ssu-ma Kuang, and Su Shih outside the fold and thus placed Ch'eng I at odds with the intellectual trends that had begun in the late eighth century. One answer to the question posed by Hoyt Tillman—"How did Tao-hsueh evolve out of Sung learning and in the context of struggles with rival schools of Sung learning?"[23]—is that it evolved from a rejection of prevailing assumptions: that men could determine values through the study of texts, that conclusions about how men should proceed to learn for themselves could be arrived at through the study and interpretation of texts, that scholars without political power could most effectively serve moral ends by writing about what they had learned, and that literary composition (whether relevant to government or not) had a valid function in shih life. Ch'eng I insisted that literary composition was unnecessary to moral learning.[24] He could do this while accepting the need for wen as cultural forms, of course, and he did claim that his brother and he were finding the tao in the Classics. Still, I would suggest that he intended Tao-hsueh to be an alternative to wen-hsueh as a general term for the enterprise of shih learning and that he self-consciously grounded his opinions in an understanding of heaven-and-earth rather than of the cultural tradition.

To put my position in the strongest possible terms: in contrast to all the scholars dealt with in this book, Ch'eng I did not think that culture should or could mediate man's search for true values. This was not mysticism. Ch'eng did not attack the validity of language—men who knew tao could say things that were true—nor was he denying the possibility of creating models for the present. The great paradox of Tao-hsueh was that through his oral teachings—which his disciples recorded and studied but which he avoided transmitting as wen-chang—Ch'eng created a doctrine of how men could learn that came to mediate the search for values for many serious intellectuals in the twelfth century. Ch'eng I's aspiration to "revive This Culture of Ours" was realized. But his foundation was not the one that had served those who claimed responsibility for This Culture during the preceding centuries; nor was the intellectual culture that his teachings supported the same as theirs.

Culture and Heaven-and-Earth

Culture

Ch'eng I's oral teachings contain a fairly coherent view of the functions and grounds of cultural forms in antiquity and the reasons why that culture cannot be restored in the present. In antiquity, ritual, music, dance, and poetry were all in tune, so to speak, and they were effective devices for tuning up men. The following passage is repeated in several records.

Master Ch'eng said: For the ancients learning was easy. In their eighth year they entered the minor school and in their fifteenth the greater school. There were decorations [wen-ts'ai] to nurture their sight, sounds to nurture their hearing, majestic ceremonies to nurture their four limbs, song and dance to nurture their circulation. . . . Today these are all lost, there is only moral principles [i-li] to nurture the mind. Must we not make an effort?[25]

The cultural forms necessary to cultivate the whole man were lost, leaving men no choice but to proceed by nurturing their minds with moral principles, but they had worked in antiquity. They worked, Ch'eng explains elsewhere with reference to music, because the sages who created them apprehended perfectly what was "so-of-itself." Later men may take the measure of the natural in constructing pitch pipes or weights and measures, but "these sorts of things, although they come from what is so-of-itself, still require humans to do them. But when the ancients did them, they apprehended what was so-of-itself, and when they [made] the compass and the square, they realized all possible squares and circles."[26] In this sense, the cultural objects created by the sages were not really "man-made" since "the fact that things can be made edible by cooking or useful by a certain construction is not man-made but so-of-itself."[27]

Cultural forms have value insofar as they are functionally effective in manifesting patterns that are so-of-themselves for men to accord with. In antiquity, they served to cultivate correctly the physical condition and faculties of perception of students. Ancient students were trained, it appears; they did not have to think. This worked because the media of their training were gauged to the state of their *ch'i*, their physical being.[28] But taken as the record or legacy of the past, as a remnant of the past rather than as something functioning in the present, cultural forms have lost real value. As a heritage culture belongs to the category of acquaintance with facts acquired by "seeing and hearing"; it is not real knowledge. Faced with two passages from the *Analects* that suggest otherwise—Yen Hui's statement that Confucius "broadens me with culture [*wen*] and brings me back to the essentials by means of the rites" and the statement that Confucius "has broadened learning with culture and brought it back to the essentials by means of the rites"[29]—Ch'eng finds in the first a correct distinction between factual knowledge and "knowing the essentials." The second conflates the two; it is said of those who do not "know tao" but "having extensive knowledge of past sayings and former practices, are able not to transgress ritual, but this is not what is meant by Yen-tzu's reasons for learning from Confucius [in the first passage]. . . . Facts and knowledge are very different."[30]

The sages spoke and they wrote, Ch'eng holds, not because they wanted to be *wen* but because they needed a device to convey something real.

When the sages and worthies spoke, it was because they had to. It must have been that these sayings were necessary for the patterns to be clear, without these sayings the patterns for the world under heaven would be incomplete. It is like the tools for cultivation, ceramics, and metallurgy: were one not constructed, the tao for mankind would be inadequate. Although the sages wished to stop speaking, could they? But while what was contained [in what they said] fully expressed the pattern for the world under heaven, it was still very concise. Later men, when they first held a writing scroll, thought literary composition was the priority, and they wrote far more in their lifetimes than did the sages. Yet having [their compositions] remedies nothing; being without them would not mean a lack of anything. They are useless, excess speech. They are not merely excess, since they do not get the essentials, they depart from the true and lose the correct. That they instead harm tao is inevitable.[31]

The sages spoke, and thus there are the Classics, because they felt compelled to make the inherent and normative patterns for life clear to men. This recalls a claim Ch'eng made in 1057: "The Classics are that by which tao is conveyed,"[32] similar to Chou Tun-i's assertion that "Wen is [merely] a means for conveying the tao."[33] (In studies of Ch'eng I, the term "li" is usually translated as "principle." I have translated it as "pattern," in accord with usage in earlier chapters; see below for a more complete discussion.)

Literary scholars had often supposed that the sages had made their language wen, thus interposing a literary surface between their own ideas and their readers' minds. Such was not the case in Ch'eng's view, and for him the fact that writers attend to the literary is a sign of their failure to understand anything significant. Since writing should be a medium to illuminate pattern, those who read should be able to see the meaning immediately: "Whenever you are trying to understand writings, just ease your mind and naturally you will see the pattern. The pattern is simply the pattern for man; it is very clear, it is like a level, flat road."[34] This is true, however, only when the language itself presents no problems. The Classics are ancient, and usage has changed. Anyone who had to study them to know tao would get stuck in the medium. Ch'eng concludes that modern men must know before they can: "Those who learned in antiquity proceeded from the Classics to know moral principles; it must have been that when they began to learn everything was transmitted [orally?]. Those who learn in later times, however, must first know moral principles; only then can they look at the Classics."[35] The true meaning of the Classics can be understood only by those who know the truth already.

The Classics are worth study; they are the surviving link with the sages. A reader, however, must find a way around the difficulties presented by their antiquity; he must know which portions are incoherent or intellectually suspect and, when he had gotten past the language, try to imagine the original situation in which the sages spoke; then he may illuminate pattern directly.[36] Ch'eng dismisses literary writing as useless verbiage, although he did find the histories of some use. Ch'eng tells students to praise and blame historical figures according to moral principles and to appreciate how much better the sages were at managing affairs. It is said that he himself used the histories to test his insight into li: he would read part of the way, figure out what should happen according to the inherent pattern, and then read the rest. Outcomes contrary to his expectations he dismissed as the result of coincidence.[37] He did not, in short, join Ssu-ma Kuang and judge men by the consequences of their deeds or seek to infer timeless principles from political history.

Yet Ch'eng I recognized historical change and the "decline" of antiquity. Early T'ang scholars had accounted for decline as a failure to maintain cultural forms; ku-wen writers had blamed it on a failure to maintain the sages' values; and Ou-yang Hsiu in the New T'ang History had had it both ways. Ch'eng found an ingenious way to account for historical change and license the changing of cultural forms while avoiding the implication that the sages' culture or values were in any sense artificial social constructions. He does this by appealing to the pattern of changes in ch'i.

Why is it that the atmosphere [*feng-ch'i*] and leading men are different in past and present? Variation in the quality of ch'i is a pattern of what is so-of-itself. If there is a rise, there must be a decline; if there is an end, there must be a beginning; if there is day, there must be night. It is analogous to a piece of land. When it is first cultivated, the harvest is many times the planting, but after a time it is ever less; the reason is also that ch'i rises and declines. As in the case of the Eastern and the Western Han, human talent and literary forms all diverged, what was valued was different. The reason what was valued was different was due to how the mind acted. The reason the mind was that particular way was simply because it had been born that way. As with spring, summer, fall, and winter, the things born differ [according to the season of birth]; the proper modes of cultivation and care also must accord with the season, they cannot be uniform; it is necessary to accord with the season. Even of all the things born in spring, those born at the beginning of spring differ from those born in the middle or end of spring. What is appropriate in ritual [changes] according to the times; that is, it is a matter of correctly apprehending what is appropriate to the times. What I call "being [in accord with] the times" requires illuminating tao for later men.[38]

What men value changes because the mind changes; the mind changes because ch'i changes. The moral decline after antiquity can thus be accounted for by the decline in ch'i. It follows, then, that since ritual is a device for orchestrating the ch'i of men, it must change to take into account their present condition.

Cultural forms cannot be constant because they must be capable of affecting man's ch'i, which is not constant. The cycle of ch'i also explains the lack of sages in the present.

It appears to be the case that the life span and the physical size of the ancients and men today are not the same. Those who wore the clothes and caps in antiquity were great of stature and thick of body; their physical appearance [*ch'i-hsiang*] was different. Were men today to be made to wear the ceremonial caps of antiquity, [the caps] would not match their affective character [*hsing-ch'ing*]. This must be due to the quality of the ch'i. Just as those things born when spring ch'i is rising necessarily differ from those things born when spring ch'i is declining. . . . This is a constant pattern [*ch'ang-li*]. Consider how many sages were born during the Three Eras; what is the reason they have been silent since then? It must be that if ch'i has a rise, it must have a decline; if it declines, then in the end it certainly will rise again. When winter does not give way to spring, nor night to day, the transforming of ch'i will have ceased.[39]

This argument implies that since men are determined by their ch'i, they are condemned to endless decline until ch'i improves. Ritual forms that fit their state would seem to do little to change the situation. Ch'eng, however, does not accept this conclusion. The sages drew on a source apart from ch'i and could orchestrate the ritual order perfectly. This was not a historical process of cumulative change (as Wang An-shih had thought), although they incorporated past forms.

When sages are in charge of transformation, then, as with Yü putting in order the waters, when they followed [earlier practice] it was proper to follow it, when they put it in order [i.e., revised earlier practice] then it was necessary to put it in order. How could it have been that Fu Hsi of antiquity was unable to let the upper and lower garments hang down [and men] had to wait for Yao and Shun to let the upper and lower garments hang?[40] On the basis of such matters, [we can conclude that] a single sage made everything, but it required several generations before [what he began] was completed; this was also going according to the times. This is called [in the "Doctrine of the Mean"] "having an all-embracing deep source and bringing it forth according to the times"[41]—first there must be an all-embracing and deep source, only then can it come out according to the times. If you lack the all-embracing deep source, how can you bring it forth according to the times? In general, ch'i transformation is the same in heaven [i.e., nature] and in man [i.e., society]. The sage is the mean [of ch'i transformation] and simply makes it work. Fang Hsun [Yao] said, "Encourage it and make it happen; correct it and make it straight; aid it and help it."[42] This is precisely how it must be. To go along with custom is not according with the times; knowing affairs that can be corrected and intrepidly taking an independent position—this is according with the times. When you take up the forms of ritual, you are engaged in a matter of a particular historical moment; what you add must be significant, capable of affecting later ages. Then you are illuminating *tao*. Mencius said, "Every five hundred years a true King should arise, and in the interval there should arise one from whom an age takes its name."[43] That number is about right, but it is not necessary to hurry things up."[44]

Thus, although culture must fit ch'i cycles, it can also be adjusted to affect ch'i. It is not necessary to go along with convention and accept decline. But making the changes necessary for a morally efficacious culture requires possessing a true basis. Ch'eng has redefined "according with the times" so that the cumulative historical change does not figure in thinking about values.

We shall see shortly, however, that it is not necessary to proceed through ritual and culture to improve the state of one's ch'i. Men can improve their ch'i by nurturing their minds with moral principles, since the decline in their ch'i has only obscured the moral nature, not harmed it. Mencius had seen that human nature was good and that ch'i could be improved; the failure of transmission after Mencius thus had left people without an escape from the cycles of ch'i.[45] From this perspective, the effect of ch'i cycles on history is due to a human failure to maintain correct ideas about learning. This is a "cultural" view in that it supposes that how men act is a function of what they believe to be true. I think Ch'eng does at times find himself saying this, although he wishes to avoid it.[46] In any case, he is sure that the mind's ability to know tao makes possible an escape from the determinism of ch'i. But if perfection was achieved in antiquity, why was there a decline? The best explanation I can infer from Ch'eng's comments is that the sages, who knew tao instinctively, created a culture that accorded with the pattern for man and thus prevented a decline in ch'i. However, because they were working through culture and ch'i, not through the mind, once a ruler lost the way, culture went out of tune with ch'i and man fell victim to its natural decline. The ruler who failed to adjust ritual correctly is to blame. It is significant, I think, that the decline first affected the natural world and then the human: "When King Yu [of the Chou, r. 781–771 B.C.] lost the tao, first the myriad creatures did not fulfill their natures, then [his] grace declined among the feudal lords, [and this decline] spread to their entire clans, and then, worst of all, he regarded the populace as birds and beasts."[47]

It seems to me that Ch'eng I found a way to avoid the conclusion that morality was a product of human history, that the culture of antiquity could guide the present, and that moral ideas were inferences drawn from culture. His teachings are not, in fact, much concerned with the problem of culture but with the real foundation for human life.

Heaven-and-Earth

To see Ch'eng's explanation of how men can escape from decline, it is necessary to consider the context in which he prefers to see man. This is heaven-and-earth, and he has much more to say about it than about culture and history. In contrast to those who ask how civilization began, Ch'eng I asks how man came into being as one of the myriad creatures. Here he is discoursing on birth through the spontaneous transformation of ch'i (ch'i-hua) and through procreation.

Question: In greatest antiquity did men come into being [sheng] together with things or not?
Answer: Together.
[Question:] Was it that pure ch'i made man, whereas impure ch'i made insects?
Answer: Yes. Man is the refined ch'i of the five phases; this [refined ch'i] is brought into being by the clear and pure ch'i of heaven-and-earth.
Question: When mankind first came into being, was it through the [spontaneous] transformation of ch'i or not?
Answer: On this we must illuminate the pattern; we should discuss it carefully. For example, when a sandbar suddenly appears in the sea, plants come into being. That when there is earth [it] gives birth to plants is not to be wondered at. Since there are plants, naturally birds and beasts will come into being there.
[Question:] Someone said: In your Record of Sayings it says, "How can we know

that on an island in the sea there are not men [born of] the [spontaneous] transformation of ch'i."[48] How about this?

Answer: Right. Certainly not in places near other men; it would have to be in a most distant place, but we cannot know.

Question: In the world today there are no men without a father and mother; in antiquity there was the [spontaneous] transformation of ch'i; today there is not the [spontaneous] transformation of ch'i. Why?

Answer: There are two kinds. There is what comes into being completely out of [spontaneous] transformation of ch'i. For instance, decaying grass becomes fireflies. Since [in this case birth is entirely due to] the [spontaneous] transformation of ch'i, when it reaches the time for transformation, it transforms of itself. Then there is what comes into being through seeds [i.e., procreation] after it has first come into being through the [spontaneous] transformation of ch'i. For example, when a man puts on new clothes, after several days lice will come into being in them; this is the [spontaneous] transformation of ch'i. But [in the case of lice], once the ch'i has transformed [into lice], it does not transform again; henceforth [the lice] come into being by seed. This pattern is very clear.[49]

And although man, having been spontaneously generated out of the ch'i of heaven-and-earth, continues to exist through procreation, at a certain level of analysis it can be said he continues to be born of heaven-and-earth. "Within heaven-and-earth there is only birth. Man being born from male and female is heaven-and-earth giving birth; how can they be taken as different?"[50]

Ch'eng points out the various ways in which man is essentially the same as heaven-and-earth. In a series of passages, he argues that if heaven-and-earth is the great creative force, then man must have the same independent ability to generate ch'i as heaven-and-earth. This leads him to conclude that we are not really inhaling when we breathe.

If you say ch'i that has been exhaled becomes the ch'i that [in the next breath] is being generated, and that one depends upon this [exhaled ch'i to breathe], then truly [man] would not resemble the transforming process of heaven-and-earth. The transforming process of heaven-and-earth [t'ien-ti chih hua] is continual generation without exhaustion [that is] so-by-itself. How could it rely on forms that are already dead or ch'i that has already reverted for creation [tsao-hua]? Finding it in the body as that which is close at hand: the opening and shutting and going and coming are evident in breathing. But it is not necessary that one inhale it once again in order to exhale. Ch'i comes into being by itself. As for the coming into being of man's ch'i, it comes into being in the primal source [chen-yuan]. The ch'i of heaven also continually generates of itself without exhaustion, just as the water of the ocean dries up when yang peaks and comes into being when yin peaks. It does not take the ch'i that is already dried up and bring water into being. It is able to come into being by itself. Going and coming and exhaling and generating are inherent patterns. When there is a rise, there will then be a decline; when there is day, there will then be night; when there is going, there will then be coming. Between heaven-and-earth it is like a great furnace: everything gets smelted.[51]

In short, the cycle of rise and fall is not a recycling but a constant generation of the new to replace the old and worn out. Ch'i reaches its maturity, dissipates, and disappears. For example, what we speak of as the tide is actually the ocean drying up and then replenishing itself. It is simply breathing, in Ch'eng's sense of that process. The importance of this theory lies, I think, in the implication that because man shares heaven-and-earth's ability to generate ch'i, he can also improve the quality of his ch'i.

Heaven-and-earth provides the context for understanding man's role in the universe. Heaven-and-earth brings about orderly and correct transformation and creation; man can as well, for there is only one tao and one inclusive pattern: "The mind of one man is the mind of heaven-and-earth. The pattern of one thing is the pattern of all things. The cycle of one day is the cycle of the year."[52] Thus it is mistaken to suppose that there is a distinction between man and heaven.

How could there be someone who knew the tao of man but did not know the tao of heaven? Tao is one. How could it be that the tao for man was only the tao for man and the tao for heaven only the tao of heaven? The "Doctrine of the Mean" says, "If they fulfill their own nature, they can fulfill the nature of others. If they can fulfill the nature of others, they can fulfill the nature of things. If they can fulfill the nature of things, they can assist in the transformative nurturing of heaven-and-earth."[53] These sentences are worth attention. Master Yang [Hsiung] said, "Comprehending [t'ung] heaven-and-earth and man is called being a ju; comprehending heaven-and-earth without comprehending man is called being a technician [chi]." This is the saying of one who does not know tao. How could one comprehend heaven-and-earth but not comprehend man? If this is referring only to comprehending the manifest forms of heaven [i.e., astronomy] and the manifest configurations of earth [geography], then even though you are not capable of these, it will not stop you from being a ju. Heaven-and-earth and man are but one tao. As soon as you comprehend one of them, then the rest is also comprehended. When later explicators of the Change say that ch'ien is the tao of heaven and k'un is the tao of man, it is nonsense. If we are speaking of their normative forms [t'i], then "heaven is honorable and earth is humble."[54] If we are speaking of their tao, how could they be different?[55]

Basic values for man are those things he shares with heaven-and-earth as something that is so-of-itself, but comprehending this one tao does not require drawing inferences from accumulated knowledge of the phenomena of heaven-and-earth. Ch'eng is interested not in the facts but in the universal process of integrated but dynamic creation.

By fulfilling his nature, man can, in the human realm, realize the pattern that is common to man and heaven-and-earth, for "the nature is pattern [*hsing* is *li*]. What is called pattern is the nature."[56] The sage is one who fulfills his nature perfectly and thus most fully resembles heaven-and-earth. As Ch'eng explains, the sage and "the tao of heaven" do not differ.[57] And "only the capacity of heaven-and-earth is limitless. Therefore the sage is the capacity of heaven-and-earth. The capacity of the sage is tao."[58] He came into being "when heaven and earth stimulated each other, [creating] refined [ch'i] of the five phases; then they gave birth to the sage."[59] The sage can be like heaven-and-earth because he was born with innate conscious knowledge (*sheng-chih*);[60] that is, "he was born consciously knowing moral principles; he did not depend on learning to know."[61] Ch'eng understands the innate knowledge of the sage as that which enables him to "fulfill all the patterns under heaven"[62] and "fulfill the tao for man" and "pattern for man."[63] "Heaven has this pattern; the sage accords with and practices it. This is what is meant by tao."[64] This knowledge can be called moral knowledge, but rather than thinking of it as a set of ideas, Ch'eng appears to understand it as instinctively knowing the structuring principles of heaven-and-earth. He distinguishes it from the knowledge of phenomena or the ability to do things, for these must be acquired.[65] Confucius was a sage; thus he must have had innate knowledge, his own protestations that he had made mistakes and had acquired knowledge of tao to the contrary.[66]

The sage is on a par with heaven-and-earth, but he is still a man, and all men are of a category, with a single nature and pattern. But as far as Ch'eng I knows, the rest of mankind has not "fulfilled the pattern for man" because later men have not been born with complete conscious knowledge. Ch'eng accounts for this on the basis of the quality of the ch'i a man is born with. "If the ch'i is pure, then the talent is good; if the ch'i is turbid, then the talent is evil. Those born receiving entirely clear ch'i are sages. Those born receiving entirely turbid ch'i are stupid people. . . . But this pertains to the sage being born with conscious knowledge. Those who know [values] through learning, irrespective of whether their ch'i is clear or turbid, can all attain goodness and restore the original of the nature."[67] Ch'i, rather than culture, mediates consciousness of innate guides. Thus developing awareness requires working through the ch'i that mediates access. Men can make the ch'i transparent, so that it cannot interfere with attaining consciousness of the good. "Ch'i has good and not good. The nature is without not-good. The reason men do not know good is that ch'i obscures and blocks it. The reason Mencius nurtured ch'i was that when he nurtured it fully, it became transparent and pure and the problem of obscuration and blockage was gone."[68] It follows that when ch'i is transparent, it becomes one with moral guides. "When it has not yet been cultivated, then ch'i is ch'i and moral principle is moral principle. When he has cultivated this pure, transparent [hao-jan] ch'i, then ch'i and moral principle are united."[69]

Ch'eng's understanding of ch'i as that which mediates the relationship between innate values and man's consciousness allows him to account for all that is not good. When men do evil, it can always be traced to the interference of turbid ch'i. "The nature is free of the not-good; what has the not-good is talent [ts'ai]. The nature is pattern. Pattern, from Yao and Shun to the man on the street, is one. Talent is endowed by ch'i. There is pure and turbid ch'i. Those who are endowed with the pure are wise; those who are endowed with the turbid are stupid."[70] The existence of mediating ch'i also accounts for the fact that men have different skills and interests; it explains why individuals are partial rather than complete. But the quality of talent is not the issue, for all men possess the ability to make their talent good by bringing it into accord with their nature.

Question: What sort of thing is "talent"?

Answer: It is like timber. Taking a piece of wood as an analogy: whether it is straight or bent is its nature, and it can be used [for different purposes accordingly]. . . . When people today say "he has talent" they are talking about the best sort of talent. The "talent" is the material of man; cultivate it according to the nature [of man] and even the entirely evil can be overcome and be good.

The nature is the same for everyone, it is pattern itself. No matter what the quality of a man's ch'i, he can clarify his ch'i and become conscious of pattern.

Further question: Can the stupid change?

Answer: Yes. Confucius said those of superior intelligence and greatest stupidity do not change. However, there is also a pattern of being able to change. It is only that those who are self-destructive do not change. . . . The nature is of a single kind. How could [men] be unchangeable? But because they have brutalized it and cast it aside and are unwilling to learn, therefore [they] are unchangeable. If they are at a point when they are willing to learn, then there is a pattern of being able to change.[71]

Learning should be directed at attaining consciousness of the pattern that man has as his nature. He can use his mind to accomplish this because "the mind is the nature. In heaven it is decree, in man it is the nature; in terms of what he takes as master it is the mind. In reality these are simply a single tao. . . . Under heaven there are no things outside the nature."[72] But when the mind responds to things and expresses itself, what emerges is not necessarily good.

Question: Does the mind have good and bad?

Answer: In heaven it is decree; in moral principle it is pattern ([original note:] I
suspect this should read "in things it is pattern"); in man it is the nature, and the
ruler in the body is mind. In fact these are one. The mind is originally good; in
the process of thinking there is good and not good. If it has found expression,
then we may call it the emotional responses [ch'ing]; we cannot call it mind. As
with water, we call it water, but when it flows and branches, some going west
and some east, we call it the streams.[73]

The mind must be cultivated. A saying by one of the Ch'eng brothers
defines the problem: "Mind and pattern are one, but men are unable to
bring them together so that they are one."[74]

Men fail to keep mind and nature and pattern one because ch'i is not
pure and transparent. Thus there is not-good, wayward emotional responses, and reliance on partial qualities and talents. What is to be done? A
true method of learning would enable men to purify their ch'i, thus
making it a transparent medium for fulfilling their nature. The methods
of ancient learning trained the ch'i through culture. But, as Ch'eng told
his students over and again: "For those who learn today, there are only
moral principles [i-li] to nurture their minds."[75]

"Nurturing the Mind with Moral Principles"

Ch'eng I's philosophical achievement was to explain how it was possible
to gain moral knowledge. To see the nature of his achievement—and the
difficulty of it—we need only recall the manner in which early T'ang
scholars dealt with heaven-and-earth as the original grounds for a unified
sociopolitical order and the cultural tradition. The T'ang scholars supposed that the Former Kings had replicated the manifest images of heaven-
and-earth in creating an integrated social, political, and cultural order.
This being so, they supposed that men could turn to the Classics and the
textual-cultural tradition that elaborated upon the Classics for guidance.
By virtue of their origin, cultural forms had value and efficacy. By not
granting authority to the cultural tradition as the necessary link between
morality and the cosmic grounds for morality, Ch'eng I creates three
problems. What is it that is "of" heaven-and-earth that one is apprehending? How it is possible to find what one is seeking, that is, to know real
values? And how can things that do not exist as cultural forms in the first
place be translated, so to speak, into guides to social life? Ch'eng explains
the nature of real values, those stemming from heaven-and-earth, through
the concept of inherent normative patterns (li). But li, although Ch'eng
contends they are real, are not images "out there" visible for all to see.
They are accessible to the mind, which "illuminates" (*ming* and similar

terms) them, but they are visible only to the individual mind; li are something that must be "apprehended for oneself" (*tzu-te*). What it means to illuminate li, why the individual is innately capable of becoming fully conscious of li, and why one who does so becomes capable of responding morally to human events are related issues.

For Ch'eng, learning in a fallen age is a moral enterprise that proceeds not by cultivating one's ch'i but by concerning itself with the mind and will (*chih*). Learning gets at that which controls the ch'i. "The will is the director of the ch'i," he asserts, and when properly set so that it is the ruler of "the ch'i that is pure and transparent [*hao-jan*]," one is then "able to generate ch'i that is pure and transparent. Where the will goes, the ch'i follows; they have this sequence of themselves."[76] Thus the first task is to nurture the mind. But this requires knowing what is good, and this, in turn, requires becoming aware of li. "Men fear that they will become entangled by affairs and that their cogitation will be hindered, simply because they have not apprehended the essentials [of affairs]. The essentials lie in clarifying the good. Clarifying the good lies in fully realizing the patterns of things [*ko-wu ch'iung-li*]. When you have fully realized the pattern of a thing, then, gradually, it will be possible to fully reach all things under heaven; they are a single pattern."[77]

Having insight into li is knowing the good, first, because every single thing has its inherent standard or li: " 'If there is a thing, there must be a norm.' For one thing there must be one pattern."[78] And, second, because the norms for all particular things come together to form a single integrated whole or all-inclusive pattern: "For the world under heaven there is only one pattern."[79] "One phrase says it all: the myriad patterns revert to a single pattern."[80] In the perfectly good person, the sage, "pattern and self become one." He thus does not have to rely on any external standards to judge himself or things; for him "the self is the measuring stick, the measuring stick is the self."[81] Unlike Su Shih, Ch'eng I does worry about uniting himself with things in order that his spontaneous response is also the correct response, for by realizing li he becomes the living embodiment of correct standards. Others might speak of acting according to ritual, but for Ch'eng I "ritual is pattern"; one needs only act according to li. Not to do so is immoral. "If it is not heaven's pattern, then it is selfish desire."[82]

When Su Shih, who also recognized the ultimate oneness of li, warned that "all the patterns under heaven have always been one, but the one cannot be held fast," he was objecting to attempts to define a single ultimate value.[83] Ch'eng I does not do this. What he holds fast is the idea that all patterns are one. This allows him to collapse the various entities that embody inherent norms into the same thing. "If you fulfill the self, then everything is fulfilled, as in what Mencius called 'fulfilling the mind.' . . . In general, what is received from heaven is called the nature and that which rules is in the mind. As soon as you fulfill the mind, you know the nature; knowing the nature is knowing heaven."[84] The mind is a source of real values because it is of the nature,[85] or "the mind is the nature,"[86] and the nature is a source of values because it is from heaven. What, then, is heaven? "Heaven is the pattern of what is so–of–itself."[87] Li exists independently of human consciousness and intention. It is not controlled or constructed by men. "If it happens without anyone making it happen and comes without anyone making it come, then it is heaven's pattern."[88] Thus to accord with li is to be on a par with heaven-and-earth and to achieve a state of perfectly moral certainty and spontaneity. I think Ch'eng accounts for evil—which, because it exists, must also have its li— by supposing that when men are not conscious of li they let their ch'i take charge. They then do things for which there are li, but they do them without cognizance of the unity of li. To maintain the unity of pattern, men must nurture the mind so that it remains in control.[89]

Wing-tsit Chan, in his influential article "The Evolution of the Neo-Confucian Concept of Li as Principle," finds precedents for the concept of li, as the idea of many patterns being of a single pattern, in Wang Pi's commentary on the *Book of Change* and in Buddhist philosophy. I can add that this concept was accepted in intellectual culture throughout the T'ang and Northern Sung. But, Professor Chan argues, no one before Ch'eng I made li the basis of a philosophy. Li can be the basis of Ch'eng I's philosophy, I would suggest, because Ch'eng I is willing to make three claims. First, li is real. "Under heaven there is nothing more real than li," as Ch'eng puts it.[90] Second, when men illuminate li, they do so perfectly for "li is very manifest"; although some may be slower at illuminating li than others, the perception is always the same.[91] Su Shih could agree with the first proposition but would have difficulty with the second; he thought it difficult to be certain that what one saw was what was actually there. Third, all li are one li. For Ch'eng the fact of one li is the same as the fact that there is one tao that includes heaven and man, the internal self and external things. "Things and self are one li; when you are illuminating [li] then you are seeing it here; [this is] the tao of uniting internal and exter-nal."[92] In contrast to Su Shih's understanding of unity as the source of differentiation, however, Ch'eng's unity of pattern is the universal pattern of spontaneous operation. The li of vastly different things are thus the same. He did not have to look beyond this for a source, for, as one of the Ch'eng brothers said, "Pattern comes into being of itself."[93] There is no ultimate reality beyond li. "A question was asked about the Buddhist theory that pattern is an obstacle. Answer: The Buddhists have this theory; they mean that when one has illuminated this pattern, he then holds fast to this pattern, and therefore it is an obstacle. This misunderstands the word "li." For the world under heaven there is only one pattern. Since you have illuminated this pattern, how could it be an obstacle? If you treat pattern as an obstacle, then self and pattern are two [separate things]."[94] Uniting self and pattern, an action that makes one the measure of and for things, is premised on the claim that there is only one pattern. From Ch'eng's perspective, the perception of li can be absolute because li is of the mind as well and, as I shall argue later, li is the principles of coherent, integrated organization and process inherent to thinking and evident in the structure of things and affairs.

At least since Chu Hsi, students of Ch'eng I's philosophy have divided his ideas about uniting self and li into an internal, spiritual aspect and an external, intellectual aspect, joined together by the simultaneous existence of li, which is unitary, in the self ("nature is pattern") and in things ("each thing has a pattern"). As a doctrine, the first aspect, "internal cultivation" (han-yang), calls for arriving at a psycho-physical state of ching (composure, reverence, or seriousness) through allowing "integrity" (ch'eng), the innate integrated state, to emerge into consciousness. Mental acts then accord with li, the will (chih) is in control of the ch'i, the pure ch'i comes into being, and one is in a state of unadulterated goodness. The following is one of several statements of this.

If you shut out deviance, then integrity will be preserved of itself. It is not that you catch an "integrity" on the outside and preserve it. Today people are caught up in not-good on the outside; how could there be a pattern for entering goodness that involved seeking a "good" [on the outside] in the midst of the not-good? Simply shut out deviance, and integrity will be preserved of itself. Thus when Mencius spoke of the nature being good, he always [spoke of it] as coming from inside. It is simply because integrity then exists that shutting out deviance requires no effort. Just move your expression and posture and adjust your cogitation, and composure will come into being so-of-itself. Composure is simply taking unity as the ruler. If you take unity as the ruler, then you go off neither east nor west. When you are like this, then you are centered. When you are going off neither that way nor this way, then you are internal. *Preserve this, and of itself the pattern of heaven will be clear.* Those who learn must use composure to straighten the internal. Cultivate this intention; straightening the internal is the basis.[95]   (My emphasis)

Ch'eng contends that innate integrity leads to composure as a state in which he is unaffected by external things and, thus, the t'ien-li, pattern of heaven, will appear. Taking unity as the mental guide, he promises, results in seeing the unity of pattern.

The second doctrine, an external orientation toward things, is summed up in a sentence from the "Great Learning": chih-chih (attaining, making arrive, extending knowledge) tsai (is present in, exists, depends upon) ko-wu (arriving at, attaining a thing or affair). Whether extended from the internal to external affairs or extended from external observation to internal consciousness, "knowledge" pertains to li. Ch'eng glossed the phrase "ko-wu," the linchpin in this formula, as "*Ko* is to arrive at; it means fully arrive at the pattern for a thing [*ch'iung-chih wu-li*],"[96] or simply as *ch'iung-li*, a phrase from an appendix to the *Change*: "*Ch'iung-li*, fulfill the nature, and attain the decree." In practice I think Ch'eng's use of *ch'iung* can be translated as "fully realize" in two senses: to become fully aware of something (e.g., he realized what he meant) and to fulfill something (he realized his intent). Thus Ch'eng's understanding of the sentence from the "Great Learning" combines extending knowledge as seeing how things conform to the pattern one has in mind and attaining knowledge as becoming fully aware of the patterns as one sees them in things. The li is the same in both cases. Men see it or they do not; it does not vary with perception.

Although it is common to translate "ko-wu" as "investigating things" and "ch'iung-li" as "investigating the li to the utmost," I am not sure that "investigate" describes the sort of mental work Ch'eng I intends. His mind is capable of illuminating the li of something; he does not have to figure it out.[97] Ch'eng I acknowledges that natural phenomena have li, just as do human affairs.[98] This was not new. Wang An-shih used a similar formulation in explaining to the emperor why government should legislate all affairs: "Heaven-and-earth create the myriad things, yet each thing, even something as small as a blade of grass, has its pattern."[99] "Investigate" is far more appropriate for what Wang An-shih was doing, because Wang accepted that things and texts mediated knowledge of values. What is notable about Ch'eng I's approach to knowledge is that he does not accept that perception of li is mediated by other kinds of thinking about things, numerology being one example, for if seeing li were dependent on first knowing something else, one would only have derived an idea about the li of something; li itself would not be known absolutely.[100] Clearly Ch'eng I was not content with the received exegesis of *chih-chih tsai ko-wu*, in which one's knowledge of received moral ideas is tested against the things one does.[101] As the verbs Ch'eng uses with reference to pattern illustrate—to see (*chien*), to illuminate (*ming*), to light (*chu* and *chao*), and to recognize (*shih*)—the mind perceives li directly.

In Ch'eng I's vision of learning, it is not necessary to say one should begin either from self or from things; rather, one should illuminate li so as to move on to fully realizing the unity of pattern. He sees that since the various patterns are one pattern, it is necessary only to become fully conscious of the pattern of one thing to see the same pattern for all.

As for arriving at things and fully realizing the pattern, it is not so that one must fully realize [the patterns of] all things under heaven. Just fully realize one pattern; the rest can be realized by extending by categorical similarity [*i lei t'ui*]. For example, that by which one is filially pious. If you can't fully realize [the pattern] for one thing, then fully realize it with another . . . just as a multitude of roads lead to the capital, find one road that leads in and it will do. The reason that one is able to fully realize [pattern] is that all things are one pattern, so that every single thing and affair, however, minor, each has this li.[102]

There are many ways to train oneself to realize the pattern: "For everything there is a pattern; you must fully realize its pattern. There are many methods for fully realizing pattern. One may read books and elucidate moral principles. One may discuss past and present figures and distinguish right and wrong. One may respond to affairs and things and arrange them as they should be. All are [methods of] fully realizing pattern." But Ch'eng is then asked: "In realizing [the pattern of] things [ko-wu], is it necessary to realize it thing by thing, or do you just realize one thing and then the myriad patterns are known?" His answer suggests that each pattern is unique and that since the single all-embracing, integrated pattern is constituted by all the various patterns, one must gradually accumulate knowledge in order to see the unified whole: "How can you then inclusively comprehend? Even Yen-tzu would not have dared say that if you arrived only at one thing, you would comprehend the multitudinous patterns. You must arrive at one item today and another tomorrow; once cumulative practice is much, then, as if released, there will be a point where all is coherently connected."[103] It seems to me that Ch'eng wants to say that of course you have to pay attention to everything in order to see how things and affairs fit together, but fully realizing the pattern of one thing teaches you how to realize pattern in everything. He says as much in another dialogue. "Question: Are we only to fully realize a single thing and, seeing this one thing, then see the many patterns? Answer: You must seek everywhere. Even Yen-tzu was only able to know ten on hearing one. If later you catch on to pattern [ta li], then even a million can be comprehended [as one]."[104]

Making "fully realized pattern" an intellectual goal, however, even if it involves learning to see patterns in things, suggests not only that "straightening the internal is the basis," as Ch'eng once said, but also that it is sufficient.[105] Do men really need more than "composure" to see "heaven's pattern?" Ch'eng addresses this by pointing to the connection between two phrases from Mencius's discussion of how to make the ch'i pure and translucent: "there must be an affair there" (pi yu shih yen) and "accumulate principles [of right behavior]" (chi i).[106] The point of the first phrase, Ch'eng explains, is that one must "accumulate principles."

Question: How are composure and principles [of right behavior] different?
Answer: Composure is simply the tao for holding onto yourself [ch'ih chi], and being principled is knowing that there is a right and there is a wrong. Acting according to the pattern is being principled. If you just maintain composure and

do not know [you should] accumulate principles [of right behavior], then there will be no affair at all. For example, if you wish to engage in filial piety, how could this mean simply maintaining the words "filial piety" [in your mind]? You must know the tao through which one is filially pious—how to wait in attendance and how to make [parents] feel comfortable—only then will you be able to realize the tao of filial piety.[107]

In other words, one should conceive of affairs such as filial piety in the mind and know how to do them. "Ethical conduct" serves, I think, as a kind of testing ground on which the individual tries to make the connection between fully realizing pattern and behaving morally.

But what precisely is the connection between learning to realize the pattern of things and behaving ethically? The passage above defines "being principled" as according with the pattern, but it is not clear that pattern is necessary to being filial unless it simply means to go beyond imitating the form to comprehending in one's mind how it works. This is part of Ch'eng's point, for Ch'eng responds to the follow-up question: "Being principled lies only in affairs—what do you think of that [proposition]?" by insisting "The internal and external are one pattern; how could you seek to be in agreement with principles [of right behavior] only in affairs?"[108] Still, I think this leads to a significant problem. If Ch'eng is contending that all moral values and virtues stem from li and if li are ultimately "so-of-themselves," how does Ch'eng posit universality for historically contingent examples of moral behavior and what does this have to do with the unity of li?

One answer (and escape from) these questions would be to interpret Ch'eng's claim that all li are one li as meaning that the ultimate pattern is simply the fact that each thing has its own pattern, in which case the student's task would simply be to see how the principles for any single affair form a coherent unity. This would make Willard Peterson's proposal to translate li as "coherence" in Ch'eng-Chu doctrine appealing.[109] I shall suggest a more involved alternative, one that helps explain how Ch'eng may have been getting around the dilemma of claiming universality for the historically bound affairs of morality. My account is derived from Ch'eng's account of Mencius's "four beginnings"—*jen* (benevolence), *i* (principles [of right behavior]), *li* (ritual or propriety), and *chih* (knowledge)—and his location of them in human nature.[110]

It is important to keep in mind that Ch'eng I repeatedly collapses various terms for the innate and cosmic sources of values. On the mind, human nature, and heaven's decree, for example, he states: "The mind is the nature. In heaven it is decree; in man it is the nature; in terms of that which is ruler [in the body], it is the mind. In reality this is just a single tao."[111] Li, nature, and decree are also one and the same: "Pattern, nature, decree. The three have always been the same. When a man is fully realizing pattern, he is fulfilling the nature; when he is fulfilling the nature, he is knowing heaven's decree. Heaven's decree is like heaven's tao. In terms of its function it is called decree; decree means *tsao-hua* [ongoing process of creation]."[112] On nature and li: "The nature is pattern. What is called pattern is the nature. When the patterns under heaven are traced back to where they come from, [you will find that] they have always been good."[113] One who is fulfilling his mind is coming to know the nature and heaven, as Mencius claimed, and one who is fully realizing pattern is fulfilling his nature.

[Shao] Po-wen asked: What about "Fulfill this mind, then know this nature; know this nature, then know heaven."[114]

Answer: Fulfilling this mind [means] I myself fulfill this mind. If I am able to fulfill the mind, then naturally [*tzu-jan*] I will know the nature and know heaven. It is like saying "Fully realize pattern, fulfill the nature, and arrive at the decree."[115] It is spoken of as a sequence; this cannot be avoided. But in reality you can fully realize only pattern; then you are fulfilling the nature and arriving at the decree.[116]

In short, everything reduces to li. The mind that is fully realizing pattern is fulfilling nature, arriving at the decree, knowing nature, and knowing heaven. It is useful to turn this back onto the concept of li. If "heaven is the pattern of what is so-of-itself"[117] and "the ongoing process of creation" is what is meant by decree,[118] then the li the mind is realizing (and the mind's process of realizing li) would appear to be of the same order as the spontaneous creative process of heaven-and-earth. The li also constitute the innate knowledge of the sage, which it will be recalled, had no factual content yet enabled him to fulfill the nature of himself and all things.

I shall argue that Ch'eng's views on the four beginnings help (1) define his understanding of li, (2) explain why all li are one li, (3) explain how moral virtues can ultimately be "so-of-themselves," and (4) show that fully realizing the pattern is a cumulative enterprise yet always the same.

Two analogies bear on the relationship between mind and the four beginnings. First, mind is to the four beginnings as the body is to the four limbs. "Mind is like the body; the four beginnings are like the four limbs. The four limbs are what the body employs [or: makes function], they are merely called the four limbs of the body. The four beginnings are all fully present in the mind, but we cannot then call them the function of mind." Here Ch'eng conceives of the four beginnings both as properties of the mind and the means the mind as the ruler employs to work. Second, jen is to the mind as the nature of growth is to the seed. "The mind is like a grain seed; the nature [*hsing*] of growth is jen."[119] Here the mind is something whose full development is made possible by its inherent qualities (presuming this is to apply by extension to all four beginnings). To me these analogies suggest that the four beginnings are ingrained in the mind. They can guide the development of the mind and are employed by the mind; they enable it to fully realize pattern and to accord with pattern in action. They provide a possible gloss on Ch'eng's claim that "mind is that in which tao is present" unless we obscure it and let it go astray.[120]

Ch'eng I understood the four beginnings in fairly abstract terms, not merely as four categories of ethical behavior or virtue but also (for at least two of the four) as aspects of coherent organization. He distinguishes between the beginnings as innate characteristics and the categories of affairs he thinks others (including Mencius) have seen.

If one is to discuss the five matters of jen, principles, ritual, knowledge, and belief in terms of the nature, it is necessary to distinguish them. As for jen, it is certainly unity [*i*]. Unity is how one is jen. Commiseration [which Mencius said was the starting point of jen] belongs under love, which is an emotion rather than the nature. Altruism approaches jen, but is not jen. It is on account of a man's "attitude of commiseration" that we know he has jen. Only four have beginnings; belief has no beginning. There is only not believing; there is no believing. As with east, west, south, and north, they already have fixed normative forms [*ting-t'i*]; so we cannot speak of believing. If you think east is west and south is north, then there is unbelief. But if east is east and west is west, then there is nothing to believe.[121]

Before the lesson shifts to the irrelevance of "belief," Ch'eng does distinguish jen as a highly abstract unity from the social affairs that pertain to jen. Ch'eng has another abstract, structural definition of jen. In the following passage he is answering a query about the possibility of a difference between sagehood and jen.

I would say that jen can be spoken of as integrating above and below [*t'ung shang-hsia*]; sagehood then is the ultimate attainment of this. The sage is the perfection [*chih*] of human relations; relations are patterns. Since he is the ultimate of integrating human pattern [*jen-li*], there is nothing to add. Now, a person today may be jen in a single matter, and it is possible to call him jen; when it comes to fully realizing the tao of jen, we also call him jen; by this we mean he integrates above and below.[122]

This suggests when speaking of jen as something innate, rather than as an affair, Ch'eng looks for "structural" properties that can both describe mental operation and serve as a root concept for such affairs as love, altruism, and inclusive moral leadership associated with jen. Wholeness and interconnectedness, I suggest, are essential qualities of the kind of thinking that seeks to see patterns in things and the unity of all patterns.

Ch'eng also conceives of ritual in the abstract, as in his assertion "Ritual is pattern."[123] In the following dialogue on ritual and music, he again differentiates affairs from the origin. "Earlier ju often said: 'For securing the superior and governing the people, ritual is best; for shifting the tone and changing customs, music is best.' This certainly is the great function of ritual and music, but in terms of their origins ritual is simply proper sequence [hsu; or: hierarchy] and music is simply harmony." In fact harmony seems to be derived from sequence (although Ch'eng later denies it): "Question: Is ritual not the sequence of heaven-and-earth and music the harmony of heaven-and-earth? Answer: Certainly. There is not a single thing under heaven that does not have ritual and music. For example, when you place two chairs, as soon as they are not correctly positioned, they lack proper sequence; when there is not proper sequence, they are distorted; when distorted they are not harmonious."[124] Hierarchy or sequence is also a basic quality of pattern and of coherent social organization. For Ch'eng ritual is universal; for robbers to succeed as robbers, he notes elsewhere, they too must have ritual. "There is no place where ritual is not."[125]

I have not found similar abstractions for principles (i) and knowledge (chih), but in these cases too Ch'eng distinguishes between the innate and the historical. For example, "Isn't moral principle seen with reference to affairs? Answer: No. It exists of itself in the nature."[126] And "Being i is knowing that there is a right and a wrong. Acting according to pattern is being i."[127] For knowledge, of course, we need only refer to Ch'eng's distinction between innate knowledge and the factual knowledge of hearing and seeing.[128]

The four beginnings are, I suggest, integrally connected to Ch'eng's view of pattern. Although he acknowledges the value of the various forms of conduct that have accreted to them through history, he attributes their value not to tradition or social utility but to their function as structuring principles of integrative thinking. This explains, I think, why Ch'eng can speak of the "natures" of the four beginnings as present in all men. Although their force within men differs with the individual, they can be developed to equal fullness. "The desires of the mouth, eye, ear, nose, and the four limbs are inborn, but there are allotments; you cannot say I must get them [all]. It is fate [ming]. Jen, i, li, and chih are heaven's tao in man. They are received from [heaven's] decree [ming] in stronger or weaker degree, but they have natures there; one can learn. Therefore the superior man does not call them fate."[129] We are not fated to be more jen than i, in the sense that some men are fated to be clearer sighted or stronger by virtue of their physical endowment. It is the existence of this nature, as the nature of pattern itself, that makes it possible to realize the pattern.

This leads me to suppose that Ch'eng means that man develops his mind and fulfills his nature by realizing patterns because the innate structure of the mind is itself the very structure of all integrated organization and coherent process. Man's task is to ensure that the mind continues to be conscious of pattern as his awareness of the world around him increases, for by doing so and acting accordingly he maintains the integrated whole or unity of pattern innate to him as a man. Thus as he becomes fully conscious of pattern and acts accordingly, he fulfills his nature and knows his nature as something that is entirely so-of-itself. The pattern of the mind is the pattern of heaven-and-earth, whether he wishes it or not. To remain ignorant of pattern and not accord with it is thus to thwart the guides to the moral world that heaven has endowed in man. Maintaining the original unity of the self in a world in which the self is constantly being jarred by things and maintaining the integrity of the nature in a body stuffed with partial and impure ch'i is hard work. It requires a constant effort to expand, develop, or fulfill the innate potential for integration to the point that it encompasses the whole world. Extending and including throughout one's life is necessary to keeping the mind in control of the ch'i and the self in control of things. But unceasing practice brings real rewards.

At various places in his teachings Ch'eng promises that pursuing his approach to learning will transform the individual. First, in achieving a state of mental coherence, "the point where all is coherently connected,"[130] "your thinking will become clearer by the day and after a while there will be enlightenment."[131] Second, knowledge attained guarantees that practice will succeed. "There is no one who knows it but is not able to practice it."[132] Third, one attains a state in which one does not have to force oneself to behave ethically; "according with pattern is happiness."[133] The fourth promise deserves some attention. Ch'eng asserts that cumulative learning can improve the quality of the physical constitution (ch'i chih). "Only when you have accumulated learning for a long time will you be able to change your physical constitution; then the dull will necessarily become bright, and the weak will necessarily become strong."[134] He is less sure that it leads to any real change in talent, but he finds evidence for physical change: "Man is but learning. See how ju ministers [i.e., civil officials] have one kind of physical appearance [ch'i-hsiang], whereas military ministers have another kind of physical appearance, and aristocrats [of the imperial clan] have yet another kind of physical appearance. They were not born this way; it is simply due to learning."[135] The body does tire, Ch'eng admits, but as long as the will is settled in its control of the ch'i there will be no decline in one's ethical behavior.[136] Ch'eng offers himself as evidence that learning leads to good health and a long life and at least once affirms the possibility of near-immortality.[137]

Finally, the improvement of one's ch'i has consequences for the universe. Ch'eng accepted cosmic resonance. "Between heaven and earth there is only a stimulation and a response; what else is there?"[138] He believes that the ch'i of heaven-and-earth respond to human activity, because human activity involves the emanation of a ch'i with particular qualities. This ch'i then stimulates the equivalent ch'i in heaven-and-earth. This accounts for portents and natural disasters.[139] Individuals who do bad emanate bad ch'i and stimulate a response. Thunder kills people; it is not that they die of fright on hearing thunder: "When people are doing bad, there is bad ch'i that strikes with the bad ch'i of heaven-and-earth and then brings on death by shock. Thunder is the angry ch'i of heaven-and-earth."[140] Worse yet: "When a man has an attitude that is not good and accumulates it over a long time, it is also capable of moving the ch'i of heaven-and-earth. The ch'i of epidemics is also like this. . . . A long or a short life is brought about by good or bad ch'i."[141]

Learning is thus a means by which the individual can directly affect the lives of the many. He can improve his ch'i and affect the ch'i of heaven-and-earth. I can only speculate that Ch'eng envisions a cumulative effect: if present men fulfill their natures, then the ch'i of those born later will be more pure, making it easier for later men to fulfill their natures, and once again it will be possible to have sages, who are born of the pure ch'i of heaven-and-earth. The downward cycle of ch'i can be changed. Just as Ch'eng envisions the process of knowing values as occurring without the mediation of culture, so does he envision the possibility of directly affecting society and heaven-and-earth without the mediation of social, political, and cultural institutions. His practice, however, was more practical.

Conclusion: A Historical Perspective on the New Culture of Tao-hsueh

"When those who know tao are many, tao is illuminated," Ch'eng I once said, "but how many know is due to teaching."[142] Ch'eng I set out to teach the shih how to know tao through learning. Learning was as vital to the shih, he explained, as agriculture was to the farmers.[143] It was the heart of their identity and the essence of their role in society. But Ch'eng also recognized the shih as a distinct, self-perpetuating social group, and at times he spoke nostalgically of the clan system of the T'ang as being in accord with heaven's pattern and of the prospect of once more having a court with hereditary ministers and families with "sons and younger brothers who obeyed their fathers and elder brothers."[144] But whether or not Ch'eng was defending the interests of old bureaucratic families such as his own, his learning made family and ethical conduct rather than government service more important to realizing the tao. Society required institutions for the people to follow, he granted,[145] but the kinds of institutions that most interested Ch'eng I were the rituals for family life.[146] He saw no shame in not serving in government and clearly did not accept that a lack of literary skill and failure in the examinations had anything to do with the worth of an individual. "How can being unable in a skill be worth being ashamed about? Those who act as shih ought to know tao; when one does not know tao, he may be ashamed."[147] Knowing tao was something all shih could do, irrespective of passing the examinations and serving in government.

Ch'eng sought to spread his message through teaching and eventually through writing on the Classics. "Benefit from [my] achievements does not reach the people, and I have not done anything else. Only in repairing the surviving books of the sages have I contributed something."[148] His commentary on the *Change*, however, was still in rough form when he died in 1107, and the real vehicle of his teachings was the "records of speech" his followers recorded. For some, Ch'eng I's teachings had the same status as the words of the sages: they were the expression of a perfectly cultivated mind. As Ch'eng said, "When a man is cultivated within, his words will accord with pattern of themselves."[149] And, as a disciple said on his death, Ch'eng's "mind and tao were in perfect agreement."[150] During the nearly six decades between his death and Chu Hsi's (1130–1200) emergence on the scene as the leading theoretician of the Tao-hsueh movement, the records of Ch'eng's teachings were disseminated and studied. This itself was a sign that thinking about tao no longer entailed wen-hsueh. The tao could be conveyed without making the language wen; Chou Tun-i had miscalculated.

Ch'eng's sayings thus served as a kind of cultural foundation for Tao-hsueh. I am not sure that this was problematic from Ch'eng's perspective. If he was one who "knew tao," his words illuminated li for the world. His sayings should be followed, and the speaker should be imitated. He tells his disciples:

The disciples of Confucius and Mencius were not all worthies and wise men; there were certainly many common folk. When common folk observed sages and worthies, many did not understand. It was precisely because they did not believe themselves but believed their teacher that on seeking they found. Now, you gentlemen, as soon as you are not in accord with my words, you set them aside and ignore them. Thus in the end you will be different from me. You must not put them aside; you must think about them again. This is the method of attaining knowledge.[151]

But why did shih intellectuals increasingly accept the authority of the teachings of the Ch'eng brothers rather than following the learning of

Wang An-shih, Ssu-ma Kuang, Ou-yang Hsiu, or Su Shih? This did not happen immediately. Almost to the end of the Northern Sung in 1127, the court continued to disseminate Wang An-shih's curriculum through a school system that examination candidates were required to attend. At the same time it suppressed the writings of Su and his circle and of Ssu-ma Kuang, as well as the teachings of the Ch'eng brothers. A more accommodative policy during the first years of the Sung restoration in the south gave opponents of Wang a chance to speak out at the highest levels once again, yet the learning of Wang An-shih, supported by the powerful Ch'in Kuei (1090–1155) against proponents of the Ch'eng brothers' learning, and Su Shih's ideas still had enough currency that Chu Hsi felt compelled to attack them. Scholars in the north, who eventually enjoyed their Jurchen rulers' patronage through an expanded examination system, found their intellectual guides in Ou-yang Hsiu and Su Shih and continued to associate morally committed learning with wen-hsueh.[152] But by the end of the twelfth century in the south, proponents of Tao-hsueh were defining the vocabulary and the issues of intellectual culture to such an extent that men with little interest in moral philosophy chose to argue for their positions within the framework of Tao-hsueh. Ch'en Liang (1143–94) is an example of this.

Southern Sung Tao-hsueh was a cultural, social, and political movement and was thus far broader than Ch'eng I himself. The following account, quoted in a miscellany by Chou Mi (1232–1308+), gives a good sense of the movement and its rhetoric, in spite of the author's dyspeptic view of the motives of those involved.

The name "Tao-hsueh" began in the Yuan-yu reign period [1086–93] and became popular during the Ch'un-hsi period [1174–89]. Some of its followers pretended to the name to fool others; they really could blow life into the dead. All who managed resources and revenues, they regarded as amassing wealth; those who served [as attendants] in the palace or [as soldiers] at the borders, they regarded as scum; those who read books and did literary composition, they regarded as fooling around and losing their will; and those who devoted their attention to the affairs of government, they regarded as petty clerks. They read only the *Four Books*, *Reflections on Things at Hand*, *Penetrating the Book of Change*, *Diagram of the Supreme Ultimate*, *Eastern and Western Inscriptions*, and "records of speech." They pretended that their learning was correcting the mind, cultivating the self, ordering the state, and bringing peace to the world. Therefore they took the following slogan as their guide: "Be the ultimate standard for the populace, establish the mind of heaven-and-earth, inaugurate the Great Peace for a myriad generations, and continue the lost learning of the former sages." When they served as prefects and intendants, they always established academies and shrines to the various worthies of their school or published and wrote commentaries on the *Four Books* and compiled "records of speech" in excess. Then they were called "worthies" and could gain great fame and a fat salary. The examination compositions of the literati would quote [their writings], and then they would take high-ranking degrees and become famous. [In their view] to be otherwise, by having the qualities of person of [the Duke of] Wen-kuo [Ssu-ma Kuang] or by having the literary attainments and courage of the immortal [Su Tung-]p'o, was not to be true to one's original character. With that, everyone began to imitate them, and when there was the slightest criticism of them, the faction classed [the critics] as morally inferior. Even the ruler could not dispute them; so compelling was their influence.[153]

This tells of a movement whose members set themselves apart from others involved in government and scholarship and followed a particular curriculum for a kind of learning they believed cultivated the self and benefited the world. It speaks also of how schools devoted to their learning and shrines to its founders were established and how scholarly contributions were made through commentaries and teaching. Eventually being part of Tao-hsueh came to be a way to fame and, when sympathetic scholars controlled the examinations, an advantage in passing the exams. At the same time, adherents denied the value of Ssu-ma Kuang and Su Shih as models and attacked the worth of all who disagreed with them.

The problem, as I see it, is a historical one. Why did Tao-hsueh become a movement? The preceding chapters have shown that Ch'eng I's philosophy was originally only one of several ways the search for values had been resolved during the latter half of the eleventh century. How should we account for the fact that increasing numbers of shih chose this rather than something else? A persuasive answer will require detailed studies of the lives and times of those who participated in the Southern Sung Tao-hsueh movement. The present account of T'ang and Sung intellectual and social change can, however, suggest a perspective on Tao-hsueh as a movement within shih society not provided by the internal history of the movement itself.

A historical perspective on Tao-hsueh can begin with a basic similarity between it and earlier definitions of good learning. Tao-hsueh, like the court scholarship of the early T'ang and the ku-wen movement of the late eighth century and the Northern Sung, was a successful attempt to redefine learning (hsueh) as one of the criteria for shih identity. However, Tao-hsueh spread during a period when learning had become far more essential than before to the efforts of the shih to maintain their identity as shih (and thus their claim to membership in the elite).

The major categories of shih identity did not change between the T'ang and Sung dynasties, although the understanding of what each category entailed did. These were (cultural) learning, ethical behavior, and public service. They were directly related to what we have come to think as defining characteristics of imperial China: a cumulative cultural-textual tradition (learning), a society based on the family system (ethical behavior), and a centralized political system that recruited its officials from a broader elite (public service). Shih identity thus involved claims to historical responsibility for culture, society, and government. And the shih justified their almost continual monopoly of elite status by claiming that they alone were capable of fulfilling these scholarly, familial, and governmental responsibilities.

Culture, family, and government were the three legs of a tripod. Each was a value in itself, and each had its own traditions and rationales. Learning could be seen as a discrete endeavor, particularly when in practice it meant a knowledge of ancient texts and an ability to compose wen-chang. Similarly, those who equated ethical conduct with the virtues of normative family life could distinguish it from the traditions and practices of governing. It is possible to see the shih world strictly in terms of its compartments and to suppose that scholars who redefined learning had at best some influence on the general practice of learning as one kind of shih activity. Learning was thus not the only source of values in shih life. It was a core value for a group that continued to believe that the business of government and ethical familial relations were also essential. But the T'ang and Sung scholars in this study shared—as one might expect of men who gained fame for scholarship—a conviction that they needed to define good learning for their times because they supposed that it had (or ought to have) bearing on the social and political activities of the shih. The early T'ang scholars who saw learning as the acquisition of cultural forms supposed, after all, that through learning men knew the proper forms of social relations and the models and methods of good government. Ku-wen intellectuals were no less concerned with making connections between learning from the cultural tradition and personal behavior and political policy. As was later the case with Tao-hsueh, both earlier groups supposed that learning was the most essential aspect of shih identity.

T'ang-Sung socio-intellectual history offers two related stories. From the first, an intellectual account, we learn that the definition of learning itself changed over time: from the culturalist and synthetic approach of early T'ang court scholarship to the search for the tao of the sage in the wen of antiquity by eighth- and eleventh-century literary intellectuals to the cultivation of the moral self in the Tao-hsueh movement. From the second story, one of social change, we learn that learning as one kind of shih activity eventually became in practice the pre-eminent criterion of elite identity, just as scholars had always thought it should be.

Tao-hsueh thus came at the end of a period during which learning gradually became, for the majority, the most important criterion for claiming to be a shih, at the expense of claims based on family pedigree and service in government. There is a rough correlation between the three intellectual periods in this study and moments when the makeup of elite identity was changing. I am arguing not that social and political change determines intellectual content but that an understanding of why the identity of the shih was becoming problematic can contribute to the way we explain the appeal of certain redefinitions of learning. At the same time, explanations for particular intellectual transitions must take into account the expectations of the intellectual culture of the time. To some extent this is a distinction between asking why the broader audience felt a need for new ideas and why the scholars who spoke to that audience thought particular ideas more appropriate than others.

The process of change began, certainly, in the seventh century, when the T'ang government began to insist that service to the newly unified empire should count more than family pedigree in ranking the great clans and in recruiting officials. Early T'ang court scholars, who did not object to great clans as far as I know, called for a style of scholarship that would further the unity of the state by synthesizing the disparate traditions of the past. Their concern with cultural unity—and their belief that unity was the opposite of decline—was reaffirmed by later ku-wen and Tao-hsueh thinkers. Indeed, with the exception of Su Shih, the scholars in this study saw the intellectual diversity of the Eastern Chou (which we have come to see as the flourishing of Chinese thought) as a mark of the Chou's decline. The An Lu-shan rebellion of the mid–eighth century launched the T'ang empire on a course of decentralization and regionalization that, among other things, made aristocratic pedigree irrelevant. Before then the popularity of learning as a means of gaining eligibility to enter office had been increasing, for on eve of the rebellion some 60,000 men were registered as examination candidates. Han Yü's generation of ku-wen intellectuals, although from more or less illustrious clans themselves, shared the conviction that learning, not pedigree, made the man. In their view the restoration of a unified society could be achieved not by relying on men who had merely acquired the proper cultural form but by turning to those who sought the tao of the sage for themselves—a view Sung ku-wen and Tao-hsueh thinkers would share.

By recruiting its officials from the shih through blind literary examinations, the Sung government institutionalized the primacy of learning relative to family status in entering government. But government—whether it was working either simply to maintain the dynasty or, as ku-wen thinkers proposed, to transform society into an integrated order that secured the welfare of all—was the focus for Ou-yang Hsiu, Wang An-shih, Ssu-ma Kuang, and (to a lesser extent) Su Shih, and how men learned mattered because it had bearing on what they would try to accomplish in government. In its effort to privilege the shih, however, the Sung government undermined this focus on government. It discontinued all the various T'ang official status groups except the examination candidate group—these groups had absorbed over 120,000 men in the mid-T'ang, placing them in official positions that led to eligibility to enter regular bureaucratic office—without adequately increasing the size of the bureaucracy. The Sung system thus made it impossible for most shih, once they gained office, to make office holding the long-term family occupation. Wang An-shih saw the problem, but the New Policies did not solve it. In effect, this meant that by the end of the eleventh century two of the criteria for maintaining shih status—family pedigree and some form of government service—were no longer available to the vast majority of shih. This left the sons of shih families and those who wished to join the elite with only one means of certifying their elite status over successive generations: learning.

We can suppose that Tao-hsueh had some appeal to shih who found themselves in this situation. By explaining why self-cultivation and ethical conduct were of real and primary importance, it directed attention away from government and ideas for transforming society that could be effected through government, a mainstay of ku-wen thought from the eighth century on. And it denied both the value of learning to compose in the literary style of the day, a necessity for all those who hoped to pass the examinations, and the notion that wen-chang was the most appropriate medium for manifesting what one had learned. Although almost all Southern Sung Tao-hsueh spokesmen were officials, few made government their full-time career. They spoke to a larger audience of shih, who participated in the examinations with ever less chance of passing and for whom government service was seldom a career possibility. Tao-hsueh set goals that examinations could not test and whose ultimate realization did not require service in government. In short, what others might see as a lack of worldly success was made irrelevant to success in learning. And those who joined in learning the tao were told that they were the best of all possible shih and they alone had real worth, for they were on the road to becoming sages. At the same time, Tao-hsueh did provide a kind of political involvement, for it created a community for newcomers to join that included scholars of national renown and high officials. And during the twelfth-century Southern Sung, its members took a highly visible political position against what they saw as a nefarious court that sacrificed the recovery of the north to its self-interested attempt to stay in power. As we shall see shortly, it also created a cultural tradition of its own.

Yet I think it is mistaken to suppose that Tao-hsueh was popular only because it provided a form of learning that allowed shih to claim to be shih without attainments in government and culture. This is because, as both Ch'eng I and Chu Hsi realized, the examination system also provided this. Indeed, both men objected to the examination system in part because it allowed shih to think that they needed only an examination education.[154] Examination participation had increased greatly during the course of the eleventh century, although more competition reduced the chance of success. During the first decade of the twelfth century, when the New Policies required candidates to attend government schools, about 200,000 were registered; perhaps 400,000 were involved in the examinations by the middle of the thirteenth century.

The shih continued to flock to the examinations during the Sung because, I suggest, examination candidacy was a viable means of maintaining a claim to shih status. And the reason it was viable was that it implied possessing not only the requisite culture and learning but the two other legs of the tripod of shih identity as well. By granting the candidate permission to take the examinations, the government simultaneously recognized his eligibility to serve as an official (since anyone who passed was eligible for appointment) and his claim to ethical behavior and good family background (since participation required certification of these qualities). Because legally the examinations were open only to shih, participation (whether one failed or passed) meant one must be a shih. Acquiring the necessary learning did not, of course, mean that the candidate was doing anything to fulfill the political and ethical responsibilities of a shih. Candidacy did not imply, then, that one was a good shih, but only that one was a shih. The difference between the social functions of the examinations and of Tao-hsueh is that the latter not only provided a definition of learning as part of shih identity but also promised that learning the tao was tantamount to fulfilling the ethical, cultural, and political responsibilities of the shih. In other words, Tao-hsueh was more than a means of being a shih; it was a means of being a good shih.

To me the most useful perspective on both the ku-wen movement and Tao-hsueh is to see their redefinitions of learning as redefinitions of what it meant to be a good shih. For the T'ang ku-wen intellectuals, being a good shih meant seeking values for oneself and acting according to what one learned, even if it put one at odds with contemporary society. The good shih aimed to serve in government; if it was impossible to accomplish anything in government, he could manifest what he had learned through his wen-chang. Ku-wen told shih to seek the tao of the sage, rather than devoting themselves to mastering tradition and received forms. Yet it also defined the parameters for what could easily become an open-ended search for meaning and values. Han Yü and others told shih where to look, what to look for, and how to express what they found. Shih should seek the tao in the wen of antiquity, they should find guides to reintegrating society and guiding government to serve the common good, and they should reveal what they had apprehended for themselves through writing that resonated with the wen of the ancients. Government and wen-chang were to be vehicles for realizing the tao of the sage in the present. To a great extent, however, being a good shih meant being able to compose wen that was "ancient," for the ability to compose in this fashion was evidence that one had apprehended something of the sages and integrated it into one's own being. Ku-wen was, in spite of itself, a product of aristocratic culture, which placed great store in having the proper appearance and demonstrating one's synthesis and refinement of past traditions through literary composition.

But by conceiving of the tao of the sage as ideas that transcended their particular expression in the past, ku-wen created a new kind of problem. On the one hand, if individuals were truly to be guided by this tao, they had to discover it for themselves—to reduce it to statements or proper forms made it something one could imitate without absorbing. On the other hand, if shih were to guide society and establish standards for others, they had to create new models to replace meaningless conventions and establish their own moral authority as teachers to others. Perhaps for men of the late eighth century, who came from families that had participated in metropolitan culture for generations, it was sufficient to demand that individuals show that they were personally committed to treating as real the values they already knew they ought to share. But the tension between knowing for oneself and establishing new models was implicit in the ku-wen position.

During the eleventh century, advocates of the ku-wen style of learning and writing came to dominate intellectual culture. But they now addressed a new public: men from provincial families that had forgotten T'ang culture and whose families in recent times had attainments in scholarship or experience at court. They were told that learning and composing wen made them eligible to enter government and that by learning from antiquity they would know what to do and how to act. There was a tao, they were told; if they could know it, they could manifest it in writing and transform society accordingly. The good shih aimed to unify the customs and values of all in order to improve the lives of all. The best shih were the ones who could tell others how to do so. For many eleventh-century intellectuals, the idea of unity was at the heart of the idea of morality. Ku-wen was a most secular movement at mid-eleventh century, an attempt to find in the realm of purely human affairs the guides to an integrated human order.

Within the intellectual culture of ku-wen, the two strands of finding it for oneself and setting models for others were played out. Fan Chung-yen had clear ideas about what the proper models were, and many found him persuasive. But Wang An-shih and Ssu-ma Kuang fully realized the possibility of providing the shih with a curriculum to learn, rules for behavior, and programs for government. They had found the tao for themselves. To be sure, each believed that others could adopt their own method of learning and reach the same conclusions, yet each had figured out what others should know. Wang and his successors used their political power to create a national curriculum for the shih. Both Wang and Ssu-ma doubted the importance of literary composition for the shih because, I think, encouraging individuality of expression simply did not serve the goal of training shih to be officials. But for many, Wang's was not a convincing curriculum, even if he saw it as a means of encouraging men to transform themselves into shih. As Su Shih put it, it produced students in a fashion analogous to striking prints; each one came out the same.

Ou-yang Hsiu and Su Shih spoke for the "find it oneself" strand of ku-wen thought. Su saw that insisting on finding it for oneself meant ultimately that those who did would not end up being the same. He accepted this conclusion and tried to persuade others to share it. The good shih learned in a manner that enabled him to experience the underlying unit of himself and the things he met in life. He cultivated in himself the process of responding to things, combining the acquisition of knowledge of how things worked and what the past had achieved with his own ineffable intuition of fundamental commonalities. In a world of inevitable individuality, wen-chang remained a useful way of practicing the art of learning, but learning was an art, not a science. A shih did his best to see beyond the surface; he tried to ensure that his responses to things would be of real value. But certainty was elusive, and knowledge required finding one's way through the cumulative accomplishments of the past. The models one created for others could be imitated, yet they were never more than provisional solutions in a changing world.

Ch'eng I denied that moral knowledge was mediated by culture, yet he generally held that shih could illuminate the li of things and fulfill their own moral nature only through their own efforts. Real values were of heaven-and-earth and inherent in things, but they had a real locus in the self as well, so that learning could be seen as the extension and enlargement of that which was of the self.[155] Yet I suspect he saw the realm of li not unlike Wang An-shih saw the Classics: the meanings were obvious to one who knew how to look. Ch'eng offered the shih certainty, not in the sense of providing a set of definitions, but in the form of a promise that those who thought in the correct manner would know for themselves, find it in themselves, and still reach the same conclusions as everyone else. All could match the clarity and moral assurance of the sages; all could be men of real worth. There was no need in principle to rely on wen-chang to show others one's progress in learning or to communicate ideas that would otherwise not be clear. Values were accessible directly and absolutely; one who saw them acted accordingly. The goal—and the proof of one's attainments—lay in practicing the virtues of the sages oneself and being able to respond to things spontaneously yet correctly. Individuals might differ according to where they started from and in how far they had gone, but they were traveling the same network of paths, and when they arrived at the same place, they could expect to see the same thing and respond in the same way. Yet since the network could expand to accommodate everything, there was no situation that a truly cultivated man could not sort out.

Ch'eng's learning was open-ended, and his ideas were open to various interpretations. Once Ch'eng was no longer there to set his students straight, some even began to think that Buddhist enlightenment was a way of thinking about the illumination of the unity of li. Ch'eng's ideas about how the individual should learn assumed that the necessary guides existed in the mind; there were no real cultural parameters. Ch'eng did see that ethical conduct provided a clearly bounded area for training oneself in thought and practice, but he himself could conceive of virtues as highly abstract structural principles. The key to the success of the Tao-hsueh movement, I believe, was that it maintained the open-endedness of its philosophical foundation but found a way to introduce the cultural parameters necessary to channel thought in socially responsible directions.

This is not to underestimate the importance of the promise of certainty. Tao-hsueh held, after all, that there was no ultimate reality or source beyond what men could know with their minds. We can suppose that the shih of the Southern Sung were burdened with considerable angst. The survival of the dynasty was at times uncertain; the Jurchens threatened, and after the 1230's the Mongols prepared to invade. The Southern Sung as a "southern dynasty" confronted a history that located the center of legitimate power in the north. Above all, for shih families their own survival as shih was increasingly contingent on circumstances. Without office they depended to a great extent on other shih agreeing that they belonged and on maintaining the resources necessary to keep up appearances. Tao-hsueh told them that their worth as men did not depend on others, and it showed them a way to learn that proved that they could know what was right and good for themselves.

For all its epistemological optimism, however, learning the tao was difficult in practice. No one became a sage in the Southern Sung. It seems to me that the Tao-hsueh movement asked shih to try to learn in the right way and provided them with a context in which to pursue self-cultivation. In effect it created a new shih culture for men to join. Now the literary activities that had been so much a part of elite social life and scholarship during the preceding centuries played a minimal role. Perhaps we can say that Tao-hsueh replaced the literary culture of the past with a culture of ethical practice or discipline. In this ethical culture men made themselves known to others and expressed what was on their minds through their acts rather than through their poems. Men who learned the tao were to put into action the principles of right behavior the mind had realized and to comprehend the ultimate coherence of the tao. They were not looking for good ideas for a poem or essay, nor were they agitating to increase the power of government to transform society from above.

What strikes me as important about this Tao-hsueh culture, especially as Chu Hsi and his collaborators contributed to it, was that it replaced the old cultural-textual tradition with a new version. The new cultural tradition included a body of texts students could study in order to fulfill their moral nature. Southern Sung thinkers extended the process of re-evaluating the textual tradition that began with Ch'eng I's work on the Classics, and they transformed parts of it into the media for true learning. In *Reflections on Things at Hand* (*Chin-ssu lu*), Chu Hsi and Lü Tsu-ch'ien (1137–81) selected passages from the works and sayings of the Ch'engs, Chang Tsai, and Chou Tun-i to show how the founding thinkers as truly moral men dealt with all aspects of shih life, from, among other things, thinking about cosmology to learning to relating to family members to participating in government.[156] Chu collated and published editions of the writings and records of speech of Northern Sung and early Southern Sung thinkers. He adopted and encouraged new commentaries on the Five Classics. And, above all, he defined the Four Books (the *Analects*, *Mencius*, *Great Learning*, and *Doctrine of the Mean*) as the essence of the sages' teachings and, through commentaries and teaching, explained what they meant.[157] Northern Sung thinkers had treated the sages as historical figures and had fathomed the constants in the Classics from a historical perspective. Tao-hsueh adherents dehistoricized the Classics and the sages and resacralized them.

Following Hu Hung (1105–55) and others, Chu Hsi adopted Ch'eng I's revision of the ku-wen view of China's intellectual history (but placed Chou Tun-i first), calling it the *tao-t'ung* ("the [line of] continuity with the Way") in his preface to the *Doctrine of the Mean*, so that only those who participated in the *tao-t'ung* were true successors to the sages. And in the *Record of the Origins of the Ch'eng School* (1173), he decided who had been part of the beginnings of the movement in the Sung: Chou Tun-i, Ch'eng Hao and Ch'eng I, Chang Tsai, Shao Yung, and 41 friends and followers (but not Ssu-ma Kuang).[158]

Chu Hsi continued the philosophical inquiries of the eleventh-century masters in his own teachings and worked to clarify the intellectual problems the Ch'engs had created and to unify the divergent lines of thought that traced their origins back to the Ch'engs.[159] To a considerable degree he established the conceptual language of Tao-hsueh as a philosophical "system" to be understood through its own vocabulary, as Ch'en Ch'un's (1159–1223) *Pei-hsi tzu-i* (Neo-Confucian terms explained) illustrates.[160] The records of Chu Hsi's own oral teachings, the greatest of all the Sung "records of speech," amply demonstrates his desire to bring the entire cultural tradition under review—and to show that there was no question he could not answer. He was far broader than the thinkers he looked back to. He and his school produced their own version of the political history of the Northern Sung with a series of biographies of major officials, the *Ming-ch'en yen-hsing lu* (Record of the words and deeds of famous ministers), and they revised and abridged Ssu-ma Kuang's *Comprehensive Mirror* as the *Tzu-chih t'ung-chien kang-mu* (Digest of the *Comprehensive Mirror for Aid in Government*), to create a history of China that would teach ethical lessons rather than Ssu-ma's political principles. Chu also addressed the foundations of the literary tradition, with works on the *Songs* and the *Ch'u tz'u*, and reviewed the history of literature in his teachings.[161]

The body of authoritative texts, the vocabulary of thought, and the correct interpretations of Chinese intellectual and political history provided Tao-hsueh followers with a curriculum. The movement also created institutions in which communities of scholars could learn the tao together. Private academies that did not orient themselves toward the examinations spread. There were shrines to past masters, devotional rituals, public lectures, discussion meetings, and time for reading and reflection.[162] Like Ch'eng I, Chu Hsi and others created a new set of family rituals. As Ch'eng I had argued, those who "knew tao" could create rituals that embodied the normative patterns of moral order yet make them accord with times.[163] Chu Hsi and his fellows also envisioned ways in which shih could take responsibility for the moral and economic welfare of local society. The "community compact," for example, would institutionalize mutual ethical supervision at the local level, making state-imposed mutual surveillance units unnecessary,[164] and the "community granary" would see to local relief.[165] Not a few of the ideals of Wang An-shih are evident in these institutions, but generally Tao-hsueh proponents wanted the government not to interfere in matters that good shih at the local level could manage.

The culture of Tao-hsueh in the twelfth century, despite its claim to "orthodoxy," was not so much the orthodox culture as a counterculture that thought of itself as transmitting true values. Like so many literary intellectuals from the late eighth century on, Chu Hsi and his allies presented themselves as a embattled minority struggling against a self-interested mainstream. They claimed This Culture of Ours as theirs, but in doing so they tailored and redyed its fabric. As with the early T'ang scholars, the cultural tradition they envisioned was ultimately based on heaven-and-earth, but now it was mediated by their own minds and was a far narrower tradition than it had been in the early T'ang. They did not have to try to synthesize received traditions. They selected those pieces they believed gave the best access to the sages' minds and principles, and they interpreted them for others.

With Tao-hsueh Sung intellectuals claimed authority to a degree unusual before. Moral thinkers like Ch'eng I were certain that they did "know tao," could pronounce absolutely on all aspects of life, and could lead lives beyond any possible reproach. From the eighth century on, intellectuals rather than the court had defined the terms of intellectual debate, and certainly the literary intellectuals of the past had begun to develop a rhetorical style that tended to pronounce. Yet it seems to me that even Wang An-shih and Ssu-ma Kuang were more likely to cast themselves as students rather than knowers of the tao. The fact that moral thinkers claimed authority and others thought them right to do so encouraged students to see themselves not as students of the distant sages with indistinct messages but of the Sung thinkers who taught them how to learn to be sages. Tao-hsueh teachers lectured or preached, a custom that was rare indeed in earlier centuries. And they made it possible to think what their predecessors had never been quite able to believe: that they had launched a new beginning and were liberated from history. Claims to such absolute authority had political implications, of course, for those who knew tao were not anxious to be co-opted and saw little reason to compromise with central authority; yet they were beyond the power of the court to suppress, as it discovered during its attack on "false learning" at the end of the twelfth century.

The willingness of moral thinkers to claim authority went together with the unwillingness and inability of scholars from other lines of thought to do so. Those such as Ch'en Liang who were not inclined to moral philosophy found themselves in the difficult situation of having to argue their position on philosophical grounds. There were many poets and literary men in the Southern Sung, yet no great writer established himself as a major force in intellectual culture. The wen-shih seem generally to have been content to be merely doing literary writing, without making larger claims by virtue of their literary accomplishment. They also began to spend more time writing about the craft of composition and the details of writing, in contrast to their Northern Sung counterparts, who rarely addressed such practical matters and spoke instead of the larger significance of wen.

Tao-hsueh provided an alternative culture for the shih by showing them how they could be members of the elite and good men at the same time. It treated "ethical conduct" seriously as the primary concern of the shih in a society that was coming to be dominated by local elites of shih families. Southern Sung intellectuals, I suggest, could reflect on the Northern Sung and conclude that their predecessors had tried to make the world a better place. They had put their trust in wen-hsueh to recruit civil officials through examinations to govern the state and had attempted to transform men through morally serious writing. Then they had tried to perfect institutions and transform society through government. Neither had worked. But ethical conduct had not been tried, although its importance had been mentioned. For Chu Hsi the core of Tao-hsueh ethical practice lay in the mind, in a struggle between the "mind of tao" and the "mind of man," in which the first enabled one to be aware of heaven's pattern (t'ien-li) and the second made the mind susceptible to human desires. At least for Chu the distinction between heaven's pattern and human desire was absolute. In every instance one was acting according to either one or the other; morally ambiguous choices were not possible.[166] (Chu distinguished jen-ch'ing, human emotional response, from desire—he thought Ch'eng I had lumped the two together—thus validating the emotions to refer to responses to things guided by Heaven's pattern.)

The Ch'eng-Chu idea that there was an absolute distinction between t'ien-li and desire meant that any actions motivated by desire were immoral. This ran counter to critical thinking: Han Yü had argued that the sages in fact had fulfilled general human needs and desires, an idea that Su Shih still held to. For thinkers in this line, this meant that contrary to Buddhist and some ju beliefs, a moral world and human desires were not incompatible; thus it was not necessary to demand either adherence to ritual as a way of thwarting the dangers of desire or withdrawal from society in an effort to be pure. It is true, of course, that these same men also believed that scholars themselves had to transcend partiality and selfishness as best they could, if only to see the real interests of the people. Ssu-ma Kuang, for example, assumed that one had to manage the bureaucracy by channeling the self-interest of bureaucrats, although he was concerned with attaining a state of impartiality within his own mind. The Ch'eng-Chu position is extreme, but perhaps it was aimed at a different issue. Earlier thinkers had asked how government could profit society, but for Chu Hsi the issue was not political in the first place but how people, especially the shih, behaved.

One of the consequences of the Sung government's inability to provide shih families with long-term careers in government was a lessened willingness on the part of those families to maintain the standards expected of officials in private life and, for various reasons, a growing incapacity on the part of government to exercise institutional discipline over them. At the same time, the social circumstances of the shih—downward mobility and the need for land and other resources to support the family, for example—pressed them to further their interests at the expense of others. It was into this world of a self-aggrandizing elite relatively immune to government control that Tao-hsueh came. It offered a vision of learning that helped the shih learn to survive without office and thus supported the independence of the shih from the government, but at the same time it explained how it was possible and why it was necessary for the shih as individuals to discipline themselves.

Appendix

The Ch'ao Family of the Northern and Southern Sung

1. Family members are listed by generation, in the order in which they appear on the chart (see pp. 348–49).

2. Cases where entry by the yin privilege has been surmised on the basis of career are noted by "YIN?" Chin-shih degree holders are denoted by "CS."

3. The highest office held has been converted to a rank grade following Umehara, "Civil and Military Officials" (e.g., R2B).

4. I state that the subject did not serve only when the sources specify that he did not.

5. When only part of a career can be reconstructed from the available sources, information is dated to a particular year if possible.

6. Family members whose direct ancestry cannot be traced are excluded from the genealogical chart and are listed in the appropriate generation here under "Others."

7. Letters in brackets indicate sources (see pp. 353–54).

8. The following abbreviations are used: d., died; m., married; PT, posthumous title; R, rank.

Ch'ao Hsien 晁憲, father of Ch'üan [a]

Generation I (10th c.)

Ch'üan 佺 (ca. 904–?), m. (1) Keng 耿, (2) Sun 孫, and (3) Fu 傅 [a,b]

Generation II Ch'ao 之 (10th–early 11th c.)

Branch A
Ti 迪, did not serve [b,m,i,q]

Branch B
Chiung 迥 (951–1034), CS 980, PT: Wen-yuan 文元, R2B, m. Chang 張 [b,f,m,n]

Branch C

Kou 遘, YIN, R7A, m. Chang 張 (983−1069) [a,b,ap]

Generation III   Ch'ao Tsung-　宗 (early−mid 11th c.)

Branch A

Tsung-chien 簡 (d. 1044), CS 992, R6B, m. Kung-sun 公孫 [i,j,s,y]

Branch B

Tsung-ch'ueh 懃 (d. before 1042), YIN, CS equivalency, R4A, PT: Wen-chuang 文莊, m. Wang 王 [f,o,ac]

Tsung-ts'ao 操, YIN, R9B in 1044, m. (1) Chao 趙, (2) Chao 趙 [h,n,au]

Branch C

Tsung-yueh 曜 (d. before 1069), CS, R? [ap]

Tsung-ko 恪 (1007−69), YIN, R6A, m. Lü-ch'iu 閭丘 [a,ap]

Tsung-yuan 愿 (d. before 1069) YIN?, R *hsuan-jen*, m. Huang 黃 (1016−1107+) [b,m,ap]

Tsung-i 懿 (d. after 1069), YIN, R7A [ap]

Generation IV   Ch'ao Chung-　仲 (mid- to late 11th c.)

Branch A

Chung-yen 匽, YIN, R7A, m. (1) Hsu 許, (2) Liu 劉 [i,s,y]
son [y]
son [y]
son [y]
Chung-ts'an 參 (1013−67) YIN, R6B, m. Kung-sun 公孫 [m,j,t,y,ar,ao(?)]

Branch B

Chung-yen 衍 (1012−53), YIN, CS equivalency, R7A, m. Wang 王 [f,l,av]
Chung-wei 劌, YIN, R7B in 1053 [f,x]
Chung-hsi 熙 (1019−86), YIN, R6A, m. Chang 張 [a,h]

Branch C

(N.B.: in 1069 Branch C had 30 sons and daughters [ap])
Chung-yueh 約, CS 1034?, R7A in 1061 (son of either Tsung-yueh or Tsung-i) [x,av,aw]
Chung-hung 紘, YIN?, R9B (son of either Tsung-yueh or Tsung-i) [x]
Chung-ch'o 綽, YIN, CS equivalency 1044, R6A in 1060's [x,ax]
Chung-ching 景, YIN?, R *hsuan-jen* in 1069 [a]
Chung-ju 孺, YIN, R9B in 1069 [a]
6 daughters, 4 m. to officials as of 1069 [a]
Chung-k'ang 康, YIN?, R *hsuan-jen* [m]

Chung-mou 謀 [m]
son [m]
Chung-hsun 詢 (1057–1115), did not serve [b,m]

Generation V   Ch'ao Tuan- 端 (mid-11th–early 12th c.)

Branch A

Tuan-yu 友 (1029–75), CS 1052, R8A, m. Yang 楊 [g,as]
Tuan-chung 中 (1051–1100), CS, R *hsuan-jen*, m. (1) Hu 胡, (2) Lü-ch'iu 閭丘 [i]
Tuan-pen 本, YIN, R8A, m. Yen 閻 [k]
Tuan-jen 仁 (1035–1102), CS, R6B, m. Yeh 葉 (1034–80) [j,aq]
Tuan-i 義, YIN, R8A [t,w]
Tuan-li 禮 (1046–1113), CS 1073, R9B [c,t,w,ay]
Tuan-chih 智, CS?, R7A [t,m,ao(?)]
5 daughters, 4 m. to officials as of 1068 [t]

Branch B

Tuan-yen 彥 (1035–95), YIN, then CS in 1059, R6B [f,v,c,z,ac]
Tuan-fang 方, no rank as of 1053 [f]
Tuan-ling 棐 (1045–90), YIN, R *hsuan-jen*, m. Wang [f,l]
3 sons died at birth [f]
2 daughters unmarried as of 1053 [f]
Tuan-pi 弼, CS, R7A in 1096 [h]
Tuan-chieh 介, YIN?, R8A in 1096 [h]
Tuan-hsiu 修, YIN?, R *hsuan-jen* in 1096 [h]
Tuan-ts'ui 粹, YIN?, R9B in 1096 [h]
Tuan-hou 厚, YIN, R *hsuan-jen* in 1096 [h]
4 daughters m. to officials [h]

Branch C

Tuan-fu 復, rank by YIN but not yet serving in 1069 [a]
Tuan-yen 儼, rank by YIN but not yet serving in 1069 [a]
Tuan-?, no rank as of 1069 [a]
Tuan-kuei 規 [b]
Tuan-chü 矩 [b]
Tuan-chun 準 [b]
6 of 8 daughters survived and m. officials [b]

Others

Tuan-te 德, R *hsuan-jen* in 1088 [az]
Tuan-ch'eng 誠, prefect by 1116 [ba]
Tuan-k'uei 揆 [an]
Tuan-chin 晉 ⎫
Tuan-ch'ang 常 ⎬ brothers [r]
Tuan-lin 臨 ⎪
Tuan-i 頤 ⎭

Genealogy of the Ch'ao Family

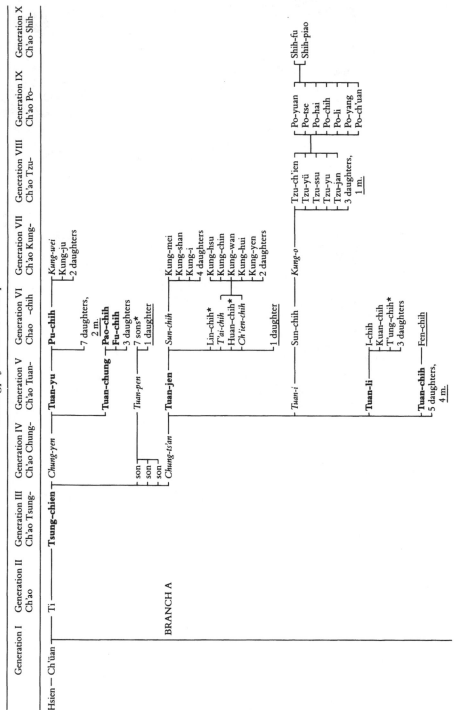

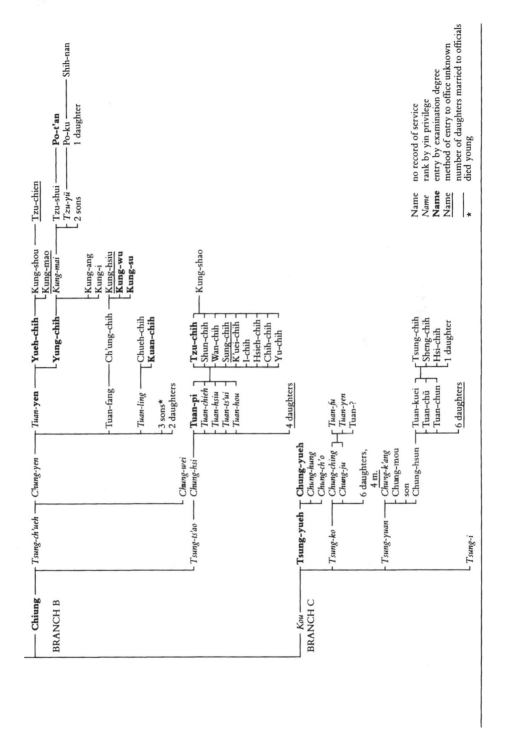

Generation VI   Ch'ao   -chih 之 (mid-11th–mid-12th c.)

Branch A

Pu-chih 補 (1053–1110), CS 1079, R6A, m. Tu 杜 [p,s]
4 of 7 daughters m. in 1075, 2 to officials [q,as]
Pao-chih 保, CS by 1100 [i]
Fu-chih 付, CS by 1100 [i]
3 unmarried daughters in 1100 [i]
7 sons died young [k]
1 daughter m. official [k]
Sun-chih 損 (1059–1122), YIN, R *hsuan-jen*, m. (1) Li 李, (2) Chang 張, (3) Liu 劉 [j,aq]
Lin-chih 臨, died young [j,aq]
T'ai-chih 泰, YIN?, R *hsuan-jen* in 1102 [j,aq]
Huan-chih 渙, died young [j,aq]
Ch'ien-chih 謙 (?–1154), YIN, R4A [j,af]
1 daughter m. official [j]
Sun-chih 巽, did not serve, m. Lü-ch'iu 閭丘 [w]
I-chih 益, exam candidate in 1113 [c,u]
Kuan-chih 觀, exam candidate in 1113 [c,u]
T'ung-chih 同, died young [c,u]
3 daughters, married in 1113 [u]
Fen-chih 賁, R6A in 1142 [ao]

Branch B

Yueh-chih 說 (1059–1129), CS 1082, R5, m. Sheng 盛 [e,ac,ak]
Yung-chih 詠, CS, R7A [v]
Ch'ung-chih 沖 (d. 1141), did not serve [aa,ah]
Chueh-chih 覺, no rank as of 1107 [l]
Kuan-chih 貫, CS, R *hsuan-jen* in 1107 [l]
Tzu-chih 資, CS, R *hsuan-jen* in 1096 [h]
Shun-chih 順, no rank as of 1096 [h]
Wan-chih 完 [h]
Sung-chih 頌, subprefect in 1135 [h,bb]
K'uei-chih 葵 [h]
I-chih 疑 [h]
Hsieh-chih 頡 [h]
Chih-chih 藄 [h]
Yu-chih 栖 [h]

Branch C

Tsung-chih 宗, no rank as of 1128 [b]
Sheng-chih 勝 [b]
Hsi-chih 曦 [b]
1 daughter in 1128 [b]

Others

Lung-chih 隆 [x]
Tsai-chih 載, CS [x]
Sheng-chih 升 [x]
Chiang-chih 將, vice-prefect in 1116 [bc]

Generation VII   Ch'ao Kung-   公 (late 11th–late 12th c.)

Branch A

Kung-wei 爲, YIN, R7A in 1129 [s,al]
Kung-ju 汝, no rank in 1110 [s]
2 daughters, 1 married in 1110 [s]
Kung-mei 美, no rank in 1122 [d,j]
Kung-shan 善 [d,j]
Kung-i 儀 [d,j]
4 daughters m. in 1122 [d]
Kung-hsu 序, no rank in 1102 [j]
Kung-chin 謹 [j]
Kung-wan 捥 [j]
Kung-hui 惠 [j]
Kung-yen 琰 [j]
2 daughters, 1 married in 1102 [j]
Kung-o 諤 (1105–65), YIN, R *hsuan-jen*, m. Chiang 姜 [w]

Branch B

Kung-shou 壽 (1085–1107) [ab]
Kung-mao 苊, an official [e,x]
Kung-mai 邁 (d. before 1180) YIN, R7A [v,ad,ae]
Kung-ang 昂, no rank in 1202 [v]
Kung-i 逸 [v]
Kung-hsiu 休, sub-prefect [x,aa,aj]
Kung-wu 武, CS of 1132, R7A in 1150's [w,aa,ah,at]
Kung-su 遡, CS of 1138, R6A [aa,ai]
Kung-shao 紹, only son as of 1096 [h]

Others

Kung-ch'ing 慶, son of Sheng-chih [x]
Kung-yü 愚, mining official in 1167 [bd]
Kung-i 裔, CS by 1141 [ag]
Kung-chih 志 [am]
Kung-ping 秉 [x]
Kung-tsan 贊 [x]
Hui 會, *tzu* Kung-hsi 公錫 (the source probably confused the *ming* and *tzu*)
  [bg]

Generation VIII   Ch'ao Tzu-   子 (12th–early 13th c.)

Branch A

Tzu-ch'ien 騫 (d. 1207) no rank [w]
Tzu-yü 與 (d. before 1207) [w]
Tzu-ssu 思 (d. before 1207) [w]
Tzu-yu 游 (d. after 1207) [w]
Tzu-jan 冉 (d. before 1207) [w]
3 daughters, 1 m. to an official [w]

Branch B

Tzu-chien 健 (1107–?), R6 in 1172 [e,ab,be]
Tzu-shui 誰 [v,ad]
Tzu-yü 與 (1114–1201), given honorary rank in the 1190's [v]
2 sons [v]

Generation IX   Ch'ao Po-   百 (mid-12th–early 13th c.)

Branch A

Po-yuan 源, no rank in 1207 [w]
Po-tse 則 [w]
Po-hai 海 [w]
Po-chih 制 [w]
Po-li 利 [w]
Po-yang 揚 [w]
Po-ch'uan 川 [w]

Branch B

Po-t'an 談, CS 1175, prefect [v,ad]
Po-ku 谷, exam candidate in 1202 [v]
1 daughter, m. [v]

Others

Po-k'uei 揆 [bf]

Generation X   Ch'ao Shih-   世 (late 12th–13th c.)

Branch A

Shih-fu 黻   [w]
Shih-piao 表 [w]

Branch B

Shih-nan 南, from 1202 [v]

Sources (for full citations of the works cited here, see the Bibliography, pp. 449–81; "d.," or dated, indicates year referred to in the source)

a.   Tseng Kung, *Tseng Kung chi* 46.629, d. 1069.

b.   Ch'ao Yueh-chih, *Sung-shan Ching-yü sheng chi* 19.24a, d. 1128.

c.   Ibid. 19.20b, d. 1128.

d.   Ibid. 20.21a, d. 1122.

e.   Ibid., appendix 2b, d. 1129+.

f.   Wang Kuei, *Hua-yang chi* 50.5b.

g.   Ch'ao Pu-chih, *Chi-pei Ch'ao hsien-sheng Chi-le chi* 60.464, d. 1095.

h.   Ch'ao Pu-chih, *Chi-le chi* 64.498, d. 1096.

i.   Ibid. 68.548, d. 1100.

j.   Ibid. 67.535, d. 1102.

k.   Ibid. 68.553, d. 1103.

l.   Ibid. 63.492, d. 1107.

m.   Ibid. 31.209, d. 1107.

n.   *Sung shih* 305.10085–87.

o.   Ibid. 305.10087–88.

p.   Ibid. 444.13111–12.

q.   Huang T'ing-chien, *Yü-chang Huang hsien-sheng wen-chi* 23.250, d. 1084.

r.   Ibid. 16.153, n.d.

s.   Chang Lei, *K'o-shan chi* 12.748, d. 1110.

t.   Wang An-shih, *Lin-ch'uan hsien-sheng wen-chi* 96.994, d. 1068.

u.   Li Chao-ch'i, *Le ching chi* 28.15a.

v.   Chou Pi-ta, *P'ing-yuan hsu-kao* 35.1a, d. 1202.

w.   Lou Yueh, *Kung-kuei chi* 108.8a, d. 1207.

x.   See appropriate entry in *Sung jen chuan-chi tzu-liao so-yin*, pp. 1946–58.

y.   Ch'ao Pu-chih, *Chi-le chi* 31.211, d. 1110.

z.   Ibid. 40.464, d. 1095.

aa.   Ch'ao Ch'ung-chih, *Ch'ao Chü-tz'u shih-chi*, preface, d. 1141.

ab.   Ch'ao Yueh-chih, *Sung-shan Ching-yü sheng chi* 19.16b, d. 1107.

ac.   *Sung jen i-shih hui-pien*, pp. 220–23.

ad.   Lu Yu, *Lu Fang-weng ch'üan-chi* 14.79–80, d. 1180.

ae.   *Chien-yen i-lai hsi-nien yao-lu* 29.12b, 13a, 136.13b, d. 1129–40.

af.   Ibid. 119.2b, 128.2a, 136.13b, 140.11a, 157.6a, 167.13a, d. 1138–54.

ag.   Ibid. 162.2b, d. 1141.

ah.   Ibid. 156.3a, 13a, 178.15b, d. 1147–57.

ai.   Ibid. 190.8a, d. 1161.

aj.   Ibid. 34.7a, d. 1130.

ak.   Ibid. 6.13b, 19.4a, d. 1127–29.

al.   Ibid. 31.1a, 46.5a, 47.11a, 57.1b, 65.5a, 74.3a, 88.6b, 95.6b, d. 1130–35.

am.   Ibid. 190.6a, d. 1161.

an.   Hung Mai, *I Chien chih* 15.665.

ao.   Wang Tsao, *Fu-ch'i chi* 28.13a, d. 1142.

ap. Tseng Kung, *Tseng Kung chi* 45.622, d. 1069.

aq. Ch'ao Pu-chih, *Chi-le chi* 64.507, d. 1086.

ar. Ibid. 62.490, d. 1086.

as. Ibid. 65.510, d. 1093.

at. *Sung Yuan hsueh-an pu-i* 2.163b.

au. *Hsu tzu-chih t'ung-chien ch'ang-pien* 83.14a, d. 1014.

av. *Sung hui-yao: hsuan-chü* 3.18a, d. 1034.

aw. *Hsu tzu-chih t'ung-chien ch'ang-pien* 145.5ab, d. 1043.

ax. *Sung hui-yao: hsuan-chü* 9.10b, d. 1044.

ay. *Hsu tzu-chih t'ung-chien ch'ang-pien* 349.9a, d. 1084.

az. Ibid. 408.18b, d. 1088.

ba. *Sung hui-yao: chih-kuan* 68.36a, d. 1116.

bb. Ibid. 61.48a, d. 1135.

bc. Ibid. 68.32a, d. 1116.

bd. Ibid. 43.159a, d. 1167.

be. Ibid. 35.44b, d. 1172.

bf. *Sung shih i-wen-chih kuang-pien*, p. 83.

bg. Yuan Hao-wen, *Chung-chou chi* 8.5b.

Reference Matter

Notes

For complete authors' names, titles, and publication data for the works cited here in short form, see the Bibliography, pp. 449–81. The following abbreviations are used in the Notes:

CTS	*Chiu T'ang shu*
CTW	*Ch'üan T'ang wen*
ECC	Ch'eng Hao and Ch'eng I, *Erh Ch'eng chi*
FWKC	Fan Chung-yen, *Fan Wen-cheng kung chi*
HCLC	Han Yü, *Han Ch'ang-li chi*
HTS	*Hsin T'ang shu*
IS	*I-shu*, in *ECC*, vol. 1
LCWC	Wang An-shih, *Lin-ch'uan hsien-sheng wen-chi*
LTYC	Liu Tsung-yang, *Liu Tsung-yuan chi*
LWKC	Li Ao, *Li wen kung chi*
OHCC	Ou-yang Hsiu, *Ou-yang Hsiu ch'üan-chi*
SHY	*Sung hui-yao*
SMWC	Ssu-ma Kuang, *Ssu-ma Wen-cheng kung ch'uan-chia chi*
SS	*Sui shu*
STPC	Su Shih, *Su Tung-p'o chi*
TCTC	Ssu-ma Kuang, *Tzu-chih t'ung-chien*
TPWC	Su Shih, *Chiao-cheng ching-chin Tung-p'o wen-chi shih-lueh*

Chapter 1

1. For brief notes on the emergence in the Eastern Chou (770–256 B.C.) of the shih as a distinct group that combined both official service with intellectual leadership, see Schwartz, *World of Thought*, pp. 44, 57–59, 238, 278, 353. For a far more extensive account of the shih, particularly in their role as intellectuals in Chinese history from ancient times through the Period of Division, see Yü Ying-shih, *Shih yü Chung-kuo wen-hua*. It is clear that in early times the shih were a subordinate group within the political hierarchy, men who made their careers by serving the political powers with their talents. It is my view, detailed in Chapter 2,

that by the early T'ang the term had come to refer to a sociopolitical elite assumed to be largely hereditary. David Johnson (*Medieval Chinese Oligarchy*, p. 16) distinguishes the aristocracy and ruling class from the shih as all those who held official rank. He concludes, however, that although he sees the shih as a conventional term for a loose category of people with earned rather than ascribed status (as with aristocrats), "as time passed people began to think of the group of office and rank holders as a kind of hereditary class." The use of "shih" to refer to the elite of Sung society is not problematic.

2. For Yen Chih-t'ui's work, see *Family Instructions for the Yen Clan*, trans. Teng Ssu-yü. For the Chinese text of the *Yen-shih chia-hsun*, I have followed Yen Chih-t'ui, *Yen-shih chia-hsun chi-chieh*. For a more detailed account of the *Family Instructions*, its contents, and Yen Chih-t'ui's life, see Utsunomiya, *Chūgoku kodai chūsei-shi kenkyū*, pp. 451–557. For an interpretation of Yen's attitudes toward Buddhism and Confucianism, see Dien, "Yen Chih-t'ui." Patricia Buckley Ebrey has translated and discussed in depth Yuan Ts'ai and his book in her *Family and Property*. For the Chinese text of the *Yuan-shih shih-fan*, I have followed the *Chih-pu-tsu chai ts'ung-shu* edition. Yuan's work was written in 1178 and reissued by the author in 1190. I have benefited from reviews of Ebrey's study by Joseph P. McDermott, *Harvard Journal of Asiatic Studies* 47, no. 1 (1987): 314–40; and Metzger, "Was Neo-Confucianism 'Tangential'?"; with a response by Ebrey, "Neo-Confucianism and the Chinese *Shih-ta-fu*." Also of interest is Ch'en Chih-ch'ao, "*Yuan shih shih-fan*."

3. Yen Chih-t'ui, *Family Instructions*, pp. xiv–xxv.

4. For a discussion of the great clans, their claims to office, and the various lists of great clans drawn up in the Southern and Northern Dynasties, see D. Johnson, *Medieval Chinese Oligarchy*, pp. 19–43. Although Johnson distinguishes the great clans from the shih, Yen Chih-t'ui uses the term "shih-ta-fu" to refer to families with long pedigrees, distinguishing them from others who serve but whose families have been *hsiao-jen* for ages (see Yen Chih-t'ui, *Family Instructions*, pp. 54, 115–16; idem, *Yen-shih chia-hsun* 3.145, 4.292).

5. Ebrey, *Family and Property*, pp. 14–18.

6. Yen Chih-t'ui, *Family Instructions*, p. 127 (see also pp. 18–25); idem, *Yen-shih chia-hsun* 5.317–19.

7. "Our branch" translates *wu fu*; those relatives included within either the five degrees of mourning or, as Teng translates, "within five generations." I take the mourning circle to be the group or branch within a larger clan that has a distinct ritual identity.

8. Yen Chih-t'ui, *Family Instructions*, p. 210, trans. modified; idem, *Yen-shih chia-hsun* 7.534.

9. Yen Chih-t'ui, *Yen-shih chia-hsun* 7.541; cf. idem, *Family Instructions*, p. 211.

10. Ebrey, *Family and Property*, pp. 233–34, trans. modified; Yuan Ts'ai, *Yuan-shih shih-fan* 2.2b.

11. Ebrey, *Family and Property*, pp. 232–35, 262; Yuan Ts'ai, *Yuan-shih shih-fan* 2.1b–4a, 20b. The role of "fate" is treated again below.

12. Ebrey, *Family and Property*, pp. 263–64, trans. revised; Yuan Ts'ai, *Yuan-shih shih-fan* 2.21b.

13. Yuan Ts'ai, *Yuan-shih shih-fan* 2.23a; Ebrey, *Family and Property*, pp. 267–68, trans. revised. I take document writing in this case to refer not to serving as a clerk but to preparing documents for submission by others (note the use of the term *tai*, "in place of"), for example, by working at a shop that prepares documents for submission in court cases. On such shops, see the early twelfth-century guide for subprefects, Li Yuan-pi, *Tso-i tzu-chen* 8.40a–41b.

14. Lu Yu, "Record of Mr. Ch'en of Tung-yang's Charitable Estate," *Lu Fang-weng ch'üan-chi* 21.124.

15. Yen Chih-t'ui, "Chieh ping," *Yen-shih chia-hsun* 5.320. Teng (Yen Chih-t'ui, *Family Instructions*, p. 129), translates: "For generations they were elegant Confucian scholars" (*i ju-ya wei yeh*). For the references to status, see pp. 42–53.

16. Yen Chih-t'ui, *Family Instructions*, pp. 54, 115–16; idem, *Yen-shih chia-hsun* 3.145, 4.292.

17. Patricia Ebrey uses Yuan's *Social Precepts* to describe shih-ta-fu life. McDermott (see note 2 to this chapter) challenges this, supposing that Yuan's audience includes the local educated peasantry, a possibility raised by Yuan's postface to the 1190 edition (translated below). I conclude that Yuan is speaking to locally dominant families because he keeps speaking about families with "wealth" and families with "honor" (i.e., official rank), the latter being by definition official (and necessarily shih-ta-fu) families. He distinguishes the two (e.g., Yuan Ts'ai, *Yuan-shih shih-fan* 2.1b, 2.15a, 2.21a), but he also recognizes that these go together when men gain office and that his audience (to his dismay) desires wealth and honor more than anything else. His references to wealthy and honored families are, by my count, more frequent than his references to shih-ta-fu families. This does not undercut Ebrey's introduction because, as men with families tied to localities, shih-ta-fu had the same problems as the larger audience. Any confusion caused by Yuan's social terminology can be accounted for by noting that his ethical precepts are not supposed to be status-group specific (he simply applies them to the situations of families similar to his) and that he has a lingering awareness that traditionally the term "shih-ta-fu" referred most exactly to those with official status.

18. Ebrey, *Family and Property*, pp. 191, 232, 267–68; Yuan Ts'ai, *Yuan-shih shih-fan* 1.7b, 2.1b, 2.23b–24a.

19. Yuan's work is not, however, "vulgar" or colloquial. He draws on past texts, especially the *Analects*, and writes in an easily comprehensible style. It is still more "literary," for example, than Li Yuan-pi's guide to local administration, the *Tso-i tzu-chen* (author's preface dated 1117, published in 1177), which was intended for subprefects.

20. Yen Chih-t'ui, *Family Instructions*, pp. 131–52; Yen reduces Taoism to nourishing life. His chapter on Buddhist teachings is a defense of the reality of the transmigration of souls and karmic retribution. As I read it, Yen sees that Buddhist doctrine gives people a reason to behave ethically. Albert Dien ("Yen Chih-t'ui," p. 55) writes: "Yen's commitment to the Confucian canon was limited, since he saw the perfect society of the future achieved through Buddhism rather than the works of Confucius." I see Yen's commitment as being to the broader cultural

tradition, not to Confucius and the Classics alone. I find no sign that he perceived a tension between his cultural concern and his beliefs in the Buddha's spiritual powers and retribution.

21. Yen Chih-t'ui, *Family Instructions*, see sections 8–10, 18.

22. Ibid., p. 54.   23. Ibid., sections 5–6.

24. Ibid., p. 22.   25. Ibid., sections 17–18.

26. Ibid., p. 95; Yen Chih-t'ui, *Yen-shih chia-hsun* 4.249.

27. Yen Chih-t'ui, *Family Instructions*, sections 1, 8, 11, 14. Both northern and southern aristocrats are faulted on these grounds.

28. Pan Ku, "Liang tu fu hsu," in *Wen hsuan*: "Therefore, officers who attended and served the emperor by virtue of their skill with words . . . day and night deliberated and thought, monthly and daily presented and offered compositions" (trans. David Knechtges, "*Wen xuan*," 1: 95).

29. *Lun yü* 17.4; trans. following Lau, *The Analects*, p. 143. Confucius went to Wu-ch'eng, where his disciple Tzu-yu was steward; he regretted his criticism of a grandiose performance when Tzu-yu reminded him that one learned in the tao loves his fellow men.

30. The allusion here is to Confucius's statement that in the past men learned for their own benefit, whereas modern men learn for others or to please others. Chu Hsi interpreted this to mean that true learning was "for" one's own ethical cultivation; Liu Chen accepts this, but takes "for others" to be for the good of others. See Bol, "Chu Hsi's Redefinition of Literati Learning," pp. 156–58.

31. *Meng-tzu* 7A.9, "In obscurity a man makes good his own person, but in prominence he makes perfect all under heaven as well" (trans. following Lau, *Mencius*, p. 183).

32. Yuan Ts'ai, *Yuan-shih shih-fan*, introduction; cf. Ebrey, *Family and Property*, pp. 175–76.

33. Yuan protested Liu's change of his original title *Su hsun* (Instructions for customs) to the grander *Shih-fan* (model for the age), although both titles imply ethical concerns. Yuan's paragraph titles regularly involve such normative locutions as "should," "must," "may not" that are dropped in Ebrey's translation. For example: Ebrey's 1.1 "Personality differences" vs. original "Personalities cannot be forced to agree"; 1.2 "The value of reflection" vs. "Men must value reflection"; 1.3 "Parental kindness and filial obedience" vs. "Fathers and sons are to value kindness and filial piety"; 1.4 "Tolerance" vs. "In living at home value tolerance"; 1.5 "Submission" vs. "With fathers and older brothers you should not argue over who is right."

34. Yuan, however, also shied away from the kinds of practical communal projects Chu Hsi favored. He appears to be much closer to Lu Chiu-yuan in regard to community; see Hymes, "Lu Chiu-yüan." Note that Ebrey (*Family and Property*, p. 31) contrasts Yuan with the Ch'eng-Chu philosophers and the "Classicist" approach to family precepts she associates with Ssu-ma Kuang.

35. Yuan Ts'ai, *Yuan-shih shih-fan* 3.28b–29a; cf. Ebrey, *Family and Property*, pp. 177–78.

36. Yuan Ts'ai, *Yuan-shih shih-fan* 1.3b; cf. Ebrey, *Family and Property*, p. 185.

37. See, e.g., Yuan Ts'ai, *Yuan-shih shih-fan* 1.1a–6b; cf. Ebrey, *Family and Property*, pp. 181–89.

38. Yuan Ts'ai, *Yuan-shih shih-fan* 2.5a; cf. Ebrey, *Family and Property*, p. 237.

39. Yuan Ts'ai, *Yuan-shih shih-fan* 2.2a; cf. Ebrey, *Family and Property*, p. 233.

40. Yuan Ts'ai, *Yuan-shih shih-fan* 2.3b; cf. Ebrey, *Family and Property*, p. 235.

41. Yuan Ts'ai, *Yuan-shih shih-fan* 1.7b; cf. Ebrey, *Family and Property*, pp. 191–92.

42. Phrases from *Chung-yung* 12; cf. Wing-tsit Chan, *Source Book*, p. 100.

43. Yuan Ts'ai, *Yuan-shih shih-fan* 3.28b–29a; cf. Ebrey, *Family and Property*, pp. 177–78.

44. See, e.g., *Liang shu* 49.685; the use of the term "chin-shen" in discussions of learning in *Sui shu* 75.1705, and *Chin shu* 91.7345–46; Li O's letter to the Sui emperor in *Sui shu* 66.1544–45; and the preface to the *Wen-ssu po-yao* in *Wen-yuan ying-hua* 699.3606b–7b.

45. *Lun yü yin-te* 11.3. Without elaboration, the passage assigns ten disciples of Confucius to the various fields. The "four fields" may be implied by the "four teachings" (*ssu chiao*) of *Lun yü* 7.25: *wen, hsing* (conduct), *chung* (loyalty), and *hsin* (trustworthiness). Loyalty could refer to the affairs of government, and trustworthiness to speech. Cf. Lau, *Analects*, p. 89.

46. Liu I-ch'ing, *New Account of Tales of the World*. These are the first four categories in Liu's work. Much of Yen Chih-t'ui's *Family Instructions* fits into these categories as well.

47. In Sung times "speech" was often treated as a subcategory of wen-hsueh, but *A New Account of Tales of the World* and Yen's *Family Instructions* give it separate attention as the art of conversation and as correct pronunciation and nomenclature, respectively. Proper speech was one of the four tests applied to those seeking appointment in the T'ang. Note that the rules for selection specified that when the quality of their appearance, speech, calligraphy, and formulaic legal decisions were equal, candidates would be ranked according to the following priorities: ethical conduct, "talent" (i.e., learning), and service. See Tu Yu, *T'ung tien* 15.3a. Often the term "ssu k'o" referred to a variation on the four fields discussed here, as its use in many T'ang edicts concerning recruitment and examinations collected in Hsu Sung, *Teng-k'o chi k'ao*, indicates.

48. For the events of 619, see *Ts'e-fu yuan-kuei* 50.1a–1b. For those of 720, see McMullen, *State and Scholars*, p. 45.

49. See the question asked of Po Chü-i by the Buddhist representative; Po Chü-i, *Po Chü-i chi* 68.1435.

50. McMullen, *State and Scholars*, p. 61.

51. The essay theme for the departmental examination of 983 was "Which of the four fields has priority in selecting shih?" (Wang Yü-ch'eng, *Hsiao-ch'u chi, wai-chi* 9.459). Fan Chung-yen (*FWKC* 5.10a), for example, cites the four fields in support of his contention that "the way to seek men does not have only one starting point." Ssu-ma Kuang (*SMWC* 20.298, 21.315, 53.653, 54.661) uses them and various subcategories in discussing categories for recommendation (see also idem, 63.772, for use in a begging letter).

52. Li Hua (ca. 710–ca. 767) mourns the fact that none can be equally good in all four fields; Liang Su (753–93) notes the difficulty of being complete in three (leaving out speech), but claims that after Tu-ku Chi (725–77) "had governed through ethical conduct and wen-hsueh for a year the methods of the ju flourished" (see *CTW* 315.9a, 518.2b, 518.24a). For the Duke of Chou, see *Lun yü* 18.10.

53. See the discussion of T'ang T'ai-tsung's (r. 627–49) family background in Wright, "T'ang T'ai-tsung," pp. 239–42. Hsuan-tsung's (r. 712–56) early chief ministers had examination degrees; his later ones did not.

54. Wu Ching, *Chen-kuan cheng-yao* 7.219–20. T'ai-tsung's minister, however, seems not to have agreed that te-hsing was as vital: "If they do not have the legacy of learning [*hsueh-yeh*], they will be unable to know 'former sayings and past deeds' and that will make them incapable of great responsibilities" (citing Ta-ch'u hexagram, *Chou-i yin-te*, p. 17).

55. *Lun yü* 1.6; Wu Ching, *Chen-kuan cheng-yao* 7.222.

56. Letter to K'ung, *SMWC* 60.718. See also Wang Yü-ch'eng's essay on the examination theme for 983 (*Hsiao-ch'u chi, wai-chi* 9.459–60). For an earlier discussion of the relative value of the ssu k'o, see the dialogue attributed to Han Yü and Li Ao in Hartman, *Han Yü*, pp. 188–90.

57. See, e.g., Chu Hsi's famous rules for the White Deer Grotto Academy (*Hui-an hsien-sheng Chu Wen-kung wen-chi* 74.17a).

58. Kuo Shao-yü, *Chung-kuo wen-hsueh p'i-p'ing shih*, pp. 40–46.

59. Thus, e.g., both the Wei-Chin period ideologies Richard B. Mather describes as conformity to moral teachings (*ming-chiao*) and naturalness (*tzu-jan*) could claim wen (see Liu I-ching, *New Accounts of Tales of the World*, pp. xvii–xxii).

60. McMullen, *State and Scholars*, p. 33. McMullen notes that the removal of the Duke of Chou from the Confucian Temple reflected a desire to increase the distinction between scholars and the imperial clan.

61. Alluding to *Lun yü* 9.5.

62. *Chung-yung*, section 30.

63. *CTW* 136.18b–19a.

64. McMullen, *State and Scholars*, chap. 2. Timothy Hugh Barrett ("Buddhism, Taoism and Confucianism," pp. 1–11) makes the same point.

65. Wu Ching, *Chen-kuan cheng-yao* 7.215.

66. *Ts'e-fu yuan-kuei* 50.1b–2b.

67. *CTW* 162.2b.

68. Introduction to the *Ju-lin* biographies, *SS* 75.1705.

69. In the Han dynasty "salt and iron debates," the side now referred to as "Confucian" was called wen-hsueh. Note also the association of wen ("elaborated phrasing") with ju in the *Han Fei tzu* (*Han Fei tzu chi-shih*, pp. 1057–58).

70. Wu Ching, *Chen-kuan cheng-yao* 7.220.

71. Those whose interests did not go much beyond literary skill were at times labeled wen-jen. See, e.g., Hsiao Ying-shih's contrast between wen-ju and wen-jen, quoted in Lo Lien-t'ien, *Sui T'ang Wu-tai wen-hsueh p'i-p'ing*, p. 70.

72. An example of the distinctions between ju-shu ("ju techniques") and other

types of scholarly attainment can be found in an edict on recruitment for the decree examination (*chih-k'o*) of 660 (see Hsu Sung, *Teng-k'o chi k'ao*, p. 49).

73. Wu Ching, *Chen-kuan cheng-yao* 7.215. An earlier example of wen-ju: Ko Hung in his preface to the outer collection of the *Pao-p'u-tzu* (p. 378) writes, "I have perfectly mastered the Five Classics and written a work of philosophy, just so that later ages will know that I was a wen-ju." A later example: after Ou-yang Hsiu directed the metropolitan examinations in 1057, the emperor bestowed on him a scroll bearing these two characters in the imperial hand (see "Nien-p'u," p. 12, in *OHCC*).

74. *CTS* 97.3059. Further examples include the existence of a decree examination category of wen-ju, Hsiao Ying-shih's use of the term, cited above, and Liu Tsung-yuan's (*Liu Tsung-yuan chi* 21.583) reference to a family that had been wen-ju for successive generations. Writing in 806, Yuan Chen (*Yuan Chen-chi*) proposed to ensure the flourishing of ju-shu by creating one examination for *hsueh-shih* (academicians) testing the Classics and histories and one for wen-shih testing literary composition; here we see the sense of division between wen and hsueh typical of his generation.

75. *CTS* 189A.4939.

76. For a brief account of these debates and books on the Three Teachings, see Yoshioka, "*Sangō shiiki*."

77. In 739 there were 3,245 Buddhist monasteries and 2,113 Buddhist nunneries compared with 1,137 Taoist monasteries and 550 Taoist nunneries (Barrett, "Taoism Under the T'ang," p. 52).

78. For an account of the 662 debate, involving some 900 officials, over whether monks could be required to do obeisance to laymen, see Weinstein, *Buddhism*, p. 33.

79. Zürcher, "Buddhism and Education in T'ang Times," pp. 23–26. See also Vande Walle, "Lay Buddhism." Chih-i (538–97), the founder of the T'ien-t'ai sect, is a good example; see Weinstein, "Imperial Patronage," pp. 274–91.

80. For a survey of the relationship between pre-T'ang Taoism and great clans, see Barrett, "Taoism Under the T'ang," pp. 2–4.

81. Fujiyoshi, "Kanri toyō," p. 31. In the late T'ang failed examination candidates were a particularly rich source of postulants.

82. I have followed Ch'üan Te-yü's biography of Wu Yun (*CTW* 508.1a–2a), which stresses Wu's continued commitment to wen and ju values without denying his role as a tao-shih. Wu's writings show that his Taoist expertise was quite real; see Schafer, "Wu Yun's 'Cantos on Pacing the Void'"; and Barrett, "Taoism Under the T'ang," pp. 66–67.

83. *CTS* 135.3728–29; discussed in Fujiyoshi, "Kanri toyō," p. 31.

84. Gregory, "Tsung-mi and Neo-Confucianism."

85. Important texts were translated and entered into the canon under T'ai-tsung and Kao-tsung (r. 649–83), Empress Wu (r. 684–705), Hsuan-tsung (r. 712–56), Tai-tsung (r. 762–79), and Te-tsung (r. 779–804) (Weinstein, *Buddhism*, pp. 24–25, 30–31, 44, 55–57, 78–81, 97–98). See also Zürcher, "Perspectives," pp. 162–64.

86. Barrett, "Taoism Under the T'ang," pp. 27–31. Copies of the Taoist canon were ordered again in 749; see idem, p. 55.

87. The three textual traditions had different origins. With some contrivance, all genres of shih texts could be traced back to the Classics and thus to the sages of China's antiquity. Buddhist texts, whether the work of Chinese or not, were ultimately founded on Indian texts. The bulk of Taoist scriptures copied in the 670's must have derived from the various bodies of revealed scriptures that had appeared since the Han. This is not to say that boundaries were not crossed. Under Hsuan-tsung the pre-Han "Taoist" texts, the *Tao te ching*, *Chuang-tzu*, and *Lieh-tzu*, were given special attention in conjunction with the creation of an examination field based on Taoist texts. The decision to remove the *Tao te ching* from the list of required texts for the other examination fields, while illustrating the effort to keep the traditions distinct, reminds us that some texts had a place in different traditions simultaneously (see Barrett, "Taoism Under the T'ang," pp. 55–63). In 754 the *Tao te ching* was replaced with the *I ching* in the Taoist examination field, a mark of the *Change's* privileged place. On the post-Han Taoist textual tradition, see Ninji, "Formation of the Taoist Canon." Moreover, one need not have the formal status of Buddhist monk, Taoist priest, or official to write something that could be included in a particular tradition. Thus although the early T'ang catalogue of the four fields of bibliography (Classics, histories, philosophical treatises, and literature) was meant primarily for shih learning and treated the Buddhist and Taoist textual traditions as separate, some writings of Buddhist monks and Taoist priests found their way into the Imperial Library and were included in catalogues, just as the Taoist and Buddhist canons included works by shih.

88. Some did write persuasive texts aimed at other traditions. See the discussion below of Tsung-mi's "On the Origin of Man" ("Yuan jen lun") for an example. However, Tsung-mi, who identified with the Southern lineage of Ch'an, put more effort into criticizing the Hung-chou school of Ch'an, the line founded by Ma-tsu Tao-i (709–88), for proposing a doctrine that led, in his view, to the conclusion that enlightenment did not require adherence to ethical standards. As Peter Gregory ("Buddhist Antecedents," pp. 11–19) notes in his study of this case, Tsung-mi's views were similar to Chu Hsi's critique of Buddhism. The fact that Tsung-mi was a Ch'an Buddhist who grounded his arguments in textual traditions quite different from Chu Hsi's reminds us that value orientations could be similar within different traditions. The values he defended—the importance of ethical norms, the need for self-discipline in social conduct, respect for authority, and so on—made him more like some contemporary ju than like some monks, yet he seems not to have directed this argument at the shih.

89. Weinstein, "Imperial Patronage."

90. This point is made by Erik Zürcher ("Perspectives," pp. 164, 176n14).

91. For an example of a Buddhist's sense of what elite society and ju learning were about, see the Japanese monk Kūkai's *Introduction to the Three Teachings* (*Sangō shiiki*; trans. in Hakeda, *Kūkai: Major Works*). The work, based on what Kūkai had read and heard by age 24 (A.D. 797), before he went to China, uses the literary device of a ju (followed by a tao-shih and then a monk) trying to persuade

a hedonistic young man of how to be a moral person. He should learn the Classics and histories, discipline himself in the virtues of filial piety and loyalty, live frugally and with proper decorum, and devote himself to study and perfecting his literary abilities. On this basis he will garner influential friends and gain office. If he does well, he will become famous, be remembered, and secure the prosperity of his descendants. He can enjoy the worldly pleasures of marriage and of wine and poetry parties. In short, scholarship, ethical conduct, and political service are his means to wealth, honor, and the satisfaction of desires. This is a stereotype, of course, but a telling one.

92. Zürcher, "Perspectives."

93. Ch'üan Te-yü, farewell preface for Wang Chung-shu, *CTW* 492.15a.

94. Tsung-mi asserts further that the moral teachings of Confucius and Lao-tzu were merely provisional (*ch'üan*) and lacking substance (*shih*); they could not logically link their ideas about how humans came into being with morality. Tsung-mi lumped the "external teachings" of the ju and Taoists together: both held that "tao models itself on what is spontaneous [*tzu-jan*]," that humans and animals alike were born of primal *ch'i*, that status, wealth, and talent were fated, and that on death humans returned to heaven-and-earth and vacuity. I have followed the text of the "Yüan jen lun" in *Chung-kuo fo-chiao ssu-hsiang tzu-liao hsuan-pien*, pp. 386–92, and the translation in de Bary, *Buddhist Tradition*, pp. 180–207.

95. These comments are based on Weinstein, *Buddhism*, pp. 106–44.

96. Compare Reischauer's translation in Ennin, *Ennin's Diary*, pp. 331–54, entry for 843/6/13; I have followed the text in vol. 3 of Ono Katsutoshi, "*Nittō guhō junrei kōki*" no kenkyū.

97. Yet we have every reason to think that shih families continued to supply clergy in the Sung and that Sung monks did find audiences among the shih. Note that in 1221 there were over 450,000 monks and nuns (K. Chen, *Buddhism*, p. 401). Northern Sung emperors also patronized Taoist texts. For an account of Hui-tsung's (r. 1100–25) attempt to use a Taoist sect to take over Buddhist institutions, see Strickmann, "Longest Taoist Scripture."

98. The best short survey of this period in English is still Pulleyblank, "Neo-Confucianism and Neo-Legalism."

99. Hartman, *Han Yü*. For examples of the study of Han Yü as a thinker alone, see below. For a treatment of Han Yü from a literary perspective, see Owen, *Meng Chiao and Han Yü*. Liu Tsung-yuan's multi-sidedness has been noted, although I am not sure that the connections between his literary and intellectual concerns have received great attention. See, e.g., Gentzler, "Literary Biography"; Jo-shui Chen, "*Dawn of Neo-Confucianism*," which argues that Liu marks the liberation of the Confucian revival from literature; and Nienhauser et al., *Liu Tsung-yuan*. For a discussion of Han and Liu that also focuses on the relation between wen and tao, see Ch'en Yu-shih, *Han Liu Ou Su ku-wen lun*.

100. See, e.g., Fung, *History of Chinese Philosophy*, 2: 408–13; T'ang Chün-i, *Chung-kuo che-hsueh yuan-lun*, pt. 3, pp. 1368–71; and Hou Wai-lu et al., *Chung-kuo ssu-hsiang t'ung-shih*, vol. 4, pt. 1, pp. 319–42.

101. De Bary, "Reappraisal of Neo-Confucianism," pp. 83–88. Pulleyblank ("Neo-Confucianism and Neo-Legalism," p. 96) seems somewhere in between, characterizing Han Yü's attitude as one of "militant Confucian orthodoxy" but claiming that he lacked originality except in assuming the role of teacher in the line of Mencius.

102. Yao Chi-kuang, "T'ang-tai wen-shih."

103. This is the textbook account. See, e.g., the histories of Chinese literary criticism by Kuo Shao-yü, *Chung-kuo wen-hsueh p'i-p'ing shih*; and Lo Ken-tse, *Wan T'ang Wu-tai wen-hsueh p'i-p'ing shih*. See also Ch'ien Mu, "Tsa lun t'ang-tai ku-wen yun-tung"; and Ch'ien Tung-fu, *T'ang Sung ku-wen yun-tung*. For the Li Hua group, see Pulleyblank, "Neo-Confucianism and Neo-Legalism," pp. 85–88; and McMullen, "Historical and Literary Criticism."

104. See Owen, *Meng Chiao and Han Yü*, pp. 2–14; see also his further use of the concept in *Poetry of the Early T'ang* and *The Great Age of Chinese Poetry*.

105. Yuan Chieh, *Yuan Tz'u-shan chi*, p. 1.

106. According to his biography in *HTS*, Li Kuan was a nephew of Li Hua. However, Li Hua was a Chao-chün Li, but, according to Han Yü's funerary biography, Li Kuan was a Lung-hsi Li (the imperial clan); see Hsu Sung, *Teng-k'o chi k'ao* 13.465. I suspect Li Kuan has been confused with Li Han, who was a Chao-chün Li (Tsan-huang branch); see Liang Su's highly laudatory introduction to his collected writings (*CTW* 518.5b–7b).

107. *CTW* 532.6a. Compare Li Po's first *ku-feng* poem, "This Sage's [i.e., this Emperor's] era returns to primal antiquity"; quoted in Lo Lien-t'ien, *Su T'ang Wu-tai wen-hsueh p'i-p'ing*, p. 65. According to Hartman (*Han Yü*, pp. 167–68, 217, 220), the term appears only once in Han Yü's works, and then to refer to returning to the good government of antiquity.

108. For example, the poet-monk Chiao-jan (ca. 734–ca. 791) criticizes Ch'en Tzu-ang for fu-ku at the expense of change (cited in Lo Lien-tien, *Sui T'ang Wu-tai wen-hsueh p'i-p'ing*, p. 100; cf. Hartman, *Han Yü*, p. 220). Liu Mien, writing ca. 800, speaks of having the intent of fu-ku as a literary project (*CTW* 527.12b–13a). In 820 Yuan Chen (*Yuan Chen chi* 40.442) explains that he has written rescripts so as to "make apparent the Son of Heaven's fu-ku," thus referring to both the political and literary projects.

109. Examples include Sun T'i's answer for the decree examination of 722 in which studying antiquity and being in harmony with tao is paired with ethical conduct and personal improvement (*CTW* 310.18b); Li Lin-fu's (d. 752) *sung* glorifying the emperor, although here the *hsuan* aspect of tao receives much more attention (*CTW* 345.16a–18b); Fang Kuan's letter to Chief Minister Chang Yueh (667–730), the great patron of scholars, which speaks of turning to the *ku-tao* as opposed to conforming to men of the present (*CTW* 332.13b–15b). As chief minister himself in 756, Fang gave scholars leading roles in the campaign to retake the capital and employed ox-drawn carts in conformity with Spring and Autumn period models (*CTS* 111.3321). He was defeated, yet was apparently not criticized for his tactics. This suggests a kind of literalism about ancient practices similar to the restoration of the "monthly ordinances" in the state ritual program in the 740's

under Li Lin-fu. Finally, Yin Fan's preface to an anthology of High T'ang poetry has a line that could have been taken directly from early T'ang historiography. The recent achievements in poetry under Hsuan-tsung, he explains, were attributable to the ruler's "dislike of ornament and preference for the simple, getting rid of the false and following the authentic, so that all writers honored antiquity" (Lo Lien-tien, *Sui T'ang Wu-tai wen-hsueh p'i-p'ing*, pp. 59–60).

110. Note that Hartman (*Han Yü*, p. 14) and Nienhauser et al. (*Liu Tsung-yuan*) avoid this, translating "ku-wen" as "the literature of Antiquity." Han Yü, the champion of ku-wen, included men famous for poetry in listing his peers past and present. See, e.g., his farewell for Meng Chiao (*HLCL* 5.19.7–8; trans. Hartman, *Han Yü*, pp. 230–32). A similar point can be made for Liu Tsung-yuan; see the comment in Nienhauser et al., *Liu Tsung-yuan*, p. 109, that "poetry also had its *ku-wen* movement." Hartman writes, "For Han Yü poetry as well as prose is *ku-wen* . . . *ku-wen* can embrace all subjects, styles and genres" (p. 14), yet in most of this work ku-wen is taken to be a prose movement.

111. For an example of a prose/poetry (wen/shih) dichotomy, see Liu K'ai, *Ho-tung hsien-sheng chi* 5.13a–15b. Note also Wang Yü-cheng, *Hsiao-ch'u chi* 18.252, where Han Yü and Liu Tsung-yuan as models for wen are contrasted with others as models for shih poetry and *fu* (rhapsodies). By the end of the eleventh century, a dichotomy between prose and poetry was current; see the various comments on Han Yü by Su Shih and his followers in the introduction to Han's collected works, *Han Ch'ang-li chi*.

112. See the section devoted to ku-wen in Yao Hsuan, *T'ang wen-ts'ui*, *chüan* 43–50. Note that Yao treated the stele (*pei*), the proposal (*i*), and the essay (*lun*) as separate categories.

113. See Chapter 4 for discussion of Li Hua, Hsiao Ying-shih, Tu-ku Chi, and others active before the 790's.

114. On this and other efforts to reform the exams, see McMullen, *State and Scholars*, pp. 287–90. See also Ch'eng Ch'ien-fan, *T'ang-tai chin-shih hsing-chüan yü wen-hsüeh*, pp. 9–13.

115. *CTW* 337.12a–b. Yen also lists the various genres in which the man composed. We do find instances of an opposition close to a prose/poetry dichotomy; e.g., Li Hua cites Hsiao Ying-shih's objection that shih and fu had lost the connection to the *ya* and *sung* of the *Songs* and that *chu-lun* (narrative forms) were no longer grounded in political concerns. Similarly, Ts'ui Yu-fu (721–80) notes that a man's writings include almost 300 shih in addition to over 50 pieces in other genres. He includes the sung among them, a genre that would fall under poetry if a prose/poetry division was made, yet further on he speaks of making one's words wen through use of the *tien-mo* (i.e., forms stemming from the *Documents*) and *ko-yung* (forms stemming from the *Songs*; *CTW* 409.9a). Po Chü-i (*Po Chü-i chi* 65.1369), writing in 806, divides "wen of praise and blame, shih of admiration and criticism," with reference to biographical stele inscriptions and poetry. At the same time he uses *wei wen* for composition in general while distinguishing *shih-jen* (poets) in particular. But does "wen" here mean "prose" or simply "literary writing?"

116. Liu Tsung-yuan, preface to Yang Ling's collection, *Liu Tsung-yuan chi* 21.578–79.

117. See, e.g., P'ei Tu's letter to Li Ao; I have followed the annotated version in Kuo Shao-yü and Wang Wen-sheng, *Chung-kuo li-tai wen-lun hsuan*, 2: 158–60.

118. *CTW* 332.15b.

119. *CTW* 430.8b–9a. The "august ultimate" (*huang-chi*) is a key symbol in the creation of an integrated order in the "Hung-fan" (Great plan) chapter of the *Documents*.

120. This examination field was established in 822. Su Mien's compilation of documents on institutions, the *Hui-yao*, does continue Tu Yu's interests; see McMullen, *State and Scholars*, pp. 197–99, 201–5. Some historical writing was done by men who appear to have seen themselves as literary men rather than as historians; Liu Tsung-yuan's critique of the *Kuo yü* and Liu K'o's historical writings are examples (on the latter, see Pulleyblank, "Liu K'o," pp. 149–50).

121. This discussion is based on a perusal of a number of works from the last half-century of Chinese, Japanese, and Western scholarship: Wing-tsit Chan, *Source Book*; idem, "Completion"; Chang, *Development of Neo-Confucian Thought*; Ch'en Chung-fan, *Liang Sung ssu-hsiang shu-p'ing*; Ch'ien Mu, *Sung Ming li-hsueh kai-shu*, vol. 1; de Bary, "Reappraisal of Neo-Confucianism"; idem, "Some Common Tendencies in Neo-Confucianism"; idem, *Neo-Confucian Orthodoxy*; idem, *Liberal Tradition*; Fumoto, *Hoku-sō ni okeru jugaku no tenkai*; idem, *Sō Gen Min Shin*; Fung, *History of Chinese Philosophy*; Graham, *Two Chinese Philosophers*; Hartwell, "Historical Analogism"; Hou Wai-lu et al., *Chung-kuo ssu-hsiang t'ung-shih*; Hsiao Kung-ch'üan, *Chung-kuo cheng-chih ssu-hsiang shih*, vol. 4; Huang Kung-wei, *Sung Ming Ch'ing li-hsueh t'i-hsi*; Jen Chi-yü, *Chung-kuo che-hsueh shih*; Kusumoto, *Sō Min jidai jugaku shisō*; Lin K'o-t'ang, *Sung ju yü fo-hsueh*; James T. C. Liu, *Reform in Sung China*; idem, *Ou-yang Hsiu*; idem, "How Did a Neo-Confucian School Become the State Orthodoxy?"; Lo Ken-tse, *Chung-kuo wen-hsueh p'i-p'ing shih*, vol. 3; Morohashi, *Jugaku mokuteki to Sō ju*; Nivison, "'Knowledge' and 'Action'"; idem, "Introduction"; Okada, *Sō Min tetsugaku josetsu*; *Shushi no senku*; Takahashi Susumu, *Mui shizen kara sakui sekkyoku e*; T'ang Chün-i, *Yuan chiao*; idem, *Yuan tao*; idem, "Spirit and Development of Neo-Confucianism"; Tillman, *Utilitarian Confucianism*; Uno, *Shina tetsugakushi*; Watanabe, *Shina tetsugakushi gairon*; and Yamamoto, *Sō jidai jugaku rinrigakuteki kenkyu*.

122. See, e.g., Chu's preface to the *Doctrine of the Mean* from 1189; in *Chung-kuo che-hsueh shih tzu-liao hsuan-chi*, vol. 4, pt. 2, pp. 268–71.

123. Wing-tsit Chan, "Completion," pp. 72–81. For an explanation of Chu's insistence on the primacy of Chou Tun-i, see Graham, *Two Chinese Philosophers*, pp. 152–75. Chu first used "tao-t'ung" in his 1189 preface to the *Doctrine of the Mean*, citing only Chou and the Ch'engs. Huang Kan adopted this scheme but included Chu Hsi; for a formal account, see his "General Introduction to the Tao-t'ung Transmission of Sages and Worthies," in *Shushigaku taikei*, 10: 432–33. Elsewhere Chu included Shao Yung, Chang Tsai, and Ssu-ma Kuang as secondary contributors, but Huang Kan left out Shao and Ssu-ma. For Chu's inclusion of

Shao, Chang, and Ssu-ma as a second rank, see Chu Hsi, *Hui-an hsien-sheng Chu Wen-kung chi* 86.12a–b. Huang (*Mien-chai hsien-sheng chi* 8.37a, 5.9a) included Chang Tsai in two important instances. Hu Hung (*Hu Hung chi*, p. 167; see also Graham, *Two Chinese Philosophers*, p. 167) treated Chou, Shao, the Ch'engs, and Chang as the Sung founders. Chen Te-hsiu thought only Chou, the Ch'engs, and Chu had illuminated the Way of Confucius (see the commemorative inscription for them in *Hsi shan hsien-sheng Chen kung wen chi* 26.448–50).

124. See Wing-tsit Chan, "Completion," pp. 78–79, on the philosophical nature of this arrangement. James T. C. Liu ("How Did a Neo-Confucian School Become the State Orthodoxy?", pp. 490–91) notes the parallel to "cheng-t'ung." Chu Hsi was a participant in the centuries-long discussion of cheng-t'ung; for an account of other Sung statements, see Jao Tsung-i, *Chung-kuo shih-hsueh shang chih cheng-t'ung lun*, pp. 28–37, 71–109, 273–83, 301–14. The concept of cheng-t'ung in the legitimation of political authority is discussed in Hok-lam Chan, *Legitimation in Imperial China*, pp. 19–48. This derivation for the term "tao-t'ung" is made explicit by Huang Kan's (*Mien-chai hsien-sheng chi* 8.37a) comment: "I have heard of the cheng-t'ung of the tao, it is transmitted according to the man." Note also the phrase "*ch'uan tao cheng-t'ung*" ("orthodox succession in the transmission of the tao") in the first chart of Li Yuan-kang, *Sheng-men shih-yeh t'u*.

125. Chu Hsi, *Chu-tzu yü-lei* 129.3089–90. Note also the following: "Sun [Fu] and Shih [Chieh] suddenly appeared and enjoyed discovering true principles [*tao-li*]. For ages there had not been men of such rank. Someone like Han [Yü] T'ui-chih was, half of the time, just talking about literary composition. If the gentlemen from Kuan [Chang Tsai] and Lo [the Ch'engs] had not appeared, Sun and Shih would be of the first rank" (idem, 129.3091). Adjacent passages show that Chu Hsi saw many faults in these early figures.

126. Ibid., 129.3090–92. See also Fumoto, *Hoku-sō*, pp. 61–62.

127. *Sung Yuan hsueh-an*. In noting Ch'üan's justifications for this arrangement, I am following his introductory comments (pp. 1–11).

128. See, e.g., de Bary, "Reappraisal of Neo-Confucianism"; and Yü Ying-shih, "Some Preliminary Observations," pp. 118–19. For reasons not to be persuaded that the *t'i-yung-wen* formulation represents Hu Yuan's ideas about learning, see Bol, "Reflections on Sung Literati Thought," pp. 93–94. Ch'üan Tsu-wang suppresses the literary perspective in his quotation of the dialogue between Liu I and Emperor Shen-tsung (r. 1067–85), the source of the account. The *Case Studies* version was taken from Chu Hsi, *Ming-ch'en yen-hsing lu* 10.6b–7b (pp. 336–38). Ch'üan changed the question from "Whose writings were better, Wang An-shih's or Hu Yuan's?" to "Who was better, Wang or Hu?" (see *Sung Yuan hsueh-an*, p. 17). Chu notes his source as a "Li Chih letter," which Fumoto (*Hoku-sō*, pp. 63–64) and Kusumoto (*Sō Min jidai jugaku shisō*, pp. 21–22) have mistaken as a reference to Li Chih's *Shih-yu t'an-chi*, where it is not found; nor is it in Li's present collection, the *Chi-nan chi*.

129. De Bary has defended the use of "Neo-Confucianism" in a broad sense. In "Reappraisal of Neo-Confucianism," a study that introduced Hu Yuan, Sun Fu, Shih Chieh, Fan Chung-yen, Ou-yang Hsiu, and Wang An-shih, he noted that

"Neo-Confucianism is now used to cover any new developments in Confucian thought which derive from the metaphysical speculation of early Sung" (p. 108n17). Yet there is little evidence that Hu, Sun, Shih, Fan, and Ou-yang engaged in metaphysical speculation. De Bary's "Some Common Tendencies in Neo-Confucianism" offers a new definition that makes metaphysical thought unnecessary. These common tendencies, "fundamentalism, restorationism, historical-mindedness, rationalism, and humanism," are said to constitute a definition of Neo-Confucianism (pp. 34–36). In this regard, note Nivison's suggestion of an alternative derived from an Ou-yang Hsiu essay ("Introduction," pp. 4–9). In *Neo-Confucian Orthodoxy*, de Bary uses "Neo-Confucianism" to include what was meant by Tao-hsueh, *li-hsueh*, *hsin-hsueh*, and *sheng-hsueh* and "Neo-Confucian orthodoxy" to refer to the Ch'eng-Chu school (see pp. xiii–xiv). This may reflect later attitudes toward the past, but it does not make sense as a historical description. How could there be a Neo-Confucian orthodoxy before Chu Hsi in the absence of a Neo-Confucianism to be orthodox about? However, in *Liberal Tradition*, where de Bary urges that we see Neo-Confucianism as something broader than the Ch'eng-Chu school, Neo-Confucianism is equated with Huang Tsung-hsi's use of the term "li-hsueh" (see pp. 3–6). That would seem to disqualify many of the figures classed as Neo-Confucians in the earlier articles. James T. C. Liu has also adopted a broad use of the term. Speaking of the mid-eleventh century, he asserts that "all Confucians at the time agreed upon a common basis" (*Reform*, p. 22). In *Ou-yang Hsiu* (p. 18), he uses "Neo-Confucianism" "to designate an extensive, pervasive intellectual system and way of life, a system based on key Confucian precepts that were developed at the beginning of the eleventh century to meet the changing needs of a more complex society." A definition of the common basis and intellectual system necessary to test this proposition is not given. In "Neo-Confucian School" (pp. 483–84), the term is said to denote a "broad spectrum of concerns with the heritage." But a broad spectrum of concerns with the heritage would include most scholars in all periods rather than only those concerned with a particular ideology.

130. See, e.g., Fumoto, *Hoku-sō*, pp. 5–12; his periodization is unique and his use of the term *cheng-hsueh* ("correct learning") for the beginning period is not justified by reference to contemporary usage. See also Huang Kung-wei, *Sung Ming Ch'ing li-hsueh*; Kusumoto, *Sō Min jidai jugaku*, pp. 21–28, which also uses "cheng-hsueh"; Morohashi, *Jugaku mokuteki*, p. 23, which also recognizes the literary nature of the 1030's and 1040's; *Shushi no senku*; T'ang Chün-i, *Yuan chiao*, chap. 1; idem, *Yuan tao*, pp. 1372–73; Uno, *Shina tetsugakushi*, pp. 1–6.

131. Graham, *Two Chinese Philosophers*, app. II.

132. Ibid. For an analysis of Chang Tsai, his relation with the Ch'engs, and an account of the moral issues of the day, see Kasoff, *Thought of Chang Tsai*.

133. For surveys of the period, see Tillman, *Utilitarian Confucianism*, pp. 30–53; James T. C. Liu, *Reform*, pp. 23–28; Lo Ken-tse, *Chung-kuo wen-hsueh*, pp. 66–69, on Wang, Su, and Ch'eng I; Hartwell, "Historical Analogism," for a discussion of the different attitudes toward history represented by Wang and Ssu-ma and, to a lesser extent, by Ch'eng I; Hsiao Kung-ch'üan, *Chung-kuo cheng-chih*, pp.

452–61, for an account of Li Kou (1009–59), Wang, the Sus, Shao Yung, and the Ch'engs; Li Kou and Wang are seen as materialists by Jen Chi-yü, *Chung-kuo che-hsüeh shih*, chap. 2, and Hou Wai-lu et al., *Chung-kuo ssu-hsiang t'ung-shih*, chaps. 8–9; Hou also treats Su Shih in chap. 12; Fumoto, *Hoku-sō*, chap. 7, treats Ssu-ma Kuang and Wang; Morohashi, *Jugaku mokuteki*, also treats Wang; Ch'en Chung-fan, *Liang Sung*, chap. 11, discusses Wang; de Bary, "Reappraisal," pp. 100–106, discusses Wang; T'ang Chün-i discusses Wang and Su Shih in *Yuan chiao*, pp. 19–23; Ch'ien Mu, *Sung Ming li-hsüeh*, discusses Wang, Ssu-ma, and the Su brothers as part of his "first period." Studies on Wang, the Sus, Ssu-ma, and other eleventh-century figures as individuals will be noted in later chapters. Even in the late Southern Sung, Tao-hsueh had not excluded different voices from scholarly attention. A 1235 edict on the Confucian Temple honors treats not only the five Tao-hsueh masters (Chou, Chang, the two Ch'engs, and Chu) but also Ou-yang Hsiu, Ssu-ma Kuang, Su Shih, Hu Yuan, and Sun Fu (*Sung shih* 40.807).

134. James T. C. Liu, *Ou-yang Hsiu*, pp. 87–89; Fan was the patron of Hu and Sun rather than their student, see idem, "Fan Chung-yen," pp. 109–10.

135. Ch'ien Mu, *Sung Ming li-hsüeh*, pp. 23–25. T'ang Chün-i (*Yuan tao*, p. 1372; *Yuan chiao*, pp. 11–17) also sees the early period as one concerned with preserving the unity of the cultural tradition, a time when men were still largely engaged in the study of the classics and history.

Chapter 2

1. For a discussion of the kind of analysis that can be used to examine the foundings of dynasties, with the T'ang case as an example, see Somers, "Time, Space, and Structure."

2. SS, 33.990, from the Treatise on Bibliography, introduction to the section on clan genealogies.

3. Given that a distinction did appear between the shih and the great clan aristocracy, there is much to be said for David Johnson's argument in *The Medieval Chinese Oligarchy* that the great clans, not the shih, were recognized in the T'ang as the sociopolitical elite. The alternative proposed in this chapter allows the possibility that the T'ang discriminated among the clans in the Wei manner and that the national-clan rankings may have included only those great clans the court chose to recognize as having national stature. I use "great clans" to denote a system in which the state formally recognized the shih by recognizing clans.

4. There was debate over whether to continue the centralized selection system for office instituted under T'ai-tsung. Herbert ("T'ang Dynasty Objections") argues persuasively that those proposing a return to a decentralized system were proposing a return to the system in the Period of Division.

5. D. Johnson, *Medieval Chinese Oligarchy*, p. 113. In the imperial clan, noble titles were granted because of the relationship to the emperor; however, the rank diminished with inheritance. See also Utsunomiya, *Chūgoku kodai chūseishi ken-kyū*, pp. 618, 621–25.

6. It has been argued that during the Period of Division, men known to be shih

were registered separately from other population groups, exempted from certain tax obligations, given the right to commute punishments, and forbidden to intermarry with the *shu-min* (common people). For a statement of this view, see Twitchett, "Composition," p. 49. David Johnson (*Medieval Chinese Oligarchy*, pp. 5–17), in his discussion of the documentary basis for this view, reaches the conclusions cited here.

7. *HTS*, 71A.2179.

8. D. Johnson, *Medieval Chinese Oligarchy*, pp. 121–39.

9. Liu Mien, letter to Ch'üan, *CTW* 527.5a.

10. *CTW* 545.16a, 17b.

11. This description is drawn from D. Johnson, *Medieval Chinese Oligarchy*, pp. 47–51, 91–99, 107–10, 113–14. Segmentation helps explain why, for example, the government could register 49 "branch lineages" of the Lu clan in 812 (Twitchett, "Composition," p. 57n12). On the early T'ang clan rankings, see Twitchett, "Composition," pp. 62–64; and Utsunomiya, *Chūgoku kodai chūseishi kenkyū*, pp. 625–30, 660–62.

12. D. Johnson, *Medieval Chinese Oligarchy*, pp. 91–99; idem, "Last Years," pp. 23–39; Ebrey, *Aristocratic Families*, pp. 90–93. On the distinction between great clans and later "lineages," see J. L. Watson, "Chinese Kinship"; and Ebrey and Watson, "Introduction."

13. D. Johnson, *Medieval Chinese Oligarchy*, pp. 99–104, 109–19; idem, "Last Years," pp. 40–48.

14. Ebrey, *Aristocratic Families*, p. 95; D. Johnson, *Medieval Chinese Oligarchy*, pp. 48–50; idem, "Last Years," pp. 40–48; Twitchett, "Composition," pp. 50–51.

15. Sun Kuo-tung, "T'ang Sung," pp. 225–30. See also Utsunomiya, *Chūgoku kodai chūseishi kenkyū*, p. 645.

16. Ebrey, *Aristocratic Families*, pp. 96–100.

17. The use of clan rankings to further the institutional interests of the center is apparent in the account of the Later Wei and Northern Chou from the *Sui shu*, cited above. Utsunomiya (*Chūgoku kodai chūseishi kenkyū*, pp. 623–24) argues that the attempt to deprive clans of their ability to certify their members for office began in the Northern Chou as well, but did not succeed until the Sui. The Sui examinations were thus an important symbol of the court's claim to be able to recruit for high office without deferring to clan status.

18. D. Johnson, *Medieval Chinese Oligarchy*, pp. 48, 138–39 (by Johnson's calculation Kao-ts'u's reign had the highest proportion of leading ministers from great clans of all T'ang reigns); Ebrey, *Aristocratic Families*, pp. 87–88; Twitchett, "Composition," pp. 48–51.

19. D. Johnson, *Medieval Chinese Oligarchy*, pp. 47–51. A reference to the difference between the 638 list and a later list notes that the former included shih-ta-fu of the four quarters; see *CTS* 82.2769.

20. D. Johnson, *Medieval Chinese Oligarchy*, pp. 51–53; *CTS* 82.2769. The reasons for this increase are not clear. It may have resulted from treating the immediate descent group of all those who had reached the fifth rank as *chia*, from further segmentation of clans, and from the appearance of new claimants to great clan status.

21. Ebrey (*Aristocratic Families*, p. 143n5) notes such uses of "shih" in funerary inscriptions. Utsunomiya (*Chūgoku kodai chūseishi kenkyū*, pp. 637–39) makes a similar case.

22. Li Lin-fu's list of 749 apparently did not list families (Twitchett, "Composition," p. 66). The Tun-huang lists that Twitchett discusses add hundreds more, revealing, he suggests, the existence of a large pool of provincial clans. Although the totals for the list of 713, in 200 *chüan*, are unknown, the criteria for inclusion were much looser than they had been in 659. It ranked the families of men with reputations for virtue, from good families, of scholarly talent or military bravery, and those admired at court (D. Johnson, *Medieval Chinese Oligarchy*, p. 54).

23. Utsunomiya, *Chūgoku kodai chūseishi kenkyū*, pp. 625–37. Utsunomiya makes the point that lists from after the era of Hsuan-tsung are not rankings but listings of the known clans by place or name according to pronunciation. In the Hsuan-tsung era he includes those post-755 rankings by men who established themselves under Hsuan-tsung. The issue here is not the continuing idea of a social elite of families but of the breakdown of a hierarchy of clans. Once the court's imprimatur was not necessary for families to claim to be "clans," they could do as they pleased, as the appearance of lists with numerous provincial clans suggests, but this also diminished the value of clan status. David Johnson (*Medieval Chinese Oligarchy*, p. 63) thinks the fact that less than half of the prefectures were included on any listing by place indicates the existence of a national ranking of some kind.

24. Ebrey (*Aristocratic Families*, pp. 103–4) notes that 91 percent of the Po-ling Ts'ui males mentioned in inscriptional records only (i.e., without biographies in formal historical sources) had rank.

25. My understanding of the T'ang bureaucratic system and its size in the 730's is taken, with some qualifications, from Twitchett, "The Bureaucracy," esp. pp. 1–9, 52–53. I have also drawn on Ch'ing-lien Huang, "Recruitment and Assessment," chap. 2 and his discussion of the eligibility list of 737 in sect. 2 of chap. 4. For an early discussion of the unimportance of the examinations in staffing the bureaucracy relative to recruitment through the *yin* privilege and from the ranks of minor officials "outside the stream," see Sun Kuo-t'ing, "T'ang Sung," pp. 246–50.

26. Note that this figure also corresponds to the 2,287 families on the clan list of 659.

27. This group is listed as *na-k'o p'in-tzu* in the eligibility list of 737 (*HTS* 45.1180). Ch'ing-lien Huang ("Recruitment and Assessment," p. 248) translates this as "the sons of ranking officials entered by paying taxes." My understanding of this term follows Twitchett, "The Bureaucracy," p. 19. Although T'ang rules limited yin privilege for appointment to office within the stream to officials in the first through fifth ranks, it is not certain that this restriction was always observed. In Sung, yin could be used, by those in the seventh rank and above, for brothers, cousins, nephews, and affines.

28. Ebrey, *Aristocratic Families*, p. 151n84.

29. *T'ang hui-yao* 74.1334–35. In 657 over 1,400 men "entered the stream" annually, although there were only 13,465 posts. In 681 it was noted that 60–80

percent of those eligible for posting by either the Ministry of [Civil] Personnel or the Ministry of War were being turned away.

30. Tu Yu, *T'ung tien* 15.3a–b. This situation favored those with family connections; cf. Herbert, "Civil Service," pp. 2–5.

31. If we also include the 10,000 listed in 737 as being "officers and clerks in the two main offices of the kingdom" and the 1,782 "lowest-ranking officers and clerks in local military units," we arrive at 18,000 clerical positions with eligibility to enter the stream (*HTS* 45.1180; Tu Yu, *T'ung tien* 15.3b). Translations following Ch'ing-lien Huang, "Recruitment and Assessment," p. 249. Ou-yang Hsiu (*HTS* 45.1180) notes that the number of clerical positions in this list does not include the unranked prefectural and subprefectural clerks.

32. Ch'ing-lien Huang, "Recruitment and Assessment," p. 37. Officials outside the stream are not given for local government, whose clerical staff were referred to as "special duty officials."

33. Twitchett ("The Bureaucracy," p. 2), however, suspects that these clerks were also liu-wai kuan.

34. Ibid., p. 3.

35. Ebrey, *Aristocratic Families*, pp. 103–8.

36. Both Twitchett ("The Bureaucracy") and Ch'ing-lien Huang ("Recruitment and Assessment") take Yang Ch'iang's (or Yang T'ang's) mention in 729 of over 2,000 men entering service as referring to the liu-wai kuan. Even assuming that *liu-wai* refers to liu-wai kuan, I am fairly confident that the text in question includes other categories of eligibility. The figure of 2,000 agrees with a reference to the selection process in 710: "Those assembled were over 10,000 men. As for those who were kept, the three selections did not exceed 2,000" (*TCTC* 211.6660). In 657 over 1,400 men were said to "enter the stream" annually (*T'ang hui-yao* 74.1334).

The confusion stems from the different formulations found in the six versions of Yang Ch'iang's text. The *T'ang hui-yao* (75.1376) and *Ts'e-fu yuan-kuei* (639.22b–23a) identify the 2,000 as "those in all categories of eligibility [*tsa-se ch'u-shen*] entering service [*ju-shih*]." Tu Yu (*T'ung tien* 17.5a) has "all categories of eligibility" (*chu-se ch'u-shen*). A Sung edition of the *T'ung tien* reprinted in Japan has the same formulation (Denis Twitchett, pers. comm.). None of these texts use the term "liu-wai," but three other texts do. The *CTW* version (298.18b–20a) identifies the 2,000 as "those outside the stream entering service, all categories of eligibility." The *HTS* (130.4496) version has "those outside the stream entering service *and* all categories of eligibility" (my italics). The *TCTC* (213.6784) has "those with eligibility [by service] outside the stream." The last two texts are abridged and obvious rewritings. Yang is objecting to a decision to cut back on the number of examination degrees granted in an effort to reduce the numbers seeking appointment. He objects to this on the grounds that "empty types [*fu-hsu chih t'u*] and clerks" are not as good as those devoted to learning. He concludes with "if those with eligibility are too many, it is necessary to reduce all categories of eligibility. Why should only the *ming-ching* and *chin-shih* degrees be cut back." "Empty types" usually meant those who were superficially cultured but lacking in substance (perhaps including the sons of good families with nominal positions in the guards who hung around the capital). I follow the *T'ung tien*, which also discusses the different eligibility groups, and conclude that the figure of 2,000 refers to all categories on the eligibility list of 737, of which the liu-wai kuan were one. I am indebted to Denis Twitchett for references to the alternative texts.

37. Ch'ing-lien Huang, "Recruitment and Assessment," p. 38; Twitchett, "The Bureaucracy"; and Herbert, "Civil Service." In contrast to Huang and Twitchett, I am not convinced that "entering the stream" refers to transfer from the "office outside the stream." Rather, following Tu Yu's discussion of eligibility (*T'ung tien* 15.3b), I take it to refer to eligibility for selection from all statuses.

38. For the entire eligibility list, see Ch'ing-lien Huang, "Recruitment and Assessment," pp. 248–49; and *HTS* 45.1180. Huang's total of 160,000 appears to be a typo.

39. Niida, *Tōryō shūi*, pp. 244–45, citing a passage in the *Liu tien* from 738 or 739; cf. Ch'ing-lien Huang, "Recruitment and Assessment," p. 20.

40. Twitchett, "The Bureaucracy," pp. 48–49; Ch'ing-lien Huang, "Recruitment and Assessment," p. 34.

41. See the discussion of Yang Ch'iang's comments, note 36 above.

42. Twitchett ("The Bureaucracy," pp. 27–31) notes that after 737 the prefectures were allowed to exceed their assigned quota of candidates.

43. Twitchett, "Composition," pp. 76–79.

44. Ebrey (*Aristocratic Families*, pp. 104–5) found that 30 to 50 percent of the known Ts'uis took examination degrees.

45. Pulleyblank (*Background of the Rebellion*, pp. 47–59) documents the political hostilities between officials with great clan pedigrees and men of obscure social background who had risen to high office through the literary examinations. For a more recent treatment of the issue, see Twitchett, "Hsüan-tsung." For the seventh-century origins of this debate, see Herbert, "Civil Service."

46. *CTS* 97.3049; cf. Pulleyblank, *Background of the Rebellion*, p. 50.

47. As Denis Twitchett has written, "The change from T'ang to Sung was essentially that claims to privilege on the basis of pedigree were gradually eroded"; see his response to J. L. Watson, "Chinese Kinship," p. 626.

48. For these and related developments, see C. A. Peterson, "Court and Province."

49. Twitchett, *Financial Administration*, p. 17.

50. All these matters are discussed in detail in ibid.; see also Twitchett, "Provincial Autonomy."

51. Numerous examples of the migration of rich families and aristocrats south are given in Aoyama Sadao's studies of Sung bureaucratic families; this research is discussed in the next section.

52. D. Johnson, *Medieval Chinese Oligarchy*, pp. 138–39.

53. D. Johnson, "Last Years," pp. 42–43.

54. Ibid., p. 48.

55. Ebrey, *Aristocratic Families*, p. 119; Utsunomiya (*Chūgoku kodai chūseishi kenkyū*, pp. 618–54) makes a similar argument.

56. Wang Gungwu, *Structure of Power*; for a brief statement of his conclusions, see pp. 2–6, 205–6; for the parallels between a governor's staff and an emperor's palace commissioners, see p. 153.

57. Worthy, "Founding of Sung China"; see chap. 5 for the history of the most important palace commission, the Shu-mi yuan, a military secretariat or privy commission prior to the Sung; the effective limitation of its authority reduced it to being the Bureau of Military Affairs (the standard translation for this organ in the Sung); see chaps. 3–4 for the Emperor's Army and the use of the Palace Army or Palace Corps for control; see chap. 6 for local government and finance.

58. Ibid., pp. 138–81.   59. Ibid., pp. 181–95.

60. Ibid., pp. 238–45.   61. Ibid., p. 272.

62. Ibid., pp. 296–311.

63. Ibid., pp. 298–311, on the basis of work by Sun Kuo-tung and Nishikawa Masao.

64. The major thesis of Nishikawa Masao's studies of Five Dynasties and Northern Sung dynastic biographies is that Northern Sung civil officials were descended from Five Dynasties civil officials (see "Kahoku Godai ōchō no bunshin kanryō" and "Kahoku Godai ōchō no bunshin to bushin"). Wang Gungwu (*Structure of Power*, pp. 164–76) distinguishes three major groups at court: the palace commissioners, military men, and the "bureaucrats." Both Nishikawa and Wang take the view that the bureaucrats were an important force with considerable prestige if limited power. Further support for Nishikawa's conclusions about the origins of the Sung shih-ta-fu can be inferred from Sun Kuo-tung's account ("T'ang Sung") of the demise of the great clans, which is based on a study of dynastic history biographies from the T'ang through the Northern Sung. Suzuki Takayuki's study of Five Dynasties degree holders ("Godai no bunkan jinjisei-saku") is also of value. Numerous examples appear in Aoyama Sadao's regional studies of Northern Sung officials and Kinugawa Tsuyoshi's study of early Northern Sung chief councillors; these are discussed in the next section.

65. An example of this distinction appears in an entry for A.D. 911 in the *Comprehensive Mirror*. Ssu-ma Kuang writes that when Liu Yen became governor of Kuang-chou he "invited many shih-jen from the north [*chung-kuo*] to serve in his secretariat and he sent them out as prefects; for prefects he did not use *wu-jen* [military men]" (*TCTC* 268.8742). Plentiful evidence from the *Old History of the Five Dynasties* indicates that this was not simply a Sung perspective; see Nishikawa, "Kahoku Godai ōchō no bunshin to bushin," pp. 292–94, 297–99. It may be objected that in biographies written by shih statements attributed to military men showing they did not think of themselves as shih were self-serving. The qualities associated with shih in these passages are, however, distinctly civil, and, as we shall see, the Sung examination system, expressly intended to recruit shih, tested those qualities.

66. D. Johnson, "Last Years," pp. 67–73; Sun Kuo-tung, "T'ang Sung," pp. 232–42; Nishikawa, "Kahoku Godai ōchō no bunshin kanryō," p. 205.

67. On the disruption of the genealogical tradition from the T'ang to the Sung,

see D. Johnson, "Last Years," pp. 51–59; and Morita Kenji, "Sō Gen jidai," pp. 515–16.

68. For an account of how dynastic biographies reflect this, see Sun Kuo-tung, "T'ang Sung," pp. 245, 272, 278.

69. This case is made in Suzuki, "Godai no bunkan jinjiseisaku"; note in particular the increase in examination degree totals (p. 31).

70. Nishikawa, "Kahoku Godai ōchō no bunshin to bushin," pp. 291–99. Wang Gungwu (Structure of Power, pp. 169–71) also notes examples of men recycling their sons as bureaucrats. For counterexamples, see Worthy, "Founding of Sung China," pp. 299–300.

71. Sun Kuo-tung ("T'ang Sung," pp. 251–57) argues that the spread of printing, together with the disappearance of great clan families, made education more public and less of a private family tradition, thus opening careers as shih to those not from shih families.

72. Cited in Lin Jui-han, "Nan-t'ang," p. 190. This article provides numerous examples of the identification of the shih with the civil pursuits of literary and Classical studies. For a brief description of Southern T'ang court culture, see Bryant, Lyric Poets, pp. xvi–xxvii. Roles for shih existed in the contemporary Min kingdom in Fukien as well, we may presume, if only to provide the documentary and ritual basis for its extensive foreign relations; on the latter, see Clark, "Trade and Economy," pp. 9–12.

73. Nishikawa's list of 33 civil officials who served outside their home prefectures can be taken as evidence that this was unusual ("Kahoku Godai ōchō no bunshin kanryō," pp. 247–48).

74. Fan Tsu-yü (Ti hsueh 3.1a–3b), for example, records such signal events as the emperor's visits to the State Academy in 960/1 and 963/4, his order to military ministers to "read books and value understanding the way of governing" in 966/6, his interview of a private scholar in 968, his announcement that chief ministers should henceforth be "men who read books," and his own study of the Documents in 968. A more extensive and anecdotal account of the Northern Sung, Chiang Shao-yü's Sung-ch'ao shih-shih lei-yuan (1145), gives a fuller record of T'ai-tsu's military achievements but arranges the material to suggest that these were, from the start, subordinated to his civil and cultural interests; see chüan 1. Araki Toshikazu accepted, and elaborated on, this view in "Sō Tai-so kakyo seisaku."

75. Furugaki, "Tai-so Tai-sō jidai," pp. 115, 119–20.

76. Worthy, "Founding of Sung China," pp. 280–88.

77. Furugaki, "Tai-so Tai-sō jidai," p. 103.

78. Ibid., p. 104.

79. On restrictions in yin during the first reign, see Ma Tuan-lin, Wen-hsien t'ung-k'ao 35.324b–c. On restrictions on transfers from the clerical service into ranked offices, the dismissal of 400 "men outside the stream," and a proposal to use shih-jen as clerical administrators in the secretariat-chancellery (t'ang-hou kuan), see idem, 35.332c–333a.

80. SHY: hsuan-chü 3.2b–3a, for 970/1/19; cf. Furugaki, "Tai-so Tai-sō jidai,"

p. 105. Note that at the same time stand-in officials (*she-kuan*), who had been appointed locally without central authorization, were ordered dismissed and prefectures were forbidden to use this method of filling vacancies (Ma Tuan-lin, *Wen-hsien t'ung-k'ao* 38.357c).

81. *SHY: hsuan-chü* 3.3b–4a, for 975/10/13.

82. Furugaki, "Tai-so Tai-sō jidai," p. 106.

83. *SHY: hsuan-chü* 3.1b–2a, dated 962/9/1.

84. Araki, "Sō Tai-so kakyo seisaku." Araki (p. 485) makes the point that T'ai-tsu himself read books but did not favor literary composition (the most prestigious test of learning). Araki's assertion that T'ai-tsu wished to favor the "common people" over aristocrats ignores the use of exams to recruit shih exclusively.

85. During the ten years of the Later Chou, 104 chin-shih degrees were given and 659 degrees in the various other fields. During the first decade of T'ai-tsu's reign, there were 104 chin-shih degrees; the figures for the various fields are unknown. The numbers begin to increase slightly in 973. For Sung degree totals, see Chaffee, *Thorny Gates*, pp. 192–95. For the Later Chou, see Ma Tuan-lin, *Wen-hsien t'ung-kao* 30.282c.

86. Ma Tuan-lin, *Wen-hsien t'ung-k'ao* 30.284c, 32.305a; cf. Chaffee, *Thorny Gates*, p. 49.

87. Ma Tuan-lin, *Wen-hsien t'ung-k'ao* 20.282c; cf. Furugaki, "Tai-so Tai-sō jidai," p. 112.

88. For a discussion of the administrative/executory division, introduced in E. A. Kracke's work, see Lo, *Civil Service of Sung China*, pp. 51–60.

89. Chaffee, *Thorny Gates*, p. 50.

90. Ma Tuan-lin, *Wen-hsien t'ung-k'ao* 35.322a.

91. James T. C. Liu, "Sung Views," pp. 321–23.

92. For a discussion of the role of military officials (men with military rank, many of whom never served in the army) in the civil administration, see Lo, "New Perspective." On the diminished status of the military in relation to the civil bureaucracy, see Liu Tzu-chien, "Lueh-lun Sung-tai wu-kuan-ch'ün."

93. See Furugaki, "Shin-sō chōchū ikō."

94. Umehara, *Sōdai kanryō seido*, pp. 423–500. The discussion that follows is based entirely on Umehara's work. For an English version of Umehara's account of the Sung system of official ranks, see "Civil and Military Officials."

95. Thus, the complaint in the early Southern Sung that up to 4,000 men were given rank through yin at each triennial sacrifice (see Umehara, *Sōdai kanryō seido*, p. 448).

96. Furugaki, "Tai-so Tai-sō jidai," p. 107, citing Chiang Shao-yü, *Sung-ch'ao shih-shih lei-yuan*, chüan 1.

97. *Sung shih* 155.3614–15. The 1059 figures, however, show a return to the old system; the 1057 precedent was not institutionalized until 1070 (see Chaffee, *Thorny Gates*, p. 193). For a discussion of the 1057 examination, see Chapter 5 below.

98. For this view and its origins in the work of Naitō Konan, see Miyakawa Hisayuki, "Outline." The view is further developed in the writings of Aoyama Sadao, Kinugawa Tsuyoshi, Nishikawa Masao, and Umehara Kaoru cited below.

99. Hartwell, "Demographic, Political, and Social Transformations."

100. Kinugawa, "Sōdai no meizoku."

101. See Twitchett, "Fan Clan's Charitable Estate."

102. The reverse, court leaders as leading intellectuals, is not true. Still, the scholarly concern with public service meant that the Northern Sung court still had more influence over intellectual life than its Southern Sung counterpart.

103. Aoyama does not ask how many male offspring attained office but whether those who did were related to officials. For Aoyama's articles, see the Bibliography, pp. 457–58.

104. Hymes, *Statesmen and Gentlemen*, pp. 34–41. For Kracke's argument, see "Family vs. Merit."

105. I have chosen the Ch'ao family because it is one of the best-documented examples of a great bureaucratic family with a strong tradition of literary scholarship. Wang Te-i ("Sung-tai Shan-chou Ch'ao shih-tsu hsi-k'ao") credits much of the Ch'aos' success to their intellectual tradition. Several of the points made in this discussion are also evident in the genealogical charts of eight prominent bureaucratic families in Lee, *Government Education and Examinations*, pp. 293–99.

106. These figures are based on Yang Yuan, "Pei-sung tsai-fu jen-wu," pp. 165, 186. Yang distinguishes only north and south, taking the Huai and Han rivers as the boundary (Szechuan falls in the south). The Council of State included the chief councillors, assisting civil councillors, and commissioners and assistant commissioners of the Bureau of Military Affairs.

107. In a review of the over 200 sons of chief councillors with biographical references in the dynastic history, Umehara (*Sōdai kanryō seido*, p. 476) found that 90 percent of the sons that survived took office through yin; only ten sons took degrees.

108. Ibid., pp. 470–73.

109. Aoyama, "Kahoku kanryō," pt. 3. This article includes an entry on the Ch'ao family. In all his articles, Aoyama stresses the combined role of examinations and yin in the perpetuation of office holding. It is possible that some Ch'aos did take degrees in one of the "various fields" and that we simply lack a reference for that individual. But the lack of any mention of such a degree in the cases we do have (most of the fourth and some of the fifth generation were beginning their careers when the "various fields" still existed) is unusual.

110. Yang Yuan, "Pei-sung tsai-fu jen-wu," pp. 150–53.

111. For more examples of elite marriage practices, see Hartwell, "Demographic, Political and Social Transformations," pp. 411–13.

112. Hymes, *Statesmen and Gentlemen*, pp. 116–23. The need to find sponsors (who in turn became liable for the misconduct of those they sponsored) for promotion from *hsuan-jen* rank to "capital rank" is one example of the importance of bureaucratic networks.

113. Ch'ao Pu-chih, *Chi-le chi* 65.510, dated 1093.

114. Sun Kuo-tung, "T'ang Sung," p. 257; Pan Mei-yueh, *Sung-tai ts'ang-shu chia k'ao*, pp. 129–30.

115. *Sung shih* 305.10087; *Sung-jen i-shih hui-pien* 6.220.

116. Ch'ao Kung-wu, *Chün-chai tu-shu chih*.

117. Hartwell, "Financial Expertise."

118. Kinugawa, "Sōdai no meizoku," p. 159.

119. For a discussion of the long-term development with a particular focus on the role of family rituals in providing the basis for the new attitudes toward kinship, see Ebrey, "Early Stages." For specific examples of the new Sung practices, see D. Johnson, "Last Years," pp. 75–97.

120. Examples of these numerical markers are found in the titles for poems in the collections of Ch'ao Pu-chih, Ch'ao Ch'ung-chih, and Ch'ao Yueh-chih.

121. Twitchett, "Fan Clan's Charitable Estate."

122. Ch'ao Pu-chih, "Chi shan chi," *Chi-le chi* 31.209.

123. In the Southern Sung both Ch'ao Kung-wu and Ch'ao Kung-mai referred to themselves as Chao-te Ch'ao, after the Kaifeng residence of Ch'ao Chiung and Tsung-ch'ueh in the Chao-te district of Kaifeng. See, e.g., the introduction to Kung-wu's *Chün-chai tu-shu chih*, where the point is to highlight kinship with Chiung and Tsung-ch'ueh.

124. Hartwell, "Demographic, Political, and Social Transformations," pp. 406–7; cf. pp. 411–12.

125. Kinugawa, "Sōdai saishō kō."

126. A closer examination of the sources will show that the very cases Hartwell cites as evidence for claims to T'ang great clan descent disprove his case. A critical examination of his evidence will appear elsewhere. For the moment it should be adequate to note David Johnson's investigation of Sung claims to Chao-chün Li clan ancestry. Johnson found three cases in which men claimed the Chao-chün Li choronym. The case of Li Ping (?–976), a censor, is a clear claim, but later writings on the family (even when descent from the Chao-chün Lis is not in question) use the placename of later residences rather than the T'ang choronym. A 1085 text on Li Hsiu (1049–68) assigns him the Chao-chün Li choronym, but it is not used for other members of the family. Li Chih, a follower of Su Shih, adopted the Tsan-huang subchoronym (a very sophisticated tactic), but this was a symbolic and personal gesture. Johnson also notes that no Hsiang claims the Ho-nei Hsiang choronym for himself until a Southern Sung fifth-generation descendant of the early Sung founder of the family ("Last Years," pp. 53–54, 81–85, 90–92, 95–97). In these instances, the adoption of a great clan choronym is consciously used to identify the individual with the illustrious T'ang clan, but in each case it is clear that the family as a whole did not use the T'ang choronym in practice.

The failure of families who claimed descent from T'ang great clans (Johnson identifies five or seven such families) to maintain the currency of the clan's choronym is strong evidence, I believe, for their own sense of discontinuity with the past and, given their tendency to confuse a choronym with family residence, the weakness of their understanding of the function of the choronym itself. Thus even when a family might be descended from a T'ang family with legitimate great clan status, its efforts were directed at showing that it was an illustrious and ancient family that had produced high officials, not at showing that this particular family was one of the constituent families of an existing great clan. Johnson shows, for example, that the Chao-chün Li claimants in the Sung were concerned with their particular descent group or lineage; in no case do we find the family in question thinking in terms of the other possible Chao-chün Li families or lineages and seeking to establish their common identity. An example of the view of the great clans as an anachronism is found in Shen Kua's *Meng-ch'i pi-t'an*; translated in Twitchett, "Composition," pp. 54–56. Shen's assertion that great clans were non-Chinese in origin suggests his hostility toward them as a model for social-political organization.

127. Kinugawa's study ("Sōdai saishō kō," pp. 140–47) of the first 40 Sung chief councillors shows that of the 15 who claimed T'ang official ancestry only four to six were descended from high court bureaucrats or aristocratic families, six were local officials (a different group), two were from the staffs of military governors, and one was a low-ranking army officer. Of the rest, twelve recorded fathers or grandfathers who had established the family during the Five Dynasties, six began in the Sung, and the origins of seven were obscure. Aoyama Sadao ("Kahoku kanryō," pt. 1) divides north China bureaucrats into three groups: those claiming T'ang official ancestry, subdivided into claims to court and local officials; those descended from Five Dynasties officials; and those beginning in the Sung. In his studies of Fukien, Chiang-hsi, Szechuan, and Chiang-nan bureaucrats, he follows the same procedure, repeatedly stressing the weakness of most claims to descent from T'ang aristocratic families; claims of descent from late T'ang local officials are more reliable. In some places, Szechuan (the last refuge of the T'ang court) for example, many aristocratic families did survive.

128. D. Johnson, "Last Years," pp. 48–59.

129. This is clearly the case for many of those claiming Chao-chün Li ancestry; in at least one instance the account of the T'ang forebears comes from an introduction to a genealogical table in the *New T'ang History*. Aoyama Sadao (see his "Shisen kanryō"; "Kahoku kanryō," pt. 1; "Kanan kanryō"; "Kōsei kanryō"; and "Newly Risen Bureaucrats in Fukien") also provides numerous cases in which biographies of earlier figures give no T'ang ancestry while biographies of later figures do. He also dates this to the mid-eleventh century.

130. The late tenth-century administrative geography, the *T'ai-p'ing huan-yü chi*, did include a listing of the famous clans by prefecture. This is thought to be a replication of a T'ang list; see Twitchett, "Composition," pp. 73–75. This information was not included in the administrative geography of the 1080's, the *Yuan-feng chiu yü chih*.

131. For a typical example of the Northern Sung Ch'ao view of their ancestry see Ch'ao Pu-chih, *Chi-le chi* 65.510, dated 1093. This funerary biography of a Ch'ao woman married into the Yeh family suggests how the Ch'aos wanted others to view them at the time. For a claim to T'ang forebears, see Lou Yueh, *Kung-kuei chi* 35.1a, dated 1207.

132. In an effort to improve the military after the loss of the north, the Southern Sung attempted to recruit shih sons by promising eventual transfer to civil rank to those recommended by three civil officials. This is indicated by an edict of 1132 temporarily forbidding such transfers on the grounds that examination candidates had taken military rank but then avoided going to war (*Chien-yen i-lai hsi-nien yao-lu*, 1132/7/i-yu).

133. There is a possible exception to this in the person of the Chin dynasty official Ch'ao Hui, said to have been a descendant of Ch'ao Chiung (Gen. II) and a Northern Sung military chin-shih. If so, the record has confused his personal name with his *tzu*, given as Kung-hsi. See Yuan Hao-wen, *Chung-chou chi* 8.5b.

134. These means included the metropolitan schools and less competitive qualifying examinations for the sons of officials (see Chaffee, *Thorny Gates*, pp. 61–65).

135. Kracke, *Civil Service*, pp. 164–66.

136. Ibid., pp. 146–52.

137. Equating the lack of mention of immediate ancestors with non–official family status, Ch'en I-yen ("Ts'ung pu–i ju-shih") has argued that 55 percent of the 1,953 Northern Sung men with biographies in the *Sung History* were new men. Thomas Lee (*Government Education and Examinations*, pp. 211–13) asserts that the number of new men should be recalculated as 32.5 percent.

138. In Fu-chou, as Robert Hymes (*Statesmen and Gentlemen*, p. 63) has shown, families were establishing themselves as members of the local shih elite during the eleventh century and during the first three decades of the Southern Sung. Aoyama Sadao's studies, which focus on the emergence of bureaucratic families in the Northern Sung, also contain numerous examples of "new" families in the eleventh century who could reasonably claim pre-Sung officials as ancestors; see his "Newly Risen Bureaucrats in Fukien"; "Kanan kanryō"; and "Kōsei kanryō."

139. The percentages of southerners serving as assisting civil councillors and commissioners and vice-commissioners of military affairs were somewhat lower (Yang Yuan, "Pei-sung tsai-fu jen-wu," pp. 165, 186).

140. Hartwell, "Demographic, Political, and Social Transformations," p. 414; see pp. 414–16 for his figures and analysis.

141. Chaffee, *Thorny Gates*, pp. 129–34.

142. On the basis of biographies in the *Sung History* for men active during the second half of the Northern Sung, Nishikawa ("Kahoku Godai ōchō no bunshin kanryō," p. 217) concludes that 110 of the 123 military men with biographies came from the north. Altogether the north accounted for 391 of 690 men from this period with biographies.

143. Aoyama, "Kahoku kanryō," pt. 1.

144. Yang Yuan, "Pei-sung tsai-fu jen-wu," pp. 150–53, based on the literary biographies in *Sung shih*, *chüan* 439–45.

145. I am not suggesting that the reform programs can be accounted for purely in terms of competition for office, for the policies had to be justified on grounds other than self-interest, but in the 1040's and 1070's reform leaders had built up reputations as men who stood apart from the court and were on the side of those who had been wrongly ignored.

146. James T. C. Liu, "Fan Chung-yen," pp. 108, 112–14.

147. Lee, *Government Education and Examinations*, p. 225.

148. Hartwell, "Demographic, Political, and Social Transformations," pp. 409–11; Hartwell stresses the role of New Policies–period factionalism in the demise of the professional elite.

149. *Sung shih* 282.9548.

150. *Hsu tzu-chih t'ung-chien ch'ang-pien* 34.757.

151. Ch'en P'eng-nien, *Kung-chü hsu-lueh*, p. 2008. Ch'en noted the danger of excessive reliance on literary skills but argued that this was not an inevitable result of the examination system.

152. Chaffee, *Thorny Gates*, pp. 39–42, 55–61, 66–73; Lee, *Government Education and Examinations*, pp. 150–51.

153. *SMWC* 40.517–22.

154. Funerary biography, *LCWC* 94.974; Yang Shih, letter, *Yang Kuei-shan hsien-sheng ch'üan-chi* 18.8a; Cheng Kang-chung, essay, *Pei-shan chi* 5.14a; Lu Yu, record for a charitable estate, *Lu Fang-weng ch'üan-chi* 21.124. Parts of these passages are discussed in a somewhat different context in Ch'eng Yun, "Sung-tai chiao-yü," p. 93.

155. Ch'ao Pu-chih, an active writer of funerary biographies, took this to the extreme, repeatedly noting origins of a surname in antiquity and finding at least one famous ancient of that surname. These documents are collected in his *Chi-le chi*.

156. See Fan Chung-yen's and Fan Ch'un-jen's rules in Twitchett, "Fan Clan's Charitable Estate," pp. 106, 110. By the 1073 rules, payment was made only for the first and second attempts (the reward was reduced by half for the second). In 1073 provisions were also made to employ either retired Fan officials or exam candidates as family tutors.

157. Morita, "Sō Gen jidai," pp. 515–17.

158. Lee, *Government Education and Examinations*, p. 166; citing Yeh Meng-te.

159. Chaffee, *Thorny Gates*, p. 35. For a discussion of the importance of examination participation to maintaining shih status, see Bol, "Examination System."

160. Lee, *Government Education and Examinations*, p. 176.

161. Chaffee, *Thorny Gates*, p. 77, notes that 210,000 students were recorded as registered in state schools in 1104, but only 167,622 in 1108. Whether the latter number marked a decline in interest or a change in registration procedures is not clear.

162. Davis, *Court and Family*.

163. See Hymes, *Statesmen and Gentlemen*, pp. 82–123, for a detailed account of the change in marriage patterns and their significance. See also Hartwell, "Demographic, Political, and Social Transformations," p. 423. Hartwell was one of the first to note this change.

164. Walton, "Kinship, Marriage, and Status."

165. Chaffee (*Thorny Gates*, chaps. 5 and 6) documents the increasing number of candidates and their regional distribution. Chaffee points out that these increases occurred even though regular degree holders were declining as a proportion of the bureaucracy and the chances of passing were becoming even slimmer.

166. Hung Mai, *I-chien chih*, chia 15.129. The story refers to the Ch'aos as a "great lineage of Teng-chou" and dates the event to 1128. I have found no other mention of Ch'aos in Teng-chou, but all known Ch'aos were of the same family

and Teng-chou is on the road connecting Chü-yeh to the tip of Shantung; thus my speculation.

167. The Chin dynastic history mentions only two Ch'aos. One was a general, the other a member of an embassy from the Tangut state of Hsia; their names do not accord with the family naming sequence (*Chin shih* 73.1681, 61.1443).

168. Hymes, *Statesmen and Gentlemen*, pp. 71–73, 293–94n35, 297n43.

Chapter 3

1. *CTS* 198.5641–42; McMullen, *State and Scholars*, pp. 73, 119, 164.

2. These phrases, from the *Change* and the *Tso chuan* respectively, will be discussed at length later in this chapter.

3. See, e.g., the late Howard Wechsler's study, *Offerings of Jade and Silk*, particularly his distinction between symbols to be believed and symbols as foci for the emotions (p. 7), his discussion of ideas about ritual (pp. 23–30), and his account of *hsiang*, "symbol" (pp. 31–36).

4. All these matters are discussed in greater detail in McMullen, *State and Scholars*, pp. 13–26, 35–42.

5. For a more detailed account, see ibid., pp. 67–81. William Hung ("Bibliographic Controversy") discusses a debate over which commentaries to use in which it was explicitly decided to be inclusive rather than to choose just one.

6. For further details, see McMullen, *State and Scholars*, pp. 162–72.

7. On ritual, see ibid., pp. 113–22. On the *Code*, see W. Johnson, *T'ang Code*, pp. 5–8, 49–54.

8. Preface by Kao Shih-lien in *Wen-yuan ying-hua* 699.3606b–7b.

9. McMullen, *State and Scholars*, pp. 218–19.

10. *TCTC* 123.3868. This corresponds to the four divisions of bibliography discussed below, with the exception that *hsuan-hsueh* alone represents the philosophical-schools division (*tzu*).

11. *SS* 32.906–7.

12. For a discussion of *fang-wai* and *fang-nei* (within the bounds) in mapping intellectual distinctions in past and present, see W. J. Peterson, "Squares and Circles." *Fang*, as Peterson notes, can also be taken as square (the square of earth in contrast to the circle of heaven and the square as a kind of boundary qualitatively different from that of the circle).

13. *SS* 35.1099.

14. *SS* 34.1003. A similar attitude is brought to bear on apocryphal texts such as "Yellow River Chart" and "Lo River Writing" (see 32.940–41).

15. For the development of the classification system and a comparison of the *Ch'i lu* and *Sui History* categories, see Yao Ming-ta, *Chung-kuo mu-lu-hsueh shih*, pp. 94–97. The compilers may not have been entirely persuaded that this arrangement reflected the realities of elite interests. The final lines of their general introduction place "the occult arts [*fang-chi*] and numerological techniques [*shu-shu*]" on a par with the four categories as "tools for establishing order" on the grounds that they can be used to "order the body" (*SS* 32.909).

16. *SS* 32.947.
17. *SS* 32.948.
18. *SS* 33.992.
19. *SS* 34.1050.
20. *SS* 35.1090–91.
21. *SS* 32.903.

22. *SS* 32.903; this passage is followed by the discussion of continuation and transformation in the preceding quotation.

23. From *Lun yü* 6.17.

24. Cited in Hsu Sung, *Teng-k'o chi k'ao* 8.263.

25. *SS* 32.948.

26. Following the text in *Wen hsuan* 52.7b, and borrowing from Owen, *Readings*.

27. *Lun yü* 8.19.

28. For a discussion of the etymology and use of these terms, see James J. Y. Liu, *Chinese Theories of Literature*, pp. 7–8, 100–101.

29. This usage is found in the *Tso chuan* Yin 5/1, Chao 15/*fu* 3.

30. *Lun yü* 5.13.

31. This is implied by the next passage, *Lun yü* 5.15, "Before he could put into practice something he had heard, the only thing Tzu-lu feared was that he should be told something further."

32. What Confucius meant by "wen" is difficult to say, although he clearly assigned considerable value to it. Both D. C. Lau (*Analects*, pp. 37–39) and Arthur Waley (*Analects*, pp. 39–41) have tried to sort this out. Both begin from the idea of "pattern" as attractive, external adornment and take it to include the various arts or accomplishments associated with the cultured aspect of the gentleman (poetry, literature, music, writing). It may be correct to see poetry as part of what one learns when one learns wen (*Lun yü* 1.6, one learns wen after one has learned to put ethical norms into practice), but learning the *Songs* could well be learning an oral tradition. On these matters, see also Holzman, "Confucius and Ancient Chinese Literary Criticism." Note also the exploration of the ancient significance of the term "wen" in Chow Tse-tsung, "Ancient Chinese Views on Literature."

33. See, e.g., *SS* 35.1090.

34. *CTW* 138.11a, in an entry entitled "The Origin in Antiquity," part of a discussion of why calligraphy is important.

35. *Han shu* 30.1755–56.

36. Cited in Hightower, "The *Wen hsüan* and Genre Theory," p. 513. For the text, see Ou-yang Hsun, *I-wen lei-chü* 56.1017.

37. For a discussion of the emergence of genres, see Hightower, "The *Wen hsüan* and Genre Theory"; and Knechtges, "*Wen xuan*," 1: 1–4, 21–22.

38. *SS* 35.1081, 1089.

39. See, e.g., the introduction to the ju biographies in *SS* 75.1705–7 and the introductions to the literary biographies in *Liang shu* 49.685–86; *Ch'en shu* 34.453–54; *Chou shu* 41.472; and *Pei Ch'i shu* 45.601–4.

40. The court of the Liang dynasty is the best-known case; see Marney, *Liang Chien-wen Ti*.

41. This became the Japanese view of how the elite participated in learning. For

this and how the literary history of China appeared from this perspective, see McCullough, *Brocade by Night*, chap. 1.

42. *Lun yü* 12.24; I have modified Lau's translation (*Analects*, p. 117).

43. This theme runs through McMullen, *State and Scholars*; for the early T'ang in particular, see pp. 206–17.

44. From the "Commentary on the Decision." *Chou I yin-te*, p. 15. Cf. Wilhelm, trans., *The I Ching*, p. 495.

45. For the text, see *Ch'üan Liang wen* (in Yen K'o-chün, *Ch'üan shang-ku . . . wen*) 12.1a–1b. I have modified the translation in James J. Y. Liu, *Chinese Theories of Literature*, p. 26.

46. *Tso chuan*, Hsiang 25/*fu* 2; *Ch'un-ch'iu ching-chuan yin-te*. Also discussed in Owen, *Readings*. The passage begins "Chung-ni said, 'A record [*chih*] has it.' " Given that "chih" (record) is used in the following sentence to signify what one is intent on or the will ("the language is to be adequate to the *chih*"), one wishes that the commentators would take the first chih for the will or intent as well.

47. My sense of the tradition of literary thought in which these works figure has been greatly informed by Owen, *Readings*; and James J. Y. Liu, *Chinese Theories of Literature*. Studies of particular works are noted below.

48. Knechtges, "*Wen xuan*," 1: 18. For the *Wen hsuan* preface, I follow principally Knechtges ("*Wen xuan*," 1: 73–91); see also his introductory comments. For the Chinese text I have followed *Wen hsuan Li chu i-shu*, annotated by Kao Pu-ying. I am also indebted to Hightower, "The *Wen hsüan* and Genre Theory"; Hughes, "Epistemological Methods," pp. 80–83, 90–91; and James J. Y. Liu, *Chinese Theories of Literature*, pp. 25–26.

49. *Wen hsuan Li chu i-shu*, preface 2a–3a. I have used many lines from Knechtges's translation, "*Wen xuan*," 1: 73–75.

50. Ou-yang Hsun, *I-wen lei-chü*, preface, p. 27.

51. For the five teachings, see the *Chou li*; for the six kinds of conduct, see the "Canon of Shun" in the *Documents*.

52. Yang Hsiung (53 B.C.–A.D. 18) used the term "insect carving" (*tiao-ch'ung*) to denigrate the composition of rhapsodies, a pursuit of his youth; it became a standard pejorative for literary embellishment (see Yang's *Fa-yen i-shu* 3.1a).

53. *SS* 66.1544; trans. Owen, *Poetry of the Early T'ang*, pp. 17–18, modified. Discussed in Chang Ch'eng-shou, "Sui-ch'ao ju-sheng."

54. This was not a polarity of form and content. In traditional usage, a piece of writing should capture the reader's senses through its skillful use of images and the patterning of its language, while saying something true about the world either through its affirmation of ethical constants or, at a more sophisticated level, through establishing the parallel between the organization of the piece and the world. Li pertains to that which is true about the world yet transcends particular forms. It is a pattern one makes apparent through the skillful use of language. It is descriptive of what is inherent in things and thus normative, assuming that there is a real correspondence between the constant patterns of human and natural activity and a moral life. Yet it cannot be reduced to a simple declaration of principle. It became a philosophical term of great importance in Wei-Chin period *hsuan-hsueh*

and in Buddhist thought. This account of the polarity between wen or tz'u and li draws heavily on Liu Hsieh, who uses "li" about 150 times (*Wen-hsin tiao-lung hsin-shu*, pp. 279–81). For Liu's insistence that li are illuminated with the mind as opposed to the senses, see Liu Hsieh, *Wen-hsin tiao-lung chu* 10.715. This follows directly from the understanding of the term in Wei-Chin hsuan-hsueh; T'ang Chün-i contrasts this usage with the use of the term in Warring States period texts to refer to the organization and ordering of external phenomena. For his comparison and discussion of the Buddhist polarity between li and phenomena (*shih*), see *Chung-kuo che-hsueh yuan-lun*, pt. 1, pp. 5–49. See also Wing-tsit Chan, "Evolution of the Neo-Confucian Concept of *Li*." Liu Hsieh and other writers use both the *wen/li* and *shih/li* polarity. Those using the wen/li polarity in theoretical writing include Lu Chi (the *Wen fu*), Ts'ao P'i (Ou-yang Hsun, *I-wen lei-chü* 56.1017), Chih Yü (*I-wen lei-chü* 56.1018), the early T'ang court scholars, the historian and critic Liu Chih-chi (661–721) (see the passage in Kuo Shao-yü and Wang Wen-sheng, *Chung-kuo li-tai wen-lun hsuan*, 2: 27), and the mid-eighth-century anthologist Yin Fan (see Lo Ken-tse, *Sui T'ang Wu-tai wen-hsueh p'i-p'ing*, p. 50). Further examples, principally from the Liang dynasty, can be found in some of the prefaces to literary collections in the *Wen hsuan, chüan* 46. In the mid-eighth century, the term "li" seems to have been used extensively in discussions of the phenomena and processes of heaven-and-earth; see, e.g., Liu Chih-ku's treatise "On Illuminating the Original Pivot," *CTW* 334.12a–14b. It is usually clear when T'ang writers substitute the character li for the taboo *chih* (to order), the personal name of Kao-tsung.

55. *CTW* 141.9a–11a.

56. *Lun yü* 3.14; trans. Lau, *Analects*, p. 69.

57. *Lun yü* 6.18; trans. Lau, *Analects*, p. 83, modified.

58. The section of Ou-yang Hsün's *I-wen lei-chü* on this theme (22.409–12) contains two essays on the topic.

59. *Lun yü* 6.27; trans. Lau, *Analects*, p. 85.

60. *Lun yü* 1.6; trans. Lau, *Analects*, pp. 59–60.

61. *Lun yü* 17.9; trans. Lau, *Analects*, p. 145.

62. *Lun yü* 13.5; trans. Lau, *Analects*, p. 119. For a more detailed examination of Confucian ideas and literature, see Holzman, "Confucius and Ancient Chinese Literary Criticism"; and James J. Y. Liu, *Chinese Theories of Literature*, pp. 107–11. Both conclude that Confucius has a pragmatic or utilitarian attitude toward literature.

63. The materials used here to identify the views of early T'ang court scholars include the "Treatise on Bibliography," discussed above, the introductions to the biographies of ju and literary men in the eight dynastic histories composed in the seventh century, introductions and covering material for the *Correct Significances of the Five Classics*, and introductions to some of the major compilations sponsored by the court. I have chosen not to stress particular authors for several reasons. First, committees were involved in most of these projects. Second, not only are the views on wen adopted in different works quite similar but in some instances lines are lifted from earlier texts, suggesting that the point is not to create an

individual statement. The *Northern and Southern Histories*, for example, borrow introductory material from the *Sui History* and *Chou History*. Third, all the works cited here are official works; the normative statements made in introductions stand as the officially sanctioned views of the scholarly community at court. Although drawing primarily on the eight histories, I shall not refer to the authors as historians, literary men, or ju. They were all of these, of course, and the term "wen-ju" used at times to refer to them is appropriate. But above all, as Howard Wechsler (*Mirror to the Son of Heaven*) convincingly demonstrated in his study of Wei Cheng, one of the foremost court scholars, they were men who sought to bring the lessons of the past and ideals of textual tradition to bear on political power in the interests of moral government and political unity.

64. *SS* 35.1081, 1090–91. Although the eleven prefaces to literary collections from which Ou-yang Hsun (*I-wen lei-chü*, pp. 995–1001) quotes range in date from the Wei through the Sui, only one Sui period preface approaches making a T'ang-style conceptual connection between the larger vision of wen as *the* textual tradition and as literary composition. Neither do the unabridged prefaces included in the *Wen hsuan* (45.28a–46.20a), although Huang-fu Mi's introduction to the "Rhapsody on the Three Capitals" (45.28a–30b) has a similar sense of historical decline.

65. I suspect this was a valid historical assessment, despite the implications of the *Wen hsuan* preface. The encyclopedias compiled by literary men during the previous century had drawn on the entire textual tradition to provide accounts that would guide both the conduct of affairs and the composition of wen-chang. See, e.g., the only extant pre–T'ang encyclopedia, the *Pei-t'ang shu-ch'ao*, compiled in the Sui under the direction of Yü Shih-nan (558–638), who also served the T'ang.

66. The first five histories written dealt with the dynasties in the north and south during the previous century, but the introductions to the biographies in the Ju-lin and Wen-yuan or Wen-hsueh sections give both summary accounts covering all of Chinese history (the *Liang shu* is less comprehensive) and general statements of principle. For the south, see *Liang shu* 48.661–62 (ju) and 49.685–86 (wen); and *Ch'en shu* 33.433–34 (ju) and 34.453 (wen). For the north, see *Chou shu* 45.805–6 (ju) and 41.742–45 (wen); *Pei Ch'i shu* 44.581–84 (ju) and 45.601–4 (wen); and *Sui shu* 35.1705–7 (ju) and 36.1729–31 (wen). The *Chou shu* does not have a section devoted to literary biographies; however, it appends the equivalent of such an introduction (in format and content) to the biography of a literary scholar. Three later histories covered earlier centuries: see *Chin shu* 91.2345–46 (ju) and 92.2669–70 (wen); *Pei shih* 81.2703 (ju) and 83.2777–83 (wen); and *Nan shih* 71.1729 (ju) and 72.1961–62 (wen).

67. *Liang shu* (wen), *Pei Ch'i shu* (ju), *Chou shu* (ju).

68. *Ch'üan T'ang shih* 1.1a.

69. Probably the best statement of this view is found in the *Sui shu* introduction to literary biographies; see also the corresponding introductions in *Pei Ch'i shu*, *Chou shu*, and *Ch'en shu*.

70. *Chou shu* 41.742. For other mentions of the patterns of heaven and of man, see *SS* 76.1729; *Pei Ch'i shu* 45.601; and *Pei shih* 83.2777. In some cases only the pattern of man is cited; see *Ch'en shu* 34.453; *Nan shih* 72.1761; and *Chin shu* 92.2369.

71. *Chou i yin-te*, p. 45, HTC B2.

72. This comes from *Hsi-tz'u chuan* A11. It is adopted in Ch'ang-sun Wu-chi's memorial submitting the *Wu ching cheng-i* (*CTW* 136.7a) and K'ung Ying-ta's introduction to the commentary on the *Change* (*Shih-san ching chu-shu*, p. 7). The preface to the *Wen-ssu po-yao* compromised: the trigrams came from the River Chart, but wen was inspired by bird and animal tracks (*Wen-yuan ying-hua* 699.3606b).

73. Pauline Yu, *Reading of Imagery*, pp. 39–40. This is also a major theme in Owen, *Traditional Chinese Poetry*; and the subject of Jullien, "L'Oeuvre et l'univers."

74. *SS* 76.1729; *Ch'en shu* 34.453; *Nan shih* 72.1761.

75. *SS* 76.1729; cf. *Chin shu* 93.2369. "In perfect agreement with heaven-and-earth" translates the phrase *ching-wei t'ien-ti* (*Tso chuan* Chao 28/*fu* 2). Read as "give woof and warp to (or regulate) heaven-and-earth," the phrase fits the cosmic resonance theory of Han correlative thought. That is, since the wen has the true pattern of heaven-and-earth, Culture serves to keep heaven-and-earth on its correct course. The T'ang subcommentary, however, glosses the passage as meaning that the sage is able to accord perfectly with heaven, so that his actions form an integrated pattern, just like the crossing of woof and warp in cloth (*Shih-san ching chu-shu*, p. 2119). The same reading is applied to a similar passage in *Tso chuan* Chao 25.

76. *Chou shu* 41.742; alluding to *Hsi-tz'u chuan* A4 (*Chou-i yin-te*, p. 40).

77. *Pei Ch'i shu* 45.601.

78. "*Chou-i* cheng-i hsu," in *Shih-san ching chu-shu*, p. 6.

79. *Ch'en shu* 34.453.

80. *Chin shu* 92.2406–7.

81. Lu's composition is dated to 303 in Ch'en Shih-hsiang, "Riku Ki."

82. An earlier title of Ch'en Shih-hsiang's translation of the *Wen fu*, "Literature as Light Against the Darkness," is thus partly apt (A. Fang, "Rhymeprose on Literature"). For the published version of Ch'en Shih-hsiang's translation, see "Essay on Literature." I have followed the Chinese text in Fang's article.

83. In his notes to his translation, Achilles Fang ("Rhymeprose on Literature") shows that the terms "wen," "yen" (language), and "tz'u" (elaborations in language) are consistently paired with words such as mind, idea, intent, pattern, and so on. The translations from the *Wen fu* that follow draw on both Fang's translation and Owen's discussion and translation in *Readings*. My reading is also informed by Takahashi Kazumi, "Riku Ki."

84. Owen, *Traditional Chinese Poetry*, pp. 18–27. I am also indebted to Owen's discussion of Liu Hsieh in *Readings*.

85. Liu Hsieh, *Wen-hsin tiao-lung chu* 1.3. See Vincent Shih, trans., *The Literary*

Mind, p. 12. In the *Hsi-tz'u chuan* (*Chou i yin-te*, p. 44, HTC A12) the term "tz'u" refers to the words of judgment attached to the hexagram; I follow Shih in supposing that Liu has the tz'u of literary composition in mind.

86. For a clear statement of this view, see Wei Cheng's introduction to the *Ch'ün shu chih yao*, *CTW* 141.9a–11a.

87. For a discussion of this in philosophical terms, see the entry on Taoists in the "Treatise on Bibliography," *SS* 34.1003.

88. See, e.g., the introductions to the commentaries on the *Documents*, *Spring and Autumn Annals*, and the *Change* in *Shih-san ching chu-shu*, pp. 110, 1698, 7. Also see Ch'ang-sun Wu-chi's covering memorials for the Five Classics and legal code, *CTW* 136.7a, 19b. In some cases the cosmic grounds are downplayed; for references to the pattern of man only that illustrate this, see *Ch'en shu* 34.453; *Nan shih* 72.1761; and *Chin shu* 92.2369.

89. *Pei Ch'i shu* 45.601.

90. *Chin shu* 92.2369.

91. *Chou shu* 41.742.

92. *SS* 76.1729; *Pei Ch'i shu* 45.601; *Nan shih* 72.1761; *Pei shih* 83.2777; *Chin shu* 92.2369.

93. *Ch'en shu* 34.453; cf. *SS* 76.1729 and *Liang shu* 49.685.

94. Liu Hsieh's preface notes, "The functions of wen-chang are in truth outgrowths of the Classics. For completion the five rituals draw on them [i.e., literary compositions]; for realization the six functions of government proceed through them. They are how the relationship between ruler and ministers is illuminated and the relation between state and armies is kept clear. . . . But as the distance from the sages increased, the normative form for wen [wen-t'i] came undone. The tz'u-jen loved the unusual; in their language they valued the superficial" (*Wen-hsin tiao-lung chu* 10.726). I have borrowed from translations by both Vincent Shih (*The Literary Mind*, p. 4) and Stephen Owen (*Poetry of the Early T'ang*, p. 15). Chih Yü's essay for the *Wen-chang liu-pieh chi* makes a similar point; see Ou-yang Hsun, *I-wen lei-chü* 56.1018.

95. *SS* 76.1729; *Pei Ch'i shu* 45.601; *Chou shu* 41.743. For the *Documents*, see *Shih-san ching chu-shu*, p. 110.

96. *Liang shu* 50.727–28, citing Ts'ao P'i.

97. For a discussion of all these works, see Owen, *Readings*; and James J. Y. Liu, *Chinese Theories of Literature*, esp. pp. 67–77. On Ts'ao P'i and the use of ch'i, see David Pollard, "Ch'i in Chinese Literary Theory." Ts'ao's claim appears in his "Discourse on *Wen*"; see Ou-yang Hsun, *I-wen lei-chü* 56.1017.

98. *Chou shu* 41.744–45. Not all the introductions to the literary biography sections in the eight histories adopt precisely the same formulation or give it equal attention, but all accept the general thesis. In two cases it appears in the postscript to the biographies; see *Liang shu* 50.727–28 and *Chin shu* 92.2406–7.

99. *Shih-san ching chu-shu*, p. 261.

100. Ibid., p. 1222. Their discussion is certainly informed by the discussion of ritual in chap. 19 of the *Hsun-tzu*.

101. *Shih-san ching chu-shu*, p. 1529.

102. Ibid., p. 261.

103. Ibid., p. 270. See the discussion of the "Great Preface" in Owen, *Readings*.

104. *Shih-san ching chu-shu*, p. 261.

105. See, e.g., *SS* 76.1730.

106. Ibid., 76.1729. I have made some use of the translation in Owen, *Poetry of the Early T'ang*, pp. 33–34.

107. *Chou shu* 41.743.   108. *Ch'en shu* 34.453.

109. *Shih-san ching chu-shu*, p. 110.   110. *Chin shu* 92.2406–7.

111. *Chou shu* 41.743. See also *Pei Ch'i shu* 45.601 and *Chin shu* 93.2396. Note that these accounts of literary history bypass the writings of the philosophical schools; not till the early ninth century would they begin to figure in such lineages.

112. *P'ei Ch'i shu* 45.602; cf. *Pei shih* 83.2777 and Lu Te-ming's preface to the *Ching-tien shih-wen*.

113. *Shih-san ching chu-shu*, p. 261.

114. *Pei Ch'i shu* 45.602.

115. Owen and others have argued that by T'ang times this sublimation of the emotional self through adaption to rules of composition and transformation of conflict and dissonance into polite forms had become characteristic of court poetry. See Owen, *Poetry of the Early T'ang*, pp. 1–76.

116. *SS* 76.1730. Cf. *Chou shu* 41.743.

117. The histories equate political decline with splintering, one-sidedness, and a loss of rootedness in origins. For a good development of this theme, see *Chou shu* 41.742–45.

118. Together with Lo Pin-wang (ca. 640–84), these men came to be known as the Four Talents of the Early T'ang. Owen (*Poetry of the Early T'ang*, pp. 77–150) notes that they had greater reputations for writing in genres other than poetry. They were, in my terms, men who had made reputations for wen-chang. Their posthumous fame suggests that later men saw them as predecessors in some sense. If so, they provide a historical link between the early T'ang credo of learning and the early eighth century. For locating these texts, I am indebted to Lo Lien-t'ien, *Sui T'ang Wu-tai wen-hsueh p'i-p'ing*.

119. This section of the preface is translated in Owen, *Poetry of the Early T'ang*, pp. 79–80.

120. Yang Chiung, *Yang Chiung chi* 3.34–38.

121. See, e.g., the various prefaces to collections of poetry in ibid., 3.40–44.

122. Wang Po, *Wang Tzu-an chi* 8.62–64. This is from a begging letter to a court official.

123. Ibid., 10.81. Yang Ch'iung's preface to Wang's works say the "P'ing-t'ai pi-lueh," of which this is part, was composed on command.

124. Ibid., 4.31–32.

125. Lu Chao-lin, *Lu Chao-lin chi* 6.69–75. Note 6.69, where Lu reformulates the ssu-wen passage in the *Analects* to read, "With King Wen dead, is not tao here with me?"

126. *CTW* 238.4a–5a. Ch'en Tzu-ang had already said this himself; see Lo Lien-t'ien, *Sui T'ang Wu-tai wen-hsueh p'i-p'ing*, p. 33.

127. Owen, *Great Age of Chinese Poetry*, p. xiv.

Chapter 4

1. Po Chü-i, "On Wen-chang," *Po Chü-i chi* 65.1368.

2. There were objections, e.g., Tu Yu in the *T'ung tien* related decay in government to the popularity of *i-wen* (artful literature; cited in Ch'ien Mu, *Kuo-shih ta-kang*, p. 328).

3. See comments by Liang Su on Tai-tsung's and Te-tsung's reigns (*CTW* 518.7a, 518.1a–b), Ch'üan Te-yü on Te-tsung's reign and the T'ang in general (*CTW* 490.6b–7a, 489.15a), Yü Shao on events ca. 780 (*CTW* 427.10b), Po Chü-i writing in 806 on the T'ang in general (see note 1 to this chapter), Liu Tsung-yuan on the T'ang in general and the situation from 785 on (*LTYC* 21.577, 30.789), and Yuan Chen on Hsien-tsung (*Yuan Chen chi* 40.442).

4. Wang Chen in a discussion of the *Tao te ching* on war (*CTW* 683.21a) and Liang Su (*CTW* 518.14a). See also *LTYC* 21.575–77; and Yü Shao (*CTW* 427.1a–b). A dichotomy between civil and military modes of exercising political power, not remarked upon by early T'ang scholars, had already appeared under Hsuan-tsung when "the court esteemed wen" and shih pursued examination education in increasing numbers. Tu-ku Chi claims the court esteemed wen with reference to the year 748 (*CTW* 388.13a). In the decree examination of 714 candidates were asked to compare wen and wu. Sun T'i wrote: "Wen virtue is that which governance takes as its single concern; military might is that which aids wen" (*CTW* 310.20b). Yuan Chieh saw the popularity of wen in the examinations as symptomatic of its decline and refused to compete (*Yuan Tz'u-shan chi* 5.74–75, dated 753).

5. Liu Yü-hsi (772–842) is particularly explicit on this (*Liu Yü-hsi chi* 19.162–63, 19.171). See also *LTYC* 30.789.

6. McMullen, *State and Scholars*, pp. 237–41.

7. This is the point of Lü Wen's (772–811) essay "On Transformation Through the Wen of Man" (*CTW* 623.17a–18b).

8. Hsuan-tsung's ritual program, adopted at the beginning of the T'ien-pao period (742–56), centered around the adoption of the "Monthly Ordinances" ("Yueh ling") chapter of the *Book of Rites*; see the Basic Annals of his reign for the years 742 and later (*CTS* 9.214 ff). This went together with greater honors for Lao-tzu, proclamation of four Taoist texts as "true classics," distribution of the *Classic of Filial Piety* (which relates filial piety to the tao of heaven-and-earth) with the emperor's own commentary, and so on; see McMullen, *State and Scholars*, pp. 99–106, 174–86, on Hsuan-tsung's reign and on the collapse of state ritual and Tu Yu's treatment of ritual in the *T'ung tien*.

9. Preface to Hsiao's collection, *CTW* 315.7b–9a.

10. Preface to Li Hua's collection, *CTW* 388.11b–16a. See also Tu-ku's commemorative text for Chia, *CTW* 393.18b–19b.

11. See, e.g., Li Chou in his preface to Tu-ku's collection (*CTW* 443.16a–18a) and Liang Su in his preface to Li Han's collection (*CTW* 518.5b–7b).

12. Li Chou, preface to Tu-ku Chi's collection, *CTW* 443.16a–18a.

13. The phrase here is *ts'ao wen-ping*; Ch'üan Te-yü, preface to Yang Ning's works, *CTW* 489.14b–16b.

14. Ch'üan's father had received extraordinary praise from Li Hua after the rebellion (see *CTS* 148.4001–2); he married his daughter to Tu-ku's son (*HTS* 162.4994).

15. For studies of Li Hua and his successors, see Yao Chi-kuang, "T'ang-tai wen-shih"; Pulleyblank, "Neo-Confucianism and Neo-Legalism"; and esp. McMullen, "Historical and Literary Theory." See also Nienhauser et al., *Liu Tsung-yuan*, pp. 15–25; and Yu-shih Chen, *Images and Ideas*, pp. 4–7. McMullen's study of Li, Hsiao, Tu-ku, Yen Chen-ch'ing (709–84), and Yuan Chieh (719–72) treats the five men as a group. Although Li Hua much admired Yuan's cousin, Yuan Te-hsiu, I do not think Yuan Chieh (whom Han Yü praised) took part in the intellectual project of Li and Tu-ku. I have not found texts by later men that identify Yuan Chieh or Yen Chen-ch'ing (who echoes some of their ideas) as part of the lineage discussed here. Yuan Chieh is frequently seen as a prototypical ku-wen writer, in part because Han Yü listed him as a predecessor (ignoring Li Hua et al.). But Han may have admired Yuan for reasons that would not have appealed to the Li Hua line. Some of Yuan's pre-755 writings were pointedly unconventional and self-consciously archaic. Examples include Yuan's creation of poems to fit the title of poems mentioned in the *Documents* but no longer extant and his introduction to them, his series on the five human relationships, and series of *yueh-fu* (*Yuan Tz'u-shan chi* 1.1, 5.77, 2.18–19). In contrast to Li Hua and others, who looked to the "mid-antiquity" of Confucius, Yuan spoke of "high antiquity" (*t'ai-ku*), a time when men lacked self-consciousness. On the issue of self-consciousness, see also Yuan's "An Account of Myself" (ibid. 5.73–76). These efforts, together with his creation of the persona of "Master Yuan," as he styled himself before 755, seem to have been intended to depict as farce the self-serving use of "antiquity" by political authority; see his introduction to a collection of his literary works (ibid. 8.113, 10.154). The device of stylistic unconventionality for expressing intent sets Yuan apart from Li Hua et al.; I think it also distinguishes him from Han Yü's desire to see style as truly reflecting the self. Han may have taken Yuan at face value or have seen him through the prism of Yen Chen-ch'ing's commemoration of him: "His mind was ancient, his conduct was ancient, and his language was ancient" (ibid., p. 168). In Yuan's post-755 writing unconventionality is less of an issue; Yuan worried that the serious intent of his earlier work would be misconstrued (ibid. 10.154). After 755 he does take up some themes found in Hsiao Ying-shih, Li Hua, and Chia Chih; see his introduction of 761 to his anthology of recent poetry, which speaks both of restoring literary composition and the role of the outsider (ibid. 7.100; in Owen, *Great Age of Chinese Poetry*, pp. 225–26). Cf. *Yuan Tz'u-shan chi* 3.37, an essay from 766.

16. An example of Chang Yueh's adoption of early T'ang ideas about wen-hsueh is an inscription on Lu Ssu-tao (an ancestor of Lu Ts'ang-yung), which defines the "hegemon of wen" as one who "sings of his emotions and character, records affairs, gives an attractive appearance to the Kingly tao, and elucidates the gate of the sages." Chang also lists those famed for wen-hsueh from Confucius

through the Six Dynasties (text in Kao Pu-ying, *T'ang Sung wen chü-yao*, pp. 43–54). Chang Chiu-ling's comments can be found in the grave inscription (*CTW* 292.15a). A few years before the rebellion Yin Fan had restated some of the old attitudes in introducing his anthology of poetry, but, in contrast to the post-rebellion scholars, Yin's aim was to assert that the present moment had succeeded in recuperating those ideas while incorporating recent literary innovations (see Pauline Yu, "Poems in Their Place," pp. 183–90).

17. Li Hua, citing Hsiao, *CTW* 315.7b–9a; see especially Yen Chen-ch'ing writing in 765 (preface to Sun T'i's collection, *CTW* 337.10b–12b). Later, e.g., in Yuan Chen's (779–831) 815 letter to Po Chü-i, Ch'en Tzu-ang's *kan-yü* poems become more important than his role as savior of wen; I have followed the text of the letter in Kuo Shao-yü and Wang Wen-sheng, *Chung-kuo li-tai wen-lun hsuan*, pp. 111–12. For the same reasons, perhaps, Liang Su the insider recognized Chang Yueh, a chief minister, as a precedent in addition to Ch'en Tzu-ang (*CTW* 518.5b–7b).

18. Ch'eng Ch'ien-fan, *T'ang-tai chin-shih hsing-chuan yü wen-hsueh*. The practice of submitting writings before (and even after) the examination to examiners and others apparently dates from the 740's or 750's. Ch'eng's findings have influenced a much longer study: Fu Hsuan-tsung, *T'ang-tai k'o-chü yü wen-hsueh*; see pp. 247–87 for further discussion of the submission of writings outside the examination.

19. *CTW* 323.12a.

20. Li Hua, preface to Hsiao's works, *CTW* 315.8a–9b.

21. In this sense he is close to the early T'ang scholars; see, e.g., his treatment of the "pattern of heaven and man" theme in a piece written before 742 (*CTW* 322.15a).

22. Li Hua, *CTW* 317.7a.

23. Li Hua, preface to Ts'ui Mien's collection (composed after 755), *CTW* 315.4b–5a.

24. Li Hua, *CTW* 317.2b–3a.

25. *CTW* 317.1b–2a. This essay is discussed at greater length in McMullen, "Historical and Literary Theory," pp. 323–24. The inequality between chih and wen is a new conception, one that implies the need for a change of culture rather than the mere addition of balancing interests. Others at the time still spoke in terms of achieving the proper balance of the two, the traditional idea; see, e.g., Yen Chen-ch'ing (*CTW* 337.10b–12b) and Hsiao Ying-shih's clansman Hsiao Li, as cited by Tu-ku Chi (*CTW* 388.2b–4a).

26. His nephew Li Han later called on scholars to use Tu Yu's work as a basis for wen-hsueh (*CTW* 430.8a–10a).

27. *CTW* 477.13a.

28. *CTW* 316.5a.

29. Li Hua, preface to Yang Chi's collection, *CTW* 315.9a. Note also his reference to "*tz'u-jen*" (literary men) who made reputations during Hsuan-tsung's reign for either wen-hsueh or *te-hsing* (*CTW* 315.11a), Hsiao Ying-shih being his example for textual studies and Yuan Te-hsiu for ethical conduct.

30. Li Hua, preface to Ts'ui Mien's works, *CTW* 315.4b–5a. The reference to conduct and wen may allude to *Mencius* 7B.37, on the discrepancy between speech and behavior.

31. For the 735 examination, see Hsu Sung, *Teng-k'o chi k'ao*, p. 275. For Li Hua's appreciation, see "On the Three Worthies," *CTW* 317.3a–7a.

32. Chia Chih, preface to Li Shih's works, *CTW* 368.3a–4b. I have followed the annotated version in Kao Pu-ying, *T'ang Sung wen chü-yao*, pp. 72–78.

33. For Chia's role, see *CTS* 190B.5029–31; for Yang's proposal, see *CTW* 368.1a–3b.

34. Citing Ssu-ma Ch'ien's comments at the end of the Basic Annals of Han Kao-tsu (*Shih chi* 8.393–94).

35. *CTW* 368.1a. The version in Chia's biographhy in *CTS* (190B.5029–31) abridges the text and has the alternative reading: ". . . used wen to choose shih, it was based on conduct."

36. *CTW* 368.1a–3b. I have not covered all parts of Chia's argument. Fifty years later, Po Chü-i and Yuan Chen would develop the idea of returning poetry to its ancient role in transforming society.

37. This problem seems to have thwarted other writers of the day. See, e.g., Ku K'uang's (727–815) essay "On Wen" and Shang Heng's on "The Ultimate Guide to Wen['s] Tao" (*CTW* 529.11a–13a and 394.19a–20b, respectively).

38. Tu-ku names Kao Hsi (Shun's minister for law, Kao Yao) and Shih K'o, whom I cannot identify except as a possible reference to the early Chou sage Shih I.

39. *CTW* 388.11b–12a.

40. *Ch'un-ch'iu ching-chuan yin-te*, Hsiang 25/*fu* 2.

41. Note that Tu-ku did not reject modern literary conventions absolutely, but granted, for example, that the regulated-verse form was an achievement. See his discussion of modern poetics in his preface to Huang-fu Jan's works (*CTW* 388.1a–2b; discussed in Owen, *Great Age of Chinese Poetry*, pp. 254–55).

42. *CTW* 388.12a–b.

43. *CTW* 388.15a.

44. The survival of the High T'ang style in poetry during this period illustrates this, I think, and it is evident that many of the writings found in *CTW* for this period do not serve the reformist cause. For those who saw poetry as the best of literature, the idea of the decline and restoration of wen-chang may well have appeared to deny the value of recent achievements; Chiao-jan's (ca. 734–ca. 791) criticism of Ch'en Tzu-ang and his appreciation for High T'ang poets is a case in point (see Lo Ken-tse, *Sui T'ang Wu-tai wen-hsueh p'i-p'ing shih*, pp. 83–104). Writing about 785, the court literary scholar Yü Shao, while acknowledging the idea of the decline of wen, protests against the denial of value to Hsuan-tsung-era writing it implies and criticizes current literary practice (*CTW* 426.9a–10b). Although at one point (*CTW* 427.17a–b) Yü takes up the writing/conduct problem (perhaps to deny that it is a problem), I take his "admonition for writers" (*CTW* 429.9a) to be more representative of his attitude. Here he argues against trying to give priority to substance over appearance ("How could chih prevail

over wen? How could the wen ever be like the chih?") and asserts the priority of language ("If shih are to establish virtue, they first must refine their use of language [hsiu tz'u]"). This may not be far from Tu-ku's belief that the will must be given particular form through language, but it lacks the kind of tension between moral purpose and acquired forms that informs Tu-ku's work.

45. See the grave stele for Tu-ku written by Ts'ui Yu-fu (721–80), who became a chief minister in 779 (CTW 409.16a–20a). Both Li Chou's preface and Liang Su's postface quote Ts'ui's evaluation of Tu-ku (see CTW 443.16a–18a, 518.3a–5b).

46. For example, see Ts'ui Yuan-han's (ca. 735–ca. 805) letter to Tu-ku, CTW 523.23b–24b.

47. Li Chou, preface to Tu-ku's works, CTW 443.16a–18a.

48. Liang Su, preface to Li Pi's works, CTW 518.1a; cf. preface to Li Han's works, CTW 518.7a.

49. Liang Su, preface to Li Pi's works, CTW 518.1a–b; cf. Liang Su, preface to Pao Chi's works, CTW 518.2b.

50. CTW 518.7a.

51. CTW 518.5b.

52. CTW 518.5b–6a. Liang's reference to ch'i alludes to Ts'ao P'i's slogan, "In wen take ch'i as the main thing"; he thus makes it into a sign of the loss of tao.

53. CTW 518.6a; cf. 518.3b, preface to Tu-ku's works.

54. The phrase "men outside the square" is used by Li Lin-fu, one of Hsuan-tsung's chief ministers (CTW 345.16a–18b). Official patronage of Taoist and Buddhist interests under Hsuan-tsung make clear that such interests were not exceptional. (The use of hsuan for the emperor's posthumous title is a further illustration.) See also the sections on the "three teachings" in answers for the 714 decree examination by Sun T'i and Li Yuan-ch'eng (CTW 310.18b, 331.12b). On the Buddhist-Taoist interests of the Li Hua group, see McMullen, "Historical and Literary Theory," pp. 312–13. See also the contrast between Yao and the Yellow Emperor in a stele by Wang Yen (late eighth century; CTW 545.14b).

55. For an extensive discussion of Liang's Buddhist connections, see Barrett, "Buddhism, Taoism, and Confucianism," pp. 162–80.

56. CTW 519.19a, 520.1a, 518.23a, 520.3a.

57. For example, while acknowledging the value of learning from Taoists how ch'i ties all things together and its role in man, he ridiculed alchemy and immortality practices (CTW 518.25a–26a, 519.10a–11a).

58. CTW 519.10a–b.

59. See Fang Kuan's comments, cited in Chapter 1 as an example of parallel prose (CTW 332.15b).

60. Liang Su, CTW 517.15a–20a; for the reference to Confucius, see 517.19a.

61. CTW 520.1b–2a.

62. CTW 518.23a.

63. Trans. Lau, Lao Tzu, p. 99. The passage ends with a line that Liang apparently ignores: "The rites are the wearing thin of loyalty and good faith."

64. CTW 518.3b–4a.

65. CTW 518.4b.

66. CTW 518.5a–b.

67. My impression is that Ch'üan defends the importance of wen in politics—insisting, for example, that good government "uses the wen of man to transform the world"—and in shih life. He subscribes generally to the notion of decline and restoration and frequently uses the term "ssu-wen" to refer to morally concerned writing both of the Chou and Han periods and of his own times. He does not, however, particularly support the criticism of testing literary craft in the examinations. He is aware of various issues, such as unifying writing and conduct and finding a common moral basis for wen, but does not try to formulate a doctrine of his own. He has an interest in Buddhist and Taoist traditions and in hsing-ming, but apparently does not adopt Liang's idea of wen based in tao. Instead, he tends to focus on the way in which the writing of a particular man reveals to others the character of the author, his tao and "mind source" (hsin yuan). He is conservative and accommodative, choosing to defend the value of wen-hsueh and cultured shih-ta-fu in general and avoiding the divisiveness that would come with a more polemical stance. For his views on decline and restoration, see his prefaces to the collections of Yang Ning (CTW 489.14b–16b), Ts'ui Yuan-han (489.16b–19a), Ts'ui Yu-fu (489.9a–11a), Li Hsi-yun (493.15b–17a), Chang Chien-feng (489.13a–14b), Yao Nan-chung (489.11a–12b), and Ch'üan Jo-na (493.18b–21a). Ch'üan Te-yü's collection includes examination questions, which take up several of the literary and intellectual issues discussed here.

68. My point is that the new "lineage" of literary/moral authority centered on Han Yü ignored Li Hua et al., although Han Yü and members of his circle acknowledged the importance of Li Hua and Liang Su, and there is some debate whether Li taught Han's uncle and brother (see Hartman, Han Yü, pp. 22, 284n22).

69. Owen, Meng Chiao and Han Yü, p. 27.

70. Po Chü-i, "Ts'e lin" no. 61, Po Chü-i chi 65.1361–62.

71. Li Ao, letter to Chu Tsai-yen, in Kuo Shao-yü and Wang Wen-sheng, Chung-kuo li-tai wen-lun hsuan, pp. 164–66.

72. CTW 483.6b–8a.

73. CTW 684.26a–27b.

74. Li Ao, CTW 640.8a–b; Huang-fu Shih, in Kuo Shao-yü and Wang Wen-sheng, Chung-kuo li-tai wen-lun hsuan, p. 121, cf. pp. 134–35.

75. This can be traced through the comments on Han Yü collected in Wu Wen-chih, Han Yü tzu-liao hui-pien, I: 1–68.

76. With regard to both these matters, I am deeply indebted to Hartman, Han Yü.

77. See ibid., chap. 4; and more recently, Yu-shih Ch'en, Images and Ideas, pp. 15–70.

78. Owen, Meng Chiao and Han Yü, p. 44 ("Poem of Hsieh Tzu-jan").

79. Ibid., p. 46 ("Thick Clouds: A Poem to Li Kuan Who Is Sick," ca. 792).

80. See, e.g., ibid., p. 75 ("How Sad This Day: A Poem to Chang Chi") and p. 251 ("Song of the Stone Drums").

81. See, e.g., ibid., pp. 190–95 ("Answering Chang Ch'e") and pp. 198–205 ("South Mountains"); cf. pp. 213–23. See also "Explaining Progress in Learning" (dated 812), in HCLC 3.12.77–79; and Hightower, "Han Yü as a Humorist."

82. Han Yü rejected claims to status by birth in his other writings as well; see

Ge Xiaoyin, "Relationship," pp. 176–80. For a poem on this theme, see Owen, *Meng Chiao and Han Yü*, pp. 271–73 ("[My Son] Fu Is Reading Books South of the City").

83. For a thorough discussion of the many ways in which Han Yü was not exceptional, see McMullen, "Han Yü," pp. 603–57. McMullen effectively challenges the Sung Neo-Confucian qualities attributed to Han in Hartman's *Han Yü*. Han was friends with Li Hua's son Li Kuan, passed the 792 examination in which Liang Su served as advisor, was acquainted with Hsiao Ying-shih's son, and had connections with Ch'üan Te-yü. The language of his brother Han Hui's (739–80) essay "Balance of Wen" (dated 780) has many similarities to Liang Su's preface to Tu-ku Chi's collection and Liang's discussion of *chih kuan* meditation. It also suggests a discomfort with the implications of basing wen on a tao located outside the cultural tradition. For the text of the essay and an account of Han Hui's life, see *Ch'üan T'ang wen chi-shih* 39.504; for a translation, see Hartman, *Han Yü*, pp. 228–29.

84. Reply to Liu Cheng-fu, *HCLC* 18.81.

85. "Sheng-jen chih tao" can mean the way of the sages (the way that is known from the cumulative accomplishments of all the sages) and the way of the sage (referring either to Confucius as the sage or to the values that were common to all the sages and that thus guide any sage). For Han Yü the way is singular, but in later periods some did mean "the ways of the sages" and suppose that the sages had various ways.

86. Farewell preface for Ch'en T'ung, *HCLC* 5.20.23; cf. Hartman, *Han Yü*, pp. 221–22. The key verb here is *wei* (to do, engage in, realize).

87. Han's answer on the decree examination of 794 that uses the phrase "sheng-jen chih tao" still seems to be somewhat in the thrall of the idea that to be a sage means that no error arises in the mind (*HCLC* 4.14.32–33; cf. Hartman, *Han Yü*, pp. 200–202).

88. *CTW* 684.26a–27b.

89. *HCLC* 4.14.38–40; cf. Hartman, *Han Yü*, pp. 37, 161–62.

90. *HCLC* 4.14.20–21. See also his letter to Meng Chien (*HCLC* 4.18.83–86), defending the analogy between Yang and Mo and Taoism and Buddhism.

91. *HCLC* 3.12.75–77; cf. Hartman, *Han Yü*, pp. 162–64, who translates tao as "tradition" in this text.

92. The phrase "sheng-jen chih tao," in Han's sense, does not appear in early T'ang writing or in the writings of Li Hua et al. Nor is the phrase common in late Chou doctrinal texts. Yang Hsiung's *Exemplary Sayings* does, however, often discuss the sages in conjunction with tao and contains at least one instance in which the phrase is used in a manner close to Han's: "Those who like to give all their attention to the sheng-jen chih tao are superior men" (Yang Hsiung, *Fa-yen i-shu* 10.2a). I have seen the phrase used in earlier times for the way of the Buddha (Mather, *Poet Shen Yüeh*, p. 164). Liu Mien uses the phrase in a letter to Ch'üan Te-yü, but it is not clear that this written before 798.

93. These points are made in Ge Xiaoyin, "Relationship," pp. 180–82.

94. *HCLC* 5.20.23–24; cf. Hartman, *Han Yü*, pp. 179–80.

95. *HCLC* 3.11.74; cf. Hartman, *Han Yü*, pp. 152–53.

96. *HCLC* 3.11.72–73; cf. Hartman, *Han Yü*, pp. 181–82.

97. This is stated in the essay "Finding the Source for Tao," discussed below.

98. *HCLC* 3.12.76; cf. Hartman, *Han Yü*, p. 164.

99. *HCLC* 4.18.80–81; cf. Hartman, *Han Yü*, pp. 253–56.

100. *HCLC* 3.11.59–63; discussed in Hartman, *Han Yü*, pp. 145–62, who sees 805 as the probable date of the essay; most of the text is translated in de Bary, *Sources of Chinese Tradition*, 1: 376–79. For a thoroughly annotated discussion, see Kao Pu-ying, *Tang Sung wen chü-yao*, pp. 143–56.

101. *HCLC* 3.11.60.

102. Yang Hsiung, *Fa-yen i-shu* 6.4b.

103. See, e.g., various writings by Ch'üan Te-yü, *CTW* 490.4a, 491.5a–b, 494.13a, 495.12a.

104. *LTYC* 21.569–71.

105. Han's pairing in 798 of Tu Fu (712–70) with the better-known Li Po (705–62) as the two great poets is an example; see Hartman, *Han Yü*, pp. 38–39; Kuo Shao-yü and Wang Wen-sheng, *Chung-kuo li-tai wen-lun hsuan*, pp. 129, 131.

106. *HCLC* 5.19.7–8; cf. Hartman, *Han Yü*, pp. 230–32.

107. *HCLC* 8.*i-wen*.21; following Hartman, *Han Yü*, pp. 199–200. "Fulfill the body" is from *Mencius* 7A.38; Han insists the process is cumulative and gradual, against Mencius's claim that only the sage can accomplish this.

108. Preface for the monk Kao-hsien, *HCLC* 5.21.28–29; cf. Hartman, *Han Yü*, pp. 222–23.

109. *HCLC* 5.20.19; cf. Hartman, *Han Yü*, pp. 147–50. The account of the sheng-jen chih tao in this piece corresponds to "Finding the Source for Tao."

110. *HCLC* 4.15.44–45; trans. Hartman, *Han Yü*, pp. 218–19, modified.

111. At various points throughout his study, Hartman argues that ch'eng occupies a central place in Han's understanding of how wen and tao can be unified. Han's gloss on the term, *pu-ch'i* (not deceiving), suggests to me that Han did not reify the concept to the degree Li Ao did in "Returning to the Innate Nature" (discussed below). For Han's gloss and a further example of the internal/external polarity, see *HCLC* 4.16.62–63.

112. *HCLC* 3.12.76–77; cf. Hartman, *Han Yü*, p. 164.

113. See, e.g., *HCLC* 4.16.61–62, 5.22.47; cf. Hartman, *Han Yü*, pp. 221, 213. I disagree with the claim (Hartman, p. 213) that Han is proposing a dialectic between style and tao, preferring to translate "One who comprehends their style has grounded his will in the ancient tao" (vs. Hartman's "Mastery of their style is basic for those whose goal is the Ancient Way").

114. Hartman, *Han Yü*, p. 248.

115. *HCLC* 4.16.58–59; cf. Hartman, *Han Yü*, pp. 241–47. A simpler version, from 798, appears in Han's letter to Feng Su (see Hartman, pp. 37–38).

116. *HCLC* 4.18.80–81; cf. Hartman, *Han Yü*, pp. 254–55.

117. *Lun yü* 4.15; cf. 15.3.

118. Preface, *HCLC*.

119. Second letter to Hou Kao, *LWKC* 7.51a.

120. Letter to his nephew, *LWKC* 8.63b–64b.

121. "Miscellaneous Theories," *LWKC* 5.32b–33a.

122. Ibid.

123. Barrett, "Buddhism, Taoism, and Confucianism," pp. 212, 278–88. My comments are based on Barrett's translation and commentary, pp. 217–73; for the original, see *LWKC* 2.1a–13b.

124. "On Getting Rid of Buddhist Masses," *LWKC* 4.23a.

125. See, e.g., "On Following Tao" (*LWKC* 4.20a–21b); Li's letter to the official Lu (8.59b); and his letter to Huang-fu Shih (6.38b–40b).

126. Letter to Huang-fu Shih, *LWKC* 6.40a.

127. I have followed the text in Kuo Shao-yü and Wang Wen-sheng, *Chung-kuo li-tai wen-lun hsuan*, pp. 164–66.

128. Ibid., p. 166.

129. Ibid.

130. The case for the influence of Tan Chu (725–70) and his successors on Liu is made in Tozaki, "Ryō Sō-gen." Lu Ch'un writes, for example, that "the mind of Confucius was the mind of Yao and Shun; the tao of Confucius was the tao of Yao and Shun" to explain that the wen of the *Annals*, even when at odds with the rules of ritual, was still the product of a "will that agrees with tao" (*CTW* 618.4a–5a). One of Liu's letters suggests that he began to take Lu Ch'un's work seriously well after he had first seen it, at which point he already knew Han Yü (letter to Yuan on the *Ch'un-chiu*, *LTYC* 31.818–20.

131. See Ch'en Jo-shui, "Dawn of Neo-Confucianism."

132. Letter to Yang P'ing, *LTYC* 30.789–91.

133. Ibid.

134. *LTYC* 34.871–74.

135. Letter to Lü Wen (809), *LTYC* 31.822–23. Two letters suggest Liu was not entirely persuaded that Lü's manner of "speaking about tao" in doctrinal terms was appropriate; see letter to Wu Wu-ling (*LTYC* 31.824–25) and letter to Yen Hou-yü (*LTYC* 34.878–80).

136. On Liu's use of the latter terms, see Ch'en Jo-shui, "Dawn of Neo-Confucianism," pp. 121–22. For an example of his interchangeable use of these terms, see his letter to Lü Wen, *LTYC* 31.822–23.

137. See Lamont, "Early Ninth Century Debate"; and Ch'en Jo-shui, "Dawn of Neo-Confucianism," pp. 129–55.

138. Liu did think that the church should stay out of politics and Ch'an monks should adhere to the rules of discipline (Ch'en Jo-shui, "Dawn of Neo-Confucianism," pp. 231–41).

139. *LTYC* 44.1265.

140. *LTYC* 31.822–25.

141. "Rhapsody on Correcting Faults," *LTYC* 2.54; cf. Gentzler, "Literary Biography," pp. 140–44.

142. "Rhapsody on Correcting Faults," *LTYC* 2.54; cf. Gentzler, "Literary Biography," pp. 140–44.

143. Second letter to Yang Hui-chih, *LTYC* 33.852–83.

144. First letter to Yang Hui-chih, *LTYC* 33.848.

145. Second letter to Yang Hui-chih, *LTYC* 33.850–51.

146. Letter to a friend on literary practice, *LTYC* 31.829–30.

147. Letter to Ts'ui An on doing wen, *LTYC* 34.886–87.

148. *LTYC* 34.871–74; for an account of the letter, see his reply to Yüan Chün-ch'en, *LTYC* 34.880–81.

149. *CTW* 527.14b–15a. Liu Mien is usually treated as a predecessor of Han Yü; he was perhaps contemporary with Liang Su. How much of his writing on wen and tao dates from before the late 790's is unclear. In any case, he lived through the years in which the new rhetoric was spreading and illustrates one possible response to it.

150. Liu Mien, letter to Ch'üan Te-yü (806), *CTW* 527.5a.

151. Liu Mien, letter to Yang, *CTW* 527.18a.

152. Liu Mien, letter to P'ei, *CTW* 527.14b.

153. Liu Mien, letter to Chief Minister Tu Huang-shang (ca. 806), *CTW* 827.7a–9a.

154. Liu Mien, letter to Cheng, *CTW* 527.18a–b.

155. *CTW* 527.6a–b. For Ch'üan's reply, rejecting the ignoring of the commentaries, see *CTW* 489.9b.

156. Liu Mien, reply to Yü-wen, *CTW* 527.9a–12a. Ssu-ma Ch'ien is Liu's example of someone who has not done it. Ssu-ma may have continued the "will of the sage," but "he did not apprehend the tao of the sage" because he did not follow the *Spring and Autumn Annals* in writing his history. "He did not base it in the moral instructions of the ju and unify the rules for the true king." Whereas the *Annals* "valued antiquity," Ssu-ma "transformed antiquity."

157. Liu Mien, reply to P'ei, *CTW* 527.13a.

158. *LTYC* 31.823–24.

159. *CTW* 625.3a.

160. Quoting *Ta hsueh* 3.

161. Lü Wen, letter to his cousin on the *Annals*, *CTW* 627.15b.

162. Ibid.

163. *CTW* 628.17b–18a.

Chapter 5

1. T'ien Hsi, *Hsien-p'ing chi* 2.13a; Hsia Sung, *Wen-chuang chi* 15.4b; and Hsu Hsuan, *Hsu ch'i-sheng chi* 23.230.

2. *IS* 18.239; Yu Tso, *Yu Chih-shan chi* 1.7b.

3. *Sung shih* 439.12997. With the exception of Liu K'ai and Mu Hsiu, the figures mentioned here do not have biographies in this section. The point of view of this introduction is restated in the introduction to the "Treatise on Bibliography" (202.5031–34). The *Sung Shih* does not introduce the collected ju biographies, but it does the Tao-hsueh biographies. One twelfth-century history—Wang Ch'eng's *Tung-tu shih-lueh*—still understood learning in terms of wen and ju and gives ku-wen the major role in early Sung intellectual trends (see 113.1a–b, 115.1a–b).

4. Fumoto, *Hoku-sō*, p. 33, quoting Yeh Meng-te. Note a 963 edict stipulating that henceforth military governors could recommend personal staff for entry into ranked office only if they had served two terms and "had wen-hsueh" (Ma Tuan-lin, *Wen-hsien t'ung-k'ao* 38.357c).

5. *Hsu tzu-chih t'ung-chien ch'ang-pien* 18.394; cf. Chaffee, *Thorny Gates of Learning*, p. 179. Yeh Meng-te (*Shih-lin yen-yü* 5.12a) also attributes the expansion of the examinations to T'ai-tsung's "intention to pursue wen." Note also Wang Ch'eng's comment (*Tung-tu shih-lueh* 3.103) that T'ai-tsung had "broadened the wen influence and finished the military achievement, thus enlarging the unification." The identification of T'ai-tsu with military achievement and T'ai-tsung with wen is found in eleventh-century sources as well; see Han Ch'i, *An-yang chi* 41.1b, in the eulogy for Jen-tsung, and idem, 22.6b, on the theme of military founding and civil preservation in "Preface to the Record of Three Reigns of Sage [Emperors]."

6. *SHY*, "ch'ung ju" 18.50a, for 978/2. This was in imitation of the T'ang's Ch'ung-wen kuan (see Chapter 3). On the early Sung academic institutes, see Ch'en Le-su, *Ch'iu shih chi*, 2: 4–5.

7. Cited in *Yü hai* 38.31.

8. *SHY*, "hsuan-chü" 7.3b–4a. For a list of palace examination themes from the beginning of the dynasty through the 1060's, see Chin Chung-shu, "Pei-sung k'o-chü chih-tu yen-chiu tsai-hsu," pp. 142–48.

9. Yao Hsuan, *T'ang wen ts'ui*, preface 1a.

10. Examples of the patronage of court scholarship follow. For surveys including useful material on the first half-century of the Sung, see Fumoto, *Hoku-sō*; Liu Po-chi, *Sung-tai cheng-chiao shih*; and Chang Shun-hui, "Lun Sung-tai hsueh-che." For a chronology of early court scholarship, see Mai Chung-kuei, *Sung Yuan li-hsueh*, pp. 1–43.

11. Fan Tsu-yü, *Ti hsueh* 3.1a–3b. Chiang Shao-yü's more extensive and anecdotal account of the Northern Sung, *Sung-ch'ao shih-shih lei-yuan* (1145), gives a fuller record of T'ai-tsu's military achievements but arranges the material to suggest that these were from the start subordinated to his civil and cultural interests (see *chüan* 1).

12. For the book-collecting program, see *SHY*, "ch'ung ju" 4.15a–16b. For the start of this program, see 4.15b for 966/*jun*8; painting and calligraphy, see 4.15b for 977/10 and 981/12; libraries of conquered states, see 4.15b for 976/9; rewards, see 4.15a for 966/*jun*8 and 4.15b for 981/12; T'ang model, see 4.16a for 984/1; T'ai-tsung's comments, see 4.16a–b for 984/1. For the history of the library and its contents, see in *SHY*, "chih-kuan" 18.50a. Aspects of this are mentioned in Haeger, "Significance of Confusion."

13. Liu Po-chi, *Sung-tai cheng-chiao shih*, pp. 1168–70. For a brief account of Five Dynasties (and Sung) period printing, see Tsien, *Paper and Printing*, pp. 151–63. See also Chang Shun-hui, "Lun Sung-tai hsueh-che," pp. 79–105. For a somewhat more detailed account of Sung publishing, see Li Chih-chung, "Sung-tai k'o-shu shu-lueh."

14. See Mai Chung-kuei, *Sung Yuan li-hsueh*, under these dates.

15. Loon, *Taoist Books*, pp. 29–35.

16. All these works are extant. For a full account of all except the *Prescriptions*, see Kuo Po-kung, *Sung ssu ta-shu k'ao*. For a summary account of all five, see Fumoto, *Hoku-sō*, pp. 24–29. Haeger ("Significance of Confusion") discusses the preparation of the *Imperial Reader* and its sources. Haeger (pp. 406–8) suggests the work (which was not published until 1023) was a manifestation of T'ai-tsung's "bibliomania." I suggest that the Sung, like the T'ang, was trying to sort out the cultural tradition. Plans were made to print the *Extensive Accounts* immediately on completion, but publication was halted by objections that the material was not of the first importance for students (see Kuo, p. 66). The *Ts'e-fu yuan-kuei* was printed in 1015 (Kuo, p. 129). The *Finest Blossoms* was not published until the Southern Sung (Kuo, p. 95). There seems to have been some dissatisfaction with the contents of this anthology, for a revision was ordered in 1007 (see Mai Chung-kuei, *Sung Yuan li-hsueh*, under 1007).

17. *Ts'e-fu yuan-kuei*, introductory material, p. 9.

18. Fan Tsu-yü, *Ti hsueh* 3.3b–4.5b. Chiang Shao-yü's *Sung-ch'ao shih-shih lei-yuan* gives a richer account of T'ai-tsung as a cultured man.

19. *SHY*, "ch'ung ju" 6.5a, for 1014/11.

20. For the gifts of calligraphy, see ibid., 6.4a; for a listing of his works, see 6.5b–6a.

21. Ibid., 6.4b.

22. For the contents of the exams in all fields, the Five Dynasties models, and the earliest Sung changes, see Chin Chung-shu, "Pei-sung k'o-chü chih-tu yen-chiu," pt. I, pp. 2–12; and idem, "Pei-sung k'o-chü chih-tu yen-chiu hsu," pt. I, pp. 105–6. The most notable change was the addition of factual questions on the law. These comments apply to the department examination; the palace exam tested only the ability to compose a poem, rhapsody, and essay.

23. The candidates' mastery of the tradition is not clear, nor do we know what they were expected to know about non-classical texts. Hung Mai (*Jung chai sui-pi* 3.31) notes that early Sung candidates did not always understand the point of the assigned theme or recognize its original context (they were allowed to ask the examiner) and in some cases they brought books into the examination hall. This is confirmed by an edict from 1005 (*SHY*, "hsuan-chü" 1.7b–8a). Yeh Meng-te (*Shih-lin yen-yü* 8.3a–b) notes that eventually the passages from the histories and Classics that provided the themes were printed and distributed to candidates before the test. Both Yeh and Hung were speaking of the palace exam.

24. For the changes of the 1070's and later restorations of the poetry requirement, see Chaffee, *Thorny Gates of Learning*, pp. 213–18; and Chin Chung-shu, "Pei-sung k'o-chü chih-tu yen-chiu," pt. I, pp. 47–70, and pt. II; and idem, "Pei-sung k'o-chü chih-tu yen-chiu hsu," pt. I, pp. 107–10. For most of the Southern Sung, a literary and a Classics chin-shih examination were held simultaneously; the first attracted the vast majority of candidates (Chaffee, p. 217).

25. This list is found in *Wen-hsieh t'ung-k'ao* 30.284a, and elsewhere; cf. discussions in Araki, *Sōdai kakyo seido*, p. 286; Chin Chung-shu, "Pei-sung k'o-chü chih-tu yen-chiu," pt. I, pp. 3–8; and idem, "Pei-sung k'o-chü chih-tu yen-chiu hsu," pt. I, pp. 110–23. There are no figures for the "various fields" as a whole before 972.

26. Chin Chung-shu, "Pei-sung k'o-chü chih-tu yen-chiu," pt. I, pp. 10–12; idem, "Pei-sung k'o-chü chih-tu yen-chiu hsu," pt. I, p. 124. The rules are given in the edict promulgating the new field in 1057/12; see *Hsu tzu-chih t'ung-chien ch'ang-pien* 186.4496.

27. Chaffee, *Thorny Gates of Learning*, pp. 51–52. The policy of covering the candidate's name began at the palace exam in 992, at the department exam in 1007, and in the prefectures in 1032. The recopying of papers to prevent the examiners from recognizing a candidate by his handwriting began at the palace and depart-ment levels in 1015 and in the prefectures in 1037. See also Araki, *Sōdai kakyo seido*, pp. 243–64.

28. See *Sung shih* 155.3607; and the discussion in Chin Chung-shu, "Pei-sung k'o-chü chih-tu yen-chiu," pt. I, pp. 9–10.

29. Chaffee, *Thorny Gates of Learning*, p. 34.

30. Much of this section is based on the extant literary collections from the per-iod. I have not tried to spell out the intellectual positions of figures for whom an adequate body of writings is lacking, for example, Wang Ch'in-jo (962–1025), Ting Wei (962–1033), and K'ou Chun (961–1023), all of whom served as both polit-ical and intellectual leaders. I was led to many of these texts by the selections in Huang Ch'i-fang, *Pei-sung wen-hsueh p'i-p'ing*. Many of the same texts appear in full in T'ao Ch'iu-ying and Yü Hsing, *Sung Chin Yuan wen-lun*. Some of the figures discussed are also treated in Chin Chung-shu, "Sung-tai ku-wen yun-tung." A particularly useful study of this period is Shang T'ao, "Pei-sung shih-ch'i."

31. Examples include Liang Chou-han's twenty "Wu-feng-lou fu" from 963–68, cited in *Yü hai* 59.25b (one of which is in *Sung wen hui*, pp. 127–28), for which he was promoted; Tiao K'an's "Sheng-te sung" of 977 or 978, cited in *Yü hai* 60.28b, for which he was reinstated in office; various commemorations of the conquest from 979 cited by Mai Chung-kuei, *Sung Yuan li-hsueh*, including works by Wang Ch'in-jo (then in his eighteenth year), T'ien Hsi, and Sung Po (these are noted in *Sung shih* 283.9559; *Yü hai* 59.12b and 60.28b, respectively); and works by Liang Ting and Ts'ui Tsun-tu from 988 cited in *Yü hai* 60.28b–29a.

32. Examples cited by Mai Chung-kuei, *Sung Yuan li-hsueh*, include Chang Chi-hsien, who submitted ten proposals in 977/1; Sun Ho's five proposals of 997/9; Ch'en P'eng-nien's five-point memorial of 1001; and Wang Yü-ch'eng's five-point memorial of 997/12 (I have been unable to locate the text of Chang's proposals; for the others, see *Hsu tzu-chih t'ung-chien ch'ang-pien* 42.881–83, 48.1046–50, and 42.896–900, respectively).

33. Examples cited by Mai Chung-kuei, *Sung Yuan li-hsüeh*, include T'ien Hsi's 981/9 remonstrance (see *Sung shih* 293.9787–88), for which he was given a large cash reward; Wang Yü-ch'eng's remonstrance of 988 (*Yü hai* 59.39b), and Chu Ang's three-*chüan* critique of 1001 (*SHY*, "ch'ung ju" 5.20).

34. See memorials by Chao P'u, T'ien Hsi, and Chang Chi-hsien in *Sung wen hui*, pp. 453, 456, and 458.

35. Examples include T'ien Hsi in 984, Wang Yü-ch'eng in 988, Wang Hua-chi in 991, and Lü Meng-cheng in 994 (see Shang T'ao, "Pei-sung shih-ch'i," pp. 550–51).

36. T'ien Hsi, famed for his frank advice, modeled himself on Wei Cheng, the noted counselor of T'ang T'ai-tsung (*Sung shih* 293.9787–92); Wang Yü-ch'eng also looked to T'ang (ibid. 293.9799–800).

37. Although in 981 T'ien Hsi was rewarded for remonstrating with the emperor, in 982 his comments were not even acknowledged. Wang Yü-ch'eng was demoted in 998 for the judgments he injected into the Veritable Record of T'ai-tsu's reign (*Hsu tzu-chih t'ung-chien ch'ang-pien* 43.923).

38. A case has been made for seeing Sun Shih (962–1033) as a link between the ku-wen writers active in the 990's and the ku-wen reformers of the 1030's and 1040's. Sun's proposals on ritual, his attack on Chen-tsung's Taoistic interests, his short commentary on the *Mencius* (done at imperial command), and his establishment of an endowed local school can all be seen as precursors of mid-eleventh-century trends. However, Sun Shih, who specialized in ritual, was not among those the famous men of the 1030's looked back to; by their own account they drew inspiration from Liu K'ai, Mu Hsiu, T'ien Hsi, Chang Yung, and Wang Yü-ch'eng. On Sun, see Yoshihara, "Sōgaku hattenjo." Although much research remains to be done on Classical studies during the first half of the Northern Sung, Chin Chung-shu has surveyed numerous developments in his four-part series "Sung-tai ching-hsueh tang-tai-hua."

39. The role of officials excelling in wen-hsueh in the Northern Sung government was substantial. Taking the two positions normally filled by men with reputations for wen-hsueh, academician (*hsueh-shih*) and rescript writers (*chih-chih-kao*), we find that 2 of T'ai-tsung's 9 chief councillors held these posts, as did 7 of Chen-tsung's 12, and 14 of Jen-tsung's 23. These figures are based on the listing of high-office holders in Li Chih, *Huang Sung shih ch'ao kang-yao*, chüan 2–4.

40. T'ai-tsung's was "a court that valued wen," in the eyes of Wang Yü-ch'eng (*Hsiao ch'u chi*, 19.5b). Others described the first two reigns as eras of "transformation through *wen-ming*" (see, e.g., Hsu Hsuan, *Hsu ch'i-sheng chi* 23.230; T'ien Hsi, *Hsien-p'ing chi* 3.14a; and Chang Yung, *Kuai-yai chi* 10.11a).

41. *Hsu tzu-chih t'ung-chien ch'ang-pien*, 71.2a–b; cf. Shang T'ao, "Pei-sung shih-ch'i," p. 553.

42. Hsu Hsuan, preface to poems, *Hsu ch'i-sheng chi* 18.185–86.

43. Ibid. 18.185.

44. See, e.g., Ch'en P'eng-nien's (961–1017) evaluation of Hsu in his 993 preface to Hsu's collected literary writings, the "record of conduct," and Li Fang's (925–96) funerary biography of Hsu (all in front matter, *Hsu ch'i-sheng chi*). For Hsu's own concern with saving This Culture of Ours, see the various prefaces in *chüan* 18 of his collection.

45. Hsu Hsuan, preface to Wang's collection, *Hsu ch'i-sheng chi* 23.230.

46. T'ien Hsi, *Hsien-p'ing chi* 9.2a–b.

47. Chang Yung, "Recorded Sayings," *Kuai-yai chi* 12.1a.

48. For their biographies, see *Sung shih* 293.9787–92, 9800–804. Fan Chung-yen wrote T'ien Hsi's funerary biography, and Su Shih later wrote a preface to his collection comparing him to Chia I (see *Hsien-p'ing-chi*, front matter). Han Ch'i (1008–75) wrote a grave stele for Chang Yung; see *Kuai-yai chi*, appendix. For

evidence of their acquaintance, see Chang's "farewell preface" for T'ien, *Kuai-yai chi* 8.13a.

49. T'ien Hsi, letter to Ch'en Chi-ho, *Hsien-p'ing chi* 2.9a–10b; Chang Yung, preface to a poetry collection, *Kuai-yai chi* 8.14b–16b.

50. Chang Yung, reply to a student's query on wen, *Kuai-yai chi* 7.14b–15a.

51. Chang Yung, memorial submitting his writings, *Kuai-yai chi* 10.11a.

52. Chang Yung, reply to the chin-shih Feng Hua, *Kuai-yai chi* 7.3a–b. For the self-image, see his accounts of himself in letters to the Chief Councillor and Su yuan-wai-lang, ibid. 7.1a–2b, 3b–5a. His biography explains that the title he selected for his collection meant that he "went against the crowd" (*kuai*) and "did not seek personal gain" (*yai*, i.e., keeping within bounds).

53. Chang Yung, *Kuai-yai chi* 7.3a–b. Chang's "Biography of Earl Tree" (ibid., 6.6a–7b) is an imitation of Han Yü's "Biography of Fur-point."

54. T'ien Hsi, letter to Tu, *Hsien-p'ing chi* 3.1a–2b. Chang seems to be less willing to accept a disjunction between "conduct" and wen, asking that one "practice what he says"; see Chang Yung, *Kuai-yai chi* 10.11a.

55. T'ien Hsi, letters to Sung Po, Ho Shih-tsung, and Liang Chou-han, *Hsien-p'ing chi* 2.11b–12a, 3.14b, 15a.

56. Chang Yung, *Kuai-yai chi* 7.15a.

57. Ibid. 8.15a.

58. For the new *Imperial Reader* and a shorter collection of aphorisms for the emperor, see *Sung shih* 293.9787–92. For T'ien's own learning, see letter to Ho Shih-tsung, *Hsien-p'ing chi* 3.12b–14b.

59. T'ien Hsi, *Hsien-p'ing chi* 2.9b.

60. Ibid. 2.10b–13a.

61. Examples of younger men with such views include Lo Ch'u-yueh (960–92), from a T'ang official family that had served the state of Shu in Szechuan, who advocated discarding the institutions the Sung had inherited from the late T'ang and Five Dynasties period military governments and returning to antiquity (see the memorial attacking the Finance Commission in his biography in the *Sung shih* 440.13033–35). Yet his essay "On Huang-Lao Being Prior to the Six Classics" asserted the equality of the Yellow Emperor and Lao-tzu with the Duke of Chou and Confucius and defined tao as "a term for nothingness [*wu*]: that which nothing does not proceed through" to make the point that men should recognize a common and universal basis rather than arguing over particularistic definitions or "traces of tao" (*Sung shih* 440.13032–33). The essay argues that this was Ssu-ma Ch'ien's position, but Lo was also defending the Shu court tradition of Taoist learning, in which Taoist masters such as Tu Kuang-t'ing had played leading roles. Note also Hsia-hou Chia-cheng's (ca. 953–ca. 989) rhapsody on Tung-t'ing lake and Ts'ui Tsun-tu's (954–1020) essay on the lute (*Sung shih* 440.13028–31, 441.13063–65). A short book by Ch'ao Chiung (951–1034), the literary court scholar and founder of the Ch'ao family discussed in Chapter 2, is even clearer. Ch'ao writes for those "learning tao." In the introduction he states his desire to draw on both ju and Buddhist traditions and, the content shows, the Taoist tradition as well. For, as he asserts later, the Three Teachings may be separate

traditions, but "their content is all tao" (*Chao-te hsin-pien*, A.3a, cf. 9b, 19a). In this work one learns tao to achieve internal stability in a world that cannot satisfy one's desires. To act impartially and responsibly requires detachment from things in order to control one's emotional responses.

62. On the issuing of the edict, see *Hsu tzu-chih t'ung-chien ch'ang-pien* 60.1342–44. For the edict itself, see *SHY*, "hsuan-chü" 1.7b–8a. For a contemporary discussion of the edict and one response to it, see Hsia Sung, *Wen-chuang chi* 24.3a–5b.

63. For the edict of 1009 see *Sung ta-ch'ao-ling chi* 101.701. According to Shih Chieh (*Ts'u-lai Shih hsien-sheng wen-chi* 18.219), this was issued in response to the increasing literary influence of Yang I. On the heavenly letters and related matters, see Cahill, "Taoism at the Sung Court." The tenor of the court is suggested in Chen-tsung's commission of the *Treasured Canons of Ch'ien and K'un* (*Ch'ien k'un pao-tien*), a record of cosmological affairs.

64. Yang's biography, *Sung shih* 305.11083.

65. Yang I, farewell preface for Ch'en Tsai-chung and preface for Sung Po's (Kuang-p'ing kung) collection of poems, *Wu-i hsin-chi*, 7.3a–5a, 13b–14a.

66. Yang I, farewell preface for Yuan Tao-tsung and preface to Nieh Mao-yuan's "Yun-t'ang" collection, *Wu-i hsin-chi* 7.21b–23a, 1a–3a.

67. See Yang's preface to his *Wu-i hsin-chi* and the *Hsi-k'un ch'ou-ch'ang chi*.

68. Yang I, preface to Nieh Mao-yuan's "Yung-chia" collection, *Wu-i hsin-chi* 7.8a–9b.

69. See, e.g., his discussion of examinations in a question for the decree examination of 1101; *Wu-i hsin-chi* 12.2b–3a.

70. The attack on the Hsi-k'un style as crafted elegance bereft of moral content is part of most accounts of Sung ku-wen, thanks largely to Shih Chieh's outlandish attack on Yang. The weakness of this story as an account of Sung poetry (but not of Sung prose) has been most recently noted by Michael Fuller ("Review of Ronald C. Egan"). A sensible early account of the entire affair, touching on Yang's anthology, his contribution as a literary scholar, Ch'eng Ts'ung-i's criticism of Yang's influence on wen in 1019, and Shih Chieh's later attack, is a short entry in T'ien K'uang (1003–61), *Ju-lin kung-i* 3a–3b. For an account of the figures included in the *Hsi-k'un Collection*, see Ch'en Chih-o, "Hsi-k'un ch'ou-ch'ang shih-jen."

71. For Hsia's 1007 decree examination, see Wang Te-i, "Sung-tai hsien-liang fang-cheng k'o k'ao," p. 180. For the question and answer, see Hsia Sung, *Wen-chuang chi* 12.1a–3a.

72. Hsia Sung, *Wen-chuang chi* 24.3b–5b.

73. Ibid. 25.8b.

74. Hsia Sung, answer for the decree examination of 1007, *Wen-chuang chi* 12.1a.

75. See his biography in *Sung shih* 440.13023–28.

76. Liu K'ai, *Ho-tung hsien-sheng chi* 2.1a–5a.

77. Ibid. 2.5a–9a, quoting 2.5b.

78. Liu's addition of Wang T'ung may have occurred after his next name change, see letter to Tsang Ping, in ibid. 6.1a.

79. This chronology of Liu's early writing is based on the record of conduct by his disciple Chang Ching and Liu's 972 letter to Liang Chou-han; see *Ho-tung hsien-sheng chi*, appendix and 5.13a–15b. Liu's two youthful books were no longer extant when Chang wrote the biography.

80. Liu K'ai, third letter to Wang Hu, *Ho-tung hsien-sheng chi* 5.5a–8a.

81. Liu K'ai, fourth letter to Wang Hu, *Ho-tung hsien-sheng chi* 5.8a–9b.

82. Liang Chou-han (929–1009) objects on these grounds; see Liu's reply to Liang, dated 972, in *Ho-tung hsien-sheng chi* 5.13a–15b. His disciple and biographer's insistence that Liu had mastered the Classics before he encountered Han Yü, even if he ignored the commentaries, the hundred schools, and literary and historical writing of the Han through the T'ang, suggests a need to forestall the objection that Liu's position was narrow, derivative, and uninformed by the cultural tradition (Chang Ching, record of conduct [1b], in Liu K'ai, *Ho-tung hsien-sheng chi*, appendix).

83. See the memorial included in his biography in *Sung shih* 440.13025–27.

84. Liu K'ai, *Ho-tung hsien-sheng chi* 1.10b–11b.

85. For this argument, see Ch'en Chih-o, "Lueh-lun Sung ch'u ku-wen yun-tung." My reading of Wang owes much also to Huang Ch'i-fang, "Wang Yü-ch'eng p'ing-chuan." The most detailed study of Wang to date is Hsu Kuei, *Wang Yü-ch'eng*.

86. Wang Yü-ch'eng, farewell preface for Sun Ho, *Hsiao-ch'u chi* 19.266–67.

87. Wang Yü-ch'eng, farewell preface for T'an Yao-sou, *Hsiao-ch'u chi* 19.269.

88. Wang Yü-ch'eng, letter to Cheng Pao, *Hsiao-ch'u chi* 18.252.

89. Wang Yü-ch'eng, letter to Chang Fu, *Hsiao-ch'u chi* 18.153–54.

90. The ku-wen advocate Mu Hsiu (979–1032) is a case in point; his fame was posthumous. See, e.g., his letter on ku-wen to Ch'iao Shih in Mu Hsiu, *Ho-nan Mu kung chi* 2.1a–3a.

91. Yao Hsuan, *T'ang wen ts'ui*, preface. Yao treated ku-wen as one category of prose genres. He placed Han in the line of Ch'en Tzu-ang, Chang Yueh, Li Hua, Hsiao Ying-shih, and others. He notes the importance of Chia Chih, Li Han, Yuan Chieh, Tu-ku Chi, Lü Wen, Liang Su, Ch'üan Te-yü, Liu Yü-hsi, Po Chü-i, and Yuan Chen.

92. Chih-yuan held that the Three Teachings were essentially compatible and particularly favored the Doctrine of the Mean. He noted that there were Buddhists who, in imitation of Han Yü's wen, "attacked their own teaching and honored ju" (see Chiang I-pin, *Sung-tai ju shih t'iao-ho-lun*, pp. 10–12).

93. Chih-yuan, farewell preface for Shu-chi, following the text in T'ao Ch'iu-ying and Yü Hsing, *Sung Chin Yuan wen-lun*, pp. 16–18.

94. See James T. C. Liu's influential article "Fan Chung-yen."

95. *FWKC* 7.5b–11b.   96. *FWKC* 7.6b.

97. *FWKC* 8.5b.   98. *FWKC* 8.10a–b.

99. *FWKC* 9.2b.

100. Wang and Ting had been closely associated with the "heavenly letters" of Chen-tsung's reign. Fan approved of their political rivals, the northerners Wang

Tan and K'ou Chun; see *FWKC* 5.19a–b. For an explicit statement of Fan's desire to get ahead in the world (in his words, to understand the "tao of the world" in addition to the "tao of the sage"), see his begging letter to Chang Chih-po dated 1022 (*FWKC* 8.1a–2b). In 1002 Chang Chih-po had himself proposed to give prose sections priority in the examinations (Chin Chung-shu, "Pei-sung k'o-chü chih-tu yen-chiu," pt. I, p. 19).

101. *FWKC*, "nien-p'u" 7a. It is said that students came from the four quarters to study with Fan and that many later gained renown for "wen-hsueh in the examination halls and at court," but I know of no record of these students with exception of an anecdote that claims one of them was Sun Fu, later famous as a scholar of the *Spring and Autumn Annals*. As a teacher, Fan prepared an anthology, in twenty categories, of rhapsodies in the current examination style, referring to them as part of This Culture of Ours. These included not only hymns to the sages' virtues but also such traditional literary offerings as "songs of things" (*yung-wu*) and, in the category "illuminating tao," works that "illuminated the pattern of nothingness." Fan was also trying to redefine the focus of the genre so that, he said, men of narrow horizons would see more while those who "prefer the lofty" would not feel compelled to look down on it. I am struck, in looking over his categories, by the absence of categories devoted to self-expression; "tracing the feelings," for example, is defined as "tracing the intents of the ancients." See the preface in *FWKC*, "pieh-chi" 4.6b–8a. Perhaps we should also see Fan's praise for Yang I as one who "took This Culture of Ours as his personal responsibility" (*FWKC* 5.19a–b) as a compromise with current literary standards.

102. *FWKC* 8.18a–23a.

103. *OHCC*, "wai-chi" 18.478–80; Shih Chieh, *Ts'u-lai Shih hsien-sheng wen-chi* 12.129.

104. For an account of these events, see James T. C. Liu, *Ou-yang Hsiu*, pp. 29–34.

105. *Tao te ching* 57; cf. Lau, *Lao Tzu*, p. 118.

106. This is a close paraphrase of "Yueh chi" 25, *Li chi*.

107. *Lun yü* 13.4; trans. Lau, *Analects*, p. 119, slightly modified.

108. *FWKC* 5.9b. The other essays, "On Selecting and Encharging the Worthy and Able," "On Fame," and "On Delegating to Ministers" (*FWKC* 5.10a–13b) similarly argue for activist leadership.

109. For an example of the defense of imperial non-action, see Hsia Sung's essay "Shun's Non-action and Yü's Attending to Affairs: Which Is Better, Achievement or Virtue?" (*Weng-chuang chi* 20.4a–6a). For examples of memorials warning the emperor that his ministers have taken control at his expense, see the submissions by Su Shen and Yeh Ch'ing-ch'en in 1038 (*Hsu tzu-chih t'ung-chien ch'ang-pien* 121.2857–60). The association of Shun with non-action is from *Analects* 15.5. Su Shun-ch'in's critique (*Su Shun-ch'in chi* 13.169) of Wang Pi's interpretation of the hexagram *fu* may also be an attack on the idea of non-action as a political value.

110. *OHCC*, "wai chi" 17.488–89. In various other writings at the time, Ou-yang claimed that punishment had not made him contrite; see the letter to Yin

Shu and reflections on reading Li Ao's writings (*OHCC*, "wai-chi" 17.490–91, 23.532–33) and "chi" 39.269–70.

111. Ts'ai Hsiang, *Tuan-ming chi* 1.5a–10a.

112. Li Kou, *Li Kou chi* 27.292–93.

113. *Hsu tzu-chih t'ung-chien ch'ang-pien* 121.2851–54.

114. First, many officials of the same generation as the majority of Fan's followers did not support him. Second, his followers were evenly divided between north and south. Third, the group included men from non-official families who did not succeed in the examinations (e.g., Li Kou) and men from very successful official families (Su Shun-ch'in), as well as men from families that had only recently begun to produce officials and/or whose members in service had only provincial careers (e.g., Ou-yang Hsiu). These comments are based on thirteen individuals: the northerners Han Ch'i (1008–75), Fu Pi (1004–83), Shih Chieh, Sun Fu, the 1043–44 policy critic Wang Su (1007–73), and Yin Shu; the southerners Ou-yang Hsiu, Ts'ai Hsiang, Yü Ching, Hu Yuan, Mei Yao-ch'en (1002–60), and Li Kou; and the Szechuanese Su Shun-ch'in. I have not included Su Hsun (1009–66) because he did not become part of the intellectual scene until the 1050's.

115. The works of Chang Fang-p'ing (1007–91) and Wen Yen-po (1006–97) are exceptions. Chang Fang-p'ing does address issues close to the heart of Fan's group, some of these are cited below. Wen Yen-po's collection, *Lu-kung wen-chi*, is weakest on this early period. Wen served on the Council of State off and on after the reform, until he was replaced by Han Ch'i in 1058. He appears to have been an associate of Kao Jo-na, a bitter enemy of Fan's faction; see his biography in the *Sung shih* (313.10258–64).

116. Yü Ching, inscription for the new school at Hung-chou (Chiang-nan West), dated 1036, *Wu-ch'i chi* 6.2b–4b.

117. See, e.g., Shih Chieh's attack on Buddhism and Taoism and on Yang I's literary values in "On What Is Really Strange" and "On the Central State" (*Ts'u-lai Shih hsien-sheng wen-chi* 5.60–64, 10.116–17), Sun Fu's essays "On the Implications of Non-Action" and "The Ju Insulted" (*Sun Ming-fu hsiao-chi* 19a–20b, 37a–38b), and Tsu Wu-tse's inscription for a school at Ts'ai-chou (*Lung-hsueh chi* 7.3a–4b).

118. The best example in Ou-yang Hsiu's writing is his three-part essay "On the Basis" (*OHCC*, "wai-chi" 8.411–13 [pt. I], and "chi" 17.121–24 [pts. II, III]).

119. Yin Shu, letter to Wang Chung-i (Wang Su), *Ho-nan hsien-sheng chi* 11.2a; "On Liking and Disliking," ibid. 3.8b–9b.

120. See the account of Hsia Sung's fabrication of a letter from Shih Chieh to Fu Pi suggesting the overthrow of the emperor (James T. C. Liu, *Ou-yang Hsiu*, p. 49), and the claim that Shih faked his death in 1045 in order to join the Khitans (*Sung-shih* 432.12833–36; *OHCC*, "tsou-shih lu," pp. 969–70).

121. I have followed Fan's summary account of his ten-point program in *FWKC*, "Cheng-fu tsou-i" 1.14a–15a; for the long version, see ibid. 1.1a–14a. The reform program is discussed in greater detail in James T. C. Liu, "Fan Chung-yen."

122. James T. C. Liu, *Ou-yang Hsiu*, pp. 40–48.

123. See, e.g., letters from Su Shun-ch'in (*Su Shun-ch'in chi* 10.117–25) and Li Kou (*Li Kou chi* 27.299) to Fan in 1044 and Ou-yang Hsiu's inscription for the school at Chi-chou (*OHCC* 39.274).

124. Sun Fu, *Sun Ming-fu hsiao-chi* 23b.

125. Chaffee, *Thorny Gates of Learning*, p. 75. The data on 1022–40 is drawn from a table on construction of 64 prefectural and 104 subprefectural schools in idem, "Education and Examinations in Sung Society," p. 170.

126. Yü Ching, inscriptions for schools at Hung-chou (Chiang-nan West, 1036), Jao-chou (Chiang-nan East, 1046), K'ang-chou (Kuang-nan East, 1043), and Hsing-kuo chün (Chiang-nan West, 1044), *Wu-ch'i chi* 6.2b–11a; Yü argues that before 1044 there was little interest in school building within the bureaucracy. Fan Chung-yen, inscription for the school at Fen-chou (Ho-tung, 1044), *FWKC* 7.4a; Fan also taught at the well-established school at Ying-t'ien in the north, established a school at Hu-chou in the south, and supported the school at Su-chou. Yin Shu, inscription for the Kung-hsien school (Ho-nan-fu, ca. 1040), and for the school at Yueh-chou (Ching-hu North, 1046), *Ho-nan hsien-sheng chi* 4.2a, 9a. Ts'ai Hsiang, inscription for the school at Fu-chou (Fu-chien, 1037), *Tuan-ming chi* 28.14a. Shih Chieh, inscriptions for the temple for Confucius at Sung-ch'eng hsien (Ching-tung West, 1037), the school at Ch'ing-chou (Ching-tung East, ca. 1038), and Sun Fu's private academy (1040), *Ts'u-lai Shih hsien-sheng wen-chi* 19.221–24. Ou-yang Hsiu, inscription for the Ku-ch'eng hsien school (Ching-hsi South, 1038), *OHCC* 39.273; and for the school at Chi-chou (Chiang-nan West, 1044), *OHCC*, "wai-chi" 9.425. Tsu Wu-tse, inscription for the school at Ts'ai-chou (Ching-hsi North, 1035), *Lung-hsueh chi* 7.3a.

127. *OHCC* 39.274–75.

128. Tsu Wu-tse, *Lung-hsueh chi* 7.3a–4b.

129. Han Ch'i, inscription for the school at Ting-chou (ca. 1050), *An-yang chi* 21.4a–6a.

130. Yin Shu, *Ho-nan hsien-sheng wen-chi* 4.8a–9b.

131. Sung Ch'i, "On Providing a Basis for Customs," *Ching-wen chi* 25.9b–13b.

132. Ts'ai Hsiang (*Tuan-ming chi* 23.12a–14a), for example, asks no more than that schools be allowed. For the rules on establishing schools as finally adopted, see *SHY*, "hsuan-chü" 3.23b–29a, under 1044/3.

133. Yin Shu, "On Strengthening Learning," *Ho-nan hsien-sheng chi* 2.6b–7a.

134. Li Kou, *Li Kou chi* 27.292–93.

135. This had been ordered in 1017, 1027, 1034, and 1038 (*SHY*, "hsuan chü" 3.11b, 15b–16b, 17b–18a, 19a). Ou-yang Hsiu later wrote that during the T'ien-sheng period (1023–32) an imperial edict had encouraged scholars to take the ancient as a model (preface to Su Shun-ch'in's collection and letter to Candidate Lo, *OHCC* 41.287–88, 47.320–21); I think this refers to the edict of 1027.

136. *OHCC*, "tsou-i" 8.827–28; Ts'ai Hsiang, *Tuan-ming chi* 23.12a–14a; both from 1044. For the procedural details, see *SHY*, "hsuan-chü" 3.23b–29a.

137. See the detailed proposal by Sung Ch'i and others in summary form

and the imperial edict effecting the policy, in *SHY*, "hsuan-chü" 3.23b–25a, 29 (1044/3). Ou-yang Hsiu was the strongest supporter of Fan on the nine-member committee; senior to him were Sung Ch'i, Wang Kung-ch'en (who would soon play a leading role in bringing down Fan's regime), and Chang Fang-p'ing (who helped undo the examination reform two years later, see ibid. 3.30a–b). For the other members, see *OHCC*, "tsou-i" 8.830.

138. Ou-yang's comments are cited in Ch'eng Yun, "Sung-tai chiao-yü," p. 93.

Chapter 6

1. Ou-yang's introduction to his catalogue of peonies in Loyang (*OHCC*, "wai-chi" 22.526), which is not only about peonies as flowers but also about peonies as a metaphor for excellent men, argues that true beauty comes not from "central and harmonious ch'i," which can produce only blossoms neither very good nor very bad, but from one-sided ch'i. The problem, he notes, is that one-sidedness produces both the best and the worst of blossoms.

2. Ts'ai Hsiang, *Tuan-ming chi* 27.7b.

3. Ibid. The views of Ts'ai's correspondent, Hsieh Po-ch'u, are cited in Ts'ai's letter. For the expression of a similar view, see Su Shun-ch'in, letter to Sun, *Su Shun-ch'in chi* 9.102.

4. Ts'ai, *Tuan-ming chi* 27.9b–10a.

5. Tsu Wu-tse, *Lung-hsueh chi* 8.4a. For a similar view, see Sun Fu, letter to Chang Tung, *Sun Ming-fu hsiao-chi* 31b.

6. *OHCC* 47.321–22.

7. For Ou-yang's rejection of his past, see his letter to Sun Mou (dated 1038), *OHCC*, "wai-chi" 18.496. For examples of his literary-aesthetic tendencies, see the various inscriptions from the period (*OHCC*, "wai-chi" 13.450–56). To my mind much of the interest in Ou-yang's writing stems from a tension between his literary and intellectual concerns. In Loyang his best friends were two fellow officials who represented those poles: Mei Yao-ch'en, whose poetry Ou-yang greatly admired, and Yin Shu, whose interest in historical and classical scholarship and whose spare style of intellectual writing also influenced Ou-yang. On Ou-yang's regard for Mei, see his postscript to a manuscript of Mei's from 1032 (*OHCC*, "wai-chi" 23.531–32). For this piece and the Loyang years, see Chaves, *Mei Yao-ch'en*, pp. 4–12. The two sides of Ou-yang are also represented by two major studies of Ou-yang in English, to both of which I am greatly indebted. These are James T. C. Liu, *Ou-yang Hsiu* (the earlier Chinese version has been of great value as well: Liu Tzu-chien, *Ou-yang Hsiu*); and Egan, *Literary Works of Ou-yang Hsiu*. Note also the review of Egan's work by Michael Fuller, "Review." On Ou-yang's literary values, see also Chang Chien, *Ou-yang Hsiu*. My understanding of Ou-yang's position on the realm of human affairs versus the realm of heaven-and-earth owes much to Teraji, "Ō-yō Shū." For Ou-yang's own account of the contemporary changes in literary values, especially in views of antiquity, see his introduction to Su Shun-ch'in's collection and his reply to student Lo (*OHCC* 41.287–88, 47.320–21).

8. Yin Shu, inscription for "Committed to Antiquity Hall," *Ho-nan hsien-sheng chi* 4.5a–5b. See also his essay "Likes and Dislikes" (ibid. 3.8b–9b), which contrasts those who judge a man in terms of their immediate reaction to his appearance and those who ignore his appearance in favor of asking whether the man internally is proceeding through the "tao of the ancient sages."

9. Ts'ai Hsiang, second letter to Hsieh Ching-shan (Hsieh Po-ch'u), *Tuan-ming chi* 27.10a–b. Dated on the basis of Ou-yang's letter cited in note 10 below.

10. Letter to Hsieh Ching-shan (dated 1037), *OHCC*, "wai-chi" 18.495.

11. For a definitive statement of the view that scholars should, like the sages, concern themselves with the realm of the human rather than the heavenly, see Ou-yang Hsiu, *Hsin wu-tai shih* 59.705–6. Both James T. C. Liu and Teraji Jun have developed this point at greater length. I discuss this in my "Sung Context," pp. 33–42.

12. *Sung shih* 157.3658.

13. *Chung-yung* 13, "Tao is not distant from man. When men enact tao and are distant from other men, it cannot be tao [they are enacting]."

14. *Chung-yung* 1.

15. Second letter to degree candidate Chang, *OHCC*, "wai-chi" 16.481.

16. This appears to be an allusion to *Meng-tzu* 4B.13.

17. *OHCC*, "wai-chi" 16.482.

18. By 1033 Shih Chieh had been studying Han Yü's collection and Yao Hsuan's T'ang anthology; see his letter to Chao and also his comments on Han's "Finding the Source for Tao" and his "Honoring Han" (which also notes Liu K'ai) (*Ts'u-lai Shih hsien-sheng wen-chi* 12.135–39, 7.28–80).

19. *Chou i yin-te*, "Hsi-tz'u chuan" A1.

20. Ibid. A11.

21. *Chou i yin-te*, p. 15, "Pi hexagram."

22. Shih Chieh, *Ts'u-lai Shih hsien-sheng wen-chi* 13.143.

23. Ibid. 13.143–44.

24. See, e.g., various letters in ibid., pp. 138, 141, 145, 153, 168, 188.

25. Ibid. 5.60–64.

26. Shih Chieh, inscription for a Confucian temple, *Ts'u-lai Shih hsien-sheng wen-chi* 19.221.

27. See, e.g., his description of the ancient system in "The Origins of Disorder" and "Returning to the Ancient Systems," *Ts'u-lai Shih hsien-sheng wen-chi* 5.64–66, 6.68–69.

28. For a discussion of this debate and additional translations, see Egan, *Literary Works of Ou-yang Hsiu*, pp. 17–20.

29. *OHCC*, "wai-chi" 16.482–83. Either this letter or Shih's reply may have been edited later; Shih's reply cites a sentence on writing giving the semblance of the author that does not appear here.

30. Shih Chieh, *Ts'u-lai Shih hsien-sheng wen-chi* 15.176.

31. *OHCC*, "wai-chi" 16.483–84.

32. Sun Fu, letter to K'ung Tao-fu (ca. 1037), *Sun Ming-fu hsiao-chi* 29a–30b.

33. For the lecture hall, see Shih Chieh, *Ts'u-lai Shih hsien-sheng wen-chi* 19.222.

34. Sun Fu, *Sun Ming-fu hsiao-chi* 35a–36a.

35. His commentary on the *Annals, Ch'un-ch'iu tsun wang fa-wei*, is extant. My understanding of this work follows Wood, "Politics and Morality," pp. 140–65. Sun's commentary on the *Spring and Autumn Annals* argued that the point of the work as a whole was to teach two essential political principles: defending the authority of the ruler against the feudal lords, which I take to be a call for further centralization of authority at the expense of the great ministers at court, and defending the integrity of the Central State from barbarian encroachment, which I read as a justification for greater mobilization against the Tanguts. The assumption behind his exegesis is that the general principles the ancients had in mind can be inferred from their writings.

36. Sun Fu, *Sun Ming-fu hsiao-chi* 31b–32a.

37. *OHCC*, "wai-chi" 18.490–91.

38. *OHCC* 17.121–24.

39. Li Kou, *Li Kou chi* 29.326.

40. Li Kou, letters to Li and Sung (1036), *Li Kou chi* 27.288–90. For a detailed account of Li's life and writings, see Shan-yuan Hsieh, *Life and Thought of Li Kou.* My interpretation of Li's essays on ritual follows Teraji, "Ri Kō."

41. Li Kou, fifth essay, *Li Kou chi* 2.15.

42. Second essay, ibid. 2.8.

43. First essay, ibid. 2.7.

44. Ibid.

45. Sixth essay, ibid. 2.19.

46. Fifth essay, ibid. 2.13.

47. Fourth essay, ibid. 2.11–12.

48. Sixth essay, ibid. 2.18.

49. Fifth essay, ibid. 2.16.

50. Sixth essay, ibid. 2.17–18.

51. Chang Wang-chih's critique of Li Kou is known only through the portions quoted in Li's rebuttal; see *Li Kou chi* 2.24–26. This is apparently the same "Master Chang" who attacked Ou-yang Hsiu's essay on legitimate succession; see Su Shih's rebuttal from 1055 (*STPC* 2.5.21.5–9). According to Ch'en Shun-yü, Chang and Li Kou were leading ku-wen teachers in the southeast during the Ch'ing-li period (see Ch'en's introduction to Ch'i-sung's literary collection, *T'an-chin wen-chi.*

52. Ch'i-sung, *T'an-chin wen-chi* 10.4a. A Ch'an monk from the far south, he began to address the issues of shih intellectual culture in the 1040's. Ch'i-sung's literary writings are collected in the *T'an-chin wen-chi.* Ch'en Shun-yü's biography of the monk is included as a preface. I have followed Ch'en's biography and Jan Yun-hua, "Ch'i-sung."

53. See, e.g., the long essay "On the Origins of Instruction" (Ch'i-sung, *T'an-chin wen-chi* 1.1a–12a). This dates from 1049. An "expanded version" is said to have been written seven years later (*T'an-chin wen-chi* 2.1b).

54. There are various accounts of Hu's career as a provincial teacher; see Chin Chung-shu, "Sung-tai hsueh-shu fa-chan," pp. 14–18. For an anecdote about Hu, see Lü Hsi-che's account of Hu's teaching methods in the capital during the 1050's, in Li Chih, *Shih-yu t'an-chi* 23a–b. Hu says, for example "Thus what is able to continue the goodness of heaven-and-earth is the *hsing* [nature] of man" (Hu Yuan, *Chou I k'ou i* A.36b); discussed in Bol, "Sung Context," pp. 37–39. For a study of Hu's lectures, see Lin I-sheng, *Hu Yuan.*

55. Ou-yang understood *shuai* as "guide" or "lead"; proponents of innate morality usually took *shuai* as "follow."

56. Reply to Li Hsu, *OHCC* 47.320.

57. Ch'i-sung, comments on two exchanges with Chang Wang-chih, *T'an-chin wen-chi* 7.13a–15b.

58. For the series "In Criticism of Han," see Ch'i-sung, *T'an-chin wen-chi, chüan* 14–16.

59. Ch'i-sung, *T'an-chin wen-chi* 7.13a.

60. *Meng-tzu* 4B14; trans. Lau, *Mencius*, p. 130. The passage is an explanation of why the gentleman should "find tao in himself."

61. Ch'i-sung, "On Wen," *T'an-chin wen-chi* 7.14b–15a; cf. "On Human Wen," ibid. 6.6a–7b.

62. Yin Shu, Fan preface, *Ho-nan hsien-sheng chi*. The appendix contains Han Ch'i's grave declaration.

63. Ou-yang's grave record for Yin and his explanation of it are included in the appendix to Yin Shu, *Ho-nan hsien-sheng chi*.

64. In taking this view, Ou-yang was in fact returning to the idea that one could discuss tao separately from excellence in wen, a position he had spelled out in 1034 in a discussion of the passage "If the language lacks wen, it will not go far" (letter to Vice-Commissioner Wang, dated 1034, *OHCC* 17.486).

65. "Strange Bamboos," *OHCC* 19.136–37.

66. The two exceptions are Yang Chieh and Cheng Hsieh. Examples of the 1020's generation whose official careers began only in the 1050's are Yang Chieh (ca. 1020–ca. 1090, chin-shih [c.s.] 1059), Cheng Hsieh (1022–77, c.s. 1053), Wen T'ung (1019–79, c.s. 1049), Su Hsun (1009–66), and two men who passed the examination of 1057, Tseng Kung (1019–83), and Chang Tsai (1020–77); see the Bibliography for the titles of these men's works. Tseng had made connections to Ou-yang Hsiu and other leading Ch'ing-li reform figures and Chang to Fan Chung-yen before 1044. Men who entered the bureaucracy through the yin privilege whose careers began at this time include Chou Tun-i (1017–73), Han Wei (1017–98), Sung Min-ch'iu (1019–79), and Ssu-ma Kuang (1019–86). Both Sung and Ssu-ma passed the chin-shih examination as well, taking degrees in 1038. The following passed the examination of 1042: Ch'en Hsiang (1017–80), Wang An-shih (1021–86), Wang Kuei (1019–85), and Su Sung (1020–1101). Passing in 1046 were Ch'en Shun-yü (ca. 1020–74), Ch'iang Chih (1022–76), and the brothers Liu Ch'ang (1019–68) and Liu Pin (1023–89).

67. The editors of the *Sung History* made this point with reference to Yang I and Ch'ao Chiung (*Sung shih* 305.10091).

68. Letter to Sung, *SMWC* 58.696; letter to Chang from 1045, *LCWC* 77.810.

69. Letter to Wu, *SMWC* 77.810. Ssu-ma wrote in 1062 that he began his career with the aim of making a name for ku-wen (letter to P'ang Chi, *SMWC* 59.712–13). There is little question about Wang's reputation as a ku-wen stylist. For the relations of Ou-yang, Tseng Kung, and Wang An-shih, see Ts'ai Shang-hsiang, *Wang Ching-kung nien-p'u k'ao-lueh*, 2.47–48. 3.52, 3.56, 3.83. Ssu-ma

eventually rejected his ku-wen past (see the letter to P'ang cited above); Wang did not (see letters to Shao and to Sun Chang-ch'ien, *LCWC* 75.798–99, 76.802).

70. Ssu-ma's foremost patron was P'ang Chi (980–1063), whom he followed into local government in 1054–56 (the only time Ssu-ma served outside the capital between 1046 and 1071), when P'ang was forced out of the chief councillorship. For a discussion of Ssu-ma's factional connections in the 1040's, see Bol, "Government, Society, and State."

71. Tseng Kung, *Tseng Kung chi* 15.237, 239.

72. "Farewell to Tseng Kung," *LCWC* 71.755.

73. Letter to Chang, *LCWC* 77.810.

74. *LCWC* 77.812. For a similar statement on composing wen that can be applied to the present, see *LCWC* 77.811.

75. Letter to the chief councillors, *LCWC* 74.780.

76. Record for a dike in Yü-yao subprefecture, *LCWC* 82.866. In this passage Wang is approvingly quoting a colleague.

77. In an article tracing Ssu-ma Kuang's acquaintance with Ou-yang Hsiu and the intellectual similarities and differences between them, Ch'en Kuang-ch'ung ("Ssu-ma Kuang yü Ou-yang Hsiu") points out that the two both wrote poems to friends in common but not to each other.

78. Preface to the collection of Yen T'ai-ch'u (1039), *SMWC* 69.851. This plays on *Analects* 1.6, which says to study wen only if one has strength to spare after learning to behave ethically.

79. *SMWC* 65.302; cf. "On Virtue and Talent" (dated 1045) and "Yü jen chuan" (*SMWC* 64.797–98, 72.882).

80. Essay on Chia I (1042), *SMWC* 65.806–7; cf. essay on Lien P'o (*SMWC* 65.805–7).

81. "On the Four Heroes," *SMWC* 65.802–4.

82. Essay on Ho-chien Hsien-wang, *SMWC* 66.825.

83. "On the Spring and the Balance" (or "On the Timely and Irregular Use of Power") (dated 1045), *SMWC* 64.790.

84. Wu Ch'ung, "Record of Conduct" for Ou-yang, cited in Ho Tse-heng, *Ou-yang Hsiu*, pp. 28–29.

85. *Sung shih* 155.3614. This is also evident from the figures for departmental and palace graduates (Chaffee, *Thorny Gates of Learning*, p. 193).

86. See the discussion of preventing candidates from using stand-ins and smuggling in miniature texts, in *OHCC*, "tsou-i chi" 15.872.

87. This is the interpretation of Yueh K'o's *T'ing shih* (1214); cited in James T. C. Liu, *Ou-yang Hsiu*, pp. 150–51. Ou-yang was not the first to pose questions on statecraft in the examination, as Liu suggests; the departmental chin-shih examination had such questions from the beginning of the dynasty. The confusion stems from an edict issued in 1057 after the exam announcing that henceforth the palace examination would pose three treatises on statecraft. However, it was not until 1070 that the treatise was adopted at the palace exam (*Hsu tzu-chih t'ung-chien ch'ang-pien* 186.4496). Traditionally candidates were passed on the basis of the

poetic sections, but the final rankings took the prose sections into account. Ou-yang may have arbitrarily decided to carry out the aborted Ch'ing-li proposal to pass students on the basis of their prose. There are conflicting reports on Ou-yang's standards. The official version states simply that he cut those who competed to be "eccentric" (*kuai-p'i*) (Wu Ch'ung, "Record of Conduct" for Ou-yang, cited in Ho Tse-heng, *Ou-yang Hsiu*, pp. 28–29). For the official version I have used *Hsu tzu-chih t'ung-chien ch'ang-pien* 185.4467, which follows Wu Ch'ung's biography closely. Ou-yang's biographer adds that in failing such men, Ou-yang "sought the even and bland, the normative and essential." This suggests a standard for the poetic sections, "even and bland" (*p'ing-tan*) being a label for the poetic values Ou-yang associated with Mei Yao-ch'en; the standard for the prose sections, "normative and essential" (*tien-yao*), refers to writing on political norms. Yeh Meng-te's note on this event (cited in Chaves, *Mei Yao-ch'en*, p. 37) is ambiguous unless he means that polishing led to abstruseness. Yeh states that candidates were writing in such novel and abstruse manners that their writing was difficult to read (a critique that recalls Ou-yang's attack on Shih Chieh), but he has Ou-yang rejecting all writings that showed signs of excessive polishing, a seeming reference to writing in the manner of Yang I. For a similar anecdote, see *OHCC*, appendix 5.1377. Su Shih, in a stele inscription for Ou-yang's grave, (*OHCC*, appendix 2.1349), says he failed "all those who had reputations for strangeness [in writing]" and passed those whose "language and meaning was close to the ancient." Elsewhere Su writes that from this time on ku-wen was esteemed and prose writing flourished at the expense of poetry (*TPWC* 21.330).

88. *OHCC* 48.328–29.

89. *OHCC* 48.328.

90. See his biography in *Sung shih* 318.10366–69.

91. Hu Su, *Wen-kung chi* 29.4a.

92. The nine sections of the "Great Plan" refer to the nine sets of affairs discussed in that text. It reads: "Heaven then gave Yü the Great Plan in nine sections, whereby the constant norms get their proper order. The first is called the five elements [i.e., five phases]" (trans. Karlgren, "The Book of Documents," p. 30).

93. Hu Su, *Wen-kung chi* 29.5a–b.

94. Ibid. 29.5b–6a. For the other view, see Yü Ching's discussion of the Ch'in dynasty (*Wu-ch'i chi* 4.4b).

95. This information (without the political interpretation) is found in Ho Tse-heng, *Ou-yang Hsiu*, pp. 105–11. Apparently Sung Ch'i had already prepared tables, annals, and treatises, but these were not used (Rotours, *Le Traité des examens*, pp. 56–64).

96. The revision of the treatises resulted in thirteen treatises in 50 *chüan* (counting divided *chüan*). Ou-yang added treatises on the imperial rest and progress (Treatise 2), official recruitment (no. 8) and the armies (no. 10). He joined the treatises on music and ritual together. He renamed the treatise "Official Functions" as "The Hundred Offices" and the "Classical Records" (i.e., bibliography)

as "Literary Texts" ("I-wen"). He shifted the treatise on carriages and garments from eighth to third place and that on bibliography from ninth to last place. He variously expanded and abridged and wrote new introductions, but left unintroduced the treatise on official recruitment, which included an account of the examination system. Below I note the significance of beginning with ritual and ending with literature.

97. The idea of using the treatises to address Ou-yang's thought is inspired by David S. Nivison's use of the "Treatise on Ritual and Music" to discuss assumptions underlying the "Neo-Confucian vision" ("Introduction" to *Confucianism in Action*, pp. 4–9). Nivison notes (1) the assumption of an integrated human order in which the state is one with society and form and function are one; (2) a contradiction between this order and the actual political order, which makes it unlikely that men can be both politically successful and moral; (3) a stress on rites that predicated the integrated order on the individual's commitment to his own moral cultivation, and (4) an implicit organic analogy.

98. In translating this passage, I have lumped together the names for various objects. The use of the conditional form in the last sentence stems from Ou-yang's use of *kai* (translated as "it must have been so") in the third sentence from the end and *shih* (here translated as "if," in the sense of "supposing that," rather than as "to cause"). In my reading, Ou-yang is explaining what he thinks "antiquity" as an ideal ought to have been like rather than claiming that it was thus.

99. *HTS* 11.307–8.

100. See, e.g., Ou-yang's explanation of his conduct in attacking Kao Jo-na in 1036 (*OHCC* 17.490–91) and his letters to Yen Shu and Ting (*OHCC* 17.493–94). See also his introduction to "Biographies of [Men Who] Made Their Conduct One" ("I hsing chuan"), a revision of the traditional "singular conduct" (*tu hsing*) section of histories, in his *New History of the Five Dynasties* (trans. and discussed in Mote, "Confucian Eremitism," pp. 206–12). In short, Ou-yang holds that in contrast to earlier periods when morally committed men took independent action during times of disorder, the Five Dynasties saw the emergence of men whose moral commitment took the form of withdrawal; in other words, they would act only if they did not have to adopt a different set of standards more appropriate to political life. As Mote points out, Ou-yang both lauds and denigrates this attitude; he still wants scholars to serve. Looking at other chapters, Kobayashi Yoshihiro ("*Godai shiki* no shijin kan") has made a strong case for seeing this history as addressing the question of the proper relation between autocratic rulers and the shih and arguing for the need for independence from the imperial interest.

101. *HTS* 11.308.

102. *HTS* 11.309.

103. Ou-yang Hsiu, *Hsin Wu-tai shih* 59.706.

104. "Treatise on Calendars," *HTS* 25.533.

105. "Treatise on Astronomy," *HTS* 31.805–6.

106. "Treatise on the Five Phases," *HTS* 34.871–73. Ou-yang objects strongly to the five-phases interpretation of the "Great Plan" and the *Spring and Autumn Annals*.

107. "Treatise on Geography," "Treatise on Armies," "Treatise on Finances," *HTS* 37.959, 50.1323, 51.1341.

108. "Treatise on Imperial Rest and Progress," *HTS* 23A.481.

109. "Treatise on Astronomy," *HTS* 31.805.

110. "Treatise on the Hundred Offices," *HTS* 46.1118.

111. "Treatise on the Armies," "Treatise on Calendars," *HTS* 50.1323, 31.803.

112. Hu Su, first examination question, *Wen-kung chi* 29.4a.

113. "Treatise on the Hundred Offices," "Treatise on Finances," *HTS* 46.1118, 51.1341.

114. "Treatise on Geography," *HTS* 37.959.

115. "Treatise on Armies," "Treatise on Penal Codes," *HTS* 50.1323, 56.1407.

116. *CTS* 21.815.

117. "Treatise on Bibliography," *HTS* 57.1421–22.

118. My understanding of the *Shih pen-i* is based largely on Van Zoeren, "Poetry and Personality," pp. 210–78.

119. For Ou-yang's writings on the *Change*, see Bol, "Sung Context." For Ou-yang's writings on the *Spring and Autumn Annals*, see Ho Tse-heng, *Ou-yang Hsiu*, pp. 77–87. On his attitude toward the Classics in general, see James T. C. Liu, *Ou-yang Hsiu*, pp. 85–99. Note also Ch'ien Mu, *Sung ming li-hsueh*, pp. 10–14, which uses a series of short quotations to present Ou-yang as a critical, historically minded thinker who rejects a moralistic position. Ch'ien notes that Ou-yang treats the refutation of Buddhism as a secondary affair, rejects "holding to the constant" and the "return to antiquity," argues that all inferences about heaven-and-earth must be drawn from what is knowable (i.e., from human affairs), denies the importance of human nature, and treats the *Doctrine of the Mean* as a vain attempt to escape from effort and thought and as exemplifying "doubting the Classics."

120. Ou-yang Hsiu, *Shih pen-i* 14.7a.

121. Ibid. 14.8a.

122. Ibid. 14.7a–b.

123. Ibid. 14.9a.

124. Van Zoeren, "Poetry and Personality," pp. 239–55.

125. See ibid., pp. 260–62, for comments on Ou-yang's interpretations and criticisms.

126. "On the Release of Prisoners" (1037), *OHCC* 19.136.

127. Chaffee, *Thorny Gates of Learning*, pp. 61–65.

128. For the Ch'engs' family background, see Bol, "Ch'eng Yi and Cultural Tradition." For the Ch'eng brothers' careers, I am indebted to Yao Ming-ta, *Ch'eng I-ch'uan nien-p'u*. On Chang Tsai's career, see Lü Ta-lin's "Record of Conduct," in Chang Tsai, *Chang-tzu ch'üan-shu* 15.11a–12a.

129. The history of the Su family is based on the comments of Su Hsun and his sons. I have followed the account drawn from this material in Tseng Tsao-chuang, *Su Hsun p'ing-chuan*, pp. 170–73, 186–87, 196–97, 206–20. See also Hatch, "Su Hsun."

130. See, e.g., his essay "Broadening the Shih" (*Chia-yu chi* 4.9b–11b).

131. Ou-yang's remark is cited in a letter from Su Hsun to Ou-yang (*Chia-yu*

chi 11.4b). These essays, as well as such essay series as "Great Plan," "On History," "Book of *Ch'üan* [expediency, power, balancing]," and "On Weighing," predate Su Hsun's arrival in the capital; see the references in the letters collected by Tseng Tsao-chuang, *Su Hsun p'ing-chuan*, pp. 211–17. It is not possible to say with any accuracy when between 1047 (when Su rethought his ideas) and 1056 these essays were written. My reading of "On the Six Classics" (Su Hsun, *Chia-yu chi, chüan* 6) owes much to Hsiao Kung-ch'üan, *Chung-kuo cheng-chih*, pp. 485–88; and Hatch, "Thought of Su Hsun," pp. 240–66 and 166–74. In Hatch's analysis, the concept of "historical contingency" is central to Su Hsun's thought; see his "Historical Thought in the Statecraft of Su Hsun."

132. Su Hsun presented himself as a student of Ou-yang's *wen-chang*, which, he claimed, had the stature of the *wen* of Mencius and of Han Yü (*Chia-yu chi* 11.1a–3b).

133. Ibid. 6.1a–2b. Hsiao and Hatch (see *n*131 above) argue that "On *Ritual*" should precede "On *Change*," on the grounds that ritual was the first creation and that the essay ends with a reference to "On *Change*." I have followed the order found in all editions because the essays form a polarity.

134. Su Hsun, *Chia-yu chi* 6.2b–4a.   135. Ibid. 6.4b–6b.
136. Ibid. 6.6b–7a.   137. Ibid. 6.8a–10a.

138. *STPC* 6.18.6.45–48. In this edition "On *Chung-yung*" appears between the policy proposals and the essays on historical figures. For a translation and study of the entire essay, which, in addition, places it in the context of Su Shih's involvement in art, see Murck, "Su Shih's Reading of the Chung-yung." See also Bol, "Culture and the Way," pp. 175–87.

139. Su accuses his contemporaries of treating *chung-yung* as innate to "exculpate their own lack of ability" (Proposal 4, *STPC* 6.18.1.8).

140. "On *Chung-yung*," pt. I, *STPC* 6.18.6.45–46.

141. Proposal 4, *STPC* 6.18.1.8. Su is speaking of the patterns of all things together as the one harmonious pattern.

142. Ibid. The "village worthy" (*hsiang-yuan*) appears in *Lun yü* 17.13 and *Meng-tzu* 7B37. Su is noting that whereas Confucius (*Lun-yü* 6.29) called chung-yung a rare virtue, later men (e.g., Han writers) took it to mean "average," which was what Confucius meant by "village worthy."

143. *Chung-yung* 21. Su's essay deals only with those passages from the *Chung-yung* noted here and below; all else in the text he dismisses as elaborations of later *ju*.

144. This part interprets *Chung-yung* 12: "The way of the superior man is repetitive yet hidden. Men and women of simple intelligence can share its knowledge, and yet in its utmost reaches, there is something that even the sage does not know. Men and women of simple intelligence can put it into practice; and yet in its utmost reaches there is something that even the sage is unable to put into practice" (trans. Wing-tsit Chan, *Source Book*, p. 100, modified).

145. *STPC* 6.18.6.47.

146. Ibid.: "The tao of the superior man can be stated succinctly when it is stated by inferring that out of which it comes into being, and being succinct, it is

clear [*ming*]. Perceived through inference from its manifestations in practice, its expression in language will be prolix, and being prolix it is hidden."

147. *Chung-yung* 2 and parts of 11, 4, and 9; in that order.

148. *STPC* 6.18.6.48.

149. Ibid. Citing *Meng-tzu* 7A26 (trans. Lau, *Mencius* p. 188, modified). In this passage the middle is the position between the extremes of egoism and love without distinction. Lau translates "ch'üan" as "proper measure." Su Shih follows Su Hsun's understanding of the term; see his discussion of the term in Proposal 23 and his usage in "On Sun Wu," "On Emperor Wu of Wei," and "On the Great Minister, II" (discussed in Chapter 8).

150. *STPC* 6.18.6.48.

151. Su Hsun, *Chia-yu chi* 14.6b–7b.

152. Ibid. 2.1a.

153. *STPC* 2.5.24.35.

154. "Yen-tzu so hao ho hsueh," *ECC*, "wen-chi" 8.578; trans. Wing-tsit Chan, *Source Book*, p. 550, slightly modified.

155. Wing-tsit Chan (*Source Book*, pp. 547–48) notes that the phrase I translate as "making his emotional responses [agree with his] nature" comes from Wang P'i's commentary on the hexagram *ch'ien*. Both this phrase and its counterpart ("making the natures [agree with their] emotional responses") were deleted by Chu Hsi; see Wing-tsit Chan, "Chu Hsi's Completion of Neo-Confucianism," pp. 64–65. It is used by the T'ang writer Liang Su in at least one instance (see *CTW* 518.10).

156. Ch'eng I, *ECC*, "wen-chi" 8.577. For an alternative translation, see Wing-tsit Chan, *Source Book*, pp. 547–48.

157. Ou-yang Hsiu, "Treatise on the Five Phases," *HTS* 34.871.

158. Liu Mu, *I shu kou yin t'u* A.31. Chou Tun-i adopts this view as well in his "Explanation of the Diagram of the Great Ultimate."

159. Li Kou, for example, bought a copy of the work solely in order to write a critique (*Li Kou chi* 4.52–66). Yü Ching (*Wu-ch'i chi* 3.7b–9a) is also critical of Liu Mu's work.

160. Chin Chung-shu has argued, on the basis of Hu Yuan's lectures on the *Change* at the Imperial University, that ideas in Ch'eng's essay stem from Hu Yuan (see his "Sung-tai hsueh-shu fa-chan"; for his discussion of the Yen-tzu essay, see pp. 21–24). Chin's argument depends on a reading of Hu Yuan's lectures on the *Change* as a case of heaven-and-earth and hsing-ming thought; I am not persuaded of this.

161. Chang Tsai, *Chang Tsai chi*, p. 4. The lack of dates for Chang's writings is one of the reasons for not treating him here. For a systematic analysis of his thought, see Kasoff, *Thought of Chang Tsai*.

162. Ch'eng Hao, *ECC*, "wen-chi" 2.460; I have borrowed from the translation in Wing-tsit Chan, *Source Book*, p. 525.

163. This follows Hu Yuan, who spoke of "imitating the function of heaven" rather than the "formal appearance of heaven" (see Chin Chung-shu, "Sung-tai hsueh-shu fa-chan," p. 32).

164. Ch'eng Hao, *ECC*, "wen-chi" 2.460–1; cf. Wing-tsit Chan, *Source Book*, p. 526.

165. "Ten Thousand Word Memorial," *LCWC* 39.410.

166. Reply to Ming T'ai-chu, *SMWC* 59.707.

Chapter 7

1. First letter to Wang, *SMWC* 60.725; Wang An-shih, *LCWC* 73.773.

2. I discuss some comparative studies of Ssu-ma and Wang in "Government, Society, and State." This chapter gives greater attention to the thought of the two men but draws extensively on that paper. In both cases James T. C. Liu, *Reform*, is my starting point for Wang. For Ssu-ma, it is Anthony Sariti, "Monarchy, Bureaucracy, and Absolutism." An influential comparative interpretation is Hartwell, "Historical Analogism."

The primary biographical sources are: for Wang, Ts'ai Shang-hsiang, *Wang Ching-kung nien-p'u k'ao-lueh*, and Higashi, *Ō An-seki jiten*; and, for Ssu-ma, Ku Tung-kao, *Ssu-ma t'ai-shih Wen-kuo Wen-cheng kung nien-p'u*. Higashi is the author of a popularized study of Wang and Ssu-ma, *Ō An-seki to Shi-ba Kō*, a work that is in fact largely devoted to Wang. Higashi has also written the most extensive account of the New Policies, *Ō An-seki shimpō no kenkyū*. Chi P'ing, *Ssu-ma Kuang hsin-lun*, is probably the best of the recent critical studies of Ssu-ma Kuang's political and intellectual views from the PRC. Although I do not accept Teraji Jun's argument that Ssu-ma's views are based on cosmology and Wang's are based on ideas about man, I have found much of value in his "Tenjin sōkansetsu."

There is a large and growing body of secondary scholarship on Wang. See, e.g., the bibliography in Wang Chin-kuang, *Wang An-shih shu-mu*. Growing attention to Ssu-ma's views beyond his historiographical contributions is evident in *Chi-nien Ssu-ma Kuang Wang An-shih*, a conference volume. Of particular interest has been the re-evaluation of Wang and Ssu-ma as historical figures in PRC scholarship. It cannot be said that Ssu-ma has won the day, but many have criticized Wang and the New Policies. The opening shot in the re-evaluation of Wang and the New Policies was Wang Tseng-yü, "Wang An-shih pien-fa chien-lun." For a defense, see Chou Liang-hsiao, "Wang An-shih pien-fa tsung-t'an." For an account of the re-evaluation of Ssu-ma, see Huo Ch'un-ying, "Chin-nien lai Ssu-ma Kuang yen-chiu"; and the monograph by Chi P'ing noted above. I hope to provide a more detailed account of this debate in a future issue of the *Bulletin of Sung and Yuan Studies* under the title: "1086 and 1986: Reversing the Verdict?"

3. Third question, *LCWC* 70.747.

4. See, e.g., Wen Yen-po's attempt to dissuade Shen-tsung from this position ("On Order Through Non-Action," *Lu-kung wen-chi* 9.11b–13b).

5. Record of a court debate between Wang and Ssu-ma in 1068/8, in *SMWC* 42.543–45.

6. For a detailed account of the controversy, see Fisher, "Ritual Dispute of Sung Ying-tsing." Fisher divides the factions into pragmatic statesmen (Ou-yang, Han Ch'i, the Council of State) and idealists (Ssu-ma Kuang, the censors, and academi-

cians). I see the dispute as an attempt to overturn the Council (dominated by ku-wen men who argued from "human feeling") by their traditional opponents, who now depicted themselves as upholding the morally correct structure of government.

7. In letters to Wang, Ssu-ma accused him of staffing the Financial Planning Commission with "shih of literary talent" as well as fiscal experts and of being inspired by the very literary to desire to "change all the old models and make everything new and unique [*hsin-ch'i*]" (*SMWC* 60.720, 726). In *TCTC* (3.100, 6.221–22) Ssu-ma lambasted "persuaders" who use rhetoric to guide political action.

8. *Hsu tzu-chih ch'ang-pien: Shih-i* 4.3b, in *Hsu tzu-chih t'ung-chien ch'ang-pien.*

9. *SMWC* 21.314–16; *LCWC* 62.667.

10. *LCWC* 39.410–23. For Wang's restatements, see *LCWC* 39.423, 41.438. For a translation of the memorial, see Williamson, *Wang An-shih*, 1: 48–84.

11. For a more extensive discussion of the policy differences between the two men, see Bol, "Government, Society, and State."

12. *LCWC* 39.410–11.

13. *LCWC* 39.411.

14. Against the argument that Wang is simply assuming the imperial system, consider the indispensable centrality of the emperor in Ssu-ma Kuang's scheme of things as discussed below.

15. For an explicit statement of this, see the essay "The Duke of Chou," *LCWC* 64.677–78.

16. The 1058 memorial brings together much that Wang said in bits and pieces elsewhere. As early as 1047 (letter to Vice-Prefect Ma, *LCWC* 75.795) he had spoken of the need for the state to play a greater role in the economy and lead the way in "creating wealth" (*sheng-ts'ai*). In 1060 (wall inscription for office of the vice-supervisor of funds, *LCWC* 82.860–61), he argued that "managing wealth" was essential to keeping private wealth from making the common people dependent on it, thus irreversibly dividing authority and hindering the uniform implementation of policy. He also advanced the idea that local schools should be the nexus of society, government, and culture, places where "day and night everything shih saw and heard was the way with which one orders society and government," as had been the practice in antiquity (school inscription for Tz'u-ch'i hsien, *LCWC* 83.870).

17. "Wang chih" chapter, *Li chi.*

18. Second letter to Wang Shen-fu, *LCWC* 72.768, for the 1058 case and response. I have translated a similar but more elaborate passage from the letter to Ting Yuan-chen (*LCWC* 75.794).

19. School inscription for T'ai-p'ing chou (1066), *LCWC* 82.862–63; cf. the inscription for Ch'ien-chou school (1064–65), *LCWC* 82.858.

20. See, e.g., Ssu-ma's three letters to Wang An-shih in 1070 (*SMWC* 60.719–27). In 1056 he had already argued that the difference between a superior man and lesser man was that the former was accommodative (*kung*) and the latter was "single-minded" (*chuan*) and concerned only with his own tao (*SMWC* 69.856–57). However, he wrote this when his patron had been forced to leave court.

21. *SMWC* 75.920–21.
22. Inscription for the temple to Confucius in Wen-hsi hsien, *SMWC* 71.872.
23. *SMWC* 71.871.
24. "Chang Hsun," *SMWC* 67.832.
25. An early example of this is his criticism in 1050–51 of using honorary titles to show the emperor's personal favor rather than as a reward for real accomplishments (*SMWC* 18.275–80).
26. Reading through "T'ien fei" (1057–58), *SMWC* 74.905–7. My comments are an interpretation of the first ten sections. Ssu-ma Kuang does qualify this. On the one hand, he recognizes that the world is made predictable in large part because men continue to follow desire and are usually incapable of following advice that requires subordinating the private to the public. On the other hand, he points out that accepting one's role does not prevent one from continuing to learn, and learning leads to an ever broader perspective (even to the point that one may realize one's past has been a mistake).
27. "On Factions" (1058) contends that "good" factions defend the public quality of the state (as opposed to being the party of idealists of Ou-yang Hsiu's famous essay from the 1040's) (*SMWC* 64.793). "Knowing Men" (1057) argues that the ruler's task is to know which men will maintain a unified hierarchy of political authority (*SMWC* 65.799–801). "On Merit and Fame" (1057) urges the ruler to find men truly committed to the survival of the state (rather than men who have achieved fame in elite opinion) and to employ them fully and trust them completely, defending them against criticism, so that they will not be afraid to do what is necessary to preserve the state (*SMWC* 65.787–90).
28. *SMWC* 21.307–14, citing the introduction (21.307).
29. "Explaining Fate," *SMWC* 67.833.
30. *SMWC* 21.309–10.
31. Later memorials often cite earlier memorials; see *SMWC* 20.296 (memorial of 1061), 24.346 (1062), 27.275 (1063), 27.383 (1063), 28.381 (1063), 31.417 (1064), 32.427 (1064), 38.493 (1067), 46.568 (1085).
32. Note the similarity between this triad and that in Wang An-shih's essay "Three Non-deceptions" (*LCWC* 67.712), which argues that benevolence, knowledge, and policy characterized the sages' tao of governing (vs. the "virtue," supervision, and punishment of later ages).
33. *SMWC* 20.296.
34. Memorial from 1061, *SMWC* 20.297–98.
35. Memorial on policy critics, *SMWC* 20.297–98.
36. *SMWC* 21.312.
37. For Ssu-ma's awareness of the fiscal and military problems, see a 1061 memorial in *SMWC* 20.298. In relations with the Hsia, he opposes attempts to increase the size of the military, conscript northern farmers, and establish a more aggressive posture on the borders. He argues that a large military depletes the treasury, thus making the military itself a threat to the state and calls for better training and better selection of the officer corps (see memorials of 1061, 1064, 1065, and 1065 in *SMWC* 20.298, 34.449–59, 35.461, 35.464).

"On Wealth and Profit" (1061; *SMWC* 25.353–62) is his most extensive memorial on fiscal affairs from this period. He opposes reforms aimed at increasing the state's share of the national wealth and calls instead for improving fiscal administration by filling posts with fiscal specialists and creating a special career path for financial offices, separate from the career path of "literary talent." He proposes attracting the common people back to farming by reducing the tax burden on the farmers, increasing the burden on urban wealth, and providing for the hiring of *ya-ch'ien* servicemen. The latter two measures were adopted with the New Policies. However, Ssu-ma's account of how to make farming more profitable, thus returning the people to their proper role and restoring production and revenue, is devoted largely to measures to ensure competence in local administration, rather than increasing investment. He calls too for a reduction in expenses, including the stipends of the imperial clan and gifts to officials, but identifies the real problem as an increase in officialdom and the military. Here, as later, he supposes that "the production of heaven-and-earth is constant" (*SMWC* 25.361), that agricultural production cannot be raised.

38. *LCWC* 70.747.

39. *SMWC* 24.347–51.

40. *SMWC* 24.349.

41. *SMWC* 24.348.

42. *SMWC* 24.349.

43. See Ssu-ma's introduction to the *Li-nien t'u*, 16.83a–88b.

44. Reply to Wu Hsiao-tsung, *LCWC* 74.786.

45. Reply to Ch'en Ch'ung, *SMWC* 59.707; cf. "Is the learning of the superior man for tao or for wen?" ("Criticizing Chuang-tzu," in "Impractical Writings," *SMWC* 74.914.

46. See, e.g., Wang's essay "Selecting Talent" (*LCWC* 69.734–35).

47. *SMWC* 74.910.

48. Reply to K'ung Wen-chung, citing *Analects* 15.41, *SMWC* 60.718–19, Ssu-ma writes further: "You say that when learning accumulates within, then wen is expressed without. If what is accumulated within is deep and broad, then what is expressed outside will be pure and profound. In that case, wen can be gotten even if you do not learn it. If learning does not fill the inside but one only externally tends to his wen, then wen will flourish outside while the substance will be encumbered within and thus he will be discarding both aspects of what he has learned."

49. Letter to an unnamed man, *LCWC* 77.811.

50. Ssu-ma's work on the proper forms for public and private letters, the *Ssu-ma shih shu-i*, makes this kind of wen an aspect of ritual. See Ebrey, "Education Through Ritual," pp. 287–93.

51. See the three prefaces to collections of poetry in *SMWC* 69.854–55; two of these date from 1085.

52. *Lun-yü* 7.1.

53. Reply to Ch'en Ch'ung, *SMWC* 59.707.

54. Inscription for T'ai-p'ing chou school (1066), *LCWC* 82.863.

55. Reply to Wu Hsiao-tsung, *LCWC* 74.786.

56. The context for this is Ssu-ma's objection to the simultaneous establish-

ment of "schools" of Neo-Taoism (*hsuan-hsueh*), ju, history, and wen under the Liu-Sung dynasty in the fifth century. Quoted in Lin Jui-han, "Ssu-ma Kuang," pp. 59–60. The passage is found in *TCTC* 123.3868.

57. Hou Wai-lu (*Chung-kuo ssu-hsiang t'ung-shih*, pp. 421–22) suggests that many of the essays in Wang's collection are from the *Huai-nan* collection, but it has yet to be determined which are. Lu Tien (*T'ao shan chi* 15.164–65) saw these works in the early 1060's and felt they represented a kind of learning different from Hu Yuan's, then current among southeastern shih-ta-fu. Liu An-shih (1048–1125) later recalled that in the early 1060's Wang's essays were circulating and "all admired him and compared him to Mencius" (see Ma Yung-ch'ing, *Yuan-ch'eng yü-lu* 1.6). In 1070 some examination candidates were already citing Wang's commentary, the *Hung-fan chuan* (see *Hsu tzu-chih t'ung-chien ch'ang-pien* 215.5246).

58. The remnants of the *Songs* commentary are collected in Ch'iu Han-sheng, *Shih i kou-shen*.

59. For Wang An-shih's writings, see Yü Ta-ch'eng, "Wang An-shih chu-shu k'ao." Although Wang's commentary on the *Change* is lost, his collected writings contain essays on the *Change*.

60. Wang An-shih, *Wang An-shih Lao-tzu chu chi-pen*.

61. On Wang's commentaries, see Chikusa, "Ssu-ma Kuang Wang An-shih yü fo-chiao." Wang gained the court's permission to convert his estate into a monastery in 1084. Whether he converted to Buddhism is unclear. Andō Tomonobu ("Ō An-seki to bukkyō") notes that no compelling explanation exists for a presumed conversion. A convincing case has yet to be made for Buddhist inspiration in Wang's political vision. Chikusa argues that Wang was not a Buddhist layman, that his creation of a monastery was a common act of filial piety among well-to-do literati, and that his interest in Buddhist texts proceeded from an interest in supporting his Confucian views. Chiang I-pin (*Sung-tai ju shih t'iao-ho-lun*, pp. 22–58) has suggested the likelihood that some philosophical ideas in Wang's essays are derived from Buddhist sources. His point is not to make Wang a Buddhist, but to show that Wang was synthesizing Buddhism and Confucianism. I would restate this: in formulating what he saw as an inclusive and coherent vision, Wang included aspects of Buddhism and Taoism.

62. For this polarity, together with the inner-outer and knowledge-action polarities, see Schwartz, "Some Polarities in Confucian Thought." Winston Lo ("Wang An-shih") demonstrates that Wang was indeed committed to self-cultivation.

63. *LCWC* 68.722–23.

64. Reply to Wang Shen-fu, *LCWC* 72.766–67, citing *Meng-tzu* 7A19.

65. See, e.g., "About Inferring Destiny," "Response to Objections," and "Method of Conduct," *LCWC* 70.741, 68.728, 67.718.

66. *LCWC* 67.710–11, citing the "Way of Heaven" chapter; Watson, *Complete Works of Chuang Tzu*, pp. 146–47.

67. See, e.g., "Explaining Destiny," "On Succeeding," "Selecting Talent," "Promoting Worthies," and "Assigning Responsibilities," *LCWC* 64.682, 69.733–37.

68. *LCWC* 68.713.

69. *LCWC* 69.731.

70. Inscription for the T'ai-p'ing chou school, *LCWC* 82.863.

71. See, e.g., Wang's discussion of Heaven and man with regard to sacrifices (*LCWC* 66.660).

72. Reply to Han Ch'iu-jen (mid-1060's), *LCWC* 72.763.

73. *Lun-yü* 17.2.

74. Reply to Kung Shen-fu, *LCWC* 72.765–66. In another edition of Wang's collection (noted in *LCWC*, appendix, pp. 1081–82), this is given as a letter to Wang Shen-fu. In either case, the letter probably dates from the mid-1050's.

75. *LCWC* 64.679–80.

76. *LCWC* 67.715; 68.726–27; appendix, pp. 1064–65.

77. Speaking of Wang Shen-fu in his reply to Kung Shen-fu, *LCWC* 72.765.

78. Reply to Han Ch'iu-jen, *LCWC* 72.763, citing *Lun-yü* 4.15.

79. Ibid., citing *Lun-yü* 6.7, 12.1.

80. Reply to Kung Shen-fu, *LCWC* 72.765.

81. *LCWC* 68.725–26.   82. *LCWC* 67.717–18.

83. *LCWC* 67.716.   84. *LCWC* 67.715.

85. *LCWC* 67.714. Ssu-ma Kuang did not share this Mencian view, seeing only a difference of degree. He argued that political order under any circumstances depended upon the same principles; if order had been achieved by a hegemon, he must have been following the same principles as kings (see "Doubts About Mencius" [1055], *SMWC* 73.896). For a discussion of Sung debates on differences between king and hegemon, see Tillman, *Utilitarian Confucianism*, pp. 46–53.

86. "An Official and Recluse," *LCWC* 69.730–31.

87. *LCWC* 69.737.   88. *LCWC* 69.738.

89. *LCWC* 67.713–14.   90. *LCWC* 70.748 (sixth question).

91. *LCWC* 67.711–12.

92. Hsia Ch'ang-p'u ("Wang An-shih," p. 315) has argued that after 1068 Wang changed his view of human nature to argue that good values were innate. I think this mistakes Wang's point that men are capable of doing good if the environment is correctly structured. "On Ritual" (*LCWC* 66.701), for example, argues both that the "intent" of ritual was to transform human character and that ritual accomplished this by guiding innate tendencies toward socially constructive ends. "On the Origin of Excessiveness" (*LCWC* 69.732) argues that a true order returns men to the constants when they have gone to an extreme. In both cases, the burden lies with the external order.

93. *LCWC* 69.734.

94. *LCWC* 73.779.

95. "On the Great Man," *LCWC* 66.707.

96. *LCWC* 66.701. Shimizu Kiyoshi ("Ō An-seki") makes this point in his discussion of the "Explanation." See also Wang's "Explanation of the Airs of the States" (*LCWC*, appendix, pp. 1071–72) and his discussion of the *Songs* in the reply to Han Ch'iu-jen (*LCWC* 72.761–62).

97. *LCWC* 84.878–79.

98. Reply to Wu Hsiao-tsung, *LCWC* 74.786.

99. "Explanation of the Images in the *Change*," *LCWC* 65.697–700, presents the 64 hexagrams as a coherent sequence teaching the "way of the superior man." See also *LCWC* 63.668, 63.671, 66.708. Wang disavowed some of his earlier writing on the *Change* as having failed to grasp the proper sequence and discourages a student from studying the *Change*; it is not clear whether these writings are meant (see reply to Han Ch'iu-jen, *LCWC* 72.764).

100. *LCWC* 71.759.

101. Preface to the commentary on the *Institutes of Chou*, LCWC 84.878.

102. *LCWC* 65.685–97.

103. *Chou i*, "Hsi-tz'u chuan" A11.

104. This refers to "in heaven it becomes [= brings about] images" and "what brings about the image is called *ch'ien* [the first hexagram, associated with heaven]" (ibid. A1, A5).

105. Referring to ibid. A5: "What imitates the model is called *k'un* [the second hexagram, opposite of *ch'ien*, thus here representing man (otherwise earth)]."

106. "On the Significance of the River Chart and Lo Writing," *LCWC* 63.673. This text is also found in *chüan* 9 of Lu Tien, *T'ao-shan chi*. If it is by Lu, then, Lu being Wang's student, we might take it as an example of imitation returning as parody.

107. Inscription for the school at Ch'ien-chou, *LCWC* 82.859.

108. "On Ritual and Music," *LCWC* 66.706.

109. Ibid.

110. *LCWC* 66.708. Both Winston Lo ("Wang An-shih") and K'o Ch'ang-i in his account of Wang's philosophical thought (*Wang An-shih p'ing-chuan*, pp. 194–196) treat "On Attaining Unity" as a statement of Wang's basic philosophy.

111. *LCWC* 66.708.   112. *Chou i*, "Hsi-tz'u chuan" B3.

113. Ibid. A9.   114. Ibid. B3.

115. *LCWC* 66.707.

116. The *Tzu shuo* is now lost. Fifty-two entries (some of which may be incomplete) have been collected in K'o Chang-i, *Wang An-shih p'ing chuan*, pp. 242–47. Further quotations can be found in the reconstructed commentary on the *Lao-tzu* and in Wang's *Chou kuan hsin i*. Winston Lo ("Wang An-shih"; "Philology") has written on the importance of this work in Wang's thought. For Wang's introduction to the *Tzu shuo*, see *LCWC* 84.879; for the memorial of presentation, see *LCWC* 56.608–9 (translated in Williamson, *Wang An-shih*, pp. 308–10).

117. Wang An-shih, *Chou kuan hsin i* 1.3a.

118. *Lun-yü* 13.3.

119. Wang An-shih, *LCWC* 84.880. The submission material (*LCWC* 56.608–9) elaborates in particular on the claim that the "so-of-itself moral significance" can still be known in spite of changes in writing and language.

120. For the *Li-nien t'u* record of events, see *Chi-ku lu* 11.63b–15.39a.

121. These interjections were compiled by Wu Yao-kuang into a separate text in the Ch'ing period; see Ssu-ma Kuang, *T'ung-chien lun*. I thank James H. Zimmerman for providing this text.

122. For the primary intent of the *Tables* (also known as the *Chronological Tables of the Hundred Offices and Court Ministers* [*Pai-kuan kung-ch'ing nien-piao*]), see the general introduction in *SMWC* 68.841–42. For the inclusion of its events in the *Chi-ku lu*, see the request for the appointment of editors, in *SMWC* 52.647–48. The events are in *Chi-ku lu* 17.89a–20.116a.

123. Ssu-ma also produced a "private" historical work, the *Su-shui chi-wen* in 16 *chüan*, a collection of fairly detailed accounts of Sung events based on his own first-hand knowledge, the oral accounts of others, and, in some instances, textual sources.

124. For a discussion of the various areas of Ssu-ma Kuang's interests and the works he produced in these areas, see Fumoto, "Shi-ba On-kō no gakugyō ni tsuite."

125. Patricia Ebrey discusses Ssu-ma's approach to family rituals in her introduction to Yuan Ts'ai's *Precepts for Social Life* in her *Family and Property*. For some remarks on Ssu-ma's work in relation to the historical genre of *shu-i*, see Ebrey, "T'ang Guides to Verbal Etiquette." The text and the rituals are treated most extensively in four articles by Yamane Mitsuyoshi (see the Bibliography, p. 468).

126. See, e.g., his preface to the *Garden of Names* (*Ming yuan*), *SMWC* 68.846. For a general account of his involvement in these projects, see Fumoto, "Shi-ba On-kō no gakugyō ni tsuite," pp. 38–44.

127. *SMWC* 75.917–19.

128. He requested in 1050 that the government print Yang's *Exemplary Sayings* and the *Hsun-tzu* (*SMWC* 18.276).

129. *SMWC* 73.854–96. Ssu-ma did not accept that human nature was inherently good, but he does not make this an issue in his critique.

130. Ssu-ma selected what he thought of value in the *Chung shuo* and included it in a biography of Wang T'ung (*SMWC* 72.886–90). The views cited here appear in the evaluation (*SMWC* 72.888–90).

131. "No One Knows Me," in the *Foolish Writings*, *SMWC* 74.911.

132. Ssu-ma did occasionally disagree with Yang. See, e.g., "On the Three Efforts," *SMWC* 65.801.

133. Ssu-ma Kuang, *Fa-yen chi-chu* and *Chi-chu T'ai-hsüan*, both in 10 *chüan*.

134. Su Hsun (*Chia-yu chi* 7.1b–2a), for example, criticized Yang for being more interested, in the *Supreme Mystery*, in numerology than the tao and for failing to grasp the intentions of the sages in creating the *Change*. In the next generation both Su Shih and Ch'eng I rejected Yang Hsiung.

135. "On Mystery," *SMWC* 67.834–35. This essay appears in the commentary as "On Reading the *Mystery*." Something of this goal was evident in Ssu-ma's 1057 commentary on the *Classic of Filial Piety* (*Ku-wen Hsiao ching chih-chieh*). See the introduction and memorial of submission in *SMWC* 68.847 and 17.253, in which he supposes a connection between political principles and filial piety as something "so-by-itself."

136. Ssu-ma Kuang, *I Shuo*; see the introduction.

137. Ssu-ma Kuang, *Ch'ien-hsu*. Known editions of this unfinished work include later elaborations; I have not used it because I do not know which parts are from Ssu-ma's hand.

138. See, e.g., "Tao Is Great" (1078) in the *Foolish Writings* (*SMWC* 74.911) and, to an extent, "Systematic Account of [My] Four-Sentence Inscription" (*SMWC* 67.836).

139. *SMWC* 20.301.

140. *SMWC* 58.649.

141. *SMWC* 67.853.

142. For an account of Loyang as a capital of the intellectual opposition to the New Policies, see Freeman, "Loyang and the Opposition to Wang An-shih." Ssu-ma's assertion that moral principles (*i*) derive from "number" (glossed as yin and yang and the five phases in Ssu-ma Kuang, *I shuo*, introduction 2a) can be seen as agreement with Shao Yung against Ch'eng I, but I do not think Ssu-ma proceeded, in the style of Shao Yung, to use a coherent numerological system as a basis for defining social values. My understanding of Shao Yung and Ch'eng I's objections to the priority of number come from Kidder Smith and Wyatt, "Shao Yung and Number."

143. *SMWC* 74.910, from "Ordering the *Ming*" in the *Foolish Writings*. Note that in 1085 he changed the title of his standard memorial on the emperor's duties as ruler to include "cultivating the mind," but did not change its content.

144. See, e.g., "Standards for Shih" (1057) and "Heaven and Man" (1074) in the *Foolish Writings*, *SMWC* 74.906–7; and "Heaven and Man" (1085) in "Appreciations of Non-action," *SMWC* 74.916.

145. "Seeking to Be Used" in the *Foolish Writings*, *SMWC* 74.912–13.

146. See, e.g., "On Centrality and Harmony," *SMWC* 64.793–96; and his correspondence with Fan Chen and Han Wei in *SMWC* 62.752–69. On *chung-ho* and ritual, see *TCTC* 192.6051–53.

147. These comments are based on two letters to Han Wei (*tzu* Ping-kuo), *SMWC* 62.766–69.

148. Ssu-ma Kuang, *Tao-te chen-ching lun* 1a.

149. *Chou i*, "Shuo kua" 1.

150. "Pattern and Nature" (1079) in the *Foolish Writings*, *SMWC* 74.909.

151. "Attaining Knowledge Lies in Restraining Things," *SMWC* 65.808–9.

152. "Bringing the Mind Back" (1081) and "Cutting Off Four Things" (1083), both in the *Foolish Writings*, *SMWC* 74.910–12.

153. *SMWC* 66.821–22.

154. Ssu-ma Kuang, *Li-nien t'u* 16.83a.

155. *SMWC* 17.254.

156. Preface to the *Tables of the Hundred Offices* and memorial submitting the *Comprehensive Mirror*, *SMWC* 68.841–42, 17.262–63.

157. Ssu-ma Kuang, *Li-nien t'u* 16.86a–b.

158. See, e.g., the discussion of Eastern Han, Northern Wei, Sui, and T'ang, *Li-nien t'u* 13.112a–13b; 14.26a–28a, 14.37a–38a, 15.68a–72b.

159. For a discussion of Ssu-ma's methods, see Pulleyblank, "Chinese Historical Criticism," p. 151–66; and Wang Te-i, "Ssu-ma Kuang."

160. These are also available separately in Ssu-ma Kuang, *T'ung-chien lun*. Part of the *Mirror* has been translated into English and annotated by Achilles Fang; see *Chronicle of the Three Kingdoms*.

161. See, e.g., Ming K. Chan, "Historiography of the *Tzu-chih t'ung-chien*"; Huang Sheng-hsiung, "*T'ung-chien*" *shih-lun*; Lin Jui-han, "Ssu-ma Kuang"; Chi P'ing, *Ssu-ma Kuang hsin-lun*, pp. 49–90; the various articles in Liu Nai-ho and Sung Yen-shen, "*Tzu-chih t'ung-chien*" *ts'ung-lun*; Tanaka Kenji, "*Shiji tsugan*"; and Chang Yuan, "*T'ung-chien* chung te nan-pei chan-cheng," which is notable for its careful analysis of Ssu-ma's relation of events and his use of primary sources.

162. *TCTC* 291.9510–13, 192.6051–53.

163. *TCTC* 220.7064–65, entry for A.D. 757.

164. Ssu-ma Kuang, *I shuo* 5.23a–25a.

165. *TCTC* 291.9510.

166. *TCTC* 244.7874–75; cf. 7.234, 244.7880–81.

167. *TCTC* 244.7880–81.

168. See, e.g., Ssu-ma's praise for Emperor Shih-tsung of the Later Chou (*TCTC* 294.9599–600).

169. *SMWC* 27.881.

170. *TCTC* 69.2185–88.

171. *TCTC* 11.375–76, 22.742, 27.881.

172. *Chou i*, "Hsi-tz'u chuan" IA.

173. Ssu-ma Kuang, *I shuo* 1.10b–11b.

174. *TCTC* 291.9510.

175. *TCTC* 73.2329; cf. 28.916, 79.2503, 104.3295, 220.7064–66.

176. Two examples of good rulers are Kuang-wu of the Han (*TCTC* 40.1285, cf. 68.2173–74 for contrasts with his successors), and Shih-tsung of the Later Chou (*TCTC* 294.9599–600).

177. *TCTC* 51.1648–50, 220.7050, 291.9510–13.

178. *TCTC* 12.416; cf. 11.370, 159.4954–55.

179. Ssu-ma Kuang, *I shuo* 2.5b–7b.

180. *TCTC* 51.1648, 149.4353.

181. *TCTC* 291.9510–13. On the difference in office holding, see 73.2329–31.

182. *TCTC* 159.4945.

183. *TCTC* 28.916, 79.2503.

184. Sariti, "Monarchy, Bureaucracy, and Absolutism"; he takes issue with Hsiao Kung-ch'üan's interpretation of Ssu-ma Kuang's political thought. Ming K. Chan, "Historiography of the *Tzu-chih t'ung-chien*," is closer to Hsiao.

185. *TCTC* 56.1823, 245.7899–900; cf. 1.14–15, 11.375–76, 40.1285, 51. 1648–50, 139.4353.

186. *TCTC* 22.742.

187. *Tso chuan*, Ch'eng 2; cf. Legge, *Chinese Classics*, 5: 344.

188. *Lun-yü* 13.3; cf. Lau, *Analects*, p. 118.

189. *I ching*, k'un; trans. Wilhelm, *I Ching*, p. 13. *Shang shu*, "Kao-yao mo"; trans. James Legge, *Chinese Classics*, 3: 73.

190. *Shang shu*, "I Chi"; trans. Legge, *Chinese Classics*, 3: 88.

191. *TCTC* 192.6052–53, quoting *Li chi*, "Li ch'i" 2.

192. *Tso chuan*, Hsi 25; trans. Legge, *Chinese Classics*, 5: 196. The last sentence of the quote is Ssu-ma Kuang's addition.

193. *TCTC* 68.2173–74.

194. *TCTC* 4.121.

195. *TCTC* 1.14–15.

196. *TCTC* 28.917.

197. *TCTC* 2.48–49, 286.9191.

198. *TCTC* 23.773, 197.6201–2.

199. *TCTC* 56.1817.

200. *TCTC* 1.1–6.

201. *TCTC* 14.482; cf. 17.577, 53.1725–26, 57.1837.

202. *TCTC* 22.723, 106.3348–49, 192.6029, 220.7050–51 (read with 218.6994), 245.7916, 291.9510–13.

203. *TCTC* 73.2329–31, 192.6051–52.

204. For a fuller treatment of Wang An-shih's New Policies and Ssu-ma Kuang's criticisms, see Bol, "Goverment, Society, and State," pt. IV.

205. "Pen-ch'ao pai nien wu shih cha-tzu," *LCWC* 41.444.

206. *SMWC* 42.543–45, from 1068/8. Whether this is a true version of the debate (the text is out of place in Ssu-ma's collection), it does accurately reflect the positions of both men.

207. Of particular interest is the examination of the effects of the new economic policies in Szechuan and the northwest in Paul J. Smith, "State Power and Economic Activism."

208. *Hsu tzu-chih t'ung-chien ch'ang-pien: Shih-i* 4.3b–4a (1070/2) and 5.19 (1070/9).

209. For an overview of most of the New Policies, see James T. C. Liu, *Reform*, pp. 4–7; and Higashi, *Ō An-seki jiten*, pp. 43–90. For a chart with institutional details of the various policies, see *Wang An-shih yen-chiu tzu-liao hui-pien*, pp. 357–70.

210. *Hsu tzu-chih t'ung-chien ch'ang-pien* 224.5442–43 (1071/6).

211. Ibid. 215.5232 (1070/9); cf. 225.5474–75 (1071/7), 250.6089–90 (1074/2), and 251.6129 (1074/3).

212. Ibid. 236.5742 (1072/interc.7).

213. Ibid. 240.5827 (1072/11).

214. Ibid. 220.5334 (1071/2).

215. Ibid. 248.6056 (1073/12).

216. Ibid. 237.5764 (1072/8); cf. 215.5230–31 (1070/7).

217. Ibid. 214.5223 (1070/8).

218. Ibid. 240.5829 (1072/11).

219. This view of Wang is close to that of many PRC scholars (although in recent years this view has come to be seen as bad). This is often discussed under the rubric of Wang's attitude toward "engrossers" (*chien-ping*). I was not convinced of the accuracy of this portrayal, however, until reading the passages in the *Hsu tzu-chih t'ung-chien ch'ang-pien*, discussed below, and the discussion of engrossers in Paul J. Smith, "State Power and Economic Activism."

220. *Hsu tzu-chih t'ung-chien ch'ang-pien: Shih-i* 4.5 (1069/2); cf. *Hsu tzu-chih t'ung-chien ch'ang-pien* 223.5433–34, 223.5419 (1071/5); 232.5640–41 (1072/4); 240.5828–29 (1072/11); and 262.7407 (1075/4).

221. *Hsu tzu-chih t'ung-chien ch'ang-pien* 218.5299–300 (1070/12), 237.5764 (1072/7); for the initial regulations, see 218.5297. For a full account of Wang's plans and the emperor's doubts, see Teng Kuang-ming, "Wang An-shih."

222. *Hsu tzu-chih t'ung-chien ch'ang-pien* 235.5697 (1072/7). Regular military training took place mainly in the northern border *lu*.

223. Ibid. 218.5297 (1070/10). The rules required that pao-chia leaders be men of ability and intelligence from landowning households of any grade.

224. Ibid. 263.6436–37, 6451 (1075/interc.4).

225. Ibid. 215.2312 (1070/9).

226. Memorial (1069/8), *SMWC* 43.547–50; cf. letter to Wang (1070/2), *SMWC* 60.719.

227. Memorial (1074/8), *SMWC* 45.572; final testament (1082), *SMWC* 17.258. See also his letters to Wang, *SMWC* 60.719–27.

228. *SMWC* 60.719–24, 726–27.

229. *SMWC* 41.523–24 (1067/9).

230. Memorial (1070/2), *SMWC* 44.559–63. Although Ssu-ma was predicting consequences, some of these problems did emerge. For example, the need to meet loan quotas and secure the loans led officials to force the rich to borrow (see Paul J. Smith, "State Power and Economic Activism").

231. *SMWC* 17.258–59, 45.575–77.

232. *SMWC* 17.259, 45.575.

233. *SMWC* 17.259.

234. Memorial (1069/2), *SMWC* 40.517–22.

235. For a general statement, see the 1085 request to abolish the New Policies, *SMWC* 46.588–91. This is detailed in memorials on the pao-chia, military, and hired service (*SMWC* 46.591–94, 48.611–13, 47.608–9). Not everyone was persuaded that the hired service system should be abolished (see *SMWC* 49.626–28, 55.669–71).

236. *SMWC* 46.586–88.

237. *SMWC* 50.638–40, 51.641–42, 54.661–67, 55.671–75, 57.685–90, all dating from 1086.

238. *SMWC* 46.624–26 (dated 1085).

Chapter 8

1. For Su Shih's literary writings I have followed *Su Tung-p'o chi* (*STPC*), a set of seven collections of Su's prose, poetry, and documentary writing; and the Southern Sung anthology of Su's prose, *Chiao-cheng ching-chin Tung-p'o wen-chi shih-lueh* (*TPWC*). A new six-volume edition of Su's prose, *Su Shih wen-chi*, compiled and edited by K'ung Fan-li, was published in 1986. For poetry, I have followed *Su Shih shih-chi*, annotated by Wang Wen-kao. There are numerous anthologies of Su's prose and poetry, a recent example being *Su Shih hsuan-chi*, compiled and annotated by Wang Shui-chao. Some of the most famous prose pieces are translated and discussed in Ogawa and Yamamoto, *So Tō-ba shū*. See also Le Gros Clark, *Selections from the Works of Su Tung-p'o*; (for *fu*) idem, *Prose-Poetry of Su Tung-p'o*; and Shih Shun Liu, *Classical Chinese Prose*, pp. 225–86. Ogawa and Yamamoto are publishing a complete, annotated translation of Su's poetry: *So Tō-ba shishū*. Fuller, *Road to East Slope*, translates and critically discusses Su's poetry and some prose written before and during the Huang-chou exile

period. For the exile in Huang-chou, see also Ginzberg, "Alienation and Reconciliation." For a selection from all periods, see Watson, *Su Tung-p'o*.

For Su's writings on literature and art, see *Su Shih lun wen-i*, compiled by Yen Chung-ch'i. Many of Su's comments on painting are included in Bush and Shih, *Early Chinese Texts on Painting*. For an early discussion of Su's place in the history of Sung poetry, see Yoshikawa, *Introduction to Sung Poetry*, pp. 97–112. For a study of Su Shih as a literary critic and theorist, see Chang Chien, "Su Shih wen-hsueh p'i-p'ing." Su has begun to receive considerable scholarly attention, especially in the PRC. See, e.g., Liu Nai-ch'ang's collected articles on Su, *Su Shih wen-hsueh lun-chi*; and two collections of articles by various authors: *Su Shih yen-chiu chuan-k'an*, and *Su Tung-p'o yen-chiu lun-ts'ung*. These three works are not limited to literature and art. Two articles by Ronald C. Egan, "Poems on Paintings" and "Ou-yang Hsiu and Su Shih on Calligraphy," explore Su Shih's aesthetics. Note also Diana Yu-shih Chen, "Change and Continuation." My interpretation of Su Shih has been enriched through discussions with Michael Fuller.

2. After reading Su Shih and Su Ch'e, Ch'ien Mu (*Sung ming li-hsueh*, pp. 29–30) concludes that they were good at synthesis but offered no guiding principles.

3. Chou Tun-i, *T'ung shu* 28, in *Chou Lien-hsi chi* 6.117–18; trans. Wing-tsit Chan, *Source Book*, p. 476, modified.

4. *IS* 18.239; see the discussion of this passage in Owen, *Remembrances*, pp. 131–33.

5. Letter to the rescript writers ("Shang liang-chih shu"), *TPWC* 42.729.

6. Quoted in Li Chih, *Shih-yu t'an-chi* 30a. Su himself notes that not all literati who had gained fame for *wen* in the eleventh century had been willing to act as "leaders of the alliance"; see his comment on Ts'ai Hsiang, in Su Shih, *Tung-p'o t'i-pa* 4.85.

7. Ch'in Kuan, letter to Fu Pin-lao (1086), *Huai-hai chi* 14.1.

8. George Hatch ("Su Shih") notes that Su has come to be seen more as a beloved cultural figure than as a serious thinker. Lin Yu-tang, *The Gay Genius*, certainly the most charming biography of a Sung figure yet written, incorporates many of these anecdotes. His sources are annotated in the Japanese translation by Goyama Kiwamu (Lin Yü-t'ang, *So Tō-ba*). For Su Shih anecdotes, see *Su Tung-p'o i-shih hui-pien*.

9. *STPC* 1.2.0.42.

10. Su Ch'e's biography was the basis for the *Sung shih* account, the longest and most detailed biography in that text and evidence of the high estimation of his political role by later historians. Modern biographies include Hatch, "Su Shih"; Lin Yü-t'ang, *Gay Genius*; Tseng Tsao-chuang, *Su Shih p'ing-chuan*; Chikusa, *So Tō-ba*; and Tanaka Katsumi, *So Tō-ba*. For a chronology of Su's career, see Wang Pao-chen, *Su Tung-p'o nien-p'u*.

11. Su Shih's ideas have occasionally been taken seriously in literary studies, the best example being Fuller, *Road to East Slope*. Intellectual historians have attended to him as well; he appears in some surveys of Sung thought. In English, see March, "Self and Landscape"; and especially George Hatch's discussions of Su

Shih's various writings in *Sung Bibliography*, pp. 4–9, 14–19, 247–48, 331–32, 396–98, 459–61. Other sources are cited below.

12. *TPWC* 41.715. A more elaborate and profound version of Su's thesis is found in his 1089 introduction to Ou-yang's collected works (*TPWC* 59.903, trans. in Shih Shun Liu, *Chinese Classical Prose*, pp. 280–85). Su claimed to have first heard of Ou-yang Hsiu in 1043 in connection with the Ch'ing-li reform and said that in 1057 Ou-yang introduced him to Han Ch'i and Fu Pi, the two other survivors of the Ch'ing-li leadership, who proceeded to treat Su as a *kuo-shih* (a shih with the potential for national leadership); see Su's introduction to Fan Chung-yen's collection, *TPWC* 56.906).

13. Commemorative text for Ou-yang, *STPC* 2.6.35.56.

14. "A Great Sigh: For Ch'in Shao-chang," *STPC* 3.8.9.18. Ch'in Kou (T. Shao-chang) stayed with Su while the latter was prefect of Hang-chou in 1089–90; see Chang Lei's farewell preface in *K'o-shan chi* 40.475; this edition misprints "Shao-chang" as "Shao-yu."

15. Hu Hung, *Hu Hung chi*, p. 156.

16. *Shih ching*, Hsiao ya, "T'ien pao." See Waley, *Book of Songs*, p. 125.

17. It is not clear to what extent Su Hsun's work on the *Change* was taken over by Su Shih; most take the commentary as a statement of Su Shih's ideas. Su Shih himself claimed that he first gained insights into the text on his own and "then following the learning of my late father, composed the *Commentary on the Change* in nine *chüan*" (letter to Wen Yen-po written in Huang-chou, *STPC* 2.5.29.110.

18. *STPC* 1.2.0.49–50.

19. Once his readers, Han-lin academicians and rescript writers of the Secretariat (one of whom was Wang An-shih), passed his 50 essays, Su sat for two one-day examinations, the first administered by academicians and the second by the emperor. Su Ch'e also passed this examination, having been recommended for it by Ssu-ma Kuang, but Su Shih placed in the third grade, the highest rank ever allowed in the Sung. The immediate reward was a promotion, and success in this examination marked Su as a future candidate for policymaking offices. He was one of a total of only 35 men who passed the decree examination in the Sung. For a full account of the institution of the decree examination, see Wang Te-i, "Sung-tai hsien-liang fang-cheng k'o k'ao."

20. *TPWC* 42.725.   21. *TPWC* 42.726.

22. *TPWC* 42.726–27.   23. *TPWC* 42.727.

24. *TPWC* 42.728.

25. Letter to Chief Councillor Tseng Kung-liang, *TPWC* 41.723. This letter was written after the 50 essays had been accepted but before the two examinations. Su sent "ten pieces" with the letter but does not mention their titles.

26. This discussion of Su's approach to pattern and change is based primarily on his use of the terms in the 1061 essays. For "change," see "On Ch'ao Ts'o" (*STPC* 6.18.10.68) and Proposal 16 (*STPC* 6.18.4.27) for examples of changes that destroy the equilibrium (*chih-p'ing*) of organisms. See "On Kuan Chung"

(6.18.8.57) for the sense of "variations," in this case variations resulting from numerical operations. In Proposal 17 (6.18.4.29) "knowing the theory of change" is shown to mean understanding that a minor element can become larger and more destructive. "On I Yin" (6.18.7.55) warns that change cannot be precluded, and the present is susceptible to the types of changes found in the past. Proposal 23 (6.18.5.39) suggests blocking the route through which change takes place "while the whole is still flourishing," i.e., keeping any political element from gaining such strength as would enable it to disturb the entire matrix of relationships.

"Pattern" appears far less frequently in these essays. After explaining that something will turn into the opposite of that for which it was originally intended, Su often comments "its pattern is so" or "evident" (e.g., Proposal 24 [6.18.5.4] and "On the Great Minister," pt. II [6.18.6.50]). I have found no further use of *tzu-jan chih li* in these essays, but the term *shih* carries the same idea, albeit stronger (men can change their minds about keeping to a principle, but they succumb to the situation and the force of events). I have taken note of Su's discussion of "pattern" in policy in a draft answer for the palace exam from about 1070 (*TPWC* 21.333), which elaborates on a sentence from the letter under discussion: "When the pattern cannot be transformed, then they wish to do it through coercion."

27. *STPC* 6.18.1.8.   28. Proposal 16, *STPC* 6.18.4.27.

29. Proposal 8, *STPC* 6.18.2.15.   30. Proposal 4, *STPC* 6.18.1.7.

31. *STPC* 6.18.1.1–2; the introduction is lines 1–9 of Proposal 1.

32. Hereafter the policy proposals are referred to in the text by their number. For the texts of the proposals and their order, I have followed *STPC* 6.18.1.1–5.45. For a brief discussion of their institutional content, see Ch'en Ch'i-han, "Lun Su Shih te Chia-yu 'chin-ts'e.' "

33. That there are three divisions does not contradict the claim of a dualistic nature. Proposal 23 concerns China and barbarians in general, and Proposals 24 and 25 deal with relations with small and large barbarian states, respectively. Su is referring to relations between the Sung and the small Hsi Hsia state and the large Liao state, but he does not name them.

34. For 20 essays on historical figures, see *STPC* 6.18.7.51–10.73. In the text they are referred to by title and number.

35. "On Tzu-ssu," *STPC* 6.18.8.60.

36. *STPC* 9.18.8.60.

37. "On Meng K'o," *STPC* 6.18.8.61; citing *Lun-yü* 15.3, cf. Lau, *Analects*, p. 132.

38. "On Yueh I," *STPC* 6.18.9.63.

39. Su cites Han Yü's attempt to unify Mencius, Hsun-tzu, and Yang Hsiung (the sources of the three views on human nature) in Han's "On the Origin of the Nature." There Han cites Confucius's claim (*Analects* 17.2) that the "average" man, in contrast to the superior/wise and the inferior/stupid man, is indeed capable of either moral improvement or degeneration.

40. "On Chu-ko Liang," *STPC* 6.18.10.72.

41. "On Han Yü," *STPC* 6.18.10.73.

42. Su's major critique of the New Policies came in a "myriad-word memorial"

to Sheng-tsung (*TPWC* 24.369–96). His objections were put more directly and starkly in 1070/2 in a second letter to the emperor (here he changes his mind on the military policy; see *STPC* 5.14.1.55–57). Also of value is his draft question and answer for the palace examination of 1070 (*TPWC* 21.329–41). Parts of the first memorial are translated in de Bary, *Sources of Chinese Tradition*, 1:426–31, and by J. K. Rideout in Birch, *Anthology of Chinese Literature*, pp. 370–80. The dating of Su's major attacks on the New Policies has been the source of some confusion (the dates in standard collections are inappropriate). This has now been resolved, and the correct dates (followed here) determined; see Huang Jen-k'o, "Su Shih lun hsin-fa wen-tzu."

43. For the record of Su's prosecution, see P'eng Chiu-wan, *Tung-p'o wu-t'ai shih-an*; 6a refers to Su's collection, *Yuan-feng hsu-t'ien Su Tzu-chan hsueh-shih Ch'ien-t'ang chi*. The case record is discussed by Hatch in Hervouet, *Sung Bibliography*, pp. 448–49. A recent discussion is Hartman, "Su Shih and Literary Persecution." The case record includes Su's explanation of the criticisms implied by his poems and prose pieces.

44. For some of the proposals made in the debate over the proposed reform, see Lee, *Government Education and Examinations*, pp. 205, 240–45.

45. Memorial on schools and examinations (1069/5, dating following Huang Jen-k'o, "Su Shih lun hsin-fa wen-tzu"), *TPWC* 29.493–98.

46. Preface to Ou-yang Hsiu's literary collection, *TPWC* 56.906.

47. *TPWC* 29.497–98.

48. *TPWC* 21.329–41, dated to 1070/3 (following Huang Jen-k'o, "Su Shih lun hsin-fa wen-tzu").

49. Farewell preface, full text (undated), *STPC* 4.12.8.43.

50. *STPC* 2.6.30.11.

51. *TPWC* 23.366.

52. *TPWC* 22.344.

53. Preface to Ou-yang's literary collection, *TPWC* 56.903–6.

54. Record for a Buddhist temple in Hang-chou (1075), *TPWC* 54.863–64. Su's preface to Yen T'ai-ch'u's literary collection (1074) has similar remarks (*TPWC* 56.911–12).

55. *Sun-tzu* 6.2b.

56. *Lun-yü* 19.7; trans. Lau, *Analects*, p. 154, modified.

57. *TPWC* 57.931–32.

58. *TPWC* 50.829. For a translation and discussion, see Fuller, *Road to East Slope*, pp. 210–12.

59. *TPWC* 60.992.

60. *Tao te ching* 12; trans. Lau, *Lao Tzu*, p. 68.

61. *TPWC* 53.857. Fully translated in Egan, "Ou-yang Hsiu and Su Shih on Calligraphy," pp. 404–5. Egan discusses Su's use of *yü-i* and *liu-i*, which he translates as "lodge his mind in" and "fix his mind upon."

62. *TPWC* 60.986.

63. Record for a Buddhist temple in Ch'eng-tu, *TPWC* 54.866.

64. *TPWC* 50.827.

65. Record for a painting by Wen T'ung at Ching-yin Cloister, *TPWC* 54.874–75; trans. Bush, *Chinese Literati on Painting*, p. 42, modified.

66. See Su's reflections on this problem in his record for Sun Chueh's pavilion for calligraphy (1072), *TPWC* 48.810–11.

67. Shao Yung, *Huang-chi ching-shih shu* 8B.16a. This citation and my understanding of Shao are drawn from Kidder Smith and Wyatt, "Shao Yung and Number."

68. *STPC* 2.6.32.32.

69. *Lun-yü* 4.15, trans. Waley, *Analects*, p. 105; cf. Lau, *Analects*, p. 74, who translates "loyalty" as "doing one's best" and "consideration" as "using oneself as a measure to gauge others."

70. *Lun-yü* 4.8; my translation borrows from Lau, *Analects*, p. 97, but Su interprets the passage differently.

71. *Lun-yü* 15.3.

72. Su Shih, *Tung-p'o t'i-pa* 1.10.

73. *Meng-tzu* 7A.26, trans. Lau, *Mencius*, p. 188, slightly modified.

74. I am indebted to Willard Peterson for this phrase; in "Confucianism in the Ming Dynasty," he doubts that Li Chih (1527–1602) had a "sharable ethic."

75. Reply to Li Tuan-shu, *TPWC* 47.794–96.

76. Letter to T'eng Ta-tao, *STPC* 4.11.4.15. For the dating of the *Change* commentary, see his letter to Wen Yen-po, *STPC* 2.5.29.110, noted in Tseng Tsao-chuang, "Ts'ung *P'i-ling I-chuan*," pp. 59–60.

77. Letter to Su Po-ku, *STPC* 4.12.7.29.

78. Su Shih, *Su-shih I chuan* 2.33 ("T'ung jen") and 3.59 ("Wu wang"). See further the discussion in Bol, "Su Shih and Culture."

79. For references to "recent scholars," see Su Shih, *Shu chuan* 4.3a, 6.11a, 9.14a, 12.5a, 14.11b, 16.19a, and 20.6a; for the use of a document as a false precedent, see ibid. 7.7a, 8.16b, 11.15b, 12.6b, 13.5a–b.

80. Letter to Wang Hsiang, *TPWC* 46.875.

81. See Su Shih, *Shu chuan* 3.16b–17b, on reading the *Documents* for the "intent"; Su Shih, *Su-shih I chuan* 7.163, for the *Change* and the Classics in general, and 7.156, for comprehending a hexagram as a coherent whole.

82. For more detail, see Bol, "Su Shih and Culture." I have benefited from interpretations by Hou Wai-lu et al., *Chung-kuo ssu-hsiang t'ung shih*, pp. 584–89; Hatch, "*Su-shih I-chuan*"; Tseng Tsao-chuang, "Ts'ung *P'i-ling I-chuan*"; and K'ung Fan, "Su Shih *P'i-ling I-chuan*."

83. Su Shih, *Su-shih I chuan* 6.138 ("Huan").

84. Ibid. 7.160, quoting *Lun-yü* 15.29.

85. See, e.g., his commentaries on "T'ai Chia," "The Great Announcement," and "The Canon of Yao," Su Shih, *Shu chuan* 7.13b, 11.15b, and 1.9b, respectively.

86. Su Shih, *Shu chuan* 8.2b–3a; Legge, *Chinese Classics*, 3: 223–24.

87. Su Shih, *Shu chuan* 8.3b; Legge, *Chinese Classics*, 3: 225.

88. Ibid. 8.5a–b.

89. Su Shih, *Shu chuan* 8.12a–b, 15b.

90. Ibid. 8.16a–b; Legge, *Chinese Classics*, 3: 247.

91. He finds two exceptions: "The Punitive Expedition to Yin" and "The Announcement to the Prince of K'ang" (see Su Shih, *Shu chuan* 6.8a).

92. See, e.g., Yü's doubts about Shun's virtue (ibid. 4.7a–b).

93. Ibid. 6.3a.

94. Ibid. 7.7a. See also the account of the Chou king Mu, ibid. 18.6b–7a.

95. Ibid. 7.4a–7b. Others have read the passage as referring to T'ang's fear that his unethical conduct would be discussed by later men; see Legge, *Chinese Classics*, 3: 177.

96. Su Shih, *Shu chuan* 9.10a–11a.

97. Ibid. 16.10b–11a.

98. See further "The Prince of Lü on Punishments," ibid. 19.1a–15a.

99. Su Shih, *Shu chuan* 16.13b–14a.

100. See ibid. 13.12a–13a, for a general statement.

101. See Su's discussion of the "Great Announcement," "Announcement Concerning K'ang," "Announcement Concerning Drunkenness," and "The Timber of the Tzu Tree," ibid. 13.5a–5b; cf. 20.6a. Legge, *Chinese Classics*, 3: 419.

102. Su Shih, *Shu chuan* 13.12a–b.

103. Ibid. 6.10b–11a. In this case Su argues that the document, which treats terror and love as a polarity, contradicts the teachings of the sages.

104. Ibid. 16.19a.

105. Ibid. 6.5a, 18.5b (quotation).

106. Ibid. 3.3a–b, 9.2a, 11.16a, 12.1a–b, 18.3b, 19.4b–6a.

107. Ibid. 1.9a–b; note that Su assumes that Yao's ministers were partial and self-interested to some extent. See also Su's treatment of Shun, ibid. 2.1a–17b.

108. Ibid. 20.7b; Legge, *Chinese Classics*, 3: 627.

109. See Su Shih, *Shu chuan* 6.11a, for a reference to Legalist writers.

110. Ibid. 19.4a.   111. Ibid. 16.6b–17a.

112. Ibid. 13.17b.   113. Ibid. 13.18a.

114. Su can at least envision the possibility that music (and by extension ritual perhaps) can be so totally in tune with cosmic process that it can control *ch'i* and attract things. This depends on getting the scale just right, but knowledge of the basic note on which the scale depends to be in cosmic tune was lost in antiquity; had it not been lost, everyone alike could make cosmically harmonious music (ibid. 4.9b–10a).

115. On "human affairs," see ibid. 7.11b, 8.25a, 13.11b; on the mandate, see ibid. 7.8b.

116. Ibid. 2.2b–3a.

117. Ibid. 10.2a–b, 11.8a.

118. Ibid. 10.2a–b.

119. Ibid. 8.26a–b. The remark on five phases theory is repeated at ibid. 11.8a.

120. Ibid. 4.7a–b.   121. Ibid. 4.9a.

122. Ibid. 20.7b–8a.   123. Ibid. 4.4b–5a.

124. Ibid. 7.4b–5a.

125. Ibid. 3.5a–b. I would read the reference to the sincere mind (ibid. 7.16a) in

these terms also. Cf. ibid. 15.16b, on the dependence of the moral trajectory of one's cultivation on what the mind concentrates on.

126. Ibid. 8.23b.

127. Several passages seem to affirm an innate morality: "All men possess the *hsing* of benevolence and righteousness," "The *hsing* is without not good," and the claim that the best-known virtues "all come from what is so-by-itself of the populace's *hsing*" (ibid. 7.8a, 7.16a, 3.18b–19a). In context, however, these claims are used to reach other conclusions. In the first case Su concludes that therefore rulers should stick to the "constants" of benevolence and righteousness rather than trusting to their emotions, in the second he argues that the task is therefore to "correct this [*hsing*] so as to make it even stronger," and in the third he concludes that this is how goodness is perverted and that men should attend to practice instead. It is significant, I think, that when glossing a line that privileges "rectifying virtue" over ensuring material well-being Su goes to some lengths to argue that "the virtue of the populace" can be corrected only when material well-being is secured (ibid. 3.4a).

128. Ibid. 3.16b–17b.

129. Ibid. 3.14b.

130. Ibid. 3.16b–17b.

131. Ibid. 3.9a.

132. From "The Counsels of the Great Yü"; cf. Legge, *Chinese Classics*, 3: 61–62.

133. *Chung-yung* 1.

134. Su Shih, *Shu chuan* 3.7b–8b.

135. Legge, *Chinese Classics*, 3: 216, modified. The document is entitled "Both Possessed Pure Virtue" in Legge's translation.

136. Su Shih, *Shu chuan* 7.20b–21a; the quotation at the end of the passage is from *Chung-yung* 30.

137. Su Shih, *Shu chuan* 7.6b (Shang), 16.4a (Chou).

138. Ibid. 3.14b.

139. Ibid.

140. Ibid. 16.8a.

141. Ibid. 12.12a–b.

142. See, e.g., ibid. 10.9b, 10.10a–b.

143. Ibid. 10.1a.

144. Ibid. 10.7a–11b.

145. Ibid. 10.9a.

146. Ibid. 10.9a–b.

147. Ibid. 10.10b–11a.

148. Ibid. 10.5a–6a.

149. *STPC* 1.2.0.50.

150. For a discussion of Su's four major followers, Chang Lei (1054–1114), Ch'ao Pu-chih (1053–1110), Ch'in Kuan (1049–1100), and Huang T'ing-chien (1045–1105), see Bol, "Culture and the Way," chaps. 5–9.

151. Letter to Yü Kua, *TPWC*, citing *Analects* 15.41.

152. *Tso chuan*, p. 307, Hsiang 25/*fu* 2.

153. Letter to Hsieh Min-shih, *TPWC* 46.780. A longer passage from this letter appears below.

154. *Shih chi* 84.2482.

155. Letter to Hsieh Min-shih, *TPWC* 46.780. Another passage from this letter appears below.

156. Ts'ao Pa (fl. mid-eighth century) was famous for both his paintings of

imperial horses and imperial ministers (see Acker, *Some T'ang and Pre-T'ang Texts on Chinese Painting*, p. 296). I thank Susan Bush for pointing this out. Another possibility is Ts'ao Pu-hsing of the state of Wu during the Three Kingdoms period.

157. Su Shih, colophon for Chün-mo's "flying white," *Tung-p'o t'i-pa* 4.78.

158. This contrasts with Confucius's assertion in *Lun-yü* 7.1 that "I transmit but do not innovate" (trans. Lau, *Analects*, p. 87).

159. "Carpenter Shih, whirling his hatchet with a noise like the wind," could slice the mud cleanly off a plasterer's nose (Watson, *Complete Works of Chuang Tzu*, p. 269).

160. Colophon for a painting by Wu Tao-tzu (dated 1085), *TPWC* 60.997–98.

161. See also the discussion of "innovation" in Egan, "Ou-yang Hsiu and Su Shih on Calligraphy," pp. 412–19.

162. See Watson, *Complete Works of Chuang Tzu*, pp. 162, 199–200, 152–53.

163. *TPWC* 56.913–15.

164. Trans. Bush and Shih, *Early Chinese Texts on Painting*, p. 196, modified.

165. *TPWC* 49.813–14; trans. Bush and Shih, *Early Chinese Texts on Painting*, pp. 207–8, slightly modified.

166. *TPWC* 57.947.

167. Letter to Hsieh Min-shih, *TPWC* 46.779–81.

168. *Chou shu* 41.744–45.

169. *HCLC*, preface.

Chapter 9

1. For the writings and sayings of Ch'eng I, I have followed *ECC*. Because I am primarily concerned with Ch'eng I apart from Ch'eng Hao, almost all selections from the recorded sayings (*I shu*), found in vol. 1 of *ECC*, are taken from *chüan* 15 through 24. Whether the twenty-fifth collection (*chüan* 25) records only Ch'eng I's sayings has been doubted. A number of studies have informed my discussion of Ch'eng I: Kidder Smith, "Ch'eng I"; Graham, *Two Chinese Philosophers*; idem, "What Was New in the Ch'eng-Chu Theory of Human Nature?"; Wing-tsit Chan, *Source Book*, pp. 518–71; Willard J. Peterson, "Another Look at *Li*"; Tu Wei-ming, "Neo-Confucian Ontology"; de Bary, *Neo-Confucian Orthodoxy*, pp. 1–17; and Owen, *Remembrances*, pp. 131–33. My translations are indebted to those found in Chan and Graham, cited above. For Ch'eng I's life and the dating of many of his writings, I have followed Yao Ming-ta, *Ch'eng I-ch'uan nien-p'u*. For a discussion of Ch'eng I's family background, his early aspirations, and his criticism of education, see Bol, "Ch'eng Yi and Cultural Tradition." On Ch'eng's regional following before 1086, see Yao Ming-ta, *Ch'eng I-ch'uan nien-p'u*, pp. 121, 134.

2. Ch'eng I passed the department examination but failed the palace *chin-shih* examination according to both Lü Kung-chu's 1066 memorial recommending him (see Yao Ming-ta, *Ch'eng I-ch'uan nien-p'u*, p. 134) and a memorial on schools and examinations in Ch'en Hsiang, *Ku-ling chi* 8.12a–b.

3. *IS* 15.166.

4. Yao Ming-ta, *Ch'eng I'ch'uan nien-p'u*, p. 26 (1057); letter to Emperor Jen-tsung (1057), *ECC: wen-chi* 5.515.

5. For an account of Loyang during this period, see Michael D. Freeman, "Loyang and the Opposition to Wang An-shih."

6. For a documentary account of Ch'eng I's appointment, his plans and demands, and the attacks on him, see Yao Ming-ta, *Ch'eng I-ch'uan nien-p'u*, entries for the years 1086 and 1087.

7. See ibid., pp. 247, 253.

8. *Meng-tzu* 4B22, "I have not had the good fortune to have been a disciple of Confucius. I have learned it indirectly from him through others" (trans. Lau, *Mencius*, p. 132).

9. "Ming-tao hsien-sheng mu-piao," *ECC: wen-chi* 11.640.

10. *ECC: wen-chi* 11.638. I suspect Ch'eng is trying out *ssu-li* (i.e., *t'ien-li*) as an alternative to *ssu-tao* in this passage.

11. The term "tao-hsueh" comes from the "Great Learning" chapter of the *Book of Rites*. It was used by Chang Tsai, who lamented that the court treated "tao-hsueh and administration as separate affairs." I capitalize the term Tao-hsueh because Ch'eng I apparently thought his learning was the only possible tao-hsueh as a categorical term for thinking about the cosmic and the innate. For usage of the term, see Ch'en Jung-chieh, "Tao-hsueh."

12. Yao Ming-ta, *Ch'eng I-ch'uan nien-p'u*, p. 204 (1087); text for Li Tuan-po, *ECC: wen-chi* 11.643.

13. For an admonition to his disciples to believe their teacher, see *ECC: wen-chi* 9.616–17.

14. Ibid. 6.542.

15. Ibid. 6.546.

16. Text for Liu Chih-fu, ibid. 11.643.

17. *IS* 21B.274.

18. *IS* 6.95; there are two other versions of this; see *IS* 18.187.

19. Yao Ming-ta, *Ch'eng I-ch'uan nien-p'u*, pp. 24–25 (1057); *ECC: wen-chi* 5.513. The *ECC* text has been followed.

20. Yao Ming-ta, *Ch'eng I-ch'uan nien-p'u*, p. 47 (1068); *ECC: wen-chi* 8.579–80.

21. *IS* 22A.269.

22. *IS* 18.187–88.

23. Tillman, *Utilitarian Confucianism*, p. 23.

24. *IS* 18.239. For a discussion of his critique from a literary perspective, see Owen, *Remembrances*, pp. 131–33.

25. *IS* 21A.268, emended following formulations in *IS* 15.162–63, 17.177, 18.200, and 22A.277.

26. *IS* 15.166.

27. *ECC: I chuan* 4.957; trans. Graham, *Two Chinese Philosophers*, p. 20, slightly modified.

28. Ch'eng contends that even if men recovered the ancient cultural forms they would not work, because the physical constitution of man has changed (*IS* 15.146; trans. below). See also *IS* 19.263, which holds that the medical theory of the *Su wen* was applicable only under Yao and Shun when *ch'i* was regular.

29. *Lun-yü* 9.11, 12.15; trans. for 9.11, Lau, *Analects*, p. 97.

30. *IS* 18.209.

31. *ECC: wen-chi* 9.600–601. The essence of this is also stated in *IS* 18.221.

32. Yao Ming-ta, *Ch'eng I-ch'uan nien-p'u*, p. 20 (1057). "Yü Fang Yuan-ts'ai," *ECC: i-wen* p. 671.

33. Chou Tun-i, "T'ung shu," *Chou Lien-hsi chi*, 6.117.

34. *IS* 18.205.

35. *IS* 15.164.

36. See, e.g., his account of the *Spring and Autumn Annals* (*IS* 15.163–64). See also *IS* 17.176, on the words of the sages as both immediate and far-reaching; and 22A.279, on reading the *Analects* as if one were the questioner. One passage does come close to the literary attitude of reading the text to discern the character of the author; unfortunately it falls in the highly suspect twenty-fifth collection (*IS* 25.322). Note that Ch'eng disclaims the ability (claimed by Mencius) to know men from their manner of speaking (*IS* 22A.280). *IS* 19.263 comes close, but the issue here, I think, is that Mencius was more prolix than Yen Hui. It is important to recognize that Ch'eng I distinguishes the words of the sages from the Classics; the former have authority. Thus in the case of the *Songs*, for example, he contends that the "Great Preface" could have been written only by the sage, whereas the "Minor Prefaces" are merely the works of historians of the time (*IS* 19.256).

37. *IS* 19.258; cf. 18.188, 24.213, and comments on the *Spring and Autumn Annals* in the previous note.

38. *IS* 15.156.

39. *IS* 15.146. For a more summary account of this discussion, see *IS* 15.171–72, where the central point is that changes in the times necessitate changes in the legacy of the sages.

40. *Chou i*: "Hsi tz'u chuan" B2 reads: "The Yellow Emperor, Yao, and Shun let the garments hang down, and the world was in order; they must have taken this from *ch'ien* and *k'un*."

41. *Chung-yung* 31; translated for this context. Wing-tsit Chan translates, "All embracing and extensive, and deep and unceasingly springing, these virtues come forth at all times" (*Source Book*, p. 112).

42. *Meng-tzu* 3A4; trans. following Lau, *Mencius*, p. 102. In the *Mencius*, the people are the subject of these efforts; Ch'eng takes ch'i transformation to be the subject.

43. *Meng-tzu* 2B13; trans. Lau, *Mencius*, p. 94.

44. *IS*, 15.146. For a more summary account of this discussion, see *IS* 15.171–72, where the central point is that changes in the times necessitate changes in the legacy of the sages.

45. Letter to Yang Shih, *ECC: wen-chi* 9.609.

46. This does not mean that doctrine is the source of values, for Ch'eng's doctrine is true because it based on a correct understanding of man in relation to heaven-and-earth. When Ch'eng does discuss changes in values from a cultural perspective, he explains that values changed because men were ignorant of tao and were thus left with no choice but to respond to events in terms of tradition. For "cultural" accounts of changes in values, see *IS* 18.194, 18.236. For indications

that Ch'eng still accepted the connection between ch'i cycles and historical change (although he thought it was not easy to pin down), see *IS* 18.199–200, 19.236.

47. *IS* 21B.273; cf. *IS* 15.161 on the variability of ch'i resulting necessarily in the existence of both superior men and lesser men; in antiquity, however, sage government was able to prevent lesser men from "realizing their evil."

48. See *IS* 15.161.

49. *IS* 18.198–99.

50. *IS* 18.223.

51. *IS* 15.148; cf. 15.165–67.

52. *IS* 2A.13, citing Ch'eng I.

53. *Chung-yung* 22; trans. following Wing-tsit Chan, *Source Book*, pp. 108–9. Chan translates "fully develop" rather than "fulfill." If the nature is whole from the start, men can fulfill its potential. The issue here, I think, is realizing its potential in practice.

54. *Chou i*: "Hsi tz'u chuan" A1.

55. *IS* 18.182–83; cf. 15.158. In one instance the unity between man and things (e.g., plants and animals) is based not on the equality of their natures but on the fact that the pattern of their generation is one (*IS* 24.315, 18.193). Passages discussed below, however, equate nature with pattern.

56. *IS* 22A.291–92.

57. *IS* 18.209.

58. *IS* 18.192.

59. *IS* 15.159.

60. *IS* 18.216.

61. *IS* 15.152; cf. 18.192, 18.226.

62. *IS* 18.226.

63. *IS* 18.211–12.

64. *IS* 21B.274.

65. *IS* 18.226, 15.152; cf. 19.256: the only innate ability man has is to suckle; all else must be acquired.

66. *IS* 18.209, 18.226; cf. 15.154.

67. *IS* 22A.291. Ch'eng I uses "the original of the nature" to refer to that part of the nature which is innately good rather than the particular character a man is endowed with; see *IS* 19.252.

68. *IS* 21A.274.

69. *IS* 18.206; referring to *Meng-tzu* 2A2.

70. *IS* 18.204.

71. *IS* 18.204–205.

72. *IS* 18.204.

73. *IS* 18.204.

74. *IS* 5.76.

75. *IS* 15.162–63; cf. 17.177, 21A.268, 22A.277. The source of this formulation is certainly *Meng-tzu* 6A7: "What is common to all minds? *Li* and *i*. The sage is simply the first to discover what is common to our minds. Thus *li* and *i* please my mind in the same way as meat pleases my palate" (trans. Lau, *Mencius*, p. 164, slightly modified).

76. *IS* 15.162.

77. *IS* 15.144.

78. *IS* 18.193; citing *Meng-tzu* 6A6.

79. *IS* 18.196; cf. 22A.293.

80. *IS* 18.195.

81. *IS* 15.156.

82. *IS* 15.144.

83. Su Shih, *Su-shih I chuan* 7.156.

84. *IS* 18.208; citing *Meng-tzu* 7A1.

85. But Ch'eng I can also say that "mind is where tao exists. . . . Mind and tao are a unity" (*IS* 21B.276, 24.312).

86. *IS* 18.204.

87. *IS* 24.313.

88. *IS* 18.215.

89. See, e.g., *IS* 19.252, 21B.274, 22A.293.

90. Graham, *Two Chinese Philosophers*, p. 125.

91. *IS* 18.224 and 22A.227: "How should we *ko-wu* [investigate things]? Answer: Just establish your sincere intent and *ko-wu*. The speed depends upon individual intelligence. The smart *ko-wu* quickly; the dim do it slowly."

92. *IS* 18.193.

93. *IS* 6.83.

94. *IS* 18.196.

95. *IS* 15.149; cf. *IS* 15.162, 15.168–69, 18.183, 18.185, 24.315.

96. *IS* 22A.277. For a more elaborate account, see *IS* 18.188.

97. In a sentence that would later become famous, Ch'eng uses a word that might be translated as "investigate": "But both the grasses and trees have pattern; you must *ch'a* [examine, check]." It appears in a discussion of Ch'eng's saying "Contemplate [the li of] a thing and check [*ch'a*] yourself." Did Ch'eng mean that one should "see the [li of a] thing and then seek it in the self"? One should not say this, Ch'eng responds, because "things and self are one li; when you are illuminating [li] there, you are seeing it here; [this is] the tao of uniting internal and external." The dialogue concludes: "Question: As for attaining knowledge: how about first seeking it in the four beginnings [of benevolence, righteousness, propriety, and wisdom]? Answer: Seeking it in nature-and-emotion [i.e., the internal, where the four beginnings exist] certainly is more immediate to the person, but each plant and each tree has pattern; it is necessary to check" (*IS* 18.193).

98. Ch'eng does see the implications for understanding natural phenomena. See, e.g., *IS* 19.247: "Anything that is before your eyes is a thing; everything has a pattern. For example, from why fire is hot and why water is cold to the relations between ruler and minister and between father and son, all is pattern." The question is whether illuminating these patterns requires investigating the phenomena in question and drawing inferences. Note *IS* 15.149: "Although the transforming process of heaven-and-earth is independent and inexhaustible, still, the degrees of yin and yang and the changes of temperature and night and day all have constants. This is how tao maintains a constant mean [*chung-yung*]."

99. Quoted in *Hsu tzu-chih t'ung-chien ch'ang-pien* 240.5827 (1072/11).

100. The tradition of calendrical studies, which measured these phenomena, apparently held little interest for Ch'eng. See, e.g., *I shu* 15.150. He was, however, concerned with numerology, an integral part of calendrical science and one tradition of *Change* interpretation, and those who used it to make connections between heaven-and-earth and human affairs. His comments on Shao Yung reveal that Ch'eng was concerned primarily with denying that number could be used in place of pattern to understand heaven-and-earth. Shao's achievement, he says in one instance, was his seeing that pattern was prior to number (*IS* 18.197). For the priority of pattern to number and image in the *Change*, see *IS* 21A.271. There are

two issues here: proponents of numerology, as a way of knowing the constants of heaven-and-earth, in effect made pattern a function of number, whereas Ch'eng wants pattern to be directly accessible. He denies that any form of knowledge mediates between the mind and seeing li. An amusing example of this stance is evident in the following anecdote. "Shao Yung said to Master Ch'eng, 'Although you are very smart, given how many affairs there are in the world, can you know them all?' The Master answered, 'Certainly there are many affairs under heaven that I do not know, but what are you referring to by "not knowing"?' At that moment there was a clap of thunder. Shao Yung said, 'Do you know where thunder comes from?' The Master replied, 'I know it, but you don't know it.' Shao Yung was startled: 'What do you mean?' The Master said, 'If you knew it, would you have to use number to make inferences? It is because you do not know that you depend upon inference to know.' Shao Yung said, 'Where do you think [thunder] comes from?' The Master said, 'It comes from where it comes from.' Shao Yung was taken aback and offered his praise" (IS 22A.270).

101. For the T'ang exegesis, see Li chi cheng i 60.445, in Shih-san ching chu-shu, p. 1673.

102. IS 15.157; cf. 15.152, 17.175.

103. IS 18.188. For a somewhat different translation, see Wing-tsit Chan, Source Book, pp. 560–61. Graham's translation is preferable; see Two Chinese Philosophers, p. 76. Cf. IS 18.193, 19.247.

104. IS 19.247.

105. IS 15.149.

106. Meng-tzu 2A2; Mencius says that floodlike ch'i is "born of accumulated rightness" (trans. Lau, Mencius, p. 78).

107. IS 18.206; cf. 18.193.

108. IS 18.206; cf. 18.193.

109. W. J. Peterson, "Another Look at Li."

110. In an essay on Yen-tzu, Ch'eng had treated the five virtues (the four plus hsin, good faith or belief) as five natures, parallel to the five phases; his mature teachings allow for only the four beginnings. "In the nature there are only the four beginnings but no belief" (IS 18.184).

111. IS 18.204. Cf. "But [man's] nature is good. It can be fulfilled through learning. Therefore it is called the nature. What is received from heaven is called the nature. Stimulated, it becomes emotional response. Acting, it becomes the mind" (IS 24.312).

112. IS 21B.274.   113. IS 22A.292.

114. Meng-tzu 7A1.   115. Chou i, "Shuo Kua."

116. IS 22A.292.   117. IS 24.313.

118. IS 21B.274.   119. IS 18.183–84.

120. IS 21B.276.   121. IS 15.168.

122. IS 18.182.   123. IS 15.144.

124. IS 18.225–26; quoting Chung-yung 26, trans. following Wing-tsit Chan, Source Book, p. 109.

125. IS 18.225.

126. IS 18.185.

127. *IS* 18.206.

128. This distinction also appears in the suspect twenty-fifth chapter; see *IS* 25.317: "Knowledge from hearing and seeing is not knowledge from the moral nature. If you know it by having compared things, it is not internal. . . . Knowledge from the moral nature does not draw upon hearing and seeing."

129. *IS* 19.257.

130. *IS* 18.188.

131. *IS* 18.186.

132. *IS* 15.164.

133. *IS* 18.186.

134. *IS* 18.191.

135. *IS* 18.190.

136. *IS* 18.190.

137. *IS* 21A.269, 18.195.

138. *IS* 15.152.

139. *IS* 18.224, 225, 237, 238.

140. *IS* 18.237.

141. *IS* 18.224.

142. *IS* 17.175–76.

143. *IS* 18.189.

144. On the distinction between shih and others, see *IS* 18.243–44. Ch'eng granted that in antiquity, but not the present, the distinction had been made according to the person after schooling; see *IS* 15.166. For the T'ang clan system, see *IS* 18.242; cf. *IS* 15.150.

145. *IS* 18.220.

146. See *IS* 18.239–40, on the project, and 18.241–45, on specific issues.

147. *IS* 18.189.

148. *IS* 17.174–75.

149. *IS* 18.204.

150. Cited in Yao Ming-ta, *Ch'eng I-ch'uan nien-p'u*, p. 262.

151. *ECC: wen-chi* 9.616–17.

152. On Chu's critiques of Wang and Su, see Bol, "Chu Hsi's Redefinition of Literati Learning"; on intellectual trends under the Jurchens, see Bol, "Seeking Common Ground."

153. Chou Mi, *Kui-hsin tsa-shih*, p. 169.

154. For Chu's objections, see Bol, "Chu Hsi's Redefinition of Literati Learning," pp. 151–60.

155. For a statement of this view, see Tu Wei-ming, "Neo-Confucian Religiosity and Human-relatedness."

156. Chu Hsi and Lü Tsu-ch'ien, *Reflections on Things at Hand*. Ch'eng I was the major source of quotes.

157. Daniel K. Gardner has written extensively on Chu's work on the Classics and Four Books; see, e.g., *Chu Hsi and the "Ta-hsueh"*; and Gardner's introduction to his translation of Chu Hsi, *Learning to Be a Sage*, pp. 23–56.

158. Chu Hsi, *I-lo yuan-yuan lu*. Even Chu recognized that some of those he included could not be counted as "members" of the Ch'eng school; see his comments on Fan Tsu-yü (7.6a) and Yang Kuo-pao (7.7a).

159. For an example of Chu Hsi dealing with problems left by the Ch'engs, see the account of Chu's work on the *Change* and his ideas about self-cultivation in Adler, "Chu Hsi and Divination." For Chu's disputes with other lines of Tao-hsueh thought, see Tillman, "Southern Sung Confucianism."

160. See Ch'en Ch'un, *Neo-Confucian Terms Explained*.

161. For Chu's views on literature, see Lynn, "Chu Hsi as Literary Theorist

and Critic." Note also Lü Tsu-ch'ien's anthology of ku-wen style prose, the *Ku-wen kuan-chien*, and his imperially commissioned anthology of Northern Sung literature, the *Huang Sung wen-chien*. A preface to the latter by Chou Pi-ta defined wen in terms of li and ch'i.

162. On academies and their activities, see Walton, "Institutional Context of Neo-Confucianism"; Wing-tsit Chan, "Chu Hsi and the Academies"; and Hymes, "Lu Chiu-yuan." See also Chaffee, *Thorny Gates of Learning*, pp. 89–94; and idem, "Chu Hsi and the Revivial of the White Deer Grotto Academy."

163. For a translation and discussion of the *Chu-tzu chia-li* (The family rituals of Master Chu), see Ebrey, *Chu Hsi's "Family Rituals."* Also dealing with rituals is Kelleher, "Chu Hsi and Public Instruction."

164. For the compact, see Übelhör, "Community Compact."

165. Von Glahn, "Community and Welfare." For Lu Chiu-yuan's lack of interest in community organizations, see Hymes, "Lu Chiu-yuan."

166. For a summary of Chu's views on the minds of tao and man, see de Bary, *Message of the Mind*, pp. 9–12. Chu's most definitive statement is in his introduction to the *Doctrine of the Mean* (see *Chung-kuo che-hsueh shih tzu-liao hsuan-chi*, pp. 286–88; partially translated in de Bary, *Message of the Mind*, pp. 28–29; and Gardner, "Transmitting the Way," pp. 169–71). Wing-tsit Chan ("The Principle of Heaven vs. Human Desires") argues that Chu Hsi was opposed only to selfish desires, not to desire per se.

Bibliography

This bibliography is divided into three sections: Primary Sources (pp. 449–57); Secondary Sources in Chinese and Japanese (pp. 457–69); and Works in Western Languages (pp. 469–81).

Primary Sources

The following abbreviations are used in this section:

KHCT   *Kuo-hsueh chi-pen ts'ung-shu* 國學基本叢書
SKCS   *Wen-yuan ko Ssu-k'u ch'üan-shu* 文淵閣四庫全書
SPPY   *Ssu-pu pei-yao* 四部備要
SPTK   *Ssu-pu ts'ung-k'an* 四部叢刊
TSCC   *Ts'ung-shu chi-ch'eng ch'u-pien* 叢書集成初編

Chang Lei 張耒. *K'o-shan chi* 柯山集 (Literary collection of Chang Lei). *TSCC*.
Chang Tsai 張載. *Chang Tsai chi* 張載集 (Collected works of Chang Tsai). Peking: Chung-hua, 1978.
———. *Chang-tzu ch'üan-shu* 張子全書 (Complete works of Chang Tsai). *SPPY*.
Chang Yung 張詠. *Kuai-yai chi* 乖崖集 (Literary collection of Chang Yung). *SKCS*.
Ch'ao Chiung 晁迥. *Chao-te hsin-pien* 昭德新編 (The new collection on illuminating virtue). *Ch'ao shih ts'ung-shu* 晁氏叢書.
Ch'ao Ch'ung-chih 晁冲之. *Ch'ao Chü-tz'u shih-chi* 晁具茨詩集 (Collected poetry of Ch'ao Ch'ung-chih). *Ch'ao shih ts'ung-shu* 晁氏叢書.
Ch'ao Kung-wu 晁公武. *Chün-chai tu shu chih* 郡齋讀書志 (Bibliographic notes of Ch'ao Kung-wu). Reprinted—Taipei: Shang-wu, 1978.
Ch'ao Pu-chih 晁補之. *Chi-pei Ch'ao hsien-sheng Chi-le chi* 濟北晁先生雞肋集 (Literary collection of Ch'ao Pu-chih). *SPTK*.
Ch'ao Yueh-chih 晁說之. *Sung-shan Ching-yü sheng chi* 嵩山景迂生集 (Literary collection of Ch'ao Yueh-chih). *Ch'ao shih ts'ung-shu* 晁氏叢書.
Chen Te-hsiu 真德秀. *Hsi-shan hsien-sheng Chen kung wen-chi* 西山先生真公文集 (Literary collection of Chen Te-hsiu). *KHCT*.

Ch'en Hsiang 陳襄. *Ku-ling chi* 古靈集 (Literary collection of Ch'en Hsiang). *SKCS*.

Ch'en P'eng-nien 陳彭年. *Kung-chü hsu-lueh* 貢舉紋略 (Brief account of examinations). *Hsueh-hai lei-pien* 學海類編. Reprinted—Shanghai: Han-fen lou, 1920.

Ch'en shu 陳書 (History of the Ch'en dynasty). Yao Ssu-lien 姚思廉. Peking: Chung-hua, 1972.

Ch'en Shun-yü 陳舜俞. *Tu-kuan chi* 都官集 (Literary collection of Ch'en Shun-yü). *SKCS*.

Cheng Hsieh 鄭獬. *Yun-ch'i chi* 郇溪集 (Literary collection of Cheng Hsieh). *SKCS*.

Cheng Kang-chung 鄭剛中. *Pei-shan chi* 北山集 (Literary collection of Cheng Kang-chung). *SKCS*.

Ch'eng Hao 程顥 and Ch'eng I 程頤. *Erh Ch'eng chi* 二程集 (Collected works of the two Ch'engs). 4 vols. Peking: Chung-hua, 1981.

Ch'i-sung 契嵩. *T'an-chin wen-chi* 鐔津文集 (Literary collection of Ch'i-sung). *SPTK*.

Chiang Shao-yü 江少虞. *Sung-ch'ao shih-shih lei-yuan* 宋朝事實類苑 (Facts about the Sung dynasty, by category). Shanghai: Shang-hai ku-chi, 1981.

Ch'iang Chih 強至. *Chi-pu chi* 祁部集 (Literary collection of Ch'iang Chih). *TSCC*.

Chien-yen i-lai hsi-nien yao-lu 建炎以來繫年要錄 (Chronological record of important events since the Chien-yen era). Li Hsin-ch'uan 李心傳. Reprinted—Taipei: Wen-hai, 1980.

Chin shih 金史 (History of the Chin dynasty). T'o-t'o 脫脫. Peking: Chung-hua, 1975.

Chin shu 晉書 (History of the Chin dynasty). Fang Hsuan-ling 房玄齡. Peking: Chung-hua, 1974.

Ch'in Kuan 秦觀. *Huai-hai chi* 淮海集 (Literary collection of Ch'in Kuan). *SPPY*.

Chiu T'ang shu 舊唐書 (Old History of the T'ang dynasty). Liu Hsu 劉昫 et al. Peking: Chung-hua, 1975.

Chou I yin-te 周易引得 (Concordance to the *Book of Change*). Harvard-Yenching Institute Sinological Index Series. Peiping, 1935.

Chou Mi 周密. *Kui-hsin tsa-shih* 癸辛雜識 (*Kui-hsin* miscellany). Peking: Chung-hua, 1988.

Chou Pi-ta 周必大. *P'ing yuan hsu-kao* 平園續稿 (Literary collection of Chou Pi-ta). In *Chou I-kuo Wen-chung kung chi* 周益國文忠公集.

Chou shu 周書 (History of the [Northern] Chou dynasty). Ling-hu Te-fen 令狐德棻. Peking: Chung-hua, 1974.

Chou Tun-i 周敦頤. *Chou Lien-hsi hsien-sheng ch'üan-chi* 周濂溪先生全集 (Complete works of Chou Tun-i). *TSCC*.

Chu Hsi 朱熹. *Chu-tzu yü-lei* 朱子語類 (Conversations of Chu Hsi, topically arranged). Edited by Li Ching-te 黎靖德. Peking: Chung-hua, 1986.

———. *Hui-an hsien-sheng Chu Wen-kung wen-chi* 晦庵先生朱文公文集 (Literary collection of Chu Hsi). *SPPY*.

———. *I-lo yuan-yuan lu* 伊洛淵源錄 (Records on the origin of the school of the two Ch'engs). Reprinted—Taipei: Wen-hai, 1968.

————. *Ming-ch'en yen-hsing lu* 名臣言行錄 (Record of the words and deeds of famous ministers). In *Ming-ch'en yen-hsing lu wu chi* 名臣言行錄五集. Reprinted—Taipei: Wen-hai, 1967.

Ch'üan T'ang shih 全唐詩 (Complete T'ang poems). Compiled by Ts'ao Yin 曹寅 et al. Shanghai: T'ung-wen, 1898.

Ch'üan T'ang wen 全唐文 (Complete T'ang prose). Compiled by Tung Kao 董誥. Reprinted—Peking: Chung-hua, 1983.

Ch'üan T'ang wen chi-shih 全唐文紀事 (Material relating to the *Complete T'ang Prose*). Compiled by Ch'en Hung-ch'ih 陳鴻墀. 3 vols. Peking: Chung-hua, 1959.

Ch'un-ch'iu ching-chuan yin-te 春秋經傳引得 (Combined concordances to *Ch'un-ch'iu, Kung-yang, Ku-liang,* and *Tso-chuan*). Harvard-Yenching Institute Sinological Index Series. Peiping, 1937.

Chung-yung 中庸 (Doctrine of the mean). In *Hsüeh Yung chang-chü yin-te* 學庸章句引得 (Concordance to the *Great Learning* and *Doctrine of the Mean*). Taipei: Chung-hua min-kuo K'ung Meng hsüeh-hui, 1970.

Fan Chung-yen 范仲淹. *Fan Wen-cheng kung chi* 范文正公集 (Literary collection of Fan Chung-yen). *SPTK.*

Fan Tsu-yü 范祖禹. *T'ang chien* 唐鑑 (Mirror of the T'ang). *Chin-hua ts'ung-shu* 金華叢書.

————. *Ti hsüeh* 帝學 (The learning of emperors). Seikado Library edition.

Han Ch'i 韓琦. *An-yang chi* 安陽集 (Literary collection of Han Ch'i). *SKCS.*

Han Fei-tzu chi-shih 韓非子集釋. Shanghai: Jen-min, 1974.

Han shu 漢書 (History of the Han dynasty). Pan Ku 班固. Peking: Chung-hua, 1962.

Han Wei 韓維. *Nan-yang chi* 南陽集 (Literary collection of Han Wei). *SKCS.*

Han Yü 韓愈. *Han Ch'ang-li chi* 韓昌黎集 (Literary collection of Han Yü). Edited by Chu Hsi 朱熹. Hong Kong: Shang-wu, 1964.

Hsia Sung 夏竦. *Wen-chuang chi* 文莊集 (Literary collection of Hsia Sung). *SKCS.*

Hsin T'ang shu 新唐書 (New history of the T'ang dynasty). Sung Ch'i 宋祁 and Ou-yang Hsiu 歐陽修. Peking: Chung-hua, 1975.

Hsin Wu-tai shih 新五代史 (New history of the Five Dynasties). Ou-yang Hsiu 歐陽修. Peking, Chung-hua, 1974.

Hsu Hsuan 徐鉉. *Hsu ch'i-sheng chi* 徐騎省集 (Literary collection of Hsu Hsuan). *KHCT.*

Hsu Sung 徐松. *Teng-k'o chi k'ao* 登科記考 (Study of the records of examination graduates [in the T'ang]). Peking: Chung-hua, 1984.

Hsu tzu-chih t'ung-chien ch'ang-pien 續資治通鑑長編 (Long draft of the continued *Comprehensive Mirror for Aid in Government*). Li T'ao 李燾. Vols. 2–20. Peking: Chung-hua, 1979–86.

Hsu tzu-chih t'ung-chien ch'ang-pien: Shih-i 續資治通鑑長編拾遺 (Addenda to the *Long Draft of the Continued Comprehensive Mirror for Aid in Government*). In *Hsu tzu-chih t'ung-chien ch'ang-pien*. Reprinted—Taipei: Shih-chieh, 1964.

Hu Hung 胡宏. *Hu Hung chi* 胡宏集. (Collected works of Hu Hung). Peking: Chung-hua, 1987.

Hu Su 胡宿. *Wen-kung chi* 文恭集 (Literary collection of Hu Su). *SKCS.*

Hu Yuan 胡瑗. *Chou I k'ou i* 周易口義 (Lectures on the *Change*). *SKCS*.

Huang Kan 黃幹. *Mien-chai hsien-sheng chi* 勉齋先生集 (Literary collection of Huang Kan). *Cheng i t'ang* 正誼堂.

Huang T'ing-chien 黃庭堅. *Yü-chang Huang hsien-sheng wen-chi* 預章黃先生文集 (Literary collection of Huang T'ing-chien). *SPTK*.

Hung Mai 洪邁. *I-chien chih* 夷堅志 (I-chien's record). 4 vols. Peking: Chung-hua, 1981.

———. *Jung-chai sui-pi* 容齋隨筆 (Hung Mai's literary miscellany). Shanghai: Ku-chi, 1978.

Ko Hung 葛洪. *Pao-p'u-tzu nei-p'ien chiao-shih* 抱朴子內篇校釋 (Critical annotated edition of *Pao-p'u-tzu nei-p'ien*). Edited by Wang Ming 王明. Peking: Chung-hua, 1985.

Ku Tung-kao 顧棟高. *Ssu-ma t'ai-shih Wen-kuo Wen-cheng kung nien-p'u* 司馬太史溫國文正公年譜 (Chronological biography of Ssu-ma Kuang). 1917.

Li Ao 李翱. *Li wen kung chi* 李文公集 (Literary collection of Li Ao). *SPTK*.

Li Chao-ch'i 李昭玘. *Le ching chi* 樂靜集 (Literary collection of Li Chao-ch'i). *SKCS*.

Li Chih 李廌 (1059–1109). *Chi-nan chi* 濟南集 (Literary collection of Li Chih). *SKCS*.

———. *Shih-yu t'an-chi* 師友談記 (Records of conversations with teachers and friends). *Hsueh-chin t'ao-yuan* 學津討源. Reprinted—Shanghai: Shang-wu, 1972.

Li Chih 李塦 (1161–1238). *Huang Sung shih ch'ao kang-yao* 皇宋十朝綱要 (Essentials of ten reigns of the Sung). Reprinted—Taipei: Wen-hai, 1980.

Li Kou 李覯. *Li Kou chi* 李覯集 (Collected works of Li Kou). Peking: Chung-hua, 1981.

Li Yuan-kang 李元綱. *Sheng-men shih-yeh t'u* 聖門事業圖 (Charts for sage learning). *Po-ch'uan hsueh-hai*. 百川學海.

Li Yuan-pi 李元弼. *Tso-i tzu-chen* 作邑自箴 (Self-admonitions for the subprefect). *SPTK*.

Liang shu 梁書 (History of the Liang dynasty). Yao Ssu-lien 姚思廉. Peking: Chung-hua, 1973.

Liu Ch'ang 劉敞. *Kung-shih chi* 公是集 (Literary collection of Liu Ch'ang). *SKCS*.

Liu Hsieh 劉勰. *Wen-hsin tiao-lung chu* 文心雕龍註 (The literary mind and the carving of dragons, with commentary). Hong Kong: Shang-wu, 1960.

———. *Wen-hsin tiao-lung hsin-shu* 文心雕龍新書 (The literary mind and the carving of dragons, new edition). Taipei: Ch'eng-wen, 1968.

Liu K'ai 柳開. *Ho-tung hsien-sheng chi* 河東先生集 (Literary collection of Liu K'ai). *San Sung jen chi* 三宋人集.

Liu Mu 劉牧. *I shu kou yin t'u* 易數鈎隱圖 (Charts for investigating the numerology of the *Change*). *SKCS*.

Liu Pin 劉攽. *P'eng-ch'eng chi* 彭城集 (Literary collection of Liu Pin). *SKCS*.

Liu Tsung-yuan 柳宗元. *Liu Tsung-yuan chi* 柳宗元集 (Collected works of Liu Tsung-yuan). Peking: Chung-hua, 1978.

Liu Yü-hsi 劉禹錫. *Liu Yü-hsi chi* 劉禹錫集 (Collected works of Liu Yü-hsi). Shanghai: Jen-min, 1975.

Lou Yueh 樓鑰. *Kung-kuei chi* 攻媿集 (Literary collection of Lou Yueh). *SKCS.*

Lu Chao-lin 盧照鄰. *Lu Chao-lin chi* 盧照鄰集 (Collected works of Lu Chao-lin). Peking: Chung-hua, 1980.

Lu Te-ming 陸德明. *Ching-tien shih-wen* 經典釋文 (Explanations of the characters in the Classics). Reprinted—Peking: Chung-hua, 1983.

Lu Tien 陸佃. *T'ao-shan chi* 陶山集 (Literary collection of Lu Tien). *Ts'ung-shu ch'i-ch'eng.*

Lu Yu 陸游. *Lu Fang-weng ch'üan-chi* 陸放翁全集 (Complete works of Lu Yu). Peking: Chung-kuo shu-tien, 1986.

Lun yü yin-te 論語引得 (A concordance to the *Analects* of Confucius). Harvard-Yenching Institute Sinological Index Series. Peiping, 1940.

Ma Tuan-lin 馬端臨. *Wen-hsien t'ung-k'ao* 文獻通考 (Comprehensive examination of the documentary record). *Shih t'ung* 十通.

Ma Yung-ch'ing 馬永卿. *Yuan-ch'eng yü-lu* 元城語錄. *TSCC.*

Meng-tzu yin-te 孟子引得 (A concordance to the *Mencius*). Harvard-Yenching Institute Sinological Index Series. Peiping, 1941.

Mu Hsiu 穆修. *Ho-nan Mu kung chi* 河南穆公集 (Literary collection of Mu Hsiu). *SPTK.*

Nan shih 南史 (History of the Southern Dynasties). Li Yen-shou 李延壽 et al. Peking: Chung-hua, 1975.

Ou-yang Hsiu 歐陽修. *Ou-yang Hsiu ch'üan-chi* 歐陽修全集 (Complete literary collections of Ou-yang Hsiu). Reprinted—Taipei: Shih-chieh, 1961.

———. *Shih pen-i* 詩本義 (The original significances of the *Songs*). *SKCS.*

Ou-yang Hsun 歐陽詢. *I-wen lei-chü* 藝文類聚 (Selections from literature, by category). Shanghai: Shang-hai ku-chi, 1965.

Pei Ch'i shu 北齊書 (History of the Northern Ch'i dynasty). Li Po-yao 李百藥. Peking: Chung-hua, 1972.

Pei shih 北史 (History of the Northern Dynasties). Li Yen-shou 李延壽. Peking: Chung-hua, 1974.

Pei-t'ang shu-ch'ao 北堂書鈔 (Digest of books in the Sui Imperial Library). Compiled by Yü Shih-nan 虞世南. Reprinted—Taipei: Wen-hai, 1962.

P'eng Chiu-wan 朋九萬. *Tung-p'o wu-t'ai shih-an* 東坡烏臺詩案 (Record of Su Shih's trial). *Han-hai* 涵海.

Po Chü-i 白居易. *Po Chü-i chi* 白居易集 (Collected works of Po Chü-i). Peking: Chung-hua, 1979.

Shao Po-wen 邵伯溫. *Wen chien lu* 聞見錄 (A record of things heard and seen). *Hsueh-chin t'ao-yuan* 學津討原. Reprinted—Shanghai: Shang-wu, 1972.

Shao Yung 邵雍. *Huang-chi ching-shih shu* 皇極經世書 (Book for the supreme ordering of the world). *SPPY.*

Shih chi 史記 (Records of the historian). Ssu-ma Ch'ien 司馬遷. Peking: Chung-hua, 1959.

Shih Chieh 石介. *Ts'u-lai Shih hsien-sheng wen-chi* 徂徠石先生文集 (Literary collection of Shih Chieh). Peking: Chung-hua, 1984.

Shih-san ching chu-shu 十三經注疏 (The Thirteen Classics with commentaries and subcommentaries). With critical notes by Juan Yuan 阮元. Reprinted—Peking: Chung-hua, 1980.

Ssu-ma Kuang 司馬光. *Chi-chu T'ai-hsuan* 集註太玄 (Collected commentaries on the *Supreme Mystery*). *SPPY*.

——. *Ch'ien-hsu* 潛虛 (Hidden vacuity). *SPTK*.

——. *Fa-yen chi-chu* 法言集註 (Collected commentaries on the *Exemplary Sayings*). *SKCS*.

——. *I shuo* 易說 (Explanations of the *Change*). *SKCS*.

——. *Ku-wen Hsiao ching chih-chieh* 古文孝經指解 (Commentary on the Old Text version of the *Classic of Filial Piety*). *SKCS*.

——. *Li-nien t'u* 歷年圖 (Chronological charts). In idem, *Chi ku lu* 稽古錄 (Record of examinations of the past). *SPTK*.

——. *Ssu-ma shih shu-i* 司馬氏書儀 (Mr. Ssu-ma's letters and ceremonies). *Ts'ung-shu chi-ch'eng*.

——. *Ssu-ma Wen-cheng kung ch'uan-chia chi* 司馬文正公傳家集 (Literary collection of Ssu-ma Kuang). *Wan-yu wen-k'u* 萬友文庫.

——. *Su-shui chi-wen* 涑水紀聞 (Record of things heard by the [man from] Su River). Taipei: Shih-chieh, 1970.

——. *Tao-te chen-ching lun* 道德真經論 (Commentary on the *Tao te ching*). *Tao-tsang* 道藏.

——. *T'ung-chien lun* 通鑑論 (Judgments in the *Comprehensive Mirror*). Compiled by Wu Yao-kuang 伍耀光. Hong Kong: T'ai-p'ing, 1963.

——. *Tzu-chih t'ung-chien* 資治通鑑 (Comprehensive mirror for aid in government). Peking: Ku-chi, 1956.

Su Hsun 蘇洵. *Chia-yu chi* 嘉祐集 (Literary collection of Su Hsun). *SPPY*.

Su Shih 蘇軾. *Chiao-cheng ching-chin Tung-p'o wen-chi shih-lueh* 校證經進東坡文集事略 (Annotated prose selections from Su Shih). Edited by Lang Yeh 郎曄. Peking: Wen-hsueh ku-chi, 1957.

——. *Shu chuan* 書傳 (Commentary on the *Documents*). *SKCS*.

——. *Su Shih hsuan-chi* 蘇軾選集 (Selected works of Su Shih). Compiled and annotated by Wang Shui-chao 王水照. Shanghai: Shang-hai ku-chi, 1984.

——. *Su-shih I chuan* 蘇氏易傳 (The Sus'commentary on the *Change*). *TSCC*.

——. *Su Shih lun wen-i* 蘇軾論文藝 (Su Shih on literature and art). Compiled by Yen Chung-ch'i 顏中其. Peking: Pei-ching ch'u-pan-she, 1985.

——. *Su Shih shih-chi* 蘇軾詩集 (Collected poetry of Su Shih). Annotated by Wang Wen-kao 王文誥. Peking: Chung-hua, 1982.

——. *Su Shih wen chi* 蘇軾文集 (Collected prose of Su Shih). Compiled and edited by K'ung Fan-li 孔凡禮. Peking: Chung-hua, 1986.

——. *Su Tung-p'o chi* 蘇東坡集 (Literary collection of Su Shih). *Kuo-hsueh chi-pen ts'ung-shu*.

——. *Tung-p'o t'i-pa* 東坡題跋 (Colophons and prefaces by Su Shih). *TSCC*.

Su Shun-ch'in 蘇舜欽. *Su Shun-ch'in chi* 蘇舜欽集 (Collected works of Su Shun-ch'in). Shanghai: Shang-hai ku-chi, 1981.

Su Sung 蘇頌. *Su Wei kung chi* 蘇魏公集 (Literary collection of Su Sung). *SKCS*.

Su Tung-p'o i-shih hui-pien 蘇東坡軼事滙編 (Collected anecdotes about Su Shih). Compiled by Yen Chung-ch'i 顏中其. Hunan: Yueh-lu shu-she, 1984.

Sui shu 隋書 (History of the Sui dynasty). Wei Cheng 魏徵 et al. Peking: Chung-hua, 1973.

Sun Fu 孫復. *Ch'un-ch'iu tsun wang fa wei* 春秋尊王發微 (The subtleties revealed of the *Spring and Autumn Annals* respect for kingship). *T'ung-chih t'ang ching-chieh* 通志堂經解.

———. *Sun Ming-fu hsiao-chi* 孫明復小集 (Literary collection of Sun Fu). *SKCS*.

Sun-tzu 孫子 (The writings of Master Sun). *SPPY*.

Sung Ch'i 宋祁. *Ching-wen chi* 景文集 (Literary collection of Sung Ch'i). *SKCS*.

Sung Hsiang 宋庠. *Yuan-hsien chi* 元憲集 (Literary collection of Sung Hsiang). *SKCS*.

Sung hui-yao chi-kao 宋會要輯稿 (Collected administrative documents from the Sung). Compiled by Hsu Sung 徐松. Reprinted—Taipei: Shih-chieh, 1964.

Sung Min-ch'iu 宋敏求. *Ch'un-ming t'ui-ch'ao lu* 春明退朝錄 (Notes made after retiring from court). Peking: Chung-hua, 1980.

Sung shih 宋史 (History of the Sung). T'o T'o 脫脫 et al. Peking: Chung-hua, 1977.

Sung shih i-wen-chih kuang-pien 宋史藝文志廣編 (The treatise on bibliography from the *Sung shih* and other bibliographies). Reprinted—Taipei: Shih-chieh, 1963.

Sung ta-chao-ling chi 宋大詔令集 (Collected major Sung edicts). Reprinted—Taipei: Ting-wen, 1972.

Sung wen hui 宋文彙 (Anthology of Sung literature). Compiled by Fang Yuan-yao 方遠堯. Taipei: Chung-hua, 1967.

Sung Yuan hsueh-an 宋元學案 (Case studies of Sung and Yuan learning). Compiled by Huang Tsung-hsi 黃宗羲 and Ch'üan Tsu-wang 全祖望. Reprinted—Taipei: Shih-chieh, 1966.

Sung Yuan hsueh-an pu-i 宋元學案補遺 (Additions to the *Case Studies of Sung and Yuan Learning*). Compiled by Wang Tzu-ts'ai 王梓材 and Feng Yun-hao 馮雲濠. *Ssu-ming ts'ung-shu* 四明叢書.

Ta hsueh 大學. In *Hsueh Yung chang-chü yin-te* 學庸章句引得 (Concordance to the *Great Learning* and *Doctrine of the Mean*). Taipei: Chung-hua min-kuo K'ung Meng hsueh-hui, 1970.

T'ai-p'ing Huan-yü chi 太平寰宇記 (Administrative geography of the T'ai-p'ing hsing-kuo era). Le Shih 樂史. *SKCS*.

T'ang hui-yao 唐會要 (Administrative documents from the T'ang). Wang Po 王溥 et al. *KHCT*.

Tao te ching 道德經. Edition: *Lao-tzu chiao-shih* 老子校釋 (Critical edition of the *Lao-tzu*). Edited by Chu Ch'ien-chih 朱謙之. Shanghai: Lung-men, 1958.

T'ien Hsi 田錫. *Hsien-p'ing chi* 咸平集 (Literary collection of T'ien Hsi). *SKCS*.

T'ien K'uang 田況. *Ju-lin kung-i* 儒林公議 (Impartial deliberations on the scholar-officials). *SKCS*.

Ts'ai Hsiang 蔡襄. *Tuan-ming chi* 端明集 (Literary collection of Ts'ai Hsiang). *SKCS*.

Ts'ai Shang-hsiang 蔡上翔. *Wang Ching-kung nien-p'u k'ao-lueh* 王荊公年譜考略 (Study of the chronological biography of Wang An-shih). Shanghai: Jen-min, 1959.

Ts'e-fu yuan-kuei 册府元龜. Compiled by Wang Ch'in-jo 王欽若 et al. Reprinted—Taipei: Chung-hua, 1967.

Tseng Kung 曾鞏. *Tseng Kung chi* 曾鞏集 (Collected works of Tseng Kung). Peking: Hsin-hua, 1984.

Tso-chuan 左傳. In *Ch'un-ch'iu ching-chuan yin-te* (q.v.).

Tsu Wu-tse 祖無擇. *Lung-hsueh chi* 龍學集 (Literary collection of Tsu Wu-tse). *SKCS*.

Tu Yu 杜佑. *T'ung tien* 通典 (Comprehensive canons of administration). Shanghai: T'u-shu chi-ch'eng, 1901.

Wang An-shih 王安石. *Chou kuan hsin i* 周官新義 (New significance of the *Institutes of Chou*). *Ching-yuan* 經苑.

———. *Lin-ch'uan hsien-sheng wen-chi* 臨川先生文集 (Literary collection of Wang An-shih). Peking: Chung-hua, 1959.

———. *Wang An-shih Lao-tzu chu chi-pen* 王安石老子注輯本 (Reconstituted text of Wang An-shih's commentary on the *Lao-tzu*). Compiled by Jung Chao-tsu 容肇祖. Peking: Chung-hua, 1979.

Wang Ch'eng 王偁. *Tung-tu shih-lueh* 東都事略 (History of the Northern Sung). Reprinted—Taipei: Wen-hai, n.d.

Wang Kuei 王珪. *Hua-yang chi* 華陽集 (Literary collection of Wang Kuei). *SKCS*.

Wang Po 王勃. *Wang Tzu-an chi* 王子安集 (Literary collection of Wang Po). *Wan-yu wen-k'u* 萬有文庫.

Wang Tsao 王藻. *Fu-ch'i chi* 浮溪集 (Literary collection of Wang Tsao). *SPTK*.

Wang Ying-lin 王應麟. *Yü hai* 玉海 (Sea of jade encyclopedia). Reprinted—Taipei: Hua-wen, 1964.

Wang Yü-ch'eng 王禹偁. *Hsiao-ch'u chi* 小畜集 (Literary collection of Wang Yü-ch'eng). *KHCT*.

Wen hsuan 文選 (Selections of refined literature). Compiled by Hsiao T'ung 蕭統. Commentary by Li Shan 李善. Reprinted—Peking: Chung-hua, 1977.

Wen hsuan Li chu i-shu 文選李註義疏 (Subcommentary on the Li commentary on the *Selections of Refined Literature*). Annotated by Kao Pu-ying 高步瀛. Reprinted—Taipei: Kuang-wen, 1964.

Wen T'ung 文同. *Hsin-k'o Shih-shih hsien-sheng Tan-yuan chi* 新刻石室先生丹淵集 (Literary collection of Wen T'ung). Reprinted—Taipei: Hsueh-sheng, 1973.

Wen Yen-po 文彥博. *Lu-kung wen-chi* 潞公文集 (Literary collection of Wen Yen-po). *SKCS*.

Wen-yuan ying-hua 文苑英華 (Finest blossoms from the park of literature). Compiled by Li Fang 李昉 et al. Reprinted—Peking: Hsin-hua, 1966.

Wu Ching 吳兢. *Chen-kuan cheng-yao* 貞觀政要 (Essentials of governance during the Chen-kuan period). Shanghai: Shang-hai ku-chi, 1978.

Yang Chieh 楊傑. *Wu-wei chi* 無為集 (Literary collection of Yang Chieh). *SKCS*.

Yang Chiung 楊炯. *Yang Chiung chi* 楊炯集 (Collected works of Yang Chiung). Peking: Chung-hua, 1980.

Yang Hsiung 楊雄. *Fa-yen i-shu* 法言義疏 (Exemplary sayings, with commentary and subcommentary). Commentary by Li Kui 李軌; subcommentary by Wang Jung-pao 汪榮寶. N.p., 1933.

Yang I 楊億. *Hsi-k'un ch'ou-ch'ang chi* 西崑酬唱集 (The Hsi-k'un poetry collection). *TSCC*.

———. *Wu-i hsin-chi* 武夷新集 (Literary collection of Yang I). *SKCS*.

Yang Shih 楊時. *Yang Kuei-shan hsien-sheng ch'üan-chi* 楊龜山先生全集 (Complete works of Yang Shih). Reprinted—Taipei: Hsueh-sheng, 1974.

Yao Hsuan 姚鉉. *T'ang wen ts'ui* 唐文粹 (Selections of T'ang literature). *SPTK*.

Yeh Meng-te 葉夢得. *Shih-lin yen-yü* 石林燕語 (Informal remarks by Yeh Meng-te). *SKCS*.

Yen Chih-t'ui 顏之推. *Yen-shih chia-hsun chi-chieh* 顏氏家訓集解 (Collected commentaries on the *Family Instructions for the Yen Clan*). Compiled by Wang Li-ch'i 王利器. Shanghai: Shang-hai ku-chi, 1980.

Yen K'o-chün 嚴可均. *Ch'üan shang-ku San-tai Ch'in Han San-kuo Liu-ch'ao wen* 全上古三代秦漢三國六朝文 (Complete collection of prose writings from high antiquity, the Three Eras, Ch'in, Han, the Three Kingdoms, and the Six Dynasties). Hupei, 1894.

Yin Shu 尹洙. *Ho-nan hsien-sheng chi* 河南先生集 (Literary collection of Yin Shu). *San Sung jen chi* 三宋人集.

Yu Tso 游酢. *Yu Chih-shan chi* 游廌山集 (Literary collection of Yu Tso). *SPTK*.

Yü Ching 余靖. *Wu-ch'i chi* 武溪集 (Literary collection of Yü Ching). *SKCS*.

Yü hai 玉海 (Sea of jade encyclopedia). Compiled by Wang Ying-lin 王應麟. Reprinted—Taipei: Hua-lien, 1964.

Yuan Chen 元稹. *Yuan Chen chi* 元稹集 (Collected works of Yuan Chen). Peking: Chung-hua, 1982.

Yuan Chieh 元結. *Yuan Tz'u-shan chi* 元次山集 (Collected works of Yuan Chieh). Peking: Chung-hua, 1969.

Yuan Hao-wen 元好問. *Chung-chou chi* 中州集 (Selected poems from the Chin dynasty). *SPTK*.

Yuan Ts'ai 袁采. *Yuan-shih shih-fan* 袁氏世範 (Mr. Yuan's precepts for social life). *Chih pu-tsu chai ts'ung-shu* 知不足齋叢書.

Secondary Sources in Chinese and Japanese

Andō Tomonobu 安藤智信. "Ō An-seki to bukkyō: Shōzan inseiki o chūshin to shite" 王安石と佛教—種山穩棲期を中心として (Wang An-shih and Buddhism, with particular attention to his retirement at Chung-shan). *Tōhō shūkyō* 東方宗教 28 (1966): 20–34.

Aoyama Sadao 青山定雄. "Godai Sō ni okeru Kōsei no shinkō kanryō" 五代宋に於ける江西の新興官僚 (The new bureaucracy and the Chiang-hsi regions during the Five Dynasties and the Sung). In *Wada hakushi kanreki kinen: Tōyōshi ronsō* 和田博士還暦記念東洋史論叢 (Oriental studies presented to Wada Sei in honor of his sixtieth birthday). Tokyo: Kodansha, 1951, pp. 19–38.

———. "Sōdai ni okeru kahoku kanryō no keifu ni tsuite" 宋代における華北官僚の系譜について (The genealogy of bureaucrats in north China in the Sung dynasty). Part I—*Seishin joshi daigaku ronsō* 聖心女子大學論叢 21 (1963): 21–41; part II—*Seishin joshi daigaku ronsō* 25 (1965): 19–49; part III—*Chūō daigaku bungakubu kiyō* 中央大学文学部紀要 45 (1967): 67–110.

———. "Sōdai ni okeru kanan kanryō no keifu ni tsuite: Toku ni Yōsukō ryūiki o chūshin to shite" 宋代における華南官僚の系譜について—特に揚子江流域を中心として (The genealogy of bureaucrats in south China in the Sung dynasty: with special reference to the Yangtze Valley). *Chūō daigaku bungakubu kiyō* 中央大学文学部紀要 72 (1974): 51–76.

———. "Sōdai ni okeru Shisen kanryō no keifu ni tsuite no ikkōsatsu" 宋代に於ける四川官僚の系譜についての一考察 (The genealogy of bureaucrats in Szechwan in the Sung dynasty). In *Wada hakushi koki kinen: Tōyōshi ronsō* 和田博士古稀記念東洋史論叢 (Oriental studies presented to Wada Sei in honor of his seventieth birthday). Tokyo: Kodansha, 1960, pp. 37–48.

———. *Tō Sō jidai no kōtsū to chishi chizu no kenkyū* 唐宋時代の交通と地誌地圖の研究 (Studies of T'ang and Sung period transportation and maps). Tokyo: Yoshikawa kōbunkan, 1963.

Araki Toshikazu 荒木敏一. *Sōdai kakyo seido kenkyū* 宋代科挙制度研究 (A study of the Sung examination system). Kyoto: Tōyōshi kenkyūkai, 1969.

———. "Sō Tai-so kakyo seisaku no ikkōsatsu" 宋太祖科挙政策の一考察 (A study of Sung T'ai-tsu's examination policy). *Tōyōshi kenkyū* 東洋史研究 24 (1966): 464–87.

Chang Ch'eng-shou 張稜壽. "Sui-ch'ao ju-sheng tui Liu-ch'ao shih-wen te p'i-p'ing" 隋朝儒生對六朝詩文的批評 (Sui dynasty Confucians' criticisms of Six Dynasties literature). *Ku-tai wen-hsueh li-lun yen-chiu ts'ung-k'an* 古代文學理論研究叢刊 6 (1985): 194–206.

Chang Chien 張健. *Ou-yang Hsiu chih shih-wen chi wen-hsueh p'i-ping lun* 歐陽修之詩文及文學批評論 (Ou-yang Hsiu's poetry and prose and literary criticism). Taipei: Shang-wu, 1973.

———. "Su Shih wen-hsueh p'i-p'ing yen-chiu" 蘇軾文學批評研究 (Study of Su Shih's literary criticism). In idem, *Sung Chin ssu-chia wen-hsueh p'i-p'ing yen-chiu* 宋金四家文學批評研究 (Studies of the literary criticism of four Sung and Chin figures). Taipei: Liao-ching ch'u-pan, 1975, pp. 2–116.

Chang Shun-hui 張舜徽. "Lun Sung-tai hsueh-che chih-hsueh te po-ta ch'i-hsiang chi t'i hou-shih Sung hsueh-shu-chieh so k'ai-p'i te hsin t'u-ching" 論宋代學者治學的博大氣象及替後世宋學術界所開闢的新途徑 (On the broad character of the scholarship of Sung period scholars and the new road they opened for later Sung scholarship). In idem, *Chung-kuo shih-lun wen-chi* 中國史論文集 (Collection of historical essays on China). Wu-han: Hu-pei jen-min, 1956, pp. 78–130.

Chang Yuan 張元. "*T'ung-chien* chung te nan-pei chan-cheng" 通鑑中的南北戰爭 (Wars between north and south in the *Comprehensive Mirror*). In *Chi-nien Ssu-ma Kuang Wang An-shih shih-shih chiu-pai chou-nien hsueh-shu yen-t'ao-hui lun-wen chi* (q.v.), pp. 65–96.

Ch'en Ch'i-han 陳啟漢. "Lun Su Shih te Chia-yu 'chin-ts'e'" 論蘇軾的嘉祐進策 (On Su Shih's Chia-yu reign period policy proposals). *Chung-kuo shih yen-chiu* 中國史研究 1985, no. 2: 31–40.

Ch'en Chih-ch'ao 陳智超. "*Yuan shih shih-fan* so chien Nan-sung min-shu ti-chu" 袁氏世範所見南宋民庶地主 (The Southern Sung commoner landlords seen in *Mr. Yuan's Family Precepts*). In *Sung, Liao, Chin shih lun-ts'ung* 宋遼金史論叢 (Collected articles on Sung, Liao, and Chin history), vol. 1. Peking: Chung-hua, 1985, pp. 110–34.

Ch'en Chih-o 陳植鍔. "Hsi-k'un ch'ou-ch'ang shih-jen sheng-tsu nien k'ao"

西昆酬唱詩人生卒年考 (Study of the dates for the Hsi-k'un poets). *Wen shih* 文史 21: 207–18.

———. "Lueh-lun Sung-ch'u ku-wen yun-tung te liang-chung ch'ing-hsiang" 略論宋初古文運動的兩種傾向 (Brief discussion of two directions in the early Sung ku-wen movement). In *Sung shih yen-chiu lun-wen chi* 宋史研究論文集 (Collection of studies on Sung history), edited by Teng Kuang-ming 鄧廣銘 and Li Chia-chü 酈家駒. Honan: Ho-nan jen-min, 1984, pp. 431–51.

Ch'en Chung-fan 陳鐘凡. *Liang Sung ssu-hsiang shu-p'ing* 兩宋思想述評 (A critical account of thought during the Sung). 1933. Reprinted—Ching-mei, Taiwan: Hua-shih, 1977.

Ch'en I-yen 陳義彥. "Ts'ung pu-i ju-shih: Lun Pei-sung pu-i chieh-shu te she-hui liu-tung" 從布衣入仕：論北宋布衣階層的社會流動 (Entering service as commoners: on the social mobility of commoners in the Northern Sung). *Ssu yü yen* 思與言 9, no. 4 (1972): 244–53.

Ch'en Jung-chieh 陳榮捷. "Tao-hsueh" 道學. In *Chung-kuo che-hsueh tz'u-tien ta-ch'üan* 中國哲學辭典大全 (The complete dictionary of Chinese philosophy), edited by Wei Cheng-t'ung 韋政通. Taipei: Shui-niu, 1983, pp. 667–71.

Ch'en Kuang-ch'ung 陳光崇. "Ssu-ma Kuang yü Ou-yang Hsiu" 司馬光與歐陽修 (Ssu-ma Kuang and Ou-yang Hsiu). *Shih-hsueh chi-k'an* 史學集刊 1985, no. 1: 11–18.

Ch'en Le-su 陳樂素. *Ch'iu shih chi* 求是集 (Collected articles of Ch'en Le-su), vol. 2. Kuangtung: Kuang-tung jen-min, 1984.

Ch'en Shih-hsiang 陳帥驤. "Riku Ki no shogai to *Bun fu* seisaku no seikaku na nendai." 陸機の生涯と文賦制作の正確な年代 (On the correct dates for Lu Chi's life and the composition of the *Wen-fu*), translated by Ikkai Tomoyoshi. *Chūgoku bungakuhō* 中國文學報 8 (1958): 50–78.

Ch'en Yu-shih 陳幼石. *Han Liu Ou Su ku-wen lun* 韓柳歐蘇古文論 (The ku-wen theories of Han Yü, Liu Tsung-yuan, Ou-yang Hsiu, and Su Shih). Shanghai: Shang-hai wen-i, 1983.

Ch'eng Ch'ien-fan 程千帆. *T'ang-tai chin-shih hsing-chüan yü wen-hsueh* 唐代進士行卷與文學 (Literature and the chin-shih candidate literary portfolios). Shanghai: Shang-hai ku-chi, 1980.

Ch'eng Yun 程運. "Sung-tai chiao-yü tsung-chih ch'an-shih" 宋代教育宗旨闡釋 (An explanation of the goal of Sung education). *Chung-cheng hsueh-pao* 中正學報 2 (1967): 90–93.

Chi P'ing 季平. *Ssu-ma Kuang hsin-lun* 司馬光新論 (A re-evaluation of Ssu-ma Kuang). Ch'ung-ch'ing: Hsi-nan shih-fan ta-hsueh, 1987.

Chi-nien Ssu-ma Kuang Wang An-shih shih-shih chiu-pai chou-nien hsueh-shu yen-t'ao-hui lun-wen chi 紀念司馬光王安石逝世九百周年學術研討會論文集 (Collected articles from the scholarly symposium commemorating the nine-hundreth anniversary of the deaths of Ssu-ma Kuang and Wang An-shih). Taipei: Wen shih che, 1986.

Chiang I-pin 蔣義斌. *Sung-tai ju shih t'iao-ho-lun chi p'ai-fo-lun chih yen-chin: Wang An-shih chih jung-t'ung ju shih chi Ch'eng-Chu hsueh-p'ai chih p'ai-fo fan-Wang* 宋代儒釋調和論及排佛論之演進—王安石之融通儒釋及程朱學派之排佛反王 (The evolution of the Confucian-Buddhist synthesis and anti-Buddhism in the Sung period: Wang An-shih's synthesis of Confucianism and Buddhism and the Ch'eng-Chu school's rejection of Buddhism and attack on Wang An-shih). Taipei: Shang-wu, 1988.

Ch'ien Mu 錢穆. *Kuo-shih ta-kang* 國史大綱 (Outline of Chinese history). Taipei: Kuo-li pien-i-kuan, 1975.

―――. *Sung Ming li-hsueh kai-shu* 宋明理學概述 (A survey of Sung and Ming Neo-Confucianism). Taipei: Chung-hua wen-hua, 1953.

―――. "Tsa lun T'ang-tai ku-wen yun-tung" 雜論唐代古文運動 (Remarks on the T'ang ku-wen movement). *Hsin-ya hsueh-pao* 新亞學報 3, no. 1 (1957): 123–68.

Ch'ien Tung-fu 錢冬父. *T'ang Sung ku-wen yun-tung* 唐宋古文運動 (The T'ang-Sung ku-wen movement). Shanghai: Shang-hai ku-chi, 1979.

Chikusa Masaaki 竺沙雅章. *So Tō-ba* 蘇東坡 (Su Tung-p'o). Tokyo: Jimbutsu ōraisha, 1967.

―――. "Ssu-ma Kuang Wang An-shih yü fo-chiao" 司馬光王安石與佛教 (Ssu-ma Kuang, Wang An-shih, and Buddhism). In *Chi-nien Ssu-ma Kuang Wang An-shih shih-shih chiu-pai chou-nien hsueh-shu yen-t'ao-hui lun-wen chi* (q.v.), pp. 477–87.

Chin Chung-shu 金中樞. "Pei-sung k'o-chü chih-tu yen-chiu" 北宋科舉制度研究 (Study of the Northern Sung examination system). Part I—*Hsin-ya hsueh-pao* 新亞學報 6, no. 1 (1964); reprinted in *Sung shih yen-chiu chi* 宋史研究集 (Collected studies on Sung history), vol. 11 (Taipei: Kuo-li pien-i kuan, 1979), pp. 1–72; Part II—*Hsin-ya hsueh-pao* 6, no. 2 (1964); reprinted in *Sung shih yen-chiu chi*, vol. 12 (1980), pp. 31–112.

―――. "Pei-sung k'o-chü chih-tu yen-chiu hsu: Chin-shih chu-k'o chih chieh-sheng shih-fa" 北宋科舉制度研究續―進士諸科之解省試法 (Study of the Northern Sung examination system continued: prefectural and departmental testing for the chin-shih and various fields). Part I—*Ch'eng-kung ta-hsueh, Li-shih-hsi hsueh-pao* 成功大學歷史系學報 5 (1978); reprinted in *Sung shih yen-chiu chi* 宋史研究集 (Collected studies on Sung history), vol. 13 (Taipei: Kuo-li pien-i kuan, 1981), pp. 61–189. Part II—*Ch'eng-kung ta-hsueh, Li-shih-hsi hsueh-pao* 6 (1979); reprinted in *Sung shih yen-chiu chi*, vol. 14 (1983), pp. 53–190.

―――. "Pei-sung k'o-chü chih-tu yen-chiu tsai-hsu: Chin-shih chu-k'o chih tien-shih shih-fa" 北宋科舉制度研究再續―進士諸科之殿試試法 (Study of the Northern Sung examination system further continued: palace examination testing for the chin-shih and various fields). Part I—*Ch'eng-kung ta-hsueh, Li-shih-hsi hsueh-pao* 7 (1980) 成功大學歷史系學報; reprinted in *Sung shih yen-chiu chi* 宋史研究集 (Collected studies on Sung history), vol. 15 (Taipei: Kuo-li pien-i kuan, 1984), pp. 125–88. Part II—*Ch'eng-kung ta-hsueh, Li-shih-hsi hsueh-pao* 9 (1982); reprinted in *Sung shih yen-chiu chi*, vol. 16. (1986), pp. 53–190. Part III forthcoming.

―――. "Sung-tai ching-hsueh tang-tai-hua ch'u-t'an" 宋代經學當代化初探 (Preliminary research on Sung neo-classicism). Part I—*Ch'eng-kung ta-hsueh, Li-shih hsueh-pao* 成功大學歷史學報 10 (1984): 71–104; part II—*Hsin-ya hsueh-pao* 新亞學報 15 (1986): 281–319; part III—*Ch'eng-kung ta-hsueh, Li-shih hsueh-pao* 11 (1985): 1–38; part IV—*Chu-hai hsueh-pao* 珠海學報 14 (1985): 133–57.

————. "Sung-tai hsueh-shu fa-chan chih chuan-kuan: Hu Yuan" 宋代學術發展之轉關—胡瑗 (The transformation in the development of the academic thought of the Sung dynasty: The influence of Hu Yuan's theory). *Ch'eng-kung ta-hsueh, Li-shih hsueh-pao* 成功大學歷史學報 13 (1987): 9–81.

————. "Sung-tai ku-wen yun-tung chih fa-chan yen-chiu" 宋代古文運動之發展研究 (A Study of the development of the Sung ku-wen movement). In *Sung shih yen-chiu chi* 宋史研究集 (Collected studies on Sung history), vol. 10. Taipei: Chung-hua ts'ung-shu, 1978, pp. 144–215.

Ch'iu Han-sheng 邱漢生, comp. *Shih i kou-shen* 詩義鉤沈 (Investigation into the *Significances of the Songs*). Peking: Chung-hua, 1982.

Chou Liang-hsiao 周良霄. "Wang An-shih pien-fa tsung-t'an" 王安石變法縱探 (On Wang An-shih's reform). *Shih-hsueh chi-k'an* 史學集刊 1985, no. 1: 19–37; 1985, no. 2: 9–17.

Chung-kuo che-hsueh shih tzu-liao hsuan-chi 中國哲學史資料選輯 (Selected materials for the history of Chinese philosophy), vol. 4, part II, *Sung Yuan Ming chih pu* 宋元明之部 (Section on Sung, Yuan, and Ming), edited by Chung-kuo she-hui k'o-hsueh yuan, Che-hsueh yen-chiu so, Chung-kuo che-hsueh shih yen-chiu shih 中國社會科學院哲學研究所, 中國哲學史研究室. 1962. Reprinted—Peking: Chung-hua, 1982.

Chung-kuo fo-chiao ssu-hsiang tzu-liao hsuan-pien 中國佛教思想資料選編 (Selected materials on Chinese Buddhist thought), compiled by Shih Chün 石峻 et al. Vol. 2, part I. Peking: Chung-hua, 1983.

Fu Hsuan-ts'ung 傅璇琮. *T'ang-tai k'o-chü yü wen-hsueh* 唐代科學與文學 (The T'ang examination system and literature). Sian: Shan-hsi jen-min, 1986.

Fujiyoshi Masumi 藤善真澄. "Kanri tōyō ni okeru dōkyo to sono igi" 官吏登用における道挙とその意義 (The Taoist examination for official recruitment and its significance). *Shirin* 史林 51, no. 6 (1981): 1–35.

Fumoto Yasutaka 麗保孝. *Hoku-sō ni okeru jugaku no tenkai* 北宋に於ける儒学の展開 (The development of Confucianism in the Northern Sung). Tokyo: Shoseki bumbutsu ryūtsūkai, 1967.

————. "Shi-ba On-kō no gakugyō ni tsuite" 司馬温公の学行について (On Ssu-ma Kuang's intellectual career). *Bōei daigakkō kiyō* 防衛大学校紀要 11 (1965): 1–79.

————. *Sō Gen Min Shin: Kinsei jugaku hensenshi ron* 宋元明清近世儒学変遷史論 (Sung, Yuan, Ming, and Ch'ing: a discussion of the transformation of Confucianism during the early modern period). Tokyo: Kokusho kankōkai, 1976.

Furugaki Kōichi 古垣光一. "Sōdai no kanryōsū ni tsuite: Shin-sō chōchū ikō no jinji gyōseijō no shinmondai" 宋代の官僚数について—真宗朝中以降の人事行政上の新問題 (The number of officials in the Sung dynasty: new problems in personnel administration from the middle of Emperor Chen-tsung's reign). In *Sōdai no shakai to shūkyō* 宋代の社會と宗教 (Sung society and religion). Tokyo: Kyūko shoen, 1985, pp. 121–58.

————. "Sōdai no kanryōsū ni tsuite: Toku ni Tai-so Tai-sō jidai o chūshin to shite" 宋代の官僚数について特に太祖太宗時代を中心として (On the number of officials during the Sung dynasty: especially during the T'ai-tsu and T'ai-tsung periods). In *Nakajima Satoshi sensei koki kinen ronshū* 中嶋敏先生古稀記念

論集 (Essays in honor of Nakajima Satoshi's seventieth birthday). Tokyo: Kyūkoshoin, 1981, pp. 97–120.

Goyama Kiwamu 合山究. "Sōshi no gakumonsei" 宋詩の学問性 (The intellectualism of Sung poetry). Chūgoku bungaku ronshū 中国文学論集 1 (1970): 3–14.

———. "So Shoku no bunjin katsudō to sono yōin" 蘇軾の文人活動とその要因 (Su Shih's activities as a literary man and their cause). Kyūshū Chūgoku gakkaihō 九州中国学会報 4 (1968): 63–77.

———, trans. Lin Yü-t'ang, So Tō-ba 蘇東坡 (Su Tung-p'o). Tokyo: Meitoku, 1978.

Higashi Ichio 東一夫. Ō An-seki jiten 王安石事典 (Historical dictionary for Wang An-shih). Tokyo: Kokusho kankōkai, 1980.

———. Ō An-seki shimpō no kenkyū 王安石新法の研究 (Studies of Wang An-shih's New Policies). Tokyo: Kazama shobō, 1970.

———. Ō An-seki to Shi-ba Kō 王安石と司馬光 (Wang An-shih and Ssu-ma Kuang). Tokyo: Chusekisha, 1980.

Ho Tse-heng 何澤恒. Ou-yang Hsiu chih ching shih hsueh 歐陽修之經史學 (Ou-yang Hsiu's classical and historical studies). Taipei: Kuo-li T'ai-wan ta-hsueh, 1980.

Hou Wai-lu 侯外廬 et al. Chung-kuo ssu-hsiang t'ung-shih 中國思想通史 (A general history of Chinese thought), vol. 4, part I. Peking: Jen-min, 1959.

Hsia Ch'ang-p'u 夏長樸. "Wang An-shih ssu-hsiang yü Meng-tzu te kuan-hsi" 王安石思想與孟子的関係 (The relationship between Wang An-shih's thought and the Mencius). In Chi-nien Ssu-ma Kuang Wang An-shih shih-shih chiu-pai chou-nien hsueh-shu yen-t'ao-hui lun-wen chi (q.v.), pp. 295–326.

Hsiao Kung-ch'üan 蕭公權. Chung-kuo cheng-chih ssu-hsiang shih 中國政治思想史 (The history of Chinese political thought), vol. 4. Reprinted—Taipei: Chung-hua wen-hua, 1964.

Hsu Kuei 徐規. Wang Yü-ch'eng shih-chi chu-tso pien-nien 王禹偁事迹著作編年 (Chronology of Wang Yü-ch'eng's life and writings). Peking: Chung-kuo she-hui k'o-hsueh, 1982.

Huang Chi-ch'ih 黃繼持. "'Wen yü tao' 'ch'ing yü hsing'" 文與道情與性 (Literature and the way, emotions and nature). Ch'ung-chi hsueh-pao 崇基學報 7, no. 2 (1968): 187–96.

Huang Ch'i-fang 黃啟方. Pei-sung wen-hsueh p'i-p'ing tzu-liao hui-pien 北宋文學批評資料彙編 (Collected materials on Northern Sung literary criticism). Taipei: Ch'eng-wen, 1978.

———. "Wang Yü-ch'eng p'ing-chuan" 王禹偁評傳 (Critical biography of Wang Yü-ch'eng). Wen shih che hsueh-pao 文史哲學報 27 (1978): 181–235.

Huang Jen-k'o 黃任軻. "Su Shih lun hsin-fa wen-tzu liu-p'ien nien-yueh k'ao" 蘇軾論新法文字六篇年月考 (On the dating of Su Shih's six writings on the New Policies). Su Shih yen-chiu chuan-k'an: Ssu-ch'uan ta-hsueh hsueh-pao ts'ung-k'an 蘇軾研究專刊:四川大學學報叢刊 6 (1980): 103–10.

Huang Kung-wei 黃公偉. Sung Ming Ch'ing li-hsueh t'i-hsi lun shih 宋明清理學體系論史 (The history of systematic theories in Sung, Ming, and Ch'ing Neo-Confucianism). Taipei: Yu-shih, 1970.

Huang Sheng-hsiung 黃盛雄. "T'ung-chien" shih-lun yen-chiu 通鑑史論研究 (Studies of the historical view of the *Comprehensive Mirror*). Taipei: Wen-shih-che, 1979.

Huo Ch'un-ying 霍春英. "Chin-nien lai Ssu-ma Kuang yen-chiu chien-shu" 近年來司馬光研究簡述 (A brief account of research on Ssu-ma Kuang in recent years). *Chin-yang hsueh-k'an* 晉陽學刊 1986, no. 3: 81–83.

Jao Tsung-i 饒宗頤. *Chung-kuo shih-hsueh shang chih cheng-t'ung lun* 中國史學上之正統論 (Legitimation theory in Chinese historiography). Hong Kong: Lung-men, 1977.

Jen Chi-yü 任繼愈. *Chung-kuo che-hsueh shih* 中國哲學史 (The history of Chinese philosophy). Shen-yang: Jen-min, 1979.

Kao Pu-ying 高步瀛. *T'ang Sung wen chü-yao* 唐宋文舉要 (Essentials of T'ang and Sung literature). 3 vols. Hong Kong: Chung-hua, 1976.

Kinugawa Tsuyòshi 衣川強. "Sōdai no meizoku: Kanan Ryoshi no baai" 宋代の名族河南呂氏の場合 (Famous clans of the Sung: the case of the Honan Lüs). *Kobe shōka daigaku jimbun ronshū* 神戸商科大学人文論集 9, no. 1/2 (1973): 134–66.

————. "Sōdai saishō kō: Hoku-sō zenki no baai" 宋代宰相考—北宋前期の場合 (Study of Sung chief councillors: the case of the early Northern Sung). *Tōyōshi kenkyū* 東洋史研究 24, no. 4 (1966): 405–42.

Kobayashi Yoshihiro 小林義廣. "*Godai shiki* no shijin kan" 五代史記の士人観 (The view of the shih in [Ou-yang Hsiu's] *Historical Record of the Five Dynasties*). *Tōyōshi kenkyū* 東洋史研究 38, no. 2 (1979): 197–218.

K'o Ch'ang-i 柯昌頤. *Wang An-shih p'ing-chuan* 王安石評傳 (Critical biography of Wang An-shih). Shanghai: Shang-wu, 1933.

K'ung Fan 孔繁. "Su Shih *P'i-ling I-chuan* te che-hsueh ssu-hsiang" 蘇軾毗陵易傳的哲學思想 (The philosophical thought in Su Shih's *P'i-ling Commentary on the Change*). *Chung-kuo che-hsueh* 中國哲學 9 (1983): 221–39.

Kuo Po-kung 郭伯恭. *Sung ssu ta-shu k'ao* 宋四大書考 (The four great works of the Sung). 1940. Reprinted—Taipei: Shang-wu, 1967.

Kuo Shao-yü 郭紹虞. *Chung-kuo wen-hsueh p'i-p'ing shih* 中國文學批評史 (History of Chinese literary criticism). 1934. Reprinted—Tainan: P'ing-p'ing, 1974.

Kuo Shao-yü 郭紹虞 and Wang Wen-sheng 王文生. *Chung-kuo li-tai wen-lun hsuan* 中國歷代文論選 (A selection of Chinese treatises on literature through the ages). Shanghai: Shang-hai ku-chi, 1979.

Kusumoto Masatsugu 楠本正継. *Sō Min jidai jugaku shisō no kenkyū* 宋明時代儒学思想の研究 (Studies of Sung and Ming period Confucian thought). Chiba: Hiroike gakuen, 1962.

Li Chih-chung 李致忠. "Sung-tai k'o-shu shu-lueh" 宋代刻書述略 (Brief account of Sung printing). *Wen shih* 文史 14 (1982): 145–73.

Li Hung-ch'i 李弘祺 (Thomas H. C. Lee). "Sung-tai kuan-yuan shu te t'ung-chi" 宋代官員數的統計 (Statistics on the numbers of Sung bureaucrats). *Shih-huo* 食貨 14, no. 5/6 (1984): 17–29.

Lin I-sheng 林益勝. *Hu Yuan te i-li I-hsueh* 胡瑗的義理易學 (Hu Yuan's moralistic interpretation of the *Change*). Taipei: Shang-wu, 1974.

Lin Jui-han 林瑞翰. "Nan-t'ang chih ching-chi yü wen-hua" 南唐之經濟與文化

(The economy and culture of the Southern T'ang). *Ta-lu tsa-chih* 大陸雜誌 29, no. 6 (1964): 183–90.

———. "Ssu-ma Kuang chih shih-hsueh chi ch'i cheng-shu" 司馬光之史學及其政術 (Ssu-ma Kuang's historiography and his politics). *Yu-shih hsueh-chih* 幼獅學誌 15, no. 2 (1972). Reprinted in *Sung shih yen-chiu chi* 宋史研究集 (Collected studies on Sung history), vol. 7. Taipei: Chung-hua ts'ung-shu, 1974, pp. 59–82.

———. "Sung T'ai-tsu chih Jen-tsung ch'ao hsiang-kung k'ao" 宋太祖至仁宗朝鄉貢考 (A study of the examinations from T'ai-tsu's to Jen-tsung's reigns). *Kuo-li T'ai-wan ta-hsueh, Li-shih-hsi hsueh-pao* 6 (1979) and 7 (1980). Reprinted in *Sung shih yen-chiu chi* 宋史研究集 (Collected studies on Sung history), vol. 15. Taipei: Kuo-li pien-i kuan, 1984, pp. 63–124.

Lin K'o-t'ang 林科棠. *Sung ju yü fo-hsueh* 宋儒與佛學 (Sung Confucians and Buddhism). 1928. Reprinted—Taipei: Shang-wu, 1966.

Liu Nai-ch'ang 劉乃昌. *Su Shih wen-hsueh lun-chi* 蘇軾文學論集 (Collected articles on Su Shih's literary writing). Chi-nan: Ch'i-Lü shu-she, 1982.

Liu Nai-ho 劉乃和 and Sung Yen-shen 宋衍申, eds. *"Tzu-chih t'ung-chien" ts'ung-lun* 資治通鑑叢論 (Collected articles on the *Comprehensive Mirror for Aid in Government*). Honan: Jen-min, 1985.

Liu Po-chi 劉伯驥. *Sung-tai cheng-chiao shih* 宋代政教史 (The history of Sung period politics and education). 2 vols. Taipei: Chung-hua, 1971.

Liu Tzu-chien 劉子健 (James T. C. Liu). "Lueh-lun Sung-tai wu-kuan-ch'ün tsai t'ung-chih chieh-chi chung te ti-wei" 略論宋代武官群在統治階級中的地位 (The position of military men within Sung China's ruling class: a brief analysis). In *Aoyama hakushi koki kinen: Sōdaishi ronsō* 青山博士古稀紀念宋代史論叢 (Collection of essays on Sung history presented to Dr. Sadao Aoyama on his seventieth birthday). Tokyo: Seishin shobō, 1974, pp. 477–87.

———. *Ou-yang Hsiu te chih-hsueh yü ts'ung-cheng* 歐陽修的治學與從政 (Ou-yang Hsiu's scholarship and political career). Hong Kong: Hsin-ya yen-chiu-so, 1963.

Lo Ken-tse 羅根澤. *Chung-kuo wen-hsueh p'i-p'ing shih* 中國文學批評史 (A history of Chinese literary criticism), vol. 3. Shanghai: Chung-hua, 1961.

———. *Sui T'ang wen-hsueh p'i-p'ing shih* 隋唐文學批評史 (A history of literary criticism in the Sui and T'ang). Reprinted—Taipei: Shang-wu, 1981.

———. *Wan T'ang Wu-tai wen-hsueh p'i-p'ing shih* 晚唐五代文學批評史 (A history of literary criticism in the late T'ang and the Five Dynasties). N.p.: Shang-wu, 1945.

Lo Lien-t'ien 羅聯添. *Sui T'ang Wu-tai wen-hsueh p'i-p'ing tzu-liao hui-pien* 隋唐五代文學批評資料彙編 (Collected materials for Sui, T'ang, and Five Dynasties literary criticism). Taipei: Ch'eng-wen, 1978.

Lo Tsung-ch'iang 羅宗強. *Sui T'ang Wu-tai wen-hsueh ssu-hsiang shih* 隋唐五代文學思想史 (A history of Sui, T'ang, and Five Dynasties literary thought). Shanghai: Shang-hai ku-chi, 1986.

Mai Chung-kuei 麥仲貴. *Sung Yuan li-hsueh chu-shu sheng-tsu piao* 宋元理學著書生卒表 (Chronology of Sung-Yuan Neo-Confucian bibliography and biography). Hong Kong: Hsin-ya, 1968.

Morita Kenji 森田憲司. "Sō Gen jidai ni okeru shūfu" 宋元時代における修譜 (Genealogy writing in the Sung and Yuan periods). *Tōyōshi kenkyū* 東洋史研究 37, no. 4 (1979): 509–35.

Morohashi Tetsuji 諸橋轍次. *Jugaku mokuteki to Sō ju Keireki shi Keigen hyaku rokujū nenkan no katsudō* 儒學目的と宋儒慶暦至慶元百六十年間の活動 (The activities of Sung Confucians during the 160 years from the Ch'ing-li to the Ch'ing-yuan era and the aims of Confucianism). Tokyo: Taishukan shoten, 1929.

Niida Noboru 仁井田陞. *Tōryō shūi* 唐令拾遺 (Collected remnants of T'ang regulations). Tokyo: Tōyō bunka gakuin, 1933.

Nishikawa Masao 西川正夫. "Kahoku Godai ōchō no bunshin kanryō 華北五代王朝の文臣官僚 (The civil bureaucracy of the Five Dynasties in North China). *Tōyō bunka kenkyūjo kiyō* 東洋文化研究所紀要 27 (1962): 211–61.

―――. "Kahoku Godai ōchō no bunshin to bushin" 華北五代王朝の文臣と武臣 (Civil officials and military officials of the Five Dynasties in North China). In *Zenkindai Ajia no hō to shakai* 前近代アジアの法と社会 (Law and society in premodern Asia). Vol. 1 of *Niida Noboru hakushi tsuitō rombun shū* 仁井田陞博士追悼論文集 (Essays in memory of Dr. Niida Noboru). Tokyo: Keisō shobō, 1967, pp. 289–314.

Ogawa Tamaki 小川環樹 and Yamamoto Kazuyoshi 山本和義, trans. *So Tō-ba shishū* 蘇東坡詩集 (The collected poetry of Su Tung-p'o). Tokyo: Chikuma shobō, 1983–).

―――. *So Tō-ba shū* 蘇東坡集 (Collection of prose writings by Su Tung-po). Tokyo: Asahi shimbunsha, 1972.

Okada Takehiko 岡田武彦. *Sō Min tetsugaku josetsu* 宋明哲学序説 (Introduction to Sung and Ming philosophy). Tokyo: Bungensha, 1977.

Ono Katsutoshi 小野勝年. *"Nittō guhō junrei kōki" no kenkyū* 入唐求法巡礼記の研究 (Studies of *The Record of a Pilgrimage to T'ang in Search of the Law*), vol. 3. Tokyo: Suzuki gakujutsu zaidan, 1967.

P'an Mei-yuch 潘美月. *Sung-tai ts'ang-shu chia k'ao* 宋代藏書家考 (A study of Sung dynasty book collectors). Taipei: Hsueh-hai, 1980.

Pei-ching ta-hsueh 北京大學. *Chung-kuo che-hsueh shih* 中國哲學史 (The history of Chinese thought). Peking: Chung-hua, 1980.

Shang T'ao 商韜. "Pei-sung shih-ch'i te cheng-chih tou-cheng yü shih wen ko-hsin yun-tung" 北宋時期的政治鬭爭與詩文革新運動 (Political struggle during the Northern Sung and the poetry and prose reform movement). In *Sung shih yen-chiu lun-wen chi* 宋史研究論文集 (Collected articles on Sung history). Shanghai: Shang-hai ku-chi, 1982, pp. 549–69.

Shimizu Kiyoshi 清水潔. "Ō An-seki no 'Shū-nan shi-ji-kai' ni tsuite" 王安石の周南詩次解について (On Wang An-shih's "The Explanation for the Sequence of the Chou-nan Poems"). In *Uno Tetsuto sensei hakuju shukuga kinen: Tōyōgaku ronsō* 宇野哲人先生白寿祝賀記念東洋学論叢 (Oriental studies in honor of Dr. Uno Tetsuto's ninety-ninth birthday). Tokyo: Uno Tetsuto sensei hakuju shukuga kinenkai, 1974, pp. 491–510.

Shushi no senku 朱子の先駆 (Chu Hsi's predecessors). Vol. 1, part II, of *Shushigaku taikei* 朱子学大系 (Outline of Chu Hsi learning), edited by Morohashi Tetsuji 諸橋轍次 and Yasuoka Masashiro 安岡正篤. Tokyo: Meitoku, 1972.

Su Shih yen-chiu chuan-k'an 蘇軾研究專刊 (Special issue of research on Su Shih). *Ssu-ch'uan ta-hsueh hsueh-pao ts'ung-k'an* 四川大學學報叢刊 6 (1980).

Su Tung-p'o yen-chiu lun-ts'ung 蘇東坡研究論叢 (Collected studies on Su Shih). *Su Shih yen-chiu lun-wen chi* 蘇軾研究論文集 (Collected research articles on Su Shih), vol. 3. Ch'eng-tu: Ssu-ch'uan wen-i, 1986.

Sun Kuo-tung 孫國棟. "T'ang Sung chih chi she-hui men-ti chih hsiao-jung: T'ang Sung chih chi she-hui chuan-pien yen-chiu chih i" 唐宋之際社會門第之消融—唐宋之際社會轉變研究之一 (The disappearance of the social elite from the T'ang to the Sung: Part one of research on social change from the T'ang to the Sung). *Hsin-ya hsueh-pao* 新亞學報 4, no. 1 (1959): 211–304.

Sung-jen chuan-chi tzu-liao so-yin 宋人傳記資料索引 (Index to biographical materials for Sung figures). Ch'ang Pi-te 昌彼得 et al. 6 vols. Taipei: Ting-wen, 1974–76.

Sung-jen i-shih hui-pien 宋人軼事彙編 (Collected anecdotes on Sung figures). Compiled by Ting Fu-ching 丁傳靖. 1935. Reprinted—Peking: Hsin-hua, 1958.

Suzuki Takayuki 鈴木隆行. "Godai no bunkan jinjiseisaku ni kansuru ikkōsatsu" 五代の文官人事政策に関する一考察 (A study of Five Dynasties policy on civil officials). *Hokudai shigaku* 北大史學 24 (1984): 25–38.

Takahashi Kazumi 高橋和己. "Riku Ki no denki to sono bungaku" 陸機の傳記とその文学 (Lu Chi's biography and his literary learning). *Chūgoku bungakuhō* 中国文学報 11 (1959): 1–57; 12 (1960): 49–84.

Takahashi Susumu 高橋進. *Mui shizen kara sakui sekkyoku e* 無為自然から作為積極へ (From non-action and naturalness to being active and positive). Tokyo: Bunri shoen, 1965.

Tanaka Katsumi 田中克己. *So Tō-ba* 蘇東坡 (Su Tung-p'o). Tokyo: Kembun shuppan, 1983.

Tanaka Kenji 田中謙二. *"Shiji tsugan"* 資治通鑑 (The *Comprehensive Mirror for Aid in Government*). Tokyo: Asahi, 1974.

T'ang Ch'eng-yeh 湯承業. *Fan Chung-yen yen-chiu* 范仲淹研究 (Studies of Fan Chung-yen). Taipei: Kuo-li pien-i kuan, 1977.

T'ang Chün-i 唐君毅. *Chung-kuo che-hsueh yuan-lun* 中國哲學原論 (Studies on the foundations of Chinese philosophy), part I. Hong Kong: Jen-sheng, 1966.

———. *Chung-kuo che-hsueh yuan-lun. Yuan tao p'ien III: Chung-kuo che-hsueh chung chih tao chih chien-li chi ch'i fa-chan* 原道篇III中國哲學中之道之建立及其發展 (The establishment and development of "tao" in Chinese philosophy). Hong Kong: Hsin-ya yen-chiu so, 1974.

———. *Chung-kuo che-hsueh yuan-lun. Yuan chiao p'ien: Sung Ming ju-hsueh ssu-hsiang chih fa chan* 原教篇宋明儒學思想之發展 (On the foundations of dogma: the development of Sung and Ming Confucian thought). Hong Kong: Hsin-ya yen-chiu so, 1977.

T'ao Ch'iu-ying 陶秋英 and Yü Hsing 虞行. *Sung Chin Yuan wen-lun hsuan* 宋金元文論選 (Selected Sung, Chin, and Yuan discussions of literature). Peking: Jen-min wen-hsueh, 1984.

Teng Kuang-ming 鄧廣銘. "Wang An-shih tui Pei-sung ping-chih kai-ko ts'o-shih chi ch'i she-hsiang" 王安石對北宋兵制改革措施及其設想 (Wang An-shih's reforms of the Northern Sung military system and their intent). In *Sung shih yen-chiu lun-wen chi* 宋史研究論文集 (Collected articles on Sung history). Shang-hai: Shang-hai ku-chi, 1982, pp. 311–20.

Teraji Jun 寺地遵. "Ō-yō Shū ni okeru ten-jin sōkansetsu e no kaigi" 歐陽修における天人相關説への懷疑 (Doubts about the connection between heaven and man in Ou-yang Hsiu). *Hiroshima daigaku, Bungakubu kiyō* 広島大学文学部紀要 28, no. 1 (1968): 161–87.

———. "Ri Kō no rei-shisō to sono rekishiteki igi: Hokusō jidai chūki no jiei jinushisō no shisō" 李覯の礼思想とその歴史的意義—北宋時代中期の自営地主層の思想 (Li Kou's conception of ritual and its historical significance: the thought of farming landowners in the mid-Northern Sung). *Shigaku kenkyū* 史学研究 118 (1973): 38–48.

———. "Ten-jin sōkansetsu yori mita Shi-ba Kō to Ō An-seki" 天人相関説より見た司馬光と王安石 (Ssu-ma Kuang and Wang An-shih from the perspective of the theory of interaction between heaven and man). *Shigaku zasshi* 史学雑誌 76, no. 10 (1967): 34–62.

Tozaki Tetsuhiko 戸崎哲彦. "Ryō Sō-gen no meidō bungaku: Riku Jun no *Shun-jū*gaku to no kankei" 柳宗元の明道文学—陸淳の春秋学との関係 (Liu Tsung-yuan's literature of illuminating tao and its relation to Lu Ch'un's studies of the *Spring and Autumn Annals*). *Chūgoku bungakuhō* 中国文学報 36 (1985): 47–80.

Tseng Tsao-chuang 曾棗莊. *Su Hsun p'ing-chuan* 蘇洵評傳 (Critical biography of Su Hsun). Ch'eng-tu: Ssu-ch'uan jen-min, 1983.

———. *Su Shih p'ing-chuan* 蘇軾評傳 (Critical biography of Su Shih), rev. ed. Ch'eng-tu: Ssu-ch'uan jen-min, 1984.

———. "Ts'ung *P'i-ling I-chuan* k'an Su Shih te shih-chieh-kuan" 從毗陵易傳看蘇軾的世界觀 (Su Shih's worldview as seen from the *P'i-ling Commentary on the Change*). *Su Shih yen-chiu chuan-k'an: Ssu-ch'uan ta-hsueh hsueh-pao ts'ung-k'an* 蘇軾研究專刊:四川大學學報叢刊 6 (1980): 59–66.

Tung-p'o yen-chiu lun-ts'ung 東坡研究論叢 (Studies of Su Tung-p'o). Third collection in the series *Su Shih yen-chiu lun-wen chi* 蘇軾研究論文集 (Collected articles on Su Shih). Ch'eng-tu: Ssu-ch'uan wen-i, 1986.

Umehara Kaoru 梅原郁. *Sōdai kanryō seido kenkyū* 宋代官僚制度研究 (Studies of the Sung bureaucratic system). Kyoto: Dōhōsha, 1985.

Uno Tetsuto 宇野哲人. *Shina tetsugakushi: Kinsei jugaku* 支那哲学史—近世儒学 (The history of Chinese philosophy: Confucianism of the early modern period). Tokyo: Hōbunkan, 1954.

Utsunomiya Kiyoyoshi 宇都宮清吉. *Chūgoku kodai chūseishi kenkyū* 中國古代中世史研究 (Studies of ancient and medieval China). Tokyo: Sōbunsha, 1977.

Wang An-shih yen-chiu tzu-liao hui-pien 王安石研究資料滙編 (Collected research materials on Wang An-shih), vol. 1. Fu-chou, Kiangsi: Wang An-shih yen-chiu hui, 1986.

Wang Chin-kuang 王晉光. *Wang An-shih shu-mu yü so-t'an* 王安石書目與瑣探 (Research notes and a bibliography on Wang An-shih). Hong Kong: Hua-feng, 1983.

Wang Ching-hung 王景鴻. "Su Tung-p'o chu-shu pan-pen k'ao" 蘇東坡著書版本考 (A study of the editions of Su Shih's writings). *Shu-mu chi-k'an* 書目季刊 4, no. 2 (1969): 13–54; 4, no. 3 (1970): 41–81.

Wang Pao-chen 王保珍. *Tseng-pu Su Tung-p'o nien-p'u hui-cheng* 增補蘇東坡年譜會證 (Supplemented chronology of Su Shih's life). Taipei: Kuo-li T'ai-wan ta-hsueh, Wen-hsueh yuan, 1969.

Wang Te-i 王德毅. "Ssu-ma Kuang yü *Tzu-chih t'ung-chien*" 司馬光與資治通鑑 (Ssu-ma Kuang and the *Comprehensive Mirror for Aid in Government*). In idem, *Sung-shih yen-chiu lun-chi* 宋史研究論集 (Collected articles on Sung history), vol. 2. Taipei: Ting-wen, 1972, pp. 1–24.

———. "Sung-tai hsien-liang fang-cheng k'o k'ao" 宋代賢良方正科考 (The Sung period decree examination). *Wen shih che hsueh pao* 文史哲學報 14 (1965). Reprinted in idem, *Sung shih yen-chiu lun chi* 宋史研究論集 (Collected articles on Sung history). Taipei: Shang-wu, 1968, pp. 111–80.

———. "Sung-tai Shan-chou Ch'ao shih-tsu hsi-k'ao" 宋代澶州晁氏族系考 (Study of the genealogy of the Ch'aos of Shan-chou). Draft. National Taiwan University, Department of History, 1987.

Wang Tseng-yü 王曾瑜. "Wang An-shih pien-fa chien-lun" 王安石變法簡論 (A brief discussion of Wang An-shih's reform). *Chung-kuo she-hui k'o-hsueh* 中國社會科學 1980, no. 3: 141–54.

Watanabe Hidekata 渡邊秀方. *Shina tetsugakushi gairon* 支那哲学史概論 (General discussion of the history of Chinese philosophy). Tokyo: Waseda daigaku, 1924.

Wu Wen-chih 吳文治. *Han Yü tzu-liao hui-pien* 韓愈資料彙編 (Collected materials on Han Yü). 4 vols. Peking: Chung-hua, 1983.

Yamamoto Mikoto 山本命. *Sō jidai jugaku rinrigakuteki kenkyū* 宋時代儒学倫理学的研究 (A logical study of Sung Confucianism). Tokyo: Risōsha, 1973.

Yamane Mitsuyoshi 山根三芳. "Shi-ba Kō konrei kō" 司馬光婚礼考 (On Ssu-ma Kuang's marriage rites). In *Tōyōgaku ronshū: Ikeda Suetoshi hakushi koki kinen* 東洋學論集：池田末利博士古稀記念 (Oriental studies in honor of Dr. Ikeda Suetoshi's seventieth birthday), edited by Ikeda Suetoshi hakushi koki kinen jigyōkai 池田末利博士古稀記念事業會. Hiroshima, 1980, pp. 673–90.

———. "Shi-ba Kō no *Kyoka zatsugi*" 司馬光の居家雜儀 (Ssu-ma Kuang's *Miscellaneous Family Rites*). In *Chūgoku tetsugakushi kenkyū ronshū: Araki kyōju taikyū kinen* 中國哲学史研究論集：荒木教授退休記念 (Collected research articles on the history of Chinese philosophy in honor of Professor Araki [Kengo]'s retirement), edited by Araki kyōju taikyū kinenkai 荒木教授退休記念會. Fukuoka, 1981, pp. 349–66.

———. "Shi-ba Kō reisetsu kō" 司馬光礼説考 (On Ssu-ma Kuang's theory of ritual). In *Mori Mikisaburō hakushi shōju kinen: Tōyōgaku ronshū* 森三樹三郎博士頌寿記念東洋学論集 (Oriental studies in honor of Dr. Mori Mikisaburō), edited by Mori Mikisaburō hakushi shōju kinen jigyōkai 森三樹三郎博士頌寿記念事業會. Kyoto: Hōyū shoten, 1979, pp. 641–57.

———. "Shi-ba Kō reisetsu kō" 司馬光礼説考 (On Ssu-ma Kuang's theory of ritual). *Tōyō gakujutsu kenkyū* 東洋学術研究 19, no. 2 (1980): 64–84.

Yang Yuan 楊遠. "Pei-sung tsai-fu jen-wu te ti-li fen-pu" 北宋宰輔人物的地理分佈

(The geographical distribution of Northern Sung councillors). *Journal of the Institute of Chinese Studies of the Chinese University of Hong Kong* 13 (1982): 147–213.

Yao Chi-kuang 姚吉光. "T'ang-tai wen-shih chih hsueh-shu ssu-hsiang" 唐代文士之學術思想 (The scholarly thought of T'ang dynasty wen-shih). *Li-shih yü wen-hua* 歷史與文化 2 (Mar. 1947): 50–53; 3 (Aug. 1947): 43–57.

Yao Ming-ta 姚明達. *Ch'eng I-ch'uan nien-p'u* 程伊川年譜 (Chronology of Ch'eng I). Shanghai: Shang-wu, 1937.

———. *Chung-kuo mu-lu-hsueh shih* 中國目錄學史 (The history of Chinese bibliography). Reprinted—Shanghai: Shang-hai shu-tien, 1984.

Yoshihara Fumiaki 吉原文昭. "Sōgaku hattenjō yori mita Son Seki no ichi ni tsuite" 宋学発展上より見た孫奭の位置に就いて (On the position of Sun Shih in the development of Sung learning). In *Uno Tetsuto sensei hakuju shukuga kinen: Tōyōgaku ronsō* 宇野哲人先生白寿祝賀記念東洋学論叢 (Oriental studies in honor of Dr. Uno Tetsuto's ninety-ninth birthday). Tokyo: Uno Tetsuto sensei hakuju shukuga kinenkai, 1974, pp. 1270–98.

Yoshioka Yoshitoyo 吉岡義豊. "Sangō shiki no seiritsu ni tsuite" 三教指帰の成立について (On the organization of the *Introduction to the Three Teachings*). *Indogaku bukkyōgaku kenkyū* 印度学佛教学研究 8, no. 1 (1960): 114–18.

Yü Ta-ch'eng 于大成. "Wang An-shih chu-shu k'ao" 王安石著書考 (On Wang An-shih's writings). *Kuo-li chung-yang t'u-shu-kuan kuan-k'an* 國立中央圖書館館刊, new series, 1, no. 3 (1968): 42–46.

Yü Ying-shih 余英時. *Shih yü Chung-kuo wen-hua* 士與中國文化 (The shih and Chinese culture). Shanghai: Jen-min, 1987.

Yuan-jen chuan-chi tzu-liao so-yin 元人傳記資料索引 (Index to biographical materials on Yuan figures). Wang Te-i 王德毅 et al. Vol. 2. Taipei: Hsin wen-feng, 1980.

Works in Western Languages

Acker, William. *Some T'ang and Pre-T'ang Texts on Chinese Painting*, vol. 2. Leiden: E. J. Brill, 1954.

Adler, Joseph A. "Chu Hsi and Divination." In *Sung Dynasty Uses of the I Ching*, by Kidder Smith, Jr., Peter K. Bol, Joseph A. Adler, and Don J. Wyatt. Princeton: Princeton University Press, 1990, pp. 169–205.

Aoyama, Sadao. "The Newly-Risen Bureaucrats in Fukien at the Five-Dynasty-Sung Period, with Special Reference to Their Genealogies." *Memoirs of the Research Department of the Tōyō Bunkō* 21 (1962): 1–48.

Barrett, Timothy Hugh. "Buddhism, Taoism and Confucianism in the Thought of Li Ao." Ph.D. dissertation, Yale University, 1978.

———. "Taoism Under the T'ang." Draft chapter for *The Cambridge History of China*. General editors Denis Twitchett and John K. Fairbank. Vol. 3, *Sui and T'ang China, 589–906, Part II*, edited by Denis Twitchett. Cambridge: Cambridge University Press, forthcoming.

Birch, Cyril, ed. *Anthology of Chinese Literature: From Early Times to the Fourteenth Century*. New York: Grove Press, 1965.

Bol, Peter K. "The Sung Context: From Ou-yang Hsiu to Chu Hsi." In *Sung Dynasty Uses of the I Ching*, by Kidder Smith, Jr., Peter K. Bol, Joseph A. Adler, and Don J. Wyatt. Princeton: Princeton University Press, 1990, pp. 26–55.

———. "Ch'eng Yi and Cultural Tradition." In *The Power of Culture: Studies in Chinese Cultural History*, edited by Willard J. Peterson and Andrew Plaks. Hong Kong: Hong Kong University Press, forthcoming.

———. "Chu Hsi's Redefinition of Literati Learning." In *Neo-Confucian Education: The Formative Stage*, edited by John Chaffee and Wm. Theodore de Bary. Berkeley: University of California Press, 1989, pp. 151–85.

———. "Culture and the Way in Eleventh Century China." Ph.D. dissertation, Princeton University, 1982.

———. "The Examination System and the Shih." *Asia Major*, 3rd series, 3, no. 2 (1990): 149–71.

———. "Government, Society, and State: On the Political Visions of Ssu-ma Kuang (1019–1086) and Wang An-shih (1021–1086)." In *Ordering the World: Approaches to State and Society in Sung Dynasty China*, edited by Robert Hymes and Conrad Schirokauer. Berkeley: University of California Press, forthcoming.

———. "Reflections on Sung Literati Thought: Review of Hoyt Cleveland Tillman, *Utilitarian Confucianism*." *Bulletin of Sung and Yuan Studies* 18 (1986): 88–97.

———. "Seeking Common Ground: Han Literati Under Jurchen Rule." *Harvard Journal of Asiatic Studies* 47, no. 2 (1987): 461–538.

———. "Su Shih and Culture." In *Sung Dynasty Uses of the I Ching*, by Kidder Smith, Jr., Peter K. Bol, Joseph A. Adler, and Don J. Wyatt. Princeton: Princeton University Press, 1990, pp. 56–99.

Bryant, Daniel. *Lyric Poets of the Southern Tang: Feng Yen-ssu, 903–960, and Li Yü, 937–978*. Vancouver: University of British Columbia Press, 1982.

Bush, Susan. *The Chinese Literati on Painting: Su Shih (1037–1101) to Tung Ch'i-ch'ang (1555–1636)*. Cambridge: Harvard University Press, 1971.

Bush, Susan, and Hsiao-yen Shih. *Early Chinese Texts on Painting*. Cambridge: Harvard University Press, 1985.

Cahill, Suzanne E. "Taoism at the Sung Court: The Heavenly Text Affair of 1008." *Bulletin of Sung and Yuan Studies* 16 (1980): 23–44.

Chaffee, John W. "Chu Hsi and the Revival of the White Deer Grotto Academy, 1179–1181 A.D." *T'oung Pao* 71 (1985): 40–62.

———. "Education and Examinations in Sung Society." Ph.D. dissertation, University of Chicago, 1979.

———. *The Thorny Gates of Learning in Sung China: A Social History of Examinations*. Cambridge: Cambridge University Press, 1985.

Chan, Hok-lam. *Legitimation in Imperial China: Discussions Under the Jurchen-Chin Dynasty (1115–1234)*. Seattle: University of Washington Press, 1984.

Chan, Ming K. "The Historiography of the *Tzu-chih t'ung-chien*: A Survey." *Monumenta Serica* 31 (1974–75): 1–38.

Chan, Wing-tsit. "Chu Hsi and the Academies." In *Neo-Confucian Education:*

The Formative Stage, edited by John Chaffee and Wm. Theodore de Bary. Berkeley: University of California Press, 1989, pp. 389–413.

————. "Chu Hsi's Completion of Neo-Confucianism." *Etudes Song* 2, no. 1 (1973): 59–90.

————. "The Evolution of the Neo-Confucian Concept of Li as Principle." *Tsing-hua hsueh-pao*, new series, 4, no. 2 (1964): 123–47.

————. "The Principle of Heaven vs. Human Desires." In idem, *Chu Hsi: New Studies*. Honolulu: University of Hawaii Press, 1989, pp. 197–211.

————. *A Source Book in Chinese Philosophy*. Princeton: Princeton University Press, 1963.

Chang, Carson. *The Development of Neo-Confucian Thought*. New York: Bookman Associates, 1957.

Chaves, Jonathan. *Mei Yao-ch'en and the Development of Early Sung Poetry*. New York: Columbia University Press, 1976.

Chen, Diana Yu-shih. "Change and Continuation in Su Shih's Theory of Literature: A Note on His *Ch'ih-pi-fu*." *Monumenta Serica* 31 (1974–75): 375–92.

————. *Images and Ideas in Chinese Classical Prose: Studies of Four Masters*. Stanford: Stanford University Press, 1988.

Chen, Jo-shui. "The Dawn of Neo-Confucianism: Liu Tsung-yuan and the Intellectual Changes in T'ang China, 773–819." Ph.D. dissertation, Yale University, 1987.

Ch'en Ch'un. *Neo-Confucian Terms Explained (The "Pei-hsi Tzu-i") by Ch'en Ch'un, 1159–1223*, translated by Wing-tsit Chan. New York: Columbia University Press, 1986.

Ch'en, Kenneth. *Buddhism in China: A Historical Survey*. Princeton: Princeton University Press, 1964.

Ch'en Shih-hsiang. "Essay on Literature." In *Anthology of Chinese Literature*, edited by Cyril Birch. New York: Grove Press, 1965, pp. 204–14.

Chow Tse-tsung. "Ancient Chinese Views on Literature, the Tao, and Their Relationship." *Chinese Literature: Essays, Articles, Reviews* 1 (1979): 3–29.

Chu Hsi. *Learning to Be a Sage: Selections from the Conversations of Master Chu, Arranged Topically*, translated, with a commentary, by Daniel K. Gardner. Berkeley: University of California Press, 1990.

Chu Hsi and Lü Tsu-ch'ien. *Reflections on Things at Hand*, translated by Wing-tsit Chan. New York: Columbia University Press, 1967.

Clark, Hugh R. "Trade and Economy in Southern Fukien Through the Thirteenth Century." Paper for the Leiden University Workshop on Fukien in the Seventeenth and Eighteenth Centuries, Dec. 1986.

Davis, Richard L. *Court and Family in Sung China, 960–1279: Bureaucratic Success and Kinship Fortunes for the Shih of Ming-chou*. Durham, N.C.: Duke University Press, 1986.

de Bary, Wm. Theodore. *The Buddhist Tradition in India, China and Japan*. New York: Vintage Books, 1972.

————. *The Liberal Tradition in China*. New York: Columbia University Press, 1983.

————. *The Message of the Mind in Neo-Confucianism*. New York: Columbia University Press, 1989.

————. *Neo-Confucian Orthodoxy and the Learning of the Mind-and-Heart*. New York: Columbia University Press, 1981.

————. "A Reappraisal of Neo-Confucianism." In *Studies in Chinese Thought*, edited by Arthur F. Wright. Chicago: University of Chicago Press, 1953, pp. 81–111.

————. "Some Common Tendencies in Neo-Confucianism." In *Confucianism in Action*, edited by David S. Nivison and Arthur F. Wright. Stanford: Stanford University Press, 1959, pp. 25–49.

de Bary, Wm. Theodore, et al. *Sources of Chinese Tradition*. New York: Columbia University Press, 1960.

Dien, Albert E. "Yen Chih-t'ui (531–591 +): A Buddho-Confucian." In *Confucian Personalities*, edited by Arthur F. Wright and Denis Twitchett. Stanford: Stanford University Press, 1962, pp. 43–64.

Ebrey, Patricia Buckley. *The Aristocratic Families of Early Imperial China: A Case Study of the Po-ling Ts'ui Family*. Cambridge: Cambridge University Press, 1978.

————. *Chu Hsi's "Family Rituals": A Twelfth-Century Manual for the Performance of Cappings, Weddings, Funerals, and Ancestral Rites*. Princeton: Princeton University Press, 1991.

————. "The Early Stages in the Development of Descent Group Organization." In *Kinship Organization in Late Imperial China*, edited by idem and James L. Watson. Berkeley: University of California Press, 1986, pp. 16–61.

————. "Education Through Ritual: Efforts to Formulate Family Rituals During the Sung Period." In *Neo-Confucian Education: The Formative Stage*, edited by John Chaffee and Wm. Theodore de Bary. Berkeley: University of California Press, 1989, pp. 277–306.

————. *Family and Property in Sung China: Yuan Ts'ai's Precepts for Social Life*. Princeton: Princeton University Press, 1984.

————. "Neo-Confucianism and the Chinese Shih-ta-fu." *American Asian Review* 4, no. 1 (1986): 34–43.

————. "T'ang Guides to Verbal Etiquette." *Harvard Journal of Asiatic Studies* 45, no. 2 (1985): 581–614.

Ebrey, Patricia Buckley, and James L. Watson. "Introduction." In *Kinship Organization in Late Imperial China*, edited by idem. Berkeley: University of California Press, 1986, pp. 1–13.

Egan, Ronald C. *The Literary Works of Ou-yang Hsiu (1007–1072)*. Cambridge: Cambridge University Press, 1984.

————. "Ou-yang Hsiu and Su Shih on Calligraphy." *Harvard Journal of Asiatic Studies* 49, no. 2 (1989): 365–420.

————. "Poems on Paintings: Su Shih and Huang T'ing-chien." *Harvard Journal of Asiatic Studies* 43, no. 2 (1983): 413–51.

Ennin. *Ennin's Diary: The Record of a Pilgrimage to China in Search of the Law*, translated from the Chinese by Edwin O. Reischauer. New York: Ronald Press, 1955.

Fang, Achilles. *The Chronicle of the Three Kingdoms.* 2 vols. Harvard-Yenching Institute Studies, 6. Cambridge: Harvard-Yenching Institute, 1952.

————. "Rhymeprose on Literature." *Harvard Journal of Asiatic Studies* 14 (1951): 527–66.

Fisher, Carney T. "The Ritual Dispute of Sung Ying-tsung." *Papers in Far Eastern History* 36 (1987): 109–38.

Freeman, Michael D. "Loyang and the Opposition to Wang An-shih: The Rise of Confucian Conservatism, 1068–1086." Ph.D. dissertation, Yale University, 1973.

Fuller, Michael. "Review of Ronald C. Egan, *The Literary Works of Ou-yang Hsiu.*" *Bulletin of Sung and Yuan Studies* 19 (1988): 50–73.

————. *The Road to East Slope: The Development of Su Shih's Poetic Voice.* Stanford: Stanford University Press, 1990.

Fung Yu-lan. *History of Chinese Philosophy,* translated by Derk Bodde. Vol. 2. Princeton: Princeton University Press, 1953.

Gardner, Daniel K. *Chu Hsi and the "Ta-hsueh": Neo-Confucian Reflection on the Confucian Canon.* Cambridge: Harvard University, Council on East Asian Studies, 1986.

————. "Transmitting the Way: Chu Hsi and His Program of Learning." *Harvard Journal of Asiatic Studies* 49, no. 2 (1989): 141–72.

Ge Xiaoyin. "The Relationship Between T'ang Literary Innovation and the Evolution of Confucianism." *Social Sciences in China,* Winter 1989: 162–90.

Gentzler, Jennings Mason. "A Literary Biography of Liu Tsung-yuan, 773–819." Ph.D. dissertation, Columbia University, 1966.

Ginzberg, Stanley M. "Alienation and Reconciliation of a Chinese Poet: The Huang-zhou Exile of Su Shi." Ph.D. dissertation, University of Wisconsin, 1974.

Graham, A. C. *Two Chinese Philosophers.* London: Lund Humphries, 1958.

————. "What Was New in the Ch'eng-Chu Theory of Human Nature?" In *Chu Hsi and Neo-Confucianism,* edited by Wing-tsit Chan. Honolulu: University of Hawaii Press, 1986, pp. 138–57.

Gregory, Peter N. "Tsung-mi and Neo-Confucianism." Paper for the Symposium on Religion and Society in China, 750–1300. University of Illinois, Champaign-Urbana, Fall 1988.

————. "Tsung-mi and the Buddhist Antecedents of Chu Hsi's Critique of Buddhism." Paper for the panel Ch'an and the Development of Neo-Confucianism. Annual Meeting of the Association for Asian Studies, Boston, 1987.

Haeger, John Winthrop. "The Significance of Confusion: The Origins of the *T'ai-p'ing yü-lan.*" *Journal of the American Oriental Society* 88 (1968): 401–10.

Hakeda, Yoshito S. *Kūkai: Major Works, Translated, with an Account of His Life and a Study of His Thought.* New York: Columbia University Press, 1972.

Hartman, Charles. *Han Yü and the T'ang Search for Unity.* Princeton: Princeton University Press, 1986.

————. "Su Shih and Literary Persecution in Northern Sung." Paper for the panel History, Poetry, and Politics in Imperial China. Annual Meeting of the Association for Asian Studies, Washington, D.C., March 1989.

Hartwell, Robert M. "Demographic, Political, and Social Transformations of China, 750–1550." *Harvard Journal of Asiatic Studies* 42, no. 2 (1982): 365–442.

———. "Financial Expertise, Examinations, and the Formulation of Economic Policy in Northern Sung China." *Journal of Asian Studies* 30 (1971): 281–314.

———. "Historical Analogism, Public Policy, and Social Science in Eleventh and Twelfth Century China." *American Historical Review* 76, no. 3 (1971): 690–727.

Hatch, George C., Jr. "Historical Thought in the Statecraft of Su Hsun." Paper for the conference volume from the Workshop on Sung Dynasty Statecraft in Thought and Action, Scottsdale, Arizona, Jan. 1986, edited by Robert Hymes and Conrad Schirokauer.

———. "Su Hsun." In *Sung Biographies*, edited by Herbert Franke. Wiesbaden: Franz Steiner Verlag, 1976, pp. 885–900.

———. "Su Shih." In *Sung Biographies*, edited by Herbert Franke. Wiesbaden: Franz Steiner Verlag, 1976, pp. 900–968.

———. "*Su-shih I-chuan.*" In *A Sung Bibliography*, edited by Y. Hervouet. Hong Kong: Chinese University Press, 1978, pp. 4–9.

———. "The Thought of Su Hsün (1009–1066): An Essay on the Social Meaning of Intellectual Pluralism in Northern Sung." Ph.D. dissertation, University of Washington, 1978.

Herbert, P. A. "Civil Service in China in the Latter Half of the Seventh Century." *Papers on Far Eastern History* 13 (1976): 1–40.

———. "T'ang Dynasty Objections to the Centralized Selection System." *Papers on Far Eastern History* 33 (1986): 83–88.

Hightower, James Robert. "Han Yü as a Humorist." *Harvard Journal of Asiatic Studies* 44, no. 1 (1984): 5–27.

———. "The *Wen hsüan* and Genre Theory." *Harvard Journal of Asiatic Studies* 20 (1957): 512–33.

Holzman, Donald. "Confucius and Ancient Chinese Literary Criticism." In *Chinese Approaches to Literature from Confucius to Liang Ch'i-ch'ao*, edited by Adele Rickett. Princeton: Princeton University Press, 1978, pp. 21–41.

Hsieh, Shan-yuan. *The Life and Thought of Li Kou (1009–1069).* San Francisco: Chinese Materials Center, 1979.

Huang, Ch'ing-lien. "The Recruitment and Assessment of Civil Service Officials Under the T'ang Dynasty." Ph.D. dissertation, Princeton University, 1986.

Huang Kan. "General Introduction to the *tao-t'ung* Transmission of Sages and Worthies." Reprinted in *Shushigaku taikei* 10: 432–33.

Hughes, E. R. "Epistemological Methods in Chinese Philosophy." In *The Chinese Mind: Essentials of Chinese Philosophy and Culture*, edited by Charles A. Moore. Honolulu: University of Hawaii Press, 1967, pp. 77–103.

Hung, William. "A Bibliographic Controversy at the T'ang Court A.D. 719." *Harvard Journal of Asiatic Studies* 20 (1957): 74–134.

Hymes, Robert P. "Lu Chiu-yüan, Academies, and the Problem of the Local Community." In *Neo-Confucian Education: The Formative Stage*, edited by

John Chaffee and Wm. Theodore de Bary. Berkeley: University of California Press, 1989, pp. 432–56.

————. *Statesmen and Gentlemen: The Elite of Fu-chou, Chiang-hsi, in Northern and Southern Sung*. Cambridge: Cambridge University Press, 1986.

Jan Yun-hua. "Ch'i-sung." In *Sung Biographies*, edited by Herbert Franke. Wiesbaden: Franz Steiner Verlag, 1976, pp. 185–94.

Johnson, David. "The Last Years of a Great Clan: The Li Family of Chao Chün in the Late T'ang and Early Sung." *Harvard Journal of Asiatic Studies* 37, no. 1 (1977): 5–102.

————. *The Medieval Chinese Oligarchy*. Boulder, Colo.: Westview, 1977.

Johnson, Wallace, trans. *The T'ang Code*, vol. 1, *General Principles*. Princeton: Princeton University Press, 1979.

Jullien, François. "L'Oeuvre et l'univers: Imitation ou déploiement (limites à une conception mimetique de la création littéraire dans la tradition chinoise)." *Extrême Orient, Extrême Occident* 3 (1984): 37–88.

Karlgren, Bernard. "The Book of Documents." *Bulletin of the Museum of Far Eastern Antiquities* 22 (1950): 1–81.

Kasoff, Ira Ethan. *The Thought of Chang Tsai (1020–1077)*. Cambridge: Cambridge University Press, 1984.

Kelleher, M. Theresa. "Chu Hsi and Public Instruction." In *Neo-Confucian Education: The Formative Stage*, edited by John Chaffee and Wm. Theodore de Bary. Berkeley: University of California Press, 1989, pp. 219–51.

Knechtges, David R., trans. Xiao Tong, comp. *"Wen xuan" or Selections of Refined Literature, Rhapsodies on Metropolises and Capitals*, vol. 1. Princeton: Princeton University Press, 1982.

Kracke, E. A., Jr. *Civil Service in Early Sung China*. Cambridge: Harvard University Press, 1953.

————. "Family vs. Merit in Chinese Civil Service Examinations Under the Empire." *Harvard Journal of Asiatic Studies* 10 (1947): 103–23.

Labadie, John Richard. "Rulers and Soldiers: Perceptions and Management of the Military in Northern Sung China (960–ca. 1060)." Ph.D. dissertation, University of Washington, 1981.

Lamont, H. G. "An Early Ninth Century Debate on Heaven: Liu Tsung-yuan's *T'ien shuo* and Liu Yü-hsi's *T'ien lun*, an Annotated Translation and Introduction." *Asia Major* 18 (1973): 181–208; 19 (1974): 37–85.

Lau, D. C., trans. *The Analects*. Harmondsworth, Eng.: Penguin Books, 1979.

————. *Lao Tzu, Tao Te Ching*. Harmondsworth, Eng.: Penguin Books, 1963.

————. *Mencius*. Harmondsworth, Eng.: Penguin Books, 1970.

Le Gros Clark, Cyril Drummond, trans. *The Prose-Poetry of Su Tung-p'o*. London: Kegan Paul, 1935.

————. *Selections from the Works of Su Tung-p'o*. London: Jonathan Cape, 1931.

Lee, Thomas H. C. (Li Hung-ch'i). *Government Education and Examinations in Sung China*. Hong Kong: Chinese University Press, 1985.

Legge, James, trans. *The Chinese Classics*. 5 vols. Oxford: Clarendon Press, 1893–95. Reprinted—Hong Kong: Hong Kong University Press, 1970.

Lin Yu-tang. *The Gay Genius: The Life and Times of Su Tungpo.* New York: John Day, 1947.

Liu I-ch'ing. *"Shih-shuo Hsin-yü": A New Account of Tales of the World, by Liu I-ch'ing with commentary by Liu Chün,* translated by Richard B. Mather. Minneapolis: University of Minnesota Press, 1976.

Liu, James T. C. "An Early Sung Reformer: Fan Chung-yen." In *Chinese Thought and Institutions,* edited by John K. Fairbank. Chicago: Chicago University Press, 1957, pp. 105–31.

———. "How Did a Neo-Confucian School Become the State Orthodoxy?" *Philosophy East and West* 23 (1973): 483–505.

———. *Ou-yang Hsiu: An Eleventh Century Neo-Confucianist.* Stanford: Stanford University Press, 1967.

———. *Reform in Sung China: Wang An-shih (1021–1086) and His New Policies.* Cambridge: Harvard University Press, 1959.

———. "Sung Views on the Control of Government Clerks." *Journal of the Economic and Social History of the Orient* 10, no. 2/3 (1967): 317–44.

Liu, James J. Y. *Chinese Theories of Literature.* Chicago: University of Chicago Press, 1975.

Liu, Shih Shun. *Classical Chinese Prose.* Hong Kong: Chinese University Press, 1979.

Lo, Winston W. *An Introduction to the Civil Service of Sung China: With Emphasis on Its Personnel Administration.* Honolulu: University of Hawaii Press, 1987.

———. "A New Perspective on the Sung Civil Service." *Journal of Asian History* 17 (1983): 121–35.

———. "Philology: An Aspect of Sung Rationalism." *Chinese Culture* 17 (1976): 1–26.

———. "Provincial Governments in Sung China." *Chinese Culture* 19, no. 4 (1978): 19–45.

———. *Szechwan in Sung China: A Case Study in the Political Integration of the Chinese Empire.* Taipei: University of Chinese Culture Press, 1982.

———. "Wang An-shih and the Confucian Ideal of Inner Sageliness." *Philosophy East and West* 26, no. 1 (1976): 41–53.

Loon, Piet van der. *Taoist Books in the Libraries of the Sung Period.* London: Ithaca Press, 1984.

Lynn, Richard John. "Chu Hsi as Literary Theorist and Critic." In *Chu Hsi and Neo-Confucianism,* edited by Wing-tsit Chan. Honolulu: University of Hawaii Press, 1986, pp. 337–54.

March, Andrew. "Self and Landscape in Su Shih." *Journal of the American Oriental Society* 86 (1966): 377–96.

Marney, John. *Liang Chien-wen Ti.* Boston: Twayne, 1976.

Mather, Richard B. *The Poet Shen Yüeh (441–513): The Reticent Marquis.* Princeton: Princeton University Press, 1988.

McCullough, Helen Craig. *Brocade by Night: Kokin Wakashū and the Court Style in Japanese Classical Poetry.* Stanford: Stanford University Press, 1985.

McMullen, David L. "Han Yü: An Alternative Picture." *Harvard Journal of Asiatic Studies* 49, no. 2 (1989): 603–57.

———. "Historical and Literary Theory in the Mid-Eighth Century." In *Perspectives on the T'ang*, edited by Arthur F. Wright and Denis Twitchett. New Haven: Yale University Press, 1973, pp. 307–42.

———. *State and Scholars in T'ang China*. Cambridge: Cambridge University Press, 1988.

Metzger, Thomas A. "Was Neo-Confucianism 'Tangential' to the Elite Culture of Late Imperial China?" *American Asian Review* 4, no. 1 (1986): 1–33.

Miyakawa Hisayuki. "An Outline of the Naitō Hypothesis and Its Effects on Japanese Studies of China." *Far Eastern Quarterly* 14, no. 4 (1955): 533–52.

Mote, Frederick W. "Confucian Eremitism in the Yuan Period." In *The Confucian Persuasion*, edited by Arthur F. Wright. Stanford: Stanford University Press, 1960, pp. 202–40.

Murck, Christian. "Su Shih's Reading of the Chung-yung." In *Theories of the Arts in China*, edited by Susan Bush and Christian Murck. Princeton: Princeton University Press, 1983, pp. 267–92.

Nienhauser, William H., Jr., Charles Hartman, William Bruce Crawford, Jan W. Walls, and Lloyd Neighbors. *Liu Tsung-yuan*. New York: Twayne Publishers, 1973.

Ninji Ōfuchi. "The Formation of the Taoist Canon." In *Facets of Taoism: Essays in Chinese Religion*, edited by Holmes Welch and Anna Seidel. New Haven: Yale University Press, 1979, pp. 253–68.

Nivison, David S. "Introduction." In *Confucianism in Action*, edited by idem and Arthur F. Wright. Stanford: Stanford University Press, 1959, pp. 3–24.

———. "The Problem of 'Knowledge' and 'Action' in Chinese Thought Since Wang Yang-ming." In *Studies in Chinese Thought*, edited by Arthur F. Wright. Chicago: University of Chicago Press, 1953, 112–45.

Owen, Stephen. *The Great Age of Chinese Poetry: The High T'ang*. New Haven: Yale University Press, 1981.

———. *The Poetry of Meng Chiao and Han Yü*. New Haven: Yale University Press, 1975.

———. *The Poetry of the Early T'ang*. New Haven: Yale University Press, 1977.

———. *Readings in Chinese Literary Thought*. Cambridge: Harvard University, Council on East Asian Studies, forthcoming.

———. *Remembrances: The Experience of the Past in Classical Chinese Literature*. Cambridge: Harvard University Press, 1986.

———. *Traditional Chinese Poetry and Poetics: Omen of the World*. Madison: University of Wisconsin Press, 1985.

Peterson, Charles A. "Court and Province in Mid- and Late T'ang." In *The Cambridge History of China*. General editors Denis Twitchett and John K. Fairbank. Vol. 3, *Sui and T'ang China, 589–906, Part I*, edited by Denis Twitchett. Cambridge: Cambridge University Press, 1979, pp. 464–560.

Peterson, Willard J. "Another Look at Li." *Bulletin of Sung and Yuan Studies* 18 (1986): 13–32.

———. "Confucianism in the Ming Dynasty." Draft chapter for *The Cambridge History of China*. General editors Denis Twitchett and John K. Fairbank. Vol. 7, *The Ming Dynasty, 1368–1644, Part II*. Forthcoming.

————. "Squares and Circles: Mapping the History of Chinese Thought." *Journal of the History of Ideas* 49, no. 1 (1988): 47–60.

Pollard, David. "Ch'i in Chinese Literary Theory." In *Chinese Approaches to Literature from Confucius to Liang Ch'i-ch'ao*, edited by Adele Rickett. Princeton: Princeton University Press, 1978.

Pulleyblank, Edwin G. *The Background of the Rebellion of An Lu-shan.* London: Oxford University Press, 1965.

————. "Chinese Historical Criticism: Liu Chih-chi and Ssu-ma Kuang." In *Historians of China and Japan*, edited by W. G. Beasley and E. G. Pulleyblank. London: Oxford University Press, 1961, pp. 135–66.

————. "Liu K'o, a Forgotten Rival of Han Yü." *Asia Major*, new series, 7 (1959): 143–60.

————. "Neo-Confucianism and Neo-Legalism in T'ang Intellectual Life, 755–805." In *The Confucian Persuasion*, edited by Arthur F. Wright. Stanford: Stanford University Press, 1960, pp. 77–114.

Rotours, Robert des. *Le Traité des examens, traduit de la "Nouvelle Histoire des T'ang."* Paris: Libraire Ernest Leroux, 1932.

Sariti, Anthony. "Monarchy, Bureaucracy, and Absolutism in the Political Thought of Ssu-ma Kuang." *Journal of Asian Studies* 32, no. 1 (1972): 53–76.

Schafer, Edward H. "Wu Yün's 'Cantos on Pacing the Void.'" *Harvard Journal of Asiatic Studies* 41, no. 2 (1981): 377–415.

Schwartz, Benjamin I. "Some Polarities in Confucian Thought." In *Confucianism in Action*, edited by David S. Nivison and Arthur F. Wright. Stanford: Stanford University Press, 1959, pp. 50–62.

————. *The World of Thought in Ancient China.* Cambridge: Harvard University Press, Belknap Press, 1985.

Shih, Vincent Yu-chung, trans. *The Literary Mind and the Carving of Dragons, by Liu Hsieh: A Study of Thought and Pattern in Chinese Literature.* New York: Columbia University Press, 1959.

Smith, Kidder, Jr. "Ch'eng I and the Pattern of Heaven and Earth." In *Sung Dynasty Uses of the I Ching*, by idem, Peter K. Bol, Joseph A. Adler, and Don J. Wyatt. Princeton: Princeton University Press, 1990, pp. 136–68.

Smith, Kidder, Jr., and Don J. Wyatt, "Shao Yung and Number." In *Sung Dynasty Uses of the I Ching*, by Kidder Smith, Jr., Peter K. Bol, Joseph A. Adler, and Don J. Wyatt. Princeton: Princeton University Press, 1990, pp. 100–135.

Smith, Paul J. "State Power and Economic Activism During the New Policies, 1068–1085: The Tea and Horse Trade and the 'Green Shoots' Loan Policy." In *Ordering the World: Approaches to State and Society in Sung Dynasty China*, edited by Robert P. Hymes and Conrad Schirokauer. Berkeley: University of California Press, forthcoming.

Somers, Robert M. "Time, Space, and Structure in the Consolidation of the T'ang Dynasty (A.D. 617–700)." *Journal of Asian Studies* 45 (1986): 971–94.

Strickmann, Michel. "The Longest Taoist Scripture." *History of Religions* 17 (1978): 331–54.

A Sung Bibliography, edited by Yves Hervouet. Initiated by Etienne Balazs. Hong Kong: Chinese University Press, 1978.

T'ang Chün-i. "The Spirit and Development of Neo-Confucianism." *Inquiry* 14 (1971): 56–83.

Tillman, Hoyt. "Southern Sung Confucianism." Draft chapter for *The Cambridge History of China*. General editors Denis Twitchett and John K. Fairbank. Vol. 4, *Sung China*, edited by Denis Twitchett. Cambridge: Cambridge University Press, forthcoming.

———. *Utilitarian Confucianism: Ch'en Liang's Challenge to Chu Hsi*. Cambridge: Harvard University, Council on East Asian Studies, 1982.

Tsien, Tsuen-hsuin. *Paper and Printing: Chemistry and Chemical Technology*, part I. Joseph Needham, *Science and Civilisation in China*, vol. 5. Cambridge: Cambridge University Press, 1985.

Tu Wei-ming. "Neo-Confucian Ontology: A Preliminary Questioning." Reprinted in idem, *Confucian Thought: Selfhood as Creative Transformation*. Albany: State University of New York Press, 1985, pp. 149–150.

———. "Neo-Confucian Religiosity and Human-relatedness." Reprinted in idem, *Confucian Thought: Selfhood as Creative Transformation*. Albany: State University of New York Press, 1985.

Twitchett, Denis C. "The Bureaucracy." 1985. Draft chapter for *The Cambridge History of China*. General editors idem and John K. Fairbank. Vol. 3, *Sui and T'ang China, 589–906, Part II*, edited by Denis Twitchett. Cambridge: Cambridge University Press, forthcoming.

———. "The Composition of the T'ang Ruling Class: New Evidence from Tunhuang." In *Perspectives on the T'ang*, edited by Arthur F. Wright and Denis Twitchett. New Haven: Yale University Press, 1973, pp. 47–85.

———. "The Fan Clan's Charitable Estate, 1050–1760." In *Confucianism in Action*, edited by David S. Nivison and Arthur F. Wright. Stanford: Stanford University Press, 1959, pp. 97–133.

———. *Financial Administration Under the T'ang Dynasty*. Cambridge: Cambridge University Press, 1970.

———. "Hsüan-tsung (reign 712–56)." In *The Cambridge History of China*. General editors idem and John K. Fairbank. Vol. 3, *Sui and T'ang China, 589–906, Part I*, edited by Denis Twitchett. Cambridge: Cambridge University Press, 1979, pp. 333–463.

———. "Provincial Autonomy and Central Finance in Late T'ang." *Asia Major*, new series, 11 (1965): 211–32.

Übelhör, Monika. "The Community Compact (*Hsiang-yüeh*) of the Sung and Its Educational Significance." In *Neo-Confucian Education: The Formative Stage*, edited by John Chaffee and Wm. Theodore de Bary. Berkeley: University of California Press, 1989, pp. 371–88.

Umehara, Kaoru. "Civil and Military Officials in the Sung: The *Chi-lu-kuan* System." *Acta Asiatica* 50 (1986): 1–30.

Vande Walle, W. "Lay Buddhism Among the Chinese Aristocracy During the Period of the Southern Dynasties: Hsiao Tzu-liang (460–494) and His Entourage." *Orientalia Lovaniensia* 10 (1979): 275–79.

Van Zoeren, Steven. "Poetry and Personality: The Hermeneutics of the Odes." Ph.D. dissertation, Harvard University, 1987.

von Glahn, Richard. "Community and Welfare: Chu Hsi's Community Granary in Theory and Practice." In *Ordering the World: Approaches to State and Society in Sung Dynasty China*, edited by Robert Hymes and Conrad Schirokauer. Berkeley: University of California Press, forthcoming.

Waley, Arthur, trans. *The Analects of Confucius*. London: George Allen & Unwin, 1938.

———. *The Book of Songs*. London: George Allen & Unwin, 1937.

Walton, Linda. "The Institutional Context of Neo-Confucianism: Scholars, Schools, and *Shu-yüan* in Sung-Yüan China." In *Neo-Confucian Education: The Formative Stage*, edited by John Chaffee and Wm. Theodore de Bary. Berkeley: University of California Press, 1989, pp. 457–92.

———. "Kinship, Marriage, and Status in Song China: A Study of the Lou Lineage of Ningbo, c. 1050–1250." *Journal of Asian History* 18, no. 1 (1984): 35–77.

Wang Gungwu. *The Structure of Power in North China During the Five Dynasties*. Kuala Lumpur: University of Malaya Press, 1963.

Watson, Burton, trans. *The Complete Works of Chuang Tzu*. New York: Columbia University Press, 1968.

———. *Su Tung-p'o: Selections from a Sung Dynasty Poet*. New York: Columbia University Press, 1965.

Watson, James L. "Chinese Kinship Reconsidered: Anthropological Perspectives on Historical Research." With comments by Denis Twitchett. *China Quarterly* 92 (1982): 589–627.

Wechsler, Howard J. *Mirror to the Son of Heaven: Wei Cheng at the Court of T'ang T'ai-tsung*. New Haven: Yale University Press, 1974.

———. *Offerings of Jade and Silk: Ritual and Symbol in the Legitimation of the T'ang Dynasty*. New Haven: Yale University Press, 1985.

Weinstein, Stanley. *Buddhism Under the T'ang*. Cambridge: Cambridge University Press, 1987.

———. "Imperial Patronage in the Formation of T'ang Buddhism." In *Perspectives on the T'ang*, edited by Arthur F. Wright and Denis Twitchett. New Haven: Yale University Press, 1973, pp. 265–306.

Wilhelm, Richard, trans. *The I Ching*. Rendered into English from German by Cary F. Baynes. Princeton: Princeton University Press, 1967.

Williamson, H. R. *Wang An-shih: A Chinese Statesman and Educationalist of the Sung Dynasty*. 2 vols. London: Probsthain, 1935, 1937.

Wood, Alan Thomas. "Politics and Morality in Northern Sung China: Early Neo-Confucian Views on Obedience to Authority." Ph.D. dissertation, University of Washington, 1981.

Worthy, Edmund Henry, Jr. "The Founding of Sung China, 950–1000: Integrative Changes in Military and Political Institutions." Ph.D. dissertation, Princeton University, 1976.

Wright, Arthur F. "T'ang T'ai-tsung and Buddhism." In *Perspectives on the T'ang*, edited by idem and Denis Twitchett. New Haven: Yale University Press, 1973, pp. 239–63.

Yen Chih-t'ui. *Family Instructions for the Yen Clan (Yen-shih chia-hsün)*, translated, with annotations and an introduction, by Teng Ssu-yü. Leiden: E. J. Brill, 1968.

Yoshikawa Kojiro. *An Introduction to Sung Poetry*, translated by Burton Watson. Cambridge: Harvard University Press, 1967.

Yu, Pauline. "Poems in Their Place: Collections and Canons in Early Chinese Literature." *Harvard Journal of Asiatic Studies* 50, no. 1 (1990): 163–96.

———. *The Reading of Imagery in the Chinese Poetic Tradition*. Princeton: Princeton University Press, 1987.

Yü Ying-shih. "Some Preliminary Observations on the Rise of Ch'ing Confucian Intellectualism." *Tsing-hua Journal of Chinese Studies* 11, no. 1/2 (1975): 105–46.

Zürcher, Erik. "Buddhism and Education in T'ang Times." *Neo-Confucian Education: The Formative Stage*, edited by John Chaffee and Wm. Theodore de Bary. Berkeley: University of California Press, 1989, pp. 19–56.

———. "Perspectives in the Study of Chinese Buddhism." *Journal of the Royal Asiatic Society* 1982, no. 2: 161–76.

Chinese Character List

An Lu-shan 安祿山
ch'a 察
ch'ai-ch'ien 差遣
Ch'an 禪
Chang Chi (T'ang) 張籍
Chang Chi (Sung) 張洎
Chang Chi-hsien 張集賢
Chang Chien-feng 張建封
Chang Chih-po 張知白
Chang Ching 張景
Chang Chiu-ling 張九齡
Chang Fang-p'ing 張方平
Chang Fu 張扶
Chang Heng 張衡
Chang Hsun 張巡
Chang Lei 張耒
Chang Te-hsiang 章得象
Chang Tsai 張載
Chang Tung 張洞
Chang Wang-chih 章望之
Chang Yueh 張說
Chang Yung 張詠
ch'ang-li 常理
Ch'ang-le Chia 長樂賈
Ch'ang-sun Wu-chi 長孫無忌
chao 照
Chao Chi 趙籍
Chao-chün Li 趙郡李

Chao K'uang-i 趙匡義
Chao K'uang-yin 趙匡胤
Chao P'u 趙普
Chao-te 昭德
Ch'ao Chiung 晁迥
Ch'ao Pu-chih 晁補之
Ch'ao Ts'o 晁錯
Che-tsung 哲宗
Chen-kuan 眞觀
Chen-tsung 眞宗
chen-yuan 眞元
Chen-yuan 貞元
Ch'en 陳
Ch'en Chi-ho 陳季和
Ch'en Ch'un 陳淳
Ch'en Ch'ung 陳充
Ch'en Hsiang 陳襄
Ch'en Liang 陳亮
Ch'en P'eng-nien 陳彭年
Ch'en Shun-yü 陳舜俞
Ch'en Tsai-chung 陳在中
Ch'en Ts'ung-i 陳從易
Ch'en Tzu-ang 陳子昂
Ch'en Yao-sou 陳堯叟
cheng-hsueh 正學
Cheng Kang-chung 鄭剛中
Cheng meng 正蒙
Cheng Pao 鄭褒

cheng-shih 政事
cheng-t'ung 正統
ch'eng (integrity, sincerity, true) 誠
Ch'eng (king) 成
Ch'eng Hao 程顥
Ch'eng Hsiang 程珦
Ch'eng I 程頤
ch'eng i-chia chih wen 成一家之文
Ch'eng-tu 成都
chi (auspicious) 吉
chi (literary collection) 集
chi (technician) 伎
chi (traces) 迹
Chi (Lu ruling family) 季
Chi Cha 季札
chi-chih 極治
Chi-chou (Ching-tung lu) 濟州
Chi-chou (Chiang-nan lu) 吉州
chi-hai 己亥
Chi-hsien yuan 集賢院
chi i 集義
chi-kang 紀網
Chi-ku lu 稽古錄
chi wu 伋物
ch'i (device) 器
ch'i (material force, vital energy) 氣
Ch'i (son of Yü, Hsia dynasty
　　founder) 啓
Ch'i (state) 齊
ch'i chih (energy and substance,
　　physical constitution) 氣質
ch'i-hsiang 氣象
ch'i-hua 氣化
Ch'i lu 七錄
Ch'i-sung 契嵩
ch'i tzu-jan chih li 其自然之理
chia 家
Chia Ch'ang-ch'ao 賈昌朝
Chia Chih 賈至
Chia I 賈誼
Chiang-hsi 江西
Chiang-nan 江南

Chiang-nan West 江南西
Chiang-nan East 江南東
Chiang-tung 江東
Ch'iang Chih 強至
chiao 教
chiao-hua 教化
Chiao-jan 皎然
Chieh 桀
chieh-tu shih 節度使
Ch'ieh yun 切韻
chien 見
Chien-ch'ang chün 建昌軍
chien-ping 兼并
Chien-wen 簡文
Chien-yü 肩愈
ch'ien 乾
Ch'ien-chou 虔州
Ch'ien hsu 潛虛
Ch'ien k'un pao-tien 乾坤寶典
Ch'ien Mu 錢穆
Ch'ien-t'ang 錢塘
chih (knowledge) 智
chih (order) 治
chih (perfection) 至
chih (point) 旨
chih (substance, substantial) 質
chih (responsibility) 職
chih (will, intent, record) 志
chih-chih-kao 知制誥
chih-chih tsai ko-wu 致知在格物
chih fa 制法
Chih-i 智顗
chih-k'o 制科
chih kuan 止觀
chih-li 至理
chih-p'ing 治平
Chih-po 智伯
Chih Yü 摯虞
Chih-yuan 智圓
ch'ih chi 持己
Chin (dynasty; feudal state) 晉
Chin (Jurchen dynasty) 金

Chin-hsiang 金鄉

chin-shen chih hsueh 搢紳之學

chin-shih 進士

Chin-ssu lu 近思錄

Ch'in 秦

Ch'in Kou 秦覯

Ch'in Kuan 秦觀

Ch'in Kuei 秦檜

ching (classic, constant) 經

ching (essential) 精

ching (reverence, composure) 敬

Ching-chao Wan-nien 京兆萬年

ching-ch'ao kuan 京朝官

ching-chi 經籍

"Ching-chi chih" 經籍志

Ching-ch'i 荊溪

Ching-hsi South 京西南

Ching-hsi North 京西北

Ching-hu North 荊湖北

ching shih-wu 經世務

ching-shu 經術

Ching-tung East 京東東

Ching-tung West 京東西

ching-wei t'ien-ti 經緯天地

Ching-yin 淨因

ch'ing (councillor) 卿

ch'ing (emotional response) 情

ch'ing (measurement) 頃

Ch'ing-chou 青州

Ch'ing-feng 清豐

ch'ing-hsing 情性

Ch'ing-li 慶曆

ch'iung-chih wu-li 窮至物理

ch'iung-li 窮理

Chou 周

Chou chih shuai 周之衰

Chou kuan hsin-i 周官新義

Chou K'ung chih chiao 周孔之教

Chou Mi 周密

Chou nan 周南

Chou Pi-ta 周必大

Chou Tun-i 周敦頤

chu (to light) 燭

Chu (feudal state) 邾

Chu Ang 朱昂

Chu Hsi 朱熹

Chu-ko Liang 諸葛亮

chu-k'o 諸科

chu-lun 著論

chu-se ch'u-shen 諸色出身

chu-shu 著述

Chu Tsai-yen 朱載言

Chu-tzu chia-li 朱子家禮

Chü-yeh 鉅野

Ch'u 楚

ch'u-ju 出入

ch'u-shen 出身

Ch'u Sui-liang 褚遂良

Ch'u tz'u 楚辭

Chü 莒

Ch'ü 懼

ch'ü pi 取必

Ch'ü Yuan 屈原

chuan 專

chüan 卷

ch'uan-tao cheng-t'ung 傳道正統

ch'üan 權

Ch'üan Jo-na 權若訥

Ch'üan Te-yü 權德輿

Ch'üan Tsu-wang 全祖望

Chuang-tzu 莊子

ch'uang-i 創意

chün-tzu 君子

Ch'un-hsi 淳熙

Ch'ün shu chih yao 羣書治要

chung (loyalty) 忠

chung (state before emotions are aroused, centrality) 中

chung-ho 中和

chung-kuo 中國

Chung-ni 仲尼

Chung-shu Yü-hsi 仲叔于奚

Chung shuo 中說

chung-tao 中道

Chung-t'u 仲塗
chung yu chu 中有主
chung-yung (centrality and
    constancy, the mean) 中庸
Chung-yung ("Doctrine of the Mean")
    中庸
Ch'ung-wen kuan 崇文觀
Ch'ung-wen yuan 崇文院
erh 二
Erh-ya 爾邪
fa 法
Fa-hsiang 法相
fa-tu 法度
Fa-yen 法言
Fan Chen 范鎮
Fan Ch'un-jen 范純仁
Fan Ch'un-ts'ui 范純粹
Fan Chung-yen 范仲淹
fan-i 番役
fan-jen 凡人
fan kuan 番官
Fan Tsu-yü 范祖禹
Fan Wen-cheng 范文正
fang 方
fang-chi 方技
Fang Hsun 方勳
Fang Kuan 房琯
fang-nei 方內
fang-wai 方外
"Fei *Kuo yü*" 非國語
fen 分
Fen-chou 汾州
feng (admonitory) 諷
feng (wind, ethos, manner) 風
feng-ch'i 風氣
feng-hua 風化
Feng Hua 馮華
feng-shan 封禪
Feng Yen-chi 馮延己
fu (a hexagram) 復
fu (rhapsody) 賦
Fu-chien 福建

Fu-chou (Chiang-nan West) 撫州
Fu-chou (Fu-chien) 福州
Fu Hsi 伏犧
"Fu hsing shu" 復性害
fu-hsu chih t'u 浮虛之徒
fu-hua 浮華
fu-ku 復古
fu kuei 富貴
Fu Pi 富弼
Fu Pin-lao 傅彬老
Han 漢
Han Ch'i 韓琦
Han Ch'ien 韓虔
Han Ch'iu-jen 韓求仁
Han Fei 韓非
Han Hui 韓會
Han I 韓億
Han Kuang-wu (ti) 漢光武(帝)
Han-lin yuan 翰林院
Han T'ui-chih 韓退之
Han Wei 韓維
han-yang 函養
Han Yü 韓愈
Hang-chou 杭州
hao-jan 浩然
ho (expression in proper measure) 和
Ho (doctor) 和
Ho-chien Hsien-wang 河間獻王
Ho-nan 河南
Ho-nan-fu 河南府
Ho-nei Hsiang 河內向
Ho-pei East 河北東
Ho Shih-tsung 何士宗
Ho-t'u 河圖
Ho-tung 河東
hou 侯
Hou Kao 侯高
Hsi Hsia 西夏
Hsi K'ang 稽康
Hsi-k'un 西崑
Hsi-tz'u chuan 繫辭傳
Hsia 夏

Hsia-hou Chia-cheng 夏侯嘉正

Hsia Sung 夏竦

hsiang (images) 象

Hsiang (king) 襄

hsiang-yuan 鄉原

hsiao-jen 小人

Hsiao Kang 蕭綱

hsiao-shuo 小說

Hsiao T'ung 蕭統

Hsiao Ying-shih 蕭穎士

Hsieh Ching-shan 謝景山

Hsieh Min-shih 謝民師

Hsieh Po-ch'u 謝伯初

hsien hou 先後

Hsien-tsung 憲宗

hsien-wei 縣尉

hsin 信

hsin-ch'i 新奇

Hsin-chou 信州

hsin fa 新法

hsin-hsueh 心學

hsin-ts'ung 信從

hsin-ts'ung-che 信從者

"Hsin-yin ming" 心印銘

hsin yuan 心源

hsing (form) 形

hsing (nature) 性

hsing (operating, conduct, practice) 行

hsing (stir) 興

hsing (surname) 姓

hsing-ch'ing 性情

Hsing-kuo chün 興國軍

hsing-ling 性靈

hsing-ming 性命

hsiu-tz'u 修辭

Hsiu-wen kuan 修文館

hsiung 凶

hsu 序

Hsu-chou 徐州

Hsu Hsuan 徐鉉

hsu-wei 虛位

hsuan 玄

hsuan-hsueh 玄學

hsuan-jen 選人

hsuan-miao 玄妙

Hsuan-tsung 玄宗

hsuan-yen 玄言

hsueh 學

Hsueh Chi 薛稷

hsueh-chiu 學究

hsueh-i 學藝

hsueh-shih 學士

hsueh-yeh 學業

Hsun Ch'ing 荀卿

Hsun Hsu 荀勗

Hsun-tzu 荀子

Hu An-ting 胡安定

Hu-chou 湖州

Hu Hung 胡宏

Hu Su 胡宿

Hu Yuan 胡瑗

Hua-lin pien-lueh 華林遍略

Hua-yen 華嚴

Huai-nan 淮南

Huai-nan tsa-shuo 淮南雜說

Huai-nan West 淮南西

Huan (doctor) 緩

Huan (hegemon) 桓

huang-chi 皇極

Huang-chou 黃州

Huang-fu Jan 皇甫冉

Huang-fu Mi 皇甫謐

Huang-fu Shih 皇甫湜

Huang Kan 黃幹

Huang lan 黃覽

Huang-lao 黃老

Huang Sung wen-chien 皇宋文鑑

Huang Ti 黃帝

Huang T'ing-chien 黃庭堅

Huang Tsung-hsi 黃宗義

Hui-tsung 徽宗

Hui-yao 會要

Hung-chou 洪州

"Hung-fan" 洪範

Hung-fan chuan 洪範傳

Hung-wen kuan 宏文館

i (intention, conception) 意

i (moral, righteousness, principle, significance) 義

i (proposal) 議

i (unity) 一

i-chia chih wen 一家之文

I ching 易經

i-feng 遺風

"I hsing chuan" 一行傳

i-hsueh (different learnings) 異學

i-hsueh (learning that defines moral principles) 義學

i ju-ya wei yeh 以儒雅爲業

i kuan 一貫

i lei t'ui 以類推

i-li 義理

i-lun 異論

I Meng 疑孟

I shu 遺書

i-tuan 異端

i-wen 藝文

I-wen lei-chü 藝文類聚

I Yin 伊尹

Jao-chou 饒州

jen 仁

Jen-ch'eng 仁城

jen-ch'ing 人情

jen-li 人理

Jen-tsung 仁宗

jen-wen 人文

jih-yung 日用

ju 儒

ju-chiao 儒教

ju-feng 儒風

ju-hsueh 儒學

Ju-lin 儒林

ju liu 入流

ju-seng 儒僧

ju-shih (enter service) 入仕

ju-shih (ju scholar) 儒士

ju-shu 儒術

ju-tsung 儒宗

ju-ya 儒雅

ju yü shen 入於神

kai 蓋

K'ai 開

Kaifeng 開封

kan-yü 感遇

kang-chi 綱紀

K'ang-chou 康州

kanryō shakai 官僚社會

Kao Hsi 皋縣

Kao-hsien 高閑

Kao Jo-na 高若訥

Kao Shih-lien 高士廉

Kao-ti 高帝

Kao-tsu 高祖

Kao-tsung 高宗

Kao Yao 皋陶

ko-wu 格物

ko-wu ch'iung-li 格物窮理

ko-yung 歌詠

K'ou Chun 冠準

ku 古

Ku-ch'eng-hsien 穀城縣

ku-feng 古風

ku-jen 古人

Ku K'uang 顧況

Ku-liang 穀梁

ku-tao 古道

ku-wen 古文

Ku-wen kuan-chien 古文關鍵

kuai 怪

kuai-p'i 乖僻

kuan 官

Kuan 關

Kuan-chung 關中

kuan jen-wen i hua-ch'eng t'ien-hsia 觀人文以化成天下

kuan tao 貫道

Kuang-chou 廣州

Kuang-nan 廣南

Kuang-nan East 廣南東
Kuang-p'ing kung 廣平公
Kuang yun 廣韻
K'uang 匡
k'un 坤
kung 公
Kung-hsien 鞏縣
kung-li 功利
Kung Shen-fu 龔深父
K'ung 孔
K'ung An-kuo 孔安國
K'ung Tao-fu 孔道輔
K'ung Wen-chung 孔文仲
K'ung Ying-ta 孔穎達
kuo 國
kuo-shih 國士
Kuo-tzu chien 國子監
Kuo yü 國語
Lang-yeh 琅琊
Lao Tan 老丹
Lao-tzu 老子
Le-ch'ing 樂清
Lei-yuan 類苑
li (clerks) 吏
li (distance measure) 里
li (pattern) 理
li (profit) 利
li (ritual, propriety) 禮
Li (king) 厲
Li Ao 李翱
Li Chih (1059–1109) 李薦
Li Chih (1527–1602) 李贄
Li Chou 李舟
li fa-tu 立法度
Li Fang 李昉
Li Han (Han Yü's son-in-law) 李漢
Li Han (of Chao-chün) 李翰
Li Ho 李賀
Li Hsi-yun 李栖筠
li hsin-fa 立新法
Li Hsiu 李修
li hsueh 理學

Li Hua 李華
Li I 李翊
Li Kou 李覯
Li Kuan 李觀
Li Lin-fu 李林甫
li min 利民
Li-nien t'u 歷年圖
Li O 李諤
Li Pi 李泌
Li Ping 李炳
Li Po 李白
"Li sao" 離騷
Li Shang-yin 李商隱
Li Shih 李適
li-shih 理事
Li Ssu 李斯
li t'ien-hsia 利天下
Li Tuan-po 李端伯
Li Tuan-shu 李端叔
li yen 立言
Li Yuan-ch'eng 李元成
Liang 梁
Liang-che 兩浙
Liang Chou-han 梁周翰
Liang Su 梁肅
Liang Ting 梁鼎
Liao 遼
Lieh-tzu 列子
Lien P'o 廉蘭
Lin-ch'uan 臨川
Liu An-shih 劉安時
Liu Ch'ang 劉敞
Liu Cheng-fu 劉正夫
Liu Chih 劉摯
Liu Chih-chi 劉知機
Liu Chih-fu 劉質夫
Liu Chih-ku 劉知古
Liu Hsiang 劉向
Liu Hsieh 劉勰
Liu Hsu 劉昫
liu i 留意
Liu I 劉彝

Liu K'ai 柳開

Liu K'o 劉軻

Liu Kung-ch'üan 柳公權

Liu Mien 柳冕

Liu Mu 劉牧

liu-nei kuan 流內官

Liu Pin 劉份

Liu Shu 劉恕

Liu tien 六典

Liu Tsung-yuan 柳宗元

liu-wai 流外

liu-wai kuan 流外官

Liu Yen 劉巖

Liu Yü-hsi 劉禹錫

Liu Yun 劉筠

Lo 洛

Lo Ch'u-yueh 羅處約

Lo Pin-wang 駱賓王

Lo shu 洛書

Lou 樓

Lou Yueh 樓鑰

Loyang 洛陽

lu 路

Lu Chao-lin 盧照鄰

Lu Chi 陸機

Lu Chih 陸贄

Lu Chiu-yuan 陸九淵

Lu Ch'un 陸淳

Lu-ling 盧陵

Lu Ssu-tao 盧思道

Lu Ts'ang-yung 盧藏用

Lu Yu 陸游

Lü-ch'iu 閭邱

Lü Hsi-che 呂希哲

Lü I-chien 呂夷簡

Lü Kung-chu 呂公著

Lü Meng-cheng 呂蒙正

Lü Ta-lin 呂大臨

Lü Tsu-ch'ien 呂祖謙

Lü Wen 呂溫

lueh 略

lun 論

Lun-yü 論語

Lung-hsi Li 隴西李

Ma-tsu Tao-i 馬祖道一

Ma Tuan-lin 馬端臨

Mei Ch'eng 枚乘

Mei-shan 眉山

Mei Yao-ch'en 梅堯臣

men-fa 門閥

Meng Chiao 孟郊

Meng K'o 孟軻

Meng-ch'i pi-t'an 夢溪筆談

Mi-chou 密州

mi-lun 彌綸

Miao 苗

min 民

Min 閩

ming (clarity, illuminate, insight) 明

ming (decree, fate) 命

ming (names) 名

Ming-ch'en yen-hsing lu 名臣言行錄

ming-chiao 名教

ming-ching 明經

Ming-chou 明州

ming-chueh 明覺

ming-fa 明法

Ming T'ai-chu 明太祝

Ming yuan 名苑

mo 謨

Mo Ti 墨翟

Mu 穆

Mu Hsiu 穆修

na-k'o p'in-tzu 納課品子

Nan ching 難經

Nan-feng 南豐

Nanking 南京

Nieh Mao-yuan 聶茂元

nien 念

Ning-po 寧波

Ou-yang Hsiu 歐陽修

Pai-kuan kung-ch'ing nien-piao
百官公卿年表

Pai-kuan piao 百官表

Pan Ku 班固
Pan Piao 班彪
P'an-keng 盤庚
P'ang Chi 龐籍
pao-chia fa 保甲法
pei (fully available) 備
pei (stele) 碑
Pei-hsi tzu-i 北溪字義
P'ei Tu 裴度
pen-chen 本眞
pen-hsin 本心
pen mo 本末
"Pen mo lun" 本末論
P'eng-ch'eng 彭城
pi (compare) 比
pi (a hexagram) 賁
pi-chi 筆記
pi hsing 比興
pi-jan 必然
pi-jan chih li 必然之理
Pi-shu sheng 秘書省
pi yu shih yen 必有事焉
pieh 別
pien 變
pien feng-su 變風俗
pien-ku 變古
p'in 品
p'in-tzu 品子
Ping-kuo 秉國
p'ing-tan 平淡
Po Chü-i 白居易
Po-kung 白公
Po-ling Ts'ui 博陵崔
pu-ch'i 不欺
pu-lo ta-jen 部洛大人
pu-wang 補亡
Pu-wang hsien-sheng 補亡先生
P'u 濮
san chiao 三教
San-chiao chu-ying 三教珠英
San-ch'ü 三衢
san ssu 三司

Shan-chou 澶州
Shang 蔺
Shang Heng 尙衡
shang-hsia chih fen 上下之分
shang-ku 上古
Shantung 山東
Shao-hsien 紹先
Shao Po-wen 邵伯溫
Shao Yung 邵雍
she-kuan 攝官
shen 神
Shen Kua 沈括
shen-ming 神明
Shen Nung 神農
Shen-tsung 神宗
sheng 生
sheng-chih 生知
sheng-hsueh 聖學
sheng-jen chih tao 聖人之道
sheng-ling 生靈
"Sheng-te sung" 聖德頌
sheng-ts'ai 生財
shih (clan name) 氏
shih (elite) 士
shih (facts, affairs, phenomena, serve) 事
shih (force of circumstances) 勢
shih (history) 史
shih (if) 使
shih (poem) 詩
shih (recognize) 識
shih (serve) 仕
shih (substance) 實
Shih (a surname) 史
shih che 十哲
Shih-chi 史記
shih-chia 世家
Shih Chieh 石介
shih chün-tzu 士君子
Shih I 史佚
shih-jen (a member of the shih) 士人
shih-jen (poet) 詩人

Shih K'o 史克

Shih kuan 史館

shih-liu 士流

Shih pen-i 詩本義

Shih Shou-tao 石守道

Shih Ssu-ming 史思明

shih-ta-fu 士大夫

shih-tao 師道

shih-tsu 士族

Shih-tsung 世宗

shih-wei ch'in-chün 侍衛親軍

shu (commoners) 庶

shu (methods) 術

Shu (Five Dynasties state in Szechuan) 蜀

Shu-chi 庶幾

shu-i 書儀

Shu-mi yuan 樞密院

shu-min 庶民

shu-shu 數術

shu-shu chih hsueh 數術之學

shu-wu 庶物

shuai (decline) 衰

shuai (lead) 率

Shun 舜

shun-ku 訓詁

shuo 說

Shuo-wen chieh-tzu 說文解字

ssu (private, partial) 私

ssu chiao 四教

ssu-hai ta-hsing 四海大姓

ssu k'o 四科

ssu-li 斯理

Ssu-ma Ch'ien 司馬遷

Ssu-ma Hsiang-ju 司馬相如

Ssu-ma Kuang 司馬光

Ssu-ma shih shu-i 司馬氏書儀

ssu-tao 斯道

ssu-wen 斯文

su 俗

Su Ch'e 蘇轍

Su-chou 蘇州

Su hsun 俗訓

Su Hsun 蘇洵

Su Huan 蘇渙

Su Mien 蘇冕

Su Po-ku 蘇伯固

Su Shen 蘇紳

Su Shih 蘇軾

Su Shun-ch'in 蘇舜欽

Su Sung 蘇頌

Su Tzu-chan 蘇子瞻

Su wen 素問

Su Yuan-ming 蘇源明

Su yuan-wai-lang 蘇員外郎

Sui 隋

Sun Chang-ch'ien 孫長倩

Sun Chueh 孫覺

Sun Fu 孫復

Sun Ho 孫何

Sun Ming-fu 孫明復

Sun Mou 孫侔

Sun Shih 孫奭

Sun T'i 孫逖

Sun Wu 孫武

sung 頌

Sung 宋

Sung-ch'eng hsien 宋城縣

Sung Ch'i 宋祁

Sung Min-ch'iu 宋敏求

Sung Po 宋白

Sung Yü 宋玉

Szechuan 四川

ta 達

ta-che 達者

ta-ch'u 大初

ta-chüan 大全

ta-fa 大法

ta-i 大義

ta ku-jen 達古人

ta li 達理

Ta-ming 大名

Ta T'ang shih-tsu chih 大唐氏族志

ta-t'i 大體

ta-tsu 大族

tai 代

tai-fu 大夫

Tai-tsung 代宗

T'ai-ch'ang ssu 太常寺

t'ai-chi 太極

T'ai-chou 台州

T'ai-hsuan 太玄

T'ai-hsueh 太學

t'ai-ku 太古

T'ai-p'ing chou 太平州

T'ai-p'ing hsing-kuo 太平興國

T'ai-p'ing huan-yü chi 太平寰宇記

T'ai-p'ing kuang-chi 太平廣記

T'ai-p'ing sheng-hui-fang 太平聖惠方

T'ai-p'ing yü-lan 太平御覽

T'ai-po 太伯

T'ai-shan 泰山

T'ai-tsu 太祖

T'ai-tsung 太宗

T'ai-yuan Wang 太原王

Tan Chu 啖助

T'an Yao-sou 譚堯叟

T'ang (dynasty) 唐

T'ang (Shang dynasty founder)
　湯

t'ang-hou kuan 堂後官

T'ang hui-yao 唐會要

tao 道

Tao-hsueh 道學

tao-li 道理

tao-shih 道士

tao-te 道德

Tao te ching 道德經

tao-t'ung 道統

T'ao Yuan-ming 陶淵明

te 德

te-hsing (ethical conduct) 德行

te-hsing (moral nature) 德性

Te-tsung 德宗

Teng-chou 登州

T'eng 滕

T'eng Ta-tao 滕達道

ti-tsu 帝族

t'i 體

t'i-wu 體物

t'i-wu yuan-ch'ing 骨物原情

tiao-ch'ung 雕蟲

Tiao K'an 刁衎

tien 典

tien-ch'ien chün 殿前軍

tien-li 典禮

tien-mo 典謨

tien-yao 典要

T'ien Ch'ang 田常

"T'ien-fei" 天非

T'ien Hsi 田錫

t'ien-hsia 天下

t'ien-li 天理

t'ien-li chih tzu-jan 天理之自然

T'ien-pao 天寶

T'ien-sheng 天聖

T'ien-t'ai 天台

t'ien-ti chih hua 天地之化

t'ien-wen 天文

ting 定

Ting-chou 定州

ting-ming 定名

ting-t'i 定體

Ting Wei 丁謂

Ting Yuan-chen 丁元珍

T'ing shih 桯史

T'ou-hu hsin-ko 投壺新格

tsa-se ch'u-shen 雜色出身

tsa-wen 雜文

ts'ai 才

Ts'ai Ching 蔡京

Ts'ai-chou 蔡州

Ts'ai Hsiang 蔡襄

Tsan-huang 贊皇

ts'an-chih cheng-shih 參知政事

Tsang Ping 臧丙

tsao yen 造言

tsao-hua 造化

Ts'ao 曹

Ts'ao Chih 曹植

ts'ao lü 操履

Ts'ao Pa 曹霸

Ts'ao P'i 曹丕

Ts'ao Pu-hsing 曹不興

ts'ao wen-ping 操文柄

ts'e 策

Ts'e-fu yuan-kuei 册府元龜

Tseng Kung 曾鞏

Tseng Kung-liang 曾鞏亮

Tseng-tzu 曾子

tso 作

tso-che 作者

Tso-chuan 左傳

tso wen 作文

tsu 族

Tsu Wu-tse 祖無擇

Ts'u-lai 徂徠

Ts'ui An 崔黯

Ts'ui Mien 崔沔

Ts'ui Tsun-tu 崔尊度

Ts'ui Yu-fu 崔祐甫

Ts'ui Yuan-han 崔元翰

tsung-chang 宗長

Tsung-mi 宗密

tu-chih p'an-kuan 度支判官

Tu Ch'un 杜純

Tu Fu 杜甫

tu hsing 獨行

Tu Huang-shang 杜黃裳

Tu K'ai 杜開

Tu-ku Chi 杜孤及

Tu Kuang-t'ing 杜光庭

tu-tuan 獨斷

Tu Yu 杜佑

tuan 斷

tung-chiao 東郊

Tung Chung-shu 董仲舒

Tung-t'ing 洞庭

t'ung 通

T'ung-chih 通志

t'ung-li 通理

t'ung-p'an 通判

t'ung shang-hsia 通上下

T'ung shu 通書

T'ung tien 通典

t'ung wan-wu chih li 通萬物之理

tzu (philosophical school) 子

tzu (sobriquet) 字

Tzu-chih t'ung-chien 資治通鑑

Tzu-chih t'ung-chien kang-mu
　資治通鑑綱目

Tzu-hsia 子夏

tzu-hsin 自信

tzu-jan 自然

tzu-jan chih li 自然之理

Tzu-kung 子貢

Tzu-lu 子路

Tzu shuo 字說

Tzu-ssu 子思

tzu-te 自得

Tzu-yu 子游

tz'u 辭/詞

Tz'u-ch'i hsien 慈溪縣

tz'u-jen 辭人/詞人

tz'u-yen 辭言

Wang An-shih 王安石

Wang Chen 王眞

Wang Ch'in-jo 王欽若

Wang Chung-i 王仲儀

Wang Hsiang 王庠

Wang Hu 王祜

Wang Hua-chi 王化基

Wang Kuei 王珪

Wang Kung-ch'en 王拱臣

Wang Pi 王弼

Wang Po 王勃

Wang P'u 王溥

Wang Shen 王詵

Wang Shen-fu 王深父

Wang Su 王素

Wang Tan 王旦

wang tao 王道

Wang Ts'an 王粲
Wang T'ung 王通
Wang Yao-ch'en 王堯臣
Wang Yen 王彥
Wang Yü-ch'eng 王禹偁
wei (do, engage in, realize) 爲
wei (position) 位
Wei 魏
Wei Cheng 魏徵
wei chi 爲己
Wei-Chin 魏晉
Wei Ch'ü-mou 韋渠牟
Wei Chung-li 韋鍾立
wei-jen 爲人
Wei-lieh 威烈
Wei Ssu 魏斯
wei tao 爲道
wei t'ien-hsia 爲天下
wei t'ien-hsia kuo-chia chih i 爲天下
  國家之意
Wei Tsung-ch'ing 韋宗卿
Wei-tzu 微子
wei-wen 爲文
wen (culture, literature) 文
Wen (King) 文
wen-chang 文章
Wen-chang liu-pieh chi 文章流別集
wen-chang meng-chu 文章盟主
wen-ch'en 文臣
wen-chi 文紀
wen-chiao 文教
Wen-chuang 文莊
Wen-fu 文賦
Wen-hsi hsien 聞喜縣
Wen-hsin tiao-lung 文心雕龍
Wen hsuan 文選
wen-hsueh 文學
wen-hsueh chih jen 文學之人
wen-hua 文化
wen i kuan tao 文以貫道
wen i ming tao 文以明道
wen i tsai tao 文以載道

wen-jen 文人
wen-ju 文儒
wen-ju chih shih 文儒之士
wen kuan 文官
"Wen lun" 文論
wen-ming 文明
Wen ming cheng hua 文明政化
wen-shih 文士
Wen-ssu po-yao 文思博要
wen-tao 文道
Wen-tao yuan-kuei 文道元龜
Wen-ti 文帝
wen-t'i 文體
wen-ts'ai 文采
Wen ts'ui 文粹
Wen T'ung 文同
wen-tzu 文字
wen-tz'u 文辭
wen-ya 文雅
Wen Yen-po 文彥博
Wen-yuan 文元
Wen yuan 文苑
Wen-yuan ying-hua 文苑英華
wo wu 我物
wu (military, militancy) 武
wu (nothing) 無
wu (things) 物
Wu (empress; king) 武
Wu (state) 吳
Wu-ch'eng 武成
Wu ching cheng-i 五經正義
Wu Ch'ung 吳充
"Wu-feng-lou fu" 五峰樓賦
wu-fu 五服
Wu Hsiao-tsung 吳孝宗
wu hsing 五行
wu-jen 武人
Wu Tao-tzu 吳道子
Wu Wu-ling 吳武陵
wu-wei 無爲
wu-yu 無有
Wu Yun 吳筠

ya 雅
ya-ch'ien 衙前
yai 涯
Yang Chi 楊極
Yang Ch'iang 楊瑒 or T'ang 湯
Yang Chieh 楊傑
Yang Chiung 楊烱
Yang Chu 楊朱
Yang Hsiung 揚雄
Yang I 楊億
Yang Kuo-pao 楊國寶
Yang Ling 楊凌
Yang Ning 楊凝
Yang P'ing 楊憑
Yang Shih 楊時
Yang Wan 楊縮
Yao 堯
Yao Hsuan 姚鉉
Yao Nan-chung 姚南中
Yeh 葉
Yeh Ch'ing-ch'en 葉清臣
Yeh Meng-te 葉夢得
yen 言
Yen Chen-ch'ing 顏眞卿
Yen Chih-t'ui 顏之推
yen chih wu wen hsing chih pu-yuan
　言之無文行之不遠
yen chih wu wen hsing erh pu-yuan
　言之無文行而不遠
Yen Hou-yü 嚴厚輿
Yen Hui 顏回
Yen-shih chia-hsun 顏氏家訓
Yen Shih-ku 顏師古
Yen Shu 晏殊
Yen T'ai-ch'u 顏太初
Yen-tzu 顏子
yen-wen 言文
yen-yü 言語
yin (privilege) 蔭
Yin (dynasty) 殷
Yin Fan 殷璠

Yin Shu 尹洙
yin-yung hsing-ch'ing 吟詠性情
Ying-t'ien 應天
Ying-tsung 英宗
ying wu 應物
Yu 幽
Yu Tso 游酢
yu-wei 有爲
Yü 禹
Yü Ching 余靖
yü i 寓意
Yü Kua 俞括
Yü lan 御覽
Yü Shao 于邵
Yü Shih-nan 虞世南
Yü-wen 宇文
Yü-yao 餘姚
Yuan 元
Yuan Chen 元鎭
Yuan Chieh 元結
Yuan Chün-ch'en 袁君陳
Yuan Chün-tsai 袁君載
Yuan-feng 元豐
Yuan-feng chiu yü chih 元豐九域志
Yuan-ho 元和
"Yuan-jen lun" 原人論
"Yuan ming" 原命
Yuan-shih shih-fan 袁氏世範
"Yuan tao" 原道
Yuan Tao-tsung 元道宗
Yuan Te-hsiu 元德秀
Yuan Ts'ai 袁采
Yuan-yu 元祐
Yueh-chou 岳州
yueh-fu 樂府
Yueh I 樂毅
Yueh K'o 岳珂
"Yueh ling" 月令
Yun-t'ang 雲堂
yung 用
yung-wu 詠物

Index

In this index an "f" after a number indicates a separate reference on the next page, and an "ff" indicates separate references on the next two pages. A continuous discussion over two or more pages is indicated by a span of page numbers, e.g., "57–59." *Passim* is used for a cluster of references in close but not consecutive sequence.

ch'üan (expedience), 197, 203f, 206, 365n, 421n

Ch'üan Te-yü, 21, 110–11, 122f, 125, 144, 392n, 393n, 397n, 398n, 408n

Ch'üan Tsu-wang: *Case Studies of Sung and Yuan Learning (Sung Yuan hsueh-an)*, 28, 29–30, 31, 369n

Chuang-tzu, 144, 166, 225, 257ff, 264

Ch'un-hsi reign period, 329

Chün-chai tu-shu chih, 380n

chün-tzu (ethical man), 11–12, 170–71

chung (center, centrality, mean), 138, 180f, 188, 234, 253, 319; and constancy, 141, 204–6, 259–61, 269; and Liu Tsung-yuan, 141–43, 144; and harmony, 235–36, 242; and emotions, 289–90

chung (loyalty), 15, 361n

chung-ho (centrality and harmony), 235–36, 242

Chung-shu Yü-hsi, 241

chung-tao (way of centrality), 141–43, 144

Chung yung, see Doctrine of the Mean

chung-yung (centrality and constancy), 141, 204–6, 445n; Su Shih on, 259–61, 269, 420n

Ch'ung-wen kuan (College for Honoring Wen), 78, 402n

Ch'ung-wen yuan (Court for Esteeming Wen), 151f

civil, *see wen; wen* versus *wu*

civil officials in the Sung: patronage of, 54f, 57f, 68–70, 156f, 171–72, 378n

civil policy and scholars, 150–66

clans, great, 4, 15, 32–51 *passim*, 58, 65–67, 327, 358n, 371n, 372n, 373n, 376n, 380n, 381n; Buddhist monks and Taoist priests in, 19–20. *See also shih*

Classic of Filial Piety (Hsiao ching), 152, 225, 392n

Classics (*ching*), 1, 10, 16, 27, 98f, 112, 115, 118, 121, 135f, 165, 181, 184, 203; memorization of, 63, 115, 154;

early T'ang view of, 76–84 *passim*; exegesis, 79f, 93–94, 198ff; Liu Mien on, 144–45; Lü Wen on, 145–46; Liu K'ai on, 163–64; Ou-yang Hsiu on, 191–94, 199–201; Wang An-shih on, 224–33; Su Shih on, 257f, 282–93; Ch'eng I and, 304, 307f, 316; commentaries on, 384n, 414n. *See also Change, Book of; Documents, Book of; Five Classics; Rites, Book of; Rites of Chou; Songs, Book of; Spring and Autumn Annals; Six Classics*

Classics examination (*ming-ching*), 44, 78–79, 154, 161, 374n

clerical service, 42–43, 55, 68, 374n, 377n

coherence as a value, 20–21, 186, 197, 283, 322; in thinking about *tao*, 137–40, 195–96, 197, 216–17, 230–33, 236–37, 283–84, 289–92, 312–14; in writing and *wen*, 140, 181–82, 189, 224–30; *li* and, 283, 318, 322–26. *See also* unity

community compact, 339

community granary, 339

composure (*ching*), 319, 321–22

compulsory service, rotation of, 172

conduct (*hsing*), *see* ethical conduct

Confucius/Confucianism, 1, 15–18, 169, 230, 235, 241f, 284, 359n; *Analects*, 1, 15, 92, 106, 152, 154, 223, 248, 257, 281f, 307, 360n; and *shih* learning, 15–18; and the Classics, 15–18, 85, 95, 98, 257; later T'ang interpretations of his *tao*, 115, 117, 120, 127–43 *passim*; and the *Book of Songs*, 199–200; Sung interpretations of his *tao*, 166, 180, 183f, 204f; Wang An-shih on, 225–28; Su Shih on, 264–68, 272, 280–81; Ch'eng I and, 304, 307, 314, 328

Correct Significance of the Five Classics (Wu ching cheng-i), 79, 387n, 389n

Cosmic resonance, 179–80, 193–94, 288, 327, 389n, 413n, 418n

Library of Congress Cataloging-in-Publication Data

Bol, Peter Kees.
  "This culture of ours" : intellectual transitions in T'ang and
Sung China / Peter K. Bol.
      p.   cm.
  Includes bibliographical references and index.
  ISBN 0-8047-1920-9 (cloth : alk. paper) :
    1. China—Intellectual life—221 B.C.–960 A.D.   2. China—
Intellectual life—960–1644.   1. Title.
DS747.42.B64   1992
951'.01—dc20   91-16004
                                                      CIP

⊚ This book is printed on acid-free paper